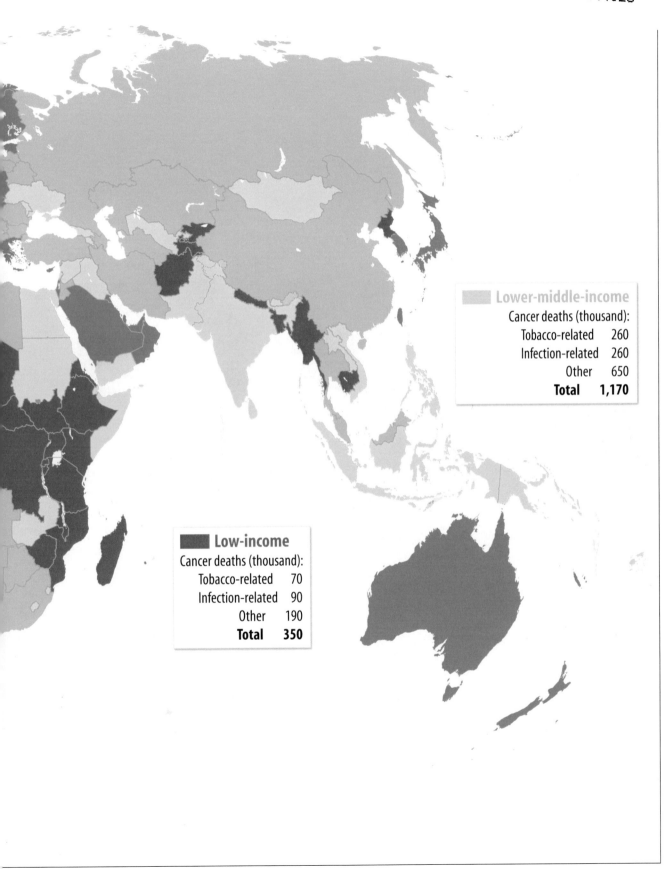

Lower-middle-income
Cancer deaths (thousand):
Tobacco-related	260
Infection-related	260
Other	650
Total	**1,170**

Low-income
Cancer deaths (thousand):
Tobacco-related	70
Infection-related	90
Other	190
Total	**350**

VOLUME **3**

DISEASE CONTROL PRIORITIES • THIRD EDITION

Cancer

DISEASE CONTROL PRIORITIES • THIRD EDITION

Series Editors

Dean T. Jamison
Rachel Nugent
Hellen Gelband
Susan Horton
Prabhat Jha
Ramanan Laxminarayan

Volumes in the Series

Essential Surgery
Reproductive, Maternal, Newborn, and Child Health
Cancer
Mental, Neurological, and Substance Use Disorders
Cardiovascular, Respiratory, Renal, and Endocrine Disorders
HIV/AIDS, STIs, Tuberculosis, and Malaria
Injury Prevention and Environmental Health
Child and Adolescent Development
Disease Control Priorities: Improving Health and Reducing Poverty

DISEASE CONTROL PRIORITIES

Budgets constrain choices. Policy analysis helps decision makers achieve the greatest value from limited available resources. In 1993, the World Bank published *Disease Control Priorities in Developing Countries* (*DCP1*), an attempt to systematically assess the cost-effectiveness (value for money) of interventions that would address the major sources of disease burden in low- and middle-income countries. The World Bank's 1993 *World Development Report* on health drew heavily on *DCP1's* findings to conclude that specific interventions against noncommunicable diseases were cost-effective, even in environments in which substantial burdens of infection and undernutrition persisted.

DCP2, published in 2006, updated and extended *DCP1* in several aspects, including explicit consideration of the implications for health systems of expanded intervention coverage. One way that health systems expand intervention coverage is through selected platforms that deliver interventions that require similar logistics but deliver interventions from different packages of conceptually related interventions, for example, against cardiovascular disease. Platforms often provide a more natural unit for investment than do individual interventions. Analysis of the costs of packages and platforms—and of the health improvements they can generate in given epidemiological environments—can help to guide health system investments and development.

DCP3 differs importantly from *DCP1* and *DCP2* by extending and consolidating the concepts of platforms and packages and by offering explicit consideration of the financial risk protection objective of health systems. In populations lacking access to health insurance or prepaid care, medical expenses that are high relative to income can be impoverishing. Where incomes are low, seemingly inexpensive medical procedures can have catastrophic financial effects. *DCP3* offers an approach to explicitly include financial protection as well as the distribution across income groups of financial and health outcomes resulting from policies (for example, public finance) to increase intervention uptake. The task in all of the *DCP* volumes has been to combine the available science about interventions implemented in very specific locales and under very specific conditions with informed judgment to reach reasonable conclusions about the impact of intervention mixes in diverse environments. *DCP3's* broad aim is to delineate essential intervention packages and their related delivery platforms to assist decision makers in allocating often tightly constrained budgets so that health system objectives are maximally achieved.

DCP3's nine volumes are being published in 2015 and 2016 in an environment in which serious discussion continues about quantifying the sustainable development goal (SDG) for health. *DCP3's* analyses are well-placed to assist in choosing the means to attain the health SDG and assessing the related costs. Only when these volumes, and the analytic efforts on which they are based, are completed will we be able to explore SDG-related and other broad policy conclusions and generalizations. The final *DCP3* volume will report those conclusions. Each individual volume will provide valuable, specific policy analyses on the full range of interventions, packages, and policies relevant to its health topic.

More than 500 individuals and multiple institutions have contributed to *DCP3*. We convey our acknowledgments elsewhere in this volume. Here we express our particular gratitude to the Bill & Melinda Gates Foundation for its sustained financial support, to the InterAcademy Medical Panel (and its U.S. affiliate, the Institute of Medicine of the National Academy of Sciences), and to the External and Corporate Relations Publishing and Knowledge division of the World Bank. Each played a critical role in this effort.

Dean T. Jamison
Rachel Nugent
Hellen Gelband
Susan Horton
Prabhat Jha
Ramanan Laxminarayan

VOLUME **3**

DISEASE CONTROL PRIORITIES • THIRD EDITION

Cancer

EDITORS

Hellen Gelband
Prabhat Jha
Rengaswamy Sankaranarayanan
Susan Horton

🌐 **WORLD BANK GROUP**

Softcover

ISBN (paper): 978-1-4648-0349-9
ISBN (electronic): 978-1-4648-0369-7
DOI: 10.1596/978-1-4648-0349-9

Hardcover

ISBN: 978-1-4648-0350-5

DOI: 10.1596/978-1-4648-0350-5

Cover photo: © IAEA Imagebank/Dana Sacchetti/IAEA. Used with permission; further permission required for reuse.
Cover and interior design: Debra Naylor, Naylor Design, Washington, DC

Library of Congress Cataloging-in-Publication Data

Cancer (Gelband)

  Cancer / editors, Hellen Gelband, Prabhat Jha, Rengaswamy Sankaranarayanan, Susan Horton.

    p. ; cm. — (Disease control priorities ; volume 3)

  Includes bibliographical references and index.

ISBN 978-1-4648-0349-9 (alk. paper) — ISBN 978-1-4648-0350-5 (alk. paper) — ISBN 978-1-4648-0369-7 (electronics)

  I. Gelband, Hellen, editor. II. Jha, Prabhat, 1965- , editor. III. Sankaranarayanan, R. (Rengaswamy), 1952- , editor. IV. Horton, Susan, editor. V. World Bank, issuing body. VI. Title. VII. Series: Disease control priorities ; v. 3

  [DNLM: 1. Neoplasms—economics. 2. Neoplasms—prevention & control. 3. Cost of Illness. 4. Developing Countries. 5. Health Services Research—economics. WA 395]

  RC262

    362.19699′400681—dc23   2015019371

Contents

Foreword

When the biopsy results confirmed that I had oral cancer, I was 18 years old. If it sounded like a death sentence, there was reason for that thought. Survival rates from cancer were very low in those days, especially in the poorer countries in the world (I was then a student in Calcutta), and statistics offered very little reason for cheer. Now, at the age of 81, I can not only celebrate the fact that I made it, with help from heavy-dose radiation, but also that the battle against cancer in the world is increasingly being won.

However, the victory is not only partial, it is also deeply uneven. With early diagnosis and effective treatment, almost two-thirds of the people who get cancer in high-income countries now survive. In low- and middle-income countries, only half of that proportion—no more than one-third—make it.

This wonderfully illuminating book tells us about the state of the battle against cancer, but it also takes on the challenge of making lives better—and longer—particularly in the poorer countries of the world. As the chapters in this state-of-the-art book on cancer show,

with extensive data and probing analyses, both mortality and suffering from cancer can be dramatically reduced, even in the less affluent countries, through a combination of *preventive measures* (of which tobacco control is the most well-known and frustratingly underused avenue), *early diagnosis* (distressingly low for cancers in which early detection is not difficult to achieve and would make a major difference, such as oral, cervical, and breast cancer as well as the cancers that afflict children), and of course *early treatment* (including well-established procedures as well as newly developed methods).

The lesson that emerges from the well-aimed empirical analyses presented in this volume is not only that a major difference can be made in the incidence, management, and elimination of cancer, even in the poorer countries of the world, but that this can be done in cost-effective and affordable ways. Understanding and determination are the deficiencies most in need of change.

This is, ultimately, a cheerful book on a very grim subject. It is also a hugely important invitation to action.

Amartya Sen
Thomas W. Lamont University Professor
Harvard University
Cambridge, Massachusetts
Nobel Laureate, Economic Sciences 1998

Preface

The burden of cancer in low- and middle-income countries (LMICs) is large and growing. By contrast, resources to control cancer in LMICs, either from domestic budgets or international aid, have not increased proportionately. Most populations in LMICs lack access to effective cancer prevention, treatment, and palliation. This volume, *Cancer*, part of the 3rd edition of *Disease Control Priorities*, provides an up-to-date review of the effectiveness, cost-effectiveness, cost, and feasibility of interventions for cancers that impose high disease burdens in LMICs.

We propose an "essential package" of feasible interventions that countries can use in cancer planning, knowing that some countries are well along in providing many of the elements. We recognize that the essential cancer package may not be immediately feasible in low-income countries and only partially so in many middle-income countries. The package is not intended to limit cancer control to these measures, but we are suggesting that these measures are likely to save large numbers of lives at an affordable cost and should be prioritized by the public sector before large investments are made in interventions that will have more limited effects. Local cancer patterns and resource availability may dictate somewhat different priorities, and these should also guide national cancer planning.

Smoking cessation reduces the risks of developing various cancers reasonably quickly, but other preventive measures, such as vaccinations against cervical or liver cancer, will take longer to manifest full effects. Many types of cancer, which are not currently preventable, will remain. Thus, the best approach to lowering the cancer burden is a system that promotes prevention as well as early detection and treatment. This volume provides evidence that policy makers at all levels can use to support the immediate ramp-up of cancer control interventions that will have near-term and long-range benefits.

Serious progress in cancer prevention and treatment began about half a century ago in high-income countries. The knowledge that has fueled progress is available immediately for LMICs. In some cases, newer and better technologies are now available: HPV testing can replace the more resource- and infrastructure-intensive Pap smear for cervical cancer screening. Newer screening tests for colon cancer have similar advantages. Increasing national incomes and broader national health coverage in middle-income countries, in particular, have already made a range of services available to a wider swath of the population. The pace needs to be accelerated and efforts can be broadened in low-income countries, where numbers of deaths from cancer are still relatively low, but increasing.

Regarding tobacco—still the single most important cancer-causing agent the world over—LMICs have the knowledge to avert the epidemic that has now begun to subside in high-income countries. At the same time, LMICs are underequipped to combat the tactics of multinational tobacco companies. In a few cases, national treasuries profit from state-owned tobacco companies.

Certain neglected areas are of special concern. Progress is all but nonexistent in providing adequate pain control and palliative care, even in middle-income countries. Limited progress has been made in cancer registration and cause of death reporting. Very little progress is evident in documenting the costs and cost-effectiveness of interventions in LMICs for even the highest-burden cancers. And very few clinical trials in cancer take place in LMICs. As a result, much of the evidence included in this volume is from high-income countries, which we and our many co-authors have reinterpreted as realistically as possible for LMICs.

We thank our dozens of co-authors for working tirelessly, responding to several reviews, and producing evidence that can be understood and acted on. We also give our thanks to the Cancer Surveillance Section of the International Agency for Research on Cancer for the custom maps and graphs in the volume and to the National Cancer Institute, particularly the Center for Global Health, for supporting the work in many ways. The Bill & Melinda Gates Foundation's core support for *DCP3*, through the University of Washington, has made the whole enterprise possible. Others in the process also deserve our thanks: the Institute of Medicine for coordinating critical reviews and the World Bank publishing staff for their wholehearted collaboration.

Sir George Alleyne, Dr. Christopher Wild, and Sir Richard Peto acted as special advisors for the volume, providing guidance and wise counsel.

Cindy Gauvreau coordinated all aspects of the volume production, including chapter content and consistency. She vastly improved the quality of the volume that you see, and we are grateful for her many contributions. Many more individuals provided thoughtful comments, guidance, and encouragement; we thank them all.

The tide has been turned against cancer in high-income countries and can be in the rest of the world, armed with evidence and bolstered by political resolve. This volume is intended to spur that effort.

Hellen Gelband
Prabhat Jha
Rengaswamy Sankaranarayanan
Susan Horton

Abbreviations

ADA	American Dental Association
ADR	adenoma detection rate
ALDH	aldehyde dehydrogenase
AML	acute myeloid leukemia
APL	acute promyelocytic leukemia
ASIR	age-specific incidence rate
BCS	breast-conserving surgery
BHGI	Breast Health Global Initiative
BL	Burkitt lymphoma
BMI	body mass index
BSE	breast self-examination
CBC	complete blood count
CBE	clinical breast examination
CEA	cost-effectiveness analysis
CI	confidence interval
CIN	cervical intraepithelial neoplasia
CISNET	Cancer Intervention and Surveillance Modeling Network
CME	continuing medical education
CMF	cyclophosphamide, methotrexate, and 5-fluorouracil
CRC	colorectal cancer
CT	computed tomography
CTC	computed tomographic colonography
CVG	cost per vaccinated girl
DALY	disability-adjusted life year
DCIS	ductal carcinoma in situ
ECEA	extended cost-effectiveness analysis
EDP	early detection and prevention
EPI	Expanded Program for Immunization
ER	estrogen receptor
FAC	5-fluorouracil, doxorubicin (®Adriamycin), and cyclophosphamide
FAP	familial adenomatous polyposis
FCTC	Framework Convention on Tobacco Control
FIT	fecal immunochemical test
FS	flexible sigmoidoscopy
Gavi	Gavi, the Vaccine Alliance
GDP	gross domestic product

gFOBT	guaiac fecal occult blood test
GICR	Global Initiative for Cancer Registry Development
GNI	gross national income
GOPI	Global Opioid Policy Initiative
GTFRCC	Global Task Force on Radiotherapy for Cancer Control
HAU	Hospice Africa Uganda
HBsAg	hepatitis B surface antigen
HBV	hepatitis B virus
HCC	hepatocellular carcinoma
HCV	hepatitis C virus
HDI	Human Development Index
HDV	hepatitis D virus
Hib	*Haemophilus influenzae* type B
HICs	high-income countries
HIV	human immunodeficiency virus
HL	Hodgkin lymphoma
HPV	human papillomavirus
HR	high-risk
HSIL	high grade squamous intraepithelial lesion
IAEA	International Atomic Energy Agency
IAHPC	International Association for Hospice and Palliative Care
IARC	International Agency for Research on Cancer
ICD	International Classification of Diseases
ICER	incremental cost-effectiveness ratio
ICRCSN	International Colorectal Cancer Screening Network
IHC	immunohistochemistry
IMRT	intensity modulated radiation therapy
INCB	International Narcotics Control Board
IT	information technology
JCI	Joint Commission International
LEEP	loop electrosurgical excision procedure
LICs	low-income countries
LLETZ	large loop excision of the transformation zone
LMICs	low- and middle-income countries
LR	low-risk
LYS	life-years saved
MICs	middle-income countries
MISCAN	microsimulation screening analysis
MMG	mammography
MRI	magnetic resonance imaging
MRM	modified radical mastectomy
NAFD	non-alcoholic fatty liver disease
NCCN	National Comprehensive Cancer Network
NCD	noncommunicable disease
NCI	National Cancer Institute
NIAAA	National Institute of Alcohol Abuse and Alcoholism
NWTS	National Wilms Tumor Study
OECD	Organisation for Economic Co-operation and Development
OSMF	oral submucous fibrosis
PAF	population attributable fraction
PAHO	Pan American Health Organization
PBCR	population-based cancer registry
PET	positron emission tomography

PODC	Pediatric Oncology in Developing Countries
PPP	purchasing power parity
PSA	prostate-specific antigen
QALY	quality-adjusted life-year
RCC	regional cancer center
RCT	randomized controlled trial
RT	radiotherapy
SEER	Surveillance, Epidemiology, and End Results
SES	socioeconomic status
SIL	squamous intraepithelial lesion
SLN	sentinel lymph node
SPS	Seguro Popular de Salud
SSP	sessile serrated polyp
TLS	tumor lysis syndrome
TNM	tumor, nodes, metastasis
TRM	treatment-related mortality
UCI	Uganda Cancer Institute
UHC	universal health coverage
UICC	Union for International Cancer Control
UMIC	upper-middle-income country
UNOP	Unidad Nacional de Oncologia Pediátrica
US	ultrasound
USMSTF	U.S. Multi-Society Task Force on Colorectal Cancer/American Cancer Society
USPSTF	U.S. Preventive Services Task Force
VAD	vascular access device
VIA	visual inspection with acetic acid
VIAM	magnified visual inspection with acetic acid
VLP	virus-like particles
VSL	value of statistical life
WBC	white blood cell
WHO	World Health Organization
WTO	World Trade Organization
YLL	years of life lost

Chapter 1

Summary

Hellen Gelband, Prabhat Jha, Rengaswamy
Sankaranarayanan, Cindy L. Gauvreau, and Susan Horton

INTRODUCTION

At the 2012 World Health Assembly, member states agreed to a goal of reducing rates of premature death from non-communicable diseases (NCDs) by 25 percent by 2025, starting from a 2008 baseline (WHO 2011a, 2011b). The United Nations (UN) Sustainable Development Goals for 2030, announced in September 2015, will include reducing premature death from NCDs, of which cancer is a substantial part (map 1.1).

This chapter summarizes the analyses and conclusions of the 79 authors of this volume on cancer, *Disease Control Priorities, 3rd edition* (*DCP3 Cancer*), and analyzes interventions for effectiveness, cost-effectiveness, affordability, and feasibility in low- and middle-income countries (LMICs; see box 1.1 for key messages). The intent is to help governments of LMICs commit to locally appropriate national cancer control strategies that will include a range of cost-effective interventions, customized to local epidemiological patterns and available funding, and to convey this commitment widely to their populations. Where affordable treatment can be provided, conveying this to the public can motivate people to seek treatment when their cancer is at an earlier, much more curable stage. Providing a package of services that addresses a large part of the cancer burden will go a long way toward helping countries reach the new NCD goals. *DCP3 Cancer* is one of nine planned volumes in the *DCP3* series (box 1.2).

The *DCP3* package includes prevention strategies, but many cancers cannot be prevented to any great extent by available methods. Some can be treated effectively (breast and childhood cancers, for example), however, and the availability of effective treatment bolsters public confidence in the overall program (Brown and others 2006; Knaul and others 2011; Sloan and Gelband 2007). Cancer control programs can mobilize broad political support, as happened in Mexico with the addition of breast cancer and childhood cancer treatment into expanded national health insurance coverage (Knaul and others 2012).

In high-income countries (HICs), most who develop cancer survive, although survival depends strongly on the type of cancer (table 1.1). In LMICs, less than one-third survive, and in some the proportion is much smaller (Ferlay and others 2015). The differences in survival are due partly to differences in the patterns of cancer incidence; some types of cancer that are common in many LMICs, such as lung, esophagus, stomach, and liver cancers, have a poor prognosis even in HICs (Bray and Soerjomataram 2015, chapter 2 in this volume). The other major contributor to poor outcomes is that many fewer people come for treatment when their cancer is at an early, curable stage than in HICs (Allemani and others 2015; Ferlay and others 2015).

The aim of *DCP3* is to identify cost-effective, feasible, and affordable interventions that address significant

Corresponding authors: Hellen Gelband, Center for Disease Dynamics, Economics & Policy, Gelband@cddep.org; and Prabhat Jha, Centre for Global Health Research, St. Michael's Hospital and Dalla Lana School of Public Health, University of Toronto, Prabhat.Jha@utoronto.ca.

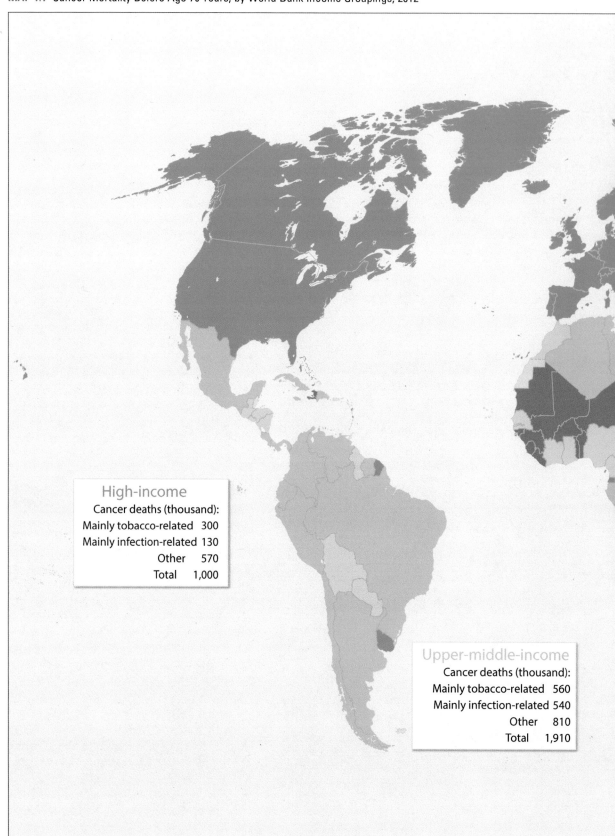

High-income
Cancer deaths (thousand):
Mainly tobacco-related 300
Mainly infection-related 130
Other   570
Total   1,000

Upper-middle-income
Cancer deaths (thousand):
Mainly tobacco-related   560
Mainly infection-related 540
Other   810
Total   1,910

Source: Based on WHO Global Health Estimates (WHO 2012)

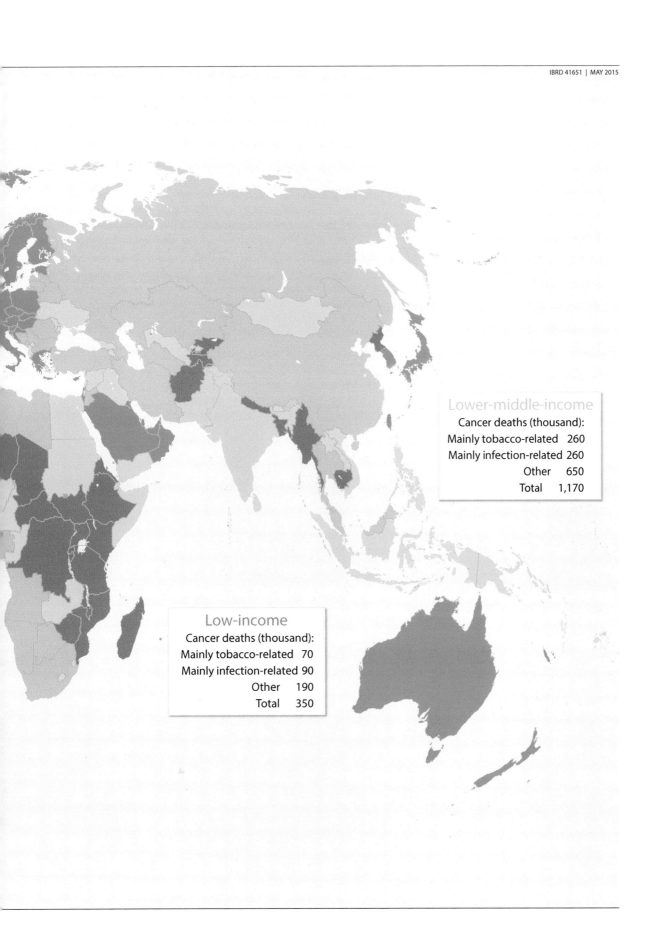

Lower-middle-income
Cancer deaths (thousand):
Mainly tobacco-related   260
Mainly infection-related 260
Other   650
Total   1,170

Low-income
Cancer deaths (thousand):
Mainly tobacco-related   70
Mainly infection-related 90
Other   190
Total   350

Key Messages

Cancer is already a major cause of death in low- and middle-income countries (LMICs), particularly in middle-income countries, and will increase as a percentage of deaths in all LMICs, driven by population aging and faster declines in other causes of death.

In most populations, helping current tobacco users to quit and young people not to start smoking are the most urgent priorities in cancer prevention (and in the control of other noncommunicable diseases), along with vaccination against hepatitis B and the human papillomavirus (HPV). Higher tobacco taxes and accompanying interventions will reduce cancer incidence and generate substantial extra revenues for governments.

Other than tobacco- and virus-related cancers, however, most of the increase in cancer incidence is not currently preventable, but many cases of cancer can be effectively treated. Early breast cancer and cervical cancer are common, and often curable; precancerous cervical lesions are even more curable. Childhood cancers are relatively rare, but some are highly curable. The interventions supported by the analyses in this *Disease Control Priorities, 3rd edition* (*DCP3 Cancer*) go beyond current World Health Organization best buys, which are limited to interventions that are deliverable in primary care settings.

The *DCP3* essential package of cost-effective and feasible interventions would, if fully implemented, cost an additional $20 billion per year, or 3 percent of total public spending on health in LMICs; 2.6 percent in upper-middle-income countries (UMICs); and 5 percent in lower-middle-income countries; but 13 percent in low-income countries (LICs). In per capita terms, this would cost $5.70, $1.70, and $1.70 annually in UMICs, lower-middle-income, and LICs, respectively. Such increases are potentially feasible in all but the LICs, which would require external support.

Cancer services that are considered appropriate for a national cancer strategy should be covered through universal health coverage as soon as countries are able to do so.

Global initiatives for cancer control in LMICs are needed to lower the costs of key inputs for the essential package, including large-scale commodity purchases; to expand technical assistance; and to promote cancer research.

---

disease burdens in LMICs (box 1.3). Accordingly, we have examined the following:

1. The avoidable burden of premature death (defined as before age 70, which approximates current global life expectancy) from cancer in LMICs (table 1.1)
2. The main effective interventions for the prevention, early detection, treatment, and palliation of cancer, and their cost-effectiveness
3. The costs and feasibility of developing health system infrastructure that could deliver progressively wider coverage of a set of cost-effective cancer services.

Using these inputs, we define an "essential package" of cost-effective interventions for cancer and discuss their affordability and feasibility, which differ markedly between low-, lower-middle-, and upper-middle-income countries. Even within the same income categories, countries may differ widely in epidemiological patterns and health systems, resulting in different country-specific essential packages. Hence, this is not intended to lead to a common cancer plan for all LMICs, but to identify elements that will be appropriate in many countries and spur discussion within countries about rational cancer control planning and implementation. The result would be national cancer plans that are tailored to local conditions but retain the characteristics of effectiveness, cost-effectiveness, feasibility, and affordability. Finally, we review some ways in which global initiatives could help LMICs to expand cancer control.

Box 1.2

From the Series Editors of Disease Control Priorities, 3rd Edition

Budgets constrain choices. Policy analysis helps decision makers achieve the greatest value from limited available resources. In 1993, the World Bank published *Disease Control Priorities in Developing Countries (DCP1)*, an attempt to assess systematically the cost-effectiveness (value for money) of interventions that would address the major sources of disease burden in low- and middle-income countries [Jamison and others 1993]). The World Bank's 1993 *World Development Report* on health drew heavily on the findings in *DCP1* to conclude that specific interventions against noncommunicable diseases were cost-effective, even in environments in which substantial burdens of infection and undernutrition persisted.

DCP2, published in 2006, updated and extended *DCP1* in several respects, including explicit consideration of the implications for health systems of expanded intervention coverage (Jamison and others 2006). One way that health systems expand intervention coverage is through selected platforms that deliver interventions that require similar logistics but address heterogeneous health problems. Platforms often provide a more natural unit for investment than do individual interventions, and conventional health economics has offered little understanding of how to make choices across platforms. Analysis of the costs of packages and platforms—and of the health improvements they can generate in given epidemiological environments—can help guide health system investments and development.

DCP3 differs substantively from *DCP1* and *DCP2* by extending and consolidating the concepts of platforms and packages and by offering explicit consideration of the financial risk protection objective of health systems. In populations lacking access to health insurance or prepaid care, medical expenses that are high relative to income can be impoverishing. Where incomes are low, seemingly inexpensive medical procedures can have catastrophic financial effects. *DCP3* offers an approach that explicitly includes financial protection as well as the distribution across income groups of the financial and health outcomes resulting from policies (for example, public finance) to increase intervention uptake (Verguet, Laxminarayan, and Jamison 2015). The task in all the volumes has been to combine the available science about interventions implemented in very specific locales and under very specific conditions with informed judgment to reach reasonable conclusions about the impacts of intervention mixes in diverse environments. The broad aim of *DCP3* is to offer, for consideration and adaptation, essential intervention packages—such as the essential cancer package in this volume—and their related delivery platforms. This information will assist decision makers in allocating budgets so that health system objectives are maximally achieved.

The nine volumes of *DCP3* are being published in 2015 and 2016 in an environment in which serious discussion continues about quantifying the sustainable development goal (SDG) for health (UN 2015). The analyses in *DCP3* are well-placed to assist in choosing the means to attain the health SDG and assessing the related costs. The final volume will explore SDG-related and other broad policy conclusions and generalizations, based on the analytic findings from the full set of volumes. Each individual volume will provide valuable, specific policy analyses on the full range of interventions, packages, and policies relevant to its health topic.

Dean T. Jamison

Rachel Nugent

Hellen Gelband

Susan Horton

Prabhat Jha

Ramanan Laxminarayan

Table 1.1 Worldwide Cancer Deaths in 2012 at Ages 0–69 by Cancer Site and Country Income Grouping, and 5-Year Survival Rates in Low-, Middle-, and High-Income Countries

Population in billions Cause of cancer and other deaths	Annual Deaths, age 0–69 years (thousands) by World Bank country income group					5-year survival (%), cancer registry data	
	Low income 0.8	Lower-middle income 2.4	Upper-middle income 2.3	High income 1.2	World (total) 6.7	Low or middle income 5.5	High income 1.2
Cancer, by site (ICD-10 C00-99)							
Lung, mouth, and esophagus	70	260	560	300	1,200	10	20
Liver	30	90	270	60	440	10	20
Breast	30	140	110	80	360	75	90
Stomach	20	80	210	50	360	20	40
Colon or rectum	20	80	120	100	310	50	60
Cervix	40	90	60	20	200	55	65
Ovary	8	30	30	30	100	25	40
Leukemia, age 0–14 years	3	10	10	2	30	65	90
age 15–69 years	10	40	60	30	140	30	50
Prostate	4	10	20	20	60	70	90
Other/unknown site	110	330	470	310	1,220	—	—
All cancers (% of all causes)	**350 (6%)**	**1,170 (6%)**	**1,920 (22%)**	**1,000 (37%)**	**4,400 (14%)**	**—**	**—**
All noncommunicable diseases	**1,660**	**6,300**	**5,950**	**2,200**	**16,070**	**—**	**—**
Communicable/external causes	**4,100**	**7,380**	**2,650**	**500**	**14,660**	**—**	**—**
All causes	**5,760**	**13,680**	**8,600**	**2,700**	**30,730**	**—**	**—**

Sources: Population and mortality based on data from the UN Population Division (UNPD 2012) and WHO Global Health Estimates (WHO 2012). Estimated 5-year survival based on Allemani and others 2015.

Note: Number of deaths above 10,000 are rounded to the nearest 10,000, so totals may differ. Estimated five-year survival rounded to the nearest 5 percent. — = Not applicable.

EVOLVING CANCER BURDEN

The WHO's International Agency for Research on Cancer (IARC) estimates that in 2012 there were 14 million new cases of cancer and 8 million deaths from cancer, more than half of them in people younger than age 70 years (table 1.1) (Ferlay and others 2015). Of the 4.4 million cancer deaths before age 70, 3.4 million were in LMICs; 1.9 million in UMICs, 1.2 million in lower-middle-income countries, and 0.3 million in LICs. Two-thirds of the cancer deaths before age 70 years in LMICs were cancers of the lung, mouth, or esophagus (0.9 million, many caused by tobacco), liver (0.4 million, many caused by vaccine-preventable hepatitis B infection), stomach (0.3 million), breast (0.3 million), cervix (0.2 million, many caused by human papillomavirus [HPV] infection), and colon or rectum (0.2 million) (See table 1.1, figure 1.1;

and Bray and Soerjomataram 2015; Ferlay and others 2015; WHO 2012).

Worldwide, cancer death rates are slowly decreasing (table 1.2). Between 2000 and 2010, age-standardized cancer death rates before age 70 years fell by about 1 percent per year, bolstered by worldwide declines in cervical cancer and stomach cancer, for reasons that are not fully understood. Male lung cancer rates decreased in some countries, but in lower-middle-income countries, the death rates from tobacco-associated cancers rose slightly.

Absolute numbers of cancer deaths and cancer as a proportion of all deaths will continue to rise because of three factors: world population is increasing, particularly in later middle age and old age; mortality from diseases other than cancer is decreasing; and in some major populations the effects of tobacco are

Box 1.3

Methods

The 79 authors of the 18 chapters in this volume surveyed the published and gray literature to identify cost-effective interventions for the cancers studied. Cancer-specific incidence and mortality data are from the International Agency for Research on Cancer's GLOBOCAN (Ferlay and others 2015). Mortality data are from the World Health Organization's Global Health Estimates (WHO 2012), and demographic estimates are from the United Nations (UNPD 2012).

The analyses were stratified by World Bank country group classifications as defined by 2013 per capita gross national income: 34 low-income countries (less than US$1,045), 50 lower-middle-income countries (US$1,046 to US$4,125), and 55 upper-middle-income countries (US$4,126 to US$12,745) (World Bank 2014a).

Cost-effectiveness estimates were compiled for each cancer and each intervention. Systematic searches were conducted in PubMed for all interventions covered in the volume, for studies in or including low- and middle-income countries (LMICs), published in 2003–13 (Horton and Gauvreau 2015). For colorectal cancer, studies from high-income Asian economies were also sought. A recent review of the cost-effectiveness of cancer interventions for high-income countries (HICs) was also useful (Greenberg and others 2010). The studies identified used various outcome measures: life years saved, quality-adjusted life years (QALYs) gained, and disability-adjusted life years averted. Evidence from studies in LMICs was preferred, but rarely available. Evidence from HICs was considered in all cases, and evidence from high-income Asian economies was particularly important. We adopted the scale used by the Commission on Macroeconomics and Health (2001) to define very cost-effective, cost-effective, and cost-ineffective as costing < 1, 1–3, and > 3 times per capita income per QALY (or other measure), respectively. (Commission on Macroeconomics and Health 2001).

The essential package includes interventions rated as very cost-effective and cost-effective and considered potentially affordable and feasible in resource-constrained environments. Costs are expressed in 2012 prices. Costs are also expressed as a percentage of national public spending on health, estimated by the World Bank (World Bank 2014b).

---

increasing (Jha 2009). Based on population growth alone (at 2010 death rates age-standardized to the expected 2030 population), more than 6 million cancer deaths are expected in 2030 in people younger than age 70 years, and an equal number in people age 70 years and older (table 1.3). Three-quarters of these future cancer deaths are expected to occur in middle-income countries (MICs).

IMPACT ON HOUSEHOLDS

Counter to common perceptions, cancer death rates are often higher in lower-income groups than high-income groups. In India, the age-standardized death rate from cancer in middle age was twice that in illiterate as in educated populations (Dikshit and others 2012). As are other NCDs, cancer is an important cause of catastrophic health expenditures that can push households into poverty (Hamid, Ahsan, and Begum 2014; Hoang Lan and others 2013; Ilbawi, Einterz, and Nkusu 2013; John and others 2011), because in many LMICs, cancer surgery, radiotherapy, and chemotherapy are paid for largely out of pocket. In Bangladesh (Hamid, Ahsan, and Begum 2014) and Cameroon (Ilbawi, Einterz, and Nkusu 2013), for example, high user fees increase the likelihood that patients will not return at all for cancer surgery. Conversely, in India, some standard types of cancer surgery (for example, mastectomy) are supposed to be provided at low, affordable cost in public hospitals; in China, the national health insurance scheme now offers standard types of cancer surgery at prices most people can afford. Nevertheless, even in China and India, cancer can still impose a major financial burden on families, especially in the lowest income groups, and in the case of India, cancer services are limited to certain large cities (Mallath and others 2014). An objective of *DCP3* is to evaluate interventions for their distributive effects, with particular emphasis on the effects on the poor and on impoverishment at any economic level because of health care expenses.

Figure 1.1 Incidence and Mortality of Selected Cancers before Age 70 Years, Low- and Middle-Income Countries, 2012

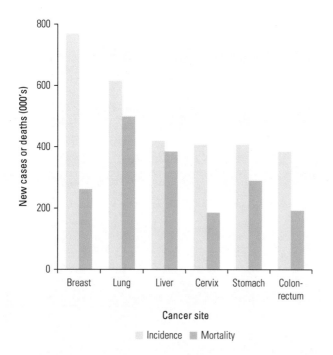

Source: Based on IARC GLOBOCAN data (Ferlay and others 2015).

ESSENTIAL PACKAGES OF INTERVENTIONS

The *DCP3* essential package of interventions for cancer is intended to be considered and modified as appropriate by governments. The specific interventions and the criteria used to choose them (effectiveness, cost-effectiveness, feasibility, and affordability) are intended to help LMIC governments decide what to support and what not to support (Jamison 2015).

For MICs that already have cancer treatment centers and clinics, the *DCP3* approach could be used to help evaluate additional interventions, now or in the future, or to re-assess some current activities; in all LMICs it could help ensure due consideration of how interventions that are considered locally appropriate can achieve high population coverage.

The WHO has formulated a list of NCD best buys for LMICs, which were limited to services considered feasible at the primary care level. Those most relevant to cancer are three preventive measures: a set of tobacco control interventions, hepatitis B vaccination to prevent liver cancer, and some form of screening and treatment for precancerous cervical lesions (WHO 2011b). The *DCP3 Cancer* essential package (table 1.4) adds HPV vaccination (also included by the Commission on Investing in Health [Jamison and others 2013]) to prevent cervical cancer. The *DCP3* also adds treatment of early-stage cervical cancer (Denny and others 2015, chapter 4 in this volume); diagnosis and treatment for early breast cancer (Anderson and others 2015, chapter 3 in this volume); diagnosis and treatment for selected, highly curable childhood cancers (Gupta and others 2015, chapter 7 in this volume); and palliative care (Cleary, Gelband, and Wagner 2015, chapter 9 in this volume), including, at a minimum, opioid drugs for severe pain control. Treating early stage breast and cervical cancer includes quality surgery, which could also be available for many other early-stage resectable cancers. The package is organized according to delivery platforms, classified as national level policy, regulation, or community information; primary health clinic or mobile outreach; first-level hospital; or specialized cancer center.

The cost of the essential package is estimated for the entire population, not restricted to age under 70 years. We estimated the global and per capita costs of each intervention in the package separately for low-income,

Table 1.2 Changes in Deaths from All Causes and Cancer, by Country Income Group, Ages 0–69, 2000–10
(Percent change in mortality rate)

	Change in % 2000–10 by World Bank country income group				
Cause of death	Low-income	Lower-middle-income	Upper-middle-income	High-income	World
All cancers	−6	−2	−12	−13	**−10**
Lung, mouth, esophagus (mainly tobacco-related)	−6	+1	−11	−12	**−9**
Cervix, liver, stomach (mainly infection-related)	−13	−2	−18	−24	**−15**
All other cancers	−4	−3	−9	−12	**−8**
All causes	−21	−15	−23	−17	**−19**

Sources: Based on data from IARC GLOBOCAN (Ferlay and others 2015) and WHO Global Health Estimates (WHO 2012).

Table 1.3 Projected Deaths from All Causes and Cancer at Ages 0–69 Years, 2030
(at 2010 death rates, thousands)

Population/Cause of death	Low-income	Lower-middle-income	Upper-middle-income	High-income	World
All Causes	8,620	18,110	11,600	2,960	41,290
Cancer	590	1,690	2,690	1,130	6,100
Lung, mouth, esophagus	130	390	820	350	1,690
Cervix, liver, and stomach	80	250	700	120	1,150
All other cancers	380	1,050	1,170	660	3,260

Sources: Based on data from UNPD 2012 and WHO Global Health Estimates (WHO 2012).
Note: All deaths are rounded to nearest 10,000. All cancer deaths (in thousands) at ages 70+ would be 240, 800, 3,110, 2,450, and 6,600 in low-income countries, lower-middle-income countries, upper-middle-income countries, high-income countries, and worldwide, respectively.

Table 1.4 Essential Cancer Intervention Package[a]

Cancer type/ Number of deaths, ages 0–69 years, 2012 (thousands)	Platform for intervention delivery			
	Nationwide policies, regulation, or community information	Primary health clinic or mobile outreach	First-level hospital[b]	Specialized cancer center/unit[c]
All cancers **3,230**	Education on tobacco hazards, value of HPV and HBV vaccination, and importance of seeking early treatment for common cancers Palliative care, including, at a minimum, opioids for pain relief[d]			
Selected tobacco-related cancers (oral, lung, and esophagus) **900**	Taxation; warning labels or plain packaging; bans on public smoking, advertising, and promotion; and monitoring	Cessation advice and services, mostly without pharmacological therapies		
Breast cancer **280**				Treat early-stage cancer with curative intent[e]
Cervical cancer **180**	School-based HPV vaccination	Opportunistic[f] screening (visual inspection or HPV DNA testing); treat precancerous lesions	Treat pre-cancerous lesions	Treat early-stage cancer
Colorectal cancer **210**			Emergency surgery for obstruction	Treat early-stage cancer with curative intent
Liver cancer **380**		Hepatitis B vaccination (including birth dose)		
Childhood cancers **80[g]**				Treat selected early-stage cancer with curative intent in pediatric cancer units/hospitals

Note: Cancer totals are rounded to nearest 10,000. Education and basic palliative care are relevant for cancers at all ages. HBV = hepatitis B virus; HPV = human papillomavirus.
a. Red type denotes emergency care.
b. First-level hospitals are referred to as district hospitals in some countries.
c. Some interventions may take place at first-level hospitals, by a specialized surgeon visiting once per month, for example.
d. Palliative care should be available at all levels specified in the table and in the home.
e. Early-stage cancer generally refers to stages I and II.
f. Screening is opportunistic when a test is requested by a patient or offered by a practitioner to a patient attending for another reason. Organized screening is a well-defined process including formal invitations to participate, recalls, reminders, tracking results, ensuring follow-up, monitoring, and reporting program performance results.
g. Including some solid tumors.

lower-middle-income, and upper-middle-income countries. Most LMICs should be able to implement a locally customized essential package that covers most of their population by 2030, given anticipated increases in public spending on health (Jamison and others 2013). The schedule of implementation will vary, however, as some interventions—in particular, higher tobacco taxes and widespread pain palliation—can begin rapidly in many countries (Foley and others 2006; Sloan and Gelband 2007). By contrast, affordable availability of treatments that require considerable infrastructure development may take many years to achieve fully after a start is made.

Prevention

Most countries (183 worldwide) now vaccinate infants against hepatitis B, with global coverage estimated at 81 percent in 2013. This will prevent many liver cancers some decades hence, but a birth dose, particularly important in countries with high mother-to-child transmission, reached only 26 percent of newborns in 2011 (WHO 2011c).

Seventy-five countries (including HICs) have begun national HPV vaccination programs and others are developing experience with the vaccine (Gavi 2013). In addition, Gavi, the Vaccine Alliance, is supporting pilot programs in several LICs in Sub-Saharan Africa. The delivery cost of reaching adolescent girls with three doses is the major barrier, as Gavi-subsidized vaccine costs only US$0.20 to US$0.40 per dose, while program costs range between US$4 and US$13 per fully immunized girl (Denny and others 2015; Gavi 2013). Hepatitis B and HPV vaccinations will have their main effect on mortality during the second half of the century, when the cohorts of immunized children reach middle age.

Tobacco control, notably much higher tobacco excise taxes (which result in marked increases in adult cessation), can have a more immediate effect: people who quit smoking before age 40 years avoid more than 90 percent of the risk they would have incurred had they continued to smoke (Jha and Peto 2014). This means a substantial saving of lives starting within 5–10 years after measures are put in place. Higher cigarette taxes also discourage youth initiation, which will prevent many deaths in the second half of the century. However, cessation remains uncommon in most LMICs, with adults quitting often as a result of cancer and other diseases, and not to avoid them. Only 28 countries are undertaking comprehensive tobacco control programs that include high taxes as a major strategy (WHO 2013). There are already some notable successes: France and South Africa used large

tax increases in the 1990s to triple the price of cigarettes; by 2005, consumption had halved, but government revenues from tobacco had doubled (Van Walbeek 2005). In France, lung cancer mortality among young adults fell shortly after the tax was raised. Brazil has also reduced smoking prevalence considerably (Monteiro and others 2007). Despite severe industry opposition, Mexico, and very recently, India and the Philippines, have levied notable increases in cigarette taxes, and in Mexico cigarette sales have already started to decline (Jha and others 2015, chapter 10 in this volume; WHO 2013). The WHO's Framework Convention on Tobacco Control, adopted by more than 180 countries, is an important enabler of country action on tobacco (Jha 2015).

Screening

The emphasis on diagnosing and treating cancers while they are still at an early stage might suggest the appropriateness of many cancer screening programs (Sullivan, Sullivan, and Ginsburg 2015, chapter 12 in this volume), but population screening is expensive (even if cost-effective, at least in some populations in HICs) and requires considerable infrastructure. Only opportunistic cervical screening (with or without some added outreach) meets the *DCP3* criteria and is a suggested component of an essential package. Screening using visual inspection with acetic acid (which makes abnormal tissue appear white) can detect precancerous lesions that can be treated inexpensively (often during the same visit) to prevent cervical cancer from developing (Denny and others 2015; Goss and others 2013). When convenient, rapid diagnostic tests for the main carcinogenic types of HPV infection become affordable and available for use by fieldworkers, they could make such screening much more effective and reliable (Sankaranarayanan and others 2009). Two or three such screenings per lifetime, starting around age 35 years, at intervals of five to10 years, should reduce lifetime cervical cancer risk by more than half (Goldie and others 2005).

The essential package does not include any type of screening for prostate or breast cancer. Both have attracted significant controversy in HICs, although for different reasons. The most widespread means of prostate cancer screening is through a blood test for prostate-specific antigen (PSA, a protein produced at elevated levels by cancerous prostate cells), with or without digital rectal examination. Although it is a simple test, PSA is not supported by national programs because it leads to overdiagnosis and overtreatment, with many more men harmed by the side effects of overtreatment than are saved from prostate cancer. The U.S. Preventive Services Task Force discourages

PSA testing (U.S. Preventive Services Task Force 2012). By contrast, screening mammography for breast cancer is supported by most HICs as an expensive but moderately effective measure, although the optimal age range for screening and screening frequency are still debated. Clinical breast examination might be a viable option in LMICs, but the effectiveness of this requires more research (Anderson and others 2015). Other common cancers with detectable precancerous stages are colorectal cancer (precancerous polyps) (Rabeneck and others 2015, chapter 6 in this volume) and oral cancer (visible lesions) (Sankaranarayanan and others 2015, chapter 5 in this volume). Eventually, screening for more cancers may be added, but it is likely to be appropriate after effective treatment is established.

Diagnosis and Treatment

Accurate diagnosis is needed for cancer treatment, but shortages of trained pathologists and other laboratory technologists and lack of facilities and supplies critically limit diagnostic capacity in many LMICs (Gospodarowicz and others 2015, chapter 11 in this volume). In addition to an initial diagnosis of cancer (often based on biopsy specimens) that can help in assessing the need for major surgery, diagnostic services can help determine treatment strategies after surgery. The status of tumors, nodes, and metastases has long been clinically useful, and other tests on the tumor itself can determine post-surgical management. In particular, breast cancer surgical specimens should undergo reliable testing to see if they carry the estrogen receptor protein; if they do (that is, if the tumor is ER+), endocrine treatment will substantially reduce the risk of recurrence and death (box 1.4).

Treatment for early breast cancer and cervical cancer includes some or all of the following: surgery, radiotherapy, chemotherapy, and targeted (for example, endocrine) therapy, that is, all the basic components of cancer care (Anderson and others 2011; Knaul and others 2011). For early cervical cancer, surgery is the primary treatment and radiotherapy is an adjunct. For whatever is considered complete treatment in a given country context, all components of care should be accessible by patients once treatment is started. Partial or incomplete treatment can cause side effects, but with less chance of clinical benefit.

Childhood cancer is rare (accounting for 1 percent of cancer deaths in HICs), representing by far the smallest burden of the cancers targeted by the essential package. Although they cannot be prevented, many common childhood cancers have high cure rates in HICs, making them feasible targets (Gupta and others 2015). Cure rates in most LMICs are far lower, but reasonably good outcomes have been achieved in specialized childhood cancer centers and through national referral and management plans, particularly for acute lymphoblastic leukemia, Burkitt lymphoma, and Wilms tumor (Gupta and others 2014).

Palliative Care

Many incurable cancers cause intractable pain. Opioid medications can generally relieve this pain, greatly improving the quality of the last few weeks or months of life for patients and families. The simplest and least expensive preparation, oral morphine, works for an estimated 90 percent of patients with severe terminal cancer pain (Foley and others 2006). It is also used by patients with HIV/AIDS and some other chronic conditions. Palliative care is widely available only in HICs, but it could be made available in LMICs quite rapidly, even before other types of treatment. Palliative care includes more than pain control and is relevant throughout the course of illness, but pain control is the core and the greatest need is at the end of life.

With appropriate organization and cooperation from the government and the health care sector, opioids can be provided even in rural areas, at home, at low cost. The current reality is, however, that few people have access to effective pain medicines because of unnecessary and ill-conceived restrictions at the country level. In 2006 (with only marginal progress since then), 66 percent of the world's population lived in countries that had virtually no consumption of opioids, 10 percent in countries with very low consumption, 3 percent in countries with low consumption, and 4 percent in countries with moderate consumption (Seya and others 2011).

Local Priority Conditions

The essential package can be customized and augmented with locally appropriate and feasible interventions. Examples include improved storage of grain and other foods to avoid fungal contamination that contributes to high liver cancer rates in parts of Africa and Asia (Gelband and others 2015, chapter 8 in this volume; Groopman, Kensler, and Wild 2008); opportunistic screening (especially of high-risk tobacco users) and treatment for precancerous lesions and early-stage oral cancer in India and other countries with high oral cancer burdens (Dikshit and others 2012; Sankaranarayanan and others 2015); screening and treatment for colorectal cancer in Argentina and Uruguay (Goss and others 2013; Rabeneck and others 2015); and elimination of liver flukes (with the drug praziquantel) to prevent bile duct cancer in the limited areas where flukes are common,

Box 1.4

Possible Strategies for Treating Early Breast Cancer in LMICs

By definition, in early breast cancer (stage I or II), all detectable disease can be removed surgically, but micrometastases may remain that, perhaps years later, cause recurrence and death. Adjuvant treatments may be given after surgery to reduce this risk. In high-income countries, most women receiving appropriate treatment for early breast cancer survive their disease (Early Breast Cancer Trialists' Collaborative Group and others 2012). The success rate of breast-conserving surgery (lumpectomy) plus radiotherapy to the conserved breast is about the same as for mastectomy (removal of the entire breast, and perhaps some local lymph nodes) and either can be offered, if safe radiotherapy is available. The most basic surgical procedure for stage II breast cancer is some form of mastectomy (Anderson and others 2015). In low- and middle-income countries (LMICs), for women with early breast cancer, the first requirement is good quality, safe surgery. In low-income countries (LICs), in particular, timely access to safe surgery is a major barrier. In middle-income countries (MICs), where there is generally better population access to surgical services, *quality* cancer surgery is the major surgical concern, particularly adequate resection of the tumor (Dare and others 2015). After technically successful surgery, treatments can be based on estrogen-receptor (ER) status, estimated recurrence risk, and general health (Anderson and others 2015).

The ER status of surgically removed breast cancers can be determined (for about US$10, in India). If the cancer is ER-positive, about five years of endocrine drug therapy substantially reduces the 15-year recurrence risk and is relatively nontoxic. Endocrine drugs, such as tamoxifen or, for post-menopausal women, an aromatase inhibitor (AI) (Early Breast Cancer Trialists' Collaborative Group and others 2015), can be dispensed safely to outpatients and are available as relatively low-cost generics (although even generic tamoxifen costs about US$15 per year in India, and generic AIs currently cost about US$50 per year). Chemotherapy also reduces recurrence but is more toxic and requires more careful medical supervision to ensure safety and efficacy. New drugs, for example, trastuzumab, that target other breast cancer receptors are not at present cost-effective in LMICs.

Relatively simple regimens of generic cytotoxic drugs (for example, four cycles of daunorubicin and cyclophosphamide with drug costs of about $200 in India) should be practicable wherever surgery is practicable (Anderson and others 2015), and could be offered to women who are otherwise in good health but whose disease has already spread from the breast to the local lymph nodes (Early Breast Cancer Trialists' Collaborative Group and others 2012). More effective cytotoxic regimens (for example, with taxanes) would increase toxicity, drug costs, and supervision costs.

Finally, global initiatives might well help to lower the cost of cancer drugs and other commodities, and develop and disseminate standardized resource-appropriate treatment protocols, such as those developed by the Breast Health Global Initiative. The successful global initiative to aid in the diagnosis and treatment of HIV/AIDS provides a model (Piot and Quinn 2013).

or treatment of schistosomiasis to prevent bladder or intestinal cancer in parts of Asia, the Middle East and North Africa, and Sub-Saharan Africa (IARC 1994). Finally, occupational hazards should be monitored and mitigated where necessary, for example, use of power tools on asbestos roofing or insulation, or heavy smoke pollution in houses (IARC 2012).

As important as what to include in a national cancer package is what to exclude. Cancer is notorious for exaggerated claims of causation (for example, nuclear power plants and folic acid) and claims of cure, even of advanced cancers and even within the health care system itself. A guidepost for the former category of claims is IARC's *Monographs on the Evaluation of Carcinogenic Risks to Humans*, which, since 1971, have evaluated more than 900 agents (http://monographs.iarc.fr/index.php). Treating advanced cancers—although a common practice in HICs—is expensive, often painful for patients, and usually futile. Countries should carefully examine the resource requirements and likely success of such treatments in deciding not only which cancers to include in a package, but the appropriate interventions by stage. For advanced cancers with little possibility of cure, palliative care may be the best alternative.

COST-EFFECTIVENESS OF INTERVENTIONS

For most types of cancer, the cost-effectiveness literature for LMICs is slim (Horton and Gauvreau 2015, chapter 16 in this volume): nine studies were identified for breast cancer, two (plus four from high-income Asian countries) for colorectal cancer, one for liver cancer prevention, and none for pediatric cancer. Seventeen studies were sourced from an expert search for cervical cancer, and a recent systematic review of vaccines (Ozawa and others 2012) identified three studies for hepatitis B vaccination. A useful benchmark was to exclude from the essential package those interventions that are not clearly cost-effective in HICs. Most new drug treatments for advanced cancer fall in this category, such as bevacizumab (a monoclonal antibody) for metastatic breast cancer, which, at current prices, does not meet cost-effectiveness criteria in the United Kingdom (Rodgers and others 2011) and other HICs (Dedes and others 2009; Montero and others 2012). Similarly, cetuximab (a monoclonal antibody for metastatic colon and lung cancers) plus irinotecan (a relatively new treatment for colon cancer) are not currently considered cost-effective in the United Kingdom (Tappenden and others 2007).

Excise taxes on tobacco (US$1–US$150 per disability-adjusted life year [DALY] averted) and hepatitis B vaccination (less than US$100/DALY averted) are very cost-effective in all LMICs. Opportunistic cervical cancer screening and treatment of precancerous lesions are likely also to be very cost-effective in all LMICs. The cost-effectiveness of HPV vaccination depends crucially on vaccine cost, but at US$15/per girl vaccinated, HPV vaccination is likely to be very cost-effective in all LMICs. Some aspects of the treatment for early breast cancer are cost-effective wherever breast cancer surgery has been performed (mainly MICs; less than US$150/DALY averted) (figure 1.2).

COSTS OF PACKAGES

To provide per capita cost estimates for an essential package, we used available information on cost combined with demographic information from three large, diverse countries (Brazil, India, and Nigeria) (expressed in 2012 U.S. dollars). Although Nigeria is a lower-middle-income country, we used its demographic structure and lack of existing facilities and human resources to represent the scenario of LICs, mainly in Sub-Saharan Africa.

Figure 1.2 Cost-Effectiveness of Selected Interventions

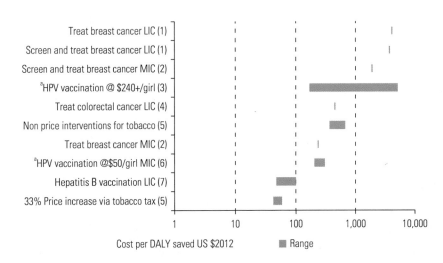

Cost per DALY saved US $2012   ■ Range

Sources: (1) Zelle and others 2012; (2) Salomon and others 2012; (3) Insinga and others 2007; Praditsitthikorn and others 2011; Termrungruanglert and others 2012; (4) Ginsberg and others 2010; (5) Jha and others 2006; (6) Kawai and others 2012; Vanni and others 2012; (7) Prakash 2003; Griffiths, Hutton, and Das Dores Pascal 2005; Kim, Salomon, and Goldie 2007.

Note: Studies used for calculations were from a systematic search, whose findings are available online (annex 16A). Cost-effectiveness has not been calculated for elements of the essential package for which relevant data were entirely lacking. DALY = disability-adjusted life year; HPV = human papillomavirus; LIC = low-income country; MIC = middle-income country; QALY = quality-adjusted life year.

a. Based on a study reporting QALYs, not DALYs (the difference is small when interventions primarily reduce mortality).

To account for training, pathology services, and other system costs, we used a multiplier, equal to 50 percent of the intervention-based costs, drawn from similar costing studies for nutrition (Bhutta and others 2013) and health systems (Rao Seshadri and others 2015). However, we did not include the one-time investment costs for building hospitals, clinics, and other infrastructure that would eventually be needed to support cancer and other clinical services (Gospodarowicz and others 2015; Sloan and Gelband 2007).

The *DCP3* essential package of cancer control interventions would cost roughly an additional US$5.70 per capita in upper-middle-income countries, and US$1.70 per capita in both lower-middle-income countries and LICs (table 1.5). The annual cost of the essential package of cancer services (table 1.6) in 2013 dollars would be about US$13.8 billion, US$4.4 billion, and US$1.4 billion in those groups of countries, respectively. There are obvious caveats on the precision of the costs, including uncertainties of these costs by 2030. Importantly, drug costs can fall substantially as drugs go off patent, and global initiatives could further reduce the prices of key generic drugs and other commodities.

Table 1.5 Approximate Per Capita Marginal Costs of the Essential Package for Low-Income, Lower-Middle-Income, and Upper-Middle-Income Countries

(2012 U.S. dollars)

Intervention	Low-income	Lower-middle-Income	Upper-middle-income
Comprehensive tobacco control measures	0.05	0.07	1.06
Palliative care and pain control	0.05	0.06	0.06
HBV vaccination	0.08	0.04	0.04
Promote early diagnosis and treat early-stage breast cancer	0.43	0.43	1.29
HPV vaccination	0.23	0.23	0.40
Screen and treat precancerous lesions and early-stage cervical cancer	0.26	0.29	0.87
Treat selected childhood cancers	0.03	0.03	0.09
Subtotal	**1.13**	**1.15**	**3.81**
Ancillary services (50% of subtotal)	**0.57**	**0.58**	**1.91**
TOTAL COSTS	**1.70**	**1.73**	**5.72**

Source: Based on online annex 1A and Horton and Gauvreau 2015, annex 16A.
Note: HPV = human papillomavirus; HBV = hepatitis B virus.

Table 1.6 Resource Requirements for the Essential Cancer Intervention Package for LMICs

Expenditures	Low-income	Lower-middle income	Upper-middle income	Total LMICs
Public spending on health as % GDP, 2013	2.0	1.8	3.1	3.0
Total public spending on health in 2013 (US$ billions)	11	89	534	634
Required amount for cancer in 2013 (US$ billions)	1.4	4.4	13.8	19.6
Cancer package as % of total public spending on health in 2013[a]	13.0	4.9	2.6	3.1

Note: GDP = gross domestic product; LMICs = low- and middle-income countries.
a. Based on spending data from World Bank 2014b.

AFFORDABILITY AND DOMESTIC FINANCING OF ESSENTIAL CANCER SERVICES

The total estimated annual cost of the essential package of cancer interventions for all LMICs is about $20 billion dollars (2013 U.S. dollars). A useful metric is the cost of the package as a proportion of current total public spending on health. This is 2.6 percent in UMICs, 5 percent in lower-middle-income countries, and 13 percent in LICs. By comparison, HICs devote 3–7 percent of their total health spending to cancer control (OECD 2013). Most LMICs allocate far less; cancer currently accounts for about 1 percent of health spending (public and private) in Brazil and India, and 2 percent in China and Mexico (Goss and others 2013; IARC 2014; Knaul and others 2011).

Financing for cancer control will have to come mainly from national health care budgets, particularly in MICs, where rising incomes are enabling expansion of public financing for health (Jamison and others 2013; Knaul and others 2015, chapter 17 in this volume). South Africa, for example, has assessed which interventions it might include in an expanded national health insurance package (Shisana and others 2006) and similar work is underway in India (Jha and Laxminarayan 2009; Rao Seshadri and others 2015). In LICs, it would be inappropriate for governments to shift to spending 13 percent of their health care dollars on cancer. External assistance will be needed in those countries to establish an expansion path for cancer control.

A clear principle to adopt is the eventual goal of coverage for every person—even if coverage expands gradually—but not coverage of everything (WHO 2000), since poorly conceived plans may provide coverage of more expensive treatments for a few, while missing the opportunity to expand cost-effective population coverage. Public finance is not necessarily synonymous with public delivery (Musgrove 1996). Properly regulated private hospitals, facilities, and providers can be contracted to deliver cancer control interventions (Jha and Laxminarayan 2009).

Several countries in Latin America are already expanding their health insurance systems from coverage limited to occupational groups or selected vulnerable groups, to more comprehensive coverage (Goss and others 2013). However, for some lower-middle-income countries and most LICs, substantial increases in public finance for health, paired with economic growth or external assistance, would be needed to adopt a full package of interventions (Jamison and others 2013). Even those countries could benefit from considering the future cancer burden, costs, and financing to project a future cancer control plan. Higher tobacco taxes are the most important single cancer prevention intervention at a practical level, and a tripling of the excise tax on tobacco (thereby approximately doubling prices) could mobilize an additional US$100 billion worldwide in annual revenue (Jha and Peto 2014). For all LMICs, the epidemiologic dividend that accrues from a decreased burden of infectious disease should generate savings that can be spent on NCD control (Jamison and others 2011).

IMPLEMENTATION CHALLENGES FOR THE ESSENTIAL PACKAGE

Within the essential package, some aspects of interventions may be implemented reasonably quickly, notably tobacco control measures that involve taxation and regulation (Jha and others 2015) and policy changes to increase access to opioids (although establishing nationwide programs and training a full cadre of providers may take years) (Cleary, Gelband, and Wagner 2015). Some interventions can be scaled to reasonably high coverage quickly with existing infrastructure, such as school-based HPV vaccination for adolescent girls, or hepatitis B vaccination for newborns. By contrast, other interventions will need expanded clinical access, most notably surgical treatment of early-stage breast cancer and cervical cancer (Dare and others 2015, chapter 13 in this volume). Increasing surgical capacity is relatively expensive but feasible from an organizational perspective, especially if existing district hospitals can be strengthened (Mock and others 2015) (paired with central cancer clinical expertise). When high quality surgery becomes available, early-stage, resectable tumors of various types, in addition to breast and cervical lesions, can be removed. Expanding chemotherapy treatment requires an extensive network of laboratories and follow-up, which in LICs and lower-middle-income countries is currently feasible only in urban areas. Scaling up radiotherapy requires large capital expenditures, and substantial attention to clinical guidelines and treatment protocols as well as safety assurances (Jaffray and Gospodarowicz 2015, chapter 14 in this volume).

Particularly for LICs where minimal cancer services exist in the public sector, the needed expertise and resources for cancer treatment will require years of steady investment to expand physical and human infrastructure. Elements that are missing or in short supply in LMICs (Bray and others 2014; Dikshit and others 2012; Gospodarowicz and others 2015) include trained professionals in oncology and relevant disciplines; appropriately-equipped facilities, including radiotherapy facilities, pathology services, and other laboratory testing services (for example, estrogen-receptor testing for breast cancer tissue; box 1.3); supplies, including chemotherapy drugs; geographic access to facilities with affordable cancer services, including surgery; public awareness of the availability and effectiveness of cancer control interventions; and cancer incidence and cause-of-death data. As more people are successfully treated and live for many years, survivorship services (for example, rehabilitation, remedies for physical deficits caused by treatment, limiting the social stigma associated with having had cancer, and follow-up for recurrence) will increase in importance (Hewitt, Greenfield, and Stovall 2005), but costs for survivorship are not included in our estimates.

The package emphasizes treatment for *early-stage* cervical and breast cancers (and similarly, early stages for other cancers included in specific country plans), because cure rates are substantially higher than they are for more advanced cancers. Surgery is particularly important, as surgery alone is curative for many early cancers. Although locally appropriate cervix screening, which will identify many precancers and early cancers, is included in the package, there is no corresponding screening intervention for breast cancer. Even without screening, however, LMICs might be able to achieve a somewhat earlier stage of presentation of common cancers by making affordable treatment available and communicating this to people. Historical evidence from HICs, illustrated by stage-shifting for cervix cancer in Sweden before organized screening began around 1960, supports this approach (Pontén and others 1995).

Cancer treatment can be organized through existing medical facilities (particularly district hospitals) or through specialized centers, but the key is to ensure good links between facilities (Sloan and Gelband 2007), which requires a centralized locus of control and the ability to adjust elements of the system that are not working to the benefit of patients (Gospodarowicz and others 2015). An example from childhood cancer illustrates this well. All children with cancer in Honduras (population 8 million) are treated in two centers that collaborate and communicate closely (Metzger and others 2003). In contrast, children with cancer in Colombia (population 48 million) are treated in more than 150 health care institutions of varying size, with little to no communication between centers (Gupta and others 2015). This adversely affects patient outcomes and costs. India, population 1.3 billion, faces more challenging coordination of care, but is building a National Cancer Grid (Pramesh, Badwe, and Sinha 2014) linking non-specialist hospitals to specialist cancer centers and providing them with current treatment protocols.

Building and improving a nation's cancer control capacity requires attention to the quality of services, from pathology and diagnosis to surgery, chemotherapy, radiotherapy, and palliative care (Gospodarowicz and others 2015). Upgrading hospitals to provide basic cancer surgical services (Mock and others 2015), developing cancer referral networks, tracking service performance, integrating the delivery of different types of services, and ensuring that financial flows accompany services are also required.

GLOBAL INITIATIVES FOR CANCER CONTROL

Only 1 percent of the US$30 billion development assistance for health in 2010 was allocated to NCDs, only a portion of which was for cancer (IHME 2012). NCD funding is likely to increase somewhat with increasing global recognition of the importance of NCDs. However, it is unlikely that significant global funds will be allocated to support national health systems to deal with cancer. As additional funding becomes available, we suggest three priorities for international support.

1. *Lower the costs to countries of key inputs for the essential package and other cost-effective interventions, such as HPV and other vaccines, cancer drugs (including generics), screening tests (for example, HPV tests), laboratory reagents and other test commodities, surgery, radiotherapy machines, and other relevant goods.* The Global Fund for AIDS, TB and Malaria; Gavi; the Clinton Health Access Initiative; and other international partnerships have developed mechanisms to reduce the price of a range of global commodities relevant to infectious disease control, utilizing economies of scale (relevant for purchases of drugs or radiotherapy machines), subsidies for reputable and affordable medicines, advanced market commitments, and similar innovations (Piot and Quinn 2013). Similar efforts for cancer are possible, for example, as has been proposed for radiotherapy by the Global Task Force on Radiotherapy for Cancer Control (Union for International Cancer Control [UICC]).

2. *Expand technical assistance in cancer control.* International and regional networks exist for many aspects of cancer care, such as treatment guidelines; networks on breast, cervical, and colorectal cancer screening; childhood cancer treatment and research; and palliative care. Other support modalities, for example, twinning institutions, have typically involved institutions in HICs and LICs (North-South collaborations), but as in other areas, the opportunities should grow to add South-South collaborations. Within countries, peer-based and professional standards of cancer care and reporting of outcomes and performance for various facilities

can improve quality of care (Peabody and others 2006; Varmus and Trimble 2011).

3. *Support for research* is a worthwhile investment for overseas developmental assistance. Research priorities include tracking national cancer burdens, clinical trials, and implementation science, including research on delivery systems; cancer epidemiology and biology; widely practicable, low-cost technologies; and economics (Trimble and others 2015, chapter 15 in this volume).

BENEFITS OF EXPANDED CANCER CONTROL

Despite substantial challenges in most LMICs, appreciable reductions in the cancer burden might well be possible by 2030, with even greater reductions by 2050 and beyond (Norheim and others 2014), particularly through treating common cancers that are detected early, tobacco control that encourages widespread adult smoking cessation, and vaccination against hepatitis B and HPV.

Global cancer death rates at ages 0–69 years were declining at about 10 percent per decade during 2000–10. If this were to continue, then from 2010 to 2030 cancer death rates will fall by almost 20 percent. A decrease of one-third in global cancer death rates by 2030, as proposed recently (Norheim and others 2014), would require faster progress in LMICs, particularly marked increases in tobacco cessation. The WHO estimates that tobacco control, HPV and HBV vaccination, and opportunistic cervical cancer screening could avoid about 6 percent of cancer deaths by 2030 (or about 200,000 deaths before age 70 years annually). The *DCP3* essential package could achieve greater reductions. If, as expected, the availability of treatment shifts diagnoses for common, treatable cancers to earlier stages, further lives could be saved. The benefits of pain relief are not measured in lives saved, but are important.

Finally, cancer control contributes to reduced inequality in health, providing relatively larger benefits to the poor. In China, increased tobacco taxes and access to cervical cancer prevention, such as screening and HPV vaccination, would disproportionately benefit those in the lowest income quintile by reducing deaths and through better financial risk protection from catastrophic health expenditures (Levin and others 2015, chapter 18 in this volume; Verguet and others 2015).

Cancer control is often approached with pessimism, but practicable, deliberate, cost-effective steps can enable many countries to reduce substantially by 2030 the suffering and premature death from cancer, with much greater improvements by 2050.

NOTES

Maps and figures in this chapter are based on incidence and mortality estimates for ages 0–69, consistent with reporting in all *DCP3* volumes. The discussion of burden (including risk factors) and interventions, however, includes all ages unless otherwise noted.

The World Bank classifies countries according to four income groupings. Income is measured using gross national income per capita, in U.S. dollars, converted from local currency using the World Bank Atlas method. Classifications as of July 2014 are as follows:

- Low-income countries = US$1,045 or less in 2013
- Middle-income countries are subdivided:
  - Lower-middle-income = US$1,046–US$4,125
  - Upper-middle-income = US$4,126–US$12,745
- High-income countries = US$12,746 or more

DCP3 CANCER AUTHOR GROUP

Issac Adewole, Hemantha Amarasinghe, Benjamin O. Anderson, Federico G. Antillon, Samira Asma, Rifat Atun, Rajendra A. Badwe, Freddie Bray, Frank J. Chaloupka, Ann Chao, Chien-Jen Chen, Wendong Chen, James Cleary, Anna J. Dare, Anil D'Cruz, Lynette Denny, Craig Earle, Silvia Franceschi, Cindy L. Gauvreau, Hellen Gelband, Ophira M. Ginsburg, Mary K. Gospodarowicz, Thomas Gross, Prakash C. Gupta, Sumit Gupta, Andrew Hall, Mhamed Harif, Rolando Herrero, Susan Horton, Scott C. Howard, Stephen P. Hunger, Andre Ilbawi, Trijn Israels, David A. Jaffray, Dean T. Jamison, Prabhat Jha, Newell Johnson, Jamal Khader, Jane J. Kim, Felicia Knaul, Carol Levin, Joseph Lipscomb, W. Thomas London, Mary MacLennan, Katherine A. McGlynn, Monika L. Metzger, Raul Murillo, Zachary Olson, Sherif Omar, Krishna Palipudi, C. S. Pramesh, You-Lin Qiao, Linda Rabeneck, Preetha Rajaraman, Kunnambath Ramadas, Chintanie Ramasundarahettige, Timothy Rebbeck, Carlos Rodriguez-Galindo, Rengaswamy Sankaranarayanan, Monisha Sharma, Ju-Fang Shi, Isabelle Soerjomataram, Lisa Stevens, Sujha Subramanian, Richard Sullivan, Terrence Sullivan, David Thomas, Edward L. Trimble, Joann Trypuc, Stéphane Verguet, Judith Wagner, Shao-Ming Wang, Christopher P. Wild, Pooja Yerramilli, Cheng-Har Yip, Ayda Yurekli, Witold Zatoński, Ann G. Zauber, and Fang-Hui Zhao.

REFERENCES

Allemani, C., H. K. Weir, H. Carreira, R. Harewood, D. Spika, and others. 2015. "Global Surveillance of Cancer Survival 1995–2009: Analysis of Individual Data for

25,676,887 Patients from 279 Population-Based Registries in 67 Countries (CONCORD-2)." *The Lancet* 385 (9972): 977–1010. doi:10.1016/S0140-6736(14)62038-9.

Anderson, B. O., E. Cazap, N. S. El Saghir, C. H. Yip, H. M. Khaled, and others. 2011. "Optimisation of Breast Cancer Management in Low-Resource and Middle-Resource Countries: Executive Summary of the Breast Health Global Initiative Consensus, 2010." *The Lancet Oncology* (4): 387–98. doi:10.1016/S1470-2045(11)70031-6.

Anderson, B. O., J. Lipscomb, R. H. Murillo, and D. R. Thomas. 2015. "Breast Cancer." In *Disease Control Priorities*: Volume 3, *Cancer*, edited by H. Gelband, P. Jha, R. Sankaranarayanan, and S. Horton. 3rd ed. Washington, DC: World Bank.

Bhutta, Z. A., J. K. Das, A. Rizvi, M. F. Gaffey, N. Walker, and others. 2013. "Evidence-Based Interventions for Improvement of Maternal and Child Nutrition: What Can Be Done and At What Cost?" *The Lancet* 382 (9890): 452–77. doi:10.1016/S0140-6736(13)60996-4.

Bray, F., and I. Soerjomataram. 2015. "The Changing Global Burden of Cancer." In *Disease Control Priorities*: Volume 3, *Cancer*, edited by H. Gelband, P. Jha, R. Sankaranarayanan, and S. Horton. 3rd ed. Washington, DC: World Bank.

Bray, F., A. Znaor, P. Cueva, A. Korir, R. Swaminathan, and others. 2014. "Planning and Developing Population-Based Cancer Registration in Low- and Middle-Income Settings." Technical Publications, International Agency for Research on Cancer.

Brown, M. L., S. J. Goldie, G. Draisma, J. Harford, and J. Lipscomb. 2006. "Health Service Interventions for Cancer Control in Developing Countries." In *Disease Control Priorities in Developing Countries*, edited by D. T. Jamison, J. Breman, A. R. Measham, G. Alleyne, M. Claeson, and others. 2nd ed. New York: Oxford University Press and World Bank.

Cleary, J., H. Gelband, and J. Wagner. 2015. "Cancer Pain Relief." In *Disease Control Priorities*: Volume 3, *Cancer*, edited by H. Gelband, P. Jha, R. Sankaranarayanan, and S. Horton. 3rd ed. Washington, DC: World Bank.

Commission on Macroeconomics and Health. 2001. *Macroeconomics and Health: Investing in Health for Economic Development.* Geneva: World Health Organization.

Dare, A. J., B. O. Anderson, R. Sullivan, C. S. Pramesh, C.-H. Yip, and others. 2015. "Surgical Services for Cancer Care." In *Disease Control Priorities*: Volume 3, *Cancer*, edited by H. Gelband, P. Jha, R. Sankaranarayanan, and S. Horton. 3rd ed. Washington, DC: World Bank.

Dedes, K. J., K. Matter-Walstra, M. Schwenkglenks, B. C. Pestalozzi, D. Fink, and others. 2009. "Bevacizumab in Combination with Paclitaxel for HER-2 Negative Metastatic Breast Cancer: An Economic Evaluation." *European Journal of Cancer* 45 (8): 1397–406. doi:10.1016/J.Ejca.2008.12.016.

Denny, L., R. Herrero, C. Levin, and J. J. Kim. 2015. "Cervical Cancer." In *Disease Control Priorities*: Volume 3, *Cancer*, edited by H. Gelband, P. Jha, R. Sankaranarayanan, and S. Horton. 3rd ed. Washington, DC: World Bank.

Dikshit, R., P. C. Gupta, C. Ramasundarahettige, V. Gajalakshmi, L. Aleksandrowicz, and others. 2012. "Cancer Mortality in India: A Nationally Representative Survey." *The Lancet* 379 (9828): 1807–16. doi:10.1016/S0140-6736(12)60358-4.

Early Breast Cancer Trialists' Collaborative Group, Writing Committee, R. Peto, C. Davies, J. Godwin, R. Gray, and others. 2012. "Comparisons between Different Polychemotherapy Regimens for Early Breast Cancer: Meta-Analyses of Long-Term Outcome among 100,000 Women in 123 Randomised Trials." *The Lancet* 379 (9814): 432–44. doi:10.1016/S0140-6736(11)61625-5.

———. Forthcoming. "Aromatase Inhibitors vs. Tamoxifen in Early Breast Cancer: Patient-Level Meta-Analysis of the Randomised Trials." *The Lancet.*

Ferlay, J., I. Soerjomataram, R. Dikshit, S. Eser, C. Mathers, and others. 2015. "Cancer Incidence and Mortality Worldwide: Sources, Methods and Major Patterns in GLOBOCAN 2012." *International Journal of Cancer* 136 (5): E359–86. doi:10.1002/Ijc.29210.

Foley, K. M., J. L. Wagner, D. E. Joranson, and H. Gelband. 2006. "Pain Control for People with Cancer and AIDS." In *Disease Control Priorities in Developing Countries*, edited by D. T. Jamison, J. Breman, A. R. Measham, G. Alleyne, M. Claeson, and others. 2nd ed. New York: Oxford University Press and World Bank.

Gavi. 2013. "Millions of Girls in Developing Countries To Be Protected against Cervical Cancer Thanks to New HPV Vaccine Deals." Gavi, the Vaccine Alliance.

Gelband, H., C.-J. Chen, W. Chen, S. Franceschi, A. Hall, and others. 2015. "Liver Cancer." In *Disease Control Priorities*: Volume 3, *Cancer*, edited by H. Gelband, P. Jha, R. Sankaranarayanan, and S. Horton. 3rd ed. Washington, DC: World Bank.

Ginsberg, G. M., S. S. Lim, J. A. Lauer, B. P. Johns, and C. R. Sepulveda. 2010. "Prevention, Screening and Treatment of Colorectal Cancer: A Global and Regional Generalized Cost Effectiveness Analysis." *Cost Effectiveness and Resource Allocation* 8: 2. doi:10.1186/1478-7547-8-2.

Goldie, S. J., L. Gaffikin, J. D. Goldhaber-Fiebert, A. Gordillo-Tobar, C. Levin, and others. 2005. "Cost-Effectiveness of Cervical-Cancer Screening in Five Developing Countries." *New England Journal of Medicine* 353 (20): 2158–68. doi:10.1056/Nejmsa044278.

Gospodarowicz, M. K., J. Trypuc, A. D'Cruz, J. Khader, S. Omar, and others. 2015. "Cancer Services and the Comprehensive Cancer Care Center." In *Disease Control Priorities*: Volume 3, *Cancer*, edited by H. Gelband, P. Jha, R. Sankaranarayanan, and S. Horton. 3rd ed. Washington, DC: World Bank.

Goss, Paul E., Brittany L. Lee, T. Badovinac-Crnjevic, K. Strasser-Weippl, Y. Chavarri-Guerra, and others. 2013. "Planning Cancer Control in Latin America and the Caribbean." *The Lancet Oncology* 14 (5): 391–436.

Greenberg, D., C. Earle, C. H. Fang, A. Eldar-Lissai, and P. J. Neumann. 2010. "When Is Cancer Care Cost-Effective? A Systematic Overview of Cost-Utility Analyses in Oncology." *Journal of the National Cancer Institute* 102 (2): 82–8. doi:10.1093/Jnci/Djp472.

Griffiths, U. K., G. Hutton, and E. Das Dores Pascoal. 2005. "The Cost-Effectiveness of Introducing Hepatitis B Vaccine into Infant Immunization Services in Mozambique."

Health Policy Planning 20 (1): 50–59. doi:10.1093/Heapol /Czi006.

Groopman, J. D., T. W. Kensler, and C. P. Wild. 2008. "Protective Interventions to Prevent Aflatoxin-Induced Carcinogenesis in Developing Countries." *Annual Review of Public Health* 29: 187–203. http://www.ncbi.nlm.nih .gov/pubmed/17914931.

Gupta, S., S. C. Howard, S. P. Hunger, F. G. Antillon, M. L. Metzger, and others. 2015. "Childhood Cancers." In *Disease Control Priorities*: Volume 3, *Cancer*, edited by H. Gelband, P. Jha, R. Sankaranarayanan, and S. Horton. 3rd ed. Washington, DC: World Bank.

Gupta, S., R. Rivera-Luna, R. C. Ribeiro, and S. C. Howard. 2014. "Pediatric Oncology as the Next Global Child Health Priority: The Need for National Childhood Cancer Strategies in Low- and Middle-Income Countries." *PloS Med* 11 (6): E1001656. doi:10.1371/Journal.Pmed.1001656.

Hamid, S. A., S. M. Ahsan, and A. Begum. 2014. "Disease-Specific Impoverishment Impact of Out-of-Pocket Payments for Health Care: Evidence from Rural Bangladesh." *Applied Health Economics and Health Policy* 12 (4): 421–33. doi:10.1007/S40258-014-0100-2.

Hewitt, M., S. Greenfield, and E. Stovall. 2005. *From Cancer Patient to Cancer Survivor: Lost in Transition*. Washington, DC: Institute of Medicine and National Research Council.

Hoang Lan, N., W. Laohasiriwong, J. F. Stewart, N. D. Tung, and P. C. Coyte. 2013. "Cost of Treatment for Breast Cancer in Central Vietnam." *Global Health Action* 6: 18872. doi:10.3402/Gha.V6i0.18872.

Horton, S., and C. L. Gauvreau. 2015. "Cancer in Low- and Middle-Income Countries: An Economic Overview." In *Disease Control Priorities*: Volume 3, *Cancer*, edited by H. Gelband, P. Jha, R. Sankaranayanan, and S. Horton. 3rd ed. Washington, DC: World Bank.

IARC (International Agency for Research on Cancer). 1994. "Mongraphs on the Evaluation of Carcinogenic Risks to Humans: Volume 61, Schistosomes, Liver Flukes and *Helicobacter Pylori*." Lyon, IARC, France.

———. 2012. "Mongraphs on the Evaluation of Carcinogenic Risks to Humans: Volume 100." Lyon, IARC, France.

———. 2014. "World Cancer Report 2014." In *World Cancer Report*, edited by B. W. Stewart and C. P. Wild. Geneva: IARC.

IHME (Institute for Health Metrics and Evaluation). 2012. *Financing Global Health 2012: The End of the Golden Age?* Seattle: IHME.

Ilbawi, A. M., E. M. Einterz, and D. Nkusu. 2013. "Obstacles to Surgical Services in a Rural Cameroonian District Hospital." *World Journal of Surgery* 37 (6): 1208–15. doi:10.1007 /S00268-013-1977-X.

Insinga, R. P., E. J. Dasbach, E. H. Elbasha, A. Puig, and L. M. Reynales-Shigematsu. 2007. "Cost-Effectiveness of Quadrivalent Human Papillomavirus (HPV) Vaccination in Mexico: A Transmission Dynamic Model-Based Evaluation." *Vaccine* 26 (1): 128–39. doi:10.1016/J .Vaccine.2007.10.056.

Jaffray, D. A., and M. K. Gospodarowicz. 2015. "Radiation Therapy for Cancer." In *Disease Control Priorities*: Volume 3,

Cancer, edited by H. Gelband, P. Jha, R. Sankaranarayanan, and S. Horton. 3rd ed. Washington, DC: World Bank.

Jamison, D. T., J. G. Breman, A. R. Measham, G. Alleyne, M. Claeson, and others. 2006. *Disease Control Priorities in Developing Countries*. 2nd ed. Washington, DC: Oxford University Press and World Bank.

Jamison, D. T. 2015. "Disease Control Priorities, 3rd edition: Improving Health and Reducing Poverty." *The Lancet* Feb 4. doi: 10.1016/S0140-6736(15)60097-6. doi: 10.1016/ s0140-6736(15)60097-6

Jamison, D. T., P. Jha, V. Malhotra, and S. Verguet. 2011. "The 20th Century Transformation of Human Health: Its Magnitude and Value." In *How Much Have Global Problems Cost The World? A Scorecard From 1900–2050*, edited by B. Lomborg. Cambridge, U.K:. Cambridge University Press.

Jamison, D. T., W. Mosley, A. R. Measham, and J. Bobadilla, eds. 1993. *Disease Control Priorities in Developing Countries*. 1st ed. New York: Oxford University Press.

Jamison, D. T., L. H. Summers, G. Alleyne, K. J. Arrow, S. Berkley, and others. 2013. "Global Health 2035: A World Converging within a Generation." *The Lancet* 382 (9908): 1898–955. doi:10.1016/S0140-6736(13)62105-4.

Jha, P. 2009. "Avoidable Global Cancer Deaths and Total Deaths from Smoking." *Nature Reviews Cancer* 9 (9): 655–64. doi:10.1038/Nrc2703.

———. 2015. "Deaths and Taxes: Stronger Global Tobacco Control by 2025." *The Lancet* 385 (9972): 918–20. doi:10.1016/S0140-6736(15)60464-0.

Jha, P., F. J. Chaloupka, J. Moore, V. Gajalakshmi, P. C. Gupta, and others. 2006. "Tobacco Addiction." In *Disease Control Priorities in Developing Countries*, edited by D. T. Jamison, J. G. Breman, A. R. Measham, G. Alleyne, M. Claeson, and others. 2nd ed. Washington, DC: Oxford University Press and World Bank.

Jha, P., and R. Laxminarayan. 2009. *Choosing Health: An Entitlement for All Indians*. Toronto: Centre for Global Health Research.

Jha, P., M. Maclennan, A. Yurekli, C. Ramasundarahettige, K. Palipudi, and others. 2015. "Global Hazards of Tobacco, Benefits of Cessation and of Taxation of Tobacco." In *Disease Control Priorities*: Volume 3, *Cancer*, edited by H. Gelband, P. Jha, R. Sankaranarayanan, and S. Horton. 3rd ed. Washington, DC: World Bank.

Jha, P., and R. Peto. 2014. "Global Effects of Smoking, of Quitting, and of Taxing Tobacco." *New England Journal of Medicine* 370 (1): 60–68. doi:10.1056/Nejmra1308383.

John, R. M., H. Y. Sung, W. B. Max, and H. Ross. 2011. "Counting 15 Million More Poor in India, Thanks to Tobacco." *Tobacco Control* 20 (5): 349–52. doi:10.1136 /Tc.2010.040089.

Kawai, K., G. T. De Araujo, M. Fonseca, M. Pillsbury, and P. K. Singhal. 2012. "Estimated Health and Economic Impact of Quadrivalent HPV (Types 6/11/16/18) Vaccination in Brazil Using a Transmission Dynamic Model." *BMC Infectious Diseases* 12: 250. doi:10.1186/1471-2334-12-250.

Kim, S. Y., J. A. Salomon, and S. J. Goldie. 2007. "Economic Evaluation of Hepatitis B Vaccination in Low-Income

Countries: Using Cost-Effectiveness Affordability Curves." *Bulletin of the World Health Organization* 85 (11): 833–42.

Knaul, F. M., E. Gonzalez-Pier, O. Gomez-Dantes, D. Garcia-Junco, H. Arreola-Ornelas, and others. 2012. "The Quest for Universal Health Coverage: Achieving Social Protection for All in Mexico." *The Lancet* 380 (9849): 1259–79. doi:10.1016/S0140-6736(12)61068-X.

Knaul, F. M., J. R. Gralow, R. Atun, and A. Bhadalia, eds. 2011. *Closing the Cancer Divide: An Equity Imperative.* Cambridge, MA: Harvard Global Equity Initiative and Harvard University Press.

Knaul, F., S. Horton, P. Yerramilli, H. Gelband, and R. Atun. 2015. "Financing Cancer Care in Low-Resource Settings." In *Disease Control Priorities*: Volume 3, *Cancer*, edited by H. Gelband, P. Jha, R. Sankaranarayanan, and S. Horton. 3rd ed. Washington, DC: World Bank.

Levin, C. E., M. Sharma, Z. Olson, S. Verguet, J. F. Shi, and others. 2015. "An Extended Cost-Effectiveness Analysis of Publicly Financed HPV Vaccination to Prevent Cervical Cancer in China." In *Disease Control Priorities*: Volume 3, *Cancer*, edited by H. Gelband, P. Jha, R. Sankaranarayanan, and S. Horton. 3rd ed. Washington, DC: World Bank.

Mallath, M. K., D. G. Taylor, R. A. Badwe, G. K. Rath, V. Shanta, and others. 2014. "The Growing Burden of Cancer in India: Epidemiology and Social Context." *The Lancet Oncology* 15 (6): E205–12. doi:10.1016/S1470-2045(14)70115-9.

Metzger, M. L., S. C. Howard, L. C. Fu, A. Pena, R. Stefan, and others. 2003. "Outcome of Childhood Acute Lymphoblastic Leukaemia in Resource-Poor Countries." *The Lancet* 362 (9385): 706–08. doi:10.1016/S0140-6736(03)14228-6.

Mock, C. N., P. Donkor, A. Gawande, D. T. Jamison, M. E. Kruk, and others. 2015. "Essential Surgery: Key Messages from Disease Control Priorities, (third edition)." *The Lancet* (Feb 4. pii: S0140-6736(15)60091-5.). doi:10.1016/S0140-6736(15)60091-5.

Montero, A. J., K. Avancha, S. Gluck, and G. Lopes. 2012. "A Cost-Benefit Analysis of Bevacizumab in Combination with Paclitaxel in the First-Line Treatment of Patients with Metastatic Breast Cancer." *Breast Cancer Research and Treatment* 132 (2): 747–51. doi:10.1007/S10549-011-1919-Y.

Monteiro, C. A., T. M. Cavalcante, E. C. Moura, R. M. Claro, and C. L. Szwarcwald. 2007. "Population-Based Evidence of a Strong Decline in the Prevalence of Smokers in Brazil (1989–2003)." *Bulletin of the World Health Organization* 85 (7): 527–34.

Musgrove, P. 1996. "Public and Private Roles in Health: Theory and Financing Patterns." Health, Nutrition and Population Discussion Paper. World Bank, Washington, DC.

Norheim, O. F., P. Jha, K. Admasu, T. Godal, R. J. Hum, and others. 2014. "Avoiding 40% of the Premature Deaths in Each Country, 2010–30: Review of National Mortality Trends to Help Quantify the UN Sustainable Development Goal for Health." *The Lancet* 385 (9964): 239–52. doi:10.1016/S0140-6736(14)61591-9.

OECD (Organisation for Economic Co-Operation and Development). 2013. *Cancer Care: Assuring Quality to Improve Survival.* Health Policy Studies, OECD.

Ozawa, S., A. Mirelman, M. L. Stack, D. G. Walker, and O. S. Levine. 2012. "Cost-Effectiveness and Economic Benefits of Vaccines in Low- and Middle-Income Countries: A Systematic Review." *Vaccine* 31 (1): 96–108. doi:10.1016/J.Vaccine.2012.10.103.

Peabody, J. W., M. M. Taguiwalo, D. A. Robalino, and J. Frenk. 2006. "Improving the Quality of Care in Developing Countries." In *Disease Control Priorities in Developing Countries*, edited by D. T. Jamison, J. Breman, A. R. Measham, G. Alleyne, M. Claeson, and others. 2nd ed. New York: Oxford University Press and World Bank.

Piot, P., and T. C. Quinn. 2013. "Response to the AIDS Pandemic: A Global Health Model." *New England Journal of Medicine* 368 (23): 2210–18. doi:10.1056/Nejmra1201533.

Pontén, J., H.-O. Adami, R. Bergstrom, J. Dillner, L-G. Friberg, and others. 1995. "Strategies for Global Control of Cervical Cancer." *International Journal of Cancer* 60: 1–26.

Praditsitthikorn, N., Y. Teerawattananon, S. Tantivess, S. Limwattananon, A. Riewpaiboon, and others. 2011. "Economic Evaluation of Policy Options for Prevention and Control of Cervical Cancer in Thailand." *Pharmacoeconomics* 29 (9): 781–806. doi:10.2165/11586560-000000000-00000.

Prakash, C. 2003. "Crucial Factors that Influence Cost-Effectiveness of Universal Hepatitis B Immunization in India." *International Journal of Technology Assessment in Health Care* 19 (1): 28–40.

Pramesh, C., R. Badwe, and R. Sinha. 2014. "The National Cancer Grid of India." *Indian Journal of Medical and Paediatric Oncology* 35 (3): 226–27. doi:10.4103/0971-5851.142040.

Rabeneck, L., S. Horton, A. G. Zauber, and C. Earle. 2015. "Colorectal Cancer." In *Disease Control Priorities*: Volume 3, *Cancer*, edited by H. Gelband, P. Jha, R. Sankaranarayanan, and S. Horton. 3rd ed. Washington, DC: World Bank.

Rao Seshadri, S., P. Jha, P. Sati, C. Gauvreau, U. Ram, and others. 2015. *Karnataka's Roadmap to Improved Health: Cost Effective Solutions to Address Priority Diseases, Reduce Poverty and Increase Economic Growth.* Report, Azim Premji University, Bangalore, India.

Rodgers, M., M. Soares, D. Epstein, H. Yang, D. Fox, and others. 2011. "Bevacizumab in Combination with a Taxane for the First-Line Treatment of HER2-Negative Metastatic Breast Cancer." *Health Technology Assessment* 15 (Suppl 1): 1–12. doi:10.3310/Hta15suppl1/01.

Salomon, J. A., N. Carvalho, C. Gutierrez-Delgado, R. Orozco, A. Mancuso, and others. 2012. "Intervention Strategies to Reduce the Burden of Non-Communicable Diseases in Mexico: Cost Effectiveness Analysis." *BMJ* 344: E355. doi:10.1136/Bmj.E355.

Sankaranarayanan, R., B. M. Nene, S. S. Shastri, K. Jayant, R. Muwonge, and others. 2009. "HPV Screening for Cervical Cancer in Rural India." *New England Journal of Medicine* 360 (14): 1385–94. doi:10.1056/Nejmoa0808516.

Sankaranarayanan, R., K. Ramadas, H. Amarasinghe, S. Subramanian, and N. Johnson. 2015. "Oral Cancer." In *Disease Control Priorities*: Volume 3, *Cancer*, edited by H. Gelband, P. Jha, R. Sankaranarayanan, and S. Horton. 3rd ed. Washington, DC: World Bank.

Seya, M. J., S. F. Gelders, O. U. Achara, B. Milani, and W. K. Scholten. 2011. "A First Comparison between the Consumption of and the Need for Opioid Analgesics at Country, Regional, and Global Levels." *Journal of Pain & Palliative Care Pharmacotherapy* 25 (1): 6–18. doi:10.3109/15360288.2010.536307.

Shisana, O., T. Rehle, J. Louw, N. Zungu-Dirwayi, P. Dana, and others. 2006. "Public Perceptions on National Health Insurance: Moving towards Universal Health Coverage in South Africa." *South Africa Medical Journal* 96 (9): 814–18.

Sloan, F. A., and H. Gelband. 2007. *Cancer Control Opportunities in Low- and Middle-Income Countries*. Washington, DC: National Academy Press.

Sullivan, T., R. Sullivan, and O. M. Ginsburg. 2015. "Screening for Cancer: Considerations for LMICs." In *Disease Control Priorities*: Volume 3, *Cancer*, edited by H. Gelband, P. Jha, R. Sankaranarayanan, and S. Horton. 3rd ed. Washington, DC: World Bank.

Tappenden, P., R. Jones, S. Paisley, and C. Carroll. 2007. "Systematic Review and Economic Evaluation of Bevacizumab and Cetuximab for the Treatment of Metastatic Colorectal Cancer." *Health Technology Assessment* 11 (12): 1–128: III–IV.

Termrungruanglert, W., P. Havanond, N. Khemapech, S. Lertmaharit, S. Pongpanich, and others. 2012. "Model for Predicting the Burden and Cost of Treatment in Cervical Cancer and HPV-Related Diseases in Thailand." *European Journal of Gynaecological Oncology* 33 (4): 391–94.

Trimble, E. L., P. Rajaraman, A. Chao, T. Gross, C. Levin, and others. 2015. "Cancer Research: The Need for National Commitment." In *Disease Control Priorities*: Volume 3, *Cancer*, edited by H. Gelband, P. Jha, R. Sankaranarayanan, and S. Horton. 3rd ed. Washington, DC: World Bank.

UICC (Union for International Cancer Control). *Global Task Force on Radiotherapy for Cancer Control*. http://gtfrcc.org/.

UN (United Nations). 2015. *Sustainable Development Goals*. http://sustainabledevelopment.un.org/?menu=1300.

UNPD (United Nations Population Division). 2012. *World Population Prospects: The 2012 Revision*. New York: UNPD.

U.S. Preventive Services Task Force. 2012. *Prostate Cancer: Screening, May 2012: Final Recommendation Statement*. http://www.uspreventiveservicestaskforce.org/page/document/recommendationstatementfinal/prostate-cancer-screening.

Van Walbeek, C. 2005. "Tobacco Control in South Africa." *Promotion and Education* 12 (Suppl 4): 25–8. doi:10.1177/10253823050120040107.

Vanni, T., P. Mendes Luz, A. Foss, M. Mesa-Frias, and R. Legood. 2012. "Economic Modelling Assessment of the HPV Quadrivalent Vaccine in Brazil: A Dynamic Individual-Based Approach." *Vaccine* 30 (32): 4866–71. doi:10.1016/J.Vaccine.2012.04.087.

Varmus, H., and E. L. Trimble. 2011. "Integrating Cancer Control into Global Health." *Science Translational Medicine* 3 (101): 101cm28. doi:10.1126/Scitranslmed.3002321.

Verguet, S., C. L. Gauvreau, S. Mishra, M. Maclennan, S. M. Murphy, and others. 2015. "The Consequences of Tobacco Tax on Household Health and Finances in Rich and Poor Smokers in China: An Extended Cost-Effectiveness Analysis." *The Lancet Global Health* 3 (4): E206–16. doi:10.1016/S2214-109x(15)70095-1.

Verguet, S., R. Laxminarayan, and D. T. Jamison. 2015. "Universal Public Finance of Tuberculosis Treatment in India: An Extended Cost-Effectiveness Analysis." *Health Economics* 24 (3): 318–32. doi:10.1002/Hec.3019.

WHO (World Health Organization). 2000. *The World Health Report 2000: Health Systems: Improving Performance*. Geneva: WHO.

———. 2011a. *Global Status Report on Non-Communicable Diseases 2010*. Geneva: WHO.

———. 2011b. *Scaling Up Action against Non-Communicable Diseases: How Much Will It Cost?* Geneva: WHO.

———. 2011c. "Final Meeting Report and Recommendations." Immunization Practices Advisory Committee, WHO, 11–13 April. http://www.who.int/immunization/policy/committees/ipac_2011_april_report.pdf?ua=1.

———. 2012. *Global Health Estimates 2012*. http://www.who.int/healthinfo/global_burden_disease/en/.

———. 2013. *WHO Report on the Global Tobacco Epidemic 2013*. Geneva: WHO.

World Bank. 2014a. *Country and Lending Groups*. http://data.worldbank.org/about/country-and-lending-groups.

———. 2014b. *World Bank Development Indicators 2014*. Table 2.15, Health Systems. http://wdi.worldbank.org/table/2.15.

Zelle, S. G., K. M. Nyarko, W. K. Bosu, M. Aikins, L. M. Niens, and others. 2012. "Costs, Effects and Cost-Effectiveness of Breast Cancer Control in Ghana." *Tropical Medicine & International Health* 17 (8): 1031–43. doi:10.1111/J.1365-3156.2012.03021.X.

The Changing Global Burden of Cancer: Transitions in Human Development and Implications for Cancer Prevention and Control

Freddie Bray and Isabelle Soerjomataram

INTRODUCTION

Changes in fertility and life expectancy are leading to major changes in the structure of the global population and, in turn, in the scale of the cancer problem worldwide and at every resource level (WHO 2011b). In addition to the increasing burden of cancer is a changing spectrum of common cancers that is in different regions correlated with levels of human development (Bray and others 2012). The ongoing cancer transition includes a reduction in infection-related cancers (for example, stomach and cervical cancer) that is offset by increases in cancers linked to a Westernization of lifestyle (for example, breast, prostate, and colorectal cancer). The transition also encompasses changes in risk behavior, including tobacco uptake, with a delayed but large impact on the burden from lung and other tobacco-related cancers (Bray and others 2012). The cancer transition is not uniform, however: in Sub-Saharan Africa, recent increases in cervical cancer are observed in Uganda and Zimbabwe; in many countries, a residual burden of cancers associated with infectious agents accompanies the increasing burden of cancers associated with economic transition (Parkin and others 2014).

This chapter presents a global overview of the cancer burden, patterns and profiles, recent trends in common cancers, and the expected future scale of the disease by 2030.

We link geographical and temporal patterns of cancer to corresponding levels of economic progress to provide an overview of the key characteristics of the global cancer transition. We use gross national income (GNI) per capita as a national indicator of societal as well as economic development (http://data.worldbank.org/news/new-country-classifications), and corresponding rates of cancer incidence and mortality as markers of the extent of the global cancer transition. We draw attention to geographical variations and trends in cancer-specific rates according to differing economic profiles and in each of the world's regions. In addition, we provide a global, trends-based projection of the likely cancer burden in 2030, based on historical trends refined by incorporating an indicator of level of development.

We also examine the number of potentially avoidable new cases and cancer deaths, assuming a reduction in risk factors (Hanley 2001). Even today, tobacco smoking is by far the most important risk factor for cancer (Lim and others 2012). Although the smoking habit is in decline in many high-income countries (HICs), tobacco consumption is still rising in many low- and middle-income countries (LMICs) (Thun and others 2012). As part of the global socioeconomic

Corresponding author: Freddie Bray, Section of Cancer Surveillance, International Agency for Research on Cancer, Lyon, France, brayf@iarc.fr.

transition, many countries presently classified as low- or middle-income are increasingly adopting Westernized diets and more sedentary and less physically active lifestyles, leading to a rapid shift in the profile of common cancers in these populations (Bray and others 2012). In view of these developments, this chapter also reviews the main causes of cancer, with an emphasis on the sources of disparities that contribute to an increasingly greater proportional burden from cancer in LMICs, and the prospects for cancer control in different settings.

We conclude by pointing to how the high-level political commitment to reduce the rising burden of cancer and other noncommunicable diseases (NCDs) can advance the measurement of cancer to inform cancer control action. There remains an overwhelming need to improve the quality and coverage of population-based cancer registration in most LMICs, as an essential component in planning and evaluating national cancer control activities.

This chapter uses the World Health Organization's (WHO) geographical regions: Africa, the Americas, South-East Asia, Europe, Eastern Mediterranean, and Western Pacific.

Figure 2.1 Top 10 Causes of Death Worldwide, 2012 *(millions of deaths)*

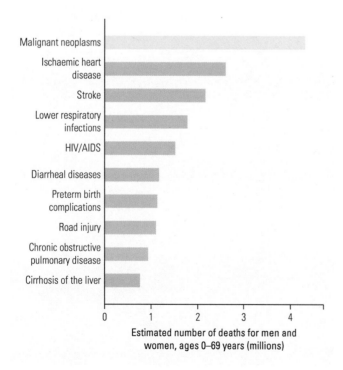

Estimated number of deaths for men and women, ages 0–69 years (millions)

Source: Global Health Observatory, WHO 2013.

CANCER IN CONTEXT: COMPARISONS WITH OTHER NONCOMMUNICABLE DISEASES BY DEVELOPMENT LEVEL

Worldwide, an estimated 38 million deaths—almost two-thirds of the annual 56 million total deaths—are caused by NCDs, principally from cardiovascular disease, diabetes, chronic respiratory disease, and cancer (WHO 2011b). In 2012, nearly 80 percent of all NCD deaths (28 million) occurred in LMICs; almost 30 percent of deaths occurred before age 60 years in these countries. Among NCDs, cancer is a leading cause of death (figure 2.1).

This observation is consistent with the global socio-economic transitions. Between 1990 and 2010, there was a 17 percent reduction in communicable maternal and neonatal and nutritional deaths, offset by a 30 percent increase in NCD-related deaths (Lozano and others 2012). This increase was greater in LMICs, compared with HICs (39 percent versus 15 percent, respectively). The shift is largely driven by population growth and improved longevity. Although the number of NCD-related deaths increased from 27 million to 34 million between 1990 and 2010, death rates declined by 19 percent (646 to 520 per 100,000) over the same period (Lozano and others 2012).

The overall statistics conceal variations among countries. Cancer is an even larger component of the NCD burden in HICs. In Japan, cancer represents over half of all NCD deaths combined; in approximately 40 countries, age-adjusted cancer mortality rates are equal to or above those of cardiovascular disease in premature mortality at ages under 70 years (WHO 2013).

KEY INDICATORS OF THE GLOBAL CANCER BURDEN

Comparisons of incidence rates can be used to investigate cancer risk factors, aid planning and prioritizing of cancer control resources, as well as facilitate monitoring and evaluating of the impact of specific primary prevention interventions. Mortality has often been considered the best means of evaluating overall success in reducing the cancer burden. An assessment of cancer-specific mortality rates is particularly useful in evaluating the effectiveness of secondary prevention, particularly where the goal is early detection of malignant tumors; it is also useful in tertiary prevention in determining the impact of cancer management and treatment. Combined successes in cancer prevention, early detection, screening, and treatment have resulted in a reduction in overall cancer mortality rates in some more developed countries, predominantly as a result of declines in the incidence and/or mortality from a number of specific types of common cancer (Doll 1990, Karim-Kos and others 2008). The broad spectrum of interventions and their tendency to produce real or artifactual changes in cancer incidence, mortality, or survival, however, lends support to combining analyses of all three measures.

Cancer is complex to monitor accurately because of its biological diversity; the underlying coding and classification issues are considerably more intricate than the other NCD categories. There has been a long history of cancer registration in many areas of the world, however, and a tradition of maintaining comparable accurate and complete global cancer incidence data that spans half a century. The serial publication, *Cancer Incidence in Five Continents* (CI5, http://ci5.iarc.fr), published by the International Agency for Research on Cancer (IARC) and the International Association of Cancer Registries, is regarded as the definitive source of local cancer data. The 10th volume of CI5, published in 2013, compiles incidence data from high-quality population-based cancer registries (PBCRs) for 2003–07.

The IARC is also the key reference source for statistics on the global, regional, and national burden of cancer; it publishes estimates of the core indicators for cancer at the country level as part of the GLOBOCAN series (http://globocan.iarc.fr). The most recent database contains estimates of the cancer incidence, mortality, prevalence, and disability-adjusted life years for all cancers combined for 2012, as well as for 27 cancer sites in 184 countries and 20 regions (Ferlay and others 2013).

The methods used to compile the GLOBOCAN estimates have evolved, but the underlying principle remains the use of the best available observed data within a country to build up the global picture. Details are provided by Ferlay and others (2015). Estimation of cancer-specific incidence and mortality rates are dependent on local data sources, and the cancer registry data from CI5 provide a key input into the compilation. Unfortunately, there remains a paucity of high-quality cancer incidence and mortality data in low-resource and medium-resource areas, and hence the accuracy of the estimates from these regions is generally lower; an alphanumeric scoring system has been introduced to provide a broad indication of the robustness of the estimation within each country (Ferlay and others 2015).

The definitions, sources, and mode of estimation of the key indicators used in this chapter are provided. Counts and rates of cancer incidence and mortality are presented; rates per 100,000 were age-standardized using the world standard population (Doll, Payne, and Waterhouse 1966).

Incidence

Cancer incidence is defined as the frequency of occurrence of new cases of cancer in a specific population over a given period of time. It can be expressed as the absolute number of cases or as a rate per unit-time, with new cancer cases the numerator and the corresponding person-time at risk the denominator.

PBCRs are the essential institutions enabling these activities (Bray 2014; Parkin 2006). They collect and classify information on all new cases of cancer within a well-defined population and provide statistics on occurrence for the purposes of assessing and controlling the impact of cancer in the community. Registries are either national or regional in their coverage, with a high degree of completeness, accuracy, and comparability of the collected data essential for making reliable inferences regarding geographical and temporal variations in the underlying rates. Although incidence trends are unaffected by the impact of changes in treatment and consequently survival, changes in registration practices, definitions of malignancy, and the International Classification of Diseases can all impact recorded incidence (Muir, Fraumeni, and Doll 1994). Inclusion in CI5 is a reliable marker of the quality of a given registry's data, in that the editorial process includes numerous assessments of the quality of the submitted data set. A substantial disparity exists in the availability of high-quality cancer registration data between HICs and LMICs. While 99 percent of the North American population is covered in the 10th volume of CI5, only 7 percent, 5 percent, and 2 percent of the respective South American, Asian, and African countries have registries that were accepted for inclusion.

Mortality

Mortality provides a unique measure of the outcome or impact of cancer and is expressed as either the number of deaths occurring or a mortality rate per unit-time. Mortality is a product of the incidence and the case-fatality of a given cancer, and fatality (1-survival) represents the probability that an individual with cancer will die from it. Mortality rates then measure average risk to the population of dying from a specific cancer. If case fatality is constant across populations or in a specified population over time, geographic or temporal comparisons of incidence can be inferred from mortality. It is evident, however, most notably in HICs and for cancers where treatment and cancer management have markedly improved, that incidence and mortality trends can be at considerable variance.

Data derive from vital registration systems, where usually a clinical practitioner certifies the fact and cause of death. The International Classification of Diseases provides the uniform system for nomenclature and coding and a suggested format for the death certificate. Mortality data are affected by the accuracy of the recorded cause of death and the completeness of registration. Errors of death certification are well documented (Doll and Peto 1981); patients diagnosed with cancer, for example, may die of the disease without this being written on the death certificate, and such inaccuracies are known to vary considerably between countries and over time.

The WHO mortality databank hosted at IARC (http://www-dep.iarc.fr/WHOdb/WHOdb.htm) contains national cancer mortality data on more than 80 countries; for many, the data cover decades. The greater availability by country and over time is confined mainly to higher-income countries; at least 15 years of data are available for 78 countries (35 in Europe, 25 in the Americas, 15 in Asia, 2 in Oceania, and 1 in Africa), but may explain its usage as a surrogate for incidence in geographic and temporal studies of cancer. In South America, mortality data are more comprehensive than incidence data, while both incidence and mortality are limited in Asia and Africa. In such settings, where deaths are often not attended by physicians, alternative methods, such as verbal autopsy, may be used to complement data collected from death certificates.

Income as a Proxy for Human Development

The remainder of this section examines cancer profiles with respect to the current burden, recent changes, and the future burden at the global, regional, and national levels. It is important to understand these patterns and trends in relation to the rapid increments in human development over recent decades. Tracking these changes helps to clarify how demographic and epidemiologic transitions impact the overall burden and the changing distribution of common cancers in different populations. In keeping with previous *DCP* volumes, we utilized national income level (GNI per capita) as a proxy for human development (UNDP 2009).

In examining aspects of the cancer burden according to resource levels, we used predefined categories of the distribution according to the World Bank classification of countries by income-group (see endnote for per capita income cut-offs). The estimated burden of cancer in 2030 is presented by gender for all cancers combined for all levels of income on the basis of the rates in 2008, assuming population growth and aging in 2030 occur according to the United Nations World Population Prospects medium-fertility variant.

Proportion of the Burden Attributable to Risk Factors

The population attributable fraction (PAF) (Hanley 2001) is a standard measure used to quantify the proportion of disease burden attributable to a risk factor. It is calculated using information on the prevalence of a risk factor in a population and the relative risk that the risk factor poses for development of disease, compared with those where the risk factor is absent. The derived proportion is indicative of the reduction in cancer incidence or mortality that would be expected if exposure to the risk factor were absent. For risk factors where zero exposure is inapplicable, such as for body weight, PAF is calculated by comparing population exposure to reported exposures at the lowest level of cancer risk.

The results presented in this chapter are largely based on a systematic search of published and unpublished reviews from major databases, censuses, health and nutrition surveys, and epidemiological studies (Lim and others 2012). Wherever possible, the data are supplemented by national, regional, or global studies with a focus on cancer (Agudo and others 2012; Boffetta and others 2006; Boffetta and others 2009; de Martel and others 2012; Ezzati and others 2005; Forman and others 2012; Goldie and others 2008; Goldstein and others 2005; McCormack and others 2012; McCormack and Schuz 2012; Renehan and others 2010). Because of the known lag time between the inception of smoking and cancer development, lung cancer mortality rates were converted into smoking impact ratios and as a proxy for exposure to smoking, thereby taking into account the duration and intensity of the exposure. To calculate PAF linked to infection, the prevalence of infection among cancer cases was used instead of the prevalence of infection in the population, because of the unreliability of population surveys on infection prevalence (de Martel and others 2012). As for effect sizes relating exposure to disease, wherever possible, the results were as reported in meta-analysis or were derived from the most up-to-date epidemiological findings.

The quality of the estimation depends largely on data availability, and a large gap remains in data availability and data quality in LMICs relative to HICs. The estimation of PAF also assumes that the association between a risk factor and cancer is causal and that a reduction in exposure to a specific risk factor will lead to a decline in the incidence of the cancer in question (Rockhill, Newman, and Weinberg 1998). To avoid an overestimation of the role of certain risk factors, we only report results for factors that have been confirmed as having sufficient evidence in causing cancer (Cogliano and others 2011). Epidemiological studies that report risk associations between exposure and cancer are prone to several limitations. In estimating PAF, studies have tried to overcome this issue by exclusively using risk estimates based on large meta-analyses that included only high-quality studies and, wherever possible, only cohort studies.

GLOBAL CANCER BURDEN AND DISTRIBUTION ACCORDING TO INCOME GROUP

For 2012, GLOBOCAN estimates indicate that there were 9.1 million new cases of cancer and 4.4 million cancer deaths between the ages of 0 and 69 years (figure 2.2). Female breast cancer is the most frequently diagnosed cancer globally (1.3 million new cases, 14.7 percent of all cancer cases), but it ranks third as the most common cause of cancer death (358,000 deaths, 8.2 percent of all cancer deaths). Lung cancer is the leading cause of death (767,000 deaths, 17.5 percent) and ranks second in incidence (1 million deaths, 10.8 percent). In terms of incidence, the most frequent cancer types thereafter are colorectal (744,000 cases, 174,000 deaths), prostate (556,000 cases, 56,000 deaths), stomach (539,000 cases, 242,000 deaths), and liver (503,000 cases, 336,000 deaths).

Four cancers constitute nearly 50 percent of the total cancer burden in HICs; for cancers of the prostate, lung, and colorectum, comparable numbers (between 350,000 and 400,000 new cases) of each type are estimated in 2012, with female breast cancer accounting for 550,000 cases (figure 2.3). Female breast cancer is also the most common form of cancer in LMICs, with almost 770,000 estimated cases in 2012. In combination, eight cancers (breast, lung, liver, cervix, stomach, colorectum, esophagus, and leukemia) account for almost two-thirds of the estimated cancer burden in LMICs. It is noteworthy that several types of cancer, more commonly associated with infection and poverty, less commonly diagnosed in HICs, are major cancers in LMICs; they include stomach and liver cancer—which are more frequently diagnosed than colorectal or prostate cancer in lower-income economies—as well as cancers of the cervix and esophagus.

In terms of risk of developing specific neoplasms worldwide, the lifetime incidence of breast cancer is highest (2.8 percent), with the lifetime risk of the next four most common cancers varying from 1 to 1.5 percent. In HICs, however, the lifetime risk exceeds 2 percent for cancers of the breast (female), prostate, lung, and colorectum.

Figure 2.2 Global Burden of Cancer: Estimated Counts of Cancer Incidence and Mortality, by Region, 2012

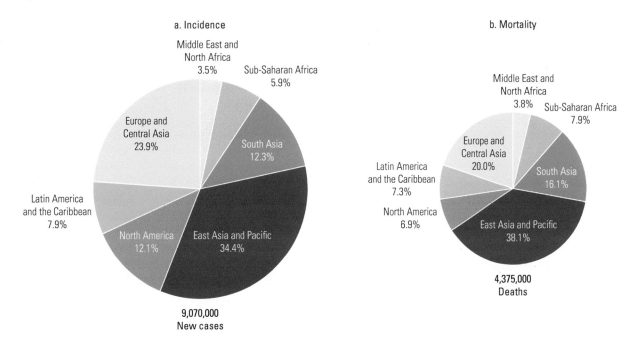

Source: Ferlay and others 2013.
Note: Data are for men and women ages 0–69 years.

Figure 2.3 Global Burden of Cancer: Cancer Incidence and Mortality by Income Level, 2012

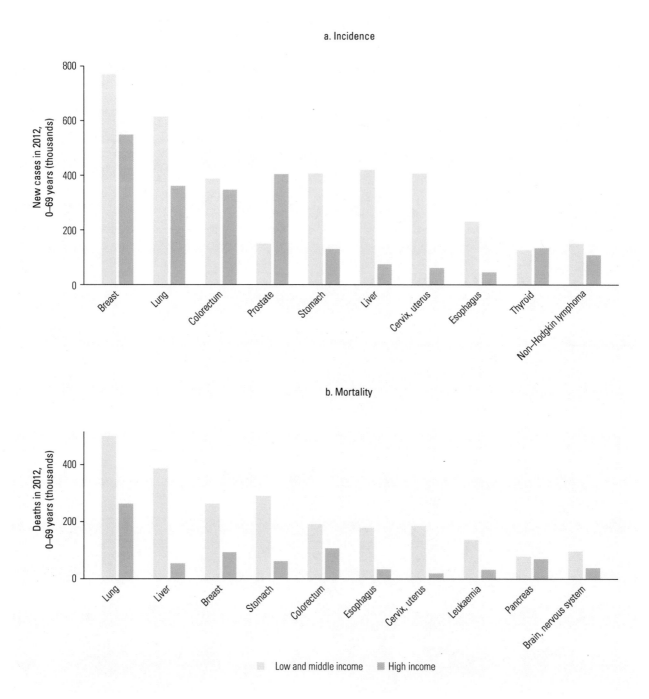

a. Incidence

b. Mortality

Low and middle income   High income

Source: Ferlay and others 2013.
Note: Values are age-standardized rates for the world population structure.

In terms of mortality, the most frequent causes of cancer death in HICs are lung, colorectum, female breast, and pancreas, which together account for about 48 percent of the total cancer deaths in 2012. Relative to incidence, a greater proportion of the mortality burden occurs in LMICs, particularly for those cancers more frequently diagnosed in LMICs, including liver and stomach (figure 2.3). Together with lung, female breast, and colorectal cancer, these neoplasms constitute half of the total cancer mortality burden in these areas. In terms of risk of death, the lifetime cumulative mortality from lung cancer and female breast cancer ranks highest in HICs (1.8 and 1.2 percent, respectively) and LMICs (1.3 and 1 percent, respectively). Colorectal cancer ranks third in HICs, and liver and cervical cancer rank third and fourth, respectively, in LMICs.

DIVERSITY OF CANCER BY TYPE: GEOGRAPHICAL VARIATIONS BY REGION

The classification of cancer patterns by broad levels of economic development draws attention to some of the key macroeconomic determinants of inequality and the variations in the risk of developing cancer globally. To underscore the diversity of cancer, it is important to show the extent to which cancer-specific patterns vary. Map 2.1, panel a, outlines the most common form of cancer among men in 184 countries in 2012. Worldwide, 10 types of cancer rank highest, with prostate cancer the most frequent cancer form in 68 countries, chiefly in HICs, but also in parts of Latin America and the Caribbean and in the southern regions of the African continent. Lung cancer is the most common neoplasm in 42 countries, mainly in Eastern Europe, Northern Africa, and Asia, including China and Indonesia. Liver cancer is the most common form in 27 countries, particularly in Western Africa and South-East Asia.

Among men, the incidence and mortality patterns vary most markedly by region in Africa (Jemal and others 2012), with liver cancer the most common cancer in 18 of the 47 Sub-Saharan African countries. Clusters of very high incidence of Kaposi sarcoma are observed in 13 countries in Eastern Africa; prostate cancer is the most frequently observed tumor in nine countries (Parkin and others 2014). In women—and in some contrast to the diversity of the highest ranking cancers in men—either breast cancer (143 countries) or cervical cancer (39 countries) ranks as the most frequent cancer diagnosed in almost all countries worldwide; exceptions include the very high female incidence rates of thyroid cancer in the Republic of Korea and liver cancer in Mongolia (map 2.1, panel b).

GLOBAL CANCER TRANSITIONS: RECENT TRENDS AND FUTURE BURDEN CIRCA 2030

The high-quality cancer registry data from CI5 (http:// ci5.iarc.fr) illustrate temporal aspects of the global cancer transition: increases in breast and prostate cancer are apparent in countries that have transitioned from low-income to middle-income or middle-income to high-income (figures 2.4 and 2.5); for colorectal cancer, the increases are more evident in registries transitioning from middle-income countries; those countries that have reached very high levels of income tend to have also attained very high incidence rates of this cancer, and a recent peak in incidence is observed in several countries (figure 2.6). Nevertheless, the trends point to a Westernization effect in countries undergoing transition. Increasing average levels of economic progress serve as a proxy for a changing population prevalence of reproductive, dietary, metabolic, and hormonal risk factors (toward levels more akin to those more commonly observed in the West) that correspondingly increase the risk of these cancers (Bray 2014).

Evidently, better diagnosis, earlier detection, and screening may have inflated the incidence burden in many settings, particularly where precursor lesions are not the target of the intervention. This includes prostate and breast cancers where prostate-specific antigen testing and mammographic screening have impacted the increasing incidence of the respective cancers in many populations (Bleyer and Welch 2012; Bray and others 2010; Bray, McCarron, and Parkin 2004). Nevertheless, such increases are countered by another hallmark of cancer transition: a reduction in infection-based neoplasms (Forman and others 2012; Vaccarella and others 2013). Most of the registries record declines in cervical and stomach cancer incidence (Bray and others 2012) (figures 2.7 and 2.8). There have been rapid increases in the incidence of breast, prostate, and colorectal cancer documented in countries in Sub-Saharan Africa with good quality incidence data; for example, rates of breast cancer have increased by 3.6 percent annually in Kampala, Uganda, and by 4.9 percent in the black population of Harare, Zimbabwe. There is little evidence of another hallmark of cancer transition—declining cervical cancer—in these populations: rather, rates exhibit persistent increases in incidence in recent years (Chokunonga and others 2013; Wabinga and others 2014).

The importance of lung cancer in the overall global burden from cancer is a reflection of the prevalence of tobacco smoking. The differences in lung cancer incidence by national income level reflect the historical and current variations of smoking habits in the underlying populations. Lung cancer rates are decreasing in men in most countries, notably in HICs and in countries where the habit has long been established, but they are increasing in women (Jemal and others 2010). Such contrasting male and female trends are consistent with the population-specific rise and fall in adult cigarette utilization over past decades (Lortet-Tieulent and others 2013). The correlation

Map 2.1 Most Common Cancers Diagnosed in Men and Women in 184 Countries, 2012, Ages 0–69 Years

a. Most common cancers among men, 2012

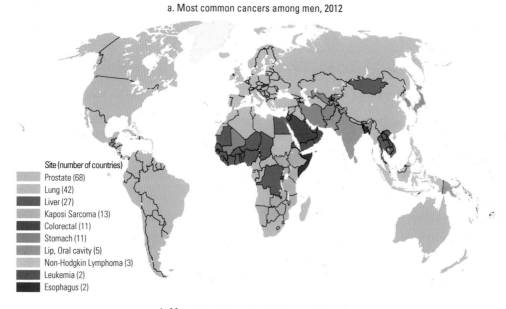

Site (number of countries)
- Prostate (68)
- Lung (42)
- Liver (27)
- Kaposi Sarcoma (13)
- Colorectal (11)
- Stomach (11)
- Lip, Oral cavity (5)
- Non-Hodgkin Lymphoma (3)
- Leukemia (2)
- Esophagus (2)

b. Most common cancers among women, 2012

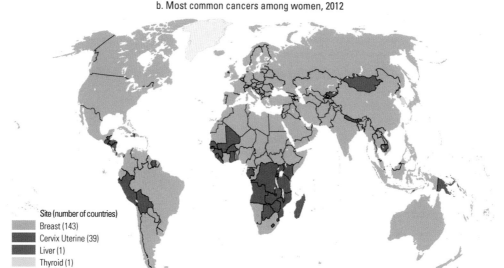

Site (number of countries)
- Breast (143)
- Cervix Uterine (39)
- Liver (1)
- Thyroid (1)

Source: Ferlay and others, 2013.

between income and male smoking prevalence has shown a curvilinear trend (Talley 2010) that mimics the smoking epidemic curve (Thun and others 2012). Smoking prevalence tends to be low in countries of low average income but rises as income increases, until it stabilizes and begins to decline as countries attain high mean income levels.

The prevalence of smoking in men has increased sharply in many middle-income countries, including China and Indonesia (Jha 2009). The future burden of lung cancer and other smoking-related cancers (IARC 2004), such as bladder, esophageal, and oral cavity in different regions and countries, will largely depend on gender-specific smoking patterns at the population level, including the duration of smoking, extent of cessation, and types of tobacco smoked (Doll and others 2004; Pirie and others 2013; Thun and others 2012).

Figure 2.4 Trends in Age-Standardized (World) Incidence Rates of Female Breast Cancer, by Income Level, 1980–2010

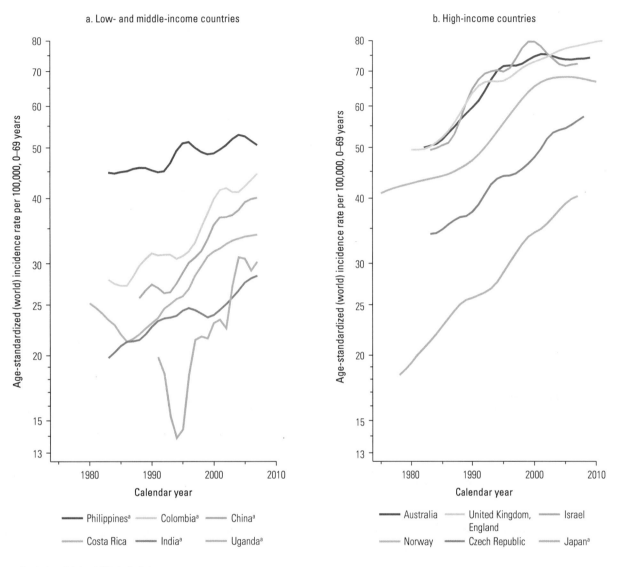

a. Low- and middle-income countries   b. High-income countries

Legend (a): Philippines[a], Colombia[a], China[a], Costa Rica, India[a], Uganda[a]

Legend (b): Australia, United Kingdom, England, Israel, Norway, Czech Republic, Japan[a]

Source: CI5*plus*, http://ci5.iarc.fr/CI5plus/Default.aspx.
Note: Estimated from selected population-based cancer registries of consistently high quality (included in successive volumes of *Cancer Incidence in Five Continents*). Data for the economies in the graphs are for China (Hong Kong SAR, China; and Shanghai), Colombia (Cali), India (Chennai and Mumbai), Japan (Miyagi, Nagasaki, and Osaka), the Philippines (Manila), and Uganda (Kampala).
a. Denotes rates based on an aggregate of one or more regional registries, as indicated.

A recent study of incidence trends in 1988–2002 for the seven most frequently diagnosed cancers worldwide (constituting more than 58 percent of the global burden) estimated the annual percentage change of trends in age-adjusted incidence using data from 101 cancer registries (Bray and others 2012). The trends were stratified by medium, high, or very high levels of the Human Development Index (HDI), a composite measure of life expectancy at birth, income as GNI per capita, and access to education. Although the HDI is highly correlated with GNI, the latter reflects average national income, whereas the former additionally provides some indication as to how income is spent, at least in the areas of health and education (UNDP 2009).

An estimated 21.6 million new cancer cases are predicted for 2030 (an increase of 53 percent from 2012), based solely on projected demographic changes and unchanged cancer incidence rates (figure 2.9). If the

Figure 2.5 Trends in Age-Standardized (World) Incidence Rates of Prostate Cancer, by Income Level, 1980–2010

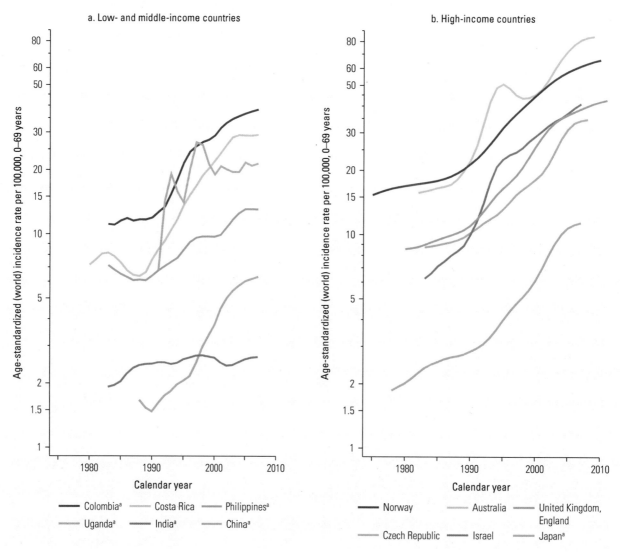

Source: CI5*plus,* http://ci5.iarc.fr/CI5plus/Default.aspx.

Note: Estimated from selected population-based cancer registries of consistently high quality (included in successive volumes of *Cancer Incidence in Five Continents*). Data for the economies in the graphs are for China (Hong Kong SAR, China; and Shanghai), Colombia (Cali), India (Chennai and Mumbai), Japan (Miyagi, Nagasaki, and Osaka), the Philippines (Manila), and Uganda (Kampala).

a. Rates based on an aggregate of one or more regional registries, as indicated.

cancer-specific incidence trends up to 2002 continue, an absolute increase of 62 percent in incidence is expected, representing an overall increase of 1.2 million new cases per year in 2012–30. The increases in cancer incidence are proportionally greatest in low HDI settings, with a predicted 77 percent increase in both genders.

Although such analyses appear to present a rather pessimistic view of the future burden of cancer, targeted interventions can significantly reduce the projected rise in the number of cancer patients through resource-appropriate interventions. Such actions include primary prevention strategies to control lifestyle factors, including tobacco avoidance and cessation foremost, a reduction in alcohol consumption and obesity, and the promotion of increased levels of physical activity. Vaccination programs for liver and cervical cancer and early detection programs for breast and cervical cancer are important.

Figure 2.6 Trends in Age-Standardized (World) Incidence Rates of Male Colorectal Cancer, by Income Level, 1980–2010

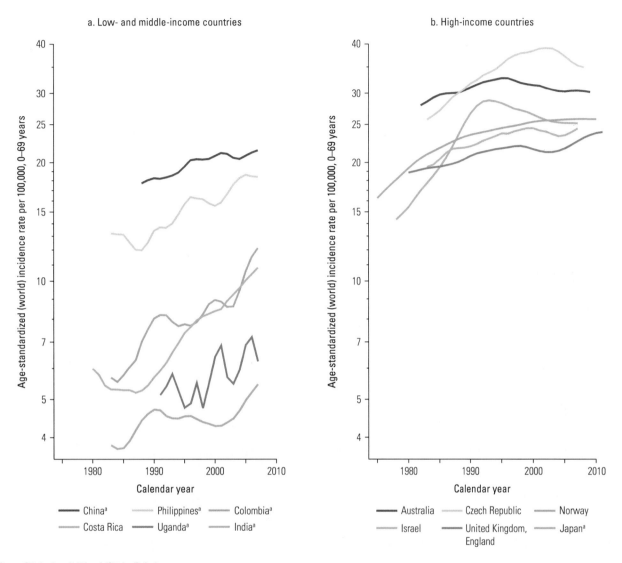

Source: CI5*plus,* http://ci5.iarc.fr/CI5plus/Default.aspx.
Note: Estimated from selected population-based cancer registries of consistently high quality (included in successive volumes of *Cancer Incidence in Five Continents*). Data for the economies in the graphs are for China (Hong Kong SAR, China; and Shanghai), Colombia (Cali), India (Chennai and Mumbai), Japan (Miyagi, Nagasaki, and Osaka), the Philippines (Manila), and Uganda (Kampala).
a. Rates based on an aggregate of one or more regional registries, as indicated.

RISK FACTORS, INTERVENTIONS AND POLICIES, AND POTENTIAL IMPACTS ON THE BURDEN OF CANCER

Approximately 30 percent of all cancers worldwide are considered preventable by modification of the predominant risk factors (Danaei and others 2005; Martin-Moreno, Soerjomataram, and Magnusson 2008).

Smoking and dietary risk factors have particularly important roles in potentially reducing the cancer burden in HICs and LMICs (Ezzati and others 2005; Jha 2009; Lim and others 2012; WCRF and AICR 2007). For cancers with strong risk modifiers, trends in risk factors are followed by trends of cancer incidence with a lag of 20–30 years (Doll and others 2004; Jha 2009). Illustrative examples include the temporal patterns of

Figure 2.7 Trends in Age-Standardized (World) Incidence Rates of Cervical Cancer, by Income Level, 1980–2010

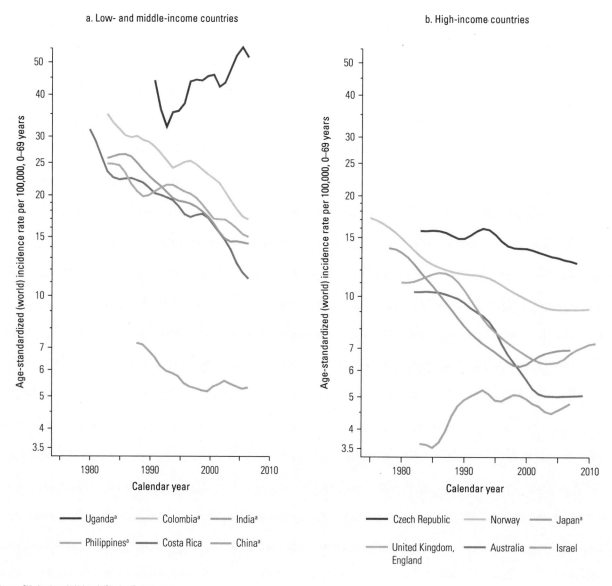

a. Low- and middle-income countries

b. High-income countries

Legend:
— Uganda[a]   — Colombia[a]   — India[a]
— Philippines[a]   — Costa Rica   — China[a]

— Czech Republic   — Norway   — Japan[a]
— United Kingdom, England   — Australia   — Israel

Source: Cl5*plus,* http://ci5.iarc.fr/Cl5plus/Default.aspx.

Note: Estimated from selected population-based cancer registries of consistently high quality (included in successive volumes of *Cancer Incidence in Five Continents*). Data for the economies in the graphs are for China (Hong Kong SAR, China; and Shanghai), Colombia (Cali), India (Chennai and Mumbai), Japan (Miyagi, Nagasaki, and Osaka), the Philippines (Manila), and Uganda (Kampala).

a. Rates based on an aggregate of one or more regional registries, as indicated.

cigarette smoking and lung cancer, and age at first child-birth and breast cancer (Jha 2009; Soerjomataram and others 2008). Unfortunately, for most risk factors, the relation to specific cancer forms is weaker than these associations. In addition, risk factors often interact, making it difficult to link directly the changing prevalence of a single risk factor to the observed trends of specific cancer types.

Tobacco

Tobacco smoking is the largest single avoidable cause of premature death. Worldwide, 70 percent of lung cancer deaths; 42 percent of cancers of the esophagus and oral cavity (Ezzati and others 2005; Lim and others 2012); a significant proportion of cancers of the larynx, urinary bladder, and pancreas; a smaller proportion of cancers of the kidney, stomach, and cervix; and myeloid

Figure 2.8 Trends in Age-Standardized (World) Incidence Rates of Men with Stomach Cancer, by Income Level, 1980–2010

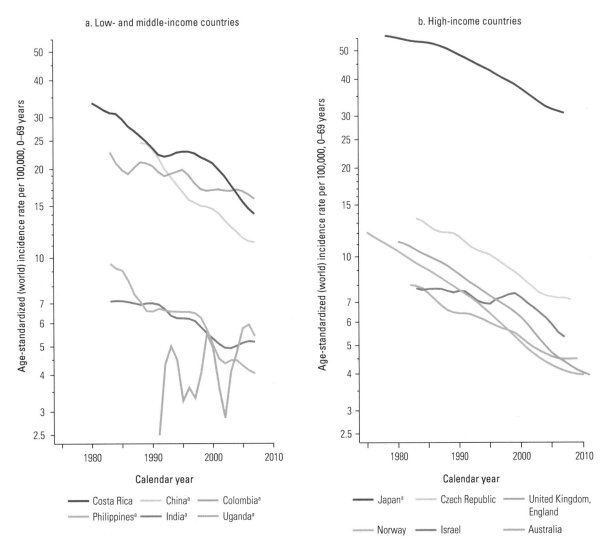

a. Low- and middle-income countries

b. High-income countries

Source: CI5plus, http://ci5.iarc.fr/CI5plus/Default.aspx.
Note: Estimated from selected population-based cancer registries of consistently high quality (included in successive volumes of *Cancer Incidence in Five Continents*). Data for the economies in the graphs are for China (Hong Kong SAR, China; and Shanghai), Colombia (Cali), India (Chennai and Mumbai), Japan (Miyagi, Nagasaki, and Osaka), the Philippines (Manila), and Uganda (Kampala).
a. Rates based on an aggregate of one or more regional registries, as indicated.

leukemia are attributable to cigarette smoking (Agudo and others 2012). Between 1990 and 2010, mortality rates from cancers related to smoking in higher resource settings decreased (Lim and others 2012), reflecting a mean decrease of smoking prevalence, especially among men. However, in countries undergoing transition, the proportion of cancer deaths attributable to smoking has increased from 12 to 14 percent (Lim and others 2012), reflecting increasing cigarette consumption (Ng and others 2014). Efforts to reduce

tobacco consumption are central to preventing deaths from cancer and other diseases.

Smoking prevalence has decreased for many decades in HICs; in LMICs, it is stable or showing only limited signs of a decline very recently. In China, for example, with one of the highest smoking rates in the world, prevalence among men dropped from 57 to 53 percent between 2002 and 2007 (Ng and others 2014). This change may represent the first impact of increasing tobacco control measures in the country. The WHO

Figure 2.9 Cancer Incidence Projected to 2030 with and without Incorporating Recent Changes in Rates by Gender, Income Level, and Age Group

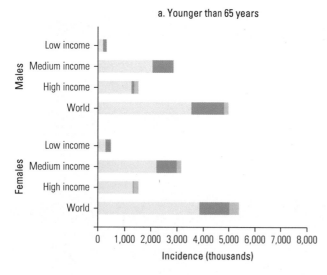

a. Younger than 65 years

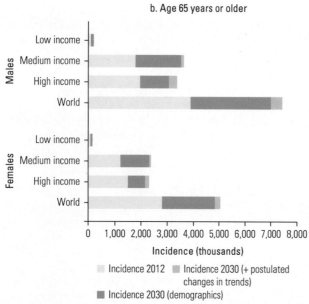

b. Age 65 years or older

Incidence 2012 ☐ Incidence 2030 (+ postulated changes in trends) ☐ Incidence 2030 (demographics) ■

Source: Bray and others 2012.

MPOWER report on the global tobacco epidemic indicated that, of the 48 countries that had implemented at least one tobacco control measure since 2007, four-fifths were LMICs (WHO 2008). The impact of such measures will not be evident in lung cancer trends for some decades, and increasing rates may continue to rise in many LMICs (McCormack and Boffetta 2011). The prevalence of women in LMICs who smoke has remained rather low, but it may be expected to rise as social and cultural prohibitions erode (Thun and others 2012). It is debatable whether the impact of tobacco on the cancer burden in some LMICs will reach the level observed in many HICs (McCormack and Boffetta 2011).

Persistent Infections

The most recent estimates state that at least 16.1 percent or two million new cases of human malignancies worldwide are attributable to persistent infections with bacteria, viruses, or parasites (de Martel and others 2012). This fraction is higher in LMICs (22.9 percent or 1.6 million new cases) than in HICs (7.4 percent or 410,000 new cases). *Helicobacter pylori*, hepatitis B and C viruses, and human papilloma viruses (HPVs) are responsible for 1.9 million cases, mainly gastric, liver, and cervical cancers. The remaining 163,000 cases are attributed to Epstein-Barr virus, human herpes virus type 8, human T-cell lymphotropic virus type 1, *Opisthorchis viverrini*, *Clonorchis sinensis*, and *Schistosoma haematobium*. By region, the attributable fraction shows marked variation (figure 2.10), from 33.2 percent of all cancers in Sub-Saharan Africa to 3.3 percent in Australia and New Zealand. The proportion of cancers associated with chronic infections ranges from 1 in 3 in Sub-Saharan Africa and 1 in 4 in China to 1 in 30 in Australia and New Zealand and 1 in 25 in North America. Awareness of the role of infectious agents in cancer has expanded rapidly, leading to the formulation of new strategies, including vaccines against hepatitis B to prevent liver cancer, and against high-risk strains of HPV to prevent cervical and other HPV-related cancer types (Beutels 2001; Harper and others 2004; Herrero and others 2013).

Increasing coverage of hepatitis B virus vaccination has been related to a decrease in the prevalence of chronic hepatitis B virus throughout the world (Goldstein and others 2005). For example, in Taiwan, China, a 75 percent decrease in the incidence of hepatocellular carcinoma in children was reported since the initiation of routine infant hepatitis B vaccination (Chang and others 1997). Gavi, the Vaccine Alliance, has subsidized vaccines in poor countries, leading to a rapid increase in coverage of hepatitis B vaccination, with a similar effort underway in implementing HPV vaccination (Kane and others 2012). Based on current epidemiologic data in 72 countries, it is predicted that we will observe a mean reduction in lifetime risk of cervical cancer of between 31 percent (for example, in Guinea and Senegal) and 60 percent (for example, in Ethiopia), assuming an increase in vaccination coverage to 70 percent (Goldie and others 2008). Differences in the results of vaccination stem from variation in risk factor prevalence and the background incidence of the cancer being targeted. Safe and effective vaccines have proven highly important in reducing infection-related cancers.

Alcohol

Excess alcohol consumption is an important risk factor for several cancers, most notably, of the oral cavity, pharynx, larynx, and esophagus, as well as for cancers of the breast, liver, and colorectum (IARC 2010). Up to 4 percent of cancer cases worldwide are attributable to alcohol intake (Boffetta and others 2006), with similar distributions in HICs and LMICs (Rehm and Shield 2013). Global alcohol consumption has been stable in recent decades, with a small decrease in countries where intake was historically high (for example, in Europe) and a small increase in countries where intake has been relatively low (for example, in South-East Asia) (Shield and others 2013). In HICs, a notable exception is an increase in consumption in the Russian Federation between 1986 and 2000, which has subsequently stabilized. Among LMICs, Uganda has the heaviest alcohol intake level (10.9 liters of pure alcohol per capita, compared with 11.3 in the Russian Federation) (WHO 2011a). This is in contrast to traditionally Muslim countries (for example, the Arab Republic of Egypt and Indonesia), where alcohol consumption is very low (0.66 and 0.67 liters of pure alcohol per capita, respectively) (WHO 2011a). Sweden is one example of a successful government policy geared toward effectively reducing alcohol intake at the population level. After restricting beer sales based on alcohol content in 1977, consumption decreased by approximately 15 percent (Makela, Tryggvesson, and Rossow 2002). Such an example points to the importance of nationwide population interventions as an effective way to reduce alcohol consumption.

Diet

Recent estimates report that about 15 percent of all cancer deaths are related to unhealthy diets, including high intake of red meat, processed meat, and sodium, as well as low intake of fruits and vegetables (Lim and others 2012). Yet, most research is still inconclusive about specific dietary items (WCRF and AICR 2007). The most recent comprehensive review of diet and cancer risks confirms an elevated risk related to red and processed meat but finds less evidence supporting the benefit of the consumption of fruits and vegetables in reducing risk (WCRF and AICR 2007). Variations in the strength of the evidence in different studies over time make the measurement of dietary intake problematic in epidemiological studies; if only well-established risk factors are included in the estimation, approximately 5 percent of

Figure 2.10 Cancer and Infection: Estimated Attributable Fraction, by Region or Country, 2008

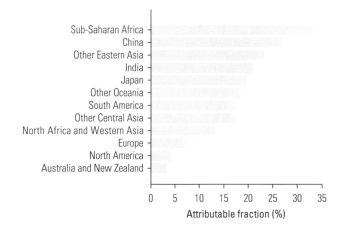

Source: de Martel and others 2012.
Note: Values are for all cancers combined, for all ages.

cancer deaths worldwide (387,000) would be attributable to dietary risk factors (Lim and others 2012).

Consumption of red meat and processed meat increases the risk of colorectal cancer by an estimated 43 percent (WCRF and AICR 2007). Consumption of red meat and processed meat is generally rising in LMICs but is stable in HICs. Another major dietary risk factor is high salt intake, which increases the risk of stomach cancer. Globally, salt intake has declined, and the associated cancer burden has declined as a result (Brown and others 2009); currently, 1.5 percent and 2 percent of all cancer deaths in HICs and LMICs, respectively, are attributed to high salt intake, compared with 2.2 percent and 2.7 percent, respectively, in 1990 (Lim and others 2012). In the United Kingdom, 10 percent of new stomach cancer cases diagnosed in 2010 may be attributable to high salt intake (Parkin 2011).

Although many of the underlying mechanisms are not yet established, food and diet are clearly important determinants of cancer risk. Over the past century, better food preservation methods, reducing the need for salt, have probably been a key factor in the decline in stomach cancer incidence. The levels of red meat consumption in recent decades may explain the low colorectal cancer rates in southern Asia (WCRF and AICR 2007), as well as the high rates in many western European countries (Center, Jemal, and Ward 2009; Center and others 2009).

Evidence linking obesity and overweight to cancer is firmer than the dietary evidence, indicating that 3 and 6 percent of cancer deaths in LMICs and HICs, respectively, can be attributed to excess weight, as quantified by the body mass index (BMI) (Bergstrom and others 2001; Lim and others 2012; Renehan and others 2010). BMI is already an important correlate of cancer incidence in

HICs, and it is likely to continue increasing in importance in some LMICs, as average BMI has increased in most Central and South American countries and also in southern Africa (Stevens and others 2012). BMI has remained low in Sub-Saharan Africa (except in southern Africa) and South and Southeast Asia. High BMI has increased as a cause of cancer deaths more substantively in LMICs, a 54 percent increase over the past 30 years, compared with a 26 percent increase in HICs over the same period (Lim and others 2012; Stevens and others 2012).

Physical Inactivity

Regular physical activity is associated with a reduction in the risk of developing colon cancer (Harriss and others 2009) and breast cancer (Monninkhof and others 2007). Many studies have suggested that regular physical activity additionally reduces the risk of cancers of the endometrium and prostate (WCRF and AICR 2007). Although this effect seems to be strongly linked to the impact of physical activity on body weight, the preventive effect of regular exercise for some cancers seems to act independently of weight control (Friedenreich and others 2006; Giovannucci and others 1995; Pischon and others 2006). In 2010, global physical inactivity was estimated to be related to 3.2 and 5.5 percent of cancer deaths in LMICs and HICs, respectively (Lim and others 2012). Motivating people to increase physical activity or reduce their body weight has proven difficult; hence, there has been a more recent emphasis on altering the built environment (Diez Roux and others 2007; Giles-Corti and others 2005). In Northern Ireland, a greenways urbanization project was considered very cost-effective at reducing major chronic diseases, including breast and colon cancer (Dallat and others 2013).

Environmental Factors

Other environmental risk factors, such as household air pollution, may have a very minor role in causing cancer in HICs, but these factors are much more important in LMICs, where they may account for about 2.4 percent of all cancer deaths (Evans and others 2013; Lim and others 2012). In China, the risk of lung cancer among smokers is three times that of nonsmokers, a risk ratio that is much lower than in other countries (Lin and others 2008), probably as a result of the common practice of cooking indoors with solid fuel—which significantly increases lung cancer risk. Some improvements in cooking conditions have already taken place and further improvements could potentially prevent a substantial number of lung cancer deaths in the future.

Many outdoor air pollutants may increase the risk of neoplasms, most notably lung cancer (Raaschou-Nielsen and others 2013). Increasing air pollution in large cities in LMICs has caused concern about links to several chronic diseases, including cancer (Evans and others 2013). Currently 3.6 percent of cancer deaths in LMICs are attributed to ambient air pollution, compared with 2.4 percent in 1990 (Lim and others 2012).

Protective measures in the workplace have led to the prevention of many cancers. A small proportion of cancer deaths are attributed to occupational risk factors (1.6 percent in LMICs and 1.3 percent in HICs). Despite the small numbers, there is cause for concern regarding occupational exposures in certain countries undergoing development, including higher industrial exposures, as well as a longer duration of exposure due to the common practice of child labor (McCormack and Schuz 2012).

Asbestos is among the best known occupational exposures and has been strongly linked to mesothelioma and lung cancer (IARC 1987). Because of past exposure, the current proportion of lung cancer attributable to asbestos is highest in the United States and the United Kingdom, ranging from 12 to 18 percent, but the future burden is likely to increase in China, India, and Russia, where current exposure to and use of asbestos are at the highest levels worldwide (McCormack and others 2012).

Exposure to the ultraviolet component of sunlight is the predominant environmental cause of skin cancer, affecting mainly fair skinned persons who live predominantly in HICs (de Vries and Coebergh 2004). A recent study predicted that protection from ultraviolet rays may reduce the incidence of melanoma by 13 to 21 percent in various Western populations over a 40-year period up to 2050 (de Vries and others 2012).

Hormonal and Reproductive Factors

Hormonal and reproductive factors play an important role in the etiology of several cancers among women, in particular, breast cancer. Established risk factors include early age at menarche, older age at first birth, low parity, and late age at menopause (Beral, Bull, and Reeves 2005; Beral and others 2007; Beral and others 2011; Reeves and others 2012; Rosner and Colditz 1996). The current changes in these factors are expected to contribute to a 25 percent increase in breast cancer incidence (McCormack and Boffetta 2011). Reversing the current trend of these factors is not commonly considered feasible or desirable; hence, breast cancer prevention must focus on other, more modifiable factors. These include reductions in BMI, physical inactivity, and alcohol consumption, and increasing the duration of breast-feeding (McCormack and Boffetta 2011).

Summary

Quantifying the totality of preventable cancers through the effects of the interventions as described above is a complicated exercise, given imprecision in the estimates and risk factor interactions that are not fully understood. One study has estimated that around 35 percent of cancer deaths are avoidable by modifying the major cancer risk factors (Danaei and others 2005).

Of seven million deaths from cancer worldwide in 2001, 0.76 million preventable deaths were in HICs and 1.67 million were in LMICs. Primary prevention would most effectively target infection and tobacco, as well as better nutrition and increased physical activity (Jemal and others 2012; Jha 2009). In more developed nations, interventions focusing on reducing smoking, improving dietary habits, and avoiding excess weight are likely to be most effective (Jha and others 2013; Murray and others 2013; Pirie and others 2013; Renehan and others 2010).

More effective early detection and better treatment will further reduce the number of deaths in LMICs (Farmer and others 2010; Sankaranarayanan and others 2011). The large burden of cancer in these regions and the great potential to prevent them call for rational and balanced investment in a broad spectrum of cancer control activities that includes primary prevention, screening, early detection, therapy, follow-up, and palliative care (Stewart 2012). In addition, surveillance of risk factor information and cancer data, particularly in LMICs, can improve global cancer risk assessment and inform national cancer control planning.

PROSPECTS FOR ENHANCING CANCER SURVEILLANCE SYSTEMS IN LMICS

Cancer is already a leading NCD at ages under 70 years worldwide and is the most common cause of death in more than 40 HICs. Global efforts are underway at a high political level to combat the rising cancer and NCD burden. The *WHO Action Plan for the Global Strategy for the Prevention and Control of Noncommunicable Diseases* provides a road map for 2013–20 that includes a target for member states of a global reduction of 25 percent in premature mortality from the four main NCD groups by 2025 ("25 by 25") (WHO 2011b). Adequate surveillance mechanisms at the country level are needed to monitor progress. With a greater number of governments adopting national cancer control plans, attention is increasingly turning to population-based cancer surveillance data as a central component in prioritizing and evaluating interventions.

Vital registration (mortality data) and population-based cancer registries (incidence and survival data) are complementary, and having the availability of both to a high standard is ideal. But for many LMICs, national vital statistics are unavailable, partial, or inaccurate. Where data are available, the coverage and completeness of the mortality data are often poor. It is thus much easier at present to quantify premature cancer mortality for higher resource countries than for those at the lower end. Efforts to develop and improve vital registration systems are being augmented by a number of verbal autopsy studies in countries and communities where many deaths occur at home and without medical attention (for example, the Million Death Study in India [Dikshit and others 2012]).

Population-based cancer registries describe the present scale and profile of cancer in the community and aid planning by assessing past and future trends. Knowing the size and nature of the cancer problem serves as an important stimulus to implement and change policy. However, although it is feasible to implement PBCRs even in the lowest income settings (Bray and others 2014), their availability is limited in most countries undergoing development, with only one in five LMICs currently predisposed with the necessary population-based data for cancer control action. This situation reflects a lack of advocacy for the value of registries historically and the subsequent lack of resources and prioritization of cancer data for cancer control among the competing demands on limited health care services (Wild 2014).

Nevertheless, positive momentum is building through the recognition of the role of cancer and other NCDs in hampering human development, changing priorities within countries at the highest political level. Importantly and as part of the global monitoring framework, WHO member states are being asked to collect *cancer incidence, by type of cancer per 100,000 population,* one of 25 indicators to monitor progress toward the 25 by 25 target, thereby obliging countries to establish and sustain population-based cancer registries.

Clearly, in aligning registries to cancer control action, technical guidance is needed to empower countries to improve their information systems so that they can be used for their vital purpose. Several technical and funding organizations are now working in a cooperative and coordinated manner under the auspices of the Global Initiative for Cancer Registry Development (http://gicr .iarc.fr) to bring about the needed improvement in the quantity and quality of data on cancer incidence through investment in PBCRs. There is a longstanding and ongoing commitment at IARC to support the development of such registries worldwide, particularly where they are in limited supply and most needed, in most LMICs.

Map 2.2 Implementing the Global Initiative for Cancer Registry through Six IARC Regional Hubs for Cancer Registration

- Central and Western Asia and Northern Africa Izmir Cancer Registry, Ismir, Turkey
- Southern, Eastern and South-Eastern Asia Tata Memorial Centre, Mumbai, India
- Caribbean (Planned)
- Latin America Instituto Nacional de Cáncer Buenos Aires, Argentina
- Sub-Saharan Africa African Cancer Registry Network, Oxfordthods
- Pacific Islands (Planned)

- Deliver standardized methods
- Allow for flexibility in style to match local context and needs
- Inspire innovation
- Generate momentum to decrease timelines
- Create linkages with partner initiatives to provide bigger impact

Source: Global Initiative for Cancer Registry (GICR).
Note: IARC = International Agency for Research on Cancer.

The presence of six recently established IARC regional hubs for cancer registration (map 2.2) across LMIC regions is providing the necessary localized support and training for cancer registries in the respective countries, as well as strengthening registry networking in each region to improve data standards and develop joint research activities.

CONCLUSIONS

This chapter has examined the increasing global importance of cancer among the major NCDs, highlighted the extent of the ongoing demographic and epidemiologic transitions, described the key risk factors involved, and highlighted the extent to which cancer deaths may be avoided.

Changing fertility patterns and increasing life expectancy are leading to major changes in the scale of the cancer problem worldwide for populations at all levels of human development. A cancer transition is clearly underway in countries transiting to high levels of income and development whereby reductions in infection-related cancers are offset by concomitant increases in cancers linked to a "Westernization" of lifestyle, including "risky" behavior. Changes in tobacco habits and the expanding tobacco markets in LMICs may have major consequences on the future burden of lung and other tobacco-related cancers in the decades that follow.

The global trends therefore place special emphasis on the need for better cancer control in LMICs and the need for expanding coverage and quality of population-based cancer registration systems in each country. Cancer statistics should also serve as a catalyst for further research on human inequality and the scale and profile of cancer from global and regional perspectives, for better determination of how and why macroeconomic determinants influence cancer indicators. It is imperative that public health clinicians and cancer control specialists are alerted to the increasing magnitude of cancer incidence and mortality worldwide. This analysis serves to highlight the need for global action to reduce the increasing incidence and mortality burden from cancer and alleviate suffering among cancer patients.

ACKNOWLEDGMENT

The authors thank Mathieu Laversanne, IARC, for statistical analysis and generation of the graphics.

NOTES

World Bank income classifications as of July 2014 are as follows, based on estimates of gross national income (GNI) per capita for 2013:

- Low-income countries (LICs): US$1,045 or less
- Middle-income countries (MICs) are subdivided:
  a) lower-middle-income: US$1,046–US$4,125
  b) upper-middle-income (UMICs): US$4,126–US$12,745
- High-income countries (HICs): US$12,746 or more

Except for figure 2.9 and estimates presented in the section Risk Factors, Interventions and Policies, and Potential Impacts on the Burden of Cancer, the maps and figures in this chapter are based on incidence and mortality estimates for ages 0 to 69, consistent with reporting in all *DCP3* volumes. Global cancer statistics are estimates for the year 2012 and have been provided by the International Agency for Research on Cancer from its GLOBOCAN 2012 database. Observable population-based data were derived from *Cancer Incidence in Five Continents, 10th edition* and for trends over time from *CI5 Plus* (http://ci5.iarc.fr/CI5plus/Default.aspx). The discussion of burden (including risk factors), however, includes all ages unless otherwise noted. Interventions also apply to all age groups, except where age ranges or cutoffs are specified.

REFERENCES

Agudo, A., C. Bonet, N. Travier, C. A. Gonzalez, P. Vineis, and others. 2012. "Impact of Cigarette Smoking on Cancer Risk in the European Prospective Investigation into Cancer and Nutrition Study." *Journal of Clinical Oncology* 30 (36): 4550–57. doi:JCO.2011.41.0183 [Pii] 10.1200 /JCO.2011.41.0183.

Beral, V., D. Bull, J. Green, and G. Reeves. 2007. "Ovarian Cancer and Hormone Replacement Therapy in the Million Women Study." *The Lancet* 369 (9574): 1703–10. doi:S0140 -6736(07)60534-0 [Pii] 10.1016/S0140-6736(07)60534-0.

Beral, V., D. Bull, and G. Reeves. 2005. "Endometrial Cancer and Hormone-Replacement Therapy in the Million Women Study." *The Lancet* 365 (9470): 1543–51. doi:S0140 -6736(05)66455-0 [Pii] 10.1016/S0140-6736(05)66455-0.

Beral, V., G. Reeves, D. Bull, and J. Green. 2011. "Breast Cancer Risk in Relation to the Interval between Menopause and Starting Hormone Therapy." *Journal of the National Cancer Institute* 103 (4): 296–305. doi:Djq527 [Pii] 10.1093/Jnci /Djq527.

Bergstrom, A., P. Pisani, V. Tenet, A. Wolk, and H. O. Adami. 2001. "Overweight as an Avoidable Cause of Cancer in Europe." *International Journal of Cancer* 91 (3): 421–30. doi:10.1002/1097-0215(200002)9999:9999<::AID -IJC1053>3.0.CO;2-T [Pii].

Beutels, P. 2001. "Economic Evaluations of Hepatitis B Immunization: A Global Review of Recent Studies (1994–2000)." *Health Economics* 10 (8): 751–74. doi:10.1002 /Hec.625 [Pii].

Bleyer, A., and H. G. Welch. 2012. "Effect of Three Decades of Screening Mammography on Breast-Cancer Incidence." *New England Journal of Medicine* 367 (21): 1998–2005. doi:10.1056/Nejmoa1206809.

Boffetta, P., M. Hashibe, C. La Vecchia, W. Zatonski, and J. Rehm. 2006. "The Burden of Cancer Attributable to Alcohol Drinking." *International Journal of Cancer* 119 (4): 884–87. doi:10.1002/Ijc.21903.

Boffetta, P., M. Tubiana, C. Hill, M. Boniol, A. Aurengo, and others. 2009. "The Causes of Cancer in France." *Annals of Oncology* 20 (3): 550–55. doi:Mdn597 [Pii]10.1093 /Annonc/Mdn597.

Bray, F. 2014. "Transitions in Human Development and the Global Cancer Burden." In *World Cancer Report 2014*, edited by C. P. Wild and B. A. Stewart. Lyon, France: International Agency for Research on Cancer.

Bray, F., A. Jemal, N. Grey, J. Ferlay, and D. Forman. 2012. "Global Cancer Transitions According to the Human Development Index (2008–2030): A Population-Based Study." *The Lancet Oncology* 13 (8): 790–801. doi:10.1016 /S1470-2045(12)70211-5.

Bray, F., J. Lortet-Tieulent, J. Ferlay, D. Forman, and A. Auvinen. 2010. "Prostate Cancer Incidence and Mortality Trends in 37 European Countries: An Overview." *European Journal of Cancer* 46 (17): 3040–52. doi:S0959-8049(10)00878-6 [Pii]10.1016/J.Ejca.2010.09.013.

Bray, F., P. McCarron, and D. M. Parkin. 2004. "The Changing Global Patterns of Female Breast Cancer Incidence and Mortality." *Breast Cancer Research* 6 (6): 229–39. doi:Bcr932 [Pii]10.1186/Bcr932.

Bray, F., A. Znaor, P. Cueva, A. Korir, R. Swaminathan, and others. 2014. "Planning and Developing Population-Based Cancer Registration in Low- and Middle-Income Settings." Technical Publication 43, International Agency for Research on Cancer, Lyon, France.

Brown, I. J., I. Tzoulaki, V. Candeias, and P. Elliott. 2009. "Salt Intakes around the World: Implications for Public Health." *International Journal of Epidemiology* 38 (3): 791–813. doi:Dyp139 [Pii] 10.1093/Ije/Dyp139.

Center, M. M., A. Jemal, R. A. Smith, and E. Ward. 2009. "Worldwide Variations in Colorectal Cancer." *CA: A Cancer Journal for Clinicians* 59 (6): 366–78. doi:59/6/366 [Pii]10.3322/Caac.20038.

Center, M. M., A. Jemal, and E. Ward. 2009. "International Trends in Colorectal Cancer Incidence Rates." *Cancer Epidemiology Biomarkers & Prevention* 18 (6): 1688–94. doi:18/6/1688 [Pii]10.1158/1055-9965.EPI-09-0090.

Chang, M. H., C. J. Chen, M. S. Lai, H. M. Hsu, T. C. Wu, and others. 1997. "Universal Hepatitis B Vaccination in Taiwan and the Incidence of Hepatocellular Carcinoma in Children. Taiwan Childhood Hepatoma Study Group." *New England Journal of Medicine* 336 (26): 1855–59. doi:10.1056/NEJM199706263362602.

Chokunonga, E., M. Z. Borok, Z. M. Chirenje, A. M. Nyakabau, and D. M. Parkin. 2013. "Trends in the Incidence of Cancer in the Black Population of Harare, Zimbabwe 1991–2010." *International Journal of Cancer* 133 (3): 721–29. doi:10.1002 /Ijc.28063.

Cogliano, V. J., R. Baan, K. Straif, Y. Grosse, B. Lauby-Secretan, and others. 2011. "Preventable Exposures Associated with Human Cancers." *Journal of the National Cancer Institute* 103 (24): 1827–39. doi:Djr483 [Pii] 10.1093/Jnci/Djr483.

Dallat, M. A., I. Soerjomataram, R. F. Hunter, M. A. Tully, K. J. Cairns, and others. 2013. "Urban Greenways Have the Potential to Increase Physical Activity Levels Cost-Effectively." *European Journal of Public Health* 24 (2): 190–95. doi:Ckt035[Pii]10.1093/Eurpub/Ckt035.

Danaei, G., S. Vander Hoorn, A. D. Lopez, C. J. Murray, and M. Ezzati. 2005. "Causes of Cancer in the World: Comparative Risk Assessment of Nine Behavioural and Environmental Risk Factors." *The Lancet* 366 (9499): 1784–93. doi:S0140-6736(05)67725-2 [Pii]10.1016 /S0140-6736(05)67725-2.

de Martel, C., J. Ferlay, S. Franceschi, J. Vignat, F. Bray, and others. 2012. "Global Burden of Cancers Attributable to Infections in 2008: A Review and Synthetic Analysis." *The Lancet Oncology* 13 (6): 607–15. doi:S1470-2045(12)70137-7 [Pii]10.1016/S1470-2045(12)70137-7.

de Vries, E., M. Arnold, E. Altsitsiadis, M. Trakatelli, B. Hinrichs, and others. 2012. "Potential Impact of Interventions Resulting in Reduced Exposure to Ultraviolet (UV) Radiation (UVA and UVB) on Skin Cancer Incidence in Four European Countries, 2010–2050." *British Journal of Dermatology* 167 (Suppl. 2): 53–62. doi:10.1111/J.1365-2133.2012.11087.X.

de Vries, E., and J. W. Coebergh. 2004. "Cutaneous Malignant Melanoma in Europe." *European Journal of Cancer* 40 (16): 2355–66. doi:S0959804904004678 [Pii]10.1016/J .Ejca.2004.06.003.

Diez Roux, A. V., K. R. Evenson, A. P. McGinn, D. G. Brown, L. Moore, and others. 2007. "Availability of Recreational Resources and Physical Activity in Adults." *American Journal of Public Health* 97 (3): 493–99. doi:AJPH.2006.087734 [Pii] 10.2105/AJPH.2006.087734.

Dikshit, R., P. C. Gupta, C. Ramasundarahettige, V. Gajalakshmi, L. Aleksandrowicz, and others. 2012. "Cancer Mortality in India: A Nationally Representative Survey." *The Lancet* 379 (9828): 1807–16. doi:10.1016/S0140-6736(12)60358-4.

Doll, R. 1990. "Are We Winning the Fight against Cancer? An Epidemiological Assessment. EACR-Muhlbock Memorial Lecture." *European Journal of Cancer* 26 (4): 500–08.

Doll, R., P. Payne, and A. J. H. Waterhouse. 1966. *Cancer Incidence in Five Continents: A Technical Report.* New York: Springer.

Doll, R., and R. Peto. 1981. "The Causes of Cancer: Quantitative Estimates of Avoidable Risks of Cancer in the United States Today." *Journal of the National Cancer Institute* 66 (6): 1191–308.

Doll, R., R. Peto, J. Boreham, and I. Sutherland. 2004. "Mortality in Relation to Smoking: 50 Years' Observations on Male British Doctors." *British Medical Journal* 328 (7455): 1519. doi: 10.1136/Bmj.38142.554479.AE Bmj.38142.554479 .AE [Pii].

Evans, J., A. Van Donkelaar, R. V. Martin, R. Burnett, D. G. Rainham, and others. 2013. "Estimates of Global Mortality Attributable to Particulate Air Pollution Using Satellite Imagery." *Environmental Research* 120: 33–42. doi:S0013-9351(12)00240-X[Pii]10.1016/J.Envres.2012.08.005.

Ezzati, M., S. J. Henley, A. D. Lopez, and M. J. Thun. 2005. "Role of Smoking in Global and Regional Cancer Epidemiology: Current Patterns and Data Needs." *International Journal of Cancer* 116 (6): 963–71. doi:10.1002/Ijc.21100.

Farmer, P., J. Frenk, F. M. Knaul, L. N. Shulman, G. Alleyne, and others. 2010. "Expansion of Cancer Care and Control in Countries of Low and Middle Income: A Call to Action." *The Lancet* 376 (9747): 1186–93. doi:S0140-6736(10)61152-X [Pii] 10.1016/S0140-6736(10)61152-X.

Ferlay, J., I. Soerjomataram, M. Ervik, R. Dikshit, S. Eser, and others. 2013. GLOBOCAN 2012 v1.0. In *Cancer Incidence and Mortality Worldwide: IARC CancerBase No. 11 [Internet].* Lyon, France: International Agency for Research on Cancer.

Ferlay, J., I. Soerjomataram, R. Dikshit, S. Eser, C. Mathers, and others. 2015. "Cancer Incidence and Mortality Worldwide: Sources, Methods and Major Patterns in GLOBOCAN 2012." *International Journal of Cancer* 136 (5): E359–86. doi:10.1002/Ijc.29210.

Forman, D., C. de Martel, C. J. Lacey, I. Soerjomataram, J. Lortet-Tieulent, and others. 2012. "Global Burden of Human Papillomavirus and Related Diseases." *Vaccine* 30 (Suppl. 5): F12–23. doi:S0264-410X(12)01080-8 [Pii] 10.1016/J.Vaccine.2012.07.055.

Friedenreich, C., T. Norat, K. Steindorf, M. C. Boutron-Ruault, T. Pischon, and others. 2006. "Physical Activity and Risk of Colon and Rectal Cancers: The European Prospective Investigation into Cancer and Nutrition." *Cancer Epidemiological Biomarkers & Prevention* 15 (12): 2398–407. doi: 15/12/2398 [Pii] 10.1158/1055-9965 .EPI-06-0595.

Giles-Corti, B., M. H. Broomhall, M. Knuiman, C. Collins, K. Douglas, and others. 2005. "Increasing Walking: How Important Is Distance to, Attractiveness, and Size of Public Open Space?" *American Journal of Preventive Medicine* 28 (2 Suppl. 2): 169–76. doi:S0749-3797(04)00298-3 [Pii] 10.1016/J.Amepre.2004.10.018.

Giovannucci, E., A. Ascherio, E. B. Rimm, G. A. Colditz, M. J. Stampfer, and others. 1995. "Physical Activity, Obesity, and Risk for Colon Cancer and Adenoma in Men." *Annals of Internal Medicine* 122 (5): 327–34.

Goldie, S. J., M. O'Shea, N. G. Campos, M. Diaz, S. Sweet, and others. 2008. "Health and Economic Outcomes of HPV 16,18 Vaccination in 72 GAVI-Eligible Countries." *Vaccine* 26 (32): 4080–93. doi:S0264-410X(08)00493 -3[Pii]10.1016/J.Vaccine.2008.04.053.

Goldstein, S. T., F. Zhou, S. C. Hadler, B. P. Bell, E. E. Mast, and others. 2005. "A Mathematical Model to Estimate Global Hepatitis B Disease Burden and Vaccination Impact." *International Journal of Epidemiology* 34 (6): 1329–39. doi:Dyi206 [Pii]10.1093/Ije/Dyi206.

Hanley, J. A. 2001. "A Heuristic Approach to the Formulas for Population Attributable Fraction." *Journal of Epidemiology and Community Health* 55 (7): 508–14.

Harper, D. M., E. L. Franco, C. Wheeler, D. G. Ferris, D. Jenkins, and others. 2004. "Efficacy of a Bivalent L1

Virus-Like Particle Vaccine in Prevention of Infection with Human Papillomavirus Types 16 and 18 in Young Women: A Randomised Controlled Trial." *The Lancet* 364 (9447): 1757–65. doi:S0140673604173984 [Pii]10.1016 /S0140-6736(04)17398-4.

Harriss, D. J., G. Atkinson, A. Batterham, K. George, N. T. Cable, and others. 2009. "Lifestyle Factors and Colorectal Cancer Risk (2): A Systematic Review and Meta-Analysis of Associations with Leisure-Time Physical Activity." *Colorectal Disease* 11 (7): 689–701. doi:CDI1767 [Pii] 10.1111/J.1463-1318.2009.01767.X.

Herrero, R., W. Quint, A. Hildesheim, P. Gonzalez, L. Struijk, and others. 2013. "Reduced Prevalence of Oral Human Papillomavirus (HPV) 4 Years after Bivalent HPV Vaccination in A Randomized Clinical Trial in Costa Rica." *Plos One* 8 (7): E68329. doi:10.1371/Journal.Pone.0068329 PONE-D-12-40404 [Pii].

IARC (International Agency for Research on Cancer). 1987. *Overall Evaluations of Carcinogenicity: An Updating of IARC Monographs 1–440*. Monographs on the Evaluation of Carcinogenic Risks to Humans, IARC, Lyon, France.

———. 2004. "Tobacco Smoke and Involuntary Smoking." Monographs on the Evaluation of Carcinogenic Risks to Humans, Volume 83, IARC, Lyon, France.

———. 2010. "Alcohol Consumption and Ethyl Carbamate." Monographs on the Evaluation of Carcinogenic Risks to Humans, IARC, Lyon, France.

Jemal, A., F. Bray, D. Forman, M. O'Brien, J. Ferlay, and others. 2012. "Cancer Burden in Africa and Opportunities for Prevention." *Cancer* 118 (18): 4372–84. doi:10.1002 /Cncr.27410.

Jemal, A., M. M. Center, C. Desantis, and E. M. Ward. 2010. "Global Patterns of Cancer Incidence and Mortality Rates and Trends." *Cancer Epidemiology Biomarkers & Prevention* 19 (8): 1893–907. doi:1055-9965.EPI-10-0437 [Pii] 10.1158/1055-9965.EPI-10-0437.

Jha, P. 2009. "Avoidable Global Cancer Deaths and Total Deaths from Smoking." *Nature Reviews Cancer* 9 (9): 655–64. doi:Nrc2703 [Pii] 10.1038/Nrc2703.

Jha, P., C. Ramasundarahettige, V. Landsman, B. Rostron, M. Thun, and others. 2013. "21st-Century Hazards of Smoking and Benefits of Cessation in the United States." *New England Journal of Medicine* 368 (4): 341–50. doi:0.1056 /Nejmsa1211128.

Kane, M. A., B. Serrano, S. De Sanjose, and S. Wittet. 2012. "Implementation of Human Papillomavirus Immunization in the Developing World." *Vaccine* 30 (Suppl. 5): F192–200. doi:S0264-410X(12)00956-5 [Pii] 10.1016/J .Vaccine.2012.06.075.

Karim-Kos, H. E., E. de Vries, I. Soerjomataram, V. Lemmens, S. Siesling, and J. W. Coebergh. 2008. "Recent Trends of Cancer in Europe: A Combined Approach of Incidence, Survival and Mortality for 17 Cancer Sites Since the 1990s." *European Journal of Cancer* 44 (10): 1345–89. doi: 10.1016/j. ejca.2007.12.015.

Lim, S. S., T. Vos, A. D. Flaxman, G. Danaei, K. Shibuya, and others. 2012. "A Comparative Risk Assessment of Burden of Disease and Injury Attributable to 67 Risk Factors and Risk Factor Clusters in 21 Regions, 1990–2010: A Systematic Analysis for the Global Burden of Disease Study 2010." *The Lancet* 380 (9859): 2224–60. doi:10.1016 /S0140-6736(12)61766-8.

Lin, H. H., M. Murray, T. Cohen, C. Colijn, and M. Ezzati. 2008. "Effects of Smoking and Solid-Fuel Use on COPD, Lung Cancer, and Tuberculosis in China: A Time-Based, Multiple Risk Factor, Modelling Study." *The Lancet* 372 (9648): 1473–83. doi:S0140-6736(08)61345-8 [Pii] 10.1016 /S0140-6736(08)61345-8.

Lortet-Tieulent, J., E. Renteria, L. Sharp, E. Weiderpass, H. Comber, and others. 2013. "Convergence of Decreasing Male and Increasing Female Incidence Rates in Major Tobacco-Related Cancers in Europe in 1988–2010." *European Journal of Cancer*. doi: S0959-8049(13)00952-0 [Pii] 10.1016/J.Ejca.2013.10.014.

Lozano, R., M. Naghavi, K. Foreman, S. Lim, K. Shibuya, and others. 2012. "Global and Regional Mortality from 235 Causes of Death for 20 Age Groups in 1990 and 2010: A Systematic Analysis for the Global Burden of Disease Study 2010." *The Lancet* 380 (9859): 2095–128. doi:S0140 -6736(12)61728-0 [Pii]10.1016/S0140-6736(12)61728-0.

Makela, P., K. Tryggvesson, and I. Rossow. 2002. "Who Drinks More or Less When Policies Change? The Evidence from 50 Years of Nordic Studies." In *The Effects of Nordic Alcohol Policies: Analyses of Changes in Control Systems*, edited by R. Room. Helsinki: Nordic Council for Alcohol and Drug Research.

Martin-Moreno, J. M., I. Soerjomataram, and G. Magnusson. 2008. "Cancer Causes and Prevention: A Condensed Appraisal in Europe in 2008." *European Journal of Cancer* 44 (10): 1390–403. doi:S0959-8049(08)00090-7 [Pii] 10.1016/J.Ejca.2008.02.002.

McCormack, V. A., and P. Boffetta. 2011. "Today's Lifestyles, Tomorrow's Cancers: Trends in Lifestyle Risk Factors for Cancer in Low- and Middle-Income Countries." *Annals of Oncology* 22 (11): 2349–57. doi:Mdq763 [Pii] 10.1093 /Annonc/Mdq763.

McCormack, V., J. Peto, G. Byrnes, K. Straif, and P. Boffetta. 2012. "Estimating the Asbestos-Related Lung Cancer Burden from Mesothelioma Mortality." *British Journal of Cancer* 106 (3): 575–84. doi:Bjc2011563 [Pii] 10.1038 /Bjc.2011.563.

McCormack, V. A., and J. Schuz. 2012. "Africa's Growing Cancer Burden: Environmental and Occupational Contributions." *Cancer Epidemiology* 36 (1): 1–7. doi:S1877 -7821(11)00146-9 [Pii] 10.1016/J.Canep.2011.09.005.

Monninkhof, E. M., S. G. Elias, F. A. Vlems, I. Van Der Tweel, A. J. Schuit, and others. 2007. "Physical Activity and Breast Cancer: A Systematic Review." *Epidemiology* 18 (1): 137–57. doi:10.1097/01.Ede.0000251167.75581.98.

Muir, C. S., J. F. Fraumeni, Jr., and R. Doll. 1994. "The Interpretation of Time Trends." *Cancer Surveys* 19–20: 5–21.

Murray, C. J., J. Abraham, M. K. Ali, M. Alvarado, C. Atkinson, and others. 2013. "The State of US Health, 1990–2010: Burden of Diseases, Injuries, and Risk Factors." *Journal of the American Medical Association* 310 (6): 591–606. doi:1710486 [Pii] 10.1001/Jama.2013.13805.

Ng, M., M. K. Freeman, T. D. Fleming, M. Robinson, L. Dwyer-Lindgren, and others. 2014. "Smoking Prevalence and Cigarette Consumption in 187 Countries, 1980–2012." *Journal of the American Medical Association* 311 (2): 183–92. doi:10.1001/Jama.2013.284692.

Parkin, D. M. 2006. "The Evolution of the Population-Based Cancer Registry." *Nature Reviews Cancer* 6 (8): 603–12. doi:Nrc1948 [Pii] 10.1038/Nrc1948.

———. 2011. "Cancers Attributable to Dietary Factors in the UK in 2010. IV. Salt." *British Journal of Cancer* 105 (Suppl. 2): S31–33. doi:Bjc2011480 [Pii] 10.1038/Bjc.2011.480.

Parkin, D. M., F. Bray, J. Ferlay, and A. Jemal. 2014. "Cancer in Africa 2012." *Cancer Epidemilogy Biomarkers & Prevention* 23 (6): 953–66. doi:10.1158/1055-9965.EPI-14-0281.

Pirie, K., R. Peto, G. K. Reeves, J. Green, and V. Beral. 2013. "The 21st Century Hazards of Smoking and Benefits of Stopping: A Prospective Study of One Million Women in the UK." *The Lancet* 381 (9861): 133–41. doi:S0140-6736(12)61720-6 [Pii]10.1016/S0140-6736(12)61720-6.

Pischon, T., P. H. Lahmann, H. Boeing, C. Friedenreich, T. Norat, and others. 2006. "Body Size and Risk of Colon and Rectal Cancer in the European Prospective Investigation into Cancer and Nutrition (EPIC)." *Journal of the National Cancer Institute* 98 (13): 920–31. doi:98/13/920 [Pii]10.1093/Jnci/Djj246.

Raaschou-Nielsen, O., Z. J. Andersen, R. Beelen, E. Samoli, M. Stafoggia, and others. 2013. "Air Pollution and Lung Cancer Incidence in 17 European Cohorts: Prospective Analyses from the European Study of Cohorts for Air Pollution Effects (ESCAPE)." *The Lancet Oncology* 14 (9): 813–22. doi:S1470-2045(13)70279-1 [Pii]10.1016/S1470-2045(13)70279-1.

Reeves, G. K., K. Pirie, J. Green, D. Bull, and V. Beral. 2012. "Comparison of the Effects of Genetic and Environmental Risk Factors on In Situ and Invasive Ductal Breast Cancer." *International Journal of Cancer* 131 (4): 930–37. doi:10.1002/Ijc.26460.

Rehm, J., and K. D. Shield. 2013. "Global Alcohol-Attributable Deaths from Cancer, Liver Cirrhosis, and Injury in 2010." *Alcohol Research* 35 (2): 174–83.

Renehan, A. G., I. Soerjomataram, M. Tyson, M. Egger, M. Zwahlen, and others. 2010. "Incident Cancer Burden Attributable to Excess Body Mass Index in 30 European Countries." *International Journal of Cancer* 126 (3): 692–702. doi:10.1002/Ijc.24803.

Rockhill, B., B. Newman, and C. Weinberg. 1998. "Use and Misuse of Population Attributable Fractions." *American Journal of Public Health* 88 (1): 15–19.

Rosner, B., and G. A. Colditz. 1996. "Nurses' Health Study: Log-Incidence Mathematical Model of Breast Cancer Incidence." *Journal of the National Cancer Institute* 88 (6): 359–64.

Sankaranarayanan, R., R. Swaminathan, K. Jayant, and H. Brenner. 2011. "An Overview of Cancer Survival in Africa, Asia, the Caribbean and Central America: The Case for Investment in Cancer Health Services." *IARC Scientific Publications* 162: 257–91.

Shield, K. D., M. Rylett, G. Gmel, T. A. Kehoe-Chan, and J. Rehm. 2013. "Global Alcohol Exposure Estimates by Country, Territory and Region for 2005: A Contribution to the Comparative Risk Assessment for the 2010 Global Burden of Disease Study." *Addiction* 108 (5): 912–22. doi:10.1111/Add.12112.

Soerjomataram, I., E. Pukkala, H. Brenner, and J. W. Coebergh. 2008. "On the Avoidability of Breast Cancer in Industrialized Societies: Older Mean Age at First Birth as an Indicator of Excess Breast Cancer Risk." *Breast Cancer Research and Treatment* 111 (2): 297–302. doi:10.1007/S10549-007-9778-2.

Stevens, G. A., G. M. Singh, Y. Lu, G. Danaei, J. K. Lin, and others. 2012. "National, Regional, and Global Trends in Adult Overweight and Obesity Prevalences." *Population Health Metrics* 10 (1): 22. doi:1478-7954-10-22 [Pii] 10.1186/1478-7954-10-22.

Stewart, B. W. 2012. "Priorities for Cancer Prevention: Lifestyle Choices versus Unavoidable Exposures." *The Lancet Oncology* 13 (3): E126–33. doi:S1470-2045(11)70221-2 [Pii]10.1016/S1470-2045(11)70221-2.

Talley, M. B. 2010. *Examining the Impact of Development, Tobacco Taxation, and Tobacco Prices on Global Adult Male Smoking Prevalence.* Altanta, GA: Georgia Institute of Technology, Georgia State University.

Thun, M., R. Peto, J. Boreham, and A. D. Lopez. 2012. "Stages of the Cigarette Epidemic on Entering Its Second Century." *Tobacco Control* 21 (2): 96–101. doi:Tobaccocontrol-2011-050294 [Pii] 10.1136/Tobaccocontrol-2011-050294.

UNDP (United Nations Develpoment Programme). 2009. *Human Development Report 2009: Overcoming Barriers: Human Mobility and Development.* New York: UNDP.

Vaccarella, S., J. Lortet-Tieulent, M. Plummer, S. Franceschi, and F. Bray. 2013. "Worldwide Trends in Cervical Cancer Incidence: Impact of Screening against Changes in Disease Risk Factors." *European Journal of Cancer* 49 (15): 3262–73. doi:S0959-8049(13)00358-4 [Pii]10.1016/J.Ejca.2013.04.024.

Wabinga, H. R., P. M. Amulen, C. Okello, L. Mbus, and D. M. Parkin. 2014. "Trends in the Incidence of Cancer in Kampala, Uganda 1991–2010." *International Journal of Cancer* 135 (2): 432–9. doi: 10.1002/ijc.28661. http://www.ncbi.nlm.nih.gov/pubmed/24615279.

WCRF (World Cancer Research Fund) and AICR (American Institute for Cancer Research). 2007. *Food, Nutrition, Physical Activity, and the Prevention of Cancer: A Global Perspective.* Washington, DC: WCRF and AICR.

WHO (World Health Organization). 2008. *Report on the Global Tobacco Epidemic, 2008: The MPOWER Package.* Geneva: WHO.

———. 2011a. *Global Status Report on Alcohol and Health.* Geneva: WHO.

———. 2011b. *Global Status Report on Non-Communicable Diseases 2010.* Geneva: WHO.

———. 2013. "Global Health Observatory Data Repository." WHO, Geneva. http://apps.who.int/gho/data/node.main.a859?lang=en.

Wild, C. P. 2014. "Foreword." In *Planning and Developing Population-Based Cancer Registration in Low- and Middle-Income Settings,* edited by F. Bray, A. Znaor, P. Cueva, A. Korir, R. Swaminathan, and others. Lyon, France: IARC.

Breast Cancer

Benjamin O. Anderson, Joseph Lipscomb, Raul H. Murillo, and
David B. Thomas

INTRODUCTION

Disparities in Global Breast Cancer Outcomes[1]

Breast cancer is the world's most common cancer among women, and it is the most likely reason that a woman will die from cancer (maps 3.1 and 3.2). Breast cancer is becoming an increasingly urgent problem in low- and middle-income countries (LMICs), where incidence rates, historically low, have been rising by as much as 5 percent per year (Bray and others 2013). High-income countries (HICs) report the highest breast cancer incidence rates (figure 3.1), but these countries have also made the most progress in improving outcomes (Jemal and others 2002). In 2010, the majority of the 425,000 global breast cancer deaths occurred in LMICs, and that percentage is expected to grow (Parkin and Fernandez 2006).

Breast cancer fatality rates are inversely correlated with per capita gross domestic product (GDP) (Greenlee and others 2000). Historically, breast cancer incidence had been low in LMICs, but these rates are rising disproportionately at the same time that mortality rates are continuing to rise or remain high (figure 3.2). The aging of current global population means that nearly 50 percent more women will develop and die from breast cancer in 2020 than in 2002. This estimate does not take into account the likely increases in age-specific breast cancer incidence and mortality rates, especially among recent birth cohorts and among urban women in

LMICs, because of changes in their childbearing patterns and their adoption of Western lifestyles (Parkin and Fernandez 2006; Porter 2008). The number of young lives lost is even more disproportionate than the total number; in 2010, breast cancer killed 68,000 women ages 15–49 years in LMICs, compared with 26,000 in this age range in HICs (Forouzanfar and others 2011).

HICs have made tremendous progress in improving outcomes (figure 3.2). Mortality rates, which had been essentially unchanged in the United States for the five decades between 1930 and 1980, have dropped nearly 2 percent each year since 1990 (Jemal and others 2009). Similar reductions have occurred in other HICs, such as Norway (Kalager and others 2010). The improvements are attributable to early detection by screening, combined with timely and effective treatment (Weir and others 2003). Randomized trials of screening mammography in the 1970s and 1980s demonstrated that early detection leads to stage shifting, improved survival, and reduced mortality (Chu, Smart, and Tarone 1988). Endocrine therapy for estrogen receptor (ER)–positive cancers and cytotoxic chemotherapy for ER-negative cancers improve survival among early and locally advanced breast cancers (Clarke 2006; Perloff and others 1988).

Low survival rates in LMICs are largely attributable to late-stage presentation and limited diagnostic and treatment capacities (Hisham and Yip 2003). In India, 50–70 percent of cases are diagnosed with locally

Corresponding author: Benjamin O. Anderson, MD, banderso@u.washington.edu

Map 3.1 Global Breast Cancer Incidence in Women in 2012

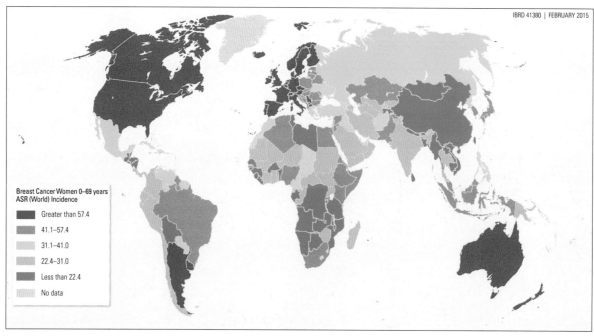

IBRD 41380 | FEBRUARY 2015

Breast Cancer Women 0–69 years
ASR (World) Incidence

- Greater than 57.4
- 41.1–57.4
- 31.1–41.0
- 22.4–31.0
- Less than 22.4
- No data

Source: Ferlay and others 2013.
Note: Values are estimated ASR per 100,000 women. ASR = age-standardized rate.

Map 3.2 Global Breast Cancer Mortality in Women in 2012

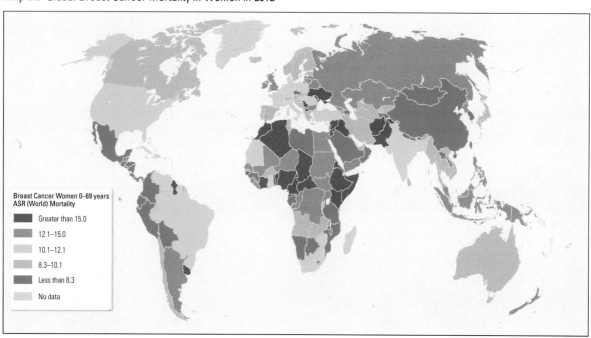

Breast Cancer Women 0–69 years
ASR (World) Mortality

- Greater than 15.0
- 12.1–15.0
- 10.1–12.1
- 8.3–10.1
- Less than 8.3
- No data

Source: Ferlay and others 2013.
Note: Values are estimated ASR per 100,000 women. ASR = age-standardized rate.

Figure 3.1 Trends in Age-Standardized Incidence Rates in Women, Selected Countries, 1975–2010

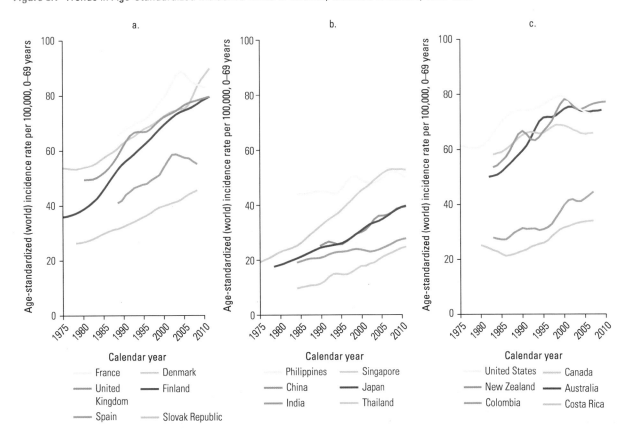

Sources: CI5 Plus (http://ci5.iarc.fr/CI5plus/Default.aspx); and Ferlay and others 2013.
Note: Values are age-standardized rates of breast cancer incidence per 100,000 women, for the world population structure.

advanced or metastatic disease (Chopra 2001); the same was true of 38 percent of European and 30 percent of American cases in the early 1990s (Sant and others 2004). Accordingly, efforts to promote early detection followed by appropriate treatment are essential components of population-based breast cancer control strategies.

The two strategies of early detection and adjuvant systemic therapy are synergistic and mutually dependent for improving outcomes; early detection only works if it can be followed by prompt therapy. Mathematical modeling suggests that between 28 percent and 65 percent of breast cancer mortality reduction can be attributed to early detection; the balance is due to pharmacotherapy (Berry and others 2005). The interdependence of early detection and treatment underscores the essential role of guidelines for administering this comprehensive strategy in limited-resource settings to shift morbidity and mortality rates at the global level.

Risk Factors and Risk Reduction Strategies

Breast cancer risk increases with some factors that cannot be modified, such as age, genetic and familial risks, younger age at menarche, and older age at menopause; some factors that are somewhat modifiable, including delayed childbearing, avoidance of lactation, radiation exposure, and use of hormone replacement therapy; and some that are more modifiable, including body mass index, sedentary lifestyle, and moderate to high levels of alcohol use (McTiernan, Porter, and Potter 2008). Modifying these behaviors to the extent possible, although not proven in clinical trials to reduce risk, is likely to be beneficial, can be good for general health and noncommunicable disease prevention, and may be of interest to policy makers in LMICs. However, because most of these factors elevate risk only marginally, even successful reduction of them may only have a small effect on overall risk. Some risk factors are not amenable to change; others are associated with

Figure 3.2 Trends in Age-Standardized Breast Cancer Mortality Rates in Women, Selected Countries, 1975–2010

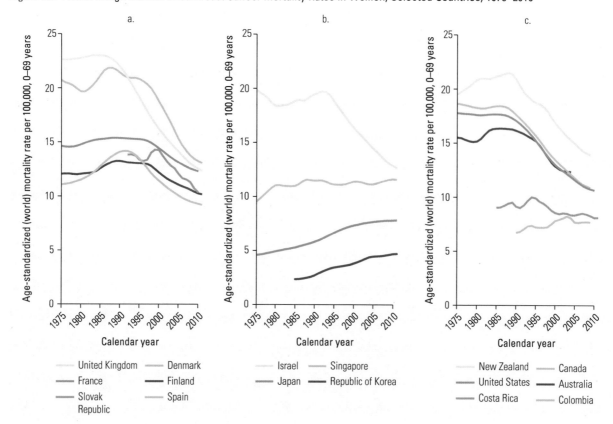

Sources: Ferlay and others 2013; WHO Mortality Database (http://www.who.int/healthinfo/statistics/mortality_rawdata/en/index.html).
Note: Values are age-standardized rates of breast cancer mortality per 100,000 women, for the world population structure.

desirable outcomes, such as the education of women, which has major societal benefits even if it tends to delay childbearing.

RESOURCE-STRATIFIED GUIDELINES

Need for Cancer Care Guidelines Explicitly Addressing Resource Limitations

Early detection and comprehensive treatment together can improve outcomes. In HICs and upper-middle-income countries, the guidelines for achieving these goals are defined, updated, and disseminated (Morrow and others 2002; Smith 2000; Theriault and others 2013). The World Health Organization (WHO) has pointed out the limited utility of these guidelines in resource-constrained countries; they fail to include implementation costs and provide no guidance as to how treatment that is effective but less than optimal (and less expensive) could be provided affordably for poorer populations (WHO 2002).

Breast Health Global Initiative

Evidence-based, economically feasible, and culturally appropriate guidelines that can be used in settings with limited resources to improve outcomes have been developed by the Breast Health Global Initiative (BHGI), an international health alliance established in 2002. The BHGI has held five global summits addressing key aspects of care:

- Health care disparities, Seattle, Washington, 2002 (Anderson and others 2003)
- Evidence-based resource allocation, Bethesda, Maryland, 2005 (Anderson and others 2006)
- Guideline implementation, Budapest, 2007 (Anderson and others 2008)
- Optimizing outcomes, Chicago, Illinois, 2010 (Anderson and others 2011)
- Supportive care and quality of life, Vienna, 2012 (Cardoso and others 2013; Cleary and others 2013; Ganz and others 2013)

Modeled after the National Comprehensive Cancer Network in the United States (Winn and Botnick 1997), the BHGI applied an evidence-based consensus panel process to build a framework defining resource prioritization for early detection (Yip and others 2008), diagnosis (Shyyan and others 2008), treatment (Eniu and others 2008), and delivery systems (Eniu and others 2008) at four levels of available resources: basic, limited, enhanced, and maximal (box 3.1). The framework is designed to facilitate strategy development and decision making by policy makers and health care administrators initiating breast cancer control programs or reviewing existing services. Different resource levels may apply to different areas of a country, because health care access and resources vary with infrastructure and geography. The same methodology has been applied to the development of guidelines for the management of hepatocellular carcinoma in Asia (Poon and others 2009), non-small cell lung carcinoma (Soo and others 2009), endometrial cancer (Tangjitgamol and others 2009), head and neck cancer (Wee and others 2009), and HER2/neu-positive breast cancer (Wong and others 2009).

BHGI GUIDELINES

Guidelines on Early Detection

Shifting the stage distribution of disease to earlier stages is a necessary step to improving outcomes in LMICs, where many women typically present with locally advanced or metastatic tumors. Achieving stage shifting is likely to reduce mortality; even if this effect is small, the quality of life will be improved. Women would no longer present with large, sometimes ulcerated masses that are painful, odiferous, ostracizing, and amenable only to palliative treatment. Breast-preserving surgery will also be possible in more cases, further reducing morbidity and enhancing the quality of life.

Early detection approaches include screening for asymptomatic disease and early diagnosis of symptomatic disease (table 3.1). As a new screening program is implemented, more cancers will be detected initially, creating an apparent increase in disease incidence. As the screening program becomes established, the detection rate will decline to a steady state. Once diagnosed, more patients will require treatment, at a cost to the health care system. This increased cost may be partially offset by lower total treatment costs, because patients with earlier stage disease require less therapy, but this model assumes that the patients would have been treated in both cases. The cost and human resource requirements of increased demand for treatment must be factored into any decision to establish a screening program.

Mammographic Screening

The efficacy of mammographic screening was established in trials in HICs that included monitoring

---

Box 3.1

Definitions of Breast Health Global Initiative Resource Levels

- *Basic.* Core resources or fundamental services that are necessary for any breast health care system to function; basic-level services are typically applied in a single clinical interaction.
- *Limited.* Second-tier resources or services that are intended to produce major improvements in outcome and are attainable with limited financial means and modest infrastructure; limited-level services may involve single or multiple clinical interactions.
- *Enhanced.* Third-tier resources or services that are optional but important; enhanced-level resources should produce further improvements in outcome and increase the number and quality of therapeutic options and patient choices.

- *Maximal.* High-level resources or services that may be used in some high-income countries and/ or may be recommended by breast care guidelines that are not adapted to resource constraints. They should be considered lower priority than those resources or services listed in the basic, limited, or enhanced categories, on the basis of cost and/or impracticality for broad use in resource-limited environments. To be useful, maximal-level resources typically depend on the existence and functionality of all lower-level resources.

Source: Anderson and others 2008.
Note: The stratification scheme implies incrementally increasing resource allocation at the basic, limited, and enhanced levels. Maximal-level resources should not be targeted for implementation in LMICs, even though they may be used in some higher-resource settings.

Table 3.1 Early Detection Resource Allocation

Early Detection	Level of available resources			
	Basic	Limited	Enhanced	Maximal
Public education and awareness	• Development of culturally sensitive, linguistically appropriate local education programs for target populations to teach value of early detection, breast cancer risk factors, and breast health awareness (education + self-examination)	• Culturally and linguistically appropriate targeted outreach/education encouraging CBE for age groups at higher risk administered at district/provincial level using health care providers in the field	• Regional awareness programs regarding breast health linked to general health and women's health programs	• National awareness campaigns regarding breast health using media
Detection methods	• Clinical history and CBE	• Diagnostic breast US ± diagnostic mammography in women with positive CBE • Mammographic screening of target group[a]	• Mammographic screening every 2 years in women ages 50–69[a] • Consider mammographic screening every 12–18 months in women ages 40–49[a]	• Consider annual mammographic screening in women ages 40 and older • Other imaging technologies as appropriate for high-risk groups[b]
Evaluation goal	• Breast health awareness regarding value of early detection in improving breast cancer outcome	• Downsizing of symptomatic disease	• Downsizing and/or downstaging of asymptomatic disease in women in highest yield target groups	• Downsizing and/or downstaging of asymptomatic disease in women in all risk groups

Source: Anderson and others 2008. Used with permission.
Note: CBE = clinical breast examination; US = ultrasound; ± = with or without.
a. Target group selection for mammographic screening should consider breast cancer demographics and resource constraints within the population.
b. Magnetic resonance imaging is more sensitive than mammography in detecting tumors in asymptomatic women who have an inherited susceptibility to breast cancer.

mammograms for image and interpretation quality. Mammography requires high-quality instrumentation and specially trained radiologists, whose performance varies substantially, depending on training and level of experience; screening efficacy is reduced if mammograms are of inferior quality, or if those who read mammograms are not adequately trained and assessed on an ongoing basis (Barlow and others 2004; Ichikawa and others 2010).

Ensuring the quality of imaging and interpretation is challenging in LMICs, due to the need to purchase machines, ensure ongoing quality control, and maintain screening registers.

Many organizations and investigators, including the International Agency for Research on Cancer (IARC) (IARC 2008) and the U.S. Preventive Services Task Force, have reviewed the evidence for the efficacy of screening with mammography (Nelson and others 2009). The evidence comes mainly from six trials, in which women were randomized to periodic mammographic screening or no screening. Based on these trials, IARC estimated a reduction in breast cancer of about 25 percent in women ages 50–69 years and about 19 percent in women ages

40–49 years. The results were consistent across studies in older women but were inconsistent for women in their forties.

Reviewing the same trials, the U.S. Preventive Services Task Force concluded that the mortality benefit is more consistent among younger women than previously described; 15 percent for ages 39–49; 14 percent for ages 50–59; and 32 percent for ages 60–69 (Nelson and others 2009). The U.S. Preventive Services Task Force withdrew a prior recommendation for routine screening for women ages 39–49 who are at average risk, based on the larger number of women who need to be screened to save a life (1,904 for ages 39–49; 1,339 for ages 50–59; and 377 for ages 60–69) (table 3.2) (U.S. Preventive Services Task Force 2009).

The positive predictive value of screening mammography increases with age. Premenopausal women tend to have denser breast tissue and a higher rate of benign lesions than postmenopausal women, resulting in greater difficulty in detecting lesions and lower sensitivity and specificity (that is, a higher rate of false-positives). Furthermore, the incidence of breast cancer increases with age in most populations.

Table 3.2 Pooled Relative Risk for Breast Cancer Mortality from Mammographic Screening Trials for Women Ages 39–74 Years

Age (years)	Trials included	Relative risk for breast cancer mortality (95% credible interval)	NNI to prevent one breast cancer death (95% credible interval)
39–49	8	0.85 (0.75–0.96)	1904 (929–6378)
50–59	6	0.86 (0.75–0.99)	1339 (322–7455)
60–69	2	0.68 (0.54–0.87)	377 (230–1050)
70–74	1	1.12 (0.73–1.72)	—

Source: Nelson and others 2009.
Note: NNI = number needed to invite to screening; — = not available.

Although it may be less cost effective to screen women in their forties than women ages 50 and older, a relatively high proportion of women with breast cancers in LMICs are ages 40–49, complicating the decision making about the parameters of a screening program. Without screening, the largest age cohort of breast cancer patients will be missed and many women will continue to present for treatment with more advanced stage disease.

Some groups question whether the demonstrated mortality benefit of mammographic screening might be outweighed by the risk of harm through false-positive studies or the potential for overtreatment of biologically favorable early-stage disease (Baum 2013; Gotzsche and others 2012). Informed consent should be provided to women so that they have an appropriate understanding of the potential risks as well as benefits of mammographic screening (Thornton 2014).

Standard practice in HICs is two-view mammography, in which the breast is imaged in two planes (MLO–medial/lateral oblique, CC–craniocaudal), which allows a more accurate reading. However, in older randomized trials, the quality of single-view mammograms was nearly equivalent to that of two-view mammograms. In LMICs with limited resources, consideration can be given to single-view mammography, if doing so will increase the coverage and the screening interval can be extended beyond one or two years. In women ages 50–69, screening every 33 months was as efficacious as screening every 18–24 months; in women ages 40–49, the reduction in mortality was inversely related to the screening interval (Breast Screening Frequency Trial Group 2002). When allocating limited resources for mammographic screening, it is more cost effective to screen a higher proportion of women less frequently than to screen a smaller proportion more frequently. The availability and cost of x-ray film may also limit the availability of screening in LMICs; digital mammography may provide an alternative, if costs are reduced to affordable levels.

Because mammographic screening is expensive and requires considerable infrastructure, consideration has been given in LMICs to screening with clinical breast examination (CBE) and breast self-examination (BSE).

Clinical Breast Examination

CBE is a basic tool in clinical management of breast cancer. However, no randomized trials to assess CBE alone as a screening tool have yet been completed, while the evidence from observational studies is inconsistent. A case-control study in Japan suggested that breast cancer deaths were reduced among asymptomatic women who underwent CBE screening (odds ratio = 0.56) (Kanemura and others 1999). A second Japanese study reported significantly greater reductions in the age-adjusted death rate from breast cancer in areas with high rates of screening coverage (principally by physical examination), compared with areas where coverage was not established (Kuroishi and others 2000). An early clinical trial conducted by the Health Insurance Plan of Greater New York demonstrated that a combination of mammography and CBE reduced the risk of breast cancer mortality; many of the tumors in the screened group were detected by CBE but not by mammography (Chu, Smart, and Tarone 1988). However, more recent randomized trials compared the combination of mammography and CBE with mammography alone, and the two approaches appeared to have equivalent outcomes (IARC 2008). As a result, IARC and the U.S. Preventive Services Task Force concluded that the evidence for the efficacy of CBE in reducing mortality from breast cancer is "inadequate" and "insufficient," respectively (U.S. Preventive Services Task Force 2009).

Most of the evidence for the efficacy of CBE has come from studies in HICs, where women typically present with relatively small tumors. CBE has been advocated for LMICs for several reasons. CBE may be more efficacious in LMICs, where women tend to present with larger tumors; CBE is less expensive than mammography because it can be performed by trained health workers who are not physicians and requires less equipment than mammography. A recent study of 1,179 screened women in Jakarta, Indonesia, compared the use of mammography and CBE in a previously unscreened population and identified 14 breast cancers. Of the 14 cancers, 13 were detected by CBE (Kardinah and others 2014).

If CBE is used for screening breast cancer in LMICs, it should be done in such a way that its effectiveness can be evaluated. A randomized trial in the Philippines was unsuccessful because too few women with positive findings on CBE consented to further diagnostic tests to determine if the findings reflected a malignant or benign finding (Pisani and others 2006). A randomized trial of CBE and visual inspection of the cervix by specially trained women with a tenth-grade education is underway in Mumbai, India. Preliminary results show more breast cancers are being detected at early stages (stages 0, I, or II) in the screening group (62 percent) than in the control group (44 percent), but breast cancer mortality results are not yet available (Mittra and others 2010).

In addition to assessments of its efficacy—sensitivity, shifted stage distribution, and reduction in breast cancer mortality—all such efforts to evaluate the usefulness of CBE should include a measure of its specificity. If large numbers of lesions detected by CBE are found not to be cancerous on further evaluation, this puts a heavy burden on local diagnostic facilities. In addition, if many women undergo unnecessary breast biopsies, this may not be acceptable, either to the women targeted for screening or to policy makers who allocate scarce resources.

CBE accuracy depends on the skill of providers, the definition of proper techniques, and the type of training received. Strategies for providing routine feedback to health care providers about the accuracy of their examinations as determined on final diagnostic work-up are integral to successful CBE programs.

Breast Self-Examination

The aim of BSE is to detect *asymptomatic* breast conditions and should be distinguished from programs that promote early treatment of *symptomatic* breast cancer. BSE is the systematic search performed regularly by the women themselves for a lump or other change in the breast that is suggestive of cancer. In formal BSE training, a woman receives instruction in the four elements of the examination: visual inspection of the breasts in a mirror to look for asymmetry and dimpling; palpation in both the standing and lying positions with the arm above the head, using a circular motion with the pads of the three middle fingers, with systematic coverage of the entire breast and axilla; squeezing of the nipple to detect discharge; and monthly BSE practice.

Most evidence for the efficacy of BSE comes from two randomized trials from Saint Petersburg (Semiglazov and others 1999) and Shanghai (Thomas and others 2002). In both studies, women were randomized to either an intervention group that received instruction in BSE and periodic reminders to practice the procedure or

to a control group that received no such education and no formal breast cancer screening. Mortality from breast cancer was unchanged by BSE instruction in these trials. Both the IARC working group and the U.S. Preventive Services Task Force concluded that the efficacy of BSE is unproven (U.S. Preventive Services Task Force 2009). However, it has been questioned if the negative findings of these BSE trials are relevant to LMICs, where women commonly present with large (> 4 cm) cancers at initial diagnosis. In the Shanghai trial, women in the control group were not taught BSE but nonetheless were largely successful in finding cancers when they were still small, that is, where 45 percent of the cancers were found as in situ or T1 invasive cancers measuring less than 2 cm (Thomas and others 2002). These favorable findings among the untrained control women from Shanghai stand in stark contrast to regions of India, where 76 percent of women present with locally advanced or metastatic (stage III or IV) disease at initial presentation (Chopra 2001). In this latter setting, the actual benefit of BSE training could potentially be much greater.

It remains unknown whether BSE could reduce mortality from breast cancer in populations in LMICs. It is not unreasonable to advocate that BSE be used as a screening tool in these settings, either alone or in combination with CBE. No new trials of BSE alone have been undertaken, but BSE instruction has been included in some of the studies of CBE. The IARC working group recommended randomized trials of BSE in conjunction with mammography. In LMICs where mammographic screening cannot be provided at least every two years, it may be particularly useful to teach BSE.

Any introduction of BSE should be accompanied by evaluation of its efficacy, including quantification of the benign lesions that must be evaluated. In both of the completed BSE trials, many more benign breast lesions were detected in the groups that received BSE instruction than in the control groups.

Breast Awareness Education

Programs to promote early diagnosis and treatment of symptomatic breast cancer are not screening programs, because they are not designed to detect asymptomatic lesions. Their purpose is to encourage women who have symptoms suggestive of breast cancer to seek medical care. Women can be educated to detect suspicious changes in their breasts and empowered to overcome social barriers that might prevent them from seeking care. Breast self-awareness programs should not be initiated unless adequate diagnostic and treatment facilities are available. And the programs should be established in such a way that they can be evaluated to determine their effectiveness.

Guidelines on Diagnosis

Diagnosis is a critical and often overlooked aspect of breast cancer management. Two key components of diagnosis are confirmation of a cancer diagnosis based on clinical evaluation and tissue sampling, and testing with the imaging and tumor markers needed for treatment planning (table 3.3).

Clinical Evaluation

A patient's history of general health and of factors specific to breast disease provides important information for clinical assessment of breast disease and comorbid conditions that might influence therapy choices. Complete physical examination performed in conjunction with CBE provides guidance on the extent of

Table 3.3 Diagnosis Resource Allocation

Diagnosis	Level of available resources			
	Basic	Limited	Enhanced	Maximal
Clinical	• History • Physical examination • CBE • Tissue sampling for cancer diagnosis (cytologic or histologic) prior to initiation of treatment	• US-guided FNAB of sonographically suspicious axillary nodes • SLN biopsy with blue dye[a]	• Image guided breast sampling • Preoperative needle localization under mammo and/or US guidance • SLN biopsy using radiotracer[a]	
Imaging and lab tests	See footnote b	• Diagnostic breast US • Plain chest and skeletal radiography • Liver US • Blood chemistry profile[b] • CBC[b]	• Diagnostic mammography • Specimen radiography • Bone scan, CT scan • Cardiac function monitoring	• PET scan, MIBI scan, breast MRI, BRCA 1/2 testing • Mammographic double reading
Pathology	• Pathology diagnosis obtained for every breast lesion by any available sampling procedure • Pathology report containing appropriate diagnostic and prognostic/predictive information to include tumor size, lymph node status, histologic type, and tumor grade • Process to establish hormone receptor status possibly including empiric assessment of response to therapy[c] • Determination and reporting of TNM stage	• Determination of ER status by IHC[c] • Determination of margin status, DCIS content, presence of LVI • Frozen section or touch prep SLN analysis[d]	• Measurement of HER2/neu overexpression or gene amplification[d] • Determination of PR status by IHC	• IHC staining of sentinel nodes for cytokeratin to detect micrometastases • Pathology double reading • Gene profiling tests

Source: Anderson and others 2008. Used with permission.

Note: BRCA1/2 = breast cancer genes 1 and 2; CBC = complete blood count; CBE = clinical breast examination; CT = computed tomography; DCIS = ductal carcinoma in situ; ER = estrogen receptor; FNAB = fine-needle aspiration biopsy; HER2 = human epidermal growth factor receptor 2; IHC = immunohistochemistry; LVI = lymphovascular invasion; mammo = mammography; MIBI = methoxy-isobutyl-isonitrile; MRI = magnetic resonance imaging; PET = positron emission tomography; PR = progesterone receptor; SLN = sentinel lymph node; TNM = malignant tumor system; US = ultrasound.

a. The use of SLN biopsy requires clinical and laboratory validation of the SLN technique.

b. Systemic chemotherapy requires blood chemistry profile and CBC testing for safety. When chemotherapy is available at the basic level, these tests also should be provided.

c. ER testing by IHC is preferred for establishing hormone receptor status and is cost effective when tamoxifen is available. When tamoxifen is available at the basic level, IHC testing of ER status should be provided.

d. If the costs associated with trastuzumab were substantially lower, trastuzumab would be used as a limited-level therapy. In this case, measurement of HER2/neu overexpression and/or gene amplification would need to be available at the limited level to properly select patients for this highly effective but expensive HER2/neu-targeted biological therapy.

disease, the presence of metastatic disease, and the ability to tolerate more aggressive therapeutic regimens.

Diagnostic Imaging

Breast imaging, initially with ultrasound and at higher resource levels with diagnostic mammography, improves preoperative diagnostic assessment and permits image-guided needle sampling of suspicious lesions. Imaging also provides important information about the extent of disease, which helps determine whether breast conservation (lumpectomy followed by radiation therapy) is an option or mastectomy is required. Ultrasound is particularly valuable as an adjunct to CBE in providing detail on the size and extent of masses and thickenings, which helps to distinguish benign cysts from solid lesions and characterizes the shape and growth pattern of lesions. Diagnostic mammography, while helpful for breast conservation therapy, is not mandatory in LMICs when these resources are lacking. However, where screening mammography is common and where nonpalpable, noninvasive cancers are often diagnosed, diagnostic mammography is critical for determining the extent of disease and properly selecting patients for breast conservation surgery versus mastectomy (Theriault and others 2013).

Tissue Sampling

Needle biopsy is preferred to surgical excision for initial diagnosis of the most suspicious breast lesions; if resource limitations preclude this option, then surgical excision is necessary. Mastectomy should never be used as a method of tissue diagnosis. Whether the tissue is obtained by needle sample or surgical excision, the sample must be processed and then evaluated by a pathologist to determine whether the disease is malignant or benign, and invasive or noninvasive (Shyyan and others 2008).

Tumor Markers

Once a cancer diagnosis is made, additional testing provides information on which to base pharmacotherapy choices. For example, tamoxifen and aromatase inhibitors are affordable generic oral medications that are quite effective in the management of ER-positive cancers with relatively manageable side effects, but these agents are relatively ineffective against ER-negative cancers (Howell and others 1998). The availability of ER testing is critical to proper selection of cancer therapy when endocrine therapies are available. Standard testing is based on immunohistochemical (IHC) methods, where quality assessment of testing methodology is important to avoid false-negative results (Hammond and others 2010; Masood and others 2008).

HER2/neu oncogene testing provides information on the relative aggressiveness of the cancer (HER2/neu-positive cancers are more aggressive), as well as on the likely drug sensitivity of the cancer (Yoo and others 2012). However, the most effective drug for HER2/neu-positive cancers is trastuzumab, which is unaffordable in most regions. Less expensive therapies are under investigation (Pinto and others 2013).

Guidelines on Treatment

Surgery

The modified radical mastectomy is the mainstay of treatment of local and regional (nodal) disease at the basic level of breast health care for early-stage (table 3.4) and late-stage (table 3.5) disease (Anderson and others 2008). The operation is not technically difficult, although surgeons must be trained to remove the breast and dissect axillary nodes properly (Thorat and others 2008).

Radiation Therapy

At increasing resource levels, the availability of radiation therapy allows for consideration of breast-conserving therapy, postmastectomy chest wall radiation, and palliation of painful or symptomatic metastases (see tables 3.4 and 3.5). Although radiation therapy requires significant infrastructure and can be cost limiting in improving treatment, the establishment of a radiation facility can be an important first step in creating an oncology center of excellence in an LMIC (Bese and others 2008).

Systemic Pharmacotherapy

Although surgery and radiation address local disease in the breast and regional disease in the lymph node beds, systemic therapy addresses microscopic disease elsewhere that can become metastases. When patients die from breast cancer, the cause is widespread metastatic disease. It is pharmacotherapy that ultimately improves breast cancer survival rates, since this is the only treatment directed at systemic disease. Pharmacotherapies for breast cancer consist of endocrine (hormonal) therapy, cytotoxic chemotherapy, and biological targeted (antibody) therapies (see tables 3.4 and 3.5).

- *Endocrine therapy* requires relatively few specialized resources, but it requires knowledge of hormone receptor status to identify the patients most likely to benefit. For ER-positive cancers, tamoxifen and aromatase inhibitors are oral drugs taken daily for five years or more that can be dispensed from

Table 3.4 Treatment Resource Allocation for Stage I and Stage II Disease

Treatment			Level of available resources			
			Basic	Limited	Enhanced	Maximal
Stage I	Local-regional treatment	Surgery	Modified radical mastectomy	Breast-conserving surgery[a] SLN biopsy with blue dye[b]	SLN biopsy using radiotracer[b] Breast reconstruction surgery	
		Radiation therapy			Breast-conserving whole-breast irradiation as part of breast-conserving therapy[a]	
	Systemic treatment	Chemotherapy		Classic CMF[c], AC, EC, or FAC[c]	Taxanes	Growth factors Dose-dense chemotherapy
		Endocrine therapy	Oophorectomy in premenopausal women Tamoxifen[d]		Aromatase inhibitors LH-RH agonists	
		Biological therapy		See footnote e	Trastuzumab for treating HER2/neu-positive disease[e]	
Stage II	Local-regional treatment	Surgery	Modified radical mastectomy	Breast-conserving surgery[a] SLN biopsy with blue dye[b]	SLN biopsy using radiotracer[b] Breast reconstruction surgery	
		Radiation therapy	See footnote f	Postmastectomy irradiation of chest wall and regional nodes for high-risk cases[f]	Breast-conserving whole-breast irradiation as part of breast-conserving therapy[a]	
	Systemic treatment	Chemotherapy	Classic CMF[c], AC, EC, or FAC[c]		Taxanes	Growth factors Dose-dense chemotherapy
		Endocrine therapy	Oophorectomy in premenopausal women Tamoxifen[d]		Aromatase inhibitors LH-RH agonists	
		Biological therapy		See footnote e	Trastuzumab for treating HER2/neu-positive disease[e]	

Source: Anderson and others 2008. Used with permission.

Note: AC = doxorubicin and cyclophosphamide; CMF = cyclophosphamide, methotrexate, and 5-fluorouracil; EC = epirubicin and cyclophosphamide; FAC = 5-fluorouracil, doxorubicin, and cyclophosphamide; HER2/neu = human epidermal growth factor receptor 2; LH-RH = luteinizing hormone-releasing hormone; SLN = sentinel lymph node.

a. Breast-conserving surgery can be provided as a limited-level resource but requires radiation therapy. If breast-conserving radiation is unavailable, then patients should be transferred to a higher-level facility for postlumpectomy radiation.

b. The use of SLN biopsy requires clinical and laboratory validation of the SLN technique.

c. Systemic chemotherapy requires blood chemistry profile and complete blood count testing for safety. When chemotherapy is available at the basic level, these tests also should be provided.

d. ER testing by IHC is preferred for establishing hormone receptor status and is cost effective when tamoxifen is available. When tamoxifen is available at the basic level, then IHC testing of ER status also should be provided.

e. If the costs associated with trastuzumab were substantially lower, trastuzumab would be used as a limited-level resource. In this case, measurement of HER2/neu overexpression and/or gene amplification would need to be available at the limited level to select patients properly for this highly effective but expensive HER2/neu-targeted biological therapy.

f. Chest wall and regional lymph node irradiation substantially decreases the risk of postmastectomy local recurrence. If available, it should be used as a basic-level resource.

pharmacies without special infrastructure and are considered very safe. Endocrine therapy could be given to all breast cancer patients, but it would be a waste of resources since it is only effective against ER-positive cancers. IHC methods involve special tissue-staining techniques with labeling antibodies, which requires pathology laboratory infrastructure; quality control is quite important to

testing accuracy. Alternative simplified techniques for ER testing are of significant interest but remain experimental.

• *Systemic cytotoxic chemotherapy* is effective in most biologic subtypes of breast cancer. It is particularly important in the management of ER-negative cancers but is resource intensive. Chemotherapy has significant side effects that must be managed

Table 3.5 Treatment Resource Allocation for Locally Advanced and Metastatic Disease

Treatment			Level of available resources			
			Basic	Limited	Enhanced	Maximal
Locally advanced	Local-regional treatment	Surgery	Modified radical mastectomy		Breast-conserving surgery Breast reconstruction surgery	
		Radiation therapy	See footnote a	Postmastectomy irradiation of chest wall and regional nodes[a]	Breast-conserving whole-breast irradiation as part of breast-conserving therapy	
	Systemic treatment (Adjuvant and neoadjuvant)	Chemotherapy	Preoperative chemotherapy with AC, EC, FAC, or CMF[b]		Taxanes	Growth factors Dose-dense chemotherapy
		Endocrine therapy	Oophorectomy in premenopausal women Tamoxifen[c]		Aromatase inhibitors LH-RH agonists	
		Biological therapy		See footnote d	Trastuzumab for treating HER2/neu-positive disease[d]	
Metastasic and recurrent	Local-regional treatment	Surgery	Total mastectomy for ipsilateral breast tumor recurrence after breast-conserving surgery			
		Radiation therapy		Palliative radiation therapy		
	Systemic treatment	Chemotherapy		Classic CMF[b] Anthracycline monotherapy or in combination[b]	Sequential single agent or combination chemotherapy: Trastuzumab Lapatinib	Bevacizumab
		Endocrine therapy	Oophorectomy in premenopausal women Tamoxifen[c]		Aromatase inhibitors	Fulvestrant
		Biological therapy	Nonopioid and opioid analgesics and symptom management		Bisphosphonates	Growth factors

Source: Anderson and others 2008. Used with permission.

Note: Treatment resource allocation table for locally advanced, metastatic (stage IV), and recurrent breast cancer. AC = doxorubicin and cyclophosphamide; CMF = cyclophosphamide, methotrexate, and 5-fluorouracil; EC = epirubicin and cyclophosphamide; FAC = 5-fluorouracil, doxorubicin, and cyclophosphamide; HER2/neu = human epidermal growth factor receptor 2; LH-RH = luteinizing hormone-releasing hormone.

a. Chest wall and regional lymph node irradiation substantially decreases the risk of postmastectomy local recurrence. If available, it should be used as a basic-level resource.

b. Systemic chemotherapy requires blood chemistry profile and complete blood count testing for safety. When chemotherapy is available at the basic level, these tests should be provided.

c. Estrogen receptor testing by immunohistochemistry (IHC) is preferred for establishing hormone receptor status and is cost effective when tamoxifen is available. When tamoxifen is available at the basic level, then IHC testing of estrogen receptor status should be provided.

d. If the costs associated with trastuzumab were substantially lower, trastuzumab would be used at a limited level. In this case, measurement of HER2/neu overexpression and/or gene amplification would need to be available at the limited level to properly select patients for this highly effective but expensive HER2/neu-targeted biological therapy.

effectively. Correct drug selection is based on the extent or stage of the cancer and on tumor markers that can predict likely drug sensitivity. Proper drug dosing is important and must be individualized to the patient's body mass index; the dosage should be sufficiently high to provide optimal effects on the cancer but as low as possible to minimize adverse events. Proper management of these agents is critical; they must be handled under sterile conditions, they must be properly and safely administered, and health care workers should not be directly exposed to these agents.

- *Biological targeted therapies* use monoclonal antibodies to control disease. HER2 neu-targeted therapy with trastuzumab is very effective in tumors that overexpress the HER2/neu oncogene, but cost largely prevents the use of this treatment in LMICs (Eniu and others 2008); a standard one-year course of treatment in the United States is approximately US$100,000. It remains unclear whether generic forms of trastuzumab will be available in the future.

IMPLEMENTATION OF BHGI GUIDELINES: AN EARLY DETECTION MODEL

Before an LMIC initiates a breast cancer control program or evaluates existing programs, careful assessment of the local situation is needed. This assessment consists of three parts:

- Breast cancer problem in the population
- Existing infrastructure that will be utilized for the program
- Social and cultural barriers to women's participation in the program

Assessing the Breast Cancer Problem

A realistic estimate of the number of women with breast cancer in the population in which screening is proposed is an essential part of the planning process; the lower the prevalence, the higher the number of women who have to be screened to detect cases and prevent deaths.

Estimating the frequency of breast cancer in LMICs can be a challenge and may require using less than ideal methods. The ideal situation is where the number of women in the target screening population is known and a reliable population-based cancer registry covers a substantial portion of the population. These elements, in conjunction with information from countries with well-developed breast cancer screening programs, would support a reasonable estimate of expected impact. In countries with poorer enumeration of the target population or cancer registration, more extrapolation is involved; estimates of breast cancer burden and expected benefit become less reliable but still useful. For example, incidence rates for populations that may be similar to populations without registries are found in *Cancer Incidence in Five Continents* (Curado and others 2007).

Accurate mortality rates can serve as good measures of the extent of the breast cancer problem. However, mortality rates can be misleading if the population size is not accurately enumerated, if many deaths are unreported, or if certification of the cause of death is not accurately recorded. In the absence of adequate information on the population to be screened, reviews of death certificates can be useful. The number of deaths certified as due to breast cancer during specific years can be obtained to provide a rough estimate of the number of annual breast cancer deaths in the population. In addition, the proportion of all deaths due to breast cancer can be calculated and compared with the proportion of deaths from other causes. If breast cancer is a small problem relative to other preventable causes of death, then a screening program may not be warranted, but if breast cancer deaths constitute a relatively high proportion of preventable deaths, this information can help to justify the costs of screening.

A review of hospital records can be useful in assessing the magnitude of the problem. If a single hospital serves all cancer patients in a defined population, then the hospital records can be reviewed to estimate the number of cases to be expected annually. A record review can provide an indication of the importance of breast cancer relative to other cancers in the population and relative to other reasons for hospitalization. If admissions for breast cancer constitute a relatively high proportion of all preventable causes of admission, or a high proportion of all admissions for cancer, then a screening program may be justifiable; if breast cancer is a rare cause of hospitalization, then it may not warrant high prioritization.

The presence of social or financial barriers that keep women from accessing services will limit the effectiveness of a screening program; it will be important to consider initiatives to overcome such barriers.

Assessing the magnitude of the problem before implementing a screening program also includes determining the disease stage distribution at diagnosis. This information would be found in population-based cancer registries or hospital-based registries. In the absence of cancer registries, the records in clinics, hospitals, and pathology laboratories can be reviewed. If a high proportion of breast cancers are diagnosed at advanced stages, then a screening program, or an educational program to encourage earlier diagnosis of symptomatic breast cancers, could have a substantial impact on the burden. Conversely, if a high proportion of breast cancers are already being diagnosed at early stages, then screening programs based on BSE, and probably also on CBE, are unlikely to have a large impact on mortality or morbidity.

Assessing the Infrastructure for Screening, Diagnosis, and Treatment

Mammography, the only screening method of proven efficacy, serves as an example for assessing infrastructure.

For a mammographic screening program to result in earlier detection of breast cancers in the population in LMICs and elsewhere, six elements need to function adequately:

- Means to recruit enough women in the target population to have a meaningful impact on the breast cancer burden
- Facilities to ensure high-quality mammograms
- Sufficient number of radiologists who can properly interpret mammograms in a timely manner
- Means to recontact women with suspicious findings and ensure that they come to facilities for further evaluation in a timely fashion
- Adequate diagnostic facilities and trained pathologists to provide timely and accurate tissue diagnoses
- Sufficient facilities and personnel to provide timely and appropriate treatment

Regardless of the screening modality used—BSE, CBE, or screening mammography—gaps in this system at any level must be identified and addressed before a program of early detection is established.

Assessing Social and Cultural Barriers

Women in LMICs may be unaware of breast cancer, or they may have misconceptions about its nature or curability or have fatalistic attitudes toward diseases in general (Yip and others 2008). Under such circumstances, programs to enhance public awareness of breast cancer and to teach that breast cancer outcomes are improved through early detection are critical to improving participation in early detection programs, regardless of the selected methods for early detection.

Cultural barriers to participation need to be identified and strategies developed to overcome them. These barriers may include the attitudes of women as well as their husbands; in some cultures, women must obtain their husbands' permission to seek medical services. Efforts to empower women and educate men may be required for programs to succeed. Cultural and social barriers are highly specific to different countries, religions, and ethnic groups and cannot be comprehensively reviewed here. However, an example illustrates how they may be addressed. In a survey in the Palestinian Authority (Azaiza and others 2010), women were more likely to undergo screening mammography if they were less religious, if they described fewer personal barriers to examinations, and if they indicated a lower degree of cancer fatalism.

Women who consented to CBE had a higher perceived effectiveness of CBE and described lower levels of cancer fatalism. Muslim women were half as likely as Christian women to participate in CBE screening. Women were more likely to perform BSE if they were more highly educated, resided in cities, were Christian, were less religious, and had a first-degree relative with breast cancer. These results suggest that participation in screening might be improved by recruiting religious leaders as spokespersons for early detection and by staffing screening clinics with women physicians and nurses sensitive to the needs of conservative Muslim women who must remain covered in public.

Women who are correctly diagnosed and properly treated for early-stage breast cancer can survive the disease and can organize breast cancer survivor groups, such as Reach for Recovery (figure 3.3). Such groups can play a vital role in educating the public about the value of early detection and in providing newly diagnosed women with practical and emotional support (Ashbury and others 1998). Survivor groups can organize into political advocacy groups that have a real and positive impact on health care policy or national cancer research agendas (Schmidt 2009; Visco 2007).

Identifying Target Groups

Identifying a target group for screening in LMICs should be based on the burden of disease in the population, the potential benefit from screening, and available resources (Humphrey and others 2002). Other than the small subset of women at very high risk of developing breast cancer due to genetic predisposition, it is very difficult to predict which women are destined to develop breast cancer. Although women with BRCA (breast cancer gene) mutations generally have a strong family history of breast and/or ovarian cancer, family history

Figure 3.3 Synergistic Relationship between Public Participation and Health Care Delivery in Downstaging Breast Cancer and Improving Outcomes

Source: Harford and others 2011. Used with permission.

is not a particularly good tool for selecting women for screening, since approximately 80 percent of breast cancers occur in women who lack a known family history of breast cancer. As a result, the only two risk factors used for determining candidacy for screening are gender and age.

In Western countries, breast cancer incidence increases sharply with age until the usual age at menopause and then increases more slowly. In LMICs, incidence increases with age until menopause but then either continues to increase less steeply with age than in Western countries, levels off, or decreases with age (Freedman and others 2006). This phenomenon is the result of an aging and growing population (Chia and others 2005; Wong, Cowling, and others 2007); over time, the age-specific incidence curves for LMICs are expected to more closely approximate those of Western countries (Yip and others 2008).

In LMICs where incidence rates in women ages 50 years and older are beginning to increase with age, the prevalence of the disease in the population may have approached a level at which establishing screening programs will be cost effective.

Considering Coverage and Impact

Coverage of the target population is also important. If screening is efficacious in reducing mortality from breast cancer, but only a small proportion of the women in the target population receives the service, then the impact of the screening program on mortality in the population will be minimal. The following simple formula illustrates the impact (Thomas and others 2013):

$$Impact = Efficacy \times Coverage$$

If we assume that mammograms reduce mortality from breast cancer by 25 percent, and if 40 percent of the women in a target population are screened, then the screening program would be expected to reduce mortality in the target population by 10 percent ($0.25 \times 0.40 = 0.10$). Mammographic screening programs in LMICs should be designed in such a way that the proportion of women in the target population who are screened can be maximized.

COST-EFFECTIVE INTERVENTIONS IN LMICs

The BHGI resource-adapted guidelines provide a sound foundation for creating intervention packages for early detection (table 3.1), diagnosis (table 3.3), and treatment by disease stage (tables 3.4 and 3.5)

at each of BHGI's four defined resource levels: Basic, Limited, Enhanced, and Maximal. By contrast, WHO's Choosing Interventions That Are Cost-Effective (WHO-CHOICE) framework provides a somewhat different and not entirely comparable set of breast cancer guidelines (Murray and Lopez 1996; Tan-Torres Edejer and others 2003). WHO-CHOICE was established as an initiative to provide evidence to policy makers who must decide on the interventions and programs that maximize health outcomes for given available resources, reporting on the costs and effects of a wide range of health interventions but without direct alignment with current stage-based treatment strategies for specific diseases.

Whether grounded in the BHGI or WHO-CHOICE framework, the development of analytical models to identify clinically effective and cost-effective approaches for improving breast health requires linking resources to interventions and patient outcomes (Brown and others 2006; Gold and others 1996). The value-for-money question can be summarized as follows: given the assumed level of resources available within a given geopolitical area, what administratively and financially feasible set of interventions has the greatest favorable impact on health outcomes? This section reviews and assesses progress to date in identifying cost-effective interventions for breast cancer in LMICs.

Appraisal of the Literature

As the recent review by Zelle and Baltussen (2013) well illustrates, substantial variations exist in the precise purpose, scope, methodology, assumptions, and technical quality of published cost-effectiveness analyses on breast cancer interventions in LMICs. The following section focuses on a selected set of studies that yields findings relevant to components of the BHGI guidelines while paying close attention to important cost-effectiveness analysis data and methods issues. Nine of the studies were among 23 selected for detailed manuscript-quality evaluation by Zelle and Baltussen and were generally among the highest rated, according to the authors' scoring scheme. The studies illustrate how cost-effectiveness analyses can be carried out in limited-resource settings.

Salient features and recommendations of these key studies are summarized in the online annex 3A to this chapter, tables 3A.1 through 3A.3. We have further mapped the study contexts to BHGI resource levels and highlighted features following methodological best-practice guidelines. Here, we focus on the cost-effectiveness results. Our conclusions about whether an intervention is cost effective were guided throughout by the following WHO recommendations (WHO 2001):

- If the intervention's applicable incremental cost-effectiveness ratio (ICER) is less than or equal to the nation's or region's GDP per capita, the intervention is "very cost effective."
- If the ICER is between one and three times the GDP per capita, it is "cost effective."
- If the ICER exceeds three times the GDP per capita, the intervention is "not cost effective."

Early Detection

Annual CBEs are very cost effective in Vietnam (Nguyen and others 2013); biennial mammography screening is cost effective in Hong Kong SAR, China (Wong, Kuntz, and others 2007). An analysis examining combinations of both screening modalities applied to different age groups in India concluded that several alternative CBE detection strategies were very cost effective, while the most efficient among various mammography screening strategies analyzed (biennial screening for women ages 40–60) was not cost effective (Okonkwo and others 2008). An analysis in the Republic of Korea determined that the most cost-efficient mammography strategy (given a prior decision to adopt this modality) is screening every three years for women ages 45–65 (Lee, Jeong, and others 2009).

Treatment

In analyses of hormonal adjuvant therapies post-surgery, Fonseca and others (2009) found that the aromatase inhibitor anastrozole was cost effective compared with tamoxifen in a Brazil-based cost-effectiveness analysis. In Korea, Yang and others (2010) calculated that tamoxifen was very cost effective compared with no hormonal therapy for hormone receptor-positive patients under a variety of assumptions; it was very cost effective or cost effective for hormone receptor-negative patients in only a subset of cases (for example, when the patient was stage III and under age 50). A self-described preliminary cost-effectiveness analysis that excluded certain cost categories found that a combination of oophorectomy and tamoxifen was very cost effective compared with "observation" in a Vietnam-based analysis (Love and others 2002).

The cost-effectiveness of alternative combination chemotherapy regimens post-surgery was investigated for China (Liubao and others 2009) and Korea (Lee, Jee, and others 2009). Liubao and others found that substituting docetaxel for doxorubicin in a treatment package that otherwise included cyclophosphamide

was cost effective; Lee and others concluded that substituting docetaxel for fluorouracil in another, more complex regimen was very cost effective. A China-based analysis (Bai and others 2012) concluded that radiation therapy following breast-conserving surgery, compared with no radiation, was very cost effective under a wide range of assumptions.

Combination Screening-Treatment Interventions

The four cost-effectiveness analyses summarized in annex table 3A.3 are all based on the WHO-CHOICE framework (Tan-Torres Edejer and others 2003); each examines alternative intervention packages involving screening and treatment for breast cancer from the perspective of a particular nation or world region. Three of the papers (Ginsberg and others 2012; Groot and others 2006; Salomon and others 2012) investigate roughly the same six options: treat only stage I, only stage II, only stage III, or only stage IV disease; treat all stages; or treat all stages, plus some variant of a breast screening and/or educational program (the "extensive program" option). Zelle and others (2012) evaluated a total of 17 options, including these six and others that differed largely on whether screening was by CBE or mammography and by the age range for screening.

Some modeling assumptions of WHO-CHOICE are not in alignment with standard stage-based treatment protocols. For example, two model options assume that early-stage breast cancer is not treated with chemotherapy when, in practice, most stage II and some stage I breast cancers do warrant chemotherapy on the basis of high-level, prospective randomized clinical trials (Theriault and others 2013). This modeling assumption could lead to incorrect cost-effectiveness conclusions, since chemotherapy is among the most expensive of the required multimodality treatments. WHO-CHOICE also assumes that lumpectomy and sentinel lymph node biopsy is the surgery for Stage I and II when, in practice, breast cancers in LMICs are often too large for breast-conserving surgery, and sentinel lymph node biopsy is often an unavailable technique in these settings such that complete axillary node dissection is routinely performed for all invasive cancers.

There is a general convergence in the recommendations, notwithstanding the diversity in geopolitical setting for these cost-effectiveness analyses. In the Asian and Sub-Saharan African regions analyzed, Groot and others (2006) concluded that the extensive program was very cost effective. For Southeast Asia and Sub-Saharan Africa, Ginsberg and others (2012) found that variants of the extensive program (differing by the assumed fraction of the female population covered) were all cost effective. Focusing on Brazil, Salomon and others (2012) calculated that the option of treating all four stages of breast cancer was very cost effective, while the extensive program that considered various screening options was cost effective. For Ghana, Zelle and others (2012) found that a variant of the extensive program defined to include biennial CBE screening for women ages 40–69 was cost effective.

Implications for Choosing Cost-Effective Breast Cancer Interventions

Although we agree with Zelle and Baltussen (2013) that many published analyses of breast cancer interventions in LMICs suffer from serious data or methods limitations, noteworthy exceptions exist, including, for the most part, the studies included in annex 3A, tables 3A.1 through 3A.3.

Yet even these conceptually strong studies reveal another important limitation: the range of intervention topics examined represents only a fraction of the important questions in prevention and control. This issue becomes evident by comparing the interventions evaluated in annex 3A, tables 3A.1 through 3A.3, with the range of BHGI-recommended interventions across the cancer continuum (tables 3.1, 3.3, 3.4, and 3.5). Although there are several well-executed cost-effectiveness analyses on early detection and screening (annex 3A, table 3A.1), we found no analyses of comparable scope and quality investigating alternative breast cancer diagnostic techniques and procedures in LMICs. In the treatment domain, we included a handful of excellent cost-effectiveness analyses examining alternative chemotherapy regimens, hormonal therapy strategies, or radiation following breast cancer surgery (annex 3A, table 3A.2); there are no cost-effectiveness analyses examining alternative multimodal adjuvant treatment *strategies* in LMICs.

The cost-effective analyses focused on combination screening-treatment interventions (annex 3A, table 3A.3), while limited, do suggest that *breast cancer intervention packages consistent with the BHGI guidelines* could be evaluated through these analyses and tailored to the resource level that best characterizes the region, nation, or subnational arena for application.

FIELD STUDIES

The summarized evidence for the efficacy of mammography, CBE, and BSE is based largely on studies in HICs and upper-middle-income countries, and the results may not be directly applicable to LMICs. We recommend strongly that early detection programs in LMICs be designed in advance in such a way that they can be evaluated during their early years (McCannon, Berwick, and Massoud 2007). Methods that have been employed for program evaluation include observational studies and randomized trials. Two types of observational studies are comparisons of screening modalities and assessments of temporal trends in stage of disease. Randomized trials may be clinic- or population-based.

Comparison of Modalities

A recent study in Indonesia that compared the use of screening mammography and CBE in a previously unscreened population found similar efficacy for breast cancer detection (Kardinah and others 2014). Midwives and trained lay health workers were trained to perform CBE; volunteers recruited women to come to the clinics for screening. Among the 1,179 previously unscreened women, 289 had a suspicious finding on CBE and/or mammogram (24.5 percent) and required further work-up: 167 had an abnormal CBE and 191 had an abnormal mammogram. After work-up and tissue sampling, 14 breast cancers (1.2 percent) were diagnosed in this unscreened population. Of the 14 cancers, 13 were detected by CBE. Mammography only identified one additional cancer not found by CBE.

These findings suggest that when starting a screening program in a previously unscreened population, most of the prevalent cancers will be found by CBE; mammography adds few additional cancer cases in the initial screening phase. The study also demonstrates that a large fraction of women (14 percent in this study) will require diagnostic evaluation beyond CBE. Screening programs based on CBE will require significant diagnostic infrastructure based on additional imaging and tissue sampling.

Temporal Trends in Stage of Disease

In Malaysia, almost all diagnosed cancers are treated in a single referral hospital in the State of Sarawak, with a population of approximately two million. By reviewing the medical records of all women with breast cancer at that hospital before and after an early detection initiative, it was possible to assess the impact of the program on breast cancer in the population (Devi, Tang, and Corbex 2007). The intervention consisted of the following elements:

- Training community nurses who worked in rural clinics to perform CBE and teach BSE
- Circulating pamphlets and posters to motivate women to go to their nearest clinic at the earliest signs of a breast problem

- Instructing community nurses to hold health education talks and discussion groups on early diagnosis during monthly visits to villages, to teach BSE and perform CBE
- Strengthening the system for referring women with signs and symptoms of breast cancer to first-level hospitals for diagnosis

The proportion of breast cancers that were diagnosed at late stages (stage III or IV) was 77 percent in 1993 before the program began and 37 percent in 1998 after the program began. Since these statistics are for nearly all women in the population who were treated for breast cancer, regardless of whether they participated in the program, they reflect the impact of the program on the population and suggest that the program had a positive impact.

Population-Based Randomized Trial

In a cluster randomized trial of CBE and cervical cancer screening by visual inspection of the cervix after acetic acid application (VIA) by lay women in Mumbai (Mittra and others 2010), 20 informal settlements (slums) were randomly allocated to screening or control groups (10 slums in each group) and women ages 35–64 years in each slum were considered eligible for the trial; more than 75,000 women were eligible for each arm of the study. Women with a tenth-grade education were trained to perform CBE and VIA; these trained workers then invited women in the screening arm of the trial for screening; women in the control arm received no screening. Three of four rounds of screening at two-year intervals were completed between 1998 and 2005.

The preliminary results showed that more breast cancers were detected in the screening arm than in the control arm (125 versus 87 cases). The proportion of cancers detected at early stages was higher in the screened arm than the control arm (62 percent versus 44 percent, stage 0, I, or II disease); this is a difference that achieved statistical difference by the third cycle of screening (p = 0.004). These results indicate that CBE performed by specially trained women may be efficacious in reducing mortality from breast cancer in the slums of India; the results clearly indicate that continuation of the trial is warranted to provide direct evidence for a reduction in breast cancer mortality by CBE. The analyses of the data from this trial include all women and all breast cancers in the screening group, whether or not the women were actually screened. The results indicate the impact of screening as it was actually implemented in the target population.

Clinic-Based Cluster Randomized Trial

The National Cancer Institute of Colombia (Instituto Nacional de Cancerología, or INC; 2006) adapted the BHGI guidelines for MICs to develop a pilot screening program in Bogotá. The INC guidelines recommend screening with annual clinical CBE and mammography every two years for women ages 50–69. Based on these guidelines, the INC designed a pilot study to evaluate opportunistic screening as a programmatic approach to improve early detection in the country (Murillo and others 2008). *Opportunistic screening* is defined as the systematic offer of CBE and mammography for all women ages 50–69 who visit health centers on their own, regardless of motivation. It implies that screening is clinic-based with no outreach outside the health centers. The primary objectives of the study are to evaluate the effect of opportunistic screening on population coverage, to determine the impact of opportunistic screening on clinical stage at diagnosis, and to identify the basic requirements for implementing opportunistic screening within the Colombian health system.

A cluster randomized trial was undertaken with health centers as the units of randomization. The screening consisted of recruitment in the clinics and follow-up by health care assistants (auxiliary nurses, backed up by registered nurses), CBE performed by general practitioners, and mammography by radiologists and radiology technicians. Mammography quality control comprises examination and adjustment of mammography machines before starting screening, quality control of mammography films, and evaluation of mammography reading according to international standards. CBE quality control was done by breast surgeons who periodically visit health centers to evaluate general practitioners' practice of CBE and differences between the diagnoses of the surgeons and general practitioners are recorded. In the control group, women who would be eligible for screening if they had been in the intervention group are given general information about breast cancer but are not offered screening.

Women attending the health centers regularly were assigned to opportunistic screening or no intervention, according to the random allocation of their clinic. Because the Colombian health system is insurance-oriented, randomization was stratified by health insurance company to control for the effect of administrative factors on access to screening and diagnosis. After the enrollment of approximately 12,000 women (about 6,000 per arm), 88.9 percent and 99.8 percent, respectively, in the opportunistic screening branch who were offered screening had a mammogram and a CBE, compared with 11.7 percent and 5 percent, respectively, of the control women. The preliminary results show a threefold greater rate of breast cancer detection in the screened group than in the control group (15 and 5 cases, respectively) and a higher proportion of cases at an early stage at diagnosis (13/15 = 86.6 percent versus 3/5 = 60 percent). Furthermore, the enrollment rate (2.9 patients per center per day) does not overburden the general practitioners or other clinic staff. At completion of follow-up, it should be possible to compare the stage of disease at diagnosis in the women screened compared with the control arm. It will also be possible to compare the stage distribution at diagnosis between the two groups, providing a measure of the impact of the screening program in the population of women served by the clinics participating in the trial.

CONCLUSIONS

Population-Based Screening Mammography

Breast cancer screening remains a major area of controversy. In HICs, the debate persists about whether mammographic screening leads to increased detection of cancers that would not become significant threats to a woman's life in her natural lifetime. Treatment of these cancers would, by definition, constitute overtreatment. Arguing against this premise is the fact that in nearly all countries where age-adjusted breast cancer mortality is decreasing, screening mammography has been established, for example, Australia, Denmark, Italy, Spain, and the United States. In contrast, Japan has not implemented screening mammography; despite adequate treatment standards, breast cancer mortality has plateaued and stabilized, but it has not yet decreased. These observations are consistent with Cancer Intervention and Surveillance Modeling Network (CISNET) modeling, which demonstrates synergy between screening and adjuvant treatment in reducing breast cancer mortality at the population level (Berry and others 2005); the modeling suggests that screening mammography will continue to be important in breast cancer control for the foreseeable future.

The effectiveness of screening mammography could be improved if it were possible to identify patients who did not need immediate treatment, even though a lesion is found. Although the debate continues regarding the age at which screening mammography should begin—age 40 years or age 50 years—new biological research on cancer progression may identify a patient subgroup warranting a wait-and-watch strategy.

Clinical Breast Examination as an Early Detection Tool

Screening mammography is unfeasible in most of the world, but CBE is a practical option in many LMICs to provide at least basic breast cancer treatment. Evidence suggests that in LMICs with rising breast cancer incidence rates, CBE will help curb the rise in mortality. What remains unknown is whether CBE, combined with highly effective treatment, can further curb breast cancer mortality and lower breast cancer mortality at the population level. The increasing use of CBE provides opportunities for research on health care delivery in limited resource settings.

Diagnosis, Treatment, and Patient Triage

Fine-needle aspiration and core needle biopsy tissue sampling techniques are necessary for diagnosing palpable lumps and distinguishing between benign and malignant lesions. However, the key systems questions go beyond selection of a tissue sampling technology. The cost of needles, availability of pathology services, and patient selection to determine which patients should be brought to second-level or third-level care centers require systematic assessment of existing resources in a health care delivery system. Before an early detection strategy is implemented, an assessment must be made of available resources, missing tools, and geographic distribution of the patient population, as well as social and cultural issues that could affect patient participation.

Once a situation-appropriate early detection, diagnosis, and patient triage strategy is devised, economic evaluation becomes relevant and important. The evolution of breast health systems will require pilot projects to determine what systems can work and, in parallel, it will require new analyses to assess economic impact. It will be important to proceed in a stepwise, systematic fashion, documenting outcomes, so that successful models can be adapted and adopted in other settings.

Economic Analyses and the Future of Breast Health Care in LMICs

The BHGI resource-stratified guideline approach can be used in priority-setting analyses in LMICs. Cost-effectiveness analyses can identify interventions yielding the greatest gain in health (for example, life years gained and disability-adjusted life years averted) per dollar spent, from which practical strategies can be built. We recognize, however, the limitations in comparing and extrapolating results from one country to another and among groups within the same population, depending on the methodology, input data, and assumptions in the studies. A core principle in developing BHGI guidelines has been to recognize that one size does not fit all.

The WHO-CHOICE framework has brought consistency, but these models are highly simplified compared with the breast cancer models used in HICs. In each case, decisions must be made:

- Determining which analytical models to use (WHO-CHOICE, CISNET, other micro-simulation models)
- Finding appropriate data that are as faithful as possible to the place of application
- Sorting out at the policy level how to work in concert with national and local health agencies so the modeling is not only academically sound but practical for local decision making

The resource-stratified approach, although enormously challenging, identifies key building blocks for cost-effectiveness analysis models that will translate resource-conditional breast health guidelines into prioritized intervention strategies.

NOTES

The annex in this chapter is as follows. It is available at http://dcp-3.org/cancer:

- Annex 3A: Summary of Salient Features and Recommendations of the Cost-effectiveness Studies Relevant to Breast Cancer Screening, Treatment, and Control in Low- and Middle-Income Countries.

World Bank income classifications as of July 2014 are as follows, based on estimates of gross national income (GNI) per capita for 2013:

- Low-income countries (LICs): US$1,045 or less
- Middle-income countries (MICs) are subdivided:
  - Lower-middle-income: US$1,046–US$4,125
  - Upper-middle-income (UMICs): US$4,126–US$12,745
- High-income countries (HICs): US$12,746 or more

1. Maps and figures in this chapter are based on incidence and mortality estimates for ages 0 to 69, consistent with reporting in all *DCP3* volumes. Global cancer statistics are estimates for the year 2012 and have been provided by the International Agency for Research on Cancer from its GLOBOCAN 2012 database. Observable population-based data were derived from *Cancer Incidence in Five Continents, 10th edition*, and for trends over time from *CI5 Plus* (http://ci5.iarc.fr/CI5plus/Default.aspx). The discussion of burden (including risk factors), however,

includes all ages unless otherwise noted. Interventions also apply to all age groups, except where age ranges or cutoffs are specified.

REFERENCES

Anderson, B. O., S. Braun, R. W. Carlson, J. R. Gralow, and M. D. Lagios. 2003. "Overview of Breast Health Care Guidelines for Countries with Limited Resources." *The Breast Journal* 9 (Suppl. 2): S42–50.

Anderson, B. O., E. Cazap, N. S. El Saghir, C. H. Yip, H. M. Khaled, and others. 2011. "Optimisation of Breast Cancer Management in Low-Resource and Middle-Resource Countries: Executive Summary of the Breast Health Global Initiative Consensus, 2010." *The Lancet Oncology* 12 (4): 387–98. doi:S1470-2045(11)70031-6 [pii]; 10.1016/S1470-2045(11)70031-6.

Anderson, B. O., R. Shyyan, A. Eniu, R. A. Smith, C. H. Yip, and others. 2006. "Breast Cancer in Limited-Resource Countries: An Overview of the Breast Health Global Initiative 2005 Guidelines." *The Breast Journal* 12 (Suppl. 1): S3–15. doi:10.1111/j.1075-122X.2006.00199.x.

Anderson, B. O., C. H. Yip, R. A. Smith, R. Shyyan, S. F. Sener, and others. 2008. "Guideline Implementation for Breast Healthcare in Low-Income and Middle-Income Countries: Overview of the Breast Health Global Initiative Global Summit 2007." *Cancer* 113 (Suppl. 8): 2221–43. doi:10.1002/cncr.23844.

Ashbury, F. D., C. Cameron, S. L. Mercer, M. Fitch, and E. Nielsen. 1998. "One-on-One Peer Support and Quality of Life for Breast Cancer Patients." *Patient Education and Counseling* 35 (2): 89–100. doi:S0738399198000354 [pii].

Azaiza, F., M. Cohen, M. Awad, and F. Daoud. 2010. "Factors Associated with Low Screening for Breast Cancer in the Palestinian Authority: Relations of Availability, Environmental Barriers, and Cancer-Related Fatalism." *Cancer* 116 (19): 4646–55. doi:10.1002/cncr.25378.

Bai, Y., M. Ye, H. Cao, X. Ma, Y. Xu, and others. 2012. "Economic Evaluation of Radiotherapy for Early Breast Cancer after Breast-Conserving Surgery in a Health Resource-Limited Setting." *Breast Cancer Research and Treatment* 136 (2): 547–57. doi:10.1007/s10549-012-2268-1.

Barlow, W. E., C. Chi, P. A. Carney, S. H. Taplin, C. D'Orsi, and others. 2004. "Accuracy of Screening Mammography Interpretation by Characteristics of Radiologists." *Journal of the National Cancer Institute* 96 (24): 1840–50. doi:10.1093/jnci/djh333.

Baum, M. 2013. "Harms from Breast Cancer Screening Outweigh Benefits If Death Caused by Treatment Is Included." *British Medical Journal* 346: f385. doi:10.1136/bmj.f385.

Berry, D. A., K. A. Cronin, S. K. Plevritis, D. G. Fryback, L. Clarke, and others. 2005. "Effect of Screening and Adjuvant Therapy on Mortality from Breast Cancer." *The New England Journal of Medicine* 353 (17): 1784–92. doi:353/17/1784 [pii]; 10.1056/NEJMoa050518.

Bese, N. S., A. Munshi, A. Budrukkar, A. Elzawawy, and C. A. Perez. 2008. "Breast Radiation Therapy Guideline Implementation in Low- and Middle-Income Countries." *Cancer* 113 (Suppl. 8): 2305–14.

Bray, F., J. S. Ren, E. Masuyer, and J. Ferlay. 2013. "Global Estimates of Cancer Prevalence for 27 Sites in the Adult Population in 2008." *International Journal of Cancer* 132 (5): 1133–45. doi:10.1002/ijc.27711.

Breast Screening Frequency Trial Group. 2002. "The Frequency of Breast Cancer Screening: Results from the UKCCCR Randomised Trial. United Kingdom Co-Ordinating Committee on Cancer Research." *European Journal of Cancer* 38 (11): 1458–64.

Brown, M. L., S. I. Goldie, G. Draisma, J. Harford, and J. Lipscomb. 2006. "Health Service Interventions for Cancer Control in Developing Countries." In *Disease Control Priorities in Developing Countries*, 2nd edition, edited by D. T. Jamison, J. G. Breman, A. R. Measham, G. Alleyne, M. Claeson, D. B. Evans, P. Jha, A. Mills, and P. Musgrove, 569–89. Washington, DC: World Bank and Oxford University Press.

Cardoso, F., N. Bese, S. R. Distelhorst, J. L. Bevilacqua, O. Ginsburg, and others. 2013. "Supportive Care During Treatment for Breast Cancer: Resource Allocations in Low- and Middle-Income Countries: A Breast Health Global Initiative 2013 Consensus Statement." *Breast* 22 (5): 593–605. doi:10.1016/j.breast.2013.07.050.

Chia, K. S., M. Reilly, C. S. Tan, J. Lee, Y. Pawitan, and others. 2005. "Profound Changes in Breast Cancer Incidence May Reflect Changes into a Westernized Lifestyle: A Comparative Population-Based Study in Singapore and Sweden." *International Journal of Cancer* 113 (2): 302–06.

Chopra, R. 2001. "The Indian Scene." *Journal of Clinical Oncology* 19 (Suppl. 18): 106S–111S.

Chu, K. C., C. R. Smart, and R. E. Tarone. 1988. "Analysis of Breast Cancer Mortality and Stage Distribution by Age for the Health Insurance Plan Clinical Trial." *Journal of the National Cancer Institute* 80 (14): 1125–32.

Clarke, M. 2006. "Meta-Analyses of Adjuvant Therapies for Women with Early Breast Cancer: The Early Breast Cancer Trialists' Collaborative Group Overview." *Annals of Oncology* 17 (Suppl. 10): x59–62.

Cleary, J., H. Ddungu, S. R. Distelhorst, C. Ripamonti, G. M. Rodin, and others. 2013. "Supportive and Palliative Care for Metastatic Breast Cancer: Resource Allocations in Low- and Middle-Income Countries: A Breast Health Global Initiative 2013 Consensus Statement." *Breast* 22 (5): 616–27. doi:10.1016/j.breast.2013.07.052.

Curado, M. P., B. Edwards, H. R. Shin, J. H. Storm, J. Ferlay, and others. 2007. "Cancer Incidence in Five Continents." Vol. 9, IARC Scientific Publication 160, IARC Press, Lyon.

Devi, B. C., T. S. Tang, and M. Corbex. 2007. "Reducing by Half the Percentage of Late-Stage Presentation for Breast and Cervix Cancer over 4 Years: A Pilot Study of Clinical Downstaging in Sarawak, Malaysia." *Annals of Oncology* 18 (7): 1172–76. doi:mdm105 [pii]; 10.1093/annonc/mdm105.

Eniu, A., R. W. Carlson, N. S. El Saghir, J. Bines, N. S. Bese, and others. 2008. "Guideline Implementation for Breast Healthcare in Low- and Middle-Income Countries: Treatment Resource Allocation." *Cancer* 113 (Suppl. 8): 2269–81. doi:10.1002/cncr.23843.

Evans, D. B., T. T. Edejer, T. Adam, and S. S. Lim. 2005. "Methods to Assess the Costs and Health Effects of Interventions for Improving Health in Developing Countries." *British Medical Journal* 331 (7525): 1137–40. doi:10.1136/bmj.331.7525.1137.

Ferlay, J., I. Soerjomataram, M. Ervik, R. Dikshit, S. Eser, and others. 2013. "GLOBOCAN 2012 v1.0, Cancer Incidence and Mortality Worldwide." IARC CancerBase No. 11 [Internet]. International Agency for Research on Cancer. http://globocan.iarc.fr.

Fonseca, M., G. T. Araujo, and E. D. Saad. 2009. "Cost-Effectiveness of Anastrozole, in Comparison with Tamoxifen, in the Adjuvant Treatment of Early Breast Cancer in Brazil." *Revista da Associação Médica Brasileira* 55 (4): 410–15.

Forouzanfar, M. H., K. J. Foreman, A. M. Delossantos, R. Lozano, A. D. Lopez, and others. 2011. "Breast and Cervical Cancer in 187 Countries between 1980 and 2010: A Systematic Analysis." *The Lancet* 378 (9801): 1461–84. doi:S0140-6736(11)61351-2 [pii]; 10.1016/S0140-6736(11)61351-2.

Freedman, L. S., B. K. Edwards, L. A. G. Ries, and J. L. Young. 2006. *Cancer Incidence in Four Member Countries (Cyprus, Egypt, Israel, and Jordan) of the Middle East Cancer Consortium (MECC) Compared with US SEER*. NIH Pub. No. 06-5873. Bethesda, MD: National Cancer Institute.

Ganz, P. A., C. H. Yip, J. R. Gralow, S. R. Distelhorst, K. S. Albain, and others. 2013. "Supportive Care after Curative Treatment for Breast Cancer (Survivorship Care): Resource Allocations in Low- and Middle-Income Countries: A Breast Health Global Initiative 2013 Consensus Statement." *Breast* 22 (5): 606–15. doi:10.1016/j.breast.2013.07.049.

Ginsberg, G. M., J. A. Lauer, S. Zelle, S. Baeten, and R. Baltussen. 2012. "Cost Effectiveness of Strategies to Combat Breast, Cervical, and Colorectal Cancer in Sub-Saharan Africa and South East Asia: Mathematical Modelling Study." *British Medical Journal* 344: e614. doi:10.1136/bmj.e614.

Gold, M. R., J. E. Siegel, L. B. Russell, and M. C. Weinstein. 1996. *Cost-Effectiveness in Health and Medicine*, 1st edition. New York: Oxford University Press.

Gotzsche, P. C., K. J. Jorgensen, P. H. Zahl, and J. Maehlen. 2012. "Why Mammography Screening Has Not Lived up to Expectations from the Randomised Trials." *Cancer Causes Control* 23 (1): 15–21. doi:10.1007/s10552-011-9867-8.

Greenlee, R. T., T. Murray, S. Bolden, and P. A. Wingo. 2000. "Cancer Statistics, 2000." *CA: A Cancer Journal for Clinicians* 50 (1): 7–33.

Groot, M. T., R. Baltussen, C. A. Uyl-de Groot, B. O. Anderson, and G. N. Hortobagyi. 2006. "Costs and Health Effects of Breast Cancer Interventions in Epidemiologically Different Regions of Africa, North America, and Asia." *The Breast Journal* 12 (Suppl. 1): S81–90.

Hammond, M. E., D. F. Hayes, M. Dowsett, D. C. Allred, K. L. Hagerty, and others. 2010. "American Society of Clinical Oncology/College of American Pathologists Guideline Recommendations for Immunohistochemical Testing of Estrogen and Progesterone Receptors in Breast Cancer." *Archives of Pathology & Laboratory Medicine* 134 (6): 907–22. doi:10.1043/1543-2165-134.6.907.

Harford, J. B., I. V. Otero, B. O. Anderson, E. Cazap, W. J. Gradishar, and others. 2011. "Problem Solving for Breast Health Care Delivery in Low and Middle Resource Countries (LMCs): Consensus Statement from the Breast Health Global Initiative." *Breast* 20 (Suppl. 2): S20–29.

Hisham, A. N., and C. H. Yip. 2003. "Spectrum of Breast Cancer in Malaysian Women: Overview." *World Journal of Surgery* 27 (8): 921–23.

Howell, A., E. Anderson, R. Blamey, R. B. Clarke, J. M. Dixon, and others. 1998. "The Primary Use of Endocrine Therapies." *Recent Results in Cancer Research* 152: 227–44.

Humphrey, L. L., M. Helfand, B. K. Chan, and S. H. Woolf. 2002. "Breast Cancer Screening: A Summary of the Evidence for the U.S. Preventive Services Task Force." *Annals of Internal Medicine* 137 (5 Part 1): 347–60.

IARC (International Agency for Research on Cancer). 2008. "Screening for Breast Cancer." In *World Cancer Report*, edited by P. Boyle and B. Levin, 296–301. Lyon: IARC.

Ichikawa, L. E., W. E. Barlow, M. L. Anderson, S. H. Taplin, B. M. Geller, and others. 2010. "Time Trends in Radiologists' Interpretive Performance at Screening Mammography from the Community-Based Breast Cancer Surveillance Consortium, 1996–2004." *Radiology* 256 (1): 74–82. doi:10.1148/radiol.10091881.

Instituto Nacional de Cancerología. 2006. *Recomendaciones para la detección temprana de cáncer de mama en Colombia.* Guía de práctica clínica No.1. Bogotá: Instituto Nacional de Cancerología.

Jemal, A., R. Siegel, E. Ward, Y. Hao, J. Xu, and others. 2009. "Cancer Statistics, 2009." *CA: A Cancer Journal for Clinicians* 59 (4): 225–49. doi:caac.20006 [pii];10.3322/caac.20006.

Jemal, A., A. Thomas, T. Murray, and M. Thun. 2002. "Cancer Statistics, 2002." *CA: A Cancer Journal for Clinicians* 52 (1): 23–47.

Johannesson, M., and M. C. Weinstein. 1993. "On the Decision Rules of Cost-Effectiveness Analysis." *Journal of Health Economics* 12 (4): 459–67.

Kalager, M., M. Zelen, F. Langmark, and H. O. Adami. 2010. "Effect of Screening Mammography on Breast-Cancer Mortality in Norway." *The New England Journal of Medicine* 363 (13): 1203–10. doi:10.1056/NEJMoa1000727.

Kanemura, S., I. Tsuji, N. Ohuchi, H. Takei, T. Yokoe, and others. 1999. "A Case Control Study on the Effectiveness of Breast Cancer Screening by Clinical Breast Examination in Japan." *Japanese Journal of Cancer Research* 90 (6): 607–13.

Kardinah, D., B. O. Anderson, C. Duggan, I. A. Ali, and D. B. Thomas. 2014. "Short Report: Limited Effectiveness of Screening Mammography in Addition to Clinical Breast Examination by Trained Nurse Midwives in Rural Jakarta, Indonesia." *International Journal of Cancer* 134 (5): 1250–55. doi:10.1002/ijc.28442.

Kuroishi, T., K. Hirose, T. Suzuki, and S. Tominaga. 2000. "Effectiveness of Mass Screening for Breast Cancer in Japan." *Breast Cancer* 7 (1): 1–8.

Lee, S. G., Y. G. Jee, H. C. Chung, S. B. Kim, J. Ro, and others. 2009. "Cost-Effectiveness Analysis of Adjuvant Therapy for Node Positive Breast Cancer in Korea: Docetaxel, Doxorubicin and Cyclophosphamide (TAC) Versus Fluorouracil, Doxorubicin and Cyclophosphamide (FAC)." *Breast Cancer Research and Treatment* 114 (3): 589–95. doi:10.1007/s10549-008-0035-0.

Lee, S. Y., S. H. Jeong, Y. N. Kim, J. Kim, D. R. Kang, and others. 2009. "Cost-Effective Mammography Screening in Korea: High Incidence of Breast Cancer in Young Women." *Cancer Science* 100 (6): 1105–11. doi:10.1111/j.1349-7006.2009.01147.x.

Liubao, P., W. Xiaomin, T. Chongqing, J. Kamon, C. Gannong, and others. 2009. "Cost-Effectiveness Analysis of Adjuvant Therapy for Operable Breast Cancer from a Chinese Perspective: Doxorubicin Plus Cyclophosphamide versus Docetaxel Plus Cyclophosphamide." *Pharmacoeconomics* 27 (10): 873–86.

Love, R. R., N. B. Duc, D. C. Allred, N. C. Binh, N. V. Dinh, and others. 2002. "Oophorectomy and Tamoxifen Adjuvant Therapy in Premenopausal Vietnamese and Chinese Women with Operable Breast Cancer." *Journal of Clinical Oncology* 20 (10): 2559–66.

Masood, S., L. Vass, J. A. Ibarra, Jr., B. M. Ljung, H. Stalsberg, and others. 2008. "Breast Pathology Guideline Implementation in Low- and Middle-Income Countries." *Cancer* 113 (Suppl. 8): 2297–304. doi:10.1002/cncr.23833.

McCannon, C. J., D. M. Berwick, and M. R. Massoud. 2007. "The Science of Large-Scale Change in Global Health." *Journal of the American Medical Association* 298 (16): 1937–39.

McTiernan, A., P. Porter, and J. D. Potter. 2008. "Breast Cancer Prevention in Countries with Diverse Resources." *Cancer* 113 (Suppl. 8): 2325–30. doi:10.1002/cncr.23829.

Mittra, I., G. A. Mishra, S. Singh, S. Aranke, P. Notani, and others. 2010. "A Cluster Randomized, Controlled Trial of Breast and Cervix Cancer Screening in Mumbai, India: Methodology and Interim Results after Three Rounds of Screening." *International Journal of Cancer* 126 (4): 976–84. doi:10.1002/ijc.24840.

Morrow, M., E. A. Strom, L. W. Bassett, D. D. Dershaw, B. Fowble, and others. 2002. "Standard for Breast Conservation Therapy in the Management of Invasive Breast Carcinoma." *CA: A Cancer Journal for Clinicians* 52 (5): 277–300.

Murillo, R., S. Díaz, O. Sánchez, F. Perry, M. Piñeros, and others. 2008. "Pilot Implementation of Breast Cancer Early Detection Programs in Colombia." *Breast Care* 3: 29–32.

Murray, C. J. L., and A. D. Lopez. 1996. "The Global Burden of Disease: A Comprehensive Assessment of Mortality and Disability from Diseases, Injuries, and Risk Factors in 1990 and Projected to 2020." In *Global Burden of Disease and Injury.* Cambridge, MA: Harvard School of Public Health.

Nelson, H. D., K. Tyne, A. Naik, C. Bougatsos, B. K. Chan, and others. 2009. "Screening for Breast Cancer: An Update for the U.S. Preventive Services Task Force."

Annals of Internal Medicine 151 (10): 727–37, W237–42. doi:10.7326/0003-4819-151-10-200911170-00009.

Nguyen, L. H., W. Laohasiriwong, J. F. Stewart, P. Wright, Y. T. B. Nguyen, and others. 2013. "Cost-Effectiveness Analysis of a Screening Program for Breast Cancer in Vietnam." *Value in Health Regional Issues* 2(1): 21–28.

Okonkwo, Q. L., G. Draisma, A. der Kinderen, M. L. Brown, and H. J. de Koning. 2008. "Breast Cancer Screening Policies in Developing Countries: A Cost-Effectiveness Analysis for India." *Journal of the National Cancer Institute* 100 (18): 1290–300. doi:10.1093/jnci/djn292.

Parkin, D. M., and L. M. Fernandez. 2006. "Use of Statistics to Assess the Global Burden of Breast Cancer." *The Breast Journal* 12 (Suppl. 1): S70–80.

Perloff, M., G. J. Lesnick, A. Korzun, F. Chu, J. F. Holland, and others. 1988. "Combination Chemotherapy with Mastectomy or Radiotherapy for Stage III Breast Carcinoma: A Cancer and Leukemia Group B Study." *Journal of Clinical Oncology* 6 (2): 261–69.

Pinto, A. C., F. Ades, E. de Azambuja, and M. Piccart-Gebhart. 2013. "Trastuzumab for Patients with HER2 Positive Breast Cancer: Delivery, Duration and Combination Therapies." *Breast* 22 (Suppl. 2): S152–55. doi:10.1016/j.breast.2013.07.029.

Pisani, P., D. M. Parkin, C. Ngelangel, D. Esteban, L. Gibson, and others. 2006. "Outcome of Screening by Clinical Examination of the Breast in a Trial in the Philippines." *International Journal of Cancer* 118 (1): 149–54.

Poon, D., B. O. Anderson, L. T. Chen, K. Tanaka, W. Y. Lau, and others. 2009. "Management of Hepatocellular Carcinoma in Asia: Consensus Statement from the Asian Oncology Summit 2009." *The Lancet Oncology* 10 (11): 1111–18. doi:S1470-2045(09)70241-4 [pii]; 10.1016/S1470-2045(09)70241-4.

Porter, P. 2008. "'Westernizing' Women's Risks? Breast Cancer in Lower-Income Countries." *The New England Journal of Medicine* 358 (3): 213–16.

Salomon, J. A., N. Carvalho, C. Gutierrez-Delgado, R. Orozco, A. Mancuso, and others. 2012. "Intervention Strategies to Reduce the Burden of Non-Communicable Diseases in Mexico: Cost Effectiveness Analysis." *British Medical Journal* 344: e355. doi:10.1136/bmj.e355.

Sant, M., C. Allemani, F. Berrino, M. P. Coleman, T. Aareleid, and others. 2004. "Breast Carcinoma Survival in Europe and the United States." *Cancer* 100 (4): 715–22.

Schmidt, C. 2009. "Komen/ASCO Program Aims to Swell Ranks of Minority Oncologists." *Journal of the National Cancer Institute* 101 (4): 224–25, 227.

Semiglazov, V. F., V. M. Moiseyenko, A. G. Manikhas, S. A. Protsenko, R. S. Kharikova, and others. 1999. "Role of Breast Self-Examination in Early Detection of Breast Cancer: Russia/WHO Prospective Randomized Trial in St. Petersburg." *Cancer Strategy* 1: 145–51.

Shyyan, R., S. F. Sener, B. O. Anderson, L. M. Garrote, G. N. Hortobagyi, and others. 2008. "Guideline Implementation for Breast Healthcare in Low- and Middle-Income Countries: Diagnosis Resource Allocation." *Cancer* 113 (Suppl. 8): 2257–68. doi:10.1002/cncr.23840.

Smith, R. A. 2000. "Breast Cancer Screening among Women Younger Than Age 50: A Current Assessment of the Issues." *CA: A Cancer Journal for Clinicians* 50 (5): 312–36.

Soo, R. A., B. O. Anderson, B. C. Cho, C. H. Yang, M. Liao, and others. 2009. "First-Line Systemic Treatment of Advanced Stage Non-Small-Cell Lung Cancer in Asia: Consensus Statement from the Asian Oncology Summit 2009." *The Lancet Oncology* 10 (11): 1102–10. doi:10.1016/S1470-2045(09)70238-4.

Tan-Torres Edejer, T., R. Baltussen, T. Adam, R. Hutubessy, A. Acharya, and others. 2003. *Making Choices in Health: WHO Guide to Cost-Effectiveness Analysis.* Geneva: WHO.

Tangjitgamol, S., B. O. Anderson, H. T. See, C. Lertbutsayanukul, N. Sirisabya, and others. 2009. "Management of Endometrial Cancer in Asia: Consensus Statement from the Asian Oncology Summit 2009." *The Lancet Oncology* 10 (11): 1119–27. doi:10.1016/S1470-2045(09)70290-6.

Theriault, R. L., R. W. Carlson, C. Allred, B. O. Anderson, H. J. Burstein, and others. 2013. "Breast Cancer, Version 3.2013: Featured Updates to the NCCN Guidelines." *Journal of the National Comprehensive Cancer Network* 11 (7): 753–60; quiz 761.

Thomas, D. B., D. L. Gao, R. M. Ray, W. W. Wang, C. J. Allison, and others. 2002. "Randomized Trial of Breast Self-Examination in Shanghai: Final Results." *Journal of the National Cancer Institute* 94 (19): 1445–57.

Thomas, D. B., R. H. Murillo, Kardinah, and B. O. Anderson. 2013. "Breast Cancer Early Detection and Clinical Guidelines." In *Cancer Epidemiology: Low and Middle Income Countries and Special Populations*, edited by A. S. Soliman, D. Schottenfeld, and P. Boffetta, 378–95. New York: Oxford University Press.

Thorat, M. A., A. Rangole, M. S. Nadkarni, V. Parmar, and R. A. Badwe. 2008. "Revision Surgery for Breast Cancer: Single-Institution Experience." *Cancer* 113 (Suppl. 8): 2347–52. doi:10.1002/cncr.23839.

Thornton, H. 2014. "Bringing an End to Mandatory Breast Cancer Screening in Uruguay." *British Medical Journal* 348: g390. doi:10.1136/bmj.g390.

U.S. Preventive Services Task Force. 2009. "Screening for Breast Cancer: U.S. Preventive Services Task Force Recommendation Statement." *Annals of Internal Medicine* 151 (10): 716–26, W-236. doi:151/10/716 [pii]; 10.1059/0003-4819-151-10-200911170-00008.

Visco, F. 2007. "The National Breast Cancer Coalition: Setting the Standard for Advocate Collaboration in Clinical Trials." *Cancer Treatment and Research* 132: 143–56.

Wee, J. T., B. O. Anderson, J. Corry, A. D'Cruz, K. C. Soo, and others. 2009. "Management of the Neck after Chemoradiotherapy for Head and Neck Cancers in Asia: Consensus Statement from the Asian Oncology Summit 2009." *The Lancet Oncology* 10 (11): 1086–92. doi:S1470-2045(09)70266-9 [pii]; 10.1016/S1470-2045(09)70266-9.

Weir, H. K., M. J. Thun, B. F. Hankey, L. A. Ries, H. L. Howe, and others. 2003. "Annual Report to the Nation on the Status of Cancer, 1975–2000, Featuring the Uses of Surveillance Data for Cancer Prevention and Control." *Journal of the National Cancer Institute* 95 (17): 1276–99.

Winn, R. J., and W. Z. Botnick. 1997. "The NCCN Guideline Program: A Conceptual Framework." *Oncology (Williston Park)* 11 (11A): 25–32.

WHO (World Health Organization). 2001. *Macroeconomics and Health: Investing in Health for Economic Development.* Geneva: WHO.

———. 2002. "Executive Summary." In *National Cancer Control Programmes: Policies and Managerial Guidelines,* 1–24. Geneva: WHO.

Wong, N. S., B. O. Anderson, K. S. Khoo, P. T. Ang, C. H. Yip, and others. 2009. "Management of HER2-Positive Breast Cancer in Asia: Consensus Statement from the Asian Oncology Summit 2009." *The Lancet Oncology* 10 (11): 1077–85. doi:10.1016/S1470-2045(09)70230-X.

Wong, I. O., B. J. Cowling, C. M. Schooling, and G. M. Leung. 2007. "Age-Period-Cohort Projections of Breast Cancer Incidence in a Rapidly Transitioning Chinese Population." *International Journal of Cancer* 121 (7): 1556–63.

Wong, I. O., K. M. Kuntz, B. J. Cowling, C. L. Lam, and G. M. Leung. 2007. "Cost Effectiveness of Mammography Screening for Chinese Women." *Cancer* 110 (4): 885–95. doi:10.1002/cncr.22848.

Yang, J. J., S. K. Park, L. Y. Cho, W. Han, B. Park, and others. 2010. "Cost-Effectiveness Analysis of 5 Years of Postoperative Adjuvant Tamoxifen Therapy for Korean Women with Breast Cancer: Retrospective Cohort Study of the Korean Breast Cancer Society Database." *Clinical Therapeutics* 32 (6): 1122–38. doi:10.1016/j.clinthera.2010.05.013.

Yip, C. H., R. A. Smith, B. O. Anderson, A. B. Miller, D. B. Thomas, and others. 2008. "Guideline Implementation for Breast Healthcare in Low- and Middle-Income Countries: Early Detection Resource Allocation." *Cancer* 113 (Suppl. 8): 2244–56. doi:10.1002/cncr.23842.

Yoo, C., J. H. Ahn, K. H. Jung, S. B. Kim, H. H. Kim, and others. 2012. "Impact of Immunohistochemistry-Based Molecular Subtype on Chemosensitivity and Survival in Patients with Breast Cancer Following Neoadjuvant Chemotherapy." *Journal of Breast Cancer* 15 (2): 203–10. doi:10.4048/jbc.2012.15.2.203.

Zelle, S. G., and R. M. Baltussen. 2013. "Economic Analyses of Breast Cancer Control in Low- and Middle-Income Countries: A Systematic Review." *Systematic Reviews* 2: 20. doi:10.1186/2046-4053-2-20.

Zelle, S. G., K. M. Nyarko, W. K. Bosu, M. Aikins, L. M. Niens, and others. 2012. "Costs, Effects and Cost-Effectiveness of Breast Cancer Control in Ghana." *Tropical Medicine & International Health* 17 (8): 1031–43. doi:10.1111/j.1365-3156.2012.03021.x.

Cervical Cancer

Lynette Denny, Rolando Herrero, Carol Levin, and Jane J. Kim

INTRODUCTION

Cervical cancer, a largely preventable disease, is one of the most common cancers found in women living in low- and middle-income countries (LMICs). A striking reduction in the incidence of and mortality from cervical cancer occurred in the past century in those countries that were able to establish successful national screening programs. These programs relied on cytology-based Papanicolaou smears to identify cervical cancer precursors that can be removed before progressing to invasive cancer. Prevention of up to 91 percent of all invasive cervical cancers has been achieved in countries able to implement widespread cytology-based screening.

However, these programs are expensive and require robust and well-funded health care systems. Few LMICs have initiated or sustained cytology-based cervical cancer prevention programs, and these countries experience very high incidence and mortality rates. The unequal burden of cervical cancer is an example of the impact of unequal access to health care. Fortunately, alternative strategies to prevent cervical cancer have been investigated and extensively evaluated in these settings. The recent introduction of two commercially available vaccines against human papillomavirus (HPV) has offered the possibility of primary prevention of cervical cancer. This chapter focuses on these innovations.

BURDEN OF CERVICAL CANCER[1]

Global Burden of Disease

Cervical cancer, caused by HPV, is the third leading malignancy among women in the world, after breast cancer and colorectal cancer, with an estimated 527,624 new cases and 265,653 deaths in 2012 (Ferlay and others 2013). Incidence and mortality rates have been declining in most areas of the world in the past 30 years, at a worldwide rate of about 1.6 percent per year (Forouzanfar and others 2011). This decline is a result of increased access to health services, reductions in some risk factors (such as fertility rates), improvements in treatment, and successful cytology-based screening programs. However, more than 80 percent of cases and 88 percent of deaths occur in LMICs. Cervical cancer is still the leading cancer in women in many LMICs; some areas report recent increases in rates, including several economies in Europe and Central Asia (Arbyn and others 2011).

A striking characteristic of cervical cancer is its variation by country, with a generally strong inverse correlation between the level of development and the incidence and mortality. Survival once the disease has developed is also much better in richer than in poorer countries. Figure 4.1 shows trends of incidence and mortality in selected countries.

Corresponding author: Lynette Denny, MBChB (UCT), MMED (O&G), PhD, FCOG (SA), lynette.denny@uct.ac.za

Figure 4.1 Trends of Age-Standardized Rates of Cervical Cancer Incidence and Mortality in Selected Countries

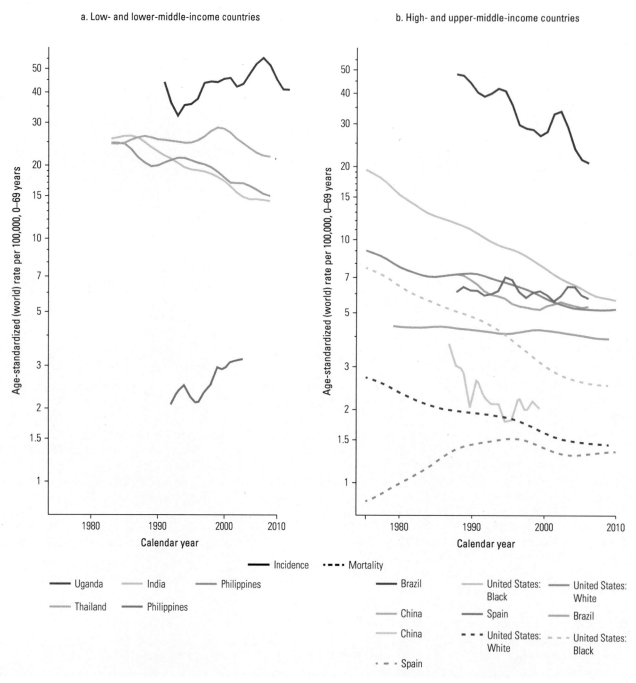

a. Low- and lower-middle-income countries

b. High- and upper-middle-income countries

Source: CI5*plus* (http://ci5.iarc.fr/CI5plus/Default.aspx) and WHO Mortality Database (http://www.who.int/healthinfo/statistics/mortality_rawdata/en/index.html).
Note: Data for the economies in the graphs are for Uganda (Kampala), Thailand (Chiang Mai), Philippines (Manila), India (Chennai and Mumbai), Brazil (Goiâna), Spain (Granada, Murcia, Navarra, and Tarragona), China (Hong Kong SAR, China, and Shanghai), and the United States (Surveillance, Epidemiology, and End Results Program). All available data for these economies are shown.

Regional Burden of Disease

Despite the declining global rates, the number of new cases and deaths has increased constantly by about 0.5 percent per year because of population aging. With no new intervention, the increase will continue, particularly in LMICs where the life expectancy of women is improving. For example, in Latin America and the Caribbean, the estimated number of new cases is likely to increase by 75 percent between 2002 and 2025 if the incidence rates remain at 2002 levels, because of population growth and aging alone (Parkin and others 2008).

The disease is strongly influenced by cultural and religious practices that govern sexual behavior and transmission of HPV. Sub-Saharan Africa has the highest estimated rates of cervical cancer; in Guinea, Malawi, and Zambia, the age-standardized incidence rate is over 50 per 100,000 (Arbyn and others 2011). In contrast, in countries in the Middle East and North Africa, such as Algeria, the Arab Republic of Egypt, Libya, Sudan, and Tunisia, where sexual behaviors are more conservative, the recorded incidence rates are below 10 per 100,000 women. In high-income countries (HICs), rates are even lower, at about 5 per 100,000 women.

In Latin America and the Caribbean, Guyana, Honduras, Jamaica, and Nicaragua have rates around 40 per 100,000. In Asia, the highest rates are in Bangladesh, Cambodia, India, and Nepal.

Map 4.1 shows the incidence of cervical cancer by country in 2012; figure 4.2 shows the contrast between the rates of incidence and mortality between national income groupings.

Even within HICs, the highest incidence and mortality rates are among the poorest or most marginalized women. For example, in the United States, where the average rates are low and cervical cancer has consistently declined in recent decades, strong disparities still exist by race and socioeconomic status (Singh 2012), reflecting the variability in accessibility of services. The other notable characteristic of cervical cancer is that it affects relatively young women who often have many children and are frequently sole providers. The median age at death for women with cervical cancer is 54 years; the burden of disease among women under age 40 years is high compared with other cancers, because of the large numbers of women in these age groups in LMICs and the fact that cervical cancer rates begin to rise at younger ages than other cancers.

Because cervical cancer affects relatively young women, it ranks highest among cancers according to a disability-adjusted life years (DALYs) metric. In a recent study, DALYs caused by cervical cancer ranged from 84 per 100,000 women in areas with a very high Human Development Index (HDI)[2] to 595 per 100,000 in areas with a low HDI (Soerjomataram and others 2012). Breast cancer DALYs ranged from a high of 566 age-adjusted DALYs per 100,000 in populations with a very high HDI to 387 in those with a low HDI.

Map 4.1 Age-Standardized Cervical Cancer Incidence Rates, 2012

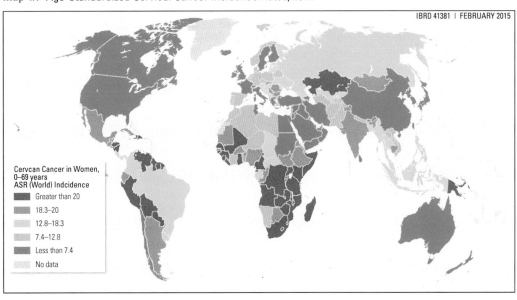

Source: Ferlay and others 2013.
Note: ASR = age-standardized rate.

Figure 4.2 Age-Standardized Cervical Cancer Incidence and Mortality Rates per 100,000 Women, by World Bank Income Group

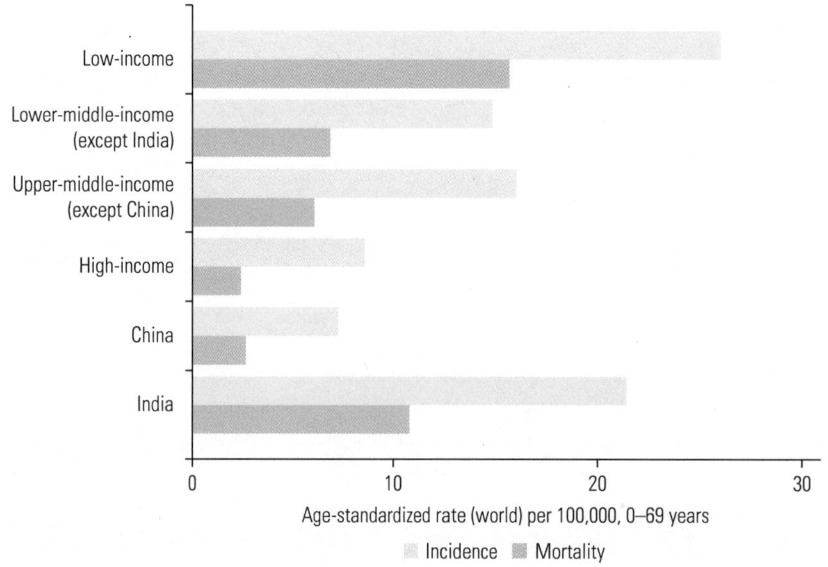

Age-standardized rate (world) per 100,000, 0–69 years

Incidence ■ Mortality

Source: Ferlay and others 2013.

NATURAL HISTORY OF CERVICAL CANCER

The natural history has been studied extensively, and persistent infection of the cervix with certain high-risk types of HPV has been well established as a necessary cause of cervical cancer (Walboomers and others 1999). HPV is a very common sexually transmitted infection, usually acquired soon after initiation of sexual activity. Most HPV infections clear spontaneously within one to two years; those that persist, particularly high-risk types of HPV (including HPV 16 and 18), may progress to cervical cancer precursors, and ultimately to invasive cervical cancer. High-risk types of HPV are identified in nearly all cancers of the cervix, and the relative risk of cervical cancer associated with persistent, ongoing infection with high-risk types of HPV is higher than the risk of lung cancer associated with smoking. HPV 16 and 18 are responsible for about 70 percent of cases worldwide (http://www.iarc.fr). There is little geographic variation in the predominant HPV types associated with cervical cancer.

A study that evaluated HPV infection in 10,575 histologically confirmed cases of invasive cancer from 38 countries in Asia, Europe, Latin America and the Caribbean, North America, Oceania, and Sub-Saharan Africa over a 60-year period found that 85 percent

(n = 8,977) of the cases were positive for HPV DNA (de Sanjose and others 2010). HPV types 16, 18, and 45 were the three most common types in each histologic form of cervical cancer (squamous cell, adenocarcinoma, and adenosquamous carcinoma), accounting for 61 percent, 10 percent, and 6 percent, respectively.

Good evidence suggests that HPV infection precedes the development of cervical cancer by decades and that persistent infection with HPV is necessary for the development and progression of precancerous lesions of the cervix, either to higher grades of precancerous disease or to cancer. Cervical cancer progresses slowly from a preinvasive state to invasive cervical cancer, a process that can take 10–30 years (Wright and Kurman 1994).

However, HPV infections are very common, particularly among young women (Herrero and others 2005), where the majority of infections are likely to regress spontaneously as a result of activation of the immune system.

Cervical Cytology Classification and Terminology

In 1988, the Bethesda classification of cytology was adopted and has been revised several times (National Cancer Workshop 1989). The latest consensus guidelines for the management of abnormal cytology in the United

States were published in 2013 (Massad and others 2013) and can be accessed at http://www.asccp.org.

Cervical Cancer and Infection with Human Immunodeficiency Virus

Women infected with human immunodeficiency virus (HIV) have an increased risk of being infected with HPV and are at increased risk for cervical cancer. Studies have consistently shown higher prevalence of HPV infection, more persistent infections with HPV, greater infections with multiple types of HPV, and higher prevalence of cervical cancer precursors in HIV-infected women (Ellerbrock and others 2000; Harris and others 2005; Palefsky and others 1999). The Rwandan Women's Interassociation Study and Assessment is an observational prospective cohort study of 710 HIV-positive and 226 HIV-negative Rwandan women enrolled in 2005 (Singh and others 2009). The prevalence of HPV was significantly higher in the HIV-positive group overall and in each 10-year age group. Forty-six percent of HIV-positive women had high-risk types of HPV and 35 percent were infected with multiple types, both of which were associated with a higher risk of abnormal cytological findings.

The association with HIV is important because integrating cervical cancer prevention strategies with chronic care for HIV-positive women is essential to maximizing the health-giving benefit of antiretroviral therapy. In many countries in Sub-Saharan Africa, antiretroviral therapy is free, but cervical cancer screening and treatment are not.

SECONDARY PREVENTION OF CERVICAL CANCER THROUGH SCREENING

Historically, cervical cancer screening, also known as secondary prevention of cervical cancer, was based on examining cells collected from the surface of the cervix by Pap smear (cytology), followed by colposcopy for women with abnormal smears and histological assessment, followed by surgical treatment for histologically proven cancer precursors. This approach resulted in dramatic reductions in cervical cancer incidence and mortality in health systems that were robust enough to support relatively complex screening programs effectively. However, very few LMICs have been able to initiate or sustain cytology-based screening programs because of lack of adequate resources or health care or laboratory infrastructure.

For screening and treatment of precancerous lesions, several new tools have been developed that are better suited to low-resource settings. Depending mainly on the target age group and frequency of screening, these tools may be effective in reducing cervical cancer rates. The new interventions include the following:

- Screening with visual inspection with acetic acid (VIA)
- Screening with HPV DNA testing
- Treatment with ablative techniques (cryotherapy and cold coagulation)
- Treatment using excisional techniques, called loop electrocautery excision procedure (LEEP), also known as large loop excision of the transformational zone (LLETZ), and cone biopsy.

Impact of Cervical Cytology-Based Screening Programs

Cytology-based cervical cancer screening, which began in the early 1960s in the Scandinavian countries, was not evaluated in randomized trials to assess the impact of screening on cervical cancer incidence or mortality. The marked reduction in cervical cancer incidence and mortality after cytology-based screening programs were initiated in a variety of LMICs was interpreted as strong nonexperimental support for organized cervical cancer screening programs.

The International Agency for Research on Cancer (IARC) conducted a comprehensive analysis of data from several of the largest screening programs in the world in 1986; the analysis showed that well-organized, cytology-based screening programs were effective in reducing cervical cancer incidence and mortality (Hakama 1986). In the Nordic countries, following the introduction of nationwide screening in the 1960s, mortality rates from cervical cancer fell between 84 and 11 percent, respectively, corresponding to the country with the shortest screening interval and widest age range (Iceland) and to the country with only 5 percent population coverage by an organized screening program (Norway) (Laara, Day, and Hakama 1987).

Further, the age-specific trends indicated that the *target age range* of a screening program was a more important determinant of risk reduction than the *frequency* of screening within that age range. This finding was in agreement with the estimates of the IARC Working Group on Cervical Cancer Screening that for interscreen intervals of up to five years, the protective effect of organized screening exceeded 80 percent throughout the targeted age group (IARC Working Group on Cervical Cancer Screening 1986a, 1986b). It is clear that the extent to which screening programs have succeeded or failed to decrease the incidence of and mortality from cervical cancer is largely a function of three factors:

- The extent of screening coverage of the population at risk
- The target age of women screened
- The reliability of cytology services in the program.

Gakidou, Nordhagen, and Obermeyer (2008) evaluated screening programs in 57 countries and found that the levels of effective screening coverage using cytology vary widely across countries, from over 80 percent in Austria and Luxembourg to less than 1 percent in Bangladesh, Ethiopia, and Myanmar. Many women in low-income countries (LICs) had never had a pelvic examination. This proportion of women is largest in Bangladesh, Ethiopia, and Malawi, where more than 90 percent of women report never having had a pelvic examination, compared with 9 percent of women living in the richest global wealth decile. Although crude coverage rates are high for women in the richest wealth deciles, effective coverage rates are overall low, with rates of around 60 percent and less than 10 percent in the poorest countries.

Screening efforts have failed to produce the expected reductions in cervical cancer mortality in many places, even when large numbers of Pap smears were performed, because the wrong women have been screened (for example, younger women attending antenatal clinics), coverage of the most at-risk population was too low (that is, women ages 35–64 years), the quality of cervical smears was poor (Irwin, Oberle, and Rosero-Bixby 1991; Lazcano-Ponce and others 1994; Sankaranarayanan and Pisani 1997), and follow-up of screen-positive women was incomplete. In all cases, funds were spent for little gain.

Alternative Approaches to Cytology for Cervical Cancer Screening

Visual Inspection with Acetic Acid

VIA involves applying a 3–5 percent acetic acid solution to the cervix and then examining it with the naked eye using a bright light source. No expensive equipment or supplies are needed, and screening takes less than five minutes. A well-defined aceto-white area close to the transformation zone indicates a positive test.

VIA is inexpensive and simple and can be carried out by primary care staff. Most important, VIA provides an immediate result that can be used to decide on treatment, usually with cryotherapy, which requires training but no surgery or anesthetic.

It is difficult to recommend VIA unconditionally, however, because its sensitivity and specificity are lower than those of other screening methods (table 4.1). VIA sensitivity and specificity are variable, because they are highly dependent on the training and skill of the staff carrying out the examinations. The accuracy of the test decreases with the increasing age of the women screened. In cross-sectional studies, the sensitivity and specificity of VIA compared favorably with cytology in detecting high-grade cervical cancer precursor lesions and cervical cancer. Sensitivity has varied from 49 to 96 percent, and specificity has varied from 49 to 98 percent (Denny, Quinn, and Sankaranarayanan 2006). However, many of these studies suffer from verification bias, where the true status of disease in test-negative women is unknown. Sauvaget and others (2011) performed a meta-analysis of 26 studies of VIA with confirmatory testing, using high-grade squamous intraepithelial lesions (HSIL) as the disease threshold. Sauvaget and others (2011) report a sensitivity of 80 percent specificity (range 79–82 percent) and 92 percent specificity (range 91–92 percent) for

Table 4.1 Performance and Characteristics of Screening Methods

Screening test	Sensitivity	Specificity	Characteristics
Conventional cytology	Moderate (44–78%)	High (91–96%)	Adequate health care infrastructure required; laboratory based; stringent training and quality control required
HPV DNA testing	High (66–100%)	Moderate (61–96%)	Laboratory based; high throughput; objective, reproducible, and robust; currently expensive
Visual inspection methods			
• VIA	Moderate (67–79%)	Low (49–86%)	Low technology; low cost
• VIAM	Moderate (62–73%)	Low (86–87%)	Linkage to immediate treatment possible; suitable for low-resource settings
Colposcopy	Low (44–77%)	Low (85–90%)	Expensive; inappropriate for low-resource settings

Source: Ranges of sensitivity and specificity adapted from Cuzick and others 2008.
Note: HPV = human papillomavirus; VIA = visual inspection with acetic acid; VIAM = magnified visual inspection with acetic acid.

VIA, with a positive predictive value of 10 percent. They conclude that in very low-resource settings where the infrastructure for laboratory-based testing is not available, VIA is a reasonable alternative to cytology. However, in more recent randomized studies, VIA has performed less well.

Despite its limitations, the possibility of immediate diagnosis and treatment makes VIA the only possible alternative in many low-resource settings. One potential use of VIA that would have a significant impact is following an HPV test, for HPV-positive women only, to make treatment decisions. The utility of VIA in this context is promising but yet to be proven.

Case Study of Upscaling VIA

From 2005 through 2009, the World Health Organization (WHO) sponsored a VIA demonstration project in six Sub-Saharan African countries: Madagascar, Malawi, Nigeria, Tanzania, Uganda, and Zambia (WHO 2012). In all, 19,579 women were screened with VIA. Of these, 1,980 were VIA-positive (11.5 percent); cancer was suspected in 326 (1.7 percent). Of the VIA-positive women, 1,737 were eligible for cryotherapy (87.7 percent); of these, 1,058 (60.9 percent) were treated, 601 (34.6 percent) were lost to follow-up, and 78 women were not treated. Of the women treated, 243 (39.1 percent) were treated during the same visit as the screening.

No information was available for 230 of the 326 women in whom cancer was suspected (70.5 percent); of the 96 women investigated, cancer was confirmed in 79, but no staging information was recorded; 77 of the women were treated, mostly with radiation.

This is an interesting study of "real world" VIA screening, with all of the difficulties of any screening program, even with a test as simple as VIA. These difficulties range from achieving adequate coverage; to losing to follow-up the large number of women needing treatment (only 60 percent of eligible women were treated); to treating women on the same day as screening ("screen and treat"), which occurred for less than 40 percent of the women. The failure to refer over 70 percent of women with suspicious lesions for further evaluation—possibly because cervical biopsy is not a free service in any of these countries and most women could not afford to pay—is disturbing. The greatest utility of VIA in countries that cannot afford any alternative is to establish the necessary infrastructure to provide health care services to older women. Once VIA becomes successfully implemented, it should be relatively easy to introduce more sensitive methods of screening into the system. In many LMICs, establishing a sustainable and appropriate infrastructure is most likely the priority.

HPV Testing

Highly sensitive and reproducible laboratory techniques to detect oncogenic HPV and cervical cancer have been developed and are being used or considered in place of cervical cytology for primary screening, in addition to other potential uses (Cuzick and others 2008). The cervix is sampled with a brush, which is inserted into the endocervix and then removed and placed in a tube containing special transport media. The U.S. Food and Drug Administration has approved five of the many tests available for routine laboratory service:

- *Hybrid Capture 2* detects 13 oncogenic types of HPV (16, 18, 31, 33, 35, 39, 45, 51, 52, 56, 58, 59, and 68).
- *Cervista HPV HR* detects 14 HPV types (16, 18, 31, 33, 35, 39, 45, 51, 52, 56, 58, 59, 66, and 68).
- *Cervista HPV 16/18* detects only HPV 16 and 18.
- *Aptima* (transcription–mediated amplification test) detects RNA from 14 HPV types (16, 18, 31, 33, 35, 39, 45, 51, 52, 56, 58, 59, 66, and 68).
- *Cobas 4800* (real-time polymerase chain reaction [PCR]–based test) detects 14 HPV types (16, 18, 31, 33, 35, 39, 45, 51, 52, 56, 58, 59, 66, and 68).

Other tests that use PCR technology are being used in many clinical studies.

HPV testing is an excellent alternative to cytology for cervical cancer screening (Arbyn and others 2012). In meta-analyses of cross-sectional studies, the sensitivity of the Hybrid Capture 2 (HC2) DNA test, the most commonly used test, was 90 percent to detect CIN2+ and 95 percent to detect CIN3+, with more heterogeneity in studies from LMICs. Compared with cytology, the sensitivity of HC2 is 23–46 percent higher on average, and the specificity is 3–8 percent lower (note we are using the terminology as reported by the authors, hence the switch between cervical intraepithelial neoplasia (CIN) and squamous intraepithelial lesion (SIL) terminology).

Another advantage of HPV testing is the possibility of linking screening to treatment without colposcopy or prior histological sampling, particularly once either simplified or point-of-care HPV tests are developed. A randomized screening trial to evaluate safety investigated the acceptability and efficacy of screening women and treating those with positive tests without colposcopy and histological sampling (Denny and others 2010). A total of 6,555 previously unscreened women, ages 35–65 years, were tested for high-risk types of HPV using HC2 (Qiagen, Gaithersburg, MD, United States) and VIA, performed by nurses in primary care settings. This study found that the HPV screen-and-treat arm was associated with a 3.7-fold reduction in the cumulative detection of CIN2 or greater by 36 months;

VIA was associated with a 1.5-fold reduction. For every 100 women screened, the HPV and screen-and-treat strategy averted 4.1 cases of CIN2 and greater compared with VIA-and-treat strategies, which averted 1.8 cases.

A further advantage of HPV testing is that specimens can be obtained by self-collection, with almost complete preservation of the sensitivity and specificity of the screening method. Self-collection, which can be done at home, is accepted by women and could significantly increase participation in screening, particularly by women who are reluctant to undergo a gynecological examination or who live in remote areas.

Another landmark study was a cluster randomized trial of villages and centers where 131,746 women ages 30–59 years were recruited and randomly assigned to one of four groups: HPV testing; cytologic testing; VIA; or the standard of care, which involved no organized or opportunistic screening (Sankaranarayanan and others 2009). The incidence rate of cervical cancer stage 2 or higher and death rates from cervical cancer were significantly higher in the cytologic, VIA, and control groups compared with the HPV testing group. Further, the age-standardized incidence rate (ASIR) of invasive cancer among women who had negative test results on cytological or VIA testing was more than four times the rate among HPV-negative women.

The high negative predictive value of HPV testing (nearly 100 percent) allows the extension of the screening interval, with consequent savings that can offset the possibly higher cost of the test compared with cytology. Screening with HPV testing under age 30 is not recommended, as HPV infection in this group of women is common, and most infections are likely to be transient with a low likelihood of developing into cancer. Screening younger women will add to the costs of the program and may result in significant overtreatment that may be associated with reproductive morbidity, in addition to significant emotional and social problems.

The HPV test is already in use for primary screening in several countries, although in the United States, primary HPV testing has been recommended only in combination with cytology in primary screening or for triage of cytologic abnormalities. A recent study including more than 300,000 women in the United States concluded that HPV testing without cytology might be sufficiently sensitive for primary screening (Katki and others 2011).

Triage of Positive HPV Tests

Even among women over age 30 years, most HPV infections regress; only a minority of women develop persistent infection with high-risk types of HPV that progresses to cervical cancer precursors and cervical cancer. HPV testing identifies women at risk, but not those HPV-positive women who are most likely to have or to develop in the near future significant disease requiring treatment. The challenge is to triage these women by further testing with visual methods, cytology, molecular biomarkers, or a combination of techniques.

Among the visual methods, colposcopy with subsequent biopsy and treatment of visible lesions is the usual procedure in cytology-based programs. However, this method requires highly specialized training and relatively costly equipment. More importantly, the colposcopic impression, colposcopically guided biopsy, and histologic diagnosis are poorly reproducible and have important limitations to the point of reducing the potential of highly sensitive screening tests. The current practice of selecting the most worrisome lesion for biopsy misses up to one-third of prevalent small HSIL lesions. The collection of multiple biopsies from aceto-white lesions can increase the sensitivity of colposcopy (Pretorius and others 2011).

Cytology of HPV-positive women is under strong consideration as a triage method in screening programs, given the high specificity of cytology and ample expertise and infrastructure existing in some areas. This method has the advantage of being highly specific, but it suffers from limited sensitivity. Sensitivity of cytology is influenced by many factors and is complex, but used as a triage test for women already identified as high risk, cytology may suffice. The reduction in the number of cytology tests required and the restriction to HPV-positive women may improve the quality of cytology by reducing the workload and the number of negative slides.

Using DNA biomarkers, limiting further follow-up to women infected with HPV 16 and 18, which are responsible for about 70 percent of cervical cancer and precursors, can reduce the number of women referred to colposcopy while maintaining adequate sensitivity (Castle and others 2011). Overexpression of certain oncoproteins is a marker for increased risk of progression to cervical cancer and may be a better predictor of cancer risk than HPV DNA testing alone, although this is yet to be confirmed (Dockter and others 2009). One biomarker under intensive study is p16^{ink4a}, which is overexpressed in cancerous and precancerous cervical cells. In a meta-analysis of studies using several detection methods, the proportion of smears overexpressing p16^{ink4a} increases with the severity of cytological abnormalities (12 percent of normals and 89 percent of HSIL) and histological abnormalities (2 percent of normals and 82 percent of CIN3) (Sahasrabuddhe, Luhn, and Wentzensen 2011). A rapid test for the E6 oncoproteins of HPV types 16, 18, and 45 is undergoing clinical trials (Schweizer and others 2010).

PRIMARY PREVENTION OF CERVICAL CANCER: HPV VACCINES

Vaccines that prevent infection with certain types of HPV are a major breakthrough in preventing cervical cancer. Monovalent (against HPV 16), bivalent (against HPV 16 and 18; Cervarix, GlaxoSmithKline Biologicals, Rixensart, Belgium), and quadrivalent (against HPV 6, 11, 16, and 18; Gardasil, Merck and Co., Inc., West Point, Pennsylvania) vaccines have been tested in randomized placebo-controlled trials and shown to be safe, immunogenic, and highly efficacious at preventing HPV infection for up to eight years after vaccination. The bivalent and quadrivalent vaccines are delivered by intramuscular injection at zero, one, and six months, with the first dose between the ages of 9 and 13 years.

Efficacy of HPV Vaccines

Evidence from well-conducted, randomized, placebo-controlled trials demonstrates that these vaccines prevent both persistent cervical infection with the types included in the vaccines in women not previously exposed to HPV infection, as well as preinvasive lesions of the anogenital tract associated with the types present in the vaccines in males and females. In addition, the quadrivalent vaccine prevents genital warts caused by types 6 and 11 (both associated with benign disease) in males and females (The Future II Study Group 2007; Harper and others 2006; Koutsky and others 2002; Mao and others 2006; Roteli-Martins and others 2012; Villa and others 2005).

Bivalent and quadrivalent vaccines appear to offer full protection against types 16 and 18, which together cause an estimated 70 percent or more of cervical cancers worldwide, and a slightly lower fraction of cervical cancer precursors. Some evidence suggests that the immune response to vaccination against types 16 and 18 also provides some cross-protection against types 45 and 31, which are important in the etiology of cervical cancer, thereby increasing the projected protection from vaccination to 75–80 percent.

However, both vaccines are prophylactic and should be administered to individuals prior to infection. HPV is the most common sexually transmitted infection in the world. Ideally, the vaccine should be administered to girls and possibly boys prior to the onset of sexual activity, the age of which varies considerably by country and culture. Vaccination of girls ages 9–12 years with high coverage will most likely be the most clinically effective and cost-effective strategy for cervical cancer prevention.

Public Health Challenges to Implementing HPV Vaccination

From the point of view of developing countries, introducing the HPV vaccine poses many challenges. The most obvious is cost. The current price of both bivalent and quadrivalent vaccines is high, although the costs have decreased considerably as a result of initiatives to enable implementation of HPV vaccination in low-resource settings. However, cost is only one aspect. Unlike the development of a platform for vaccinating infants and children against a range of diseases (the Extended Program for Immunization [EPI]), few LMICs have established pubescent/adolescent health platforms or school health systems from which to vaccinate young girls and possibly boys. The infrastructure will have to be created; for this to happen, a great deal of political will must be generated. Studies supporting the efficacy of HPV vaccines involve adolescents, so they are effective in that age group; however, no completed studies have included infants, so it would be premature to consider adding an HPV vaccine to infant EPI. Several studies including young children are ongoing.

In addition to the need to create a new infrastructure, both vaccines require a cold chain and thus a reliable source of electricity, which is absent in many LMICs, particularly in Sub-Saharan Africa. The need for three injections and follow-up poses its own challenges, as does the necessity for intramuscular injection, which requires skill and medical waste disposal. However, recent data indicate that the immunogenicity and efficacy of two doses of the vaccine may be comparable to three doses, a promising development that could simplify the logistics and reduce the cost of HPV vaccination programs. Furthermore, the vaccine is administered to young girls to prevent a disease that will manifest itself only after 30 years or more. Developing a national strategy will require those familiar with vaccination, including pediatricians and public health officials, to communicate with those who work in the adult oncology field; these two worlds rarely intersect.

A new pubescent or adolescent health platform could be used beyond HPV vaccination. Such a platform would provide an excellent opportunity to offer a range of services to young people, including booster vaccinations against hepatitis B and tetanus; possibly an anti-HIV vaccination in the future; antihelminthic medication; nutritional assessment; and education about drug, tobacco, and alcohol use and pregnancy prevention and sexuality.

Case Studies of HPV Vaccine Implementation

Rwanda, a country of 11 million people, introduced an HPV vaccination program in partnership with Merck, the manufacturer of the quadrivalent vaccine, in 2010. Merck guaranteed three years of vaccinations at no cost and concessional prices for future doses. In April 2011, 93,888 Rwandan girls in primary grade 5 received their first dose of the HPV vaccine, which represented 95 percent coverage of all Rwandan girls in the first round, followed by 94 percent in the second and 93 percent in the third (Binagwaho and others 2012). The success of this program is attributed to the school-based vaccination and community involvement in identifying girls absent from or not enrolled in school.

On World Cancer Day 2013, Gavi, the Vaccine Alliance, announced that it would provide support for the rollout of HPV vaccination in eight developing countries: Ghana, Kenya, the Lao People's Democratic Republic, Madagascar, Malawi, Niger, Sierra Leone, and Tanzania; the price has since been established at US$4.50 per dose (http://www.gavi.org). Further, Gavi plans to have one million girls vaccinated by introducing the HPV vaccine in 20 countries by 2015 and hopes to reach 30 million by 2020 by introducing the vaccine in 40 countries.

Ladner and others (2012) report on the Gardasil Access Program, managed by Axios Healthcare Development, which received a large donation of the quadrivalent vaccine from Merck. Participating projects received free vaccine and were responsible for the costs related to the importation, transportation, storage, and distribution of the vaccine, as well as the costs of community outreach, program management, and data collection. Eight programs were implemented in seven countries: Bhutan, Bolivia, Cambodia, Cameroon, Haiti, Lesotho, and Nepal. The eight programs targeted 87,380 girls, of whom 76,983 (88 percent) received three doses of the vaccine. Three vaccine delivery models were used: health facility–based, school-based, and mixed (health facility– and school-based). The mixed model resulted in the best coverage (96.6 percent); the school-based model was intermediate (88.6 percent); and the health facility model was the least effective (79.9 percent). The estimated coverage was 94.9 percent for the five programs that targeted girls ages 9–13 years, and 80.0 percent for the three programs that vaccinated girls outside that age range.

These data, which show high coverage in low-resource settings, are encouraging. They suggest that with sufficient political will, the implementation of HPV vaccination in low-resource settings should be possible in the near future.

Whether countries introduce the vaccine into the public health sector will be determined by several factors:

- Burden of HPV-associated disease in the country
- Ability to convince politicians and health officials, particularly those who work with children and vaccination, that it is worthwhile to invest in vaccinating children to prevent a disease of adulthood
- Creation of the appropriate infrastructure for the administration of the vaccine
- Cost

TREATMENT OF CERVICAL CANCER

As a result of screening, particularly at long intervals, some more advanced cancers will be detected, and some women will come for treatment because of symptoms, commonly abnormal vaginal bleeding (postcoital, irregular, or postmenopausal), offensive vaginal discharge, pelvic pain, dysuria, or symptoms of local or advanced metastatic disease.

As for all cancers, treatment of cervical cancer is determined by the stage of the disease at presentation. Cervical cancer is staged clinically, for example, through a pelvirectal examination combined with some basic tests as part of the metastatic work-up. Most institutions rely on the International Federation of Gynecology and Obstetrics (FIGO) 2009 staging.

Treatment options for most stage 1 cancers favor surgery alone and usually are curative. For women with later stage 1, stage 2, and early stage 3 cancers, primary treatment is chemotherapy and radiotherapy, with curative intent but lower success rates than for earlier stages. For stage 4 disease, treatment is usually palliative and may involve chemotherapy, radiotherapy, and surgery, although few women in LMICs are likely to have access to these services.

COST-EFFECTIVENESS ANALYSIS

Model-Based Cost-Effectiveness Analysis

In addition to the strong evidence of the clinical effectiveness of primary and secondary prevention of cervical cancer worldwide, a critical factor in decision making, particularly in resource-poor settings, is the financial impact and cost-effectiveness of alternative strategies. Most economic evaluations of cervical cancer prevention approaches have utilized mathematical models to project the long-term public health and economic impacts of prevention strategies in different populations. State-of-the-art methods, as well as the limitations of modeling, have been discussed extensively in published review papers (Brisson, Van de Velde, and Boily 2009; Canfell and others 2012; Kim, Brisson, and others 2008).

HPV Vaccination

The economic evaluations of HPV vaccination have focused primarily on vaccination of preadolescent girls prior to sexual initiation; only a handful of evaluations have addressed HPV vaccination of other targeted groups, such as preadolescent boys or older women (Tsu and Murray 2011; Tsu, Murray, and Franceschi 2012). Several regional reports published as part of an HPV monograph series have projected health benefits (for example, cancer risk reduction and life expectancy, adjusted or unadjusted for disability or quality of life) and economic outcomes of HPV vaccination of preadolescent girls in all countries in the following regions:

- East Asia and Pacific (25 countries) (Goldie, Diaz, Kim, and others 2008)
- Europe and Central Asia (28 countries) (Berkhof and others 2013)
- Latin America and the Caribbean (33 countries) (Goldie, Diaz, Constenla, and others 2008)
- Middle East and North Africa (20 countries) (Kim, Campos, and others 2013)
- Sub-Saharan Africa (48 countries) (Kim, Sharma, and others 2013)

A related analysis evaluated HPV vaccination in 72 countries eligible for support from Gavi (Goldie, O'Shea, and others 2008). A handful of country-specific analyses in these regions and economies have also been conducted, including Brazil (Goldie and others 2007; Vanni and others 2012); China (Canfell and others 2011); India (Diaz and others 2008); Malaysia (Aljunid and others 2010; Ezat and Aljunid 2010); Mexico (Reynales-Shigematsu, Rodrigues, and Lazcano-Ponce 2009); Taiwan, China (Demarteau and others 2012); and Thailand (Sharma and others 2011).

The overwhelming majority of these studies has concluded that HPV vaccination of preadolescent girls has the potential to reduce substantially the morbidity and mortality associated with cervical cancer, under assumptions of sustained, high vaccine efficacy and reasonable uptake. For example, when assuming vaccination coverage of 70 percent and complete, lifelong protection against HPV 16/18 cervical cancer, HPV vaccination was estimated to avert more than 670,000 cervical cancer cases in Sub-Saharan Africa alone over the lifetimes of women in five consecutive birth cohorts vaccinated as young adolescents (Kim, Sharma, and others 2013).

Measures of Cost-Effectiveness

Not surprisingly, HPV vaccination was cost-effective in more countries as the cost of the vaccine decreased. Consistently across the regional and country-specific studies cited, the results have suggested that for a cost per vaccinated girl (CVG) of US$50 or less, HPV vaccination of preadolescent girls was good value for money in most of the countries evaluated. In countries with a relatively lower disease burden and/or lower per capita gross domestic product, the vaccine cost threshold at which HPV vaccination was cost-effective was lower, at US$10 or US$25 CVG. One study, published by the manufacturers of the quadrivalent HPV vaccine, included strategies of vaccinating males and females up to age 24 years in Mexico; the study found that the most cost-effective strategy was vaccinating 12-year-old girls alone (Insinga and others 2007).

Generally, the factors with the greatest influence on the cost-effectiveness results were the vaccine cost and discount rate, which reflect the time preference for health benefits and costs and are important to capture, given the long time horizon between vaccine expenditure and expected cancer benefits. Vaccine efficacy and the length of vaccine protection—and the requirement for booster doses—also influence the results, with the cost-effectiveness profile diminishing greatly, assuming protection lasts only 10–20 years and/or requires at least one booster dose. Variations in cancer incidence moderately influenced the cost-effectiveness ratios.

In interpreting cost-effectiveness results, a critical distinction must be made between value for resources and affordability. Affordability will be a critical determinant for success in preventing cervical cancer in LMICs with high cervical cancer incidence (Natunen and others 2013). Despite the high value that HPV vaccination can provide at US$25–US$50 per vaccinated girl, the immediate financial expenditures required for adoption of HPV vaccination at this cost may not be attainable in many countries. For example, the financial requirements for vaccinating five birth cohorts over five years at 70 percent coverage in all of Sub-Saharan Africa will range from US$110.0 million (US$0.55 per dose) to US$2.8 billion (US$19.50 per dose) (Kim, Sharma, and others 2013). At least one HPV vaccine manufacturer has offered a price as low as US$5 per dose to Gavi, undoubtedly diminishing the financial barrier to accessing HPV vaccines. Study results suggest that the upfront financial investments in HPV vaccination may be offset by downstream savings in costs of cancer care averted at such a low vaccine price. Careful planning to ensure the sustainability of an HPV vaccination program will be as important as the decision to implement it.

Recent publications on the incremental program costs of introducing and scaling up HPV vaccination suggest that integrating HPV vaccination into existing immunization services is feasible but will likely incur an additional financial burden to countries above the cost of the vaccine (Hutubessy and others 2012; Levin and others 2013). The support by Gavi not only to fund HPV vaccines directly, but also to develop country HPV vaccination programs through demonstration projects, will be instrumental in creating sustainable programs; to date, at least 14 countries have applied for demonstration projects.

Future Directions for Cost-Effectiveness Analysis of HPV Vaccines

Head-to-head comparisons of the bivalent and quadrivalent vaccines are lacking for LICs, but such comparisons may be more relevant in the future. Economic evaluations in HICs that have introduced the HPV vaccine have been conducted comparing the bivalent and quadrivalent vaccines. To date, the results have been conflicting; three studies find that the quadrivalent vaccine is more cost-effective than the bivalent vaccine (Dee and Howell 2010; Jit and others 2011; Lee and others 2011). In contrast, two studies (Demarteau and others 2012; Ezat and Aljunid 2010) find that the cost-savings from reducing more cases of cervical cancer (bivalent vaccine) outweigh the cost-savings from reducing cases of genital warts (quadrivalent vaccine). Current studies have not yet explored the potential added benefits from broad-coverage HPV vaccines that target additional oncogenic HPV types and are anticipated to be available in the near future; these second-generation vaccines are expected to yield even greater cancer reductions and are likely further to impact optimal screening, but the efficacy and costs are unknown.

Cervical Cancer Screening

Studies evaluating screening strategies alone have primarily assessed screening tests (for example, cytology, HPV DNA tests, and VIA), frequencies (for example, one to three times per lifetime, at 3- to 10-year intervals), and ages at screening (for example, 30–50 years). In a seminal study, Goldie and others (2005) assess the cost-effectiveness of screening strategies in five LMICs with heterogeneous epidemiologic, demographic, and economic profiles. They find that strategies that required the fewest visits—and thereby minimized loss to follow-up—were consistently the most cost-effective. The reduction in lifetime cervical cancer risk was 25–36 percent, with only one screening per lifetime; 47–52 percent, with two screenings per lifetime; and 57–60 percent, with three screenings per lifetime. Taking into consideration the direct medical and patient costs

associated with screening, the authors conclude that HPV DNA testing and VIA, requiring one or two clinic visits, two to three times per lifetime, at age 35 years, are attractive alternatives to traditional three-visit, cytology-based testing programs. In a more recent study, Levin and others (2010) find that increased coverage levels of cervical cancer screening using rapid HPV tests were cost-effective for a two-visit strategy for screening and treatment of precancerous lesions in China.

The most influential factors in determining the relative value of different screening strategies include the assumptions regarding loss to follow-up between clinic visits, the clinical performance of the screening test (that is, the sensitivity/specificity), and the relative costs of the test. Patient time spent receiving interventions and traveling to clinics are also found to be influential, given the long distances to the clinics, lack of paved roads, and limited public transportation in some settings. Treatment of precancerous lesions can range from inexpensive cryotherapy to more complex and costly LEEP, cold knife conization, and simple hysterectomies. However, these costs are rarely the main drivers affecting the cost-effectiveness of cervical cancer screening strategies.

Remaining challenges include improving the acceptability and accessibility of these services among previously unscreened women. Even with the strong momentum toward introducing HPV vaccination programs, investing in expanded quality screening and treatment services and increasing demand for these services among older women remain critical, given that screening rates are very low in Asia, Latin America and the Caribbean, and Sub-Saharan Africa, irrespective of income, and that these women are not the target group for HPV vaccination.

Combined Vaccination and Screening

Increasingly, analyses are considering the potential synergies between preadolescent HPV vaccination followed by screening in adulthood. The majority of recent studies are set in upper-middle-income countries, such as Malaysia (Aljunid and others 2010; Ezat and Aljunid 2010), Mexico (Insinga and others 2007; Reynales-Shigematsu, Rodrigues, and Lazcano-Ponce 2009), Peru (Goldie and others 2012), South Africa (Sinanovic and others 2009), and Thailand (Praditsitthikorn and others 2011; Sharma and others 2011; Termrungruanglert and others 2012). Only a handful of such studies are in LICs and lower-middle-income countries, such as countries in Eastern Africa (Campos and others 2012), India (Diaz and others 2008), and Vietnam (Kim, Kobus, and others 2008).

The findings suggest an opportunity to improve on cervical cancer prevention by following preadolescent

HPV vaccination with screening (HPV DNA testing) of women one to three times per lifetime, starting at about age 40 years. For example, in Thailand, preadolescent HPV vaccination combined with screening in older women reduced the risk of cervical cancer by over 50 percent (Sharma and others 2011). In Mexico, HPV vaccination combined with cytology screening every three years reduced cancer incidence and mortality by 75 percent (Reynales-Shigematsu, Rodrigues, and Lazcano-Ponce 2009). Similar to findings in studies that explored the cost-effectiveness of HPV vaccination alone, this set of literature generally finds that adding HPV vaccination for preadolescent girls to existing or modified screening programs has the potential to be a cost-effective strategy, with the vaccine price being a key factor in determining cost-effectiveness. Despite finding that HPV vaccination is cost-effective, these studies reiterate the concern over affordability (Canfell and others 2011; Praditsitthikorn and others 2011; Sharma and others 2011).

Conclusion of Cost-Effectiveness Analysis

The findings from recent cost-effectiveness analyses clearly indicate that there are promising opportunities to prevent cervical cancer in different world settings. HPV vaccination for preadolescent girls and screening of adult women, even only three times per lifetime, can avert a significant proportion of cervical cancer cases in a cost-effective manner. In addition to many other critical inputs to health decisions, such as political will and cultural acceptability, evidence on the cost-effectiveness and affordability of HPV vaccination and screening from rigorous model-based analyses can help to inform decision makers and stakeholders in their deliberations on how best to prevent cervical cancer worldwide.

CONCLUSIONS

Cervical cancer remains one of the most common cancers among women living in LMICs, yet it is a preventable and treatable cancer. Resource-constrained countries have been unable to initiate or sustain cytology-based cervical cancer screening programs because of weak health care infrastructure and prohibitive cost. There are two new avenues for cervical cancer prevention:

- Primary prevention through prophylactic vaccination against the most common HPV types causally associated with cervical cancer.
- Use of alternative screening tests and strategies for cervical cancer prevention, namely, HPV DNA testing

and VIA. Both tests have their advantages and disadvantages, but the development of a highly reproducible, reliable, and accurate point-of-care HPV DNA test (or an alternative test yet to be developed but fulfilling these criteria) will enable women to be screened and treated in one visit and without the need for colposcopy and laboratory infrastructure. HPV DNA testing has shown very promising results; however, issues of specificity, overtreatment, and effective triage still need to be resolved.

Screening and vaccinating either separately or together are shown to be highly cost-effective public health interventions.

NOTES

The World Bank classifies countries according to four income groupings. Income is measured using gross national income per capita, in U.S. dollars, converted from local currency using the World Bank Atlas method. Classifications as of July 2014 are as follows:

- Low-income countries = US$1,045 or less in 2013
- Middle-income countries are subdivided:
  - Lower-middle-income = US$1,046–US$4,125
  - Upper-middle-income = US$4,126–US$12,745
- High-income countries = US$12,746 or more

1. The map and figures in this chapter are based on incidence and mortality estimates for ages 0–69 years, consistent with reporting in all DCP3 volumes. Cancer statistics are estimates for 2012 and have been provided by the International Agency for Research on Cancer from its GLOBOCAN 2012 database. Observed population-based cancer incidence rates were derived from *Cancer Incidence in Five Continents*, 10th edition, and for trends over time from CI5*plus* (http://ci5.iarc.fr/CI5plus/Default.aspx). The discussion of burden (including risk factors), however, includes all ages unless otherwise noted. Interventions also apply to all age groups, except where age ranges or cutoffs are specified.
2. HDI is a composite of three dimensions of human development: a long and healthy life (life expectancy at birth), access to knowledge (adult literacy and enrollment at different educational levels), and standard of living (gross domestic product adjusted for purchasing power parity).

REFERENCES

Aljunid, S., A. Zafar, S. Saperi, and M. Amrizal. 2010. "Burden of Disease Associated with Cervical Cancer in Malaysia and Potential Costs and Consequences of HPV Vaccination." *Asian Pacific Journal of Cancer Prevention* 11 (6): 1551–59.

Arbyn, M., X. Castellsague, S. de Sanjose, L. Bruni, M. Saraiya, and others. 2011. "Worldwide Burden of Cervical Cancer in 2008." *Annals of Oncology* 22 (12): 2675–86.

Arbyn, M., G. Ronco, A. Anttila, C. J. Meijer, M. Poljak, and others. 2012. "Evidence Regarding Human Papillomavirus Testing in Secondary Prevention of Cervical Cancer." *Vaccine* 30 (Suppl. 5): F88–99.

Berkhof, J., J. A. Bogaards, E. Demirel, M. Diaz, M. Sharma, and others. 2013. "Cost-Effectiveness of Cervical Cancer Prevention in Central and Eastern Europe and Central Asia." *Vaccine* 31 (S7): H71–79.

Binagwaho, A., C. M. Wagner, M. Gatera, C. Karema, C. T. Nutt, and others. 2012. "Achieving High Coverage in Rwanda's National Human Papillomavirus Vaccination Programme." *Bulletin of the World Health Organization* 90 (8): 623–28.

Brisson, M., N. Van de Velde, and M. C. Boily. 2009. "Economic Evaluation of Human Papillomavirus Vaccination in Developed Countries." *Public Health Genomics* 12 (5–6): 343–51.

Campos, N. G., J. J. Kim, P. E. Castle, J. Ortendahl, M. O'Shea, and others. 2012. "Health and Economic Impact of HPV 16/18 Vaccination and Cervical Cancer Screening in Eastern Africa." *International Journal of Cancer* 130 (11): 2672–84.

Canfell K., H. Chesson, S. L. Kulasingam, J. Berkhof, M. Diaz, and J. J. Kim. 2012. "Modelling Preventative Strategies against Human Papillomavirus-Related Disease in Developing Countries." *Vaccine* 30 (Suppl. 5): F157–67.

Canfell, K., J. F. Shi, J. B. Lew, R. Walker, F. H. Zhao, and others. 2011. "Prevention of Cervical Cancer in Rural China: Evaluation of HPV Vaccination and Primary HPV Screening Strategies." *Vaccine* 29 (13): 2487–94.

Castle, P. E., M. H. Stoler, T. C. Wright, Jr., A. Sharma, T. L. Wright, and others. 2011. "Performance of Carcinogenic Human Papillomavirus (HPV) Testing and HPV16 or HPV18 Genotyping for Cervical Cancer Screening of Women Aged 25 Years and Older: A Subanalysis of the ATHENA Study." *The Lancet Oncology* 12 (9): 880–90.

Cuzick, J., M. Arbyn, R. Sankaranarayanan, V. Tsu, G. Ronco, and others. 2008. "Overview of HPV-Based and Other Novel Options for Cervical Cancer Screening in Developed and Developing Countries." *Vaccine* 206: k29–41.

de Sanjose, S., G. V. Quint, L. Alemany, D. T. Geraets, J. E. Klaustermeier, and others. 2010. "Human Papillomavirus Genotype Attribution in Invasive Cervical Cancer: A Retrospective Cross-Sectional Worldwide Study." *The Lancet Oncology* 11 (11): 1048–56.

Dee, A., and F. A. Howell. 2010. "A Cost-Utility Analysis of Adding a Bivalent or Quadrivalent HPV Vaccine to the Irish Cervical Screening Program." *European Journal of Public Health* 20 (2): 213–29.

Demarteau, N., C. H. Tang, H. C. Chen, C. J. Chen, and G. Van Kriekinge. 2012. "Cost-Effectiveness Analysis of the Bivalent Compared with the Quadrivalent Human Papillomavirus Vaccines in Taiwan." *Value Health* 15 (5): 622–31.

Denny, L., L. Kuhn, C. C. Hu, W. Y. Tsai, and T. C. Wright, Jr. 2010. "Human Papillomavirus–Based Cervical Cancer Prevention: Long-Term Results of a Randomized Screening Trial." *Journal of the National Cancer Institute* 102 (20): 1557–67.

Denny, L., M. Quinn, and R. Sankaranarayanan. 2006. "Screening for Cervical Cancer in Developing Countries." *Vaccine* 24 (Suppl. 3): S3/71–77.

Diaz, M., J. J. Kim, G. Albero, S. de Sanjose, G. Clifford, and others. 2008. "Health and Economic Impact of HPV 16 and 18 Vaccination and Cervical Cancer Screening in India." *British Journal of Cancer* 99 (20): 230–38.

Dockter, J., A. Schroder, C. Hill, L. Guzenski, J. Monsonego, and others. 2009. "Clinical Performance of the APTIMA HPV Assay for the Detection of High-Risk HPV and High-Grade Cervical Lesions." *Journal of Clinical Virology* 45 (Suppl. 1): S55–61.

Ellerbrock, T. V., M. A. Chiasson, T. J. Bush, X. W. Sun, D. Sawo, and others. 2000. "Incidence of Cervical Squamous Intraepithelial Lesions in HIV-Infected Women." *Journal of the American Medical Association* 283 (8): 1031–37.

Ezat, S. W., and S. Aljunid. 2010. "Comparative Cost-Effectiveness of HPV Vaccines in the Prevention of Cervical Cancer in Malaysia." *Asian Pacific Journal of Cancer Prevention* 11 (4): 943–51.

Ferlay, J., I. Soerjomataram, M. Ervik, R. Dikshit, S. Eser, and others. 2013. GLOBOCAN 2012 v1.0, Cancer Incidence and Mortality Worldwide: IARC CancerBase No. 11. International Agency for Research on Cancer, Lyon, France. http://globocan.iarc.fr.

Forouzanfar, M. H., K. J. Foreman, A. M. Delossantos, R. Lozano, A. D. Lopez, and others. 2011. "Breast and Cervical Cancer in 187 Countries between 1980 and 2010: A Systematic Analysis." *The Lancet* 378 (9801): 1461–84.

Gakidou, E., S. Nordhagen, and Z. Obermeyer. 2008. "Coverage of Cervical Cancer Screening in 57 Countries: Low Average Levels and Large Inequalities." *PLoS Medicine* 5 (6): e132.

Goldie, S. J., M. Diaz, D. Constenla, N. Alvis, J. K. Andrus, and others. 2008. "Mathematical Models of Cervical Cancer Prevention in Latin America and the Caribbean." *Vaccine* 26 (Suppl. 11): L59–72.

Goldie, S. J., M. Diaz, S. Y. Kim, C. E. Levin, H. V. Minh, and J. J. Kim. 2008. "Mathematical Models of Cervical Cancer Prevention in the Asia Pacific Region." *Vaccine* 26 (Suppl. 12): M17–29.

Goldie, S. J., L. Gaffikin, J. D. Goldhaber-Fiebert, A. Gordillo-Tobar, C. Levin, and others. 2005. "Cost-Effectiveness of Cervical Cancer Screening in Five Developing Countries." *New England Journal of Medicine* 353 (20): 2158–68.

Goldie, S. J., J. J. Kim, K. E. Kobus, J. Goldhaber-Fiebert, J. A. Salomon, and others. 2007. "Cost-Effectiveness of HPV Vaccination in Brazil." *Vaccine* 25 (33): 6257–70.

Goldie, S. J., C. Levin, N. R. Mosqueira-Lovon, J. Ortendahl, J. J. Kim, and others. 2012. "Health and Economic Impact of HPV 16 and 18 Vaccination of Pre-adolescent Girls and Cervical Cancer Screening of Adult Women in Peru." *Revista Panamericana de Salud Pública* 32 (6): 426–34.

Goldie, S. J., M. K. O'Shea, N. G. Campos, M. Diaz, S. J. Sweet, and others. 2008. "Health and Economic Outcomes of HPV 16, 18 Vaccination in 72 GAVI-Eligible Countries." *Vaccine* 26 (32): 4080–93.

Hakama, M. 1986. "Cervical Cancer: Risk Groups for Screening." *IARC Scientific Publications* 76: 213–19.

Harper, D. M., E. L. Franco, C. M. Wheeler, A. B. Moscicki, B. Romanaowski, and others. 2006. "Sustained Efficacy up to 4–5 Years of a Bivalent L1 Virus-Like Particle Vaccine against Human Papillomavirus Types 16 and 18: Follow-Up from a Randomised Control Trial." *The Lancet* 367 (9518): 1247–55.

Harris, T. G., R. D. Burk, J. M. Palesky, L. S. Massad, J. Y. Bang, and others. 2005. "Incidence of Cervical Squamous Intraepithelial Lesions Associated with HIV Serostatus, CD4 Cell Counts, and Human Papillomavirus Test Results." *Journal of the American Medical Association* 293 (12): 1471–76.

Herrero, R., P. E. Castle, M. Schiffman, M. C. Bratti, A. Hildesheim, and others. 2005. "Epidemiologic Profile of Type-Specific Human Papillomavirus Infection and Cervical Neoplasia in Guanacaste, Costa Rica." *Journal of Infectious Diseases* 191 (11): 1796–807.

Hutubessy, R., A. Levin, S. Wang, W. Morgan, M. Ally, and others. 2012. "A Case Study Using the United Republic of Tanzania: Costing Nationwide HPV Vaccine Delivery Using the WHO Cervical Cancer Prevention and Control Costing Tool." *BMC Medicine* 10: 136.

IARC (International Agency for Research on Cancer) Working Group on Cervical Cancer Screening. 1986a. "Summary Chapter." In *Screening for Cancer of the Uterine Cervix*, edited by M. Hakama, A. B. Miller, and N. E. Day, 133–42. Lyon: IARC.

———. 1986b. "Screening for Squamous Cervical Cancer: Duration of Low Risk after Negative Results of Cervical Cytology and Its Implication for Screening Programmes." *British Medical Journal* 293 (6548): 659–64.

Insinga, R. P., E. J. Dasbach, E. H. Elbasha, A. Puig, and L. M. Reynales-Shigematsu. 2007. "Cost-Effectiveness of Quadrivalent Human Papillomavirus (HPV) Vaccination in Mexico: A Transmission Dynamic Model-Based Evaluation." *Vaccine* 26 (1): 128–39.

Irwin, K. L., M. W. Oberle, and L. Rosero-Bixby. 1991. "Screening Practices for Cervical and Breast Cancer in Costa Rica." *Bulletin of the Pan American Health Organization* 25 (1): 16–26.

Jit, M., R. Chapman, O. Hughes, and Y. H. Choi. 2011. "Comparing Bivalent and Quadrivalent Human Papillomavirus Vaccines: Economic Evaluation Based on Transmission Model." *British Medical Journal* 343: d5775. doi:10.1136/bmj.d5775.

Katki, H. A., W. K. Kinney, B. Fetterman, T. Lorey, N. E. Poitras, and others. 2011. "Cervical Cancer Risk for Women Undergoing Concurrent Testing for Human Papillomavirus and Cervical Cytology: A Population-Based Study in Routine Clinical Practice." *The Lancet Oncology* 12 (7): 663–72.

Kim, J. J., M. Brisson, J. Edmunds, and S. J. Goldie. 2008. "Modeling Cervical Cancer Prevention in Developed Countries." *Vaccine* 26 (11): K76–86.

Kim, J. J., N. G. Campos, M. O'Shea, M. Diaz, and I. Mutyaba. 2013. "Model-Based Impact and Cost-Effectiveness of Cervical Cancer Prevention in Sub-Saharan Africa." *Vaccine* 31 (S5): G60–72.

Kim, J. J., K. E. Kobus, M. Diaz, V. Van Minh, and S. J. Goldie. 2008. "Exploring the Cost-Effectiveness of HPV Vaccination in Vietnam: Insights for Evidence-Based Cervical Cancer Prevention Policy." *Vaccine* 26 (32): 4015–24.

Kim, J. J., M. Sharma, M. O'Shea, S. Sweet, M. Diaz, and others. 2013. "Model-Based Impact and Cost-Effectiveness of Cervical Cancer Prevention in the Middle East and Northern Africa." *Vaccine* 31 (S6): G65–77.

Koutsky, L. A., K. A. Ault, C. M. Wheeler, D. R. Brown, E. Barr, and others. 2002. "A Controlled Trial of a Human Papillomavirus Type 16 Vaccine." *New England Journal of Medicine* 372 (2): 1645–51.

Laara, E., N. E. Day, and M. Hakama. 1987. "Trends in Mortality from Cervical Cancer in the Nordic Countries: Association with Organised Screening Programs." *The Lancet* 1 (8544): 1247–49.

Ladner J., M. Besson, R. Hampshire, L. Tapert, M. Chirenje, and others. 2012. "Assessment of Eight HPV Vaccination Programs Implemented in Lowest Income Countries." *BMC Public Health* 12: 370.

Lazcano-Ponce, E., A. de Ruiz, L. Lopez-Carillo, M. Vazquez-Manriquez, and M. Hernandez-Avila. 1994. "Quality Control Study on Negative Gynecological Cytology in Mexico." *Diagnostic Cytopathology* 10 (1): 10–14.

Lee, V. J., S. K. Tay, Y. L. Teoh, and M. Y. Tok. 2011. "Cost-Effectiveness of Different Human Papillomavirus Vaccines in Singapore." *BMC Public Health* 11: 203.

Levin, C. E., J. Sellors, J. F. Shi, L. Ma, Y. L. Qiao, and others. 2010. "Cost-Effectiveness Analysis of Cervical Cancer Prevention Based on a Rapid Human Papillomavirus Screening Test in a High-Risk Region of China." *International Journal of Cancer* 127 (6): 1404–11.

Levin, C. E., H. Van Minh, J. Odaga, S. S. Rout, D. N. Ngoc, and others. 2013. "Delivery Cost of Human Papillomavirus Vaccination of Young Adolescent Girls in Peru, Uganda and Viet Nam." *Bulletin of the World Health Organization* 91 (8): 585–92.

Mao, C., L. A. Koutsky, K. A. Ault, C. M. Wheeler, D. R. Brown, and others. 2006. "Efficacy of Human Papillomavirus-16 Vaccine to Prevent Cervical Intraepithelial Neoplasia: A Randomized Controlled Trial." *Obstetrics and Gynecology* 107 (1): 18–27.

Massad, L. S., M. H. Einstein, W. K. Huh, H. A. Katki, W. K. Kinney, and others. 2013. "Updated Consensus Guidelines for Management of Abnormal Cervical Cancer Screening Tests and Cancer Precursors." *Journal of Lower Genital Tract Disease* 17 (5): S1–S27.

National Cancer Workshop. 1989. "The 1988 Bethesda System for Reporting Cervical/Vaginal Cytologic Diagnosis." *Journal of the American Medical Association* 262 (7): 931–34.

Natunen, K., T. A. Lehtinen, S. Torvinen, and M. Lehtinent. 2013. "Cost-Effectiveness of HPV-Vaccination in Medium or Low Income Countries with High Cervical Cancer Incidence—A Systematic Review." *Journal of Vaccines and Vaccination* 4 (1): 2–10.

Palefsky, J., H. Minkoff, L. Kalish, A. Levine, H. S. Sacks, and others. 1999. "Human Papillomavirus Infection and Cervical Cytology in HIV-Infected and HIV-Uninfected Rwandan Women." *Journal of Infectious Diseases* 12: 1851–61.

Parkin, D. M., M. Almonte, L. Bruni, G. Clifford, M. P. Curado, and others. 2008. "Burden and Trends of Type-Specific Human Papillomavirus Infections and Related Diseases in the Latin America and Caribbean Region." *Vaccine* 26 (Suppl. 11): L1–15.

Praditsitthikorn, N., Y. Teerawattananon, S. Tantivess, S. Limwattananon, A. Riewpaiboon, and others. 2011. "Economic Evaluation of Policy Options for Prevention and Control of Cervical Cancer in Thailand." *Pharmacoeconomics* 29 (9): 781–806.

Pretorius, R. G., J. L. Belinson, R. J. Burchette, S. Hu, X. Zhang, and others. 2011. "Regardless of Skill, Performing More Biopsies Increases the Sensitivity of Colposcopy." *Journal of Lower Genital Tract Disease* 15 (3): 180–88.

Reynales-Shigematsu, L. M., E. R. Rodrigues, and E. Lazcano-Ponce. 2009. "Cost-Effectiveness Analysis of a Quadrivalent Human Papilloma Virus Vaccine in Mexico." *Archives of Medical Research* 40 (6): 503–13.

Roteli-Martins, C., P. Naud, P. De Borba, J. Teixeira, N. De Carvalho, and others. 2012. "Sustained Immunogenicity and Efficacy of the HPV-16/18 AS04-Adjuvanted Vaccine: Up to 8.4 Years of Follow-Up." *Human Vaccine Immunotherapy* 8 (3): 390–97.

Sahasrabuddhe, V., V. P. Luhn, and N. Wentzensen. 2011. "Human Papillomavirus and Cervical Cancer: Biomarkers for Improved Prevention Efforts." *Future Microbiology* 6 (9): 1083–98.

Sankaranarayanan, R., B. M. Nene, S. S. Shastri, K. Jayant, R. Muwonge, and others. 2009. "HPV Screening for Cervical Cancer in Rural India." *New England Journal of Medicine* 360 (14): 1385–94.

Sankaranarayanan, R., and P. Pisani. 1997. "Prevention Measures in the Third World: Are They Practical?" In *New Developments in Cervical Cancer Screening and Prevention*, edited by E. Franco and J. Monsonego, 70–83. Oxford: Blackwell Science Ltd.

Sauvaget, C., J. M. Fayette, R. Muwonge, R. Wesley, and R. Sankaranarayanan. 2011. "Accuracy of Visual Inspection with Acetic Acid for Cervical Cancer Screening." *International Journal of Gynecology and Obstetrics* 113 (1): 14–24.

Schweizer, J., P. S. Lu, C. W. Mahoney, M. Berard-Bergery, M. Ho, and others. 2010. "Feasibility Study of a Human Papillomavirus E6 Oncoprotein Test for Diagnosis of Cervical Precancer and Cancer." *Journal of Clinical Microbiology* 48 (12): 4646–48.

Sharma, M., J. Ortendahl, E. van der Ham, S. Sy, and J. J. Kim. 2011. "Cost-Effectiveness of Human Papillomavirus Vaccination and Cervical Cancer Screening in Thailand." *British Journal of Obstetrics and Gynaecology* 119 (2): 166–76.

Sinanovic, E., J. Moodley, M. A. Barone, S. Mall, S. Cleary, and others. 2009. "The Potential Cost-Effectiveness of Adding a Human Papillomavirus Vaccine to the Cervical Cancer Screening Program in South Africa." *Vaccine* 27 (44): 6196–202.

Singh, G. K. 2012. "Rural-Urban Trends and Patterns in Cervical Cancer Mortality, Incidence, Stage, and Survival in the United States, 1950–2008." *Journal of Community Health* 37: 217–23.

Singh, D., K. Anastos, D. Hoover, R. Burk, Q. Shi, and others. 2009. "Human Papillomavirus Infection and Cervical Cytology in HIV-Infected and HIV-Uninfected Rwandan Women." *Journal of Infectious Diseases* 199 (12): 1851–61.

Soerjomataram, I., J. Lortet-Tieulent, D. M. Parkin, J. Ferlay, C. Mathers, and others. 2012. "Global Burden of Cancer in 2008: Systematic Analysis of Disability-Adjusted Life-Years in 12 World Regions." *The Lancet* 380: 1840–50.

Termrungruanglert, W., P. Havanond, N. Khemapech, S. Lertmaharit, S. Pongpanich, and others. 2012. "Model for Predicting the Burden and Cost of Treatment in Cervical Cancer and HPV-Related Diseases in Thailand." *European Journal of Gynaecological Oncology* 33 (4): 391–94.

The Future II Study Group. 2007. "Quadrivalent Vaccine against Human Papillomavirus to Prevent High-Grade Cervical Lesions." *New England Journal of Medicine* 356: 1915–27.

Tsu, V., and M. Murray. 2011. "Limited Benefit of HPV Vaccination for Sexually Active Women in Developing Countries." *Vaccine* 29 (50): 9290–91.

Tsu, V., M. Murray, and S. Franceschi. 2012. "Human Papillomavirus Vaccination in Low-Resource Countries: Lack of Evidence to Support Vaccinating Sexually Active Women." *British Journal of Cancer* 107 (9): 1445–50.

Vanni, T., P. Luz, A. Mendes, M. Foss, M. Mesa-Frias, and others. 2012. "Economic Modelling Assessment of the HPV Quadrivalent Vaccine in Brazil: A Dynamic Individual-Based Approach." *Vaccine* 30 (32): 4866–71.

Villa, L. L., R. L. Costa, C. A. Petta, R. P. Andrade, K. A. Ault, and others. 2005. "Prophylactic Quadrivalent Human Papillomavirus (Types 6, 11, 16, and 18) L1 Virus-Like Particle Vaccine in Young Women: A Randomised Double-Blind Placebo-Controlled Multicentre Phase II Efficacy Trial." *The Lancet Oncology* 6 (5): 271–78.

Walboomers, J. M., M. V. Jacobs, M. M. Manos, F. X. Bosch, J. A. Kummer, and others. 1999. "Human Papillomavirus Is a Necessary Cause of Invasive Cervical Cancer Worldwide." *Journal of Pathology* 189: 12–19.

WHO (World Health Organization). 2012. "Prevention of Cervical Cancer through Screening and Using Visual Inspection with Acetic Acid (VIA) and Treatment with Cryotherapy." WHO, Geneva.

Wright, T. C., and R. J. Kurman. 1994. "A Critical Review of the Morphologic Classification Systems of Preinvasive Lesions of the Cervix: The Scientific Basis for Shifting the Paradigm." *Papillomavirus Report* 5: 175–82.

Chapter 5

Oral Cancer: Prevention, Early Detection, and Treatment

Rengaswamy Sankaranarayanan, Kunnambath Ramadas, Hemantha Amarasinghe, Sujha Subramanian, and Newell Johnson

INTRODUCTION

Oral cancer is the 11th most common cancer in the world, accounting for an estimated 300,000 new cases and 145,000 deaths in 2012 and 702,000 prevalent cases over a period of five years (old and new cases) (tables 5.1 and 5.2) (Bray and others 2013; Ferlay and others 2013). For this chapter, oral cancers include cancers of the mucosal lip, tongue, gum, floor of the mouth, palate, and mouth, corresponding to the International Classification of Diseases, 10th revision [ICD-10], codes C00, C02, C03, C04, C05, and C06, respectively. Two-thirds of the global incidence of oral cancer occurs in low- and middle-income countries (LMICs); half of those cases are in South Asia. India alone accounts for one-fifth of all oral cancer cases and one-fourth of all oral cancer deaths (Ferlay and others 2013).

Tobacco use, in any form, and excessive alcohol use are the major risk factors for oral cancer. With dietary deficiencies, these factors cause more than 90 percent of oral cancers. Preventing tobacco and alcohol use and increasing the consumption of fruits and vegetables can potentially prevent the vast majority of oral cancers (Sankaranarayanan and others 2013). When primary prevention fails, early detection through screening and relatively inexpensive treatment can avert most deaths. However, oral cancer continues to be a major cancer in India, East Asia, Eastern Europe, and parts of South America (Forman and others 2013), where organized prevention and early detection efforts are lacking. This chapter discusses the epidemiology, prevention, early detection, and treatment of oral cancers, as well as the cost-effectiveness of interventions.

ORAL CANCER: INCIDENCE, MORTALITY, AND SURVIVAL

Incidence and Mortality[1]

Oral cancer incidence and mortality are high in India; Papua New Guinea; and Taiwan, China, where chewing of betel quids with tobacco or without tobacco or areca nut chewing is common, as well as in Eastern Europe, France, and parts of South America (Brazil and Uruguay), where tobacco smoking and alcohol consumption are high. The age-standardized incidence rates for men are, on average, twice as high as those for women (tables 5.1 and 5.2). Incidence rates do not follow a particular pattern from low- to high-income countries (HICs), when countries are grouped into wealth strata (figure 5.1). In selected countries where some reliable cancer registries exist, India is highest and Belarus is lowest, with incidence rates varying by more than five times in men and women.

Corresponding author: Rengaswamy Sankaranarayanan, MD, International Agency for Research on Cancer, SankarR@iarc.fr

Table 5.1 Oral Cancer in Men (All Ages): Global Incidence, Mortality, and Prevalence, World Health Organization Geographic Classification, 2012

Population	Incidence		Mortality		Prevalence	
	Number	ASR (W)	Number	ASR (W)	Number	Five-year
World	198,975	5.5	97,919	2.7	198,267	467,157
More developed regions	68,042	7	23,380	2.3	67,978	195,233
Less developed regions	130,933	5	74,539	2.8	130,289	271,924
WHO Africa region	8,009	3.4	5,026	2.2	7,763	18,446
WHO Americas region	31,898	5.9	8,532	1.5	31,805	94,953
WHO East Mediterranean region	11,601	5.1	6,185	2.8	11,533	27,236
WHO Europe region	45,567	7.1	18,621	2.8	45,499	118,151
WHO South-East Asia region	70,816	8.9	45,247	5.7	70,667	122,976
WHO Western Pacific region	31,013	2.7	14,292	1.2	30,929	85,233
Africa	10,230	3.3	6,083	2.1	9,961	23,560
Latin America and Caribbean	12,988	4.6	5,244	1.9	12,918	32,424
Asia	111,994	5.2	65,045	3	111,683	230,389
Europe	42,573	7.5	17,598	3	42,539	111,347
Oceania	2,280	9.6	661	2.7	2,279	6,908

Source: Incidence/mortality data: Ferlay and others 2013. Prevalence data: Bray and others 2013.
Note: ASR (W) = age-standardized incidence rate per 100,000 population, for the world population structure; WHO = World Health Organization.

Table 5.2 Oral Cancer in Women (All Ages): Global Incidence, Mortality, and Prevalence, World Health Organization Geographic Classification, 2012

Population	Incidence		Mortality		Prevalence	
	Number	ASR (W)	Number	ASR (W)	Number	Five-year
World	101,398	2.5	47,409	1.2	100,784	234,992
More developed regions	32,781	2.6	9,908	0.6	32,683	93,180
Less developed regions	68,617	2.5	37,501	1.4	68,101	141,812
WHO Africa region	5,475	2	3,504	1.4	5,349	12,766
WHO Americas region	17,302	2.6	4,271	0.6	17,204	48,526
WHO East Mediterranean region	9,080	4.1	4,812	2.2	8,993	21,570
WHO Europe region	20,366	2.4	6,556	0.7	20,305	51,933
WHO South-East Asia region	32,648	3.9	20,487	2.5	32,482	58,034
WHO Western Pacific region	16,511	1.3	7,776	0.6	16,435	42,123
Africa	7,046	2	4,258	1.3	6,892	16,409
Latin America and Caribbean	7,645	2.2	2,381	0.7	7,586	17,813
Asia	56,856	2.5	32,363	1.4	56,549	117,362
Europe	18,843	2.5	6,033	0.7	18,789	48,653
Oceania	1,351	5.3	484	1.9	1,350	4,042

Sources: Incidence/mortality data: Ferlay and others 2013. Prevalence data: Bray and others 2013.
Note: ASR (W) = age-standardized incidence rate per 100,000 population, for the world population structure; WHO = World Health Organization.

The estimated age-standardized incidence rates of oral cancer also vary among countries in different regions (maps 5.1 and 5.2).

The buccal (cheek) mucosa is the most common site for oral cancer in South and Southeast Asia; in all other regions, the tongue is the most common site (Forman and others 2013). Regional variations in incidence and the site of occurrence relate to the major causes, which are alcohol and smoking in Western countries, and betel quid and tobacco chewing in South and Southeast Asia (Lambert and others 2011). Oral cancer mortality rates range between 1 and 15 per 100,000 persons in different regions; mortality rates exceed 10 per 100,000 in Eastern European countries, such as the Czech Republic, Hungary, and the Slovak Republic (Ferlay and others 2013). Oral cancer mortality rates are influenced by oral cancer incidence, access to treatment, and variations in site distribution.

The observed trends in incidence and mortality among men and women are closely correlated with the patterns and trends in tobacco and alcohol use. An increasing trend in incidence has been reported in Karachi, Pakistan (Bhurgri and others 2006), and in Taiwan, China (Tseng 2013), caused by increases in tobacco and areca nut chewing and alcohol drinking. Oral cancer incidence and mortality rates have been steadily declining over the past two decades because of declining smoking prevalence and alcohol consumption in the United States (Brown, Check, and Devesa 2011).

However, a recent increase in cancers at the base of the tongue, possibly driven by the human papillomavirus (HPV), has been observed in white men in the United States (Saba and others 2011).

Oral cancer incidence and mortality rates have been declining steadily in most European countries over the past two decades; until recently, rates had been

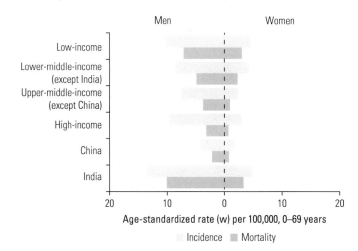

Figure 5.1 Age-Standardized Incidence and Mortality Rates of Oral Cancer, by World Bank Income Classification, 2012

Source: Ferlay and others 2013.

Map 5.1 Age-Standardized Incidence Rates of Oral Cancer in Men, 2012

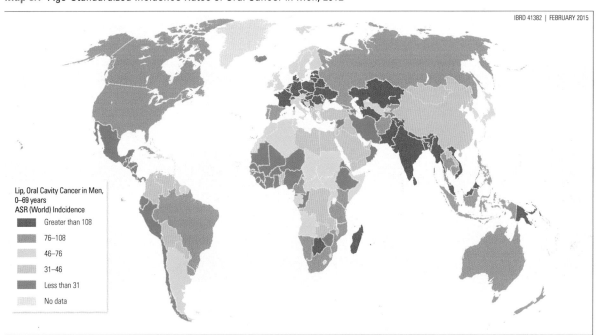

Source: Ferlay and others 2013.
Note: ASR = Age-Standardized Rate.

Lip, Oral Cavity Cancer in
Women, 0–69 years
ASR (World) Indcidence

- Greater than 38
- 28–38
- 2–28
- 1.4–2
- Fewer than 1.4
- No data

Source: Ferlay and others 2013.
Note: ASR = Age-Standardized Rate.

increasing in some Central European countries, including Hungary and the Slovak Republic, reflecting changes in alcohol and tobacco consumption (Bonifazi and others 2011). Oral cancer mortality has declined steadily in France since reaching a peak in the early 1990s, and the decline correlates with the reduction in per capita alcohol consumption. Incidence and mortality have been stable in the Nordic countries, the Russian Federation, and the United Kingdom. Mortality rates have been steadily declining in Australia and Hong Kong SAR, China, but increasing in Japan and the Republic of Korea (Yako-Suketomo and Matsuda 2010).

Survival

In the United States, five-year survival improved by more than 11 percentage points between 1992 and 2006 (Pulte and Brenner 2010) and is now approximately 65 percent (Howlader and others 2010; Ries and others 2008). In Europe, it is approximately 50 percent (Sant and others 2009). In India, five-year survival is less than 35 percent; in China, the Republic of Korea, Pakistan, Singapore, and Thailand, it ranges between 32 and 54 percent (Sankaranarayanan and others 2010; Sankaranarayanan and Swaminathan 2011). Overall, the five-year survival for early, localized cancers exceeds 80 percent and falls to less than 20 percent when regional lymph nodes are involved.

ORAL CANCER: RISK FACTORS AND PREVENTION

The major causes of oral cancer worldwide remain tobacco in its many different forms, heavy consumption of alcohol, and, increasingly, infection with certain types of HPV. Although the relative contribution of risk factors varies from population to population, oral cancer is predominantly a disease of poor people (Johnson and others 2011). Prevention of this devastating disease can come from fundamental changes in socioeconomic status, as well as from actions to reduce the demand, production, marketing, and use of tobacco products and alcohol (Johnson and others 2011). A healthy diet, good oral and sexual hygiene, and awareness of the signs and symptoms of disease are important. Success depends on political will, intersectoral action, and culturally sensitive public health messages disseminated through educational campaigns and mass media initiatives.

Smokeless and Smoking Tobacco Use

Smokeless tobacco in the form of betel quid, oral snuff, and betel quid substitutes (locally called guktha, nass, naswar, khaini, mawa, mishri, and gudakhu) increases the risk of oral precancerous lesions and oral cancer between 2-fold and 15-fold (Gupta and others 2011;

Gupta, Ariyawardana, and Johnson 2013; IARC 2004b, 2007; Javed and others 2010; Johnson and others 2011; Somatunga and others 2012). In most areas, betel quid consists of tobacco, areca nut, slaked lime, catechu, and several condiments, wrapped in a betel leaf. In recent years, small, attractive, and inexpensive sachets of betel quid substitutes containing a flavored and sweetened dry mixture of areca nut, catechu, and slaked lime with tobacco (gutkha) or without tobacco (pan masala), often claiming to be safer products, have become widely available and are increasingly used by young people, particularly in India. These products have been strongly implicated in oral submucous fibrosis (OSMF), which places individuals at high risk for malignancy.

More than 50 percent of oral cancers in India, Sudan, and the Republic of South Sudan, and about 4 percent of oral cancers in the United States, are attributable to smokeless tobacco products. Smokeless tobacco use among young people is increasing in South Asia, with the marketing of conveniently packaged products made from areca nut and tobacco; as a consequence, oral precancerous conditions in young adults have increased significantly (Gupta and others 2011; Sinha and others 2011).

Consistent evidence from many studies indicates that tobacco smoking in any form increases the risk of oral cancer by twofold to tenfold in men and women (IARC 2004a). Risk increases substantially with duration and frequency of tobacco use; risk among former smokers is consistently lower than among current smokers, and there is a trend of decreasing risk with increasing number of years since quitting. Use of smokeless tobacco and alcohol in combination with tobacco smoking greatly increases the risk of oral cancer. The biological plausibility is provided by the identification of several carcinogens in tobacco, the most abundant and strongest being tobacco-specific N-nitrosamines, such as N-nitrosonornicotine and 4-(methylnitrosamino)-1-(3-pyridyl)-1-butanone (IARC 2007). These are formed by N-nitrosation of nicotine, the major alkaloid responsible for addiction to tobacco.

The fact that more than 80 percent of oral cancers can be attributed to tobacco and/or alcohol consumption justifies regular oral examinations targeting tobacco and alcohol users, as well as prevention efforts focusing on tobacco and alcohol control (Radoi and others 2013). The World Health Organization Framework Convention on Tobacco Control, an evidence-based international treaty, aims to reduce the demand for tobacco globally by price, tax, and non-price measures. (See chapter 10 for a full discussion of tobacco control.)

Areca Nut Chewing

Areca nut or betel nut, because it is often wrapped in betel leaf, is now regarded as a type 1 carcinogen (IARC 2004b, 2007). It is chewed raw, dried, or roasted, or as part of betel quid, by millions of people in Asia; its use is spreading across the Pacific, as well as in emigrant Asian communities worldwide. Cheap, prepackaged areca nut products, such as pan masala, are of recent concern, especially among youth. The inclusion of tobacco in the betel quid adds considerably to the carcinogenicity (Amarasinghe and others 2010; Johnson and others 2011).

Alcohol Use

Epidemiological studies indicate that drinking alcoholic beverages increases the risk of oral cancer twofold to sixfold and is an independent risk factor (IARC 2010), with risk increasing with quantity consumed. The risk varies by population and individual and subsite within the oral cavity (Radoi and others 2013). The combined use of alcohol and tobacco has a multiplicative effect on oral cancer risk. The various pathways by which alcohol may exert carcinogenic influence include topical exposure leading to a direct effect on cell membranes, altered cell permeability, variation in enzymes that metabolize alcohol, and/or systemic effects, such as nutritional deficiency, immunological deficiency, and disturbed liver function. A recent review failed to identify an association between the use of mouthwash containing alcohol and oral cancer risk, or any significant trend in risk with increasing daily use of mouthwash (Gandini and others 2012).

Poor Nutrition

High consumption of fruits and vegetables is associated with a reduction of 40–50 percent in the risk of oral cancer (Lucenteforte and others 2009; Pavia and others 2006; World Cancer Research Fund/American Institute for Cancer Research 2007). In HICs, selected aspects of diet—such as lack of vegetables and fruits—may account for 15–20 percent of oral cancers; this proportion is likely to be higher in LMICs. Chemoprevention studies have not established a preventive effect of retinoid and carotenoid dietary supplements (Chainani-Wu, Epstein, and Touger-Decker 2011; Wrangle and Khuri 2007).

Other Risk Factors

Genetic Factors

Most carcinogens are metabolized through the cytochrome p450 system in the liver. If this system is defective by virtue of inheriting a particular form of the gene (a polymorphism), the risk of many cancers is enhanced. This risk is particularly important with oral and other head and neck cancers, although the relative risks are modest at 1.5 or lower (that is, less than a doubling of risk) (Lu, Yu, and Du 2011).

Polymorphisms in alcohol-metabolizing enzymes also contribute to the risk. Individuals with the fast-metabolizing version (allele) of alcohol dehydrogenase (ADH3[1-1]) have a greater risk of developing oral cancer in the presence of alcoholic beverage consumption than those with the slow-metabolizing forms; this higher risk re-enforces the role of acetaldehyde as the carcinogen involved (Harty and others 1997).

Mate Drinking

Mate, a leaf infusion that is commonly drunk many times a day in parts of South America—usually very hot—appears to enhance the risk of oral cancer by a small amount (Deneo-Pellegrini and others 2012).

Viruses

Recent evidence suggests that HPV infection may be an independent risk factor for cancer of the base of the tongue, tonsils, and elsewhere in the oropharynx. HPV may modulate the process of carcinogenesis in some tobacco- and alcohol-induced oral and oropharyngeal cancers, and it may act as the primary oncogenic agent for inducing carcinogenesis among nonsmokers (Johnson and others 2011; Prabhu and Wilson 2013). Growing evidence suggests that such oropharyngeal infections can be sexually transmitted (Heck and others 2010).

Chronic Trauma

It now seems clear that chronic trauma, from sharp teeth, restorations, or dentures, contributes to oral cancer risk, although this higher risk commonly occurs only in the presence of the other local risk factors (Piemonte, Lazos, and Brunotto 2010).

ORAL CANCER: NATURAL HISTORY

Oral cancer has a long preclinical phase that consists of well-documented precancerous lesions. The precancerous lesions include homogeneous leukoplakia, nonhomogeneous leukoplakia, verrucous leukoplakia, erythroplakia, OSMF, lichen planus, and chronic traumatic ulcers. The estimated annual frequency of malignant transformation of oral precancerous lesions ranges from 0.13 percent to 2.2 percent (Amagasa, Yamashiro, and Uzawa 2011; Napier and Speight 2008).

Very early preclinical invasive cancers (early-stage cancers without symptoms) present as painless small ulcers, nodular lesions, or growths. These changes can be easily seen and are clinically detectable through careful visual inspection and palpation of the oral mucosa. Early, localized oral cancers—less than four centimeters—that have not spread to the regional lymph nodes can be effectively treated and cured with surgery or radiotherapy alone, with no functional or cosmetic defects, resulting in five-year survival rates exceeding 80 percent.

Leukoplakia is a white plaque that may be categorized clinically as *homogeneous* or *nonhomogeneous*. Homogeneous lesions are thin, flat, uniform, smooth, and white. Nonhomogeneous lesions may have a white and red appearance or tiny, white, pinhead-size raised nodules on a reddish background or a proliferative, warty appearance. Erythroplakia presents as a red patch with smooth or granular surface that cannot be characterized clinically or pathologically as any other definable disease (Warnakulasuriya, Johnson, and Van Der Waal 2007). Erythroplakia has a higher probability than leukoplakia to harbor occult invasive cancer and to undergo malignant transformation.

Oral lichen planus may present as interlacing white lines (known as *Wickham's striae*) with a reddish border, or as a mix of reddish and ulcerated areas.

OSMF, mostly restricted to people of Indian subcontinent origin and in certain Pacific islands such as Mariana Islands, presents with a burning sensation, blanching of the oral mucosa, and intolerance to spicy food. Stiffening and atrophy of the oral and pharyngeal mucosa occurs as the disease progresses, leading to reduced mouth opening and difficulty in swallowing and speaking.

Palatal lesions are seen in populations who smoke with the lighted end of the tobacco product inside the mouth, known as *reverse smoking*, resulting in white or mixed reddish-white lesions of the palate.

A higher risk of malignant transformation may be associated with the following factors: female gender, lesions of long duration, large precancerous lesions, precancerous lesions in nonusers of tobacco, tongue and floor of mouth lesions, nonhomogeneous lesions, and lesions showing epithelial dysplasia and aneuploidy (Hsue and others 2007; Napier and Speight 2008). However, it is impossible to predict with certainty which precancerous lesion will become malignant during follow-up in patients. The malignant transformation of precancerous lesions can be prevented by interventions, such as avoiding exposure to tobacco use and alcohol drinking, and in selected instances, by excision of the lesions.

ORAL CANCER SCREENING: ACCURACY, EFFICACY, AND POTENTIAL HARMS

Although an affordable, acceptable, easy to use, accurate, and effective screening test for oral cancer is available in high-risk countries, a decision to introduce population-based screening should take into account the level of health service development and available resources to meet the increased treatment demand that screening generates. The target population for oral cancer screening consists of those age 30 years and older who use tobacco and/or alcohol.

Visual screening of the oral cavity has been widely evaluated for its feasibility, safety, acceptability, accuracy to detect oral precancerous lesions and cancer, and efficacy and cost-effectiveness in reducing oral cancer mortality (Johnson and others 2011; Sankaranarayanan and others 2005; Sankaranarayanan and others 2013). Visual screening involves systematic visual and physical examination of the intraoral mucosa under bright light for signs of oral potentially malignant disorders (OPMDs), as well as early oral cancer, followed by careful inspection and digital palpation of the neck for any enlarged lymph nodes. It is a provider-dependent, subjective test; accordingly, its performance in detecting lesions varies among providers. Comprehensive knowledge of the oral anatomy, the natural history of oral carcinogenesis, and the clinico-pathological features of the OPMDs and preclinical cancers are important prerequisites for efficient providers of oral visual screening.

The potential harms of oral visual screening may include additional diagnostic investigations, such as incisional or excisional biopsy; anxiety associated with false-positive screening tests; detection and treatment of biologically insignificant conditions that may have no impact on oral cancer incidence; and false reassurance from false-negative tests.

Visual Screening by Health Care Personnel

A variety of health care personnel—including dentists, general practitioners, oncologists, surgeons, nurses, and auxiliary health workers—may provide oral visual screening after training (Ramadas and others 2008). Sensitivity ranges from 40 percent to 93 percent, and specificity ranges from 50 percent to 99 percent for detecting precancerous lesions and early asymptomatic oral cancers (Downer and others 2004; Mathew and others 1997; Mehta and others 1986; Warnakulasuriya and others 1984; Warnakulasuriya and Nanayakkara 1991).

A significant reduction of 34 percent in oral cancer mortality among a high-risk group of tobacco or alcohol

users following three rounds of oral visual screening has been demonstrated in a cluster-randomized controlled trial in India (Sankaranarayanan and others 2005; Sankaranarayanan and others 2013). A 15-year follow-up found sustained reduction in oral cancer mortality, with larger reductions in those adhering to repeated screening rounds; there was a 38 percent reduction in oral cancer incidence (95 percent confidence interval [CI] 8–59 percent), and an 81 percent reduction in oral cancer mortality (95 percent CI 69–89 percent) in tobacco and/or alcohol users who were screened four times (Sankaranarayanan and others 2013). The studies (Sankaranarayanan and others 2005; Sankaranarayanan and others 2013) were the basis for the conclusions of the recent Cochrane Collaboration Review (Brocklehurst and others 2013) and an American Dental Association (ADA) expert panel review on population-based oral cancer screening (Rethman and others 2010). The ADA review recommended that clinicians look for signs of precancerous lesions or early-stage cancers while performing routine visual and tactile screening in all subjects, particularly in those who use tobacco or alcohol or both; the panel also concluded that the life-saving benefits for subjects with treatable lesions were more important than the potential harms incurred by those with benign or nonprogressive lesions (Rethman and others 2010). The Cochrane Review (Walsh and others 2013) concluded that evidence suggests that a visual examination as part of a population-based screening program reduces the mortality rate of oral cancer in high-risk individuals; in addition, it could result in diagnoses of oral cancer at an earlier stage of disease and improvement in survival rates across the population as a whole (Brocklehurst and others 2013).

The U.S. Preventive Services Task Force released a draft Recommendation Statement, which stated that for adults age 18 years or older seen in primary care settings, the current evidence is insufficient to assess the balance of benefits and harms of screening for oral cancer in asymptomatic adults. However, this statement overlooks the benefits of early detection of oral cancers among users of tobacco or alcohol or both, as well as other benign conditions whose early detection may improve oral health. Discouraging oral visual examination in primary care is clearly not in the interests of oral cancer control and improving oral health (Edwards 2013).

Self-Examination and Other Screening Methods

Although mouth self-examination using a mirror has been evaluated as a screening test in some studies (Elango and others 2011; Mathew and others 1995; Scott and others 2010), whether it could lead to reductions in oral cancer mortality is not known. There is insufficient evidence to recommend the routine use of other oral screening tests, such as toluidine blue staining, chemiluminescence, tissue fluorescence imaging, tissue fluorescent spectroscopy, and salivary analysis and cytology for primary screening of oral cancer (Johnson and others 2011; Patton, Epstein, and Kerr 2008; Richards 2010; Su and others 2010).

Despite the high risk of oral cancer in the Indian subcontinent, no national or regional screening programs exist in the region. The only large-scale, ongoing, national oral cancer screening programs are in Cuba and Taiwan, China.

- The Cuban program has been in existence since 1984. An evaluation conducted in 1994 indicated that 12–26 percent of the target population has been screened annually, but less than 30 percent of screen-positive individuals complied with referrals (Fernandez and others 1995). The program was reorganized in 1996, with the target age raised from 15 years to 35 years, screening intervals increased from one to three years, and the referral system revamped. No further formal evaluation has been conducted, but there has been no reduction in oral cancer incidence or mortality rates in Cuba over the past three decades. The outcomes from the Cuban program emphasize that screening programs without efficient organization and resources are not an effective use of limited resources.
- Oral cancer screening was initiated in Taiwan, China, in 2004, targeting those age 18 years and older who were smokers or betel nut chewers; the target population for oral cancer screening was revised in 2010 to cover smokers or chewers age 30 years and older. The screening program has led to almost half of the oral cancers diagnosed in stages I and II, with a declining trend in oral cancer mortality rates.

ORAL CANCER: EARLY CLINICAL DIAGNOSIS AND STAGING

Primary care dental and general practitioners should play a major role in referring patients to cancer treatment facilities for early diagnosis and treatment. Improving the skills of these primary care doctors is essential to improving prospects for early diagnosis, particularly among patients who use tobacco or alcohol in any form. Routine biopsy in those clinically presenting with features of precancerous lesions may lead to early diagnosis of underlying invasive oral cancer. In addition to history, physical examination, and biopsy, a simultaneous

assessment of the upper aerodigestive tract is necessary because patients with oral cancer have a high risk of cancers developing in other head and neck sites and in the lungs.

Once a diagnosis of oral cancer is confirmed, staging assessment is completed and treatment is planned. The Union for International Cancer Control Tumor, Nodes, Metastasis (TNM) staging system is widely used for staging oral cancer (Patel and Shah 2005; Sobin and Wittekind 2002) (table 5.3): **T** indicates the size and extent of spread of the primary tumor, **N** indicates the extent spread to the regional lymph nodes in the neck, and **M** indicates the spread to distant organs. The TNM categorization is further grouped into stages 0 through IV, which denote increasing severity of disease and decreasing survival.

Oral cancer staging involves assessing the clinical extent of disease through physical examination, biopsies, and imaging investigations, including X-rays of the mandible, maxillary sinuses, and chest; computerized tomography (CT) scans; magnetic resonance imaging (MRI); and positron emission tomography (PET) imaging, depending on what resources are available. Advanced imaging techniques such as CT, MRI, and PET may be useful in more accurately evaluating local spread, such as invasion of muscles, bone, and cartilage, and lymph node metastases, as well as in planning treatment, but these investigations are seldom feasible in LMICs.

ORAL CANCER: MANAGEMENT

Oral cancer is predominantly a loco-regional disease that tends to infiltrate adjacent bone and soft tissues and spreads to the regional lymph nodes in the neck. Distant metastasis is uncommon at the time of diagnosis. A thorough inspection and palpation of the oral cavity and examination of the neck is mandatory. CT and MRI imaging are widely used to assess the extent of involvement of adjacent structures, such as bones and soft tissues. Surgery and radiotherapy are the main treatment modalities. Given the skills, expertise, and infrastructure required for staging and treatment with minimal physical, functional, and cosmetic morbidity, oral cancer treatment is usually provided in specialized cancer hospitals, such as comprehensive cancer centers, or in hospitals at the highest level of health services, third-level centers.

Treatment of Early-Stage Oral Cancer (Stages I and II)

Surgery and radiotherapy are widely used for the treatment of early oral cancer, either as single modalities or in combination. The choice of modality depends on

Table 5.3 Clinical Staging of Oral Cancer, Treatment Modalities, and Prognosis, by Clinical Stage

Composite stage	Extent of disease	TNM category	Treatment options	Five-year survival (percent)
0	Cancer is limited to the epithelium (carcinoma in-situ) (Tis) and has not spread to deeper layers and nearby organs, regional (neck) lymph nodes (N0), or distant organs (M0)	TisN0M0	Limited surgical excision	~100
I	Primary tumor measures 2 cm or less (T1) and has not spread to regional organs, regional (neck) lymph nodes (N0), or distant organs (M0)	T1N0M0	Radical surgery or radical radiotherapy	> 90
II	Primary tumor is larger than 2 cm and smaller than 4 cm (T2) and has not spread to regional organs, regional (neck) lymph nodes (N0), or distant organs (M0)	T2N0M0	Radical surgery or radical radiotherapy; in selected cases, combination therapy	> 70
III	Primary tumor measures > 4 cm (T3) and has not spread to neck nodes (N0) or distant organs (M0); or tumor is any size (T1 to T3) and has spread to one lymph node measuring 3 cm or less on the same side of the of the neck (N1) as the primary tumor and the cancer has not spread to distant organs (M0)	T3N0M0 T1 to T3, N1, M0	Combined modality treatment with surgery and/or radiotherapy and/or chemotherapy	30–40 20–25
IV	Tumor involves nearby structures, including the mandible, tongue muscles, maxillary sinus, and skin (T4); or tumor is any size but involves one lymph node measuring 3–6 cm on the same side of the neck (N2a) or one lymph node measuring no more than 6 cm on the opposite side of the neck (N2b), or two or more lymph nodes no more than 6 cm on any side of the neck (N2c); or lymph node involvement measuring more than 6 cm (N3); or distant metastases (M1)	T4, N0, or N1, M0 Any T, N2, or N3 M0 Any T, any N, M1	Multimodality management treatment with surgery and/or radiotherapy and/or chemotherapy for cancers without distant metastases; palliative radiotherapy and/or chemotherapy and pain/symptom relief measures	5–10 < 5

Source: Staging: Sobin and Wittekind 2002.
Note: cm = centimeter; TNM = Tumor, Node, Metastasis.

the location of the tumor, cosmetic and functional outcomes, age of the patient, associated illnesses, patient's preference, and the availability of expertise.

Most early-stage oral cancers can be locally excised or treated with radiotherapy, with no or minimal functional and physical morbidity. Elective neck dissection to remove lymph nodes may be considered in selected cases, such as patients with stage I tongue cancer and stage II cancers at other oral sites, who may be at high risk of microscopic but not clinically evident involvement of the neck nodes (N0) (El-Naaj and others 2011; Hicks, Jr., and others 1997; Vijayakumar and others 2011; Woolgar 2006; Zwetyenga and others 2003).

External beam radiotherapy and brachytherapy—using radioactive sources implanted in the tumor—either alone or in combination, is an alternative to surgery for early-stage oral cancers. Excellent outcomes have been demonstrated following brachytherapy alone or in combination with external beam radiotherapy for small tumors (Fujita and others 1999; Marsiglia and others 2002; Wendt and others 1990). Deep infiltrative cancers have a high propensity to spread to regional lymph nodes; therefore, brachytherapy alone, which does not treat regional nodes adequately, is not recommended. Newer techniques, such as three-dimensional conformal radiotherapy and intensity modulated radiotherapy, can minimize the side effects of radiotherapy by delivering the radiation dose to the tumor more precisely and accurately while avoiding healthy surrounding tissues. However, these treatments require advanced equipment and are more expensive than conventional radiotherapy.

Treatment of Locally Advanced Tumors of the Oral Cavity (Stages III and IV)

Locally advanced tumors are aggressive, and locoregional treatment failure rates are high. A combined modality approach integrating surgery, radiotherapy with or without chemotherapy, and planned and executed by a multidisciplinary team is always preferred. Appropriate importance should be given to factors such as functional and cosmetic outcomes and the available expertise. Surgery followed by postoperative radiotherapy is the preferred modality for patients with deep infiltrative tumors and those with bone infiltration (Lundahl and others 1998). Postoperative concurrent chemo-radiation has been found to be superior to radiotherapy alone in those with surgical margins showing cancerous changes indicating incomplete excision of the tumor (Bernier and others 2004; Cooper and others 2004). The use of chemotherapy prior to surgery may eliminate the need to remove the mandible—a major benefit—although it does not confer a survival benefit (Licitra and others 2003).

Primary radiotherapy, with or without chemotherapy, is a reasonable option for locally advanced tumors without bone involvement, especially for patients who have inoperable disease, who are medically unfit for surgery, or who are likely to have unacceptable functional and cosmetic outcomes with surgery. Incorporating chemotherapy with surgery or radiotherapy is useful in younger patients who are in good general condition, increasing survival by about 5 percentage points at five years (Blanchard and others 2011).

Side Effects of Radiotherapy

Side effects may occur during or immediately following radiotherapy—acute reactions—or months to years after treatment. Acute reactions are self-limiting and generally resolve within two to three weeks. These reactions are caused by the inflammation of tissues within the radiotherapy treatment field. Alteration of taste, pain, difficulty in eating, mucosal ulceration of the oral cavity, bacterial and fungal infections, increased thickness of saliva, discoloration and peeling of the overlying skin, loss of hair within the field of treatment, and edema of the skin are the major side effects. Maintenance of good oral hygiene, frequent cleaning of the oral cavity with soda-saline solution, analgesics, and control of infection are recommended for conservative management of these side effects. Good hydration, a high-calorie diet, and avoidance of spicy and hot food are recommended.

Late effects of radiation are related to dose per fraction, total dose, and the type and volume of the tissue irradiated. Late effects include loss of hair within the irradiated area, dry mouth (xerostomia), thickening of the skin, dental caries, and, rarely, necrosis of the mandible or maxillary bone.

Complications of Surgery

The common complications of oral surgery are infection, collection of blood (hematoma), skin necrosis, flap failure, and wound breakdown. Resorption of bone, osteomyelitis, and salivary fistula can also occur. Complications are more frequent when neck dissection is part of the surgery. Fatal hemorrhage can occur if the carotid artery is exposed in the wound. Resection of the structures can interfere with cosmetic appearance and functions such as speech, swallowing, and airway. These complications can be minimized through reconstructive surgery and by good prosthetic rehabilitation.

Posttreatment Follow-Up

Patients with oral cancer are at risk for developing loco-regional recurrences and second malignancies. After completion of the treatment, patients should be followed up at regular intervals to detect any signs of recurrence. Patients should be encouraged to give up tobacco and alcohol and know the signs and symptoms of recurrence.

Prognosis

Lymph node involvement and tumor size are the most important prognostic factors. Data for the United States for 1975–2007 report a five-year survival for all stages of oral cancer of 60.9 percent, 82.5 percent for early-stage disease, and 54.7 percent for locally advanced oral cavity cancer (Ries and others 2008). The reported five-year overall survival rates for oral cancer for all stages combined from populations in LMICs such as China, Cuba, India, Pakistan, and Thailand ranged from 26 to 45 percent; for stages I and II, the survival rates ranged from 36 to 83 percent. The inferior survival rates in LMICs versus HICs reflect disparities in the availability, accessibility, and affordability of diagnostic and treatment services (Sankaranarayanan and others 2010; Sankaranarayanan and Swaminathan 2011).

ECONOMICS OF PREVENTING AND SCREENING FOR ORAL CANCERS IN LMICs

Cost-Effectiveness Assessments

Only a few cost-effectiveness studies of oral cancer screening focus on LMICs; therefore, we include a broader range of studies, including some from HICs. Although these studies may not be directly relevant to resource-limited settings, they provide valuable insights into the potential cost-effectiveness of interventions.

Primary Prevention

Interventions targeted at reducing or eliminating tobacco and alcohol use should be considered for implementation when shown to be cost-effective. All the interventions presented are cost-effective, even for LMICs. In the case of tobacco cessation, increasing the price of tobacco products is the most cost-effective approach, with incremental cost-effectiveness ratios ranging from US$4 to US$34 per disability-adjusted life year. Alcohol control interventions tend to have higher cost-effectiveness ratios; advertising bans and reduced access range from US$367 to US$1,307; combination strategies (including price increases, reduced access, and advertisement bans) range from US$601 to US$1,704. (Interventions to decrease tobacco use are covered in more detail in chapter 10.)

Screening

Table 5.4 summarizes findings from the relevant cost-effectiveness studies. Among the four studies of the cost-effectiveness of oral cancer screening, three—all set in HICs—used decision analytic modeling; the other, the only one from a resource-constrained environment, used data from a randomized clinical trial in India. Only the Indian study (Subramanian and others 2009) directly reflects the costs and effectiveness likely to be experienced in LMICs. In general, screening was at ages 35 or 40 years and older; three of the four studies included both high-risk and average-risk individuals. All of the studies presented incremental cost-effectiveness, compared with the scenario of no screening. A variety of interventions was assessed, using invitation and opportunistic screening; visual inspection was performed by specialists (oral cancer surgeons), dentists, or trained health care workers.

The results indicate that screening is cost-effective even in LMICs. The study from India provides evidence that oral cancer screening by visual inspection costs less than US$6 per person in a screening program; this has an incremental cost-effectiveness ratio of US$835 per life year saved. The most cost-effective and affordable option in the limited-resource setting is to offer oral cancer screening to high-risk individuals, for example, tobacco and alcohol users. The incremental cost-effectiveness ratio for screening high-risk individuals in southern India is US$156 per life year saved. There is wide variation in the incremental cost-effectiveness reported across the studies, probably because of factors such as the underlying prevalence of disease and the

Table 5.4 Oral Cancer Screening Cost-Effectiveness Studies

Study	Country	Setting/population	Methodology/ cost data	Interventions/tests compared	Cost-effectiveness assessment
Van Der Meij, Bezemer, and Van Der Waal 2002	Netherlands	Individuals with OLP	Decision analytic model: all relevant clinical costs	Screening by oral specialist or dentist versus no screening	US$53,430 per ELS or US$2,137 per QALY for screening by specialist, compared with no screening: lower cost-effectiveness ratio for screening by dentists
Speight and others 2006	United Kingdom	Screening programs for individuals ages 40 years and older in primary care settings	Decision analytic model: all relevant invitation and clinical costs	No screening compared with invitation and opportunistic screening	Opportunistic screening of high-risk individuals ages 40–60 years most cost-effective: US$19,000 per QALY
Subramanian and others 2009	India	13 clusters randomized in Kerala; those ages 35 years or older were eligible for the study	Cost-effectiveness assessment, including program and clinical costs	Visual inspection by trained health care workers compared with usual care	US$835 per LYS for all individuals; US$156 per LYS for high-risk individuals
Dedhia and others 2011	United States	Community-based screening for high-risk men (ages 40 years or older, tobacco and/or alcohol users)	Markov model: clinical costs included but no program costs	Oral exam (visual inspection and manual palpation) by trained health care workers, compared with no screening	A budget of US$3,363 per person over a 40-year cycle for screening is cost-effective

Note: ELS = equivalent life saved; LYS = life year saved; OLP = oral lichen planus; QALY = quality-adjusted life year.

local cost of cancer treatment. The cost of care related to screening, diagnosis, and treatment can differ substantially, even among countries classified as LMICs. Accordingly, it is essential to systematically assess costs at the country or even local level to analyze the cost-effectiveness and resources required to implement oral cancer screening.

Future Research Needs

Primary prevention, especially smoking cessation, and secondary prevention, focused on high-risk individuals, are likely to be cost-effective and affordable in LMICs. Additional studies are required to assess the cost-effectiveness and budget implications of visual screening for oral cancers in LMICs. These studies should focus on the screening delivery structure to identify the most cost-effective approach to provide oral cancer screening to high-risk individuals.

When cancer screening policies are implemented, the success of the program will depend on participation by the target population. Even when screening and follow-up care are free of charge, patients may not be able to afford to lose a day's wages to attend screening clinics or travel to health centers to receive follow-up diagnostic testing or treatments. The indirect costs borne by the patients may be particularly challenging among those in the lower socioeconomic strata. These are the very individuals likely to be at higher risk for developing oral cancers; it is, therefore, vital that identifying approaches to encourage and sustain participation among this potentially hard-to-reach, high-risk population be given high priority.

CONCLUSION

A multifaceted approach that integrates health education, tobacco and alcohol control, early detection, and early treatment is needed to reduce the burden of this eminently preventable cancer. How to accomplish this is known; astonishingly, it has not been applied in most countries, and not at all in the high-burden countries. Improving awareness among the general public and primary care practitioners, investing in health services to provide screening and early diagnosis services for tobacco and alcohol users, and providing adequate treatment for those diagnosed with invasive cancer are critically important oral cancer control measures. Imaging, histopathology, cancer surgery and radiotherapy infrastructure and services, trained professionals, and the availability of chemotherapeutic agents are inadequate in many LMICs, seriously compromising early detection

and optimum treatment. As this chapter has demonstrated, however, these interventions are affordable and cost-effective.

NOTES

The World Bank classifies countries according to four income groupings. Income is measured using gross national income per capita, in U.S. dollars, converted from local currency using the *World Bank Atlas* method. Classifications as of July 2014 are as follows:

- Low-income countries = US$1,045 or less in 2013
- Middle-income countries are subdivided:
  - Lower-middle-income = US$1,046–US$4,125
  - Upper-middle-income = US$4,126–US$12,745
- High-income countries = US$12,746 or more

1. Maps and figures in this chapter are based on incidence and mortality estimates for ages 0–69, consistent with reporting in all *DCP3* volumes. Global cancer statistics are estimates for the year 2012 and have been provided by the International Agency for Research on Cancer from its GLOBOCAN 2012 database. Observable population-based data were derived from Cancer Incidence in Five Continents, 10th edition and for trends over time from CI5 Plus (http://ci5.iarc.fr/CI5plus/Default.aspx). The discussion of burden (including risk factors), however, includes all ages unless otherwise noted. Interventions also apply to all age groups, except where age ranges or cutoffs are specified.

REFERENCES

Amagasa T., M. Yamashiro, and N. Uzawa. 2011. "Oral Premalignant Lesions: From a Clinical Perspective." *International Journal of Clinical Oncology* 16 (1): 5–14.

Amarasinghe, H. K., N. W. Johnson, R. Lalloo, M. Kumaraarachchi, and S. Warnakulasuriya. 2010. "Derivation and Validation of a Risk-Factor Model for Detection of Oral Potentially Malignant Disorders in Populations with High Prevalence." *British Journal of Cancer* 103 (3): 303–09.

Bernier J., C. Domenge, M. Ozsahin, K. Matuszewska, J. L. Lefebvre, and others. 2004. "Postoperative Irradiation with or Without Concomitant Chemotherapy for Locally Advanced Head and Neck Cancer." *New England Journal of Medicine* 350 (19): 1945–52.

Bhurgri Y., A. Bhurgri, A. Usman, S. Pervez, N. Kayani, and others. 2006. "Epidemiological Review of Head and Neck Cancers in Karachi." *Asian Pacific Journal of Cancer Prevention* 7 (2): 195–200.

Blanchard P., B. Baujat, V. Holostenco, A. Bourredjem, C. Baey, and others. 2011. "Meta-Analysis of Chemotherapy in Head and Neck Cancer (MACH-NC): A Comprehensive Analysis by Tumour Site." *Radiotherapy and Oncology* 100 (1): 33–40.

Bonifazi M., M. Malvezzi, P. Bertuccio, V. Edefonti, W. Garavello, and others. 2011. "Age-Period-Cohort Analysis of Oral Cancer Mortality in Europe: The End of an Epidemic?" *Oral Oncology* 47 (5): 400–07.

Bray, F., J. S. Ren, E. Masuyer, and J. Ferlay. 2013. "Estimates of Global Cancer Prevalence for 27 Sites in the Adult Population in 2008." *International Journal of Cancer* 132 (5): 1133–45.

Brocklehurst, P., O. Kujan, L. A. O'Malley, G. Ogden, S. Shepherd, and A. M Glenny. 2013. "Screening Programmes for the Early Detection and Prevention of Oral Cancer." *Cochrane Database of Systematic Reviews* 11: CD004150.

Brown L. M., D. P. Check, and S. S. Devesa. 2011. "Oropharyngeal Cancer Incidence Trends: Diminishing Racial Disparities." *Cancer Causes and Control* 22 (5): 753–63.

Chainani-Wu, N., J. Epstein, and R. Touger-Decker. 2011. "Diet and Prevention of Oral Cancer: Strategies for Clinical Practice." *Journal of the American Dental Association* 142 (2): 166–69.

Cooper, J. S., T. F. Pajak, A. A. Forastiere, J. Jacobs, B. H. Campbell, and others. 2004. "Postoperative Concurrent Radiotherapy and Chemotherapy for High-Risk Squamous-Cell Carcinoma of the Head and Neck." *New England Journal of Medicine* 350 (19): 1937–44.

Dedhia, R. C., K. J. Smith, J. T. Johnson, and M. Roberts. 2011. "The Cost-Effectiveness of Community-Based Screening for Oral Cancer in High-Risk Males in the United States: A Markov Decision Analysis Approach." *Laryngoscope* 121 (5): 952–60.

Deneo-Pellegrini, H., E. De Stefani, P. Boffetta, A. L. Ronco, G. Acosta, and others. 2012. "Mate Consumption and Risk of Oral Cancer: Case-Control Study in Uruguay." *Head & Neck* 35 (8): 1091–95.

Downer, M. C., D. R. Moles, S. Palmer, and P. M. Speight. 2004. "A Systematic Review of Test Performance in Screening for Oral Cancer and Precancer." *Oral Oncology* 40 (3): 264–73.

Edwards, C. P. 2013. "Oral Cancer Screening for Asymptomatic Adults: Do the United States Preventive Services Task Force Draft Guidelines Miss the Proverbial Forest for the Trees?" *Oral Surgery, Oral Medicine, Oral Pathology and Oral Radiology* 116 (2): 131–34.

Elango, K. J., N. Anandkrishnan, A. Suresh, S. K. Iyer, S. K. Ramaiyer, and others. 2011. "Mouth Self-Examination to Improve Oral Cancer Awareness and Early Detection in a High-Risk Population." *Oral Oncology* 47 (7): 620–24.

El-Naaj, I. A., Y. Leiser, M. Shveis, E. Sabo, and M. Peled. 2011. "Incidence of Oral Cancer Occult Metastasis and Survival of T1-T2N0 Oral Cancer Patients." *Journal of Oral & Maxillofacial Surgery* 69 (10): 2674–79.

Ferlay, J., I. Soerjomataram, M. Ervik, R. Dikshit, S. Eser, and others. 2013. *GLOBOCAN 2012 V1.0, Cancer Incidence and Mortality Worldwide: IARC Cancerbase No. 11* [Internet]. Lyon, France: International Agency for Research on Cancer. http://globocan.iarc.fr.

Fernandez, G. L., R. Sankaranarayanan, J. J. Lence Anta, S. A. Rodriguez, and D. M. Parkin. 1995. "An Evaluation of the Oral Cancer Control Program in Cuba." *Epidemiology* 6 (4): 428–31.

Forman, D., F. Bray, D. H. Brewster, C. Gombe Mbalawa, B. Kohler, and others. 2013. *Cancer Incidence in Five Continents.* Vol. 10 (Electronic Version). Lyon, France: International Agency for Cancer. http://ci5.iarc.fr.

Fujita, M., Y. Hirokawa, K. Kashiwado, Y. Akagi, K. Kashimoto, and others. 1999. "Interstitial Brachytherapy for Stage I and II Squamous Cell Carcinoma of the Oral Tongue: Factors Influencing Local Control and Soft Tissue Complications." *International Journal of Radiation Oncology Biology Physics* 44 (4): 767–75.

Gandini, S., E. Negri, P. Boffetta, V. C. La, and P. Boyle. 2012. "Mouthwash and Oral Cancer Risk Quantitative Meta-Analysis of Epidemiologic Studies." *Annals of Agricultural and Environmental Medicine* 19 (2): 173–80.

Gupta, B., A. Ariyawardana, and N. W. Johnson. 2013. "Oral Cancer in India Continues in Epidemic Proportions: Evidence Base and Policy Initiatives." *International Dental Journal* 63 (1): 12–25.

Gupta, P. C., C. S. Ray, D. N. Sinha, and P. K. Singh. 2011. "Smokeless Tobacco: A Major Public Health Problem in the SEA Region: A Review." *Indian Journal of Public Health* 55 (3): 199–209.

Harty, L. C., N. E. Caporaso, R. B. Hayes, D. M. Winn, E. Bravo-Otero, and others. 1997. "Alcohol Dehydrogenase 3 Genotype and Risk of Oral Cavity and Pharyngeal Cancers." *Journal of the National Cancer Institute* 89 (22): 1698–705.

Heck, J. E., J. Berthiller, S. Vaccarella, D. M. Winn, E. M. Smith, and others. 2010. "Sexual Behaviours and the Risk of Head and Neck Cancers: A Pooled Analysis in the International Head and Neck Cancer Epidemiology (INHANCE) Consortium." *International Journal of Epidemiology* 39 (1): 166–81.

Hicks, W. L., Jr., T. R. Loree, R. I. Garcia, S. Maamoun, D. Marshall, and others. 1997. "Squamous Cell Carcinoma of the Floor of Mouth: A 20-Year Review." *Head & Neck* 19 (5): 400–05.

Hirsch, J. M., M. Wallstrom, A. P. Carlsson, and L. Sand. 2012. "Oral Cancer in Swedish Snuff Dippers." *Anticancer Research* 32 (8): 3327–30.

Howlader, N., L. A. Ries, A. B. Mariotto, M. E. Reichman, J. Ruhl, and others. 2010. "Improved Estimates of Cancer-Specific Survival Rates from Population-Based Data." *Journal of the National Cancer Institute* 102 (20): 1584–98.

Hsue, S. S., W. C. Wang, C. H. Chen, C. C. Lin, Y. K. Chen, and L. M. Lin. 2007. "Malignant Transformation in 1458 Patients with Potentially Malignant Oral Mucosal Disorders: A Follow-Up Study Based in a Taiwanese Hospital." *Journal of Oral Pathology & Medicine* 36 (1): 25–29.

IARC (International Agency for Research on Cancer). 2004a. *IARC Monographs on the Evaluation of Carcinogenic Risks to Humans, Volume 83: Tobacco Smoke and Involuntary Smoking.* Lyon, France: IARC.

———. 2004b. *IARC Monographs on the Evaluation of Carcinogenic Risks to Humans, Volume 85: Betel-Quid and Areca-Nut Derived Nitrosamines.* Lyon, France: IARC.

———. 2007. *IARC Monographs on the Evaluation of Carcinogenic Risks to Humans, Volume 89: Smokeless Tobacco and Some Tobacco-Specific N-Nitrosamines.* Lyon, France: IARC.

———. 2010. *IARC Monographs on the Evaluation of Carcinogenic Risks to Humans, Volume 96: Alcohol Consumption and Ethyl Carbamate.* Lyon, France: IARC.

Javed, F., M. Chotai, A. Mehmood, and K. Almas. 2010. "Oral Mucosal Disorders Associated with Habitual Gutka Usage: A Review." *Oral Surgery, Oral Medicine, Oral Pathology, Oral Radiology, and Endodontics* 109 (6): 857–64.

Johnson, N. W., S. Warnakulasuriya, P. C. Gupta, E. Dimba, M. Chindia, and others. 2011. "Global Oral Health Inequalities in Incidence and Outcomes for Oral Cancer: Causes and Solutions." *Advances in Dental Research* 23 (2): 237–46.

Lambert, R., C. Sauvaget, C. M. De Camargo, and R. Sankaranarayanan. 2011. "Epidemiology of Cancer from the Oral Cavity and Oropharynx." *European Journal of Gastroenterology & Hepatology* 23 (8): 633–41.

Licitra L., C. Grandi, M. Guzzo, L. Mariani, V. S. Lo, and others. 2003. "Primary Chemotherapy in Resectable Oral Cavity Squamous Cell Cancer: A Randomized Controlled Trial." *Journal of Clinical Oncology* 21 (2): 327–33.

Lu, D., X. Yu, and Y. Du. 2011. "Meta-Analyses of the Effect of Cytochrome P450 2E1 Gene Polymorphism on the Risk of Head and Neck Cancer." *Molecular Biology Reports* 38 (4): 2409–16.

Lucenteforte, E., W. Garavello, C. Bosetti, and V. C. La. 2009. "Dietary Factors and Oral and Pharyngeal Cancer Risk." *Oral Oncology* 45 (6): 461–67.

Lundahl, R. E., R. L. Foote, J. A. Bonner, V. J. Suman, J. E. Lewis, and others. 1998. "Combined Neck Dissection and Postoperative Radiation Therapy in the Management of the High-Risk Neck: A Matched-Pair Analysis." *International Journal of Radiation Oncology Biology Physics* 40 (3): 529–34.

Marsiglia, H., C. Haie-Meder, G. Sasso, G. Mamelle, and A. Gerbaulet. 2002. "Brachytherapy for T1-T2 Floor-of-the-Mouth Cancers: The Gustave-Roussy Institute Experience." *International Journal of Radiation Oncology Biology Physics* 52 (5): 1257–63.

Mathew, B., R. Sankaranarayanan, K. B. Sunilkumar, B. Kuruvila, P. Pisani, and others. 1997. "Reproducibility and Validity of Oral Visual Inspection by Trained Health Workers in the Detection of Oral Precancer and Cancer." *British Journal of Cancer* 76 (3): 390–94.

Mathew, B., R. Sankaranarayanan, R. Wesley, and M. K. Nair. 1995. "Evaluation of Mouth Self-Examination in the Control of Oral Cancer." *British Journal of Cancer* 71 (2): 397–99.

Mehta, F. S., P. C. Gupta, R. B. Bhonsle, P. R. Murti, D. K. Daftary, and J. J. Pindborg. 1986. "Detection of Oral Cancer Using Basic Health Workers in an Area of High Oral Cancer Incidence in India." *Cancer Detection and Prevention* 9 (3–4): 219–25.

Napier, S. S., and P. M. Speight. 2008. "Natural History of Potentially Malignant Oral Lesions and Conditions: An Overview of the Literature." *Journal of Oral Pathology & Medicine* 37 (1): 1–10.

Patel, S. G., and J. P. Shah. 2005. "TNM Staging of Cancers of the Head and Neck: Striving for Uniformity among Diversity." *CA: A Cancer Journal for Clinicians* 55 (4): 242–58.

Patton, L. L., J. B. Epstein, and A. R. Kerr. 2008. "Adjunctive Techniques for Oral Cancer Examination and Lesion Diagnosis: A Systematic Review of the Literature." *Journal of the American Dental Association* 139 (7): 896–905.

Pavia, M., C. Pileggi, C. G. Nobile, and I. F. Angelillo. 2006. "Association between Fruit and Vegetable Consumption and Oral Cancer: A Meta-Analysis of Observational Studies." *American Journal of Clinical Nutrition* 83 (5): 1126–34.

Piemonte, E. D., J. P. Lazos, and M. Brunotto. 2010. "Relationship between Chronic Trauma of the Oral Mucosa, Oral Potentially Malignant Disorders and Oral Cancer." *Journal of Oral Pathology & Medicine* 39 (7): 513–17.

Prabhu, S., and D. Wilson. 2013. "Human Papillomavirus and Oral Disease: Emerging Evidence: A Review." *Australian Dental Journal* 58 (1): 2–10.

Pulte, D., and H. Brenner. 2010. "Changes in Survival in Head and Neck Cancers in the Late 20th and Early 21st Century: A Period Analysis." *Oncologist* 15 (9): 994–1001.

Radoi, L., S. Paget-Bailly, D. Cyr, A. Papadopoulos, F. Guida, and others. 2013. "Tobacco Smoking, Alcohol Drinking and Risk of Oral Cavity Cancer by Subsite: Results of a French Population-Based Case-Control Study, the ICARE Study." *European Journal of Cancer Prevention* 22 (3): 268–76.

Ramadas, K., E. Lucas, G. Thomas, B. Mathew, A. Balan, and others. 2008. *A Digital Manual for the Early Diagnosis of Oral Neoplasia.* Lyon, France: International Agency for Research on Cancer. http://screening.iarc.fr/atlasoral.php.

Rethman, M. P., W. Carpenter, E. E. Cohen, J. Epstein, C. A. Evans, and others. 2010. "Evidence-Based Clinical Recommendations Regarding Screening for Oral Squamous Cell Carcinomas." *Journal of the American Dental Association* 141 (5): 509–20.

Richards, D. 2010. "Does Toluidine Blue Detect More Oral Cancer?" *Evidence-Based Dental Practice* 11 (4): 104–05.

Ries, L. A. G., D. Melbert, M. Krapcho, D. G. Stinchcomb, N. Howlader, and others. 2008. *Cancer Statistics Review, 1975–2005.* Bethesda, MD: National Cancer Institute. http://seer.cancer.gov/csr/1975-2005.

Saba, N. F., M. Goodman, K. Ward, C. Flowers, S. Ramalingam, and others. 2011. "Gender and Ethnic Disparities in Incidence and Survival of Squamous Cell Carcinoma of the Oral Tongue, Base of Tongue, and Tonsils: A Surveillance, Epidemiology and End Results Program-Based Analysis." *Oncology* 81 (1): 12–20.

Sankaranarayanan, R., K. Ramadas, S. Thara, R. Muwonge, G. Thomas, and others. 2013. "Long Term Effect of Visual Screening on Oral Cancer Incidence and Mortality in a Randomized Trial in Kerala, India." *Oral Oncology* 49 (4): 314–21.

Sankaranarayanan, R., K. Ramadas, G. Thomas, R. Muwonge, S. Thara, and others. 2005. "Effect of Screening on Oral Cancer Mortality in Kerala, India: A Cluster-Randomised Controlled Trial." *The Lancet* 365 (9475): 1927–33.

Sankaranarayanan, R., and R. Swaminathan. 2011. *Cancer Survival in Africa, Asia, the Caribbean and Central America. Scientific Publications No. 162.* Lyon, France: International Agency for Research on Cancer.

Sankaranarayanan, R., R. Swaminathan, H. Brenner, K. Chen, K. S. Chia, and others. 2010. "Cancer Survival in Africa, Asia, and Central America: A Population-Based Study." *The Lancet Oncology* 11 (2): 165–73.

Sant, M., C. Allemani, M. Santaquilani, A. Knijn, F. Marchesi, and others. 2009. "EUROCARE-4. Survival of Cancer Patients Diagnosed in 1995–1999. Results and Commentary." *European Journal of Cancer* 45 (6): 931–91.

Satyanarayana, L., and S. Asthana. 2008. "Life Time Risk for Development of Ten Major Cancers in India and Its Trends over the Years 1982 to 2000." *Indian Journal of Medical Sciences* 62 (2): 35–44.

Scott, S. E., K. Rizvi, E. A. Grunfeld, and M. Mcgurk. 2010. "Pilot Study to Estimate the Accuracy of Mouth Self-Examination in an At-Risk Group." *Head & Neck* 32 (10): 1393–401.

Sinha, D. N., K. M. Palipudi, I. Rolle, S. Asma, and S. Rinchen. 2011. "Tobacco Use among Youth and Adults in Member Countries of South-East Asia Region: Review of Findings from Surveys under the Global Tobacco Surveillance System." *Indian Journal of Public Health* 55 (3): 169–76.

Sobin, L. H., and C. Wittekind. 2002. *UICC TNM Classification of Malignant Tumours.* Geneva: Union for International Cancer Control.

Somatunga, L. C., D. N. Sinha, P. Sumanasekera, K. Galapatti, S. Rinchen, and others. 2012. "Smokeless Tobacco Use in Sri Lanka." *Indian Journal of Cancer* 49 (4): 357–63.

Speight, P. M., S. Palmer, D. R. Moles, M. C. Downer, D. H. Smith, and others. 2006. "The Cost-Effectiveness of Screening for Oral Cancer in Primary Care." *Health Technology Assessment* 10 (14):1–144, Iii-Iv.

Su, W. W., A. M. Yen, S. Y. Chiu, and T. H. Chen. 2010. "A Community-Based RCT for Oral Cancer Screening with Toluidine Blue." *Journal of Dental Research* 89 (9): 933–37.

Subramanian, S., R. Sankaranarayanan, B. Bapat, T. Somanathan, G. Thomas, and others. 2009. "Cost-Effectiveness of Oral Cancer Screening: Results from a Cluster Randomized Controlled Trial in India." *Bulletin of the World Health Organization* 87 (3): 200–06.

Tseng, C. H. 2013. "Oral Cancer in Taiwan: Is Diabetes a Risk Factor?" *Clinical Oral Investigations* 17 (5): 1357–64.

Van Der Meij, E. H., P. D. Bezemer, and I. Van Der Waal. 2002. "Cost-Effectiveness of Screening for the Possible Development of Cancer in Patients with Oral Lichen Planus." *Community Dentistry and Oral Epidemiology* 30 (5): 342–51.

Vijayakumar, M., R. Burrah, K. S. Sabitha, H. Nadimul, and B. C. Rajani. 2011. "To Operate or Not to Operate: N0 Neck in Early Cancer of the Tongue? A Prospective Study." *Indian Journal of Surgical Oncology* 2 (3): 172–75.

Walsh, T, J. L. Liu, P. Brocklehurst, A. M. Glenny, M. Lingen, and others. 2013. "Clinical Assessment to Screen for Oral Cavity Cancer and Potentially Malignant Disorders in Apparently Healthy Adults." *Cochrane Database of Systematic Reviews* 11: CD010173.

Warnakulasuriya, K. A., A. N. Ekanayake, S. Sivayoham, J. Stjernsward, J. J. Pindborg, and others. 1984. "Utilization of Primary Health Care Workers for Early Detection of Oral Cancer and Precancer Cases in Sri Lanka." *Bulletin of the World Health Organization* 62 (2): 243–50.

Warnakulasuriya, S., N. W. Johnson, and I. Van Der Waal. 2007. "Nomenclature and Classification of Potentially Malignant Disorders of the Oral Mucosa." *Journal of Oral Pathology & Medicine* 36 (10): 575–80.

Warnakulasuriya, K. A., and B. G. Nanayakkara. 1991. "Reproducibility of an Oral Cancer and Precancer Detection Program Using a Primary Health Care Model in Sri Lanka." *Cancer Detection and Prevention* 15 (5): 331–34.

Wendt, C. D., L. J. Peters, L. Delclos, K. K. Ang, W. H. Morrison, and others. 1990. "Primary Radiotherapy in the Treatment of Stage I and II Oral Tongue Cancers: Importance of the Proportion of Therapy Delivered with Interstitial Therapy." *International Journal of Radiation Oncology Biology Physics* 18 (6): 1287–92.

Woolgar, J. A. 2006. "Histopathological Prognosticators in Oral and Oropharyngeal Squamous Cell Carcinoma." *Oral Oncology* 42 (3): 229–39.

World Cancer Research Fund and AICR (American Institute for Cancer Research). 2007. *Food, Nutrition, Physical Activity, and the Prevention of Cancer: A Global Perspective.* Washington, DC: AICR.

Wrangle, J. M., and F. R. Khuri. 2007. "Chemoprevention of Squamous Cell Carcinoma of the Head and Neck." *Current Opinion in Oncology* 19 (3): 180–87.

Yako-Suketomo, H., and T. Matsuda. 2010. "Comparison of Time Trends in Lip, Oral Cavity and Pharynx Cancer Mortality (1990–2006) between Countries Based on the WHO Mortality Database." *Japanese Journal of Clinical Oncology* 40 (11): 1118–19.

Zwetyenga, N., C. Majoufre-Lefebvre, F. Siberchicot, H. Demeaux, and J. Pinsolle. 2003. "[Squamous-cell carcinoma of the tongue: treatment results and prognosis]." *Revue de stomatologie et de chirurgie maxillo-faciale* 104 (1): 10–17.

Colorectal Cancer

Linda Rabeneck, Susan Horton, Ann G. Zauber, and Craig Earle

INTRODUCTION

Adenocarcinoma of the colon and rectum (colorectal cancer, CRC) is the third most common cancer, the fourth most common cause of cancer death, and the second most common cancer in terms of the number of individuals living with cancer five years after diagnosis worldwide. An estimated 1,361,000 people are diagnosed with CRC annually; approximately 694,000 people die from CRC annually; and 3,544,000 individuals are living with CRC (Ferlay and others 2013).

Randomized controlled trials (RCT) have shown that screening is associated with a reduction in CRC mortality; in several high-income countries (HICs), organized, population-based screening programs have been introduced, starting in 2006. Some screening tests detect cancer at an early stage when treatment is less arduous and more often results in cure. Other screening tests have the ability to detect adenomas as well as cancer. Screening provides the opportunity to identify and remove adenomas and thereby to prevent the development of the disease (Lieberman and others 2012).

In general, the burden of disease, as measured by incidence and mortality rates, tracks the World Bank grouping of countries into low-, lower-middle, upper-middle, and high-income: the lowest-income countries have the lowest burden of disease. The ability to intervene to introduce screening and offer access to high-quality treatment is a function of resource availability, which is associated with income level. The ability

of countries to develop interventions increases with income, suggesting a progression in policy options as country income increases.

The focus of this chapter is on those who are at average risk for CRC. In our discussion of policy options, we use a slightly different typology than income for resource availability, following chapter 3 in this volume (Anderson and others 2015). The resources available at a health facility can be described as basic, limited, enhanced, and maximal. The basic level corresponds approximately to the situation in low-income countries (LICs), the limited level to the situation in rural areas of lower-middle-income countries and upper-middle-income countries, the enhanced level to the situation in urban areas of lower-middle-income and upper-middle-income countries, and the maximal level to the situation in HICs. We provide suggestions for appropriate screening and treatment strategies that correspond to these resource levels for policy makers to consider.

BURDEN AND EPIDEMIOLOGY[1]

CRC is the third most common cancer in men (746,000 cases, 10.0 percent of all cancers in men worldwide); it is the second most common cancer in women (614,000 cases, 9.2 percent of all cancers in women worldwide). CRC incidence rates vary approximately tenfold in both genders worldwide and are higher in men than in women; the overall sex ratio of the age-standardized

Corresponding author: Linda Rabeneck, MD, MPH, FRCPC, Cancer Care Ontario and University of Toronto, linda.rabeneck@cancercare.on.ca.

rates is 1.44:1 (Ferlay and others 2013). CRC incidence and mortality rates vary widely across regions, with mortality highest among men in HICs (map 6.1). The distribution of incidence in men and women and mortality in women may be seen in online annex 6A (maps 6A.1, 6A.2, and 6A.3). Approximately 55 percent of persons diagnosed with CRC are in HICs. Australia, Canada, New Zealand, the United States, and Western Europe have the highest estimated incidence rates, while incidence rates are intermediate in Latin America and the Caribbean. The lowest rates are in Sub-Saharan Africa, with the exception of southern Africa, and South Asia.

CRC mortality rates are lower in women than in men. However, compared with incidence rates, variability in mortality rates worldwide is less (sixfold in men, fourfold in women). Estimated CRC mortality rates are highest in Eastern and Central Europe (20.3 per 100,000 for men and 11.7 per 100,000 for women); Western Africa has the lowest estimated mortality rates (3.5 and 3.0, respectively).

Temporal Trends in Incidence and Mortality

Temporal trends in CRC incidence and mortality in a population reflect changes in the prevalence of risk factors in the population, coupled with changes associated with the introduction of screening. CRC incidence rates have stabilized or are declining in many HICs. Initially, the stabilization or decline may have been caused by declines in some risks, such as smoking; more recently, the change is likely to be caused by increased screening. Data from the Surveillance, Epidemiology, and End Results (SEER) Program for the state of Connecticut, United States, from 1940 to 2009, is one of the longest consistent time-series available. Incidence rates increased rapidly until the 1980s and then declined. (See online annex 6A, figure 6A.1). The peak in the 1980s represents the introduction of screening (primarily with fecal occult blood tests) and is consistent with an initial increase in incidence with screening because of detection of early-stage and preclinical disease. The decline post-1985 likely represents the impact of screening, as well as a decrease in risk factors such as smoking. The inverted U-shaped curve is more pronounced for men than for women (figure 6A.1). CRC incidence rates are now declining to the lowest level since the 1940s (Edwards and others 2010).

Trends for the United States as a whole are similar to those for Connecticut, but data are not available as far back as 1940 in a continuous series. A declining trend in CRC mortality is also seen in other HICs, including Australia, Denmark, and Japan. Incidence has not yet begun to decline in these three countries, likely because

Map 6.1 Global Colorectal Cancer Mortality in Men, 2012

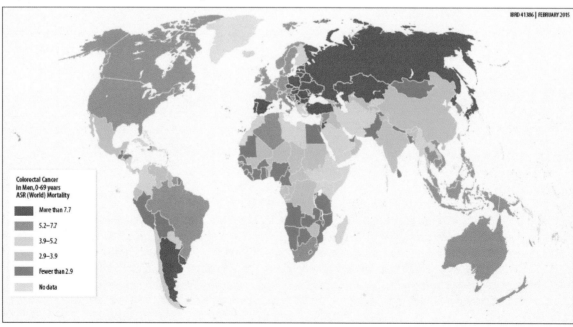

Source: Based on data from Ferlay and others 2013.
Note: ASR = Age-Standardized Rate.

a "bulge" in reported cases occurs as CRC is detected at increasingly earlier stages. One would eventually expect to see incidence rates decline as in the United States, once a steady state is reached in screening.

The increase in CRC incidence and mortality in middle-income countries (MICs), such as Brazil, China, the Philippines, and Thailand (figures 6.1 and 6.2), is occurring prior to the onset of organized screening. Even in lower-middle-income countries such as India, incidence

rates are increasing. Data from LICs are sparse, because of the limited availability and coverage of cancer registries.

Incidence and Mortality by Income Group

We classified the age-adjusted incidence and mortality rates for CRC by World Bank groupings of countries into LICs, lower-middle-income countries, upper-middle-income countries, and HICs (figure 6.3). The CRC

Figure 6.1 Trends in Age-Standardized Incidence and Mortality Rates of Colorectal Cancer in Men, Selected Countries, 1980–2010

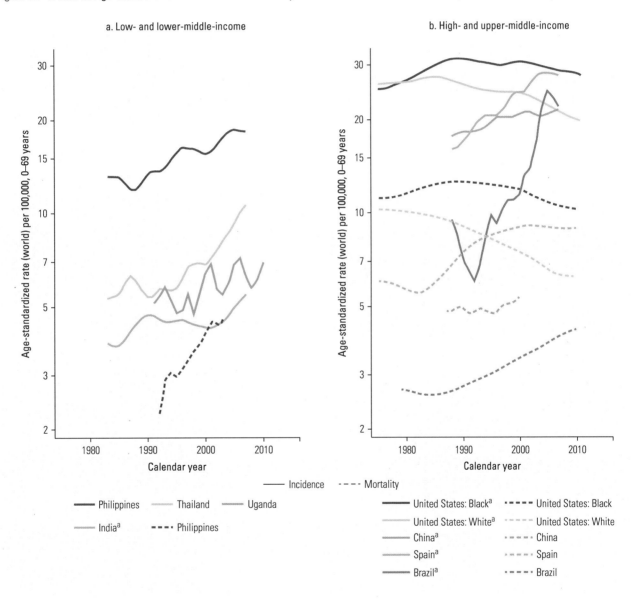

a. Low- and lower-middle-income

b. High- and upper-middle-income

Source: CI5 Plus (http://ci5.iarc.fr/CI5plus/Default.aspx) and WHO Mortality Database (http://www.who.int/healthinfo/statistics/mortality_rawdata/en/index.html).
Note: Mortality data are not available for all economies shown. Incidence estimated from selected population-based cancer registries of consistently high quality (included in successive volumes of *Cancer Incidence in Five Continents*). Incidence data for the economies in the graphs are for Brazil (Goiania), China (Hong Kong SAR and Shanghai), India (Chennai and Mumbai), Philippines (Manila), Spain (Granada, Murcia, Navarra, and Tarragona), Thailand (Chiang Mai), Uganda (Kampala), United States (SEER).
a. Denotes rates based on an aggregate of one or more regional registries, as indicated.

Figure 6.2 Trends in Age-Standardized Incidence and Mortality of Colorectal Cancer Rates in Women, Selected Countries, 1980–2010

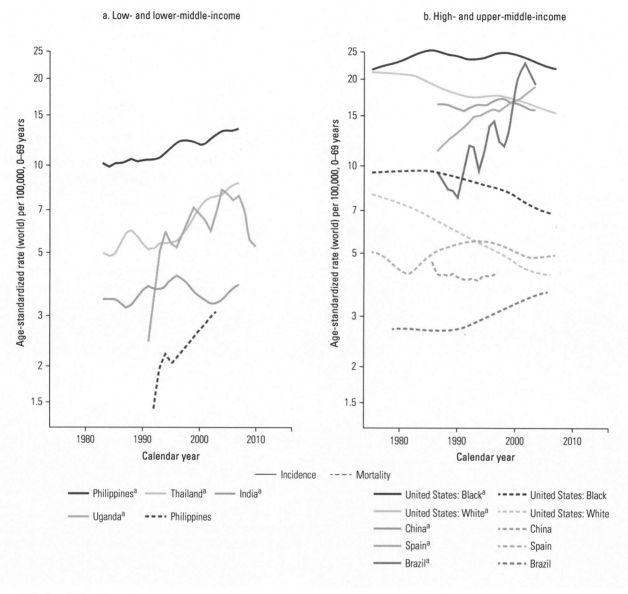

Source: CI5 Plus (http://ci5.iarc.fr/CI5plus/Default.aspx) and WHO Mortality Database (http://www.who.int/healthinfo/statistics/mortality_rawdata/en/index.html).
Note: Mortality data are not available for all economies shown. Incidence estimated from selected population-based cancer registries of consistently high quality (included in successive volumes of *Cancer Incidence in Five Continents*). Incidence data for the economies in the graphs are for Brazil (Goiania), China (Hong Kong SAR and Shanghai), India (Chennai and Mumbai), Philippines (Manila), Spain (Granada, Murcia, Navarra, and Tarragona), Thailand (Chiang Mai), Uganda (Kampala), United States (SEER).
a. Denotes rates based on an aggregate of one or more regional registries, as indicated.

incidence and mortality rates increase with increasing country income, as indicated by the World Bank income groupings.

We derived the mortality-to-incidence ratio as an approximation of the CRC-specific mortality rate using the data from figure 6.3. The mortality-to-incidence ratio roughly represents the percentage of people with CRC who die of this disease. Although the low-income

countries had the lowest CRC incidence and mortality rates, approximately 67 percent of men and 68 percent of women who develop CRC die from the disease. This is in strong contrast to the experience in HICs, where the incidence and mortality rates are much higher, but only approximately 31 percent of men and 30 percent of women with CRC die of this cancer. The corresponding figures for lower-middle-income countries are 60 percent of men and 58 percent of women; for upper-middle-income countries, they are 49 percent of men and 47 percent of women. These results indicate that better survival is associated with higher country income. For China, the mortality-to-incidence ratio is 37 percent for men and 36 percent for women who develop CRC, whereas for India, the mortality-to-incidence ratio is 70 percent for men and 68 percent for women, indicating a very high case fatality rate from CRC in India.

In summary, the current burden of disease parallels the World Bank income groupings, with the lowest-income countries having the lowest burden of disease and poorest disease-specific survival.

Risk Factors

Age, sex, and family history are independent risk factors for CRC. The incidence of CRC increases with age, with approximately 7 percent of cases occurring in those younger than 50 years. The risk is somewhat higher among men than women. About 75 percent of new cases of CRC occur in those with no known predisposing factors. Those at increased risk because of a family history of CRC but without an identifiable genetic syndrome account for 15–20 percent of cases. HNPCC (Lynch syndrome) accounts for about 5 percent of cases, and familial adenomatous polyposis (FAP) accounts for about 1 percent (Winawer and others 1997). HNPCC and FAP are genetic polyposis syndromes. Those with a family history of CRC in a parent, sibling, or child are at a twofold increased risk of the disease (Butterworth, Higgins, and Pharoah 2006; Johnson and others 2013).

In terms of modifiable risk factors, epidemiological evidence supports roles for diet, lifestyle, and medications (Chan and Giovannucci 2010). In general, diets high in red meat are associated with an increased risk. For red meat, a recent meta-analysis reported a relative risk of 1.13 for consumption of five versus no servings per week (Johnson and others 2013). In addition, smoking, obesity, and a sedentary lifestyle are associated with an increased risk. For smoking, a relative risk of 1.26 for a 30-pack per year smoker versus a non-smoker, and for obesity, a relative risk of 1.10 for body mass index greater than 30 versus 22 kg/m^2 were recently reported (Johnson and others 2013). Calcium supplements may be associated with a modest reduction in risk. Aspirin and nonsteroidal anti-inflammatory drugs and postmenopausal hormone therapy among women are inversely associated with CRC risk, although the magnitudes of these effects are uncertain. The rise in CRC incidence rates in low- and middle-income countries (LMICs) is largely attributed to the adoption of Western diets and sedentary lifestyles.

Figure 6.3 Age-Standardized Incidence and Mortality Rates of Colorectal Cancer by World Bank Income Classification, 2012

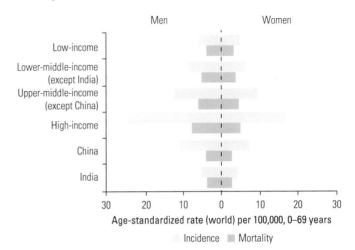

Source: Ferlay and others 2013.

INTERVENTIONS

Screening

CRC Screening Tests

Guaiac Fecal Occult Blood Test (gFOBT) gFOBT is a stool test that indirectly detects blood in the stool that may be caused by bleeding from CRC. A positive test is not specific for the presence of human blood; however, it may reflect blood from ingested animal meats, for example. gFOBT is supported by evidence from RCTs with long-term follow-up and CRC mortality as the outcome. RCTs of periodic (annual or biennial) gFOBT show a reduction in mortality from CRC of 13 to 33 percent, with up to 50 percent compliance with periodic gFOBT (Hardcastle and others 1996; Kronborg and others 1996; Mandel and others 1993; Towler and others 1998). Individuals with a positive gFOBT must be followed up by colonoscopy.

Fecal Immunochemical Test (FIT) FIT is a stool test that uses an antibody against human globin, the protein part of hemoglobin. A positive FIT is specific for human blood. There are no large-scale RCTs that have evaluated FIT with long-term follow-up and CRC mortality as the outcome, although two RCTs are underway. FIT is supported by RCTs of FIT versus gFOBT (van Rossum and others 2008) and FIT versus colonoscopy (Quintero and others 2012). These are cross-sectional RCTs with cancer detection and advanced adenoma as the outcomes. The RCT of FIT compared with gFOBT shows that the use of FIT is associated with higher adherence/compliance rates than the use of gFOBT, and also that FIT is superior to gFOBT in detection rates and positive predictive values for adenomas and cancer (van Rossum and others 2008). The RCT of FIT compared with colonoscopy showed higher participation in the FIT group than in the colonoscopy group, and that the numbers of subjects in whom CRC was detected were similar in the two groups, but a greater number of subjects with adenomas were identified in the colonoscopy group (Quintero and others 2012).

Flexible Sigmoidoscopy (FS) FS is an endoscopic procedure in which a flexible fiberoptic instrument is used to examine the rectum and lower (distal) colon, unlike colonoscopy, which examines the rectum and total (upper and lower) colon. Cancers and precancerous lesions, such as adenomas observed in this area, can be removed or biopsied. Large-scale RCTs of FS, coupled with colonoscopy for those who test positive, have shown reductions in CRC incidence (Atkin and others 2010; Schoen and others 2012; Segnan and others 2011) and CRC mortality (Atkin and others 2010; Schoen and others 2012) over a 10-year period. A meta-analysis of the results from the published RCTs of FS screening reported, in an intention-to-treat analysis, an 18 percent reduction in relative risk of CRC incidence and a 28 percent reduction in CRC mortality (Elmunzer and others 2012).

Colonoscopy Colonoscopy is an examination of the entire colon and rectum with a flexible fiberoptic endoscope. Colonoscopy detects asymptomatic cancers, and precancerous lesions can be removed. Evidence from the National Polyp Study, analyzed as an observational cohort study, indicates that colonoscopy with polypectomy is associated with a reduction in CRC incidence and mortality (Winawer and others 1993; Zauber and others 2012). No published evidence from RCTs has evaluated screening colonoscopy with long-term follow-up and CRC mortality as the outcome. However, indirect evidence to support screening colonoscopy comes from RCTs of gFOBT, in which persons with a positive gFOBT underwent colonoscopy. In these trials, colonoscopy with polypectomy was responsible for the mortality reduction associated with gFOBT screening. Further indirect evidence comes from RCTs of FS screening, which demonstrate a reduction in CRC mortality. By extrapolation, it would be expected that since colonoscopy evaluates the entire colon, screening colonoscopy would be associated with a reduction in CRC mortality that might exceed that observed for screening FS. Several large-scale RCTs of colonoscopy are underway, with CRC mortality as the primary outcome. In the NordICC trial in Europe, screening colonoscopy is being compared with usual care. In the COLONPREV trial in Spain and the CONFIRM trial by the U.S. Department of Veterans Affairs, colonoscopy is being compared with FIT.

Fecal DNA A cross-sectional study comparing the performance of a stool DNA prototype versus gFOBT versus colonoscopy reported that the stool DNA test detected a greater proportion of CRCs and CRCs plus adenomas with high-grade dysplasia than the gFOBT, 51.6 percent vs. 12.9 percent, and 40.8 percent vs. 14.1 percent, respectively (Imperiale and others 2004). However, the majority of neoplastic lesions was not detected by either test. Since then, stool DNA technology has continued to evolve (Ahlquist and others 2012). A large-scale, cross-sectional study (DeeP-C) of a next-generation stool DNA test has recently been published (Imperiale and others 2014) and indicates 92.3 percent sensitivity for the detection of CRC and 42.4 percent sensitivity for the detection of advanced adenomas.

Computed Tomographic Colonography (CTC) CTC is a computerized tomography examination of the abdomen and pelvis in which imaging information, when processed with special imaging software, provides images of the colon and rectum. Images are also produced of structures outside the colon (extracolonic findings). The technique requires bowel preparation and colonic insufflation, but not conscious sedation, as is generally required for colonoscopy. CTC does not permit biopsy or polyp removal; colonoscopy is required. The two largest reports evaluating CTC in asymptomatic persons are cross-sectional studies that compared CTC and colonoscopy for the detection of adenomas (Johnson and others 2008; Pickhardt and others 2003). Taken together, these studies found that CTC was comparable to colonoscopy for detecting adenomas ≥ 10 mm (pooled sensitivity was 92 percent), but fell short in detecting smaller adenomas (6–9 mm).

Role of Colonoscopy in Diagnosis and Surveillance

Having adequate colonoscopy resources is a key aspect in implementing CRC screening, because of the role of colonoscopy in diagnosis and surveillance. When a less invasive screening test—such as gFOBT, FIT, or FS—is used, colonoscopy is required to investigate those with a positive (abnormal) screen, and it is the final common pathway to establish a diagnosis. Colonoscopy is also recommended for surveillance, depending on the findings at the initial colonoscopy, which are used to stratify risk for subsequent colorectal neoplasia.

Guidelines for Colonoscopic Surveillance In 2012, the U.S. Multi-Society Task Force on CRC/American Cancer Society (USMSTF) published updated surveillance guidelines that take into account the serrated neoplasia pathway (Lieberman and others 2012). Based on the findings at the baseline colonoscopy, the recommended surveillance intervals are as follows: 10 years for those with no polyps or small (< 10 mm) hyperplastic polyps in the rectum or sigmoid; 5–10 years for those with 1 or 2 small (< 10 mm) tubular adenomas; three years for those with three to 10 tubular adenomas, one or more tubular adenomas ≥ 10 mm, one or more villous adenomas, or an adenoma with high-grade dysplasia; and less than three years for those with more than 10 adenomas. When serrated lesions are detected at the baseline colonoscopy, the recommended surveillance intervals are as follows: five years for those with sessile serrated polyps (SSPs) < 10 mm with no dysplasia, three years for SSPs ≥ 10 mm or SSPs with dysplasia or a traditional serrated adenoma, and one year for those with serrated polyposis syndrome.

Colonoscopy Effectiveness in Usual Practice

Large-scale, population-based studies have shown that lesions can be missed at colonoscopy, including adenomas and cancers (Baxter and others 2009; Bressler and others 2007). It is often not possible to be certain that a CRC that was not detected at the time of colonoscopy, but subsequently diagnosed, was a missed cancer. The alternative explanation is that the "new" cancer was not present at the time of the colonoscopy, but arose and grew rapidly following the procedure. These new or missed cancers have been referred to as postcolonoscopy CRCs (Rabeneck and Paszat 2010) or interval cancers.

Evidence from population-based, case-control studies shows that colonoscopy is associated with a reduction in overall CRC mortality; however, the magnitude of the effect is less in the proximal colon (Baxter and others 2009; Brenner and others 2011). This means that in usual practice, colonoscopy is less effective in the proximal colon. This finding is attributed to suboptimal colonoscopy quality or differences in tumor biology between those cancers that arise in the proximal compared with the distal colon. These findings have given rise to renewed emphasis on the critical importance of colonoscopy quality and increased attention to CRC carcinogenesis. In particular, the recognition that lesions arising in the serrated neoplasia pathway have been underdetected at colonoscopy may explain, in part, the lesser effectiveness of colonoscopy in the proximal (right) colon.

What are the possible reasons for postcolonoscopy CRCs?

- First, the lesion may not have been seen because the cecum was not reached during the procedure (reaching the cecum is more challenging technically than reaching the distal colon); the bowel preparation was not adequate and the mucosa was not fully visualized (the upper or proximal colon is more difficult to clean); or the technique was inadequate, that is, the lesion was simply not seen.
- Second, a prior polypectomy may have been incomplete. Polypectomy is the key to reducing CRC incidence following colonoscopy.
- Third, a rapidly progressing CRC may not have been present at the initial colonoscopy, which may have been truly negative.

What all of this means is that colonoscopy fails to detect a small but clinically important percentage of lesions, and this lack of effectiveness is more pronounced in the right colon, making meticulous technique paramount.

CRC Screening Guidelines

International Agency for Research on Cancer In 2010, the International Agency for Research on Cancer (IARC), an agency of the World Health Organization (WHO), published a landmark document, *European Guidelines for Quality Assurance in Colorectal Cancer Screening and Diagnosis* (Segnan, Patnick, and von Karsa 2010). The recommendations are based on a comprehensive and systematic review of the scientific evidence and are intended for organized screening programs (see below). The guidelines recommended annual or biennial screening with gFOBT, FIT screening at an interval not to exceed three years and at a minimum to include screening for those ages 60–64 years, and FS screening at an interval not less than 10 years, with the best age range for screening between ages 55 and 64 years but not exceeding age 74 years. Colonoscopy was not recommended for CRC screening in the European Union.

U.S. Preventive Services Task Force (USPSTF) USPSTF recommends routine screening for average risk persons ages 50–75 years, no routine screening for persons ages 76–85 years, and no screening for persons older than age 85 years (USPSTF 2008). USPSTF recommends annual screening with high-sensitivity gFOBT, or FS every five years with high-sensitivity gFOBT every three years, or colonoscopy every 10 years. USPSTF did not assess barium enema because of lack of evidence and declining use, and it concluded that the evidence was insufficient to assess the benefits and harms of CTC and fecal DNA for CRC screening.

U.S. Multi-Society Task Force/American Cancer Society (USMSTF)

USMSTF defines two categories of screening test (Levin and others 2008). In the first category are tests that primarily detect cancers. Tests that are recommended in this category for screening persons at average risk (age 50 years and older, no symptoms, no family history of the disease) are the following: annual high-sensitivity gFOBT, annual FIT, or stool DNA (interval uncertain). In the second category are tests that detect cancers and adenomas. Recommended tests in this category for screening persons at average risk are: FS every five years, colonoscopy every 10 years, double-contrast barium enema every five years, or CTC every five years.

Organized Versus Opportunistic Screening

Screening is not simply a test; it is a process. Chapter 12, this volume, discusses organized and opportunistic screening in detail. Compared with opportunistic screening, organized screening focuses much greater attention on the quality of the screening process, including follow-up of participants (Miles and others 2004). Thus, a key advantage of organized screening is that it provides greater protection against the possible harms of screening. Poor follow-up of those who test positive may occur, for example, when those with a positive (abnormal) FIT fail to undergo colonoscopy, the recommended next step in the screening process (Miles and others 2004).

Organized CRC Screening Worldwide The International Colorectal Cancer Screening Network (ICRCSN) is a consortium of organized initiatives delivering screening to their populations. In 2008, ICRCSN conducted a survey of full or pilot programs that fulfill at least four of the IARC criteria for an organized screening program (Benson and others 2012). At that time, 43 organized screening programs were identified, of which 35 programs had been collecting data for at least 12 months and were eligible for the survey. Of the 35 programs from 24 countries, 26 were full programs and nine were pilot programs. The majority of the programs were in Europe, with a few from North America, South America, and the Western Pacific. The majority (28) used stool-based tests as their primary screening test: 16 used gFOBT, nine used the FIT, and three used both tests. Wide variations were observed in the ability of the jurisdictions to report on performance indicators, such as the participation rate, the gFOBT or FIT positivity rate, and the cancer detection rate.

Performance of Organized Screening Programs In general, a period of at least 10 years is required to plan, pilot, and implement an organized CRC screening program (von Karsa and others 2010). The European Guidelines define key performance indicators for CRC screening, including participation, follow-up colonoscopy among those with a positive gFOBT, retention rates, cancer detection rates, and CRC mortality (von Karsa and others 2010). High performance in all of these measures is required in CRC screening programs. A few programs have published early results for participation. For example, Ontario launched its provincewide, organized screening program, ColonCancerCheck, in 2008. The program is based on gFOBT for those at average risk and colonoscopy for those at increased risk, defined by a family history of one or more first-degree relatives with the disease. The target population—men and women ages 50–74 years—is 3.4 million. Prior to launch of the program, gFOBT participation in 2003–04 was 15 percent; in 2010–11, gFOBT participation was 29.8 percent (Rabeneck and others 2014).

Some high-income Asian countries have begun to implement organized screening: Japan, the Republic of Korea, and Singapore. Currently, organized, population-based screening programs do not exist in the majority of LMICs. As MICs develop organized cancer screening programs, CRC screening is under consideration. There are or have been pilot studies of CRC screening conducted in several upper-middle-income countries and economies using gFOBT, including Thailand (Lampang province: http://www.iarc.fr/en/staffdirectory/display-staff.php?id=10114); Shanghai is embarking on a pilot study, as is Argentina (Manzur 2013). These pilot studies are important to lay the groundwork for national programs (Goss and others 2013).

Other countries offer opportunistic screening, largely restricted to the population covered by work-based health insurance. As a high-income economy, Taiwan, China, offers free screening under the national health insurance program (Ng and Wong 2013). Formal sector employees and/or government employees in much of Latin America and the Caribbean are covered for cancer screening. However, most MICs do not have organized screening programs.

International Efforts to Advance CRC Screening: IARC The vision of the Early Detection and Prevention (EDP) Section of the IARC is to serve as the major global resource for high-quality scientific and evidence-based information on cancer prevention and early detection interventions. The EDP Section evaluates and reports on interventions for early detection and prevention. The findings guide the development of public health policy, with a particular focus on cancer control in LMICs. The EDP Section's work catalyzes the implementation of CRC prevention and early detection programs that follow the principles of organized screening as outlined, to the extent feasible.

Experience from the European Union shows that a minimum period of 10 years is required to establish a population-based cancer screening program, with any impact taking even longer (Lee and others 2013). Examples of early detection and prevention work include the *European Guidelines for Quality Assurance in Colorectal Cancer Screening and Diagnosis* (Segnan, Patnick, and von Karsa 2010). In addition, a network of reference and training centers (European School of Screening Management) has been created that is developing and piloting training courses for planning, implementation, quality assurance, and evaluation of population-based cancer screening programs. The European School of Screening Management is intended to serve as a platform to connect and facilitate collaboration among relevant personnel from HICs and LMICs. Further, the EDP Section provides scientific and technical support to upper-middle-income countries, such as Albania and Belarus, to assist them in moving forward with population-based cancer screening programs.

Other International Organizations and Networks Promoting Screening The International Cancer Screening Network is a consortium of countries that have active population-based cancer screening programs and active efforts to evaluate and improve the processes and outcomes from cancer screening in practice. These programs can be national or subnational in scope, and established or pilot-based. Administered by the Applied Research Program of the U.S. National Cancer Institute, the consortium includes 33 countries and holds biennial meetings; specific activities are moved forward through working groups. Participation in the International Cancer Screening Network is open to any country that has initiated a population-based screening program.

The World Endoscopy Organization is a federation of national digestive endoscopy societies. Its mission includes the advancement of digestive endoscopy for the diagnosis and treatment of gastrointestinal diseases in underserved areas. The World Endoscopy Organization has an active CRC Screening Committee that holds annual meetings in the East Asia and Pacific region, Europe, and the United States, in conjunction with the major regional scientific meetings of gastroenterology societies. The meetings provide a forum to facilitate the presentation and discussion of new knowledge related to CRC screening and sharing of best practices across the world.

The International Digestive Cancer Alliance promotes the screening, early detection, and primary prevention of digestive cancers worldwide, including development of practice guidelines (http://www .worldgastroenterology.org/assets/downloads/en/pdf /guidelines/06_colorectal_cancer_screening.pdf). The International Digestive Cancer Alliance recommended staging the approach to screening, with respect to the choice of screening test, to the resources available in a given country (Winawer 2007).

Diagnosis

In HICs, persons with CRC can present in several ways:

- First, the cancer can be detected as a result of screening. When gFOBT, FIT, or FS is used as the initial screening test, colonoscopy is undertaken as a diagnostic test to evaluate those with an abnormal screening test. During the colonoscopy, polyps are removed and masses or other suspicious lesions are either removed or biopsied to establish a pathological diagnosis.
- Second, the cancer can be detected when an individual undergoes colonoscopy to evaluate large bowel symptoms, such as rectal bleeding, anemia, or a change in bowel habits.
- Third, some individuals may present as an emergency, such as a large bowel obstruction, in which case the cancer may be diagnosed at surgery without prior diagnostic evaluation.

Staging

When the cancer is diagnosed in nonemergency presentations, staging and complete visualization of the colon and rectum with colonoscopy are undertaken. Complete colonoscopy is also undertaken for the purpose of detecting synchronous cancers (present in 3–5 percent of cases); if not done prior to definitive treatment, it should be done within 6–12 months. Colonoscopy will also detect synchronous premalignant adenomas, which can be removed to reduce the risk of subsequent cancer. Barium enema, a radiological test, was used to diagnose CRC prior to the widespread availability of colonoscopy in HICs and may still be relevant in LMICs.

Clinical staging to determine the extent of disease focuses on imaging the liver and lungs, the two most common sites of spread. In HICs, computerized tomography is used to detect these distant metastases

(Leufkens and others 2011). Chest X-ray and abdominal ultrasound are less expensive alternative tests that can be used in lower-income settings.

Pathologic stage I refers to CRCs that are confined to the surface of the bowel. Stage II means the cancer has invaded through the muscle layer of the bowel wall. Stage III cancers involve the local lymph nodes. These stages are usually determined by examining the tumor pathologically after surgery. Stage IV cancers have spread (metastasized) into other organs.

Treatment

Surgery for Colon Cancer

The cornerstone of treatment is surgical resection. For early-stage cancers, surgery alone may cure the disease. For colon cancer, the preferred procedure is a hemicolectomy (resection of either the right or the left colon) with wide (> 5 cm) margins of normal colon. This procedure can typically be performed by a general surgeon. Where available, minimally invasive (laparoscopically-assisted) techniques have produced similar long-term results compared with an open procedure, but with shorter hospital stays and increased speed of recovery. Achieving these benefits requires an experienced surgeon and specialized instruments, however; even in HICs, the cost-effectiveness of this approach has been questioned. A minimum of 12 lymph nodes in the surgical specimen is required for adequate staging and is associated with better outcomes than a lesser dissection. In patients presenting with stage IV colon cancer where cure is not possible, if the primary (that is, the site of the original cancer) is not associated with symptoms and the metastatic disease (that is, the sites where the disease has spread) is anticipated to be controlled with chemotherapy, the primary tumor does not necessarily need to be resected.

Surgery for Rectal Cancer

Surgery for rectal cancer is much more complex. High-volume, specialized surgeons and centers have been associated with better outcomes: less likely to need an ostomy bag, lower rates of local recurrence, better overall survival.

- Mid-to-upper rectal tumors can be resected with a *low anterior resection*, which leaves the rectal sphincter intact, thereby avoiding colostomy.
- Lower-lying tumors, that is, those within 2–3 cm of the anal sphincter or levator muscles, require an *abdominal perineal resection* and creation of a permanent stoma requiring colostomy. Surgeon skill often determines how low a low anterior resection can be done.

- *Total meso-rectal excision*, the meticulous, sharp dissection of perirectal tissues with removal of the primary tumor and lymph nodes all in one piece, has been shown to decrease local relapse rates.
- To avoid a stoma, *transanal excision* of small, early-stage distal tumors with good prognostic features can be considered. (Good is defined here as T1N0, < 3 cm, < 30 percent circumference, not poorly differentiated, and no lymphovascular or perivascular invasion.)

Radiation

The availability of radiation therapy is most relevant for cancers of the rectum, as local recurrence is much more common than in colon cancer, because of the inability to obtain wide margins and the lack of a serosal barrier. Radiation therapy has improved local control for persons with stages II and III rectal cancer (Hoffe, Shridhar, and Biajioli 2010). Evidence suggests that compared with postoperative radiation, preoperative radiation is associated with improved surgical outcomes and disease-free survival (Sebag-Montefiore and others 2009). This decision depends on determining the stage of cancer preoperatively, which requires diagnostic services such as magnetic resonance imaging or specialized endorectal ultrasound capability. Where these are not available, postoperative delivery of radiation and chemotherapy still provides important benefits. In settings with access to radiation but difficulty obtaining or delivering chemotherapy, or where travel requirements preclude the 5.5 weeks of daily long-course radiotherapy, short-course radiotherapy may be a preferred option (Içli and others 2010).

Chemotherapy

Evidence-based practice guidelines recommend six months of adjuvant chemotherapy following surgery for persons with stage III colon cancer (Benson and others 2000) and stages II and III rectal cancer. FOLFOX (FOLinic acid [leucovorin], Fluorouracil, OXaliplatin) is the preferred regimen. If chemoradiotherapy is given for rectal cancer, only four months of chemotherapy are required. In addition to the cost of the drugs, however, systemic chemotherapy always requires the ability to monitor blood counts for safety and may require venous access devices.

Management of Metastatic Colorectal Cancer

Metastatic CRC is treated the same way, regardless of whether it started in the colon or rectum. Although metastatic disease is generally incurable, it is increasingly recognized that, where possible, in 10–20 percent of patients, aggressive resection of liver and lung metastases may lead to cure 20–30 percent of the time. Such surgery requires highly specialized training and centers, even in HICs. Alternatives to surgical resection, such as *radiofrequency ablation* and *stereotactic body radiotherapy*, can provide long-term control in these situations, but surgical resection is preferred where feasible. Perioperative chemotherapy with FOLFOX has been shown to improve disease-free survival in this setting. For the majority of patients with metastatic CRC, however, treatment is palliative, with an expected median survival with surgery alone of 6–12 months.

International Partnerships for CRC Care

As with CRC screening, international partnership arrangements can support diagnosis and treatment in LMICs. The American Society of Clinical Oncology (http://www.asco.org) established an International Affairs Committee in 2007 with a goal of reducing disparities in cancer care and maximizing chances of survival through the global exchange of oncologic knowledge. The National Comprehensive Cancer Network (http://www.nccn.org) provides translations of many of its guidelines into other languages, such as Chinese, Japanese, and Spanish, and has published local adaptations of guidelines, for example, for countries in the Middle East and North Africa. One National Comprehensive Cancer Network institution, the MD Anderson Cancer Center at the University of Texas, lists 28 sister institutions, as well as affiliates in at least 18 countries, 10 of these in LMICs (http://www.mdanderson.org/education-and -research/education-and-training/schools-and-programs /global-academic-programs/sister-institutions/index .html). Similar partnerships exist with other major cancer centers.

COST-EFFECTIVENESS OF CRC SCREENING AND TREATMENT

A systematic search of the literature on CRC screening and treatment was undertaken using PubMed from 2004 to 2013 to identify relevant articles for LMICs, as well as selected high-income Asian countries and economies that can help serve as regional models, principally Hong Kong SAR, China; the Republic of Korea; Singapore; and Taiwan, China. The parameters were medical subject heading terms (colorectal neoplasms, colonic neoplasms, rectal neoplasms, CRC, colon cancer, or rectal cancer); colonoscopy or sigmoidoscopy; and multiple terms related to economic evaluation, cost, cost analysis, and cost-effectiveness.

This search was supplemented by a nonsystematic search using the Internet for certain LMICs. For HICs,

a fairly recent publication, Greenberg and others (2010), was used. This is a systematic review of the cost-effectiveness literature for various cancers, primarily for industrialized countries, and has the advantage that all the costs have been standardized to those of a common year. For additional analyses, comparing the cost-effectiveness of CRC screening and treatment with screening and treatment for other cancers in LMICs, see chapter 16 in this volume (Horton and Gavreau 2015).

Screening

Cost-effectiveness studies for CRC screening in the United States, several European countries, and high-income Asian countries and economies (Hong Kong SAR, China; Korea; Singapore; and Taiwan, China) generally conclude that screening is cost-effective compared with no screening. The cost-effectiveness of several screening options can be considered. Guidelines generally recommend that screening should begin at age 50 years (except for those with strong family history of CRC), but it can stop at different ages (such as 70, 75, 80, or 85). Tests can be undertaken in combination, such as FS combined with a sensitive gFOBT. The use of an efficiency frontier for each individual country can help to identify the most appropriate screening strategy given the budget constraints (see figure 6.4 for the United States).

Studies in the United States

Cost-effectiveness studies in the United States generally have used one of a few large cancer microsimulation models. Comparative studies (for example, Pignone and others 2002 and Pignone, Russell, and Wagner 2005) suggest that results are sensitive to the parameters used, particularly cost. The models also entail different assumptions about disease progression that also affect relative test performance (Pignone, Russell, and Wagner 2005). Since the review by Pignone and others (2002), three microsimulation models for CRC have become part of the U.S. National Cancer Institute consortium for Cancer Intervention and Surveillance Modeling Network (CISNET), a consortium of National Cancer Institute-sponsored investigators that use statistical modeling to improve the understanding of cancer control interventions in prevention, screening, and treatment, and their effects on population trends in incidence and mortality. These models can be used to guide public health research and priorities.

Figure 6.4 shows the results for cost-effectiveness analysis from one CISNET model, the Microsimulation Screening Analysis model from Erasmus University Medical Center, for eight CRC screening strategies beginning at age 50 years. Figure 6.4 is a modification of

Figure 6.4 Discounted Costs and Discounted Life Years Gained for Eight Colorectal Cancer Screening Strategies and the Efficient Frontier

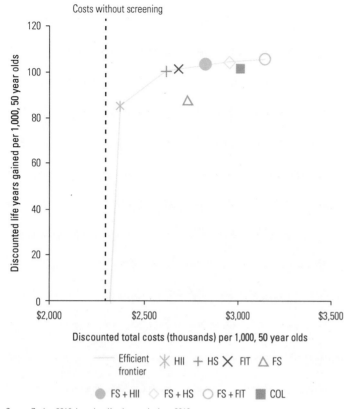

Source: Zauber 2010, based on Knudsen and others 2010.
Note: COL = colonoscopy; FIT = fecal immunochemical test; FS = flexible sigmoidoscopy; HII = Hemoccult II (fecal occult blood test, FOBT); HS = Hemoccult Sensa (FOBT). This analysis assumes 100 percent adherence with each strategy.

a larger analysis as given by Knudsen and others (2010), which assumed that subjects were 100 percent adherent to screening tests and subsequent diagnostic or treatment for those with positive tests or cancer diagnosis. Gains in life years are plotted on the y-axis and total costs are plotted on the x-axis. Each possible intervention strategy is represented by a point. The higher the point is, the more effective is the screening strategy; the further to the right the point is, the more expensive is the screening strategy (Marks 2002).

Cost-effectiveness analysis does not select which strategy is economically preferred overall, but only which strategy is the most effective in terms of life years gained for a given level of desired (or possible) expenditure. The eight CRC screening strategies are ranked in order of the procedure, with the least life years gained relative to no screening (Knudsen and others 2010). The strategies are then compared incrementally by ordering of the life years gained relative to the costs of each screening strategy. Those strategies that have the most life years gained for a given level of cost are considered

to be on the efficiency frontier. In this example, the lowest-cost option of those options on the frontier is the less sensitive gFOBT (Hemoccult II). However, if the budget available for testing increases, then a more sensitive gFOBT (Hemoccult Sensa) or FIT is the next best choice for cost relative to life years gained with screening. The next choice would be FS with some type of fecal occult blood test (FOBT). Colonoscopy lies just below the efficient frontier, with the rankings for life years gained relative to costs similar to those of FS with gFOBT or FIT. The rankings using two other models (the SimCRC model from University of Minnesota and Massachusetts General Hospital, and the CRC-SPIN model from Group Health Research Institute; see http://cisnet.cancer.gov/profiles/) were broadly similar, although the absolute cost per life year gained differed between models. All of the strategies had average costs per life year gained (compared with no screening) well within the threshold considered cost-effective in the United States (below US$50,000 per life year gained).

Taken together, the results from the U.S. analyses using simulation models suggest the following:

- Screening is cost-effective; since compliance is not 100 percent, encouraging screening by any of a small group of strategies will save life years.
- Where the total budget available is limited, the lowest-cost testing strategy involves gFOBT.
- The differences in the cost-effectiveness of some strategies are modest and susceptible to variation in assumptions.
- Knowledge of details of disease progression is limited, for example, how untreated adenomas progress to cancer or how this progression varies by individual characteristics such as age, gender, and family history. Different assumptions regarding disease progression affect the results of the simulation model.

The evidence base for different screening methods continues to evolve. FS and colonoscopy can be performed by appropriately trained nonphysicians, including nurses (Maule 1994; Wallace and others 1999). Newer generations of chemotherapy agents increase life expectancy modestly, but they considerably increase treatment costs; accordingly, most screening methods (although not colonoscopy by a narrow margin) remain cost-saving (Lansdorp-Vogelaar and others 2009).

European Studies
The European studies identified by the systematic review by Pignone and others (2002) (two studies of gFOBT and one of FS, in Denmark, Norway, and the United Kingdom) all supported the conclusion that

screening is cost-effective compared with no screening, and the cost per life year saved was lower than in the United States because of the higher overall medical costs in the United States (Gyrd-Hansen, Søgaard, and Kronborg 1998; Norum 1998; Whynes and others 1998).

Studies in High-Income Economies in Asia

Table 6.1 summarizes cost-effectiveness results for four studies of Asian economies, with the standardized model for the United States from Pignone, Russell, and Wagner (2005) for comparison. The Asian economies are Hong Kong SAR, China; the Republic of Korea; Singapore; and Taiwan, China. Observations from these results include the following:

- Screening in the four Asian economies is cost-effective, although the simpler models used in some studies may underestimate costs.

- Relative costs of procedures such as colonoscopy/FS and colonoscopy/gFOBT vary by country, which is likely to affect rankings.
- For the Republic of Korea, for example, it has been argued that colonoscopy reimbursement rates are artificially low and do not reflect cost (Park, Yun, and Kwon 2005). This is likely to affect the relative ranking of strategies for that country.

These four Asian economies do not all have published cost-effectiveness thresholds used for public decision making. However, from the WHO Commission on Health (WHO 2001), health interventions costing up to three times per capita gross domestic product per disability-adjusted life year saved should be considered. By this criterion, all the methods of CRC screening considered here (gFOBT, FS, and colonoscopy) would be acceptable in these four economies. Another study for

Table 6.1 Selected Costs and Cost-Effectiveness of Screening, Per Capita GDP, and Colorectal Cancer Incidence in Four High-Income Asian Economies Compared with the United States

Item cost or value (US$)	United States 2005[a]	Korea, Rep. 2004[b]	Taiwan, China 2004[c]	Hong Kong SAR, China 2003[d]	Singapore 2004[e]
gFOBT	10	1.91	0.60	4	5.59
Colonoscopy (diagnostic)	625	43.80	66.20	450	368.72
Colonoscopy (polyp removal)	900	—	—	830	446.93
Sigmoidoscopy	200	22.18	35.30	244	134.08
Treat CRC, local	24,000	4,291.67	3,117.60	16,552	11,173.18
Treat CRC, regional	31,000	—	7,705.90	27,321	19,553.07
Treat CRC, distant	40,000	8,583.33	7,647.10	71,751	—
Colon perforation	24,000	2,500	1,617.60	10,790	4,863.69
Cost-effectiveness versus no screening US$/LYS	gFOBT 9,676 COL 21,000 (median of 5 models, standardized assumptions)	COL (5 years) 1,142; others dominated	gFOBT 70 FS 594 COL 407	gFOBT 6,222 FS 8,044 COL 7,211	gFOBT 91 FS 190 COL 225
Per capita GDP[f]	46,760	19,028	17,461	31,426	34,466
CRC incidence[g]/100,000 (age-standardized to world population)	34.1 men 25.0 women	46.9 men 25.6 women	40.2 men 29.7 women (Taiwan, China)	50.1 (crude, men and women combined)	34.1 men 25.0 women

Note: COL = colonoscopy; CRC = colorectal cancer; FS = flexible sigmoidoscopy; GDP = gross domestic product; gFOBT = guaiac fecal occult blood test; LYS = life years saved; — = not available.
a. Pignone, Russell, and Wagner 2005.
b. Park, Yun, and Kwon 2005.
c. Wu and others 2006.
d. Tsoi and others 2008.
e. Wong, Leong, and Leong 2004.
f. World Bank 2013, except Taiwan, China, which is http://www.indexmundi.com.
g. Bray and others 2013, except Hong Kong SAR, China, which is Tsoi and others 2008.

Hong Kong SAR, China, for women only (Woo, Kim, and Leung 2007), concluded that CRC screening had higher costs than for men per disability-adjusted life year saved and would not be cost-effective (CRC incidence rates in women are lower than in men).

Studies in LMICs

Two global cost-effectiveness models report estimates of cost-effectiveness of interventions for various world regions. Ginsberg and others (2010) conclude that expanding treatment in low-income countries is a higher priority than screening. Ginsberg and others (2012) come to a similar conclusion when focusing on Southeast Asia and Sub-Saharan Africa, and they conclude that screening colonoscopy is cost-effective in Sub-Saharan Africa. However, the feasibility of implementing this approach in light of resource availability and health system infrastructure limitations was not addressed.

A systematic search did not identify other studies of the cost-effectiveness of screening in LMICs. One other study was found from an unsystematic search using the Internet for the Islamic Republic of Iran (Barouni and others 2012). From the results presented, it is possible to conclude that colonoscopy every 10 years is cost-effective, but not very cost-effective, in the Islamic Republic of Iran, but that gFOBT screening is not cost-effective. There are problems with the calculation of the incremental cost-effectiveness ratios in this study, but enough information is given to permit the reader to recalculate them.

We anticipate that CRC screening would be equally cost-effective in urban areas of other upper-middle-income countries where incidence rates approach levels similar to those in HICs (30 or more per 100,000 in men, age-standardized rates). Lambert, Sauvaget, and Sankaranarayanan (2009, 255) conclude that population screening for CRC is not the highest priority in most LMICs, but that it deserves to be developed "in limited regions of large emerging countries where there is a shift to Western lifestyle and an aging population," and they point to Mumbai; Hong Kong SAR, China; and São Paulo as examples.

Treatment

No literature on the cost-effectiveness of treatment for CRC was found for LMICs. Chapter 16 summarizes the evidence of cost-effectiveness of treatment in HICs, making the assumption that treatments that are "very cost-effective" in HICs are the first candidates for consideration in MICs, while treatments that are "not cost-effective" in HICs are unlikely to

be cost-effective in LMICs. This is likely to be a better guide if relative costs and "standard care"—the alternative to which a particular treatment is compared—are reasonably similar.

RECOMMENDATIONS

Country income level does not have to dictate the availability of screening, diagnosis, and treatment. Countries can help overcome resource constraints by accessing technical assistance from the IARC and international networks, or from partnerships with cancer centers or cancer agencies in other countries. Local champions are essential for moving CRC screening and treatment forward as a priority.

Table 6.2 summarizes the authors' recommendations on how screening and diagnosis for CRC might be implemented in four different resource environments: LICs, rural areas of MICs, urban areas of MICs, and HICs. These correspond approximately to the basic, limited, enhanced, and maximal resource environments for a similar exercise undertaken for breast cancer by the Global Breast Health Initiative and discussed in chapter 3. Recommendations for the treatment of CRC in these resource environments are found in online annex 6B (tables 6B.1 through 6B.5). These recommendations provide initial guidance only and need to be validated by a larger international expert group.

Low-Income Countries

In LICs, the incidence of CRC is relatively low; other diseases—including other cancers—are a higher priority for screening and treatment. Laying the foundation for cancer screening and treatment is important. This process includes investing in public health and primary health care where screening is initiated, in hospital systems, and in a cancer registry. Investments in health require medical personnel, as well as good systems for monitoring and evaluation and quality control. Smaller countries lacking specific resources, such as radiation facilities and specialized laboratories, may need to rely on other countries in the same region.

Even in LICs, surgery for colon cancer at a good district hospital is possible to save lives and improve the quality of remaining life. If colonoscopy is unavailable as a diagnostic tool, barium enema may be an option. Radiation therapy is available only in limited volumes, if at all, and laboratory services required for chemotherapy are not likely to be available. Pain management for late-stage cancers is an ethical imperative, since the ability to treat effectively is extremely limited.

Table 6.2 Proposed Strategies for Colorectal Cancer Screening and Diagnosis, by Country Resource Level

Level of resources	General	Detection and diagnosis
Basic	• Build capacity: human, physical (for example, radiation capacity), cancer registry	• Barium enema if colonoscopy not available; in emergency situations, may be diagnosed at surgery
Limited	• Establish capacity for colonoscopy (needed for diagnosis) • Engage in partnership arrangements with cancer centers to build capacity • Establish national guidelines • Build quality assurance for lab testing	• Opportunistic screening for those covered by health insurance • Diagnostic colonoscopy (or barium enema) for those with symptoms
Enhanced	• Join international screening networks • Provide support to less-well-resourced countries in region	• Establish organized screening in high-incidence cities/regions starting at age 50 years in persons at average risk: use annual or biennial sensitive gFOBT or FIT; FS (see text for discussion of interval); or colonoscopy every 10 years • Considerable infrastructure is required to support organized screening, including invitations, recalls, reminders, tracking screening test results, ensuring follow-up of those with an abnormal screening test, etc.
Maximal		• National (or jurisdiction-wide) organized screening: starting at age 50 years in persons at average risk: use annual or biennial sensitive gFOBT or FIT; FS (see text for discussion of interval); or colonoscopy every 10 years; in those at increased risk because of family history, consider colonoscopy

Note: Since no international consensus-setting exercise has occurred, this categorization represents a basis for further discussion and work and not a definitive analysis. The basic resource level is assumed to correspond to low-income countries (limited or no access to radiation and likely insufficient support for blood chemistry to undertake chemotherapy). The limited resource level corresponds to rural areas of middle-income countries, where distances to radiation and chemotherapy resources make their use in treatment difficult. In urban areas of middle-income countries (enhanced level), radiation therapy is available, as are many chemotherapy drugs no longer under patent. The maximal level corresponds to resource availability in high-income countries. See chapter 16 in this volume for more detailed discussion of resource levels. The recommendations are cumulative: any intervention that is feasible at a lower resource level is also an option at higher resource levels. Blank cells indicate that no additional options of a particular type of treatment are available at the particular resource level considered. FIT = fecal immunochemical test; FS = flexible sigmoidoscopy; gFOBT = guaiac fecal occult blood test.

Middle-Income Countries

In MICs, there is an increase (more pronounced initially in urban areas) in CRC incidence and the ability to intervene. Opportunistic screening increases for those covered by health insurance. Those countries that have already begun organized screening for other cancers (including countries in Latin America and the Caribbean and upper-middle-income Asia; see chapter 12 in this volume [Sullivan, Sullivan, and Ginsburg 2015]) may decide to implement screening initially as a pilot study in selected urban regions. Other regions that are beginning organized screening for other cancers may decide to incorporate screening as well, for example, by developing programs in cities in Asia.

Priority countries are those where age-standardized CRC incidence rates in men are more than 30 per 100,000 (for example, Hungary, Serbia, and other countries in Eastern Europe), in addition to those economies with existing pilot programs, such as Argentina. Countries where CRC incidence rates in men approach 20 per 100,000 may need to begin planning (for example, countries such as Cuba, Lebanon, and Malaysia). Data are not available using GLOBOCAN for individual cities, but similar CRC incidence thresholds could be used to consider when to begin to take action on CRC screening.

For CRC screening, gFOBT is inexpensive; however, additional investments are needed to implement all the components of organized screening. MICs initiating organized CRC screening may be advised to use FIT rather than gFOBT; doing so may become more attractive if a larger demand for such tests results in a decrease in the unit costs of the kits.

MICs also have more resources for treatment and can extend this to a larger proportion of the population. As cancers are detected earlier, the goal of treatment shifts from palliation to cure. MICs can be active participants in international networks and local centers of excellence and can provide support for other countries in their region.

High-Income Countries

In HICs, cost-effectiveness considerations suggest that FIT, FS accompanied by a sensitive gFOBT or FIT, or colonoscopy are options for screening. The Republic of Korea and Singapore, which started their screening programs more recently than European countries, have opted to use FIT. Adherence to screening varies; although each test has its advocates, the best test is the one that gets done, and done well. A wider range of treatment options is feasible in these countries, which typically have higher cost-effectiveness thresholds.

CONCLUSIONS

The burden of CRC is increasing worldwide. There is an unparalleled opportunity for prevention and early detection of CRC, based on our knowledge of colorectal carcinogenesis. The implementation of effective screening tests, both stool-based (gFOBT, FIT) and endoscopic (FS, colonoscopy), coupled with advances in treatment (colonoscopic polypectomy, surgery, radiation therapy, and chemotherapy) are cost-effective approaches.

Since screening is a process, it is most effective when delivered within an organized program, requiring infrastructure and resources to ensure the benefits while minimizing the harms. CRC screening and treatment are becoming priorities in an increasing number of countries, as health resources are enhanced and changes in lifestyles and risk factors lead to a rise in incidence. Research on the cost-effectiveness of options in these countries is needed, ideally adapting available, well-constructed models to these environments. The development of regional CRC screening guidelines would be helpful; the resource-based recommendations outlined in this chapter may be useful in that process.

NOTES

World Bank Income Classifications as of July 2014 are as follows based on estimates of gross national income (GNI) per capita for 2013:

- Low-income countries (LICs) = US$1,045 or less
- Middle-income countries (MICs) are subdivided:
  a) lower-middle-income = US$1,046–US$4,125
  b) upper-middle-income(UMICs)=US$4,126–US$12,745
- High-income countries (HICs) = US$12,746 or more.

1. Maps and figures in this chapter are based on incidence and mortality estimates for ages 0–69, consistent with reporting in all DCP3 volumes. Global cancer statistics are estimates for 2012 and have been provided by the International Agency for Research on Cancer from its GLOBOCAN 2012 database. Observable population-based data were derived from *Cancer Incidence in Five Continents, 10th edition* and for trends over time from *CI5 Plus* (http://ci5.iarc.fr/CI5plus/Default.aspx). The discussion of burden, including risk factors, however, includes all ages unless otherwise noted. Interventions also apply to all age groups, except where age ranges or cutoffs are specified.

REFERENCES

Ahlquist, D. A., H. Zou, M. Domanico, D. W. Mahoney, T. C. Yab, and others. 2012. "Next-Generation Stool DNA Test Accurately Detects Colorectal Cancer and Large Adenomas." *Gastroenterology* 142: 248–56.

Anderson, B. O., J. Lipscomb, R. H. Murillo, and D. B. Thomas. "Breast Cancer." In *Disease Control Priorities* (third edition): Volume 3, *Cancer*, edited by H. Gelband, P. Jha, R. Sankaranarayanan, and S. Horton. Washington, DC: World Bank.

Atkin, W. S., R. Edwards, I. Kralj-Hans, K. Wooldrage, A. R. Hart, and others. 2010. "Once-Only Flexible Sigmoidoscopy Screening in Prevention of Colorectal Cancer: A Multicentre Randomised Controlled Trial." *The Lancet* 375 (9726): 1624–33.

Barouni, M., M. H. Larizadeh, A. Sabermahani, and H. Ghaderi. 2012. "Markov's Modeling for Screening Strategies for Colorectal Cancer." *Asia Pacific Journal of Cancer Prevention* 13: 5125–29.

Baxter, N. N., M. A. Goldwasser, L. F. Paszat, R. Saskin, D. R. Urbach, and others. 2009. "Association of Colonoscopy and Death from Colorectal Cancer: A Population-Based, Case-Control Study." *Annals of Internal Medicine* 150: 1–8.

Benson, V. S., W. S. Atkin, J. Green, M. R. Nadel, J. Patnick, and others. 2012. "Toward Standardizing and Reporting Colorectal Cancer Screening Indicators on an International Level: The International Colorectal Cancer Screening Network." *International Journal of Cancer* 130 (12): 2961–73.

Benson, A. B., M. A. Choti, A. M. Cohen, J. H. Doroshow, C. Fuchs, and others. 2000. "NCCN Practice Guidelines for Colorectal Cancer." *Oncology* (Williston Park) 14: 203–12.

Bray, F., J. S. Ren, E. Masuyer, and J. Ferlay. 2013. "Estimates of Global Cancer Prevalence for 27 Sites in the Adult Population in 2008." *International Journal of Cancer* 132: 1133–45.

Brenner, H., J. Change-Claude, C. M. Seiler, A. Rickert, and M. Hoffmeister. 2011. "Protection from Colorectal Cancer after Colonoscopy: A Population-Based, Case-Control Study." *Annals of Internal Medicine* 154: 22–30.

Bressler, B., L. F. Paszat, Z. Chen, D. M. Rothwell, C. Vinden, and others. 2007. "Rates of New or Missed Colorectal Cancers after Colonoscopy and Their Risk Factors: A Population Based Analysis." *Gastroenterology* 132: 96–102.

Butterworth, A. S., J. P. T. Higgins, and P. Pharoah. 2006. "Relative and Absolute Risk of Colorectal Cancer for Individuals with a Family History: A Meta-Analysis." *European Journal of Cancer* 42: 216–27.

Chan, A. T., and E. L. Giovannucci. 2010. "Primary Prevention of Colorectal Cancer." *Gastroenterology* 138 (6): 2029–43.

Edwards, B. K., E. Ward, B. A. Kohler, C. Eheman, A. G. Zauber, and others. 2010. "Annual Report to the Nation on the Status of Cancer, 1975–2006, Featuring Colorectal Cancer Trends and Impact of Interventions (Risk Factors, Screening, and Treatment) to Reduce Future Rates." *Cancer* 116 (3): 544–73.

Elmunzer, B. J., R. A. Hayward, P. S. Schoenfeld, S. D. Saini, A. Deshpande, and others. 2012. "Effect of Flexible Sigmoidoscopy-Based Screening on Incidence and Mortality of Colorectal Cancer: A Systematic Review and Meta-Analysis of Randomized Controlled Trials." *PLOS Medicine* 9 (12): 1–9.

Ferlay J., I. Soerjomataram, M. Ervik, R. Dikshit, S. Eser, and others. 2013. *GLOBOCAN 2012 V1.0, Cancer Incidence and Mortality Worldwide: IARC Cancerbase No. 11* [Internet]. Lyon, France: International Agency for Research on Cancer. http://globocan.iarc.fr.

Ginsberg, G. M., J. A. Lauer, S. Zelle, S. Baeten, and R. Baltussen. 2012. "Cost Effectiveness of Strategies to Combat Breast, Cervical, and Colorectal Cancer in Sub-Saharan Africa and South East Asia: Mathematical Modeling Study." *British Medical Journal* 344: E614.

Ginsberg, G. M., S. S. Lim, J. A. Lauer, B. P. Johns, and C. R. Sepulveda. 2010. "Prevention, Screening and Treatment of Colorectal Cancer: A Global and Regional Generalized Cost-Effectiveness Analysis." *Cost Effectiveness and Resource Allocation* 8: 2–17.

Goss, P. E., B. L. Lee, R. Bidovinac-Cmjevic, K. Strasser-Weippl, Y. Chavani-Guerra, and others. 2013. "Planning Cancer Control in Latin America and the Caribbean." *The Lancet Oncology* 14: 391–436.

Greenberg, D., C. Earle, C. H. Fang, A. Eldar-Lissai, and P. J. Neumann. 2010. "When Is Cancer Care Cost-Effective? A Systematic Overview of Cost-Utility Analyses in Oncology." *Journal of the National Cancer Institute* 102: 82–88.

Gyrd-Hansen, D., J. Søgaard, and O. Kronborg. 1998. "Colorectal Cancer Screening: Efficiency and Effectiveness." *Health Economics* 7: 9–20.

Hardcastle, J. D., J. O. Chamberlain, M. H. Robinson, S. M. Moss, S. S. Amar, and others. 1996. "Randomised Controlled Trial of Faecal-Occult-Blood Screening for Colorectal Cancer." *The Lancet* 348: 1472–77.

Hoffe, S. E., R. Shridhar, and M. C. Biajioli. 2010. "Radiation Therapy for Rectal Cancer: Current Status and Future Directions." *Cancer Control* 17: 25–34.

IARC (International Agency for Research on Cancer). 2010. Handbook of Cancer Prevention, vol. 10, *Cervix Cancer Screening*. Lyon, France: IARC Press.

Içli, F., H. Akbulut, S. Bazarbashi, M. A. Kuzu, M. K. Mallath, and others. 2010. "Modification and Implementation of NCCN Guidelines on Colon Cancer in the Middle East and North Africa Region." *Journal of the National Comprehensive Cancer Network* 8 (Suppl. 3): S22–25.

Imperiale, T. F., D. F. Ransohoff, S. H. Itzkowitz, T. R. Levin, P. Lavin, and others. 2014. "Multitarget Stool DNA Testing for Colorectal-Cancer Screening." *New England Journal of Medicine* 370 (14): 1287–97.

Imperiale, T. F., D. F. Ransohoff, S. H. Itzkowitz, B. A. Turnbull, and M. E. Ross. 2004. "Fecal DNA versus Fecal Occult Blood for Colorectal-Cancer Screening in an Average-Risk Population." *New England Journal of Medicine* 351 (26): 2704–14.

Johnson, C. D., M. H. Chen, A. Y. Tolendano, J. P. Heiken, A. Dachman, and others. 2008. "Accuracy of CT Colonography for Detection of Large Adenomas and Cancers." *New England Journal of Medicine* 359: 1207–17.

Johnson, C. M., C. Wei, J. E. Ensor, D. J. Smolenski, C. I. Amos, and others. 2013. "Meta-Analysis of Colorectal Cancer Risk Factors." *Cancer Causes and Control* 24: 1207–22.

Knudsen, A. B., I. Lansdorp-Vogelaar, C. M. Rutter, J. E. Savarino, M. Van Ballegooijen, and others. 2010. "Cost-Effectiveness of Computed Tomographic Colonography Screening for Colorectal Cancer in the Medicare Population." *Journal of the National Cancer Institute* 102: 1238–52.

Kronborg, O., C. Fenger, J. Olsen, O. D. Jorgensen, and O. Sondergaard. 1996. "Randomised Study of Screening for Colorectal Cancer with Faecal-Occult-Blood Test." *The Lancet* 348: 1467–71.

Lambert, R., C. Sauvaget, and R. Sankaranarayanan. 2009. "Mass Screening for Colorectal Cancer Is Not Justified in Most Developing Countries." *International Journal of Circulation* 125: 253–56.

Lansdorp-Vogelaar, I., M. Van Ballegooijen, A. G. Zauber, J. D. F. Habbemaand, and E. J. Kuipers. 2009. "Effect of Rising Chemotherapy Costs on the Cost Savings of Colorectal Cancer Screening." *Journal of the National Cancer Institute* 101: 1412–22.

Lee, S. J., W. J. Boscardin, I. Stijacic-Cenzer, J. Conell-Price, S. O'Brien, and others. 2013. "Time Lag to Benefit after Screening for Breast and Colorectal Cancer: Meta-Analysis of Survival Data from the United States, Sweden, United Kingdom, and Denmark." *British Medical Journal* 346: E8441.

Leufkens, A. M., M. A. Van Den Bosch, M. S. Van Leeuwen, and P. D. Siersema. 2011. "Diagnostic Accuracy of Computed Tomography for Colon Cancer Staging: A Systematic Review." *Scandinavian Journal of Gastroenterology* 46 (7–8): 887–94. doi:10.3109/00365521.2011.574732.

Levin, B., D. A. Lieberman, B. McFarland, K. S. Andrews, D. Brooks, and others. 2008. "Screening and Surveillance for the Early Detection of Colorectal Cancer and Adenomatous Polyps, 2008: A Joint Guideline from the American Cancer Society, the U.S. Multi-Society Task Force on Colorectal Cancer, and the American College of Radiology." *Gastroenterology* 134 (5): 1570–95.

Lieberman, D. A., D. K. Rex, S. J. Winawer, F. M. Giardiello, D. A. Johnson, and others. 2012. "United States Multi-Society Task Force on Colorectal Cancer Guidelines for Colonoscopy Surveillance after Screening and Polypectomy: A Consensus Update by the US Multi-Society Task Force on Colorectal Cancer." *Gastroenterology* 143 (3): 844–57. doi:10.1053/J.Gastro.2012.06.001.

Mandel, J. S., J. H. Bond, T. R. Church, D. C. Snover, G. M. Bradley, and others. 1993. "Reducing Mortality from Colorectal Cancer by Screening for Fecal Occult Blood.

Minnesota Colon Cancer Control Study." *New England Journal of Medicine* 328: 1365–71.

Manzur, J. 2013. "Argentinean Perspectives on Cancer Control in Latin America." *The Lancet Oncology* 14: 387–88.

Marks, D. H. 2002. "Visualizing Cost-Effectiveness Analysis." *Journal of the American Medical Association* 287: 2428–29.

Maule, W. F. 1994. "Screening for Colorectal Cancer by Nurse Endoscopists." *New England Journal of* Medicine 330: 183–87.

Miles, A., J. Cockburn, R. A. Smith, and J. Wardle. 2004. "A Perspective from Countries Using Organized Screening Programs." *Cancer* 101: 1201–13.

Ng, S. C., and S. H. Wong. 2013. "Colorectal Cancer Screening in Asia." *British Medical Bulletin* 105: 29–42.

Norum, J. 1998. "Prevention of Colorectal Cancer: A Cost-Effectiveness Approach to a Screening Model Employing Sigmoidoscopy." *Annals of Oncology* 9: 613–18.

Park, S. M., Y. H. Yun, and S. Kwon. 2005. "Feasible Economic Strategies to Improve Screening Compliance for Colorectal Cancer in Korea." *World Journal of Gastroenterology* 11 (11): 1587–93.

Pickhardt, P. J., J. R. Choi, I. Hwang, J. L. Butler, M. A. Puckett, and others. 2003. "Computed Tomographic Virtual Colonoscopy to Screen for Colorectal Neoplasia in Asymptomatic Adults." *New England Journal of Medicine* 349: 2191–200.

Pignone, M., L. Russell, and J. Wagner, eds. 2005. *Economic Models of Colorectal Cancer Screening in Average-Risk Adults.* Washington, DC: National Academies Press.

Pignone, M., S. Saha, R. Hoerger, and J. Mandelblatt. 2002. "Cost-Effectiveness Analyses of Colorectal Cancer Screening: A Systematic Review for the U.S. Preventive Services Task Force." *Annals of Internal Medicine* 137 (2): 96–104.

Quintero, E., A. Castells, L. Bujanda, J. Cubiella, D. Salas, and others. 2012. "Colonoscopy versus Fecal Immunochemical Testing in Colorectal-Cancer Screening." *New England Journal of Medicine* 366: 697–706.

Rabeneck, L., and L. F. Paszat. 2010. "Circumstances in Which Colonoscopy Misses Cancer." *Frontline Gastroenterology* 1: 52–58.

Rabeneck, L., J. M. Tinmouth, L. F. Paszat, N. N. Baxter, L. D. Marrett, and others. 2014. "Ontario's Coloncancercheck: Results from Canada's First Province-Wide Colorectal Cancer Screening Program." *Cancer, Epidemiology, Biomarkers, and Prevention* 23: 508–15.

Schoen, R. E., P. F. Pinsky, J. L. Weissfeld, L. A. Yokochi, T. Church, and others. 2012. "Colorectal-Cancer Incidence and Mortality with Screening Flexible Sigmoidoscopy." *New England Journal of Medicine* 366: 2345–57.

Sebag-Montefiore, D., R. J. Stephens, R. Steele, J. Monson, R. Grieve, and others. 2009. "Preoperative Radiotherapy versus Selective Postoperative Chemoradiotherapy in Patients with Rectal Cancer (MRC CR07 and NCIC-CTG C016): A Multicentre, Randomised Trial." *The Lancet* 373: 811–20.

Segnan, N., P. Armaroli, L. Bonelli, M. Risio, S. Sciallero, and others. 2011. "Once-Only Sigmoidoscopy in Colorectal Cancer Screening: Follow-Up Findings of the Italian Randomized Controlled Trial—SCORE." *Journal of the National Cancer Institute* 103 (17): 1310–22.

Segnan, N., J. Patnick, and L. von Karsa, eds. 2010. *European Guidelines for Quality Assurance in Colorectal Cancer Screening and Diagnosis.* Luxembourg: Publications Office of the European Union.

Sullivan, T., R. Sullivan, and O. M. Ginsburg. "Screening for Cancer: Considerations in Low- and Middle-Income Countries." In *Disease Control Priorities* (third edition): Volume 3, *Cancer*, edited by H. Gelband, P. Jha, R. Sankaranarayanan, and S. Horton. Washington, DC: World Bank.

Towler, B., L. Irwig, P. Glasziou, J. Kewenter, D. Weller, and others. 1998. "A Systematic Review of the Effects of Screening for Colorectal Cancer Using the Faecal Occult Blood Test, Hemoccult." *British Medical Journal* 317 (7158): 559–65.

Tsoi, K. K. F., S. S. M. Ng, M. C. M. Leung, and J. J. Y. Sung. 2008. "Cost-Effectiveness Analysis on Screening for Colorectal Neoplasm and Management of Colorectal Cancer in Asia." *Alimentary Pharmacology and Therapeutics* 28: 353–63.

USPSTF (U.S. Preventive Services Task Force). 2008. "Screening for Colorectal Cancer: U.S. Preventive Services Task Force Recommendation Statement." *Annals of Internal Medicine* 149: 627–37.

van Rossum, L. G., A. F. Van Rijn, R. J. Laheij, M. G. Van Oijen, P. Fockens, and others. 2008. "Random Comparison of Guaiac and Immunochemical Fecal Occult Blood Tests for Colorectal Cancer in a Screening Population." *Gastroenterology* 135: 82–90.

von Karsa, L., T. A. Lignini, J. Patnick, R. Lambert, and C. Sauvaget. 2010. "The Dimensions of the CRC Problem." *Best Practice & Research Clinical Gastroenterology* 24: 381–96.

Wallace, M. B., J. A. Kemp, F. Meyer, K. Horton, A. Reffel, and others. 1999. "Screening for Colorectal Cancer with Flexible Sigmoidoscopy by Nonphysician Endoscopists." *American Journal of Medicine* 107: 214–28.

WHO (World Health Organization). 2001. *Macroeconomics and Health: Investing in Health for Economic Development.* Geneva: WHO.

Whynes, D. K., A. R. Neilson, A. R. Walker, and J. D. Hardcastle. 1998. "Faecal Occult Blood Screening for Colorectal Cancer: Is It Cost-Effective?" *Health Economics* 7: 21–29.

Winawer, S. J. 2007. "Colorectal Cancer Screening." *Best Practice & Research Clinical Gastroenterology* 21 (6): 1031–48.

Winawer, S. J., R. H. Fletcher, L. Miller, F. Godlee, M. H. Stolar, and others. 1997. "Colorectal Cancer Screening: Clinical Guidelines and Rationale." *Gastroenterology* 112: 594–642.

Winawer, S. J., A. G. Zauber, M. N. Ho, M. J. O'Brien, L. S. Gottlieb, and others. 1993. "Prevention of Colorectal Cancer by Colonoscopic Polypectomy." *New England Journal of Medicine* 329 (27): 1977–81.

Wong, S. S., A. P. K. Leong, and T. Z. Leong. 2004. "Cost-Effectiveness Analysis of Colorectal Cancer Screening Strategies in Singapore: A Dynamic Decision Analytic

Approach." *Studies in Health Technology Information* 107 (Pt 1): 104–10.

Woo, P. P. S., J. J. Kim, and G. M. Leung. 2007. "What Is the Most Cost-Effective Population-Based Cancer Screening Program for Chinese Women?" *Journal of Clinical Oncology* 25: 617–24.

World Bank. 2013. World Databank. http://databank .worldbank.org/data/home.aspx.

Wu, G. H.-M., Y.-M. Wang, A. M.-F. Yen, J.-M. Wong, H.-C. Lai, and others. 2006. "Cost-Effectiveness Analysis of Colorectal Cancer Screening with Stool DNA Testing in Intermediate-Incidence Countries." *BMC Cancer* 6: 136–48.

Zauber, A. G. 2010. "Cost-Effectiveness of Colonoscopy." *Gastroenterology Clinics of North America* 20: 751–70.

Zauber, A. G., S. J. Winawer, M. J. O'Brien, I. Lansdorp-Vogelaar, M. Van Ballegooijen, and others. 2012. "Colonoscopic Polypectomy and Long-Term Prevention of Colorectal-Cancer Deaths." *New England Journal of Medicine* 366: 687–96.

Treating Childhood Cancer in Low- and Middle-Income Countries

Sumit Gupta, Scott C. Howard, Stephen P. Hunger,
Federico G. Antillon, Monika L. Metzger, Trijn Israels,
Mhamed Harif, and Carlos Rodriguez-Galindo

BURDEN OF CHILDHOOD CANCER IN LMICs

In high-income countries (HICs), the annual incidence of childhood cancer is approximately 140 per 1 million children younger than age 15 years, although estimates vary between and within countries (Parkin and others 1998). Incidence rates from low- and middle-income country (LMIC) registries are generally significantly lower, as annual rates per 1 million children of 45.6 in Namibia and 64.4 in India, respectively, illustrate (Parkin and others 1998). Some of this variation may relate to differences in environmental exposures or to biologic susceptibility. However, deficiencies in diagnosis and registration likely contribute significantly to differences in the reported incidence of cancer, both overall and of particular subtypes, such as acute leukemias (Howard and others 2008).

Incidence data from high-quality cancer registries with complete population coverage are rare in LMICs. In 2006, only 8 percent of people in Asia and 11 percent in Sub-Saharan Africa were covered by population-based cancer registries; when only high-quality registries are considered, these rates are 4 percent and 1 percent, respectively (Ferlay and others 2010).

Multiple steps are required for children with cancer to be included in a registry (figure 7.1). Caregivers must seek medical attention for symptoms. Primary health care workers must appropriately refer patients to third-level centers capable of recognizing and diagnosing pediatric malignancies and then entering data into cancer registries. Breaks in the chain of events may occur at any step.

A comparison of leukemia and non-leukemia cancer incidence rates is instructive. Pediatric leukemia may present with a variety of nonspecific symptoms, such as fever, anemia, malaise, or hemorrhage; many of the symptoms are also associated with infections. Most non-leukemia cancers present with enlarging masses more easily recognizable as malignant. Accordingly, the magnitude of underdiagnosis would be expected to be greater in leukemia than in non-leukemia cancers; registry data bear this out. In the most recent global compilation of pediatric cancer data, leukemia incidence in low-income countries (LICs) averaged 16.4 per million children, far lower than the incidence rate of 36.5 in middle-income countries (MICs) and 40.9 in HICs (figure 7.2) (Howard and others 2008). The non-leukemia cancer incidence was broadly similar in all income groups: 85 in LICs, 70 in MICs, and 89 in HICs (Howard and others 2008). The underdiagnosis of childhood brain tumors is likely even greater; many regions report few or no incident cases of pediatric central nervous system malignancies (Parkin and others 1998).

Corresponding author: Sumit Gupta, Toronto Hospital for Sick Children, Toronto, Canada, sumit.gupta@sickkids.ca

Figure 7.1 Links in the Chain of Childhood Cancer Diagnosis and Registration with Potential Barriers in Low- and Middle-Income Countries

Source: © John Wiley and Sons. Reproduced, with permission, from Howard and others 2008; further permission required for reuse.
Note: SES = socioeconomic status.

Figure 7.2 Reported Incidence Rate of Childhood Leukemia and Its Association with 2005 Gross National Income, Selected Economies

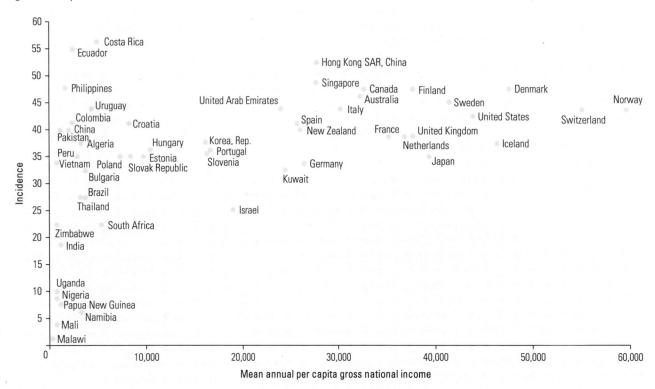

Source: © John Wiley and Sons. Reproduced, with permission, from Howard and others 2008; further permission required for reuse.
Note: Incidence rates are per 1 million children per year.

Underdiagnosis and underregistration are not uniform across all segments of the population. In Jordan and Honduras, higher leukemia incidence rates are reported in urban compared with rural districts (Al Sheyyab and others 2003; Metzger and others 2003).

Comparing Indian cancer registries, the male-to-female ratio in acute lymphoblastic leukemia (ALL) incidence ranged from 1.7 per million in Mumbai to 2.6 in Delhi, compared with 1.3 in Canada during the same time period (Parkin and others 1998). At least in some cases, underdiagnosis may affect girls and rural children disproportionately.

In addition, not only is childhood cancer severely underrepresented in LMIC cancer registration; only a proportion of the children who are registered receive appropriate treatment. From a survey of health care workers in 10 LMICs, including Bangladesh, the Philippines, Tanzania, and Vietnam, 15–37 percent of the expected patients were seen (Ribeiro and others 2008). Including children missed by registries would lower this percentage even further.

Thus, the approximately 175,000 children diagnosed with cancer globally every year are likely to represent a significant underrepresentation of the worldwide incidence. Expansion of current cancer registries, improvement in diagnosis and registration, and novel methodologies are needed to establish the true pediatric cancer burden (Ferlay and others 2010; Magrath and others 2013). The International Agency for Research on Cancer is assembling an updated volume of the *International Incidence of Childhood Cancer*, drawn predominantly from registry data. Comparisons with previous editions will allow an assessment of progress.

WHY TREAT CHILDHOOD CANCER IN LMICs?

Epidemiologic Transition

In most HICs, cancer represents the leading cause of non-accidental death in children older than age one year (Ellison, Pogany, and Mery 2007; Siegel, Naishadham, and Jemal 2013). Although infection accounted for 64 percent of global deaths in the first five years of life in 2010 (Liu and others 2012), major shifts in the magnitude and causes of childhood mortality have occurred in many LMICs, especially in MICs. In Brazil, mortality in children younger than age five years decreased from 129 per 1,000 live births in 1970 to 59 per 1,000 in 1990, and to 19 per 1,000 in 2010; cancer now leads the causes of non-accidental death in that country. Worldwide, 106 countries witnessed accelerated declines in childhood mortality from 1990 to 2011; about 80 percent of the decline was from infectious disease control (Lozano and others 2011). Consequently, noncommunicable causes represent a greater proportion than before (Liu and others 2012; Patton and others 2012). Indeed, while 3.2 percent of deaths among children ages 5–14 years in LICs are estimated to be caused by cancer, the equivalent figures for LICs and upper-middle-income countries are 6.0 percent and 18.6 percent, respectively (Magrath and others 2013).

Ineffectiveness of Prevention and Screening

Most pediatric malignancies are not caused by modifiable risk factors, and public health campaigns would have limited impact on decreasing the incidence, although impact on delayed presentation is possible. Similarly, population-based screening programs have not been shown to affect cancer mortality in children (Schilling and others 2002). Decreasing childhood cancer mortality rates requires early and accurate diagnosis followed by effective treatment.

Achievability of Cure

In HICs, over 80 percent of children with cancer are cured of their disease (Ellison, Pogany, and Mery 2007; Pui and others 2012; Smith and others 2010). Although cure rates in LMICs are much lower, there are many examples of successful treatment with less intensive regimens that can nevertheless cure a significant portion of patients in LMICs. Burkitt lymphoma (BL), the most common childhood malignancy in many parts of Sub-Saharan Africa, is cured in 90 percent of cases in HICs, using intensive regimens and intense and costly supportive care (Patte and others 2007; Woessmann and others 2005). However, up to 50 percent of Sub-Saharan African children with BL are curable with only three to six doses of single-agent cyclophosphamide and intrathecal therapy (Harif and others 2008).

Spillover Effect from Pediatric to Adult Oncology

In societies in which cancer may be seen as a death sentence, pediatric oncology offers the opportunity to demonstrate high cure rates in a manageable number of patients through the establishment of a defined and feasible cancer infrastructure. Such success can serve as powerful encouragement to governments and policy makers to create and expand programs targeting adults with cancer, in addition to ensuring that children with cancer are not neglected in the face of far greater numbers of adult patients.

PLATFORMS FOR CHILDHOOD CANCER TREATMENT DELIVERY

Dedicated Centers

Childhood cancer treatment requires specialized diagnostic and therapeutic capabilities, as well as the ability to manage potential complications. Expensive, high-technology equipment is not required, however. Although volume-outcome relationships have not been convincingly demonstrated in pediatric oncology, the dominant paradigm is to manage care through a limited number of treatment centers in which resources and expertise are concentrated. Satellite centers can deliver some treatment, decreasing the burden on families, providing rapid management of complications and, in LMICs, decreasing abandonment of treatment (Metzger and others 2003; Pediatric Oncology Group of Ontario 2012).

Tables 7.1 and 7.2 list the personnel and infrastructural requirements for an ideal LMIC center delivering pediatric cancer care; however, many institutions in LMICs deliver curative treatment in the absence of many of these elements (Harif and others 2008; Madani and others 2006; Pedrosa and others 2000). Such treatment must be adapted to local capabilities. For example, centers without an intensive care unit or ventilators will not be able to deliver as intensive chemotherapy as ones with these resources, but they will nonetheless be able to cure a portion of children.

It is worth highlighting the importance of stable drug supplies. Shortages of essential chemotherapy agents have been shown to impact pediatric survival, even in HICs (Metzger, Billett, and Link 2012). In LMICs, the impact of inconsistent chemotherapy availability is likely to be even greater.

In many LMICs, childhood cancer services are delivered through cancer hospitals serving primarily adult populations. In these instances, appropriately sized pediatric equipment and specific pediatric expertise are still required. Even when these requirements are met, the neglect of pediatric populations in the face of large volumes of adult patients may still adversely impact the quality of childhood cancer care.

Twinning Programs

"Twinning" is currently the most effective model for sustained improvement in childhood cancer care in LMICs. Twinning programs foster interactions between hospitals in LMICs and established cancer treatment centers,

Table 7.1 Examples of Essential Personnel for Ideal Pediatric Cancer Care in Low- and Middle-Income Countries[a]

Personnel	Requirements
Medical doctors	Individuals who have received training or have experience managing pediatric oncology patients are essential to lead the unit and coordinate all other personnel needed to achieve cure. In many centers, pediatricians, adult hematologists, adult oncologists, or surgeons with some degree of extra training or experience may fill this role. Training and fellowship programs now exist in several LMICs.
Surgeons	Surgery is necessary for the diagnosis and treatment of many pediatric malignancies, such as Wilms tumor. However, some cancers are curable without surgical intervention.
Radiation oncologists	Radiation therapy is used for a variety of pediatric malignancies in HICs, such as Hodgkin lymphoma, Wilms tumor, and sarcomas. However, in some cases, substituting additional chemotherapy or surgery can result in cure (Mauz-Korholz and others 2010; Nachman and others 2002).
Pathologists	Correct diagnosis is the foundation of cancer care, and a professional who has experience in the diagnosis of pediatric malignancies and who is connected with disease-specific pathology experts for difficult cases is ideal.
Nursing	Strong nursing support with additional training in safe chemotherapy administration is needed. Expertise in the recognition and management of complications related to either the malignancy or treatment is desirable. An open line of communication between nursing and medical colleagues is crucial. Models for training nurses in pediatric oncology in LMICs have been described (Day and others 2011; Day and others 2012).
Pharmacists	Dedicated pharmacists are needed to prepare chemotherapy and to facilitate the safe preparation, handling, and disposal of chemotherapeutic medications.
Social workers	Addressing the emotional, social, financial, and spiritual needs of children and families facilitates adherence to treatment, improves quality of life, and reduces the risk of abandonment.
Dieticians or nutritionists	Nutritional support is particularly important in LMICs where malnutrition at diagnosis or during treatment is prevalent (Israels and others 2009; Sala and others 2005; Viana and others 2001).

Note: HICs = high-income countries; LMICs = low- and middle-income countries.

a. This list is not meant to be exhaustive. Other personnel, including infectious disease specialists and intensive care physicians, play crucial roles but may not be available in many resource-constrained settings. All the elements listed are desirable, but a proportion of children will still be cured in their absence.

Table 7.2 Infrastructure Needed to Deliver Ideal Pediatric Cancer Care in Low- and Middle-Income Countries[a]

Infrastructure	Requirements
Inpatient and outpatient beds	Sufficient inpatient and outpatient beds are required, preferably designated for pediatric oncology patients. A hand hygiene program, isolation capabilities, and other infection control methods are desirable.
Laboratory and pathology services	Basic hematologic, biochemical, microbiologic, and pathologic laboratory services capable of timely turnaround are desirable. Although advanced diagnostic modalities, such as flow cytometry and cytogenetics, are available in HICs, their absence does not preclude the establishment of a pediatric oncology center (Hunger, Sung, and Howard 2009).
Diagnostic imaging	Basic imaging capabilities are necessary. While advanced modalities—such as computerized tomography and magnetic resonance imaging—are ideal, basic modalities, such as plain radiographs and ultrasonography are sufficient to begin treating childhood cancer (Madani and others 2006; Marjerrison and others 2012).
Chemotherapy and supportive care medications	Reliable supplies of selected chemotherapeutic agents and supportive care medications, such as antimicrobials, antiemetics, and analgesics, are crucial. The World Health Organization Model List of Essential Medications for Children provides a starting point for specific medications (WHO 2013).
Blood product availability	Treatment protocols may cause bone marrow suppression, necessitating the timely and reliable delivery of safe blood products. However, this is not the case for all chemotherapies; treatment for several malignancies requires minimal transfusion support.
Psychosocial support	Abandonment of therapy is a significant cause of treatment failure in many LMICs. The provision of financial support in case of inability to pay for medical care, and of transport and accommodation when necessary, decreases the risk of abandonment and must be considered an essential part of oncology care in LMICs.
Surgical facilities	Surgery is necessary for diagnosis and treatment of many pediatric malignancies, for example, Wilms tumor. Many cancers are curable without surgical intervention.
Radiation facilities	Radiation therapy is used for a variety of pediatric malignancies in HICs, for example, Hodgkin lymphoma, Wilms tumor, and sarcomas. However, in some cases, substituting additional chemotherapy or surgery can result in cure (Mauz-Korholz and others 2010; Nachman and others 2002).

Note: HICs = high-income countries; LMICs = low- and middle-income countries.

a. This list is not meant to be exhaustive. While all of the elements listed are desirable, a proportion of children can still be cured in their absence.

with the goal of improving survival rates among children with cancer (Ribeiro and Pui 2005). Twinning allows a bidirectional exchange and combines disease-specific multidisciplinary expertise with local knowledge and capabilities.

Twinning programs can involve the flow of financial resources, although the presence of committed individuals on both sides predicts success better than the availability of funding. Interactive online tools such as Cure4Kids (http://www.Cure4Kids.org) facilitate communication between participating centers (St. Jude Children's Research Hospital 2012). In some cases, twinning programs have been associated with rapid increases in cure rates (annex map 7A.1). The Pediatric Oncology in Developing Countries (PODC) committee of the International Society of Pediatric Oncology (SIOP) has created a forum for interested people from centers in HICs and LMICs to develop twinning programs. Indeed, the 12 working groups of PODC are exclusively dedicated to improving care for children with cancer in LMICs by fostering twinning programs,

adapting treatment regimens, improving supportive care, and reducing treatment abandonment.

Despite the success of the twinning paradigm in improving individual pediatric cancer units, improvements must be translated into national childhood cancer strategies to have the greatest impact. Most LMICs lack policies to ensure good pediatric oncology care, and many have no national cancer plan, let alone one targeting the unique needs of children. Notable exceptions include Seguro Popular in Mexico, which includes an accreditation process for hospitals treating children with cancer, and reimbursement for care provided by qualifying institutions. Since this program began, abandonment of treatment has fallen from 52 percent to 5 percent (Rivera-Luna and others 2012), although access to care and the survival of treated patients varies widely among accredited pediatric cancer units (Perez-Cuevas and others 2013). Current efforts in China to build comprehensive health insurance programs that cover childhood cancer treatment hold great promise but are in their infancy.

GENERAL PRINCIPLES OF TREATMENT

Importance of Locally Adapted Treatment Protocols

Although not true for all cancers, increasing the intensity of treatment has increased cure rates (Matthay and others 1999; Womer and others 2012; Woods and others 1996). Different childhood cancers require different treatment intensities for maximum cure rates; for example, the chemotherapy for Wilms tumor is far less intense than for acute myeloid leukemia (AML). One of the great achievements of pediatric oncology in recent decades is the refinement of risk stratification systems, allowing for an assessment of the aggressiveness of a particular child's cancer and for treatment intensity to be matched to disease risk, thereby reducing both undertreatment and overtreatment (Crawford, MacDonald, and Packer 2007; Maris 2010; Metzger and Dome 2005; Pui, Robison, and Look 2008).

Avoiding overtreatment is crucial in LMICs, since it carries with it an increased risk of treatment-related mortality (TRM), defined as death from complications of treatment, as opposed to the disease itself (Creutzig and others 2004; Ethier and others 2011; Gupta and others 2009; Gupta and others 2011; Prucker and others 2009). At some point, any benefit in disease control of intensifying treatment will be outweighed by an increase in TRM. Finding the balance point for each malignancy at each pediatric cancer center is key to optimizing therapy and curing the maximum number of children possible.

This ideal balance point depends on the malignancy in question, as well as a particular center's ability to provide supportive care to prevent and manage treatment complications. The same high intensity chemotherapy delivered at two centers, one with 24-hour availability of intensive care and the other without, will result in higher TRM rates in the latter. In HICs, advances in supportive care have allowed the delivery of ever higher intensity treatments. Even in this context, however, the ideal balance has at times been difficult to find; intensifying treatment for AML initially resulted in high TRM rates in Europe and North America, which later decreased as cancer units developed the new level of supportive care required (Creutzig and others 2004; Lange and others 2008).

In many LMIC centers, supportive care capabilities lag behind those in HICs. Transposing treatment protocols designed for HIC levels of supportive care to LMIC centers is therefore almost certain to cause high levels of TRM (Gupta and others 2009; Gupta and others 2011). The possibility of doing more harm than good is significant. An important example is described in box 7.1, where decreasing treatment intensity actually led to higher cure rates. Questions to ask when trying to determine the supportive care capabilities of an individual institution include the following:

- Are 24-hour nursing and medical coverage available for inpatients?
- How quickly can antibiotics be ordered, received, and given to patients when urgent treatment is necessary?
- How quickly can a blood transfusion be ordered, received, and given to patients when urgent treatment is necessary?

Box 7.1

Acute Promyelocytic Leukemia: Cost and Treatment Intensity

Acute promyelocytic leukemia (APL) is a subtype of acute myeloid leukemia, with cure rates of about 80 percent in high-income countries. In Guangzhou, China, Luo and others (2009b) treated 30 children with APL between 1999 and 2008. Before September 2004, children were treated on an intensive protocol including high-dose cytarabine and high cumulative doses of anthracycline. After September 2004, children were treated with a far less intensive protocol with fewer chemotherapy cycles, lower anthracycline doses, and no cytarabine. The total cost of therapy was lower, decreasing the financial burden on parents.

With the first protocol, of 16 children, six abandoned therapy and seven developed bacterial sepsis, one of whom died. With the less intensive protocol, none of the 14 children studied abandoned therapy, and there was only one episode of sepsis, with no resultant infectious deaths. The three-year, event-free survival was 37.5 percent with the more intense protocol, and 79.6 percent with the less intensive treatment. Although the number of patients is small, this example illustrates an important principle: increased intensity and cost of treatment can do more harm than good.

Sources: Ortega and others 2005; Testi and others 2005; Luo and others 2009b.

- Are basic radiographic, microbiologic, and hematologic diagnostic tests available?
- Is intensive care, including ventilator and inotropic support, available?
- What is the prevalence of malnutrition in the population? What programs are available in the pediatric cancer unit to address malnutrition?
- Are families able to reach medical attention quickly in case of a treatment complication?
- Where do outpatients go when emergencies develop after hours? Who treats them there? Are pediatric oncology professionals involved in their care after hours?

Further consequences stem from the principle that increased intensity and cost of treatment can do more harm than good. Many diagnostic modalities are utilized to classify the extent of disease, including stage and risk group, of particular patients. For example, in ALL, the most common childhood cancer in many countries, flow cytometry and cytogenetics help to identify high-risk subgroups, such as T-cell or hypodiploid ALL (Pui, Robison, and Look 2008). Children with these high-risk subgroups are treated with higher intensity protocols. In a center in which higher intensity therapy leads to unacceptable TRM rates, spending limited resources on developing these diagnostic modalities is difficult to justify. However, making a correct diagnosis (such as distinguishing between myeloid and lymphoblastic leukemia) is often life-saving and cost-effective (Howard and others 2005).

Abandonment of Therapy

Abandonment is defined as the "failure to start or complete [potentially] curative treatment" (Mostert and others 2011, 719). The phenomenon of abandonment, virtually unknown in HICs, is a significant problem in LMICs; in some contexts, it constitutes the most common cause of treatment failure (Arora, Eden, and Pizer 2007). The importance of this issue led SIOP to establish the Abandonment of Treatment Working Group (Mostert and others 2011). A systematic review of pediatric acute lymphoblastic leukemia in LMICs found that abandonment rates ranged from 3 percent to an astonishing 74 percent (Gupta and others 2013). None of 83 published reports of abandonment were from LICs, so the review likely underestimates the global incidence of abandonment.

Many reasons for abandonment have been cited, including a lack of financial resources, poor disease comprehension, cultural factors, belief in alternative medicines, fear of treatment toxicity, inadequate care on the part of health care workers, and decreased awareness of aid programs (Bonilla and others 2009; Howard and others 2004; Kulkarni and Marwaha 2010; Luo and

others 2009a; Mostert and others 2006). Interestingly, even in the context of a treatment program in which chemotherapy, supportive care, lodging, and transport were provided at no cost to families, families of low socioeconomic status were still at higher risk of abandonment (Bonilla and others 2009). Various efforts in LMICs have decreased abandonment rates, including providing financial support, adapting treatment protocols based on a family's financial resources, providing parental education, and establishing a social work program (box 7.2) (Bonilla and others 2009; Howard and others 2004; Luo and others 2008; Mostert and others 2010).

Thus, just as some level of basic supportive care capacity is necessary to treat children with cancer, basic educational and aid programs aimed at preventing abandonment are also imperative.

Outcome Evaluation

Although it is possible to theorize as to what protocol modifications are best suited to a particular LMIC institution, there is no substitute for the actual

---

Box 7.2

Examples of Successful Efforts to Decrease the Abandonment of Therapy in Children with Cancer

- In Guatemala City, Guatemala, through the establishment of a psychosocial team including both social workers and psychologists whose aim is to support families throughout the cancer experience, abandonment has decreased from 42 to 2 percent (F. Antillon, personal communication).
- In Recife, Brazil, through the provision of lodging, social work, transportation, and food subsidies, and the establishment of a parent group, a fundraising foundation, and a patient tracking system, abandonment among children with acute lymphoblastic leukemia (ALL) decreased from 16 to 1 percent from 1980 to 2002 (Howard and others 2004).
- In Yogyakarta, Indonesia, after the introduction of a parental education program, upfront treatment refusal for children with ALL decreased from 14 to 2 percent among poor parents (Mostert and others 2010).

Sources: F. Antillon, personal communication; Howard and others 2004; Mostert and others 2010.

monitoring of treatment outcomes. Collection of basic data on patient demographics, disease characteristics, and treatment outcomes, including cause of death, allows for evaluation of a specific treatment protocol, as well as the design of future interventions. For example, it is not enough to know that children with ALL in an individual center have a mortality rate of 50 percent, without evaluating the causes of death. If the predominant cause of death was TRM, then appropriate interventions would include the strengthening of supportive care, perhaps accompanied by de-intensification of treatment. However, if the predominant cause was relapse, increasing treatment intensity may be appropriate. Outcome monitoring allows for the gradual evolution of treatment strategies in a safe and efficient manner and cure of the maximum number of children possible at each stage (Hunger, Sung, and Howard 2009).

Health care workers in many LMICs lack the time to collect, review, and analyze outcome information. In most settings, a dedicated data manager with sufficient training, infrastructure, and support is needed to ensure accurate and timely data entry. It is worth emphasizing that the collection and analysis of these data are neither academic research nor a luxury. Indeed, outcome monitoring is essential to improving the care and outcomes at any pediatric cancer center, whether in LMICs or HICs. However, quality improvement efforts in LMICs often mean the difference between life and death, whereas those in HICs affect more subtle outcomes.

TREATMENT OF SPECIFIC CANCERS

The ideal malignancy targeted for treatment in LMICs would be one that accounts for a significant proportion of the local cancer burden and that is curable with either simple surgery or short-course chemotherapy alone. The treatment of this ideal target would involve minimal acute toxicity and few chronic late effects—survivorship issues specific to LMIC children are unstudied. Of course, no single malignancy perfectly fits this profile. Which malignancies should be treated in a particular LMIC center depends on the local incidence, the available treatment modalities, the institutional level of supportive care possible, and theoretically attainable cure rates.

A center that is only beginning to treat childhood cancer could start with malignancies for which cure is possible with relatively simple and low-intensity chemotherapy, such as BL or Hodgkin lymphoma (HL). A center that has achieved significant cure rates in these cancers could then address malignancies requiring more complex chemotherapy (for example, ALL) and multimodality treatment (for example, Wilms tumor) and could eventually advance to treatment of sarcomas, brain tumors, and diseases that require high levels of supportive care (for example, AML, high-risk neuroblastoma). Table 7.3 lists characteristics of 13 of the most common childhood cancers; this information should be considered before deciding which malignancies to treat and which resources to develop in a specific setting. For each type of cancer, the elements required for successful treatment may differ based on stage and risk group. For example, while intensive chemotherapy, surgery, radiation, and autologous stem cell transplantation cure only a minority of advanced-stage neuroblastoma in older children, surgery alone may cure localized and biologically favorable neuroblastoma in a younger child.

The subsequent sections discuss five childhood cancers often targeted by LMIC centers because of their high potential cure rates with relatively low intensity treatment regimens. In addition, these five cancers collectively account for a significant portion of pediatric malignancies: ALL, HL, Wilms tumor, BL, and retinoblastoma. Each section outlines aspects of diagnosis and treatment and how both may be adapted to local resource constraints.

Acute Lymphoblastic Leukemia

Stephen P. Hunger[1] and Federico G. Antillon[2]
[1]Children's Hospital Colorado and the Department of Pediatrics, University of Colorado School of Medicine, Aurora, CO, United States.
[2]Unidad Nacional de Oncología Pediátrica, Guatemala City, Guatemala.

ALL, a cancer of white blood cells (WBC), is the most common childhood cancer, accounting for 25 percent of cancers among those younger than 15 years of age, and 20 percent of those that occur before 20 years of age (Ries and others 1999). ALL is universally fatal without effective therapy. In North America and Western Europe, five-year survival rates have steadily improved, from below 10 percent in the 1960s to over 90 percent today (Hunger and others 2012; Moricke and others 2010; Pui and others 2009; Silverman and others 2010). However, most children who develop ALL do not reside in these countries. China and India are predicted to have four to five times as many pediatric ALL cases as the United States; Indonesia, Nigeria, and Pakistan are predicted to have about the same number of cases as the United States (online annex table 7A.1). Thus, it is critical to consider how pediatric ALL can be cured in countries that have very different income

Table 7.3 Characteristics of Childhood Cancers to Consider When Determining Which Malignancies Are Appropriate for Treatment in a Particular Resource-Constrained Setting

Cancer	Approximate HIC cure rate[a] (percent)	Approximate treatment duration (months)	Supportive care level required	Chemotherapy necessary?	Surgery necessary?	Radiation necessary?	Late effects/ disability
ALL	90	24–40	++	Yes	No	No	+
AML	60	5–7	++++	Yes	No	No	++
Hodgkin lymphoma	90	2–8	++	Yes	No	No[b]	++
Burkitt lymphoma	90	6–8	+++[c]	Yes	No	No	+
Medulloblastoma	75	8–10	++	Yes	Yes	Yes	++++
Neuroblastoma	65	8–10	+++	Yes	Yes	Yes	+++
Wilms tumor	90	4–8	+	Yes	Yes	No[b]	++
Rhabdomyosarcoma	70	8–12	++	Yes	Yes	No[b]	++
Osteosarcoma	70	8–12	++	Yes	Yes	No	++
Ewing sarcoma	75	8–12	++	Yes	Yes	No[b]	++
Retinoblastoma	95[d]	0–3	+	No[e]	Yes[f]	No	++
Testicular cancer	90	0–3	+	No[e]	Yes	No	–
Hepatoblastoma	85[g]	4–6	+	Yes	Yes	No	+

Note: The scale is from not very significant (–) to very significant (++++). ALL = acute lymphoblastic leukemia; AML = acute myeloid leukemia; HIC = high-income country.

a. Unless otherwise specified, HIC cure rates are taken from Surveillance, Epidemiology, and End Results Program registry data (Smith and others 2010).

b. Radiation is indicated in select cases.

c. While HIC regimens for Burkitt lymphoma require significant supportive care, lower intensity regimens requiring minimal supportive care can also be used.

d. Dimaras and others 2012.

e. Chemotherapy is required for advanced cases, although localized cases may be cured without it.

f. Local control methods, including cryotherapy and laser therapy, are often used instead of surgery in HICs, but these are unavailable in many low- and middle-income countries.

g. Perilongo and others 2009; Zsiros and others 2010.

structures and health care systems than those in North America and Western Europe.

Diagnosis of ALL

Children with ALL are commonly brought to medical attention for symptoms caused by ineffective production of normal blood cells because of replacement of the bone marrow by leukemia, including pallor, bleeding, fever, infections, and bone pain. They may also have leukemic involvement of other organs, including liver, spleen, mediastinum, central nervous system, and testicles.

ALL is diagnosed based on review of peripheral blood cell counts and a bone marrow aspirate/biopsy, tests that can be performed at most medical facilities. Simple factors predictive of outcome include age (younger is better, except for infants less than one year) and initial WBC count (lower is better). More sophisticated and often very expensive diagnostic tests readily available in HICs include immunophenotyping, to determine cell lineage,

and cytogenetic or molecular genetic studies, to define sentinel abnormalities, many of which have important prognostic implications. However, these tests are often not available in LMICs. A major prognostic factor is the rapidity of response to single-agent or multiagent therapy, which can be measured in a simple and inexpensive manner by peripheral blood or bone marrow morphology, or in a complicated and expensive manner using advanced flow cytometry and/or molecular genetic techniques.

General Concepts of Pediatric ALL Treatment

Contemporary treatment for ALL consists of complex combination chemotherapy regimens that last 2.5–3 years, with six to eight months of relatively intensive therapy, followed by 1.5–2 years of low-intensity maintenance therapy, during which most children can resume normal activities and attend school. Chemotherapy drugs included in these regimens have been widely available for decades; most are relatively inexpensive, with the exception of asparaginase preparations, which are extremely expensive (Masera and others 2004). Radiation therapy to the brain was a critical component of early effective ALL regimens, but the use of cranial irradiation has been greatly reduced in most contemporary HIC regimens (Pui and Howard 2008).

Although treatment of pediatric ALL is associated with significant risk of short- and long-term side effects, most children cured of ALL will lead healthy and productive lives. Cure rates are much lower for children with ALL that relapses, with the chance of cure related to site of relapse, ALL genetic features, and time between initial diagnosis and relapse (Nguyen and others 2008).

Because most children with ALL live in LMICs, efforts have been made to improve treatment available in those countries through partnerships with centers in HICs (Masera and others 1998). This twinning has led to major improvements in ALL survival in LMICs, often through adoption of intact or modified HIC treatment regimens (Howard and others 2004; Veerman, Sutaryo, and Sumadiono 2005). Critical to these successes has been the transfer of knowledge regarding treatment regimens, supportive care, and emotional and psychosocial support. Abandonment of care is a major issue in LMICs because of economic and social pressures on parents and cultural beliefs that a child has been healed (Sitaresmi and others 2010; Wang and others 2011). Innovative programs have been developed to support patients and families and greatly reduce abandonment; a Guatemalan program reduced abandonment rates from 42 percent to less than 2 percent (unpublished observations, Rivas and Antillon). Successful implementation and improvement of therapies also requires close tracking of patient characteristics and outcomes, necessitating access to databases and data management personnel (Ayoub and others 2007).

Specifics of Pediatric ALL Treatment

The development of large cooperative treatment groups that conduct clinical trials, which often include 70 percent or more of children with ALL in a given country (Hunger and others 2012), has been critical to improvements in survival for pediatric ALL in HICs. This development has resulted in near-universal access to effective treatments in most HICs (limited in some cases because of country-specific differences in health care financing) and the widespread availability of knowledge about the specifics of effective treatment regimens.

Twinning has provided outstanding examples of very effective transfer of knowledge and adoption of contemporary treatment regimens in LMICs, such as the Central American Association of Pediatric Hematology Oncology (AHOPCA), largely developed through collaborations with pediatric cancer programs in Monza and Milan, Italy, and St. Jude Children's Research Hospital in the United States. AHOPCA now conducts its own non-randomized clinical trials. In Guatemala, ALL survival rates now range from 50 percent (high-risk) to 90 percent (low-risk) for different patient subgroups (Antillon-Klussmann and others 2010). This strategy is possible in countries with reasonably well-developed health care systems, with infant mortality rates less than 40–50 per 1,000 live births serving as a good surrogate marker (online annex, table 7A.1).

However, high rates of ALL TRM can be a major problem (Gupta and others 2011). Regimens that are delivered safely with TRM rates less than 5 percent in North America and Western Europe can be associated with TRM rates 5–10 times higher in LMICs; the problem is much worse in countries with less developed health care systems, reflected by infant mortality rates more than 50 per 1,000 live births. High rates of TRM severely compromise cure rates and can be a major impediment to program development in LMICs. Treatment of relapsed ALL has a very low chance of success in LMICs.

One way to address these problems is through the use of graduated intensity regimens, whereby centers first implement less intensive regimens similar to those used in North America and Western Europe in the 1970s and 1980s, and increase treatment intensity only when they establish these therapies to be safe and effective in their local settings (Hunger, Sung, and Howard 2009). This strategy is attractive because it starts with regimens that are less costly, less toxic, and do not require sophisticated diagnostic tests, but that can cure about 50 percent of children with ALL if TRM can be kept low and abandonment can be minimized.

An example from the pediatric cancer program in Santo Domingo, the Dominican Republic, shows the potential benefit of this strategy. In 2005–07, a relatively intensive HIC-type treatment regimen was followed for 91 children with ALL; however, it was associated with excessive TRM. Following this experience, a less intensive regimen was used to treat 101 patients diagnosed in 2008–10. The less intensive treatment improved 24-month overall survival from 40 to 70 percent, accompanied by a decrease in TRM from 29 of 91 cases in the early period to 8 of 101 in the later period (Hunger and others 2011).

Costs of Pediatric ALL Treatment

Pediatric ALL treatment in North America and Western Europe is widely recognized to be very expensive and highly cost effective. A report from the Dutch Childhood Oncology Group showed mean total costs for treating pediatric ALL to be US$115,858–US$163,350 per case, with highly favorable costs per life year saved of US$1,962–US$2,655 (van Litsenburg and others 2011). However, effective treatments can be implemented for much lower costs. Luo and others reported in 2008 that a reduced intensity, low-cost protocol that obtained a four-year event-free survival rate of 72.8 percent could be implemented in Guangzhou, China, for a total hospital cost of US$4,300 per case; the range is from US$3,100 to US$6,800 (Luo and others 2008). More intensive regimens obtained slightly better results and could be implemented for US$9,900–US$12,500, similar to the average cost of US$11,000 per patient reported from Shanghai, China (Liu and others 2009).

Summary

ALL is the most common pediatric cancer. Five-year survival rates exceed 90 percent in HICs. Through twinning, centers in LMICs with infant mortality rates less than 40–50 per 1,000 live births have attained cure rates of about 70 percent. Outcomes for relapsed ALL are much worse, stressing the need for effective therapy at initial diagnosis. Graduated intensity regimens have the promise to decrease TRM and improve survival, and they may be particularly effective in LMICs with infant mortality rates greater than 50 per 1,000 live births.

Hodgkin Lymphoma

Monika L. Metzger[1]
[1]Division of Leukemia/Lymphoma, St. Jude Children's Research Hospital, Memphis, TN, United States.

In HICs, over 80 percent of children with HL survive long-term. In LMICs, survival has been lower because of lack of adequate staging, drug shortages, inadequate access to radiotherapy, delays in therapy, and social hardship leading to abandonment of therapy. Most children with HL in LMICs present to medical attention with advanced-stage disease and a long history of symptoms. Despite these obstacles, many LMIC patients can still be cured with basic chemotherapy, with or without consolidative radiotherapy. HL is curable, diagnosable without expensive technology, and constitutes an important portion of children with cancer.

Epidemiology and Prognostic Factors

Childhood HL rarely presents before five years of age in HICs; however, in LMICs it can be seen in children as young as age one year. In HICs, HL has a bimodal age distribution in early adulthood and after the age of 50 years. The age distribution is shifted toward younger ages in LICs, and it often occurs before adolescence. Furthermore, in LMICs, HL is most often Epstein-Barr virus-positive and of mixed cellular histology (Siddiqui and others 2006). Disease stage and bulk, as well as the presence of "B-symptoms" (fevers, drenching night sweats, or greater than 10 percent weight loss in the past six months) are established prognostic factors. Other potential prognostic factors include the erythrocyte sedimentation rate and low hemoglobin and albumin levels, although these may be less reliable indicators in children suffering from chronic malnutrition or parasitic infections.

Diagnosis of HL

An excisional lymph node biopsy is recommended, as fine-needle aspirates are often inadequate for diagnosis. This is, in fact, the only surgical procedure routinely required in the treatment of HL. Pathology is basic; the diagnosis can be confirmed with a simple hematoxylin and eosin stain without the need for immunohistochemistry.

Staging and Treatment Options

In HICs, the ideal initial evaluation of children for HL includes computed tomography of the neck, chest, abdomen, and pelvis, accompanied by FDG-positron emission tomography. Staging and the presence of B-symptoms allow risk stratification with therapy tailored according to risk of relapse and adapted based on disease response after two cycles of chemotherapy. Risk-stratified, response-adapted therapy offers the potential to maximize cure and minimize toxicity (Hodgson, Hudson, and Constine 2007).

In LMICs with limited availability of diagnostic imaging, a thorough physical examination for determination of all pathologic peripheral adenopathy, chest radiograph for extent of mediastinal involvement, and ultrasonography for intra-abdominal adenopathy can be sufficient for staging. Bone marrow biopsy is not recommended for most patients, since it is expensive, painful, and rarely affects risk classification or therapy (Hines-Thomas and others 2010). In some cases, a positive bone marrow biopsy may actually harm the patient by leading to the false perception that bone marrow involvement is incurable or that consolidative radiation therapy is not indicated.

In cases of limited staging evaluation, the treatment approach must account for incomplete ascertainment of affected areas. Accordingly, more weight must be placed on effective chemotherapy and less on local control with radiotherapy, which would not be applied to disease sites undetected by incomplete staging evaluations. Furthermore, radiation therapy is often unavailable, inconsistently available, or too toxic when given by radiation oncologists without pediatric expertise. Risk stratification in many LMICs should also be broader, similar to early HIC chemotherapy-only trials. Table 7.4 provides examples of chemotherapy-only and combined modality treatment regimens used successfully in LMICs.

During HL treatment, the minimum necessary supportive care consists of antibiotics and antiemetics, blood products are rarely needed, and therapy can be administered in the outpatient setting without the need for growth factors.

Costs of HL Treatment

The bulk of the cost of HL therapy is due to pathologic evaluation, radiation therapy, and diagnostic imaging studies; chemotherapy and supportive care constitute a far smaller portion. In a study evaluating the cost of therapy in Sub-Saharan Africa for a child with stage II disease and followed for two years, the total cost was more than US$6,500 in a continent where the annual gross domestic product (GDP) per inhabitant is usually less than US$2,000 (Stefan and Stones 2009). However, these costs can be significantly reduced by carefully choosing the minimal necessary diagnostic imaging techniques

Table 7.4 Treatment Results of Pediatric Hodgkin Lymphoma Trials in Low- and Middle-Income Countries

Chemotherapy	Stage[a]	Number of patients	Outcome % (years)		
			Event-free survival	Disease-free survival	Overall survival
Chemotherapy-only regimens					
Grupo Argentino de Tratamiento de Leucemia Aguda[b]					
CVPP x 3	IA, IIA	10	86 (7)	—	—
CVPP x 6	IB, IIB	16	87 (7)	—	—
Nicaragua[c]					
COPP x 6	I, IIA	14	100 (3)	—	100 (3)
COPP-ABV x 8–10	IIB, III, IV	34	75 (3)	—	—
Chennai, India[d]					
COPP/ABV x 6	I–IIA	10	89 (5)	—	—
COPP/ABV x 6	IIB–IVB	43	90 (5)	—	—
New Delhi, India[e]					
COPP x 6	All stages	34	—	80 (5)	—
Uganda[f]					
MOPP x 6	I–IIIA	38	—	75 (5)	—
	IIIB–IV	10	—	60 (5)	—
Combined modality trials					
New Delhi, India[g]					
4 ABVD + 25–40 Gy IFRT	I–IIA	79	—	91 (5)	—
6–8 ABVD + 25–40 Gy to bulky disease sites	IIB, III, IV	183	—	73 (5)	—

Note: ABVD = doxorubicin (Adriamycin), bleomycin, vinblastine, dacarbazine; COPP = cyclophosphamide, vincristine (Oncovin), procarbazine, prednisone; CVPP = cyclophosphamide, vincristine, procarbazine, prednisone; IFRT = involved-field radiation therapy; MOPP = mechlorethamine (Mustargen), vincristine (Oncovin), procarbazine, and prednisone; — = no information available.

a. Stage I represents involvement of a single lymph node region or extralymphatic site. Stage II represents involvement of two or more lymph nodes on the same side of the diaphragm. Stage III represents involvement of lymph node regions on both sides of the diaphragm. Stage IV represents involvement of extralymphatic organs (for example, lung). B represents the presence of B symptoms (fever, night sweats, weight loss), while A represents the absence of B symptoms.

b. Sackmann-Muriel and others 1997.

c. Baez and others 1997.

d. Sripada and others 1995.

e. Chandra and others 2008.

f. Olweny and others 1978.

g. Ganesan and others 2011.

required for staging and chemotherapy regimens that will permit the omission of radiotherapy. The most important cost to avoid is that of relapse.

Wilms Tumor

Trijn Israels[1]
[1]Department of Pediatric Hematology/Oncology, VU University, Amsterdam, The Netherlands.

Wilms tumor is relatively common, accounting for 5–7 percent of all childhood cancers (Stiller and Parkin 1996). In many settings, Wilms tumor is the most common malignant abdominal tumor. As treatment programs for pediatric oncology are developed, Wilms tumor should be one of the first tumors targeted because of its frequency and curability. Treatment also requires the development of multidisciplinary capacities that may benefit other children and programs across the hospital.

Great progress has been made in the treatment of children with Wilms tumor in recent decades. The survival rates in HICs now exceed 85 percent. Multidisciplinary treatment combines surgery and chemotherapy, with radiotherapy in a selected group of patients (Graf, Tournade, and de Kraker 2000; Green 2004). Two treatment strategies have been used for Wilms tumor worldwide. The first operates on tumors upfront, as practiced by the Children's Oncology Group in North America, followed by chemotherapy; the second starts with preoperative chemotherapy, as practiced in Europe (SIOP).

Both strategies result in similar long-term survival for HIC patients (Graf, Tournade, and de Kraker 2000; Green 2004). Preoperative chemotherapy, however, reduces surgical complications, such as tumor rupture, and downstages the tumor at surgery, thereby allowing for lower intensity, postoperative chemotherapy and reducing the need for radiotherapy. This is a sensible strategy for many LMIC patients, who often present with large tumors in settings where supportive care is limited and radiotherapy may not be available.

Survival rates in LMICs are lower than in HICs, ranging from 11 percent to 81 percent (Abuidris and others 2008; Israels 2012; Israels and others 2012; Moreira and others 2012; Wilde and others 2010). Known challenges are late presentation with advanced disease, malnutrition, abandonment of treatment, and poor facilities for specific cancer treatment and supportive care (Abuidris and others 2008; Harif and others 2005; Moreira and others 2012). Capacity building, earlier presentation, a multidisciplinary approach, social support, improved supportive care, and treatment adapted to local circumstances are key to improving results (Hadley 2010; Hadley, Rouma, and Saad-Eldin 2012; Israels and others 2012).

Treatment Settings

The facilities and resources available for the care of children with Wilms tumor vary among centers, but they can be defined using the following settings (table 7.5):

- *Setting 1* is one in which the minimal requirements for treatment with curative intent are available.

Table 7.5 Classification of Different Settings Providing Care for Children with Wilms Tumor[a]

Setting	Medical facilities	Specialists	Drugs	Supportive care	Diagnostic facilities
0				Pain medication	Physical exam
1. Minimal requirements for curative intent	Pediatric ward	Surgeon (Pediatrician) Nurse	Vincristine Actinomycin (Doxorubicin)	Antibiotics Whole blood Morphine Social support	Full blood count Chest x-ray Ultrasonography
2. Intermediate	Pediatric oncology ward Radiotherapy Pathology Multidisciplinary care	Pathologist Pediatric surgeon Pediatric oncologist Radiation oncologist Oncology nurse	Doxorubicin Cyclophosphamide Etoposide Ifosfamide Carboplatin	All blood products Central venous access	CT scan
3. State of the art	Intensive care unit	Pediatric pathologist Pediatric radiation oncologist Pharmacist (oncology) Intensivist		Mechanical ventilation Hemodialysis Pressure support	Special stains Immunohistochemistry Cytogenetics

Note: CT = computed tomography.
a. Facilities and resources mentioned are in addition to those associated with lower settings. In setting 2, mentioned facilities may or may not be available.

- *Setting 3* is one where all state-of-the-art facilities are available.
- *Setting 2* is in between.

Diagnosis

The diagnosis of Wilms tumor can be made with reasonable certainty based on history, physical examination, and ultrasonography of the abdomen. The typical presentation of a child with Wilms tumor in low-income settings is that of a malnourished young child with a large abdominal or flank mass, who is relatively well without acute pain or severe general malaise, but with hematuria and hypertension (Green 2004; Israels 2012). Ultrasonography of the abdomen is extremely useful to confirm the diagnosis (De Campo 1986; Hartman and Sanders 1982; Lowe and others 2000). An x-ray should be done to detect chest metastases.

In HICs, pathology is useful to confirm the diagnosis and, in addition to stage, to help risk stratify children and determine postoperative chemotherapy. In many LMICs, however, the availability of pathologists with pediatric expertise is limited and pathology results often are available too late to effect clinical decision making. Other challenges include the appropriate processing of specimens and the availability of special stains and immunohistochemistry, although central pathology review or telepathology may be helpful (Vujanic and others 2009). Fortunately, a diagnosis can often be made with some certainty based on clinical findings and ultrasonography. Postoperative chemotherapy can be based on surgical staging, only if needed.

A diagnostic biopsy before preoperative chemotherapy is not standard practice in current SIOP Wilms protocols; it is only recommended in LMICs when there is serious doubt about the diagnosis (Vujanic and others 2003). Such biopsies may result in bleeding, infection, or tumor spillage with consequent upstaging.

Treatment of Wilms Tumor

Preoperative chemotherapy should be used for children with Wilms tumor in LMICs, even in cases of small, seemingly easily resectable tumors (Lemerle and others 1983). Preoperative chemotherapy reduces surgical complications, downstages the tumor, and allows for less intense postoperative chemotherapy and the potential avoidance of radiotherapy (Graf, Tournade, and de Kraker 2000). Reliable and continuous access to the chemotherapeutic drugs such as vincristine, actinomycin D, and doxorubicin is essential.

Radiotherapy is used in patients with advanced-stage or unfavorable histology disease in centers with advanced capabilities. Unfortunately, safe radiotherapy for children is often unavailable in developing countries. The recent National Wilms Tumor Study and SIOP studies have shown that omitting or decreasing radiation therapy may not compromise cure rates, but these studies have not been done in children with very advanced disease or large tumors. Studies from Morocco and Nicaragua have demonstrated that cure can be achieved in some patients with advanced disease without radiotherapy (Baez and others 2002; Madani and others 2006). Higher cure rates in these populations may, however, require radiotherapy.

Table 7.6 shows some elements of the therapy used and the results from selected countries with limited resources. More detailed treatment recommendations can be found in a recently published SIOP guideline developed for use in LMICs (Israels and others 2013).

Cost of Wilms Treatment

To date, cost analyses related to the treatment of children with Wilms tumor in LMICs have not been reported. Although of relatively long duration (six months to two years), treatment is of relatively low intensity and does not involve expensive chemotherapeutic agents. The costs of surgery are likely to be high. Social support enabling parents to complete treatment is very likely to be cost-effective in LMICs.

Burkitt Lymphoma

Mhamed Harif[1]

[1]Unité Hématologie et Oncologie Pédiatrique, Centre d'Oncologie et Hématologie, Centre Hospitalier Mohammed VI, Marrakech, Morocco.

BL is a mature B-cell neoplasm that arises in lymphoid tissue, commonly in the jaw or abdomen. Described first in 1957 by Denis Burkitt in Uganda, it remains the most common pediatric cancer in malaria-endemic regions of Sub-Saharan Africa (Burkitt 1958; Lewis and others 2012). BL invariably arises from chromosomal translocations in which an oncogene (c-myc) is juxtaposed with genes encoding immunoglobulins. These translocations lead to an overexpression of monoclonal surface immunoglobulins in malignant cells, which is important for diagnosing and distinguishing it from other lymphoid cancers.

Although more than 90 percent of children with BL in HICs can be cured, doing so requires timely, accurate diagnosis and risk-directed treatment with high intensity chemotherapy and well-developed supportive care (Patte and others 2007). In many LMICs with limited supportive care, delivery of such therapy causes excessive toxic death; adapted regimens are necessary to cure as many patients as possible (Hesseling, Israels, and others 2012).

Table 7.6 Reported Outcomes of Patients with Wilms Tumor Treated in Low- and Middle-Income Countries

Country or region	Setting[a]	Numbers of patients	Chemotherapy	Radiotherapy	Event-free survival % (years)	Overall survival % (years)
Sudan[b]	1	37	Generally postoperative, based on NWTS-5, 37 percent received preoperative chemotherapy based on specific indications	No	11[c]	—
Malawi[d]	1	84	Preoperative and postoperative, modified from SIOP protocols	No	46	—
Egypt, Arab Rep.[e]	2	62	Postoperative	Yes	58 (4)	70 (4)
Central America[f]	2	374	Postoperative, based on NWTS-4	Yes	59 (3)	74 (3)
Morocco[g]	2	86	Preoperative and postoperative, based on SIOP protocols	Yes	77 (5)	79 (5)
South Africa[h]	2 (–3)	188	Preoperative and postoperative, based on SIOP protocols	Yes	75 (5)	81 (5)
Turkey[i]	2 (–3)	327	Preoperative and postoperative, based on SIOP protocols	Yes	56 (10)	61 (10)

Note: NWTS = National Wilms Tumor Study; SIOP = International Society of Pediatric Oncology; — = not available.

a. *Setting 1* is one in which the minimal requirements for treatment with curative intent are available. *Setting 3* is one where all state-of-the-art facilities are available; *Setting 2* is in between.

b. Abuidris and others 2008.

c. 89 percent of children in this study abandoned therapy prior to the completion of therapy.

d. Israels and others 2012.

e. Abd El-Aal, Habib, and Mishrif 2005.

f. Ortiz and others 2012.

g. Madani and others 2006.

h. Davidson and others 2006.

i. Kutluk and others 2006.

Nevertheless, in even the most resource-constrained environment, a simplified protocol for patients with BL can cure 50 percent (Hesseling and others 2009). Indeed, treatment of BL is likely to be highly cost-effective in all settings (Bhakta and others 2012).

Diagnosis

Suspected BL is a medical emergency. BL is the fastest growing human malignancy, in some cases doubling its volume every 24 hours. The risks of tumor lysis syndrome (TLS)—a collection of metabolic derangements caused by the rapid turnover of malignant cells, disease progression, nutritional deterioration, and concomitant infection—make diagnosis and therapy critical. Indeed, any child from an endemic region presenting with massive facial swelling or an abdominal mass requires immediate physical and laboratory evaluation for any of these complications.

Biopsy of the suspected tumor is recommended for diagnosis, but extensive surgery is contraindicated. The top priority must always be to make a diagnosis in the fastest, least invasive way possible and to initiate therapy rapidly. In rare cases, BL cells may be seen in the peripheral blood, as in Burkitt leukemia, obviating the need for a biopsy. A fine-needle aspiration may be sufficient in patients whose clinical features are consistent with BL (Razack and others 2011). When possible, the presence of mature B-cell markers (for example, CD20, immunoglobulin) and proliferative markers, such as Ki67, should be verified to differentiate BL from other small, round, blue cell tumors.

In cases in which the diagnosis is very likely and pathologic confirmation will be delayed, chemotherapy with cyclophosphamide, vincristine, and prednisone (COP) may be initiated empirically in potentially life-threatening situations. These agents have low toxicity and are active for most lymphomas. The benefits of prompt therapy initiation greatly outweigh the risks, as delayed therapy can lead to metabolic complications such as TLS that can be rapidly fatal.

Staging Evaluations and Risk Stratification

Staging evaluations in HICs includes a detailed physical examination to document peripheral adenopathy and testicular involvement; computed tomography imaging of the neck, chest, abdomen, and pelvis to define all sites of adenopathy; and the evaluation of cerebrospinal fluid, bone marrow aspirates, and biopsies.

Ideally, lumbar punctures are delayed until a diagnosis is made, so that intrathecal therapy can be administered at the time of the diagnostic puncture. The Murphy (St. Jude) staging system is most commonly used to classify the extent of disease (Murphy 1978). In LMICs, a physical examination, chest radiograph, abdominal ultrasound, bone marrow aspiration, and lumbar puncture may provide sufficient staging information (Marjerrison and others 2012).

Disease risk assignment, and thus treatment intensity, is determined mainly by disease stage. Lactate dehydrogenase level indicates disease activity and affects risk group assignment in some, but not all, HIC protocols. Inadequate response to treatment, defined in HICs as less than 20 percent reduction in tumor size after the initial chemotherapy cycle or residual cancer after the first intense blocks of therapy, require intensification of therapy. Different definitions of inadequate response have been used in resource-constrained settings (Hesseling, Israels, and others 2012). In either case, the dimensions of all masses must be documented at presentation.

Treatment

The optimal treatment regimen for a particular patient depends on disease stage, as well as the environment of care. Families with high socioeconomic status, good transportation, and proximity to a pediatric cancer unit with excellent infrastructure and supportive care can be treated on an HIC regimen, including intensive- and short-duration therapy with vincristine, cyclophosphamide, doxorubicin, cytarabine, high-dose methotrexate, and intrathecal agents. Duration and intensity vary according to risk group, but overall the therapy produces a 90 percent cure rate (Patte and others 2007). However, this treatment approach in settings with limited supportive care exposes patients to high rates of mortality and abandonment.

In LMICs and even in very poor settings, it has been shown that at least 50 percent of children with BL and up to 70 percent of children with localized stage I or stage II disease can be cured with intravenous or oral cyclophosphamide in combination with intrathecal methotrexate (Harif and others 2008; Hesseling and others 2009; Traore and others 2011). Treatment with simplified regimens is feasible everywhere and should always be attempted (table 7.7).

In all cases, optimizing supportive care includes the prevention and treatment of TLS, infection, and vomiting. TLS is the most common cause of early death in patients with BL (Howard, Jones, and Pui 2011). Aggressively hydrating (three liters/m²/day), frequently monitoring urine output and serum chemistry values, and controlling uric acid with rasburicase (where available) or allopurinol can prevent acute kidney injury in most cases. Nutritional support and the prompt diagnosis and treatment of febrile neutropenia and mucositis are the mainstays of supportive care after the first week. Family education, written care pathways, and creative nutritional supplements can

Table 7.7 Selected Cohorts and Outcomes of Children with Burkitt Lymphoma Treated in Low- and Middle-Income Countries with Locally Adapted Protocols of Lower Intensity

Study	Countries	Subgroups	Number of patients	Outcome (percent)
Hesseling, Njume, and others 2012	Cameroon	Stages I and II	18	EFS 94
		Stage III, clinical remission, or residual abdominal < 30 mL	58	EFS 76
		Stage IV, no clinical remission, or residual abdominal mass > 30 mL	45	EFS 40
Ngoma and others 2012	Tanzania, Kenya, Nigeria	All stages	326	EFS 52; OS 62[a]
Traore and others 2011	Burkina Faso, Cameroon, Côte d'Ivoire, Madagascar, Mali, Senegal	Stage I	19	EFS 44
		Stage II	23	EFS 49
		Stage III	128	EFS 30
		Stage IV	6	EFS 17

Note: EFS = event-free survival; OS = overall survival.
a. No significant differences according to stage.

produce remarkable results, even in LMICs (Gavidia and others 2012; Israels and others 2009).

Relapses are usually seen during the first six months and are rare after one year. Follow-up after one year focuses on identifying late toxicities and assisting with reintegration into society. In LMICs, recruiting survivors to improve community awareness of pediatric cancer care and the possibility of cure is essential.

More detailed treatment recommendations can be found in a published SIOP guideline developed for use in LMICs (Hesseling, Israels, and others 2012).

Costs of BL Treatment

As in other pediatric malignancies, data on the cost-effectiveness of treatment are rare. Given that a small number of doses of cyclophosphomide, a relatively inexpensive drug, can cure a significant portion of children, the treatment of BL is likely to be highly cost-effective. A paper using data from Malawi demonstrated that using the World Health Organization (WHO) definition, treatment costs under US$14,243 per case would be considered very cost-effective (Bhakta and others 2012). Actual estimated costs of treatment per case, at US$50, were far lower, although this figure only accounted for the costs of chemotherapy and is likely an underestimate.

Retinoblastoma

Carlos Rodriguez-Galindo[1]
[1]Dana-Farber/Children's Hospital Cancer Center, Harvard Medical School, Boston, MA, United States.

Retinoblastoma is the most frequent neoplasm of the eye in childhood, representing 2.5–4 percent of all pediatric cancers and 11 percent of cancers in the first year of life. Retinoblastoma presents in two distinct clinical forms.

- *Bilateral or multifocal* (25 percent of cases) is hereditary, characterized by the presence of germline mutations of the *RB1* gene. Multifocal retinoblastoma may be inherited from an affected survivor or be the result of a new germline mutation.
- *Unilateral* retinoblastoma (75 percent) is almost always nonhereditary. Retinoblastoma is a cancer of the very young; two-thirds of the cases are diagnosed before age two years, and 90 percent of the cases are diagnosed before age five years (Ries and others 1999).

Epidemiology

The incidence of retinoblastoma in the United States and Europe is 2–5 per million children (approximately one in 14,000–18,000 live births). However, the incidence is not consistent around the world, appearing higher (6–10 per million) in India, Sub-Saharan Africa, and among children of Native American descent in North America (Stiller and Parkin 1996). Whether this variation is because of ethnic or socioeconomic factors is unknown, although an environmental role has been suggested (de Camargo and others 2011; Fajardo-Gutierrez and others 2007). An estimated 8,000 children develop retinoblastoma each year worldwide. This burden is unequally distributed, with the majority of children living in LMICs; these settings witness 90 percent of metastatic cases and virtually all cases of abandonment (Chantada and others 2011).

Prevention and Early Detection

As with virtually all childhood cancers, retinoblastoma is not amenable to primary prevention. However, identification of the hereditary forms and proper counseling of these patients and their families is key to limiting the incidence and burden of retinoblastoma in those relatives.

The successful management of retinoblastoma depends on the ability to detect the disease while it is still intraocular. Disease stage correlates with delay in diagnosis; growth and invasion occur in sequence, with extension beyond the retina occurring only once the tumor has reached large intraocular dimensions. In HICs, retinoblastoma typically presents while still intraocular; in LMICs, 60–90 percent of children present with extraocular tumor. Poverty, limited health care access, poor education, and other aspects of low socioeconomic status are factors in delayed diagnosis and underdiagnosis in LMICs. The true magnitude of the problem is difficult to ascertain, given the paucity of population-based cancer registries.

Conversely, retinoblastoma educational and public awareness campaigns have been shown to increase referrals, decrease rates of advanced disease, and improve outcomes in LMICs (Leander and others 2007; Rodriguez-Galindo and others 2008). Also critical is the ability of the first health care contact to identify the problem and make the appropriate referrals. A lack of knowledge on the part of frontline health care workers has been shown to be a significant barrier, highlighting the importance of targeting educational initiatives to primary health care providers (Leal-Leal and others 2011).

Diagnosis and Staging

The diagnosis of intraocular retinoblastoma does not require pathologic confirmation. An examination under anesthesia with a maximally dilated pupil and scleral indentation is required to examine the entire retina. Additional imaging studies, including bi-dimensional ultrasound, computerized tomography, and magnetic resonance imaging, are desirable but not necessary to evaluate extraocular extension and to differentiate retinoblastoma from other causes of leukocoria.

The staging of retinoblastoma reflects the sequential nature of its progression, beginning with extension into the ocular coats (choroids and sclera) and optic nerve. Loco-regional dissemination occurs by direct extension into the orbital contents and pre-auricular lymph nodes. Extraorbital disease manifests as both intracranial dissemination and hematogenous metastases to bones, bone marrow, and liver. Patients are accordingly staged as having intraocular, orbital, or extraorbital disease (Chantada and others 2006).

For patients with intraocular retinoblastoma, dedicated staging of the eye is performed to guide treatment modalities. This classification system is based on tumor size and location within the eye, as well as the extent of tumor seeding within the vitreous cavity and subretinal space, all of which must be documented on the initial exam under anesthesia. An evaluation for the presence of metastatic disease (bone scintigraphy, bone marrow aspirates and biopsies, lumbar puncture) should be considered in patients presenting with intraocular retinoblastoma with specific high-risk features (Rodriguez-Galindo and others 2007a).

Treatment

The treatment goal is to save life and preserve vision; accordingly, treatment is individualized according to the unilaterality or bilaterality of the disease, potential for vision, and disease stage. In HICs, more than 90 percent of children present with intraocular disease; clinical and research programs aim to improve ocular salvage and preserve vision. Although surgical removal of the eye (enucleation) is commonly performed for patients with advanced intraocular unilateral disease, more conservative approaches are followed for children with bilateral and early unilateral disease. Modalities include systemic or intra-arterial chemotherapy, as well as intensive focal treatments, such as laser thermotherapy and cryotherapy (Gobin and others 2011; Rodriguez-Galindo and others 2007b).

Orbital radiation therapy is used when the preceding methods fail. For patients undergoing upfront enucleation, chemotherapy is only used in the presence of high-risk features, which in HICs occurs in 20–25 percent of cases (Rodriguez-Galindo and others 2007b). In general, the outcome for children with retinoblastoma in HICs is excellent, with survival rates in excess of 95 percent. Many of the modalities discussed require state-of-the-art equipment and expertise that are unavailable in most LMIC settings. Thus, for LMIC patients presenting with orbital disease, the use of chemotherapy, enucleation, and radiation therapy may offer the best chances of cure.

Patients presenting with metastatic disease are not curable with standard therapies in any setting; patients without central nervous system spread may benefit from intensive chemotherapy and consolidation with high-dose chemotherapy and autologous stem cell rescue (Dunkel and others 2010; Rodriguez-Galindo and others 2007b). In children in LMICs presenting with advanced extraocular retinoblastoma, measures to decrease suffering and improve quality of life may be most appropriate. Low-dose oral chemotherapy and radiation therapy may result in temporary symptom control.

More detailed treatment recommendations can be found in a published SIOP guideline developed for use in LMICs (Chantada and others 2013).

Costs of Retinoblastoma Treatment

Little is known about the cost-effectiveness of retinoblastoma treatment, but measures targeting early diagnosis are likely key. Failures in public awareness and deficiencies in education among frontline health care providers represent major barriers in early diagnosis and result in the high incidence of metastatic disease and mortality rates in LMICs (Chantada and others 2011). In LMICs, children with retinoblastoma are usually diagnosed with advanced intraocular disease; by the time leukocoria is obvious, the tumor may fill more than 50 percent of the globe, complicating ocular salvage. Delayed diagnosis remains an issue in HICs and LMICs, although with consequences on a different scale. As retinoblastoma is a cancer of the infant and young child, initiatives targeting early recognition during standard health supervision visits and immunizations should facilitate diagnosis, decrease disease and treatment burdens and costs, and increase survival (Rodriguez-Galindo 2011).

COST-EFFECTIVENESS OF TREATING CHILDHOOD CANCER

Financial objections are often raised to the treatment of childhood cancer in resource-constrained settings; policy makers and lay persons may assume that any such treatment is prohibitively expensive. However, this assumption is often unsupported.

Indeed, preliminary evidence suggests that treating childhood cancer may be highly cost-effective. Standard WHO methodology defines cost-effectiveness as the ratio of the cost required to avert one disability-adjusted life year to the annual per capita GDP of the area (WHO 2003). Ratios of 3:1 are considered cost-effective, while ratios of 1:1 are considered very cost-effective. Bhakta and others found that the amount that could be spent on a single case and still remain under the very cost-effective threshold was US$257,000 for ALL in Brazil and US$14,243 for BL in Malawi (Bhakta and others 2012). Although treatments costing these theoretical thresholds may still be unachievable for many LMICs, Bhakta and others also found that these cancers could be treated for a fraction of the threshold values: US$16,400 and less than US$50, respectively. Table 7.8 and figure 7.3 illustrate cost-effective thresholds for several malignancies in various countries and compare them with actual costs, when available. These figures, however, do not account for the initial expenditures associated with developing new pediatric oncology treatment centers, such as the initial training of personnel or acquisition of infrastructure. Further data on theoretical cost-effectiveness thresholds and real costs are needed to aid LMIC policy makers.

Discussions of cost and cost-effectiveness in pediatric oncology should consider three additional factors.

- First, adapted treatment regimens of lower intensity can cure a significant proportion of children, with further increases in intensity delivering real, but diminishing, gains. This observation suggests that in most LMICs, an initial modest commitment of funds to childhood cancer will result in a dramatic increase in survival, although further improvements will require significant additional resources.
- Second, traditional cost-effective models assume a finite resource pool; funding one intervention requires cutting another. This zero-sum assumption may not be applicable to childhood cancer. In multiple LMICs, largely through the efforts of nongovernmental organizations, private funds that otherwise may have remained outside the

Table 7.8 Comparison of Cost-Effectiveness Thresholds among Common Childhood Cancers, Selected Countries

Threshold	Brazil	Malawi	El Salvador	El Salvador	China	Brazil	United States	Brazil	Morocco
Type of pediatric cancer	ALL	BL	SR-ALL	HR-ALL	ALL	ALL	ALL	BL	Wilms
Source	Howard and others 2004	Hesseling and others 2009	Bonilla and others 2010	Bonilla and others 2010	Tang and others 2008	Brandalise and others 2010	Pui and others 2009	Sandlund and others 1997	Madani and others 2006
Event-free survival definition	5-year	1-year	5-year	5-year	5-year	5-year	5-year	5-year	5-year
Percentage abandoning treatment[a]	1	—	—	—	48.3	—	—	—	—
Percentage event-free survival[b]	63	48	56.3	48.6	38.5	83.6	85.6	39	56.0
Gross domestic product per capita	$11,900	$900	$7,600	$7,600	$8,500	$11,900	$49,000	$11,900	$5,100
Life expectancy	72.79	52.31	73.69	73.69	74.84	72.79	78.49	72.79	76.11
Age at diagnosis	5.4	6.9	4.6	7.1	4.7	5.3	5.3	5.5	3
Upper limit of very cost-effective (US$ per patient)	257,075	14,243	147,756	129,037	58,620	344,385	1,454,695	167,146	100,285
Upper limit of cost-effective (US$ per patient)	771,225	42,729	443,268	387,112	175,859	1,033,156	4,364,086	501,438	300,855

Source: Bhakta and others 2012.

Note: ALL = acute lymphoblastic leukemia; BL = Burkitt lymphoma; HR-ALL = high-risk ALL; SR-ALL = standard-risk acute lymphoblastic leukemia; — = not available.

a. When no abandonment percentage is listed, the authors included abandonment as an event when calculating event-free survival.

b. In all studies cited, relapse and abandonment were included as events when calculating event-free survival.

Figure 7.3 Cost-Effective Thresholds Compared with Actual Costs in Selected Pediatric Malignancies

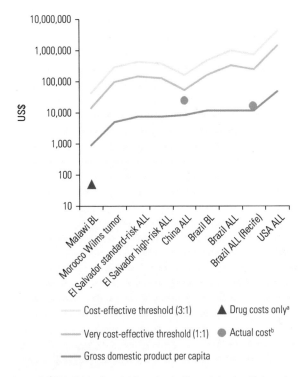

Source: © BMJ Publishing Group Ltd. Reproduced, with permission, from Bhakta and others 2012; further permission required for reuse.
Note: ALL = acute lymphoblastic leukemia; BL = Burkitt lymphoma; US$= U.S. dollars.
a. Costs only include chemotherapy and supportive care medications, such as antibiotics and antipyretics.
b. Includes total costs for the entire treatment. Not included are the costs of lost economic productivity, associated infrastructure and personnel costs, or indirect costs to parents, such as transportation, accommodation, and food.

health system have instead been allocated to pediatric oncology centers. The success of Unidad Nacional de Oncología Pediátrica (UNOP) in Guatemala provides an example of how multiple sectors can be mobilized, creating a positive-sum scenario. An initial outlay of funds to UNOP through a twinning program was leveraged into additional resources from government and private donors. The creation of an independent fundraising organization (Fundación Ayúdame a Vivir, http://ayuvi.org.gt) was essential to this outcome. Figure 7A.1 in the online annex illustrates the results of this process.

- Finally, determining whether resources should be allocated to the treatment of childhood cancer may be more complex than simple analyses of cost and cost-effectiveness. Arguments pertaining to justice, equity, and the non-monetary value of children to society may well hold resonance for governments, policy makers, health care workers, and the general public.

CONCLUSIONS AND FUTURE DIRECTIONS

Although the advances in pediatric oncology in HICs have not been fully realized in most LMICs, significant progress has been achieved in some pediatric cancer units. The challenge remains to extend this progress to all cancer centers in LMICs and to close the survival gap. The following steps are key prerequisites:

- The development of national childhood cancer strategies is needed to move beyond the twinning paradigm and to increase cure rates for entire populations. Lobbying of governments by clinicians and parent groups is required, as are strengthening links between childhood cancer advocates in HICs and LMICs.
- To better inform governments and health officials, further research into the cost and cost-effectiveness of treatment is necessary. Without such data, the misconception of childhood cancer treatment as unaffordable will persist.
- The outcomes of children with cancer should be monitored by individual treatment centers using data entry systems. These data should be used continually to evaluate and modify the local implementation of therapeutic interventions. Governments can encourage this process through national childhood cancer strategies that include high-quality pediatric registries.
- Further research is needed into how to effectively treat various different childhood malignancies in settings of different resource constraints. Studies identifying how to prevent common causes of treatment failure in LMICs should be conducted.
- The formation of cooperative groups of LMIC centers should be encouraged as forums for protocol evaluation and advocacy; AHOPCA, the French-African Pediatric Oncology Group, and the Brazilian Childhood Cooperative Group for ALL Treatment are three excellent examples. Collaborations with HIC cooperative groups may aid this process.

Pediatric oncology treatment can create a cohort of cancer survivors in LMICs while building cancer management capacity and galvanizing cancer advocacy efforts more generally. Closing the pediatric oncology survival gap will help not only the more than 150,000 children in LMICs who develop cancer every year; it will also have long-lasting benefits for the societies to which they belong.

NOTE

World Bank income classifications as of July 2014 are as follows, based on estimates of gross national income per capita for 2013:

- Low-income countries: US$1,045 or less
- Middle-income countries:
  - Lower-middle-income: US$1,046–US$4,125
  - Upper-middle-income: US$4,126–US$12,745
- High-income countries: US$12,746 or more

REFERENCES

Abd El-Aal, H. H., E. E. Habib, and M. M. Mishrif. 2005. "Wilms' Tumor: The Experience of the Pediatric Unit of Kasr El-Aini Center of Radiation Oncology and Nuclear Medicine (NEMROCK)." *Journal of the Eyptian National Cancer Institute* 17: 308–14.

Abuidris, D. O., M. E. Elimam, F. M. Nugud, E. M. Eligali, M. E. Ahmed, and others. 2008. "Wilms Tumour in Sudan." *Pediatric Blood & Cancer* 50: 1135–37.

Al Sheyyab, M., A. Bateiha, S. E. Kayed, and B. Hajjawi. 2003. "The Incidence of Childhood Cancer in Jordan: A Population-Based Study." *Annals of Saudi Medicine* 23: 260–63.

Antillon, F., F. Baez, J. C. Barrantes Zamorra, L. C. Fu, B. Moreno, and others. 2005. "AMOR: A Proposed Cooperative Effort to Improve Outcomes of Childhood Cancer in Central America." *Pediatric Blood & Cancer* 45 (2): 107–10.

Antillon-Klussmann, F., P. Valverde, C. Garrido, M. Castellanos, P. De Alarcon, and others. 2010. (abstract). "Treatment of Acute Lymphoblastic Leukemia in Limited Income Country: The Experience of the Unidad Nacional de Oncologis Pediatrica (UNOP) of Guatemala." *Pediatric Blood & Cancer* 55: 861.

Arora, R. S., T. Eden, and B. Pizer. 2007. "The Problem of Treatment Abandonment in Children from Developing Countries with Cancer." *Pediatric Blood & Cancer* 49: 941–46.

Ayoub, L., L. Fu, A. Pena, J. M. Sierra, P. C. Dominguez, and others. 2007. "Implementation of a Data Management Program in a Pediatric Cancer Unit in a Low Income Country." *Pediatric Blood & Cancer* 49 (1): 23–27. doi:10.1002/pbc.20966.

Baez, F., B. F. Fossati, E. Ocampo, V. Conter, A. Flores, and others. 2002. "Treatment of Childhood Wilms' Tumor without Radiotherapy in Nicaragua." *Annals of Oncology* 13: 944–48.

Baez, F., E. Ocampo, V. Conter, A. Flores, T. Gutierrez, and others. 1997. "Treatment of Childhood Hodgkin's Disease with COPP or COPP-ABV (Hybrid) without Radiotherapy in Nicaragua." *Annals of Oncology* 8: 247–50.

Bhakta, N., A. L. C. Martiniuk, S. Gupta, and S. C. Howard. 2012. "The Cost-Effectiveness of Treating Paediatric Cancer in Low-Income and Middle-Income Countries: A Case-Study Approach Using Acute Lymphocytic Leukaemia in Brazil and Burkitt Lymphoma in Malawi." *Archives of Disease in Childhood*. doi:10.1136/archdischild-2011-301419.

Bonilla, M., S. Gupta, R. Vasquez, S. L. Fuentes, G. deReyes, and others. 2010. "Predictors of Outcome and Methodological Issues in Children with Acute Lymphoblastic Leukemia in El Salvador." *European Journal of Cancer* 46 (18): 3280–86.

Bonilla, M., N. Rossell, C. Salaverria, S. Gupta, R. Barr, and others. 2009. "Prevalence and Predictors of Abandonment of Therapy among Children with Cancer in El Salvador." *International Journal of Cancer* 125 (9): 2144–46.

Brandalise, S. R., V. R. Pinheiro, S. S. Aguiar, E. I. Matsuda, R. Otubo, and others. 2010. "Benefits of the Intermittent Use of 6-Mercaptopurine and Methotrexate in Maintenance Treatment for Low-Risk Acute Lymphoblastic Leukemia in Children: Randomized Trial from the Brazilian Childhood Cooperative Group: Protocol ALL-99." *Journal of Clinical Oncology* 28: 1911–18.

Burkitt, D. 1958. "A Sarcoma Involving the Jaws of African Children." *British Journal of Surgery* 46: 218–23.

Chandra, J., R. Naithani, V. Singh, Y. K. Saxena, M. Sharma, and others. 2008. "Developing Anticancer Chemotherapy Services in a Developing Country: Hodgkin Lymphoma Experience." *Pediatric Blood & Cancer* 51: 485–88.

Chantada, G., F. Doz, C. B. Antoneli, R. Grundy, F. F. Clare Stannard, and others. 2006. "A Proposal for an International Retinoblastoma Staging System." *Pediatric Blood & Cancer* 47 (6): 801–05.

Chantada, G., S. Luna-Fineman, R. S. Sitorus, M. Kruger, T. Israels, and others. 2013. "SIOP-PODC Recommendations for Graduated-Intensity Treatment of Retinoblastoma in Developing Countries." *Pediatric Blood & Cancer* 60 (5): 719–27.

Chantada, G. L., I. Qaddoumi, S. Canturk, V. Khetan, Z. Ma, and others. 2011. "Strategies to Manage Retinoblastoma in Developing Countries." *Pediatric Blood & Cancer* 56 (3): 341–48.

Crawford, J. R., T. J. Macdonald, and R. J. Packer. 2007. "Medulloblastoma in Childhood: New Biological Advances." *The Lancet Neurology* 6 (12): 1073–85.

Creutzig, U., M. Zimmermann, D. Reinhardt, M. Dworzak, J. Stary, and others. 2004. "Early Deaths and Treatment-Related Mortality in Children Undergoing Therapy for Acute Myeloid Leukemia: Analysis of the Multicenter Clinical Trials AML-BFM 93 and AML-BFM 98." *Journal of Clinical Oncology* 22 (21): 4384–93.

Davidson, A., P. Hartley, F. Desai, J. Daubenton, H. Rode, and others. 2006. "Wilms Tumour Experience in a South African Centre." *Pediatric Blood & Cancer* 46: 465–71.

Day, S. W., J. Garcia, F. Antillon, J. A. Wilimas, L. M. Mckeon, and others. 2012. "A Sustainable Model for Pediatric Oncology Nursing Education in Low-Income Countries." *Pediatric Blood & Cancer* 58: 163–66.

Day, S. W., L. Segovia, P. Viveros, A. Banfi, G. K. Rivera, and others. 2011. "Development of the Latin American Centre for Pediatric Oncology Nursing Education." *Pediatric Blood & Cancer* 56: 5–6.

de Camargo, B., J. de Oliveira Ferreira, R. de Souza Reis, S. Ferman, M. de Oliveira Santos, and others. 2011. "Socioeconomic Status and the Incidence of Non-Central

Nervous System Childhood Embryonic Tumours in Brazil." *BMC Cancer* 11: 160.

De Campo, J. F. 1986. "Ultrasound of Wilms' Tumor." *Pediatric Radiology* 16: 21–24.

Dimaras, H., K. Kimani, E. A. O. Dimba, P. Gronsdahl, A. White, and others. 2012. "Retinoblastoma." *The Lancet* 379 (9824): 1436–46.

Dunkel, I. J., H. S. L. Chan, R. Jubran, G. L. Chantada, S. Goldman, and others. 2010. "High-Dose Chemotherapy with Autologous Hematopoietic Stem Cell Rescue for Stage 4B Retinoblastoma." *Pediatric Blood & Cancer* 55 (1): 149–52.

Ellison, L. F., L. Pogany, and L. S. Mery. 2007. "Childhood and Adolescent Cancer Survival: A Period Analysis of Data from the Canadian Cancer Registry." *European Journal of Cancer* 43: 1967–75.

Ethier, M-C., E. Blanco, T. Lehrnbecher, and L. Sung. 2011. "Lack of Clarity in the Definition of Treatment-Related Mortality: Pediatric Acute Leukemia and Adult Acute Promyelocytic Leukemia as Examples." *Blood* 118: 5080–83.

Fajardo-Gutierrez, A., S. Juarez-Ocana, G. Gonzalez-Miranda, V. Palma-Padilla, R. Carreon-Cruz, and others. 2007. "Incidence of Cancer in Children Residing in Ten Jurisdictions of the Mexican Republic: Importance of the Cancer Registry (A Population-Based Study)." *BMC Cancer* 19 (7): 68.

Ferlay, J., H. R. Shin, F. Bray, D. Forman, C. Mathers, and others. 2010. "Estimates of Worldwide Burden of Cancer in 2008: GLOBOCAN 2008." *International Journal of Cancer* 127: 2893–917.

Ganesan, P., L. Kumar, V. Raina, A. Sharma, S. Bakhshi, and others. 2011. "Hodgkin's Lymphoma—Long Term Outcome: An Experience from a Tertiary Care Cancer Center in North India." *Annals of Hematology* 90: 1153–60.

Gavidia, R., S. L. Fuentes, R. Vasquez, M. Bonilla, M-C. Ethier, and others. 2012. "Low Socioeconomic Status Is Associated with Prolonged Times to Assessment and Treatment, Sepsis and Infectious Death in Pediatric Fever in El Salvador." *Plos One* 7 (8): E43639.

Gobin, Y., I. J. Dunkel, B. P. Marr, S. E. Brodie, and D. H. Abramson. 2011. "Intra-Arterial Chemotherapy for the Management of Retinoblastoma: Four-Year Experience." *Archives of Ophthalmology* 129 (6): 732–37.

Graf, N., M. F. Tournade, and J. de Kraker. 2000. "The Role of Preoperative Chemotherapy in the Management of Wilms' Tumor: The SIOP Studies." *International Society of Pediatric Oncology. Urologic Clinics of North America* 27: 443–54.

Green, D. M. 2004. "The Treatment of Stages I–IV Favorable Histology Wilms' Tumor." *Journal of Clinical Oncology* 22: 1366–72.

Gupta, S., F. A. Antillon, M. Bonilla, L. Fu, S. C. Howard, and others. 2011. "Treatment-Related Mortality in Children with Acute Lymphoblastic Leukemia in Central America." *Cancer* 117: 4788–95.

Gupta, S., M. Bonilla, S. L. Fuentes, M. Caniza, S. C. Howard, and others. 2009. "Incidence and Predictors of Treatment-Related Mortality in Paediatric Acute Leukaemia in El Salvador." *British Journal of Cancer* 100 (7): 1026–31.

Gupta, S., S. Yeh, A. Martiniuk, C. G. Lam, H. Y. Chen, and others. 2013. "The Magnitude and Predictors of Abandonment of Therapy in Pediatric Acute Leukemia in Middle-Income Countries: A Systematic Review and Meta-Analysis." *European Journal of Cancer* 49: 2555–64.

Hadley, G. P. 2010. "Can Surgeons Fill the Void in the Management of Children with Solid Tumours in Not-Developing Countries?" *Pediatric Blood & Cancer* 55: 16–17.

Hadley, L. G., B. S. Rouma, and Y. Saad-Eldin. 2012. "Challenge of Pediatric Oncology in Africa." *Seminars in Pediatric Surgery* 21: 136–41.

Harif, M., S. Barsaoui, S. Benchekroun, L. Boccon-Gibod, R. Bouhas, and others. 2005. "Treatment of Childhood Cancer in Africa: Preliminary Results of the French-African Paediatric Oncology Group." *Archives de Pediatrie* 12: 851–53.

Harif, M., S. Barsaoui, S. Benchekroun, R. Bouhas, P. Doumbe, and others. 2008. "Treatment of B-Cell Lymphoma with LMB Modified Protocols in Africa: Report of the French-African Pediatric Oncology Group (GFAOP)." *Pediatric Blood & Cancer* 50: 1138–42.

Hartman, D. S., and R. C. Sanders. 1982. "Wilms' Tumor versus Neuroblastoma: Usefulness of Ultrasound in Differentiation." *Journal of Ultrasound in Medicine* 1: 117–22.

Hesseling, P., T. Israels, M. Harif, G. Chantada, and E. Molyneux. 2012. "Practical Recommendations for the Management of Children with Endemic Burkitt Lymphoma (BL) in a Resource Limited Setting." *Pediatric Blood & Cancer* 60 (3): 357–62. doi:10.1002/Pbc.24407.

Hesseling, P., E. Molyneux, S. Kamiza, T. Israels, and R. Broadhead. 2009. "Endemic Burkitt Lymphoma: A 28-Day Treatment Schedule with Cyclophosphamide and Intrathecal Methotrexate." *Annals of Tropical Paediatrics* 29 (1): 29–34.

Hesseling, P., E. Njume, F. Kouya, T. Katayi, P. Wharin, and others. 2012. "The Cameroon 2008 Burkitt Lymphoma Protocol: Improved Event-Free Survival with Treatment Adapted to Disease Stage and the Response to Induction Therapy." *Pediatric Hematology and Oncology* 29 (2): 119–29.

Hines-Thomas, M. R., S. C. Howard, M. M. Hudson, M. J. Krasin, S. C. Kaste, and others. 2010. "Utility of Bone Marrow Biopsy at Diagnosis in Pediatric Hodgkin's Lymphoma." *Haematologica* 95: 1691–96.

Hodgson, D. C., M. M. Hudson, and L. S. Constine. 2007. "Pediatric Hodgkin Lymphoma: Maximizing Efficacy and Minimizing Toxicity." *Seminars in Radiation Oncology* 17: 230–42.

Howard, S. C., D. Campana, E. Coustan-Smith, F. Antillon, M. Bonilla, and others. 2005. "Development of a Regional Flow Cytometry Center for Diagnosis of Childhood Leukemia in Central America." *Leukemia* 19: 323–25.

Howard, S. C., D. P. Jones, and C. H. Pui. 2011. "The Tumor Lysis Syndrome." *New England Journal of Medicine* 364: 1844–54.

Howard, S. C., M. L. Metzger, J. A. Wilimas, Y. Quintana, C. H. Pui, and others. 2008. "Childhood Cancer Epidemiology in Low-Income Countries." *Cancer* 112: 461–72.

Howard, S. C., M. Pedrosa, M. Lins, A. Pedrosa, C. H. Pui, and others. 2004. "Establishment of a Pediatric Oncology Program and Outcomes of Childhood Acute Lymphoblastic Leukemia in a Resource-Poor Area." *Journal of the American Medical Association* 291 (20): 2471–75.

Hunger, S. P., X. Lu, M. Devidas, B. M. Camitta, P. S. Gaynon, N. J. Winick, and others. 2012. "Improved Survival for Children and Adolescents with Acute Lymphoblastic Leukemia between 1990 and 2005: A Report from the Children's Oncology Group." *Journal of Clinical Oncology* 30 (14): 1663–69.

Hunger, S. P., D. Reyes, O. Negrin, M. Montero, L. De La Rosa, and others. 2011. "Decreased Early Mortality and Increased Survival with Less Intensive Therapy for Acute Lymphoblastic Leukemia (ALL) in the Dominican Republic." Abstract. *Pediatric Blood & Cancer* 57: 761.

Hunger, S. P., L. Sung, and S. C. Howard. 2009. "Treatment Strategies and Regimens of Graduated Intensity for Childhood Acute Lymphoblastic Leukemia in Low-Income Countries: A Proposal." *Pediatric Blood & Cancer* 52 (5): 559–65.

Israels, T. 2012. "Wilms Tumor in Africa: Challenges to Cure." *Pediatric Blood & Cancer* 58: 3–4.

Israels, T., E. Borgstein, M. Jamali, J. de Kraker, H. N. Caron, and E. M. Molyneux. 2009. "Acute Malnutrition Is Common in Malawian Patients with a Wilms Tumor: A Role for Peanut Butter." *Pediatric Blood & Cancer* 53: 1221–26.

Israels, T., E. Borgstein, D. Pidini, G. Chagaluka, J. de Kraker, and others. 2012. "Managment of Children with a Wilms Tumor in Malawi, Sub-Saharan Africa." *Journal of Pediatric Hematology/Oncology* 34: 606–10.

Israels, T., C. Moreira, T. Scanlan, E. Molyneux, S. Kampondeni, and others. 2013. "Clinical Guidelines for the Management of Children with Wilms Tumour in a Low Income Setting." *Paediatrics and International Child Health* 60 (1): 5–11.

Kulkarni, K. P., and R. K. Marwaha. 2010. "Pattern and Implications of Therapy Abandonment in Childhood Acute Lymphoblastic Leukemia." *Asian Pacific Journal of Cancer Prevention* 11: 1435–36.

Kutluk, T., A. Varan, N. Buyukpamukcu, L. Atahan, M. Caglar, and others. 2006. "Improved Survival of Children with Wilms Tumor." *Journal of Pediatric Hematology/Oncology* 28: 423–26.

Lange, B. J., F. O. Smith, J. Feusner, D. R. Barnard, P. Dinndorf, and others. 2008. "Outcomes in CCG-2961: A Children's Oncology Group Phase 3 Trial for Untreated Pediatric Acute Myeloid Leukemia: A Report from the Children's Oncology Group." *Blood* 111 (3): 1044–53.

Leal-Leal, C., H. Dilliz-Nava, M. Flores-Rojo, and J. Robles-Castro. 2011. "First Contact Physicians and Retinoblastoma in Mexico." *Pediatric Blood & Cancer* 57: 1109–12.

Leander, C., L. C. Fu, A. Pena, S. C. Howard, C. Rodriguez-Galindo, and others. 2007. "Impact of an Education Program on Late Diagnosis of Retinoblastoma in Honduras." *Pediatric Blood & Cancer* 49 (6): 817–19.

Lemerle, J., P. A. Voute, M.-F. Tournade, C. Rodary, J. F. Delemarre, and others. 1983. "Effectiveness of Preoperative Chemotherapy in Wilms' Tumor: Results of an International Society of Paediatric Oncology (SIOP) Clinical Trial." *Journal of Clinical Oncology* 1: 604–09.

Lewis, N., J. L. Young, P. Hesseling, P. Mccormick, and N. Wright. 2012. "Epidemiology of Burkitt's Lymphoma in Northwest Province, Cameroon, 2003–2010." *Paediatrics and International Child Health* 32 (2): 82–85.

Liu, Y., J. Chen, J. Tang, S. Ni, H. Xue, and others. 2009. "Cost of Childhood Acute Lymphoblastic Leukemia Care in Shanghai, China." *Pediatric Blood & Cancer* 53 (4): 557–62. doi:10.1002/pbc.22127.

Liu, L., H. L. Johnson, S. Cousens, J. Perin, S. Scott, and others. 2012. "Global, Regional, and National Causes of Child Mortality: An Updated Systematic Analysis for 2010 with Time Trends Since 2000." *The Lancet* 379 (9832): 2151–61.

Lowe, L. H., B. H. Isuani, R. M. Heller, S. M. Stein, J. E. Johnson, and others. 2000. "Pediatric Renal Masses: Wilms Tumor and Beyond." *Radiographics* 20: 1585–603.

Lozano, R., H. Wang, K. J. Foreman, J. K. Rajaratnam, M. Naghavi, and others. 2011. "Progress towards Millennium Development Goals 4 and 5 on Maternal and Child Mortality: An Updated Systematic Analysis." *The Lancet* 378 (9797): 1139–65.

Luo, X. Q., Z. Y. Ke, X. Q. Guan, Y. C. Zhang, L. B. Huang, and others. 2008. "The Comparison of Outcome and Cost of Three Protocols for Childhood Non-High Risk Acute Lymphoblastic Leukemia in China." *Pediatric Blood & Cancer* 51 (2): 204–09.

Luo, X. Q., Z. Y. Ke, L. B. Huang, X. Q. Guan, Y. C. Zhang, and X. L. Zhang. 2009a. "High-Risk Childhood Acute Lymphoblastic Leukemia in China: Factors Influencing the Treatment and Outcome." *Pediatric Blood & Cancer* 52 (2): 191–15.

———. 2009b. "Improved Outcome for Chinese Children with Acute Promyelocytic Leukemia: A Comparison of Two Protocols." *Pediatric Blood and Cancer* 53 (3): 325–28.

Madani, A., S. Zafad, M. Harif, M. Yaakoubi, S. Zamiati, and others. 2006. "Treatment of Wilms Tumor According to SIOP 9 Protocol in Casablanca, Morocco." *Pediatric Blood & Cancer* 46 (4): 472–75.

Magrath, I., E. Steliarova-Foucher, E. Sidnei, R. C. Ribeiro, M. Harif, and others. 2013. "Pediatric Cancer in Low-Income and Middle-Income Countries." *The Lancet Oncology* 14: 3104–16.

Maris, J. M. 2010. "Recent Advances in Neuroblastoma." *New England Journal of Medicine* 362: 2202–11.

Marjerrison, S., C. V. Fernandez, V. E. Price, E. Njume, and P. Hesseling. 2012. "The Use of Ultrasound in Endemic Burkitt Lymphoma in Cameroon." *Pediatric Blood & Cancer* 58 (3): 352–55.

Masera, G., F. Baez, A. Biondi, F. Cavalli, V. Conter, and others. 1998. "North-South Twinning in Paediatric Haemato-Oncology: The La Mascota Programme, Nicaragua." *The Lancet* 352 (9144): 1923–36. doi:S0140673698070779 [Pii].

Masera, G., T. Eden, M. Schrappe, J. Nachman, H. Gadner, and others. 2004. "Statement by Members of the Ponte Di Legno Group on the Right of Children to Have Full Access to Essential Treatment for Acute Lymphoblastic Leukemia." *Pediatric Blood & Cancer* 43 (2): 13–14. doi:10.1002 /Pbc.20135.

Matthay, K. K., J. G. Villablanca, R. C. Seeger, D. O. Stram, R. E. Harris, and others. 1999. "Treatment of High-Risk Neuroblastoma with Intensive Chemotherapy, Radiotherapy, Autologous Bone Marrow Transplantation, and 13-Cis-Retinoic Acid." *New England Journal of Medicine* 341 (16): 1165–73.

Mauz-Korholz, C., D. Hasenclever, W. Dorffel, K. Ruschke, T. Pelz, and others. 2010. "Procarbazine-Free OEPA-COPDAC Chemotherapy in Boys and Standard OPPA-COPP in Girls Have Comparable Effectiveness in Pediatric Hodgkin's Lymphoma: The GPOH-HD-2002 Study." *Journal of Clinical Oncology* 28 (23): 3680–86.

Metzger, M., A. Billett, and M. P. Link. 2012. "The Impact of Drug Shortages on Children with Cancer: The Example of Mechlorethamine." *New England Journal of Medicine* 367 (26): 2461–63.

Metzger, M. L., and J. S. Dome. 2005. "Current Therapy for Wilms' Tumor." *The Oncologist* 10 (10): 815–26.

Metzger, M. L., S. C. Howard, L. C. Fu, A. Pena, R. Stefan, and others. 2003. "Outcome of Childhood Acute Lymphoblastic Leukaemia in Resource-Poor Countries." *The Lancet* 362 (9385): 706–08.

Moreira, C., M. N. Nachef, S. Ziamati, Y. Ladjaj, S. Barsaoui, and others. 2012. "Treatment of Nephroblastoma in Africa: Results of the First French African Pediatric Oncology Group (GFAOP) Study." *Pediatric Blood & Cancer* 58 (1): 37–42.

Moricke, A., M. Zimmermann, A. Reiter, G. Henze, A. Schrauder, and others. 2010. "Long-Term Results of Five Consecutive Trials in Childhood Acute Lymphoblastic Leukemia Performed by the ALL-BFM Study Group from 1981 to 2000." *Leukemia* 24: 265–84. doi:Leu2009257 [Pii]10.1038/Leu.2009.257.

Mostert, S., R. S. Arora, M. Arreola, P. Bagai, P. Friedrich, and others. 2011. "Abandonment of Treatment for Childhood Cancer: Position Statement of a SIOP PODC Working Group." *The Lancet Oncology* 12 (8): 719–20.

Mostert, S., M. N. Sitaresmi, C. M. Gundy, V. Janes, Sutaryo, and A. J. Veerman. 2010. "Comparing Childhood Leukaemia Treatment before and after the Introduction of a Parental Education Programme in Indonesia." *Archives of Disease in Childhood* 95 (1): 20–25.

Mostert, S., M. N. Sitaresmi, C. M. Gundy, Sutaryo, and A. J. Veerman. 2006. "Influence of Socioeconomic Status on Childhood Acute Lymphoblastic Leukaemia Treatment in Indonesia." *Pediatrics* 118 (6): E1600–06.

Murphy, S. B. 1978. "Childhood Non-Hodgkin's Lymphoma." *New England Journal of Medicine* 299: 1446–48.

Nachman, J. B., R. Sposto, P. Herzog, G. S. Gilchrist, S. L. Wolden, and others. 2002. "Randomized Comparison of Low-Dose Involved Field Radiotherapy and No Radiotherapy for Children with Hodgkin's Disease Who Acheive a Complete Response to Chemotherapy." *Journal of Clinical Oncology* 20 (18): 3765–71.

Ngoma, T., M. Adde, M. Durosinmi, J. Githang'a, Y. Aken'Ova, and others. 2012. "Treatment of Burkitt Lymphoma in Equatorial Africa Using a Simple Three-Drug Combination Followed by a Salvage Regimen for Patients with Persistent or Recurrent Disease." *British Journal of Haematology* 158 (6): 749–62.

Nguyen, K., M. Devidas, S. C. Cheng, M. La, E. A. Raetz, and others. 2008. "Factors Influencing Survival after Relapse from Acute Lymphoblastic Leukemia: A Children's Oncology Group Study." *Leukemia* 22 (12): 2142–50. doi:Leu2008251 [Pii]10.1038/Leu.2008.251.

Olweny, C. L., E. Katongole-Mbidde, C. Kiire, S. K. Lwanga, I. Magrath, and others. 1978. "Childhood Hodgkin's Disease in Uganda: A Ten Year Experience." *Cancer* 42: 787–92.

Ortega, J. J., L. Madero, G. Martin, A. Verdeguer, P. Garcia, and others. 2005. "Treatment with All-Trans Retinoic Acid and Anthracycline Monotherapy for Children with Acute Promyelocytic Leukemia: A Multicentre Study by the PETHEMA Group." *Journal of Clinical Oncology* 23: 7632–40.

Ortiz, R., S. Abad, A. Pena, F. Spreafico, J. Wilimas, and others. 2012. "Treatment of Wilms Tumor (WT) within the Central American Association of Pediatric Hematology/Oncology (AHOPCA): Report from Guatemala, Honduras, El Salvador, and Nicaragua: Causes of Treatment Failure." *Pediatric Blood & Cancer* 59 (6): 971.

Parkin, D. M., E. Kramarova, G. J. Draper, E. Masuyer, J. Michaelis, and others. 1998. *International Incidence of Childhood Cancer.* Vol. II. Lyon, France: International Agency for Research on Cancer.

Patte, C., A. Auperin, M. Gerrard, J. Michon, R. Pinkerton, and others. 2007. "Results of the Randomized International FAB/LMB96 Trial for Intermediate Risk B-Cell Non-Hodgkin Lymphoma in Children and Adolescents: It Is Possible to Reduce Treatment for the Early Responding Patients." *Blood* 109 (7): 2773–80.

Patton, G. C., C. Coffey, C. Cappa, D. Currie, L. Riley, and others. 2012. "Health of the World's Adolescents: A Synthesis of Internationally Comparable Data." *The Lancet* 379 (9826): 1665–75.

Pediatric Oncology Group of Ontario. 2012. *Provincial Pediatric Oncology Satellite Program.* http://www.pogo.ca /care/satelliteprograms.

Pedrosa, F., M. Bonilla, A. Liu, K. Smith, D. Davis, and others. 2000. "Effect of Malnutrition at the Time of Diagnosis on the Survival of Children Treated for Cancer in El Salvador and Northern Brazil." *Journal of Pediatric Hematology/ Oncology* 22 (6): 502–05.

Perez-Cuevas, R., S. V. Doubova, M. Zapata-Tarres, S. Flores-Hernandez, L. Frazier, and others. 2013. "Scaling Up Cancer Care for Children without Medical Insurance in Developing Countries: The Case of Mexico." *Pediatric Blood & Cancer* 60: 196–203. doi:10.1002/Pbc.24265.

Perilongo, G., R. Maibach, E. Shafford, L. Brugieres, P. Brock, and others. 2009. "Cisplatin versus Cisplatin Plus Doxorubicin for Standard-Risk Hepatoblastoma." *New England Journal of Medicine* 361: 1662–70.

Prucker, C., A. Attarbaschi, C. Peters, M. Dworzak, U. Potschger, and others. 2009. "Induction Death and Treatment-Related Mortality in First Remission of Children with Acute Lymphoblastic Leukemia: A Population-Based Analysis of the Austrian Berlin-Frankfurt-Munster Study Group." *Leukemia* 23: 1264–69.

Pui, C. H., D. Campana, D. Pei, W. P. Bowman, J. T. Sandlund, and others. 2009. "Treating Childhood Acute Lymphoblastic Leukemia without Cranial Irradiation." *New England Journal of Medicine* 360: 2730–41.

Pui, C. H., and S. C. Howard. 2008. "Current Management and Challenges of Malignant Disease in the CNS in Paediatric Leukaemia." *The Lancet Oncology* 9 (3): 257–68.

Pui, C. H., D. Pei, A. S. Pappo, S. C. Howard, C. Cheng, and others. 2012. "Treatment Outcomes in Black and White Children with Cancer: Results from the SEER Database and St. Jude Children's Research Hospital, 1992 through 2007." *Journal of Clinical Oncology* 30: 2005–12.

Pui, C. H., L. L. Robison, and A. T. Look. 2008. "Acute Lymphoblastic Leukemia." *The Lancet* 371 (9617): 1030–43.

Razack, R., P. Michelow, G. Leiman, A. Harnekar, J. Poole, and others. 2011. "An Interinstitutional Review of the Value of FNAB in Pediatric Oncology in Resource-Limited Countries." *Diagnostic Cytopathology* 40 (9): 770–76.

Ribeiro, R., and C. H. Pui. 2005. "Saving the Children: Improving Childhood Cancer Treatment in Developing Countries." *New England Journal of Medicine* 352: 2158–60.

Ribeiro, R. C., E. Steliarova-Foucher, I. Magrath, J. Lemerle, T. Eden, and others. 2008. "Baseline Status of Paediatric Oncology Care in Ten Low-Income or Mid-Income Countries Receiving My Child Matters Support: A Descriptive Study." *The Lancet Oncology* 9: 721–29.

Ries, L. A., M. A. Smith, J. G. Gurney, M. Linet, T. Tamra, and others, editors. 1999. *Cancer Incidence and Survival among Children and Adolescents: United States SEER Program 1975–1995.* NIH Pub. No. 99–4649. Bethesda, MD: National Cancer Institute SEER Program.

Rivera-Luna, R., C. Correa-Gonzalez, E. Altamirano-Alvarez, F. Sanchez-Zubieta, R. Cardenas-Cardos, and others. 2012. "Incidence of Childhood Cancer among Mexican Children Registered under a Public Medical Insurance Program." *International Journal of Cancer* 132: 1646–50. doi:10.1002/Ijc.27771.

Rodriguez-Galindo, C. 2011. "The Basics of Retinoblastoma: Back to School." *Pediatric Blood & Cancer* 57 (7): 1093–94. doi:10.1002/Pbc.23305.

Rodriguez-Galindo, C., G. Chantada, B. G. Haik, and M. W. Wilson. 2007a. "Treatment of Retinoblastoma: Current Status and Future Perspectives." *Current Treatment Options in Neurology* 9 (4): 294–307.

———. 2007b. "Retinoblastoma: Current Treatment and Future Perspectives." *Current Treatment Options in Neurology* 9 (4): 294–307.

Rodriguez-Galindo, C., M. W. Wilson, G. Chantada, L. Fu, I. Qaddoumi, and others. 2008. "Retinoblastoma: One World, One Vision." *Pediatrics* 122 (3): E763–70.

Sackmann-Muriel, F., P. Zubizarreta, G. Gallo, M. Socpinaro, D. Alderete, and others. 1997. "Hodgkin Disease in Children: Results of a Prospective Randomized Trial in a Single Institution in Argentina." *Medical and Pediatric Oncology* 29: 544–52.

Sala, A., F. Antillon, P. Pencharz, R. Barr, and others for the AHOPCA Consortium. 2005. "Nutritional Status in Children with Cancer: A Report from the AHOPCA Workshop Held in Guatemala City, August 31–September 5, 2004." *Pediatric Blood & Cancer* 45: 230–36.

Sandlund, J. T., T. Fonseca, T. Leimig, L. Verissimo, C. W. Berard, and others. 1997. "Predominance and Characteristics of Burkitt Lymphoma among Children with Non-Hodgkin Lymphoma in Northeastern Brazil." *Leukemia* 11 (5): 743–46.

Schilling, F. H., C. Spix, F. Berthold, R. Erttmann, N. Fehse, and others. 2002. "Neuroblastoma Screening at One Year of Age." *New England Journal of Medicine* 346: 1047–53.

Siddiqui, N., B. Ayub, F. Badar, and A. Zaidi. 2006. "Hodgkin's Lymphoma in Pakistan: A Clinico-Epidemiological Study of 658 Cases at a Cancer Center in Lahore." *Asian Pacific Journal of Cancer Prevention* 7: 651–55.

Siegel, R., D. Naishadham, and A. Jemal. 2013. "Cancer Statistics, 2013." *CA: A Cancer Journal for Clinicians* 63 (1): 11–30.

Silverman, L. B., K. E. Stevenson, J. E. O'Brien, B. L. Asselin, R. D. Barr, and others. 2010. "Long-Term Results of Dana-Farber Cancer Institute ALL Consortium Protocols for Children with Newly Diagnosed Acute Lymphoblastic Leukemia (1985–2000)." *Leukemia* 24 (2): 320–34. doi:Leu2009253 [Pii]10.1038/Leu.2009.253.

Sitaresmi, M. N., S. Mostert, R. M. Schook, and A. J. Veerman. 2010. "Treatment Refusal and Abandonment in Childhood Acute Lymphoblastic Leukemia in Indonesia: An Analysis of Causes and Consequences." *Psychooncology* 19 (4): 361–67. doi:10.1002/Pon.1578.

Smith, M. A., N. L. Seibel, S. F. Altekruse, L. A. G. Ries, D. L. Melbert, and others. 2010. "Outcomes for Children and Adolescents with Cancer: Challenges for the Twenty-First Century." *Journal of Clinical Oncology* 28: 2625–34.

Sripada, P. V., S. G. Tenali, M. Vasudevan, S. Viswanadhan, D. Sriraman, and others. 1995. "Hybrid (COPP/ABV) Therapy in Childhood Hodgkin's Disease: A Study of 53 Cases during 1989–1993 at the Cancer Institute, Madras." *Pediatric Hematology Oncology* 12: 333–41.

St. Jude Children's Research Hospital. 2012. *St. Jude Children's Research Hospital Cure4Kids: Pediatric Oncology Education.* St. Jude Children's Research Hospital. http://www.cure4kids.org.

Stefan, D. C., and D. Stones. 2009. "How Much Does It Cost to Treat Children with Hodgkin Lymhpoma in Africa?" *Leukemia & Lymphoma* 50: 196–99.

Stiller, C. A., and D. M. Parkin. 1996. "Geographic and Ethnic Variations in the Incidence of Childhood Cancer." *British Medical Bulletin* 52: 682–703.

Tang, Y., X. Xu, H. Song, S. Yang, S. Shi, and others. 2008. "Long-Term Outcome of Childhood Acute Lymphoblastic Leukemia Treated in China." *Pediatric Blood & Cancer* 51: 380–86.

Testi, A. M., A. Biondi, F. L. Coco, M. L. Moleti, F. Giona, and others. 2005. "GIMEMA-AIEOP AIDA Protocol for the Treatment of Newly Diagnosed Acute Promyelocytic Leukemia (APL) in Children." *Blood* 106: 447–53.

Traore, F., C. Coze, J.-J. Atteby, N. Andre, C. Moreira, and others. 2011. "Cyclophosphomide Monotherapy in Children with Burkitt Lymphoma: A Study from the French-African Pediatric Oncology Group (GFAOP)." *Pediatric Blood & Cancer* 56 (1): 70–76.

Van Litsenburg, R. R., C. A. Uyl-De Groot, H. Raat, G. J. Kaspers, and R. J. Gemke. 2011. "Cost-Effectiveness of Treatment of Childhood Acute Lymphoblastic Leukemia with Chemotherapy Only: The Influence of New Medication and Diagnostic Technology." *Pediatric Blood & Cancer* 57 (6): 1005–10. doi:10.1002/Pbc.23197.

Veerman, A. J., Sutaryo, and Sumadiono. 2005. "Twinning: A Rewarding Scenario for Development of Oncology Services in Transitional Countries." *Pediatric Blood & Cancer* 45 (2): 103–06. doi:10.1002/Pbc.20390.0.

Viana, M. B., R. A. Fernandes, B. M. De Oliveira, M. Murao, C. De Andrade Paes, and others. 2001. "Nutritional and Socio-Economic Status in the Prognosis of Childhood Acute Lymphoblastic Leukemia." *Haematologica* 86 (2): 113–20.

Vujanic, G. M., A. Kelsey, C. Mitchell, R. S. Shannon, and P. Gornali. 2003. "The Role of Biopsy in the Diagnosis of Renal Tumors of Childhood: Results of the UKCCSG Wilms Tumor Study 3." *Medical and Pediatric Oncology* 40: 18–22.

Vujanic, G. M., B. Sandstedt, A. Kelsey, and N. J. Sebire. 2009. "Central Pathology Review in Multicenter Trials and Studies: Lessons from the Nephroblastoma Trials." *Cancer* 115: 1977–83.

Wang, Y. R., R. M. Jin, J. W. Xu, and Z. Q. Zhang. 2011. "A Report about Treatment Refusal and Abandonment in Children with Acute Lymphoblastic Leukemia in China, 1997–2007." *Leukemia Research* 35 (12): 1628–31.

WHO (World Health Organization). 2003. *Making Choices in Health: WHO Guide to Cost-Effectiveness Analysis*, edited by T. Tan-Torres Edejer, R. Baltussen, T. Adam, R. Hutubessy, A. Acharya, and others. Geneva: WHO.

————. 2013. *WHO Model List of Essential Medicines for Children*. WHO, Geneva. http://www.who.int/medicines /publications/essentialmedicines/en/index.html.

Wilde, J. C., W. Lameris, E. H. Van Hasselt, E. Molyneux, H. A. Heij, and others. 2010. "Challenges and Outcome of Wilms' Tumour Management in a Resource-Constrained Setting." *African Journal of Paediatric Surgery* 7: 159–62.

Woessmann, W., K. Seidemann, G. Mann, M. Zimmermann, B. Burkhardt, and others. 2005. "The Impact of the Methotrexate Administration Schedule and Dose in the Treatment of Children and Adolescents with B-Cell Neoplasms: A Report of the BFM Group Study NHL-BFM95." *Blood* 105 (3): 948–58.

Womer, R. B., D. C. West, M. D. Krailo, P. S. Dickman, B. Pawel, and others. 2012. "Randomized Controlled Trial of Interval-Compressed Chemotherapy for the Treatment of Localized Ewing Sarcoma: A Report from the Children's Oncology Group." *Journal of Clinical Oncology* 30 (33): 4148–54.

Woods, W. G., K. Kobrinsky, J. D. Buckley, J. W. Lee, J. Sanders, and others. 1996. "Time-Sequential Induction Therapy Improves Postremission Outcome in Acute Myeloid Leukemia: A Report from the Children's Cancer Group." *Blood* 87 (12): 4979–89.

Zsiros, J., R. Maibach, E. Shafford, L. Brugieres, P. Brock, and others. 2010. "Successful Treatment of Childhood High-Risk Hepatoblastoma with Dose-Intensive Multiagent Chemotherapy and Surgery: Final Results of the SIOPEL-3HR Study." *Journal of Clinical Oncology* 28 (15): 2584–90.

Liver Cancer

Hellen Gelband, Chien-Jen Chen, Wendong Chen,
Silvia Franceschi, Sir Andrew Hall, W. Thomas London,
Katherine A. McGlynn, and Christopher P. Wild

INTRODUCTION

Deaths from liver cancer are common, especially in East Asia and Pacific, South Asia, and parts of Sub-Saharan Africa, largely as a result of infection decades ago. As the toll from other cancers is likely to climb in the coming decades, however, liver cancer incidence and mortality rates should fall, as generations vaccinated against the hepatitis B virus (HBV)—the cause of most liver cancers globally—reach middle and old age. Much still needs to be done and it is feasible and affordable to hasten the decline. Much can also be done to address other causes of liver cancer—including some on the rise, in particular, obesity-related non-alcoholic fatty liver disease (NAFD)—in the coming years and decades. The latter half of the twentieth century witnessed the identification of the main causes of liver cancer and deployment of the first cancer prevention vaccine for humans. All of the risk factors that lead to cirrhosis cause at least as many noncancer deaths as cancer deaths. Controlling these risk factors would not only reduce the incidence of liver cancer; it would also reduce the incidence of cirrhosis and its other complications, notably, end-stage liver disease and portal hypertension.

GLOBAL BURDEN OF LIVER CANCER

Primary liver cancer—cancer originating in the liver—is the sixth most commonly occurring cancer in the world (782,000 cases in 2012) and the second largest cause of

cancer mortality (746,000 deaths in 2012) (Ferlay and others 2013). Incidence and mortality rates vary greatly, mirroring the uneven distribution of major risk factors. In most high-rate liver cancer areas, the dominant risk factors are chronic infection with HBV and consumption of foods contaminated with the mycotoxin aflatoxin B1. In contrast, in most low-rate areas, the major risk factors are infection with the hepatitis C virus (HCV), excessive alcohol consumption, obesity, and diabetes. HBV and HCV have been classified by the International Agency for Research on Cancer (IARC) as carcinogenic to humans (Group 1).

The most common histologic type of primary liver cancer, hepatocellular carcinoma (HCC), arises from the epithelial liver cells known as *hepatocytes*. Globally, approximately 80–85 percent of primary liver cancers are HCCs; the rates of primary liver cancer and rates of HCC are roughly equivalent. Intrahepatic cholangiocarcinoma, which arises from *cholangiocytes*—epithelial cells that line the bile duct—is the second most common type of primary liver cancer, but it accounts for only 10–12 percent of primary liver cancer worldwide. Infection with liver flukes (flatworms) is a major cause of cholangiocarcinoma in high-incidence regions.

Incidence and Mortality Rates[1]

The highest national liver cancer incidence rates in the world are found in East Asia and Pacific and Sub-Saharan Africa (maps 8.1 and 8.2). Approximately

Corresponding author: Hellen Gelband, gelband@cddep.org

Map 8.1 Age-Standardized Liver Cancer Incidence Rates for Women, 2012

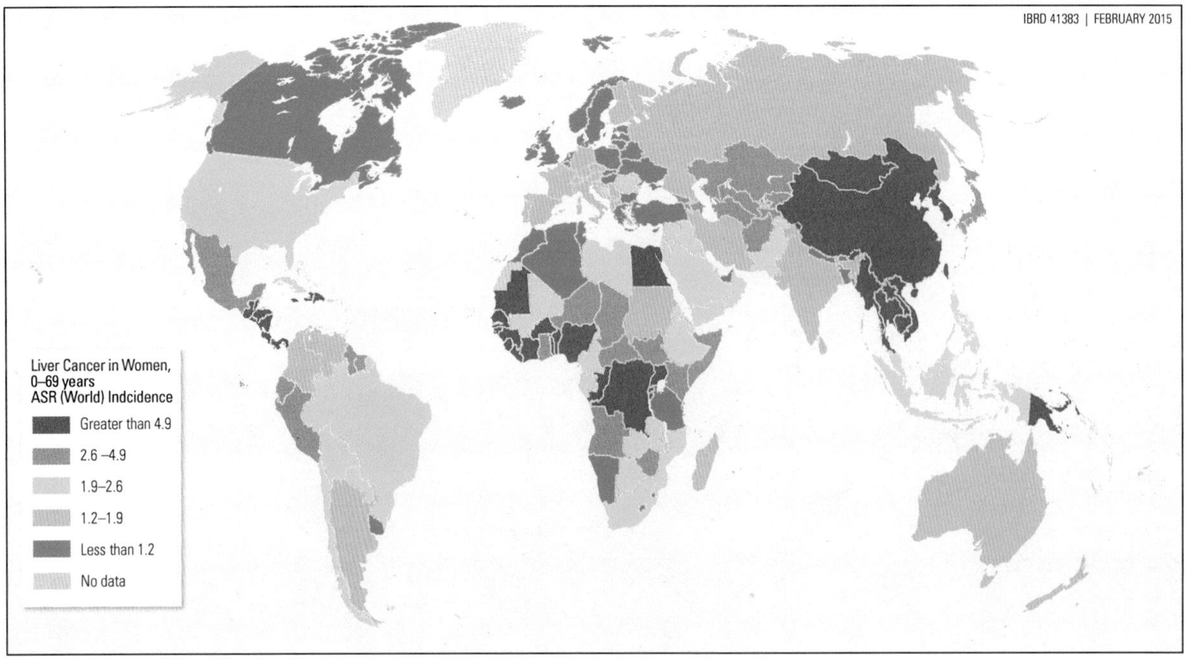

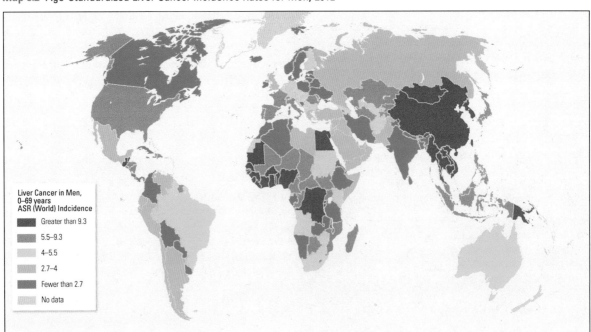

IBRD 41383 | FEBRUARY 2015

Liver Cancer in Women,
0–69 years
ASR (World) Indcidence

- Greater than 4.9
- 2.6 –4.9
- 1.9–2.6
- 1.2–1.9
- Less than 1.2
- No data

Source: Ferlay and others 2013.
Note: ASR = age-standardized rate.

Map 8.2 Age-Standardized Liver Cancer Incidence Rates for Men, 2012

Liver Cancer in Men,
0–69 years
ASR (World) Indcidence

- Greater than 9.3
- 5.5–9.3
- 4–5.5
- 2.7–4
- Fewer than 2.7
- No data

Source: Ferlay and others 2013.
Note: ASR = age-standardized rate.

85 percent of the total liver cancer burden is concentrated in these areas; China alone—because of high rates and a very large population—bears over half of the global burden (Ferlay and others 2013). Although more liver cancers occur in China than any other country, the country with the highest liver cancer incidence rate in the world is Mongolia (78.1 per 100,000 population), with an incidence rate more than three times as high as that of China (22.3 per 100,000) (Ferlay and others 2013). These exceedingly high rates are reportedly the result of high rates of infection with HBV, HCV, or both, as well as co-infection of HBV carriers with hepatitis D virus (HDV) (Oyunsuren and others 2006).

The prevalence of HBV infection in Mongolia is likely to decline as the results of a childhood HBV vaccination program that began in 1991 decrease the prevalence of new infections. However, the continued high rate of HCV infection may result in liver cancer incidence rates increasing for some years (Dondog and others 2011). Alcohol consumption rates are reportedly higher in Mongolia than in many Asian populations, a factor that may contribute to the liver cancer burden (Alcorn 2011).

In addition to China, other East Asian and Pacific countries and economies with incidence rates greater than 20 per 100,000 include Taiwan, China; the Republic of Korea; the Lao People's Democratic Republic; Thailand; and Vietnam. Thailand has high rates of both HCC and intrahepatic cholangiocarcinoma in the northeastern part of the country, where liver fluke infection is common. Countries in Sub-Saharan Africa with incidence rates greater than 20 per 100,000 include The Gambia and Guinea; rates in the Democratic Republic of Congo (10.6 per 100,000), Ghana (11.1 per 100,000), and Guinea-Bissau (13.4 per 100,000) are almost as high (Ferlay and others 2013). Although the reported incidence of liver cancer in Sub-Saharan Africa is lower than the incidence in East Asia and Pacific, at least some of the difference arises from underdiagnosis and the historic paucity of well-functioning, reliable cancer registries. Another reason for the lower incidence in Sub-Saharan Africa is that babies are less likely to become infected with HBV in the perinatal period compared with babies in Asia (Marinier and others 1985). The later age at infection results in lower HBV replication rates in Sub-Saharan Africa than in East Asia and Pacific (Evans and others 1998). Nevertheless, in both East Asia and Pacific and Sub-Saharan Africa, the major risk factor for liver cancer is chronic HBV infection. Notable exceptions are the Arab Republic of Egypt and Japan, in which HCV is the dominant risk factor.

In contrast to these high-rate areas, rates are low in North and South America and northern Europe. Incidence rates in these areas are generally less than 5 per 100,000. Rates are intermediate—typically between 5 per 100,000 and 10 per 100,000—in some countries of central Europe (for example, Greece and Italy) and central Asia (for example, Kazakhstan, the Kyrgyz Republic, Pakistan, and Turkmenistan). Not all low- and middle-income countries (LMICs) have high HBV infection rates. A prime example is India, which has historically had low HBV infection rates and, as a result, low liver cancer incidence rates.

At all incidence levels, almost all countries report rates in men that are twofold to threefold higher than rates in women. The greatest gender disparity in incidence, however, is not reported by countries with the highest liver cancer rates, such as Mongolia (where the ratio in men to women is 1.6) (men, 97.8; women, 61.1), but by countries with intermediate rates, such as France (men, 11.3; women, 2.5) and Spain (men, 9.9; women, 2.4). An exception to the general predominance in men occurs in Central America and Mexico, where the rates of both genders are low and not very different. Although the reasons for higher rates in men in most regions are not completely understood, the differences may be partly explained by the sex-specific prevalence of risk factors. Men are more likely to be chronically infected with HBV and HCV, consume alcohol, and smoke cigarettes. Whether androgenic hormones or increased genetic susceptibility also predispose men to the development of liver cancer is unclear (Hsieh and others 2007).

Age-Specific Incidence

Liver cancer incidence rates increase with age in all populations, with the highest rates in those ages 75 years and older. The age-specific curves look somewhat different in various regions, but in no area do the rates decline among older persons (men and women combined). In a low-rate area, such as northern Europe, rates are generally very low before age 40 and then rise exponentially with age. In high-rate areas of East Asia and Pacific, rates become elevated in childhood and continue to rise with age. In contrast, in the high-rate area of Sub-Saharan Africa, rates increase until age 55 years and then plateau until age 70 years. The reasons for the slightly different patterns in Asia and Sub-Saharan Africa may be related to competing causes of mortality and differences in mean ages at HBV infection and/or differences in HBV viral replication patterns (Evans and others 1998).

Incidence by World Bank Economic Group

Globally, the single greatest determinant of liver cancer prevalence in any country is the prevalence of chronic HBV infection. As chronic HBV infection has historically

Figure 8.1 Age-Standardized Liver Cancer Incidence and Mortality Rates in Men and Women, by World Bank Income Classification, 2012

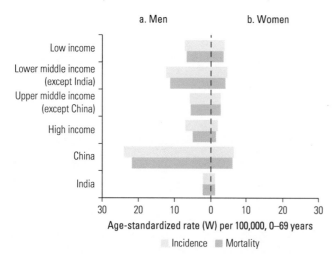

Source: Ferlay and others 2013.

been much more common in LMICs, liver cancer has been more prevalent in these countries (figure 8.1). In general, the incidence rates decrease as a country's per capita gross domestic product (GDP) increases. Among the low-income countries (LICs), 13 of the 34 (38 percent) have rates of 10 per 100,000 or greater. In the lower-middle-income group, excluding India, 18 of 49 countries (37 percent) have rates of 10 per 100,000 or higher. In the upper-middle-income group, excluding China, only 2 of 55 countries (4 percent) have rates of this magnitude; in the high-income countries (HICs), only 2 of 75 countries (3 percent) have rates of 10 per 100,000 or higher.

A rapidly expanding economy does not have an immediate effect on a country's HBV carrier rate and does not greatly alter its liver cancer incidence in the short term. For example, although China has undergone rapid economic development in the late twentieth century, it still has a high liver cancer rate. With economic growth, however, comes the ability to reduce future liver cancer rates by funding universal HBV vaccination of newborns and aflatoxin abatement programs, ensuring that the blood supply is free of HCV, and possibly treating HCV infection.

Trends

From 1983–87 through 1998–2002, liver cancer incidence increased in many areas of the world. Increases were notable in northern Europe, India, Israel, North and South America, Oceania, and most countries in southern Europe. In contrast, incidence rates declined in most eastern Asian countries. Increases in incidence in HICs and India have been linked to HCV infection, increasing rates of obesity and diabetes, and improved treatment of cirrhosis (which reduces the risk of death from cirrhosis, leaving individuals at persistent risk of HCC).

Rates have been declining in some eastern Asian countries for several reasons. In Japan, the large cohort of individuals infected with HCV in the 1930s and 1940s is dying off, and the rate of HCV-related HCC is declining accordingly (Tanaka and others 2002). In China, where HBV is the dominant risk factor, HBV vaccination of newborns was introduced in the mid-1980s but ramped up only after 2000. Vaccine recipients are still too young to have their rates greatly affect the rates in the overall population. It is more likely that the rates in China have declined because exposure to aflatoxin B1 in the diet has decreased as a result of shifting from a corn-based to a rice-based diet (Sun and others 2013). The declining rates of HCC in younger age groups reported in Jiangsu Province, a high aflatoxin B1 area, support this hypothesis (Chen and others 2006; Wang and others 2010).

Prognosis and DALYs

The prognosis for liver cancer, even in HICs, is unfavorable. In the United States, the one-year survival rate is less than 50 percent; the five-year survival rate is only 16 percent (NCI 2013). As with all cancers, survival is best when detected early—for localized liver cancer, five-year survival is 29 percent, but it falls to 3 percent for cancers detected late (NCI 2013). Survival is even less favorable in LMICs. Mortality rates in all locations are roughly equivalent to incidence rates, and the number of years lived with disability is very small. Accordingly, disability-adjusted life years (DALYs) caused by ill health, disability, or early death from liver cancer are almost identical to the years of life lost (YLLs) because of liver cancer. The age-standardized rate of DALYs is highest in the high-incidence areas of eastern Asia (744 per 100,000 for men; 277 per 100,000 for women) and western Africa (451 per 100,000 for men; 213 per 100,000 for women); it is lowest in the low-incidence areas of Europe (110 per 100,000 for men; 45 per 100,000 for women) and North America (109 per 100,000 for men; 39 per 100,000 for women).

Major Risk Factors

Hepatitis B Virus

An estimated two billion people alive today have been infected with HBV; about 360 million of these are chronically infected (carriers) (Dienstag 2008). Routes of transmission vary by life stage, but HBV is never spread by air, food, or water. Neonates may be infected by their mothers, if the mothers are infectious carriers. During childhood, transmission can occur among children living in close proximity, although the precise route is unclear. The virus is found in the blood and in most body secretions. In adult life, the virus can be spread sexually via semen and vaginal fluid or by contaminated needles, frequently the result of intravenous drug misuse. Blood transfusion was an important source of infection before the introduction of donor selection and serological screening of donated blood.

The natural history of chronic infection is the development of chronic hepatitis, then cirrhosis, and finally, liver cancer. However, especially in Sub-Saharan Africa, cancer can develop without underlying cirrhosis. Aflatoxin exposure multiplies the risk of liver cancer in chronic carriers by a factor of twofold to tenfold. The interval from the initial HBV infection to the development of cancer is in the range of 5–75 years, with most cases manifesting after several decades. In 1994, IARC declared HBV a human carcinogen (Group 1).

The age of infection is critically important in determining whether the infection becomes chronic. Newborns infected by their mothers have an 80–90 percent probability of becoming carriers. Those infected in the first five years of life beyond the perinatal period have a 20–50 percent probability; those infected in adult life have a probability of less than 10 percent. This is the inverse of the risk of developing acute hepatitis, which manifests in one-third of adult infections with the characteristic fever, jaundice, and lethargy, whereas it is very unusual following infection in children under age five years.

Acute hepatitis carries a risk of death of 1 percent or less. Chronic infection increases the risk of primary liver cancer by tenfold to fiftyfold.

In some populations in the pre-vaccination era, the prevalence of chronic HBV infection was 10–15 percent of the adult population. This was the case in China and surrounding East Asian countries, much of Sub-Saharan Africa, and the Amazon forest. These high carriage rates resulted from very high rates of infection in the early years of life, either perinatally from mothers or in early childhood from other children (WHO 2004). In China, some 40 percent of carriers were infected perinatally by their mothers. In contrast, in Sub-Saharan Africa, only 10 percent of carriers were infected perinatally and 90 percent were infected through child-to-child transmission during the first few years of life, but overall, rates were very high. These differences resulted from the fact that about half of Chinese women who were HBV-positive remained infectious into adult life, whereas only 10 percent of HBV-positive African women did so (Marinier and others 1985).

Rates of liver cancer in Chinese carriers are higher than in Sub-Saharan African carriers. The reasons for this are unclear but may be related to the differences in age at infection.

Hepatitis C Virus
HCV, a blood-borne RNA virus identified in 1988, was declared a definite human carcinogen by IARC in 1994. The World Health Organization (WHO)

estimates that about 180 million people, some 3 percent of the world's population, are infected with HCV, of which 130 million are chronic carriers. At least three million to four million people are newly infected each year; this compares with the approximately 360 million people chronically infected with HBV. HCV prevalence is highest (10 percent or more) in Pakistan (Ahmad 2004), Egypt (Attia 1998), Mongolia (Dondog and others 2011), and some parts of China (Gao and others 2011). Prevalence is also high in some parts of Italy (Fusco and others 2008) and Japan (Tanaka and others 2002). Globally, 10 million intravenous drug users are HCV-positive, with prevalence in this group exceeding 60 percent in most countries (Nelson and others 2011).

HCV transmission is primarily from contaminated blood or blood products; however, HCV can be acquired from sexual and household contacts. Acute infection with HCV is usually asymptomatic; in approximately 75 percent of people, HCV persists as a chronic infection, in which HCV RNA and serum HCV antibodies (anti-HCV) can be detected in the blood (Alter and Seeff 2000). Approximately 20 percent of individuals with chronic HCV will develop HCC by age 75 (Huang and others 2011).

Evidence suggests that HCV prevalence is substantially underestimated for several reasons:

- Country-specific data are absent, notably in LICs.
- Surveillance systems that focus on acute HCV infection are insensitive because the infection is rarely symptomatic.
- Prevalence surveys tend to include mainly young adults (for example, blood donors or pregnant women), while transmission of HCV through contaminated blood and needles is more probable in adulthood and old age than in childhood (Dondog and others 2011).

The seroprevalence of HCV and HBV in cases of HCC can be used to estimate HCV and HBV prevalence where accurate population-based data are lacking. In a large meta-analysis of seroprevalence (Raza and others 2007), a higher proportion of cases had HBV than HCV in most countries in East Asia and Pacific, Latin America and the Caribbean, South Asia, and Sub-Saharan Africa. In contrast, in most European countries, Japan, the United States, and, among low-resource countries, Egypt and Pakistan, HCV was more frequent than HBV (figure 8.2). The proportion of HCV-associated HCC cases is growing steadily in other countries and economies, for example, Taiwan, China (Lu and others 2006).

HCV epidemics have accompanied the increase in the availability of injections and blood transfusions in several countries (Prati 2006). Massive and unsafe injection campaigns have occurred in many countries, for example, the anti-schistosomal treatments in Japan

Figure 8.2 HCV and HBV Presence in HCC Cases: Countries and Economies Where HCV Predominates or Is Increasing

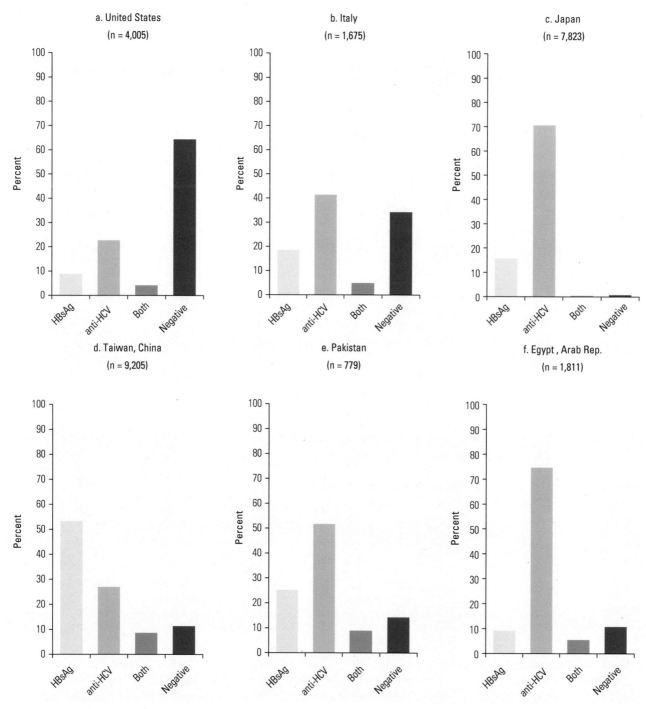

a. United States
(n = 4,005)

b. Italy
(n = 1,675)

c. Japan
(n = 7,823)

d. Taiwan, China
(n = 9,205)

e. Pakistan
(n = 779)

f. Egypt , Arab Rep.
(n = 1,811)

Source: Adapted from Raza and others 2007.
Note: Includes studies that reported seroprevalence of both hepatitis B surface antigen (HBsAg) and anti-HCV, alone and in combination, for at least 20 hepatocellular carcinoma cases; updated through 2010. HBV = hepatitis B virus; HCV = hepatitis C virus; HCC = hepatocellular carcinoma.

starting in the 1920s and in Egypt in the 1960s, and the use of intravenous stimulants starting in Japan in the 1940s (Tanaka and others 2002). Unsafe blood transfusions and medical procedures have tended to increase in times of military conflicts. By the end of the 1980s, most chronic transfusion recipients, and virtually all patients receiving clotting factor concentrates, had been infected by HCV (Prati 2006). New cases of HCV infection greatly decreased in high-resource countries in the 1990s after the introduction of HCV testing for blood donors, inactivation procedures for blood derivatives, and disposable needles and syringes.

However, HCV-related HCC continued to increase as those people who were infected decades ago aged. Trends in HCV prevalence were generally dominated by cohort effects: an estimated 73 percent of HCV infections in the United States, for example, involve individuals born between 1945 and 1965 (Smith and others 2012). In some low-resource countries, the spread of HCV has continued and may undermine the future benefits of HBV immunization (Dondog and others 2011).

Aflatoxins

Aflatoxins are secondary metabolites of the fungal species *Aspergillus flavus* and *A. parasiticus*. These toxins contaminate many staple cereals and oilseeds, with particularly high levels found on maize (corn) and groundnuts (peanuts) (IARC 2002). Contamination occurs during crop cultivation and increases postharvest under poor storage conditions, in which high humidity and temperature promote fungal growth and toxin production. An estimated 4.5 billion people worldwide are exposed to aflatoxins (Williams and others 2004); the highest exposures are in LICs in East and Southeast Asia and Sub-Saharan Africa, where regulatory control is weak.

The naturally occurring aflatoxins are aflatoxins B1, B2, G1, and G2 (AFB1, AFB2, AFG1, and AFG2, respectively). AFB1 is the most abundant, toxic, and carcinogenic. Aflatoxins M1 and M2 (AFM1 and AFM2, respectively), the hydroxylation products of AFB1 and AFB2, respectively, are found in milk and milk products (IARC 2002).

Aflatoxins induce toxicity and tumors in the liver in a wide range of animal species. Epidemiological studies in different populations have established aflatoxins as a risk factor for HCC (IARC 2002, 2012a). Prospective cohorts have provided the most convincing evidence, with the increased risk highest among individuals who were also chronically infected with HBV (Qian and others 2013; Wang and others 1996; Wu and others 2009). The effect of aflatoxins in the absence of chronic HBV infection is more difficult to assess because of their common co-occurrence in many populations. Nevertheless, some studies have reported an increased risk with aflatoxin

exposure among individuals not chronically infected with HBV (Omer and others 2004; Wu and others 2009). In contrast to aflatoxins and HBV, there has been little focus on the potential for interaction with HCV. Knowledge about aflatoxin and risk of liver cirrhosis is also limited (Kuniholm and others 2008). However, exposure to aflatoxins in childhood has been linked to hepatomegaly (enlarged liver) (Gong and others 2012).

Improved understanding of the biochemistry of aflatoxin-cell interactions strongly supports the association between aflatoxin exposure and liver cancer. Following bioactivation, AFB1 binds predominantly to guanine in DNA, leading to a mutation from guanine to thymine. In HCCs collected from areas where aflatoxin exposure is high, up to half have been shown to harbor this type of mutational change in one specific location within the tumor suppressor gene TP53. This same mutation is extremely rare in liver tumors from regions where aflatoxin exposure is low (Wild and Gong 2010).

Based on animal, epidemiological, and mechanistic data, IARC has classified mixtures of naturally occurring aflatoxins as carcinogenic to humans (Group 1) (IARC 2002, 2012a). An association between early life exposure to aflatoxins and impaired child growth has been reported and may represent a significant additional disease burden globally (Gong and others 2002, 2004).

Aflatoxin exposure is ubiquitous in many of the poorest populations worldwide and is a cause of human liver cancer. Aflatoxins appear to be more potent among HBV chronic carriers than among noncarriers, but there may also be an increased risk in the absence of HBV. Given more than 350 million chronic HBV carriers worldwide, many in areas with endemic aflatoxin consumption, the need for reduction of aflatoxin exposure is highly relevant for liver cancer prevention. Adverse effects of early life exposure to aflatoxins add to the public health concerns related to these potent, naturally occurring toxins.

Alcohol

In 1988, IARC classified alcohol as a Group 1 human carcinogen of the liver, causing HCC (IARC 2012a). The National Institute of Alcohol Abuse and Alcoholism (NIAAA) has also documented that prolonged heavy drinking is associated with primary liver cancer (NIAAA 1993), mainly through cirrhosis (Corrao and Arico 2000). The dose-response relationship for the amount of alcohol consumed and the risk of HCC has been explored in a meta-analysis (Corrao and others 2004), which produced a relative risk of liver cirrhosis of 27 and of HCC of 1.8 for the heaviest drinkers (100 grams daily) compared with non-drinkers. The incidence of liver cancer increases by 0.7 per 1,000 for every additional drink, defined as 14.0 grams (0.6 ounces) of pure alcohol by

NIAAA, regularly consumed per day (Allen and others 2009). Alcohol-associated liver cirrhosis is the most important risk factor for HCC in populations with low prevalence of HBV and HCV, as in the United States and northern Europe (Boffetta and Hashibe 2006). Alcohol-related HCC without preexisting cirrhosis is rare.

Alcohol is synergistic with tobacco consumption and chronic viral hepatitis (either HBV or HCV) in causing HCC (Haenel 1989). Alcohol as a solvent increases the exposure of hepatocytes to carcinogens such as 4-aminobiphenyl and polycyclic aromatic hydrocarbons in tobacco smoke (IARC 2012a). However, alcohol consumption remains an independent risk factor for HCC after adjustment for multiple host and viral factors (Chen, Yu, and Liaw 1997). The risk of developing HBV/HCV-related HCC is about twice as high for habitual alcohol drinkers as for non-drinkers (Chen and Chen 2002).

The carcinogenicity of alcoholic beverages does not seem to vary with the type of beverage; the effect appears to be caused by ethanol itself. After ingestion, ethanol is converted by the enzymes alcohol dehydrogenase and cytochrome P450 2E1 into acetaldehyde, which is oxidized by aldehyde dehydrogenase (ALDH) to acetate (IARC 2012b). Acetaldehyde is a plausible candidate for the carcinogenic effects of alcoholic drinks through two mechanisms. It forms adducts (bonds) with DNA, leading to mutations, and it can increase cell proliferation (Boffetta and Hashibe 2006). Ethanol-caused hepatocellular injury can result in enhanced fibrogenesis and, finally, cirrhosis. A deficiency of ALDH—and subsequent inefficient oxidation of acetaldehyde to acetate—substantially increases the risk of alcohol-related liver cancer.

Liver Flukes

Opisthorchis viverrini and *Clonorchis sinensis*—liver flukes—are the strongest risk factors for cholangiocarcinoma, accounting for about 15 percent of liver cancers globally. *O. viverrini* was classified by IARC as a human carcinogen in 1994, and *C. sinensis* was so classified in 2009. These small, but not microscopic (1–2.5 centimeters by 0.3–0.5 centimeter), worms are prevalent only in parts of eastern Asia, but infection in some places is extraordinarily common—historically reaching virtually entire populations in some areas—and possibly one-sixth of those with chronic infection develop cholangiocarcinoma, starting in middle age. The worms, protected in the bile duct, live surprisingly long lives—up to two decades or more for *C. sinensis* but possibly less than 10 years for *O. viverrini* if untreated (Sithithaworn and Haswell-Elkins 2003).

O. viverrini infects at least 10 million people in Lao PDR and Thailand and an unknown number in Cambodia and Vietnam (Sripa and others 2011). The prevalence of infection varies greatly. In Thailand in 1980–81, approximately 35 percent of the population in the northeast was infected; prevalence in the south was close to zero. The national average was 14 percent. By 2001, presumably as a result of treatment and control, prevalence in the northeast had fallen to 15 percent and the national average to 10 percent.

The variation in *O. viverrini* infection in Thailand is echoed in the variation in mortality rates from cholangiocarcinoma, which varies more than 12-fold from a low in Prachuap province in the south to a high in Nakhon Phanom province in the northeast (Sripa and others 2011).

In 2009, IARC estimated that 35 million people were infected with *C. sinensis* in China, Korea, Lao PDR, Thailand, the Russian Federation, and Vietnam (IARC 2009). Infections are occasionally reported in Malaysia and Singapore. In China, prevalence varies, with the highest rates in Guangdong (16.4 percent) and Guangxi (9.8 percent) in southern China and in Korean ethnic communities in northeastern Heilongjiang province (4.7 percent) (Shin and others 2010).

The spread of these liver flukes is restricted by the distribution of the two definitive hosts other than humans—particular species of snail (mainly of the genus *Bothynia*) and cyprinid fish—and the cultural practice of eating raw fish (either fresh or fermented fish can harbor fluke metacercariae that infect humans after ingestion). The transmission cycle also requires eggs from fish-eating hosts, which emerge in feces, to contaminate the freshwater bodies inhabited by the snails and fish—the consequences of the poor sanitation that is synonymous with poverty. Other fish-eating mammals, notably dogs and cats, play some role in maintaining the cycle, but their part is thought to be relatively unimportant.

Obesity

Obesity is discussed last because it currently is not an important risk factor in LMICs. However, like other obesity-related health problems, cirrhosis from NAFD is on the rise in HICs (Baffy, Brunt, and Caldwell 2012; Michelotti, Machado, and Diehl 2013; Vanni and Bugianesi 2014). All expectations are that in the coming decades it will have a similar impact in LMICs. HCC is the cancer most strongly affected by NAFD.

INTERVENTIONS

Hepatitis B Virus

The major intervention is primary prevention of chronic infection by vaccination (vaccination has no impact on established chronic infection). The vaccine consists of the surface antigen of the virus, an antigen that circulates in the blood of carriers. The first vaccine was made by separating this antigen from the blood of carriers and sterilizing it. Although this plasma-derived vaccine is still used in some parts of the world, in most places it has been replaced by recombinant hepatitis B vaccine, which uses a manufactured surface antigen.

The plasma-derived vaccine first became available in 1982 and initial trials in high-risk populations showed it to be safe and effective. It has subsequently been introduced in 168 countries as part of the routine childhood vaccination program. However, this has been a gradual process over the intervening 30 years. Three doses of the vaccine are required to ensure protection against acute hepatitis and chronic infection. These can be given at intervals of one month. Most countries use a schedule of doses at two, three, and four months of age, either as a separate injection or as part of a combination vaccine with diphtheria, pertussis, and tetanus. Early studies showed that administration of the vaccine in the first 24 hours of life could prevent transmission from a highly infectious mother. The recommended WHO schedule is three or four doses of vaccine, with the initial dose within 24 hours of birth (WHO 2009).

The HBV vaccine is supported by The Vaccine Aliance (Gavi) in countries eligible because of low income levels. By the end of 2011, Gavi estimated that the vaccines it has supported would save 5.5 million lives, 3.7 million of them attributable to the HBV vaccine.

Dramatic reductions in the prevalence of HBV carriage have been demonstrated in early adopters of universal vaccination. In China, for example, vaccination has reduced the prevalence of carriage from greater than 10 percent to less than 1 percent (Cui and others 2010). In Taiwan, China, mortality rates from infant fulminant hepatitis, chronic liver disease, and HCC have declined more than 90 percent among those vaccinated since a nationwide HBV immunization began (Chiang and others 2013).

Screening for and Treating HBV

In addition to vaccination, testing blood donors for chronic infection and excluding positive blood has eliminated this relatively small but important source of infection. A global program to reduce needle reuse and to ensure the safe disposal of used needles has also reduced the risk of infection.

More recently, antiviral treatment of those chronically infected has been shown to reduce the risk of liver cancer. Studies are underway in countries with a high prevalence of HBV in adults to screen for carriage, evaluate those found infected, and treat those with significant disease.

Hepatitis C Virus

Although no vaccines against HCV are available, most HCV transmission could be avoided. Needle sharing by intravenous drug users has become the predominant source of HCV acquisition in high-resource countries (Nelson and others 2011). In contrast, most infections in low-resource countries are iatrogenic, acquired through contaminated blood and contaminated injections of medications. Many low-resource countries, mostly in East Asia and Pacific, South Asia, and Sub-Saharan Africa, do not systematically screen blood donations for HCV, although screening for HBV and human immunodeficiency virus (HIV) is common (Prati 2006). Blood safety in low-resource countries is additionally threatened by lack of voluntary, nonpaid blood donors; inadequate supplies of medical instruments and laboratory reagents; and lack of infrastructure. Many transfusions could be avoided with the use of appropriate measures to optimize the patient's own blood volume before surgery and to minimize blood loss during surgery (Goodnough 2013).

More than 16 billion injections are administered annually in low-resource countries (Prati 2006). Especially high rates of injections have been reported in Mongolia and some countries of the former Soviet Union; they have also been reported in Pakistan (Ahmad 2004) and some Sub-Saharan African countries (Attia 1998). The most frequently injected medications, nearly all of which could be taken orally, include antibiotics, vitamins, iron, and analgesics, as well as treatments for nonspecific symptoms such as headache, fatigue, or fever. Injections represent an important source of revenue for providers and are encouraged by the popular belief that injections are more effective than oral administration. Insufficient hygiene, inappropriate use of multiple-dose medication vials, and sharing bottles of intravenous solution also contribute to the spread of HCV. Finally, HCV transmission can occur through traditional medicine (for example, acupuncture and scarring) and outside health care settings (for example, tattooing). Preventing infection is the most affordable option to reduce HCV-related diseases in low-resource countries (box 8.1).

Screening and Treating Chronic HCV

Much progress has been made in the management of chronic hepatitis C, in terms of eradicating the virus and reducing hepatic and extrahepatic complications and HCV-related deaths. Increasingly efficacious regimens have been developed to eradicate the virus. The first was interferon monotherapy, which was introduced in 1990; a combination of ribavirin and pegylated interferon was introduced in 2002; and in 2011, a protease inhibitor (telaprevir or boceprevir) was added to ribavirin and pegylated interferon (Morgan and others 2013).

A new generation of direct-acting antiviral drugs, the first two of which entered the market in late 2013—sofosbuvir and simeprevir—is promising. Compared with the best previous regimens, they are significantly

Interventions to Prevent Blood-Borne Infections, Including HCV

- Increase awareness of the importance of HCV and other blood-borne infections and the means of preventing them, among the population, health care workers, and traditional healers.
- Use oral treatments instead of injections and use alternatives to blood transfusions whenever possible.
- Use safe injection practices in the management of sharp waste.
- Provide services to intravenous drug users, including access to sterile needles and syringes.
- Make blood supplies safe by recruiting voluntary donors and screening all donated blood for markers of HCV, HBV, and HIV.

Note: HBV = hepatitis B virus; HCV = hepatitis C virus; HIV = human immunodeficiency virus.

more effective in clearing the virus (in trials, up to 100 percent of patients cleared, including multiple viral genotypes), are taken for half the treatment period of previous regimens (12 versus 24 weeks), have few side effects, and are taken orally (with another oral antiviral drug, ribavirin) rather than having an injectable component. At least two other similar drugs are in late-stage development. Hepatitis C medications were put on the WHO Essential Medicines List in 2015. They are all, however, priced well above what is affordable in LMICs; they would have serious budgetary implications, even in HICs. In the United States in 2014, sofosbuvir is priced at US$84,000 for a course of treatment, and simeprivir at US$66,000. Because the previous regimens are also expensive (US$25,000–US$45,000), relatively few HCV-infected people anywhere have been treated. In 2010, an estimated 7 percent of those with chronic infection in France were treated, 3 percent in the United Kingdom, and 0.3 percent in Russia (Razavi and others 2013).

The only way the new anti-HCV drugs can benefit most infected individuals is if they can be made affordable, particularly in LMICs. Patents on these drugs will not begin to expire until 2025. In the meantime, several hundred thousand deaths per year could be averted by finding an acceptable means of setting lower prices, at least for LMICs, similar to the success story of low-priced antiretrovirals for HIV.

One of the factors allowing for low-priced antiretrovirals for HIV has been the economies of scale that come with a hugely expanded market. Hill and others (2014) estimate the minimum production costs of the two available HCV drugs, the two in late-stage development, and ribavirin, using the history of HIV drugs as a guide. Using these costs, they estimate the costs of complete combination 12-week regimens at from US$78 to US$166 for the least expensive, to US$232 to US$454 for the most expensive. Recognizing that companies require compensation for their investment and profit, these are not suggested as realistic sales prices; however, with tiered pricing (charging higher prices in richer countries) and high volumes, affordable prices can be envisioned and should be pursued by the global community for this now highly curable infection.

Widespread treatment implies screening, as well, which currently is recommended for relatively few individuals. Should treatment be made affordable, the recommended populations should be expanded.

Aflatoxins

Human exposure to aflatoxins can be reduced in several ways. *Aspergillus spp.* infects crops during cultivation, but toxins accumulate postharvest under poor storage conditions. Accordingly, preharvest and postharvest interventions can contribute to controlling aflatoxins (Groopman, Kensler, and Wild 2008; Wild and Hall 2000). Aflatoxin control measures are applied to commercial crops to meet the stringent regulatory demands to limit exposure in HICs. Industrial-scale sorting, optimal storage, and extensive aflatoxin testing programs combine to limit exposure in wealthier nations. In contrast, little is done to reduce the exposure of the populations in LICs, where aflatoxin levels are high (Pitt and others 2012).

The most effective measure to reduce exposure is to avoid consumption of contaminated foods or to reduce dependence on them. In China, for example, economic development led to a shift from consumption of maize to rice, which is far less susceptible to aflatoxin contamination. This dietary shift has been linked to reduced exposure to aflatoxins and falling HCC rates (Chen and others 2013). However, many of the poorest populations remain trapped by poverty and the lack of dietary alternatives.

Preharvest mycotoxin control includes a wide range of good agricultural practices to reduce crop stress— such as irrigation; early sowing; low plant density; and the use of fungicides, pesticides, and insecticides—as well as the identification of fungus-resistant strains, genetic engineering of crop resistance, and biocontrol (Pitt and others 2012). Biocontrol is one of the most vigorously investigated approaches (Mehl and others 2012), although it is too early to know whether it will produce usable interventions (Atehnkeng and others 2008). The approach relies on competitive exclusion: strains of *Aspergillus* that do not produce aflatoxin (atoxigenic strains) are introduced into the soil, and they compete with native aflatoxin-producing spores for colonization of crops. The cost can be high; ensuring access and sustainability at the subsistence or small-farm level is critical.

Increased aflatoxin during storage is a major problem with dietary staples, such as maize and groundnuts in LMICs. Improved storage presents the simplest and most affordable opportunity for limiting exposure in such settings. In studies in West Africa, basic improvements in sorting, drying, and storing the groundnut crop in West Africa resulted in marked reductions in aflatoxin contamination, feasibly and cost-effectively (Turner and others 2013; Wu and Khlangwiset 2010a, 2010b), suggesting that simple, inexpensive approaches can offer significant benefits. Nevertheless, challenges remain in scaling up and implementing such approaches.

Once present in a food commodity, the toxins are relatively resistant to destruction during preparation and cooking. An exception is the use of alkaline methods (nixtimalization), for example, using lime for maize tortilla preparation, as is done by some populations in Latin America and the Caribbean (Pitt and others 2012).

An alternative to primary prevention is to modify the effects of toxins once ingested, either by preventing absorption or by modifying metabolism (Groopman, Kensler, and Wild 2008). Reduced absorption has been achieved in animal feeds by the incorporation of clays into feeds to bind aflatoxin in the gastrointestinal tract; this process remains at the pilot phase in humans (Wang and others 2008) and may be limited to emergency situations of high contamination and food insufficiency. In terms of altered metabolism, several compounds have been explored—including chlorophyllin, oltipraz, and broccoli sprout extract (Groopman, Kensler, and Wild 2008)—but these have not been translated to widespread application.

Alcohol

Alcohol is found in beer, wine, and liquor, as well as in some medicines, mouthwashes, household products, and essential oils (for example, scented liquids taken from plants). The alcohol content of various alcoholic beverages varies: 3–7 percent for beers and hard ciders; 9–15 percent for wines and sake; 16–20 percent for wines fortified with liquors, such as port; and 35–40 percent for liquor or distilled spirits, such as gin, rum, vodka, and whiskey (IARC 2012b). Alcohol consumption varies among adults over age 15 years in different parts of the world. From 2003 to 2005, average annual alcohol consumption per adult (over age 15) was highest in Europe and Central Asia (12.2 liters of pure alcohol); followed by North and South America (8.7 liters), the western Pacific (6.3 liters), Sub-Saharan Africa (6.2 liters), and southeast Asia (2.2 liters); it was lowest in the eastern Mediterranean (0.7 liters) (WHO 2008).

Excessive alcohol consumption can take the form of heavy drinking, binge drinking, or any drinking by pregnant women or underage youth (CPSTF 2013). Heavy drinking is defined as more than two drinks per day on average for men or more than one drink per day on average for women. Binge drinking is defined as five or more drinks during a single occasion for men, or four or more drinks during a single occasion for women.

Several interventions have been developed to reduce excessive alcohol consumption. The U.S. Community Preventive Services Task Force has reviewed the effectiveness of current intervention strategies, although not commenting on the use of interventions outside the United States. The recommended effective interventions that are most likely to be applicable in LMICs include the following:

- Increase alcohol taxes.
- Maintain limits on days of sale.
- Maintain limits on hours of sale.
- Enforce laws against privatizing retail alcohol sales.
- Regulate alcohol outlet density.
- Enhance enforcement of laws prohibiting sales to minors.

The effectiveness of other interventions, such as overservice law enforcement initiatives—efforts to increase enforcement of laws against serving intoxicated individuals—and responsible beverage service training, is not supported by sufficient evidence to recommend them. Unfortunately, very little information is available about the effects of these and alternative interventions in LMICs.

Liver Flukes

Infection with liver flukes can be prevented, and infections can be treated with a single dose of praziquantel, an inexpensive and relatively safe drug. Infections are detected by the presence of eggs excreted in stool, a standard laboratory procedure. Once cholangiocarcinoma develops, like HCC, treatment of the cancer is almost always futile.

The simplest means of preventing infection appears to be stopping the consumption of raw fish. This approach, however, has not been simple, because raw fish dishes are well-established components of the cuisine of certain cultures.

Control programs in Thailand started in the 1950s. In the late 1980s, the Thai government initiated a new three-pronged control strategy that includes screening and treatment with single-dose praziquantel (which has a cure rate of 95 percent or higher), education programs to encourage cooking fish before eating, and practicing hygienic defecation (Jongsuksuntigul and Imsomboon 2003). The large decreases in infection prevalence in Thailand are attributed to these combined efforts.

Finally, work is proceeding on a vaccine against *O. viverrini* and is considered a feasible development (Sripa and others 2011).

Treatment of HCC

Liver resection and liver transplantation are the gold standards for treating HCC, but even with the best treatment, survival is poor. In the United States, five-year relative survival from liver cancer was 16 percent during the 2000s, with a plurality of patients diagnosed with early-stage disease. Survival from late-stage disease was less than 5 percent (NCI 2013).

Some new loco-regional ablative methods, notably, percutaneous radiofrequency ablation, may represent safer and cheaper alternatives for small lesions (less than 5.0 centimeters) (Zhang and Chen 2010) and may eventually be commonly used in LMICs.

COSTS AND COST-EFFECTIVENESS OF INTERVENTIONS

Fortunately—and unlike most other major cancers—preventive interventions for all of the major risk factors are feasible. However, as is the case for other cancers and many other conditions, costs and cost-effectiveness are not well studied in LMICs. We present the evidence as documented in the literature, focusing first on prevention and then on treatment of liver cancer. We could find no economic analysis of liver fluke control. (Discussion of excessive alcohol consumption prevention is covered in *DCP3* volume 4, Mental, Neurological, and Substance Use Disorders.)

HBV Control

Vaccination against HBV is highly cost-effective in HBV-endemic countries. The economic evidence from China suggests that universal HBV vaccination is cost-saving compared with not vaccinating (Hutton, So, and Brandeau 2010). Even in India, a low HBV-endemic country, universal HBV vaccination is also highly cost-effective at US$13.22 per quality-adjusted life year (QALY) gained (Aggarwal, Ghoshal, and Naik 2003). Since the introduction of vaccines in the 1980s, more

and more countries have begun vaccinating; now, 168 of 190 WHO member countries have implemented universal hepatitis B vaccination in newborns and infants.

Chronic HBV can be treated with medications, although current therapy seldom results in a cure (Aman and others 2012). The antiviral agents currently used include lamivudine, adefovir, tenofovir, telbivudine, entecavir, and the two immune system modulators, interferon alpha-2a and pegylated interferon alpha-2a. Lifetime treatment inhibits virus replication, minimizing liver damage and reducing the risk of HCC (Matsumoto and others 2005). In an Indian study, the incremental cost-effectiveness ratio (ICER) per QALY gained associated with interferon use compared with usual care was six times the per capita GDP of India (Aggarwal, Ghoshal, and Naik 2002); this cost is not considered cost-effective according to the WHO definition of cost-effectiveness, as an ICER less than three times the per capita GDP of the country. Even if drug therapy were cost-effective in HICs, it may be unaffordable in LMICs. For example, the ICER per QALY gained for lamivudine in HICs ranged from 0.024 per capita GDP in Australia (Crowley and others 2000) to 0.819 per capita GDP in the United States (Yuan and others 2008). In LMICs, the ICER per QALY gained for lamivudine could be as high as three times the per capita GDP (Lui and others 2010). Therefore, the current strategy of treating patients from a young age is very expensive for LMICs, although this could change when the price of these drugs declines. Future studies should explore the cost-effectiveness of treating older patients before the onset of cirrhosis, possibly using on-off treatment that may be significantly less costly but have similar long-term clinical benefits.

HCV Control

There is no effective vaccine for HCV, but viral transmission can be prevented by reducing exposure to infected blood products and unsafe medical procedures, the main routes of infection in LMICs (Kermode 2004). Screening blood donors and improving the safety of medical procedures can significantly reduce HCV infection (Chanzy and others 1999; Wang and others 2013). The main laboratory test for detecting HCV in blood donations is the third-generation HCV antibody enzyme-linked immunosorbent assay, which has high sensitivity and specificity (Colin and others 2001).

Unsafe injections, which could be eliminated by single-use needles and syringes, are another important route for HCV transmission in LMICs. A recent cost-benefit analysis reported that introducing auto-disable syringes (which prevent reuse by locking mechanisms or other mechanical means) for all medical injections in India would be highly cost-effective, costing US$46–US$48 per DALY (Reid 2012).

Standard antiviral therapy for HCV before the new generation of drugs—pegylated interferon plus ribavirin—cures more than half of all patients (Hartwell and Shepherd 2009). However, the treatment takes months and is expensive, making it cost-effective only in patients in HICs who have progressive liver disease placing them at high risk of HCC (Shepherd and others 2004). The new drugs discussed earlier in this chapter are currently even more expensive, but more effective, are all oral, and are taken for a shorter duration. If costs can be brought down, they could become affordable in LMICs.

Aflatoxin Control

The economic burden of HCC in LMICs can be reduced by controlling the risk of food contamination by aflatoxin. Preharvest and postharvest interventions are possible.

Good farming practices to reduce crop stress (for example, irrigation; early sowing; low plant density; use of fungicides, pesticides, and insecticides) reduce aflatoxin production in addition to providing other more direct benefits, but the practices may be costly. For example, advanced irrigation systems cost US$740–US$940 per acre in the United States (Burt 2000).

Introducing atoxigenic strains of *Aspergillus* is potentially cost-effective in LMICs (Khlangwiset and Wu 2010; Wu and Khlangwiset 2010a, 2010b). In Nigeria, local atoxigenic strains of *A. flavus* were inoculated on maize and substantial reductions in aflatoxin levels were achieved (Atehnkeng and others 2008); data from additional field trials are awaited. Sun drying and hand sorting, together with other postharvest measures, were effective in reducing aflatoxins in the groundnut crop in Guinea and were considered cost-effective (Wu and Khlangwiset 2010b).

Postharvest interventions include sorting, adequate drying, and good storage conditions for grains. In large-scale commercial farming, mechanical blanching and sorting is highly cost-effective in the United States, completely eliminating aflatoxin at a cost of US$150–US$170 per ton (Dorner and Lamb 2006). However, their reliance on electricity and technical support puts them out of reach in many LMICs. The cost-effectiveness of artificial drying to reduce aflatoxin is highly correlated with the costs of fuel and electricity and moisture content in harvested crops.

Costs of Treating HCC

The clinical burden of HCC in LMICs is relatively well understood, but analyses of health expenditures for treating HCC are almost entirely lacking. A thorough search of the medical literature identified just three studies of health expenditures for HCC treatment, all in HICs. The average treatment cost in Russia for an HCC patient in 2008 was US$10,400, almost equal to the per capita GDP in that year. Inpatient care accounted for 90 percent of the total. The average indirect cost associated with HCC was US$707, in which productivity loss accounted for 26 percent and social welfare for disability accounted for 74 percent (Omelyanovsky and others 2010).

The second study is from Taiwan, China, and reports on national insurance claims data for 2,873 patients diagnosed between 1996 and 2002 (Lang and others 2008). More than 30 percent of the patients had died within one year of diagnosis. The highest expenditures accrued during the six months before death, equaling US$7,183, or half of Taiwan, China's per capita GDP in 2002. The projected 10-year costs were the equivalent of the per capita GDP.

A recent Canadian study investigated the health care costs of 2,341 HCC patients in Ontario, Canada, from 2002 to 2008. Average five-year net costs were US$77,509, or US$15,502 annually, about 30 percent of Canada's 2008 per capita GDP.

Without studies from LMICs, it is impossible to know what the economic burden of treating HCC would be, but we can make some inferences. First, we know that patients in LMICs are much less likely to receive treatment than patients in HICs. Most HCCs, even in HICs, are diagnosed at late stages. Second, for those who are treated, the dollar costs might be somewhat lower than in the studies cited, assuming lower input prices. However, it is likely to be an even larger fraction of per capita GDP—possibly many multiples—making the burden even heavier for what is, in most cases, treatment that does not save the patient's life.

Summary of Costs

The direct and indirect costs of HCC in LMICs are higher compared with costs in HICs because the disease is more frequent, it occurs at younger ages, and diagnosis is often delayed.

The most cost-effective approaches to preventing HCC are the following:

- Reducing the prevalence of HBV through vaccination of infants, including a birth dose, and uninfected adolescents.
- Preventing HCV transmission by blood donor screening and safe injection practices, including auto-disable syringes.

- Controlling aflatoxin through postharvest and possibly some preharvest (genetically resistant maize and/or atoxigenic strains of *Aspergillus*) practices.
- Educating people to eat fully cooked food in areas with high prevalence of liver fluke infection to prevent cholangiocarcinoma.
- Treating liver fluke infection with single-dose praziquantel.

Approaches that are not currently cost-effective are the following:

- Antiviral therapies for HBV and HCV, which are very expensive and require extended periods of treatment (HBV requires lifetime treatment). They are used by only a small fraction of infected individuals in HICs and unlikely to be cost-effective in LMICs. However, as treatment efficacy improves and prices moderate, these interventions could become more

attractive, especially if preventive measures have reduced transmission.
- HCC and cholangiocarcinoma treatments, which are usually unsuccessful for long-term survival in any country, particularly because the diseases are not usually diagnosed until late stages. Liver cancer treatment cannot be recommended as an important control strategy for LMICs.

The economic attractiveness of these interventions may change, however, as new technologies are introduced and the prices of existing effective technologies fall.

CONCLUSIONS

Liver cancer is among the least successfully treated of all cancers but among the most readily prevented. Each major risk factor is amenable to modification by feasible and cost-effective (and some effective but expensive) interventions. Some of these should become more affordable in LMICs in the medium term; for example, drugs that are currently expensive will eventually be much less expensive. All of these interventions will prevent morbidity and mortality from other liver diseases and, in the case of alcohol, from a number of other conditions. The risk factors and interventions are summarized in table 8.1.

NOTES

World Bank income classifications as of July 2014 are as follows, based on estimates of gross national income per capita for 2013:

- Low-income countries: US$1,045 or less
- Middle-income countries:
  - Lower-middle-income: US$1,046–US$4,125
  - Upper-middle-income: US$4,126–US$12,745
- High-income countries: US$12,746 or more

1. Maps and figures in this chapter are based on incidence and mortality estimates for ages 0 to 69, consistent with reporting in all *Disease Control Priorities* volumes. Global cancer statistics are estimates for the year 2012 and have been provided by the International Agency for Research on Cancer from its GLOBOCAN 2012 database. Observable population-based data were derived from *Cancer Incidence in Five Continents, 10th edition* (Forman and others 2013) and for trends over time from *CI5 Plus* (http://ci5.iarc.fr/CI5plus/Default.aspx). The discussion of burden (including risk factors), however, includes all ages unless otherwise noted. Interventions also apply to all age groups, except where age ranges or cutoffs are specified.

Table 8.1 Liver Cancer Risk Factors and Feasible Interventions

Risk factor	Intervention	Cost-effectiveness
HBV	HBV vaccine	+++
	HBV treatment	−/+
	Blood supply protection	+++
HCV	Blood supply protection	+++
	Safe medical injection	+++
	Programs to provide clean needles for injected-drug users	++
	HCV treatment	−/+
Aflatoxin	Preharvest good agricultural practices to reduce crop stress	++
	Fungus-resistant strains	++
	Biocontrol	Not yet known
	Postharvest sorting, storing, drying	+++
	Improved grain storage	+++
	Postharvest treatment of grain	+
	Postingestion effect modification	−
Alcohol	Taxation	+++
	Legal/regulatory interventions	+++
	Behavioral interventions	++
Liver flukes	Public education to avoid raw fish	++
	Screen for infection and treat with praziquantel	++

Note: Scale from not cost-effective (−) to highly cost-effective (+++) in low- and middle-income countries. HBV = hepatitis B virus; HCV = hepatitis C virus.

REFERENCES

Aggarwal, R., U. C. Ghoshal, and S. R. Naik. 2002. "Treatment of Chronic Hepatitis B with Interferon-Alpha: Cost-Effectiveness in Developing Countries." *The National Medical Journal of India* 15 (6): 320–27. http://www.ncbi.nlm.nih.gov/pubmed/12540064.

———. 2003. "Assessment of Cost-Effectiveness of Universal Hepatitis B Immunization in a Low-Income Country with Intermediate Endemicity Using a Markov Model." *Journal of Hepatology* 38 (2): 215–22. http://www.ncbi.nlm.nih.gov/pubmed/12547411.

Ahmad, K. 2004. "Pakistan: A Cirrhotic State?" *The Lancet* 364 (9448): 1843–44. doi:10.1016/S0140-6736(04)17458-8.

Alcorn, T. 2011. "Mongolia's Struggle with Liver Cancer." *The Lancet* 377 (9772): 1139–40. http://www.ncbi.nlm.nih.gov/pubmed/21465699.

Allen, N. E., V. Beral, D. Casabonne, S. W. Kan, G. K. Reeves, and others. 2009. "Moderate Alcohol Intake and Cancer Incidence in Women." *Journal of the National Cancer Institute* 101 (5): 296–305. http://www.ncbi.nlm.nih.gov/pubmed/19244173.

Alter, H. J., and L. B. Seeff. 2000. "Recovery, Persistence, and Sequelae in Hepatitis C Virus Infection: A Perspective on Long-Term Outcome." *Seminars in Liver Disease* 20 (1): 17–35. http://www.ncbi.nlm.nih.gov/pubmed/10895429.

Aman, W., S. Mousa, G. Shiha, and S. A. Mousa. 2012. "Current Status and Future Directions in the Management of Chronic Hepatitis C." *Virology Journal* 9: 57. http://www.pubmedcentral.nih.gov/articlerender.fcgi?artid=3325870&tool=pmcentrez&rendertype=abstract.

Atehnkeng, J., P. S. Ojiambo, T. Ikotun, R. A. Sikora, P. J. Cotty, and others. 2008. "Evaluation of Atoxigenic Isolates of Aspergillus Flavus as Potential Biocontrol Agents for Aflatoxin in Maize." *Food Additives & Contaminants. Part A, Chemistry, Analysis, Control, Exposure & Risk Assessment* 25 (10): 1264–71. http://www.ncbi.nlm.nih.gov/pubmed/18608502.

Attia, M. A. 1998. "Prevalence of Hepatitis B and C in Egypt and Africa." *Antiviral Therapy* 3 (Suppl. 3): 1–9. http://www.ncbi.nlm.nih.gov/pubmed/10726051.

Baffy, G., E. M. Brunt, and S. H. Caldwell. 2012. "Hepatocellular Carcinoma in Non-Alcoholic Fatty Liver Disease: An Emerging Menace." *Journal of Hepatology* 56 (6): 1384–91. doi:10.1016/j.jhep.2011.10.027.

Boffetta, P., and M. Hashibe. 2006. "Alcohol and Cancer." *The Lancet Oncology* 7 (2): 149–56. http://www.ncbi.nlm.nih.gov/pubmed/16455479.

Burt, C. M. 2000. "Selection of Irrigation Methods for Agriculture." Environmental and Water Resources Institute (U.S.). On-Farm Irrigation Committee. Reston, VA: American Society of Civil Engineers. http://mobius.missouri.edu:2082/record=b14299016~S0.

Chanzy, B., D. L. Duc-Bin, B. Rousset, P. Morand, C. Morel-Baccard, and others. 1999. "Effectiveness of a Manual Disinfection Procedure in Eliminating Hepatitis C Virus from Experimentally Contaminated Endoscopes." *Gastrointestinal Endoscopy* 50 (2): 147–51. http://www.ncbi.nlm.nih.gov/pubmed/10425404.

Chen, C. J., and D. S. Chen. 2002. "Interaction of Hepatitis B Virus, Chemical Carcinogen, and Genetic Susceptibility: Multistage Hepatocarcinogenesis with Multifactorial Etiology." *Hepatology* (Baltimore, MD) 36 (5): 1046–49. doi:10.1053/jhep.2002.37084.

Chen, C. J., M. W. Yu, and Y. F. Liaw. 1997. "Epidemiological Characteristics and Risk Factors of Hepatocellular Carcinoma." *Journal of Gastroenterology and Hepatology* 12 (9–10): S294–308. http://www.ncbi.nlm.nih.gov/pubmed/9407350.

Chen, J.-G., J. Zhu, D. M. Parkin, Y. H. Zhang, J. H. Lu, and others. 2006. "Trends in the Incidence of Cancer in Qidong, China, 1978–2002." *International Journal of Cancer* 119 (6): 1447–54. doi:10.1002/ijc.21952.

Chen, J.-G., P. A. Egner, D. Ng, L. P. Jacobson, and others. 2013. "Reduced Aflatoxin Exposure Presages Decline in Liver Cancer Mortality in an Endemic Region of China." *Cancer Prevention Research* 6: 1038. doi:10.1158/1940-6207.

Chiang, C.-J., Y.-A. Yang, S.-L. You, M.-S. Lai, and C.-J. Chen. 2013. "Thirty-Year Outcomes of the National Hepatitis B Immunization Program in Taiwan." *JAMA* 310 (9): 974–76.

Colin, C., D. Lanoir, S. Touzet, L. Meyaud-Kraemer, F. Bailly, and C. Trepo. 2001. "Sensitivity and Specificity of Third-Generation Hepatitis C Virus Antibody Detection Assays: An Analysis of the Literature." *Journal of Viral Hepatitis* 8 (2): 87–95. http://www.ncbi.nlm.nih.gov/pubmed/11264728.

Corrao, G., and S. Arico. 2000. "Alcohol and Liver Cirrhosis: Old Questions and Weakly Explored Opportunities." *Addiction* 95 (8): 1267–70. http://doi.wiley.com/10.1046/j.1360-0443.2000.958126715.x.

Corrao, G., V. Bagnardi, A. Zambon, and C. La Vecchia. 2004. "A Meta-Analysis of Alcohol Consumption and the Risk of 15 Diseases." *Preventive Medicine* 38 (5): 613–19. http://www.ncbi.nlm.nih.gov/pubmed/15066364.

CPSTF (Community Preventive Services Task Force). 2013. "Preventing Excessive Alcohol Consumption." *The Community Guide* [Internet]. U.S. Government. http://www.thecommunityguide.org/alcohol/index.html.

Crowley, S. J., D. Tognarini, P. V. Desmond, and M. Lees. 2000. "Cost-Effectiveness Analysis of Lamivudine for the Treatment of Chronic Hepatitis B." *PharmacoEconomics* 17 (5): 409–27. http://www.ncbi.nlm.nih.gov/pubmed/10977384.

Cui, F., L. Li, S. C. Hadler, F. Wang, H. Zheng, and others. 2010. "Factors Associated with Effectiveness of the First Dose of Hepatitis B Vaccine in China: 1992–2005." *Vaccine* 28 (37): 5973–78. http://www.ncbi.nlm.nih.gov/pubmed/20637773.

Dienstag, J. L. 2008. "Hepatitis B Virus Infection." *New England Journal of Medicine* 359 (14): 1486–500. doi:10.1056/NEJMra0801644. http://www.ncbi.nlm.nih.gov/pubmed/18832247.

Dondog, B., M. Lise, O. Dondov, B. Baldandorj, and S. Franceschi. 2011. "Hepatitis B and C Virus Infections in Hepatocellular Carcinoma and Cirrhosis in Mongolia." *European Journal of Cancer Prevention* 20 (1): 33–39. http://www.torna.do/s/Dondov-O/.

Dorner, J. W., and M. C. Lamb. 2006. "Development and Commercial Use of Afla-Guard(®), an Aflatoxin Biocontrol Agent." *Mycotoxin Research* 22 (1): 33–38. http://www.ncbi.nlm.nih.gov/pubmed/23605499.

Evans, A. A., A. P. O'Connell, J. C. Pugh, W. S. Mason, F. M. Shen, and others. 1998. "Geographic Variation in Viral Load among Hepatitis B Carriers with Differing Risks of Hepatocellular Carcinoma." *Cancer Epidemiology, Biomarkers & Prevention* 7 (7): 559–65. http://www.ncbi.nlm.nih.gov/pubmed/9681522.

Ferlay, J., I. Soerjomataram, M. Ervik, R. Dikshit, S. Eser, and others. 2013. "GLOBOCAN v1.0, Cancer Incidence and Mortality Worldwide: IARC CancerBase No. 11" [Internet]. International Agency for Research on Cancer, Lyon, France. http://globocan.iarc.fr.

Forman D., F. Bray, D. H. Brewster, C. Gombe Mbalawa, B. Kohler, M. Piñeros, E. Steliarova-Foucher, R. Swaminathan, and J. Ferlay, eds. 2013. Cancer Incidence in Five Continents, Vol. X (electronic version). IARC, Lyon. http://ci5.iarc.fr.

Fusco, M., E. Girardi, P. Piselli, R. Palombino, J. Polesel, and others. 2008. "Epidemiology of Viral Hepatitis Infections in an Area of Southern Italy with High Incidence Rates of Liver Cancer." *European Journal of Cancer* 44 (6): 847–53. http://www.ncbi.nlm.nih.gov/pubmed/18313290.

Gao, X., Q. Cui, X. Shi, J. Su, Z. Peng, and others. 2011. "Prevalence and Trend of Hepatitis C Virus Infection among Blood Donors in Chinese Mainland: A Systematic Review and Meta-Analysis." *BMC Infectious Diseases* 11: 88. http://www.pubmedcentral.nih.gov/articlerender.fcgi?artid=3079653&tool=pmcentrez&rendertype=abstract.

Gong, Y. Y., K. Cardwell, A. Hounsa, S. Egal, P. C. Turner, and others. 2002. "Dietary Aflatoxin Exposure and Impaired Growth in Young Children from Benin and Togo: Cross Sectional Study." *BMJ (Clinical Research Ed.)* 325 (7354): 20–21. http://www.pubmedcentral.nih.gov/articlerender.fcgi?artid=116667&tool=pmcentrez&-rendertype=abstract.

Gong, Y., A. Hounsa, S. Egal, P. C. Turner, A. E. Sutcliffe, and others. 2004. "Postweaning Exposure to Aflatoxin Results in Impaired Child Growth: A Longitudinal Study in Benin, West Africa." *Environmental Health Perspectives* 112 (13): 1334–38. http://www.pubmedcentral.nih.gov/articlerender.fcgi?artid=1247526&tool=pmcentrez&rendertype=abstract.

Gong, Y. Y., S. Wilson, J. K. Mwatha, M. N. Routledge, J. M. Castelino, and others. 2012. "Aflatoxin Exposure May Contribute to Chronic Hepatomegaly in Kenyan School Children." *Environmental Health Perspectives* 120 (6): 893–96. http://www.pubmedcentral.nih.gov/articlerender.fcgi?artid=3385435&tool=pmcentrez&rendertype=abstract.

Goodnough, L. T. 2013. "Blood Management: Transfusion Medicine Comes of Age." *The Lancet* 381 (9880): 1791–92. http://www.ncbi.nlm.nih.gov/pubmed/23706789.

Groopman, J. D., T. W. Kensler, and C. P. Wild. 2008. "Protective Interventions to Prevent Aflatoxin-Induced Carcinogenesis in Developing Countries." *Annual Review of Public Health* 29: 187–203. http://www.ncbi.nlm.nih.gov/pubmed/17914931.

Haenel, H. 1989. "Alcohol Drinking." *IARC Monographs on the Evaluation of Carcinogenic Risks to Humans.* Volume 44. IARC, Lyon, France.

Hartwell, D., and J. Shepherd. 2009. "Pegylated and Non-Pegylated Interferon-Alfa and Ribavirin for the Treatment of Mild Chronic Hepatitis C: A Systematic Review and Meta-Analysis." *International Journal of Technology Assessment in Health Care* 25 (1): 56–62. doi:10.1017/S0266462309090084.

Hill, A., S. Khoo, J. Fortunak, B. Simmons, and N. Ford. 2014. "Minimum Costs for Producing Hepatitis C Direct-Acting Antivirals for Use in Large-Scale Treatment Access Programs in Developing Countries." *Clinical Infectious Diseases* 58 (7): 928–36. doi:10.1093/cid/ciu012.

Hsieh, Y.-C., W.-S. Lee, P.-L. Shao, L.-Y. Chang, and L.-M. Huang. 2007. "The Transforming Streptococcus Pneumoniae in the 21st Century." *Chang Gung Medical Journal* 31 (2): 117–24. http://www.ncbi.nlm.nih.gov/pubmed/18567411.

Huang, Y.-T., C-L. Jen, H-I. Yang, M-H. Lee, J. Su, and others. 2011. "Lifetime Risk and Sex Difference of Hepatocellular Carcinoma among Patients with Chronic Hepatitis B and C." *Journal of Clinical Oncology* 29 (27): 3643–50. doi:10.1200/JCO.2011.36.2335.

Hutton, D. W., S. K. So, and M. L. Brandeau. 2010. "Cost-Effectiveness of Nationwide Hepatitis B Catch-up Vaccination among Children and Adolescents in China." *Hepatology (Baltimore, MD)* 51 (2): 405–14. http://www.pubmedcentral.nih.gov/articlerender.fcgi?artid=3245734&tool=pmcentrez&rendertype=abstract.

IARC (International Agency for Research on Cancer). 2002. "Some Traditional Herbal Medicines, Some Mycotoxins, Naphthalene and Styrene." *IARC Monographs on the Evaluation of Carcinogenic Risks to Humans*, Volume 82. IARC, Lyon, France.

———. 2009. "Biological Agents." *IARC Monographs on the Evaluation of Carcinogenic Risks to Humans*, Volume 100B. IARC, Lyon, France.

———. 2012a. "A Review of Human Carcinogens. E. Personal Habits and Indoor Combustions." *Monographs on the Evaluation of Carcinogenic Risks to Humans*, Volume 100: 585. IARC, Lyon, France.

———. 2012b. "A Review of Human Carcinogens: Chemical Agents and Related Occupations." *Monographs on the Evaluation of Carcinogenic Risks to Humans*, 100F. http://monographs.iarc.fr/ENG/Monographs/vol100F/index.php.

Jongsuksuntigul, P., and T. Imsomboon. 2003. "Opisthorchiasis Control in Thailand." *Acta Tropica* 88 (3): 229–32. doi:10.1016/j.actatropica.2003.01.002.

Kermode, M. 2004. "Unsafe Injections in Low-Income Country Health Settings: Need for Injection Safety Promotion to Prevent the Spread of Blood-Borne Viruses." *Health Promotion International* 19 (1): 95–103. http://www.ncbi.nlm.nih.gov/pubmed/14976177.

Khlangwiset, P., and F. Wu. 2010. "Costs and Efficacy of Public Health Interventions to Reduce Aflatoxin-Induced Human Disease." *Food Additives & Contaminants: Part A* 27 (7): 998–1014. doi:10.1080/19440041003677475

Kuniholm, M. H., O. A. Lesi, M. Mendy, A. O. Akano, O. Sam, and others. 2008. "Aflatoxin Exposure and Viral Hepatitis in the Etiology of Liver Cirrhosis in The Gambia,

West Africa." *Environmental Health Perspectives* 116 (11): 1553–57. http://www.pubmedcentral.nih.gov/articlerender .fcgi?artid=2592277&tool=pmcentrez&rendertype =abstract.

Lang, H.-C., J.-C. Wu, S.-H. Yen, C.-F. Lan, and S.-L. Wu. 2008. "The Lifetime Cost of Hepatocellular Carcinoma: A Claims Data Analysis from a Medical Centre in Taiwan." *Applied Health Economics and Health Policy* 6 (1): 55–65. http:// www.ncbi. nlm.nih.gov/pubmed/18774870.

Lu, S.-N., W.-W. Su, S.-S. Yang, T.-T. Chang, K.-S. Cheng, and others. 2006. "Secular Trends and Geographic Variations of Hepatitis B Virus and Hepatitis C Virus-Associated Hepatocellular Carcinoma in Taiwan." *International Journal of Cancer* 119 (8): 1946–52. http://www.ncbi.nlm.nih.gov /pubmed/16708389.

Lui, Y. Y., K. K. Tsoi, V. W. Wong, J.-H. Kao, J.-L. Hou, and others. 2010. "Cost-Effectiveness Analysis of Roadmap Models in Chronic Hepatitis B Using Tenofovir as the Rescue Therapy." *Antiviral Therapy* 15 (2): 145–55. http://www .ncbi.nlm.nih.gov/pubmed/20386069.

Marinier, E., V. Barrois, B. Larouze, W. T. London, A. Cofer, and others. 1985. "Lack of Perinatal Transmission of Hepatitis B Virus Infection in Senegal, West Africa." *Journal of Pediatrics* 106 (5): 843–49. http://aje.oxfordjournals.org /content/147/5/478.full.pdf.

Matsumoto, A., E. Tanaka, A. Rokuhara, K. Kiyosawa, H. Kumada, and others. 2005. "Efficacy of Lamivudine for Preventing Hepatocellular Carcinoma in Chronic Hepatitis B: A Multicenter Retrospective Study of 2795 Patients." *Hepatology Research* 32 (3): 173–84. http://www.ncbi.nlm .nih.gov/pubmed/16024289.

Mehl, H. L., R. Jaime, K. A. Callicott, C. Probst, N. P. Garber, and others. 2012. "Aspergillus Flavus Diversity on Crops and in the Environment Can Be Exploited to Reduce Aflatoxin Exposure and Improve Health." *Annals of the New York Academy of Sciences* 1273: 7–17. http://www.ncbi.nlm .nih.gov/pubmed/23230832.

Michelotti, G. A., M. V. Machado, and A. M. Diehl. 2013. "NAFLD, NASH and Liver Cancer." *Nature Reviews Gastroenterology and Hepatology* 10: 656–65. doi:10.1038 /nrgastro.2013.183.

Morgan, R. L., B. Baack, B. D. Smith, A. Yartel, M. Pitasi, and Y. Falck-Ytter. 2013. "Eradication of Hepatitis C Virus Infection and the Development of Hepatocellular Carcinoma: A Meta-Analysis of Observational Studies." *Annals of Internal Medicine* 158 (5 Pt 1): 329–37. http:// www.ncbi.nlm.nih.gov /pubmed/23460056.

NCI (National Cancer Institute). 2013. "SEER Stat Fact Sheets: Liver and Intrahepatic Bile Duct." U.S. National Institutes of Health, Bethesda, MD. http://seer.cancer.gov/statfacts /html/livibd.html#survival.

Nelson, P. K., B. M. Mathers, B. Cowie, H. Hagan, D. D. Jarlais, and others. 2011. "Global Epidemiology of Hepatitis B and Hepatitis C in People Who Inject Drugs: Results of Systematic Reviews." *The Lancet* 378 (9791): 571–83. http://www.pubmedcentral.nih.gov/articlerender.fcgi?artid =3285467&tool=pmcentrez&rendertype=abstract.

NIAAA (National Institute on Alcohol Abuse and Alcoholism). 1993. "Alcohol and Cancer." Alcohol Alert No. 21-1993. http://pubs.niaaa.nih.gov/publications/aa21.htm.

Omelyanovsky, V. V., M. V. Avksentieva, I. Krysanov, and O. Ivakhnenko. 2010. "PCN53 Analysis of Socioeconomic Burden of Hepatocellular Carcinoma in Russia." *Value in Health* 13 (7): A260–61. doi:10.1016/S1098-3015(11)71948-9. http://www.valueinhealthjournal.com /article/S1098-3015(11)71948-9.

Omer, R. E., A. Kuijsten, A. M. Y. Kadaru, F. J. Kok, M. O. Idris, and others. 2004. "Population-Attributable Risk of Dietary Aflatoxins and Hepatitis B Virus Infection with Respect to Hepatocellular Carcinoma." *Nutrition and Cancer* 48 (1): 15–21. http://www.ncbi.nlm.nih.gov/pubmed/15203373.

Oyunsuren, T., F. Kurbanov, Y. Tanaka, A. Elkady, R. Sanduijav, and others. 2006. "High Frequency of Hepatocellular Carcinoma in Mongolia; Association with Mono-, or Co-Infection with Hepatitis C, B, and Delta Viruses." *Journal of Medical Virology* 78 (12): 1688–95. doi:10.1002/jmv.20755.

Pitt, J. I., C. P. Wild, R. A. Baan, W. C. A. Gelderblom, J. D. Miller, R. T. Riley, and F. Wu. 2012. "Improving Public Health through Mycotoxin Control." *IARC Scientific Publication*, No. 158. IARC, Lyon, France. http:// apps.who.int/bookorders/anglais/detart1.jsp?codlan=1 &codcol=73&codcch=158#.

Prati, D. 2006. "Transmission of Hepatitis C Virus by Blood Transfusions and Other Medical Procedures: A Global Review." *Journal of Hepatology* 45 (4): 607–16. http://www .ncbi.nlm.nih.gov/pubmed/16901579.

Qian, G. S., R. K. Ross, M. C. Yu, J. M. Yuan, Y. T. Gao, and others. 2013. "A Follow-up Study of Urinary Markers of Aflatoxin Exposure and Liver Cancer Risk in Shanghai, People's Republic of China." *Cancer Epidemiology, Biomarkers & Prevention* 3 (1): 3–10. http://www.ncbi.nlm .nih.gov/pubmed/8118382.

Raza, S. A., G. M. Clifford, and S. Franceschi. 2007. "Worldwide Variation in the Relative Importance of Hepatitis B and Hepatitis C Viruses in Hepatocellular Carcinoma: A Systematic Review." *British Journal of Cancer* 96: 1127–34. doi:10.1038/sj.bjc.6603649.

Razavi, H., C. Estes, K. Pasini, E. Gower, and S. Hindman. 2013. "51 HCV Treatment Rate in Select European Countries in 2004–2010." *Journal of Hepatology* 58 (null): S22–23. http:// dx.doi.org/10.1016/S0168-8278(13)60053-7.

Reid, S. 2012. "Estimating the Burden of Disease from Unsafe Injections in India: A Cost-Benefit Assessment of the Auto-Disable Syringe in a Country with Low Blood-Borne Virus Prevalence." *Indian Journal of Community Medicine* 37 (2): 89–94. http://www.pubmedcentral.nih .gov/articlerender.fcgi?artid=3361807&tool=pmcentrez &rendertype=abstract.

Shepherd, J., H. Brodin, C. Cave, N. Waugh, A. Price, and others. 2004. "Pegylated Interferon Alpha-2a and -2b in Combination with Ribavirin in the Treatment of Chronic Hepatitis C: A Systematic Review and Economic Evaluation." *Health Technology Assessment* (Winchester, England) 8 (39): iii–iv, 1–125.

Shin, H.-R., J.-K. Oh, E. Masuyer, M.-P. Curado, V. Bouvard, and others. 2010. "Epidemiology of Cholangiocarcinoma: An Update Focusing on Risk Factors." *Cancer Science* 101 (3): 579–85. doi:10.1111/j.1349-7006.2009.01458.x.

Sithithaworn, P., and M. Haswell-Elkins. 2003. "Epidemiology of Opisthorchis Viverrini." *Acta Tropica* 88 (3): 187–94. http://www.ncbi.nlm.nih.gov/pubmed/14611873.

Smith, B. D., R. L. Morgan, G. A. Beckett, Y. Falck-Ytter, D. Holtzman, and others. 2012. "Recommendations for the Identification of Chronic Hepatitis C Virus Infection among Persons Born during 1945–1965." *MMWR. Recommendations and Reports: Morbidity and Mortality Weekly Report. Centers for Disease Control* 61 (RR-4): 1–32. http://www.ncbi.nlm.nih.gov/pubmed/22895429.

Sripa, B., J. M. Bethony, P. Sithithaworn, S. Kaewkes, E. Mairiang, and others. 2011. "Opisthorchiasis and Opisthorchis-Associated Cholangiocarcinoma in Thailand and Laos." *Acta Tropica* 120 (Suppl. 1): S158–68. doi:10.1016/j.actatropica.2010.07.006.

Sun, Z., T. Chen, S. S. Thorgeirsson, Q. Zhan, J. Chen, and others. 2013. "Dramatic Reduction of Liver Cancer Incidence in Young Adults: 28 Year Follow-Up of Etiological Interventions in an Endemic Area of China." *Carcinogenesis* 34 (8): 1800–05. http://www.ncbi.nlm.nih.gov/pubmed/23322152.

Tanaka, Y., K. Hanada, M. Mizokami, A. E. T. Yeo, J. Wai-Kuo Shih, and others. 2002. "A Comparison of the Molecular Clock of Hepatitis C Virus in the United States and Japan Predicts That Hepatocellular Carcinoma Incidence in the United States Will Increase over the Next Two Decades." *Proceedings of the National Academy of Sciences* 99 (24): 15584–89. http://www.pubmedcentral.nih.gov/articlerender.fcgi?artid=137760&tool=pmcentrez&rendertype=abstract.

Turner, P. C., A. Sylla, Y. Y. Gong, M. S. Diallo, A. E. Sutcliffe, and others. 2013. "Reduction in Exposure to Carcinogenic Aflatoxins by Postharvest Intervention Measures in West Africa: A Community-Based Intervention Study." *The Lancet* 365 (9475): 1950–56. http://www.ncbi.nlm.nih.gov/pubmed/15936422.

Vanni, E., and E. Bugianesi. 2014. "Obesity and Liver Cancer." *Clinics in Liver Disease* 18 (1): 191–203. doi:10.1016/j.cld.2013.09.001.

Wang, J.-F., W.-Y. Lin, F. Jiang, W. Meng, and F.-M. Shen. 2010. "Analysis of Time Trend of Hepatocellular Carcinoma Mortality in Haimen City of Jiangsu Province from 1993 to 2006." *Zhonghua Liu Xing Bing Xue Za Zhi = Zhonghua Liuxingbingxue Zazhi* 31 (7): 727–32. http://www.ncbi.nlm.nih.gov/pubmed/21162831.

Wang, J.-T., T.-H. Wang, J.-T. Lin, C.-Z. Lee, J.-C. Sheu, and others. 2013. "Effect of Hepatitis C Antibody Screening in Blood Donors on Post-Transfusion Hepatitis in Taiwan." *Journal of Gastroenterology and Hepatology* 10 (4): 454–58. http://www.ncbi.nlm.nih.gov/pubmed/8527713.

Wang, L.-Y., M. Hatch, C.-J. Chen, B. Levin, S.-L. You, and others. 1996. "Aflatoxin Exposure and Risk of Hepatocellular Carcinoma in Taiwan." *International Journal of Cancer* 67 (5): 620–25. http://www.ncbi.nlm.nih.gov/pubmed/8782648.

Wang, L., Y. Wang, S. Jin, Z. Wu, D. P. Chin, and others. 2008. "Emergence and Control of Infectious Diseases in China." *The Lancet* 372 (9649): 1598–605. doi:10.1016/S0140-6736(08)61365-3.

WHO (World Health Organization). 2004. "UNICEF/WHO Workshop on the Expanded Programme on Immunizations in the Pacific." WHO, Regional Office for the Western Pacific. http://iris.wpro.who.int/handle/10665.1/1663.

———. 2008. "Global Information System on Alcohol and Health." WHO, Geneva. http://apps.who.int/globalatlas/default.asp.

———. 2009. "Weekly Epidemiological Record: Hepatitis B Vaccines." *WHO Position Paper* 40 (84): 405–20.

Wild, C. P., and Y. Y. Gong. 2010. "Mycotoxins and Human Disease: A Largely Ignored Global Health Issue." *Carcinogenesis* 31 (1): 71–82. http://www.pubmedcentral.nih.gov/articlerender.fcgi?artid=2802673&tool=pmcentrez&rendertype=abstract.

Wild, C. P., and A. J. Hall. 2000. "Primary Prevention of Hepatocellular Carcinoma in Developing Countries." *Mutation Research/Reviews in Mutation* 462 (2–3): 381–93. doi:10.1016/S1383-5742(00)00027-2.

Williams, J. H., T. D. Phillips, P. E. Jolly, J. K. Stiles, C. M. Jolly, and D. Aggarwal. 2004. "Human Aflatoxicosis in Developing Countries: A Review of Toxicology, Exposure, Potential Health Consequences, and Interventions." *American Journal of Clinical Nutrition* 80 (5): 1106–22. http://www.ncbi.nlm.nih.gov/pubmed/15531656.

Wu, F., and P. Khlangwiset. 2010a. "Evaluating the Technical Feasibility of Aflatoxin Risk Reduction Strategies in Africa." *Food Additives & Contaminants. Part A, Chemistry, Analysis, Control, Exposure & Risk Assessment* 27 (5): 658–76. doi:10.1080/19440041003639582.

———. 2010b. "Health Economic Impacts and Cost-Effectiveness of Aflatoxin-Reduction Strategies in Africa: Case Studies in Biocontrol and Post-Harvest Interventions." *Food Additives & Contaminants. Part A, Chemistry, Analysis, Control, Exposure & Risk Assessment* 27 (4): 496–509. http://www.pubmedcentral.nih.gov/articlerender.fcgi?artid=2858428&tool=pmcentrez&rendertype=abstract.

Wu, H.-C., Q. Wang, H.-I. Yang, H. Ahsan, W.-Y. Tsai, and others. 2009. "Aflatoxin B1 Exposure, Hepatitis B Virus Infection, and Hepatocellular Carcinoma in Taiwan." *Cancer Epidemiology, Biomarkers & Prevention* 18 (3): 846–53. doi:10.1158/1055-9965.EPI-08-0697.

Yuan, Y., U. H. Iloeje, J. Hay, and S. Saab. 2008. "Evaluation of the Cost-Effectiveness of Entecavir versus Lamivudine in Hepatitis BeAg-Positive Chronic Hepatitis B Patients." *Journal of Managed Care Pharmacy* 14 (1): 21–33.

Zhang, Y.-J., and M.-S. Chen. 2010. "Role of Radiofrequency Ablation in the Treatment of Small Hepatocellular Carcinoma." *World Journal of Heptalogy* 2 (4): 146–50. doi:10.4254/wjh.v2.i4.146.

Cancer Pain Relief

James Cleary, Hellen Gelband, and Judith Wagner

INTRODUCTION

Despite substantial effort and expenditure, at least one-third of patients diagnosed with cancer in high-income countries (HICs) die of their disease within a few years of diagnosis (National Cancer Institute 2009). In low- and middle-income countries (LMICs), two-thirds succumb, because the cancer types prevalent in LMICs tend to have poor prognoses, most cancers are advanced when diagnosed, and even for curable cancers few people have access to effective cancer treatment. For rich and poor everywhere, cancer can cause pain and severe distress, especially during the last few months of life. Cancer-related pain is not the exclusive domain of those who die of cancer. Even many who are cured of their disease live with the long-term effects of the disease and its treatment; many of them live with pain, as do people with a range of chronic conditions other than cancer.

For the majority of cancer patients in LMICs, the most effective and feasible intervention for pain control is medication. For mild pain, over-the-counter, inexpensive analgesic medicines can provide adequate relief. When these nonopioids no longer relieve pain, then weak opioids, such as codeine, may work. Cancer patients most often experience worsening pain as their cancer progresses; 70–80 percent progress to severe pain, which only strong opioid medicines can relieve.

Other approaches are effective for specific pain indications; the most widely applicable are palliative radiotherapy and surgery. Chemotherapy, neurologic, psychological, and other approaches also can be effective (see Foley and others 2006 for a comprehensive listing). All but analgesic medications and psychological approaches require access to well-developed health care facilities; these are usually available in large urban areas of middle-income countries (MICs), although not necessarily in sufficient numbers, but they may not exist at all in low-income countries (LICs). For example, many countries have no radiotherapy centers, and many have only one center (International Atomic Energy Agency Directory of Radiotherapy Centres, http://www-naweb.iaea.org/nahu/dirac/default.asp). Palliative surgery and palliative radiotherapy are discussed further in chapters 13 and 14, respectively. The focus of this chapter is pain control medication, which can relieve most cancer pain and can be delivered at home, even in remote areas.

Since 1990, the World Health Organization (WHO) and other bodies have offered definitions of palliative care. These definitions differ in specifics but share a common vision of care that emphasizes effective pain relief and a team approach to care throughout the course of the illness (Cleary and Carbone 1997; Foley and Gelband 2001; Morrison and Meier 2011; WHO 1990). The primary goal of palliative care is improving the quality of life of patients and those around them; it is not the prolongation of life or the hastening of death. Access to pain relief has been declared a human right (Brennan, Carr, and Cousins 2007; Gwyther, Brennan, and Harding 2009; International Pain Summit of the International Association for the Study of Pain 2011; Lohman, Schleifer, and Amon 2010).

Corresponding author: James Cleary, MD, FRACP, FAChPM, University of Wisconsin, jfcleary@wisc.edu

From a global perspective, the growth of palliative care has been largely limited to HICs, which also rank high on the Human Development Index (HDI). The availability of palliative care—using the availability of opioid medicines as a surrogate—is correlated with a country's HDI. At the low end, the availability is almost nil, and repeated surveys have shown that this availability changed only marginally between 2006 and 2011 (Gilson and others 2013).

In the previous edition of *Disease Control Priorities in Developing Countries*, Foley and others (2006) documented the global problem of low access to adequate pain relief in LMICs. Since then, a few countries have improved access, but these accomplishments are sporadic; in many countries, the change is negligible. Now, there is both cause for optimism and the view of a long road ahead. Efforts to support leaders in reforming policy and clinical practice in LMICs have grown and provide a basis for improvements (Cherny and others 2013; Cleary, Radbruch, and others 2013).

This chapter describes the current state of pain relief in LMICs, consistent with WHO's use of opioid consumption as a surrogate for access to palliative care in the Global Monitoring Framework for Noncommunicable Diseases (WHO 2013a). We describe the gaps in pain control access across countries, analyze the barriers to improving its delivery, and describe the costs and benefits that might accrue from removing the barriers.

Evidence summarized in this chapter focuses on the modest costs and substantial benefits of providing pain control, and it supports increased efforts in the short term. Pain control medication and other aspects of palliative care can lead, rather than follow, increased efforts in cancer treatment, relying on interventions that are part of a more advanced cancer control and treatment infrastructure.

CANCER PATIENTS' NEED FOR PAIN CONTROL MEDICATION

Patients with cancer usually experience pain at some points during their illness, increasingly toward the end. Mild and moderate pain often can be controlled with commonly available analgesics, such as acetaminophen and ibuprofen, but progressively stronger medications are needed to control cancer pain as the illness progresses and pain becomes more severe. Opioids—such as codeine and morphine—are invariably needed toward the end of life. This progression is embodied in WHO's Three-Step Analgesic Ladder, developed in 1986 to guide clinicians (WHO 1986). More recently, the American

Pain Society has advocated an approach based on the mechanism of pain together with its severity, but this group also emphasized that all patients with cancer should have access to opioids, as needed (Miaskowski and others 2005).

How prevalent is the need for pain relief among cancer patients in LMICs? Cancer deaths are rising throughout the world as progress is made against infectious diseases and as the world's population ages. In 2012, 5.3 million people died of cancer in LMICs, compared with 2.9 million in HICs. In Sub-Saharan Africa, 715,000 new cases and 542,000 cancer deaths occurred in 2008; these numbers are projected to nearly double by 2030 due to population growth and aging (Ferlay and others 2010). The consensus among researchers is that 60–90 percent of patients with advanced cancer experience moderate to severe pain (Cleeland and others 1988; Cleeland and others 1996; Daut and Cleeland 1982; Foley 1979, 1999; Stjernsward and Clark 2003). The intensity, degree of pain relief, and effect of pain vary according to the type of cancer, treatment, and personal characteristics, but prevalence and severity of pain usually increase with the progression of the disease.

Foley and others (2006) estimated that about 80 percent of people dying of cancer would experience moderate or severe pain that requires opioid medication for relief for an average of 90 days before death. This estimate amounts to 425 million days of cancer pain that could be relieved by opioids in LMICs each year currently.

STATUS OF PAIN CONTROL IN LMICs

In an ideal world, palliative care and pain control would be one component of a cancer care system, but in nearly all LICs and for the rural poor in many MICs, palliative care—if it exists at all—is more likely to be independent of cancer services, and patients receive little or no primary cancer treatment. Unfortunately, despite the inclusion of morphine and codeine on WHO's essential medicines list (WHO 2013b), the programs to deliver them are likely to be undeveloped, and patients go without relief.

In 2006, 66 percent of the world's population lived in countries that had virtually no consumption of opioids, 10 percent in countries with very low consumption, 3 percent in countries with low consumption, and 4 percent in countries with moderate consumption (Seya and others 2011). Only 7.5 percent of the world's population lived in countries with consumption levels defined as adequate. The level of adequacy of access for a country was highly correlated with its HDI ($R^2 = 0.7583$) (Seya and others 2011).

To what extent is the need for cancer pain relief met under these circumstances? Even with increases in certain areas, the starting levels are so low that the most recent levels are only a fraction of the per capita use in HICs (figure 9.1).

This global assessment is supported by new data from sites in 26 countries representing all World Bank income levels. The International Association for Hospice and Palliative Care (IAHPC) conducted its first round of the Opioid Price Watch (De Lima and others 2014), which reports on availability of opioids, as well as the prices that consumers pay for those medicines. The survey was conducted in the following manner: surveyors visited the pharmacy closest to a public health facility treating patients with life-threatening conditions. If that pharmacy had no opioids in stock, or if the chief pharmacist did not wish to participate, the surveyors visited the next closest pharmacy; this process continued until at least one opioid was found or the surveyor concluded that none would be available anywhere. At least one opioid was available in the first pharmacy sampled in all seven HICs. In three of the eight low-income sites in six countries (including three sites in Tanzania), no opioids were found, even after visiting an average of 4.5 pharmacies; where they were found, many fewer kinds were available than in HICs. In three of the sample countries—Moldova, Nepal, and Sudan—opioids for outpatients were available only from hospital pharmacies with permission to dispense them, limiting access geographically. No information was available on consumption in Moldova or Sudan, and very low consumption was reported per capita in Nepal, suggesting that most cancer patients have no access.

AVAILABILITY OF BROADLY DEFINED PALLIATIVE CARE SERVICES

The level of palliative care services available to cancer patients was assessed in 2007 by the International Observatory of End of Life Care (Clark and others 2007) and again in 2011 (Lynch, Connor, and Clark 2013). Four categories were defined in 2007, and two subcategories were added in 2011 (designated 3b and 4b, following):

1. No known hospice-palliative care activity
2. Capacity-building activity
3a. Isolated palliative care provision
3b. Generalized palliative care provision

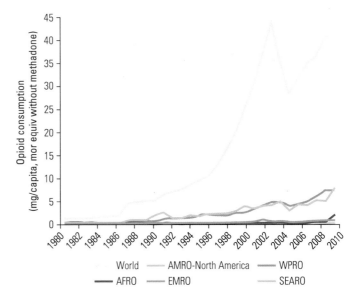

Figure 9.1 Comparison of Opioid Consumption in Morphine Equivalents without Methadone
(mg per capita)

Source: Cleary, Radbruch, and others 2013.
Note: AFRO = Africa; AMRO-North America = Latin America and Caribbean (America not including North America); EMRO = Middle East (Eastern Mediterranean); SEARO = Southeast Asia; WPRO = Western Pacific.

4a. Hospice-palliative care services at a stage of preliminary integration into mainstream service provision
4b. Hospice-palliative care services at a stage of advanced integration into mainstream service provision.

Palliative care was in stage 4a or 4b primarily in HICs, with only a handful of LMICs (mainly MICs) in the highest category. In 2011, most countries still had no services, were in a capacity-building mode, or had only isolated services.

BARRIERS TO PAIN CONTROL IN LMICs

The near-total lack of access to opioid drugs for pain relief in most LICs and many MICs is best understood by examining the barriers to their supply (Cherny and others 2013; Foley and others 2006; Sloan and Gelband 2007). In HICs, modern palliative care, including access to opioid medicines and other methods of pain control, has often developed as an adjunct to cancer care programs. In LICs and many MICs, the same pattern has been difficult to follow because care programs simply do not exist in most places. However, cancer control programs are not the only things that are absent, sparse, or overstretched. Medical and pharmacy resources are lacking in numbers and quality; medicines are costly and are most often paid for out of pocket. Patients in some places are reluctant to use addictive drugs, even in the last stages of illness, and clinicians who have received little training in appropriate prescribing for cancer patients may reinforce this reluctance.

The greatest and most widespread barrier, however—by far—comes from national regulations to control the nonmedical use of narcotics. These regulations make it difficult or impossible for clinicians to prescribe and patients to obtain opioids for relief of cancer pain. These regulations have been put in place in response to the Single Convention on Narcotic Drugs of 1961 (INCB 1961) and amended by the 1972 Protocol. The Single Convention is an international treaty to ensure the availability of opioids for medical and scientific needs while preventing the illicit production of, trafficking in, and nonmedical use of narcotic drugs. The Convention established the International Narcotics Control Board (INCB) in 1968 as an independent, quasi-judicial organization to implement the Single Convention.

The Single Convention requires that all governments, even nonsignatories, estimate the amounts of opioids needed for medical and scientific purposes and report annually on imports, exports, and consumption. It sets out the following principles on which countries can base their own policies and regulations:

- Individuals must be authorized to dispense opioids by virtue of their professional license or be specially licensed to do so.
- Opioids may be transferred only between authorized parties.
- Opioids may be dispensed only with a medical prescription.
- Security and records are required.

Despite the Convention's recognition of the need for opioid use in pain control—and the demonstration by organizations such as Hospice Africa Uganda that the needs of patients can be met even in remote areas while respecting these limits—the concern over illegal narcotics has tipped the scale against the legitimate medical needs of patients. Many countries have established regulations that go well beyond those required by the Convention. Overzealous drug controllers and poorly considered laws and regulations to restrict the diversion of medicinal opioids into illicit markets profoundly interfere with the medical availability of opioids for the relief of pain. Often, the logistics of pain treatment with opioids is so burdensome or complex for physicians, nurses, and pharmacists that they assume it is an impossible task and do not pursue it. This problem has been recognized since the 1980s by INCB, WHO, the Council of Europe, and Human Rights Watch (Cherny and others 2010).

In 2000, WHO, in collaboration with INCB, developed guidelines for national authorities to scrutinize their regulatory systems for barriers that could impede access (WHO 2000). The movement to diagnose barriers to access has led to several exemplary national reforms. It appears that the very act of diagnosing regulatory impediments to opioids for cancer pain is a strong first step toward reform.

The international organizations that have collaborated in the Global Opioid Policy Initiative (GOPI)[1] have published a detailed country-specific analysis in five regions of the world of the availability and regulatory restrictions on seven opioid analgesic formulations (Cleary, De Lima, and others 2013; Cleary, Powell, and others 2013; Cleary, Radbruch, and others 2013):

- Codeine
- Immediate-release morphine (liquid or tablet)
- Controlled-release oral morphine
- Injectable morphine
- Oxycodone
- Transdermal fentanyl
- Immediate-release methadone

IAHPC deems these agents essential for treatment of pain in palliative care (De Lima and Doyle 2007).

Respondents commonly reported that these opioids were included in national formularies. The reality, however, was substantial variation in true availability and many regulatory barriers to access.

Although the picture we present is lack of progress on a broad scale, we can point to positive developments that have improved the availability or delivery of opioid medicines in particular situations (Gilson and others 2013). Cost has been reduced by the domestic manufacture of morphine tablets or solutions in Ethiopia (2010), Jordan (2004), and Vietnam (2009). In Kenya (2010), a tax on morphine powder was eliminated. In Ethiopia, India, Kenya, and Vietnam, providers and policy makers have been educated about the use of and need for opioids.

National cancer policies or palliative care policies have been created in a number of countries, laying the groundwork for greater opioid availability. This has been the case in Ethiopia (2004), Kenya (2011), Nepal (2009), and Rwanda (2010). Jamaica took steps in 2010 and 2011 to clarify and facilitate opioid distribution through improved regulation. In Uganda (2004), the National Drug Policy and Authority statute was amended to allow specially trained palliative care nurses and clinical officers to prescribe morphine, greatly expanding the pool of providers and thus the population with access.

In Georgia (2008), Mongolia (2004), and Vietnam (2008), the number of days allowed for an opioid prescription was increased; in some cases, the eligible patient population was expanded, for example, from only patients with the most advanced cancers to those with certain types of acute and chronic pain.

ECONOMICS OF PALLIATIVE CARE IN LMICs

We consider economics from two perspectives: that of the health care system and that of the patients. In countries with comprehensive, publicly funded health care, the governments pay for all or most of the services and commodities needed for palliative care. The patients pay either nothing or a predetermined copay.

In settings in which the public sector does not yet provide or subsidize the cost of services, patients may be responsible for all costs. The costs may be mainly market-driven, but they also may include taxes, tariffs, and other government add-ons. In the case of palliative care, the cost of pain control medications is most important. Patients everywhere inevitably bear other costs, including transportation and the opportunity costs of family caregivers who miss work. How high a barrier these costs impose varies with the economic situation of the families and the support available.

Health System Perspective

Evaluating the costs and effectiveness of palliative care in LMICs presents challenges of the most basic kind. No single model of palliative care delivery can be implemented across all countries; each country presents with a unique constellation of health care resources and challenges.

Studies comparing the costs of organized palliative care programs for patients with cancer with care delivered in the absence of such programs are limited to HICs, where conventional cancer care is already well organized. Researchers reviewing such studies have concluded that organized palliative care tends to save health care costs, compared with usual cancer care, because it lowers hospitalization rates for patients who are terminally ill (Simoens and others 2010). No specific model of palliative care appears to be superior to any other (García-Pérez and others 2009).

An important difference exists in the availability of pain relief in HICs and LMICs, however. Even when palliative care programs do not exist in HICs, medications for pain relief are usually available to patients with cancer through conventional medical care. Patients in LMICs are often unable to obtain such medications in any health care setting. Yet, it is telling that even when pain medications are readily available through conventional cancer care, organized programs for palliative care can enhance the effectiveness of pain control and lower the costs to the medical care system. Health care providers who focus on and are trained in cancer pain relief can reduce health care costs, at least in HICs, and improve the quality of life for patients and their caregivers (Amery and others 2009).

Most patients in LICs and many in MICs do not routinely receive care for cancer in hospitals; many receive no cancer-specific care at all. Where this is the case, improving access to pain relief at the end of life may increase health care costs, because adding care to a baseline of little or no care clearly involves new costs. For the minority of cancer patients who receive end-of-life care in hospitals, improving the availability of pain medicine through dismantling regulatory barriers, educating professionals, and integrating palliative care programs may reduce health care costs, as such measures have done in HICs.

A useful first step in assessing the cost of palliative care to a health system is to assess the cost of the most basic oral opioid medicine—oral morphine. Foley and colleagues estimated the cost of oral morphine, and medicines to treat side effects, sufficient for pain relief in the last three months of life in three countries— Chile, Romania, and Uganda—at between US$0.48 and US$0.98 per day (US$ 2004) (Foley and others 2006).

In the United States, the average community pharmacy's acquisition cost of immediate-release oral morphine tablets sufficient for three days at 60 mcg per day was US$1.20 in 2014. More sophisticated dosing forms may cost more to manufacture; new, patented formulations include in their price a premium for intellectual property. A fentanyl patch, for example, compares at US$4.09 for similar pain relief.[2] Costs vary widely by country, depending on such factors as whether medicines can be produced within the country or must be imported, whether they face import duties, and the nature of the existing medicine distribution system. An unfortunate circumstance is that the factors that make opioids more expensive tend to be prevalent in LMICs.

In some cases, making more effective pain relief medications available to patients with cancer by removing regulatory barriers would involve no costs other than the cost of the medicine itself. Where oral morphine is already available and affordable, for example, the additional cost of providing other medicines deemed essential for palliative care by IAHPC[3] would be limited largely to the drug costs alone, since the care delivery and narcotics control mechanisms would already be in place. The training for professional staff in the appropriate use of palliative medicines would be an ongoing cost, but that cost would be spread across the population of patients with cancer who are served.

In areas with no effective access to any opioids for these patients, getting the most appropriate medicine to patients is likely to involve additional clinic or home visits with trained personnel, as well as new controls to secure the medicines from theft or abuse.

Since 1993, Hospice Africa Uganda's (HAU) model program has offered palliative care to patients with cancer, AIDS, and, increasingly, other (mainly noncommunicable) conditions. Most patients are seen at home, but HAU also provides hospice care at inpatient facilities (HAU 2013). The service is nurse-led, with physician backup. It includes basic needs support, including food, clothing, blankets, and transport costs; pain and symptom control, including morphine; and other support services. HAU estimated that the cost of adding a children's palliative care program at a hospital for children and at HAU's clinic was approximately US$75 (US$ 2007) per child per year. About one-third of that cost was for medicines and pharmacy consumables (Amery and others 2009).

Patient Perspective

For patients, the most serious problem is that opioids are not available at any price, even if prescribed. Where they are available, price is the next consideration, but reliable information on the price of pain medicines to consumers has been lacking in LMICs. This deficit was the impetus for IAHPC to begin the Opioid Price Watch, an availability and price survey in a sample of 26 low-, lower-middle-, and upper-middle-income countries and HICs (De Lima and others 2014). The endpoints were the availability and price of opioids to the consumer on a single day in each site.

The survey included five opioids (13 formulations), including those on WHO's List of Essential Medicines (17th edition, WHO 2011) and additional medicines on the IAHPC list of essential palliative care medicines:

- Fentanyl: transdermal patch
- Hydromorphone: injectable, oral liquid, oral solid immediate release, oral solid sustained release
- Methadone: oral liquid, oral solid
- Morphine: injectable, oral liquid, oral solid
- Oxycodone: oral solid immediate release, oral solid sustained release

The price of opioids, when available at all, was highest, in absolute terms, in the poorest countries, except in certain LMICs where they are free to patients; however, these are countries with extremely low consumption, meaning effectively no availability. In the Opioid Price Watch sample, these no-cost but no-availability countries were Nepal (LIC), Sudan (LMIC), and Romania (upper-middle income).

The least expensive drug globally, according to the international buyer reference price, was the immediate-release morphine oral solid; this was not the least expensive formulation (standardized to a 30-day average dose) in many countries. Fentanyl patches were less expensive in China (Chengdu), Germany, Guatemala, India, the Islamic Republic of Iran, Norway, Poland, Spain, the Philippines, and the United Kingdom, suggesting that these governments subsidize at least some of these medicines and do so differentially.

CONCLUSIONS

There is no palliative care without pain control. The benefits of opioid medicines for pain relief to patients with cancer and their families, regardless of their whereabouts, are real and universally observable. These benefits have been known for decades, yet the vast majority of those dying in pain cannot get these medicines, even though the basic forms are inexpensive, oral, and relatively easy to administer at home. The movement to declare pain relief a human right reflects the recognition that its benefits extend to the core of human dignity. The question becomes not whether pain relief with opioids is worth its cost, but what steps will most quickly and efficiently facilitate access to these medications for those who need them, even in the absence of organized cancer control efforts.

It has taken the inspired efforts of pioneers to build palliative care capacity in LMICs, mainly in the private faith and philanthropic sectors, but involving, as it must, government. According to the GOPI report, many international and regional organizations are focusing on palliative care, with efforts to find, train, and support the leaders in each country or area. The investment in leadership required to reform national and regional policies is a real cost that must be supported. The next steps identified by GOPI (Cleary, Radbruch, and others 2013), which they refer to as the "cornerstone trinity," are medication availability, education, and policy reform. The costs of policy measures are front-loaded; once policies supporting the widespread availability of pain medications to patients with cancer are in place, they will need only routine monitoring.

These conclusions are robust even in the absence of large numbers of studies and supporting data about the extent of palliative care available in LMICs. The evidence supporting the effectiveness of pain control medicines is strong and applicable worldwide, but validation in LMICs would provide support to expanded efforts. Studies detailing the lack of services, the personal consequences of dying in pain, and the increasing burden of deaths from cancer and other noncommunicable diseases will help to persuade policy makers and funders of the importance of palliative care.

It is appropriate to note that progress has been made in the past few years, but the main message remains that very few of the increasing numbers of people dying from cancer in LMICs can expect to die without debilitating pain. Yet the interventions needed could be made available affordably everywhere, in a relatively short time, if given high enough priority and modest resources.

NOTES

World Bank income classifications as of July 2014 are as follows, based on estimates of gross national income per capita for 2013:

- Low-income countries: US$1,045 or less
- Middle-income countries:
  - Lower-middle-income: US$1,046–US$4,125
  - Upper-middle-income: US$4,126–US$12,745
- High-income countries: US$12,746 or more

1. African Organisation for Research and Training in Cancer, African Palliative Care Association, Asia Pacific Hospice Palliative Care Network, Chinese Society of Clinical Oncology, Foundation Akbaraly, Madagascar, Help the Hospices, Indian Association of Palliative Care, International Association for Hospice & Palliative Care, Japanese Society of Medical Oncology, Latin American and Caribbean Society of Medical Oncology, Latin American Association for Palliative Care, Malaysian Oncology Society, Middle East Cancer Consortium, Multinational Association of Supportive Care in Cancer, Myanmar Oncology Society, Open Society Foundations, Worldwide Palliative Care Alliance.

2. Sources: Prices obtained from the April 9, 2014, Survey of Drug Acquisition Costs Paid by Retail Community Pharmacies, http://www.medicaid.gov/Medicaid-CHIP-Program-Information/By-Topics/Benefits/Prescription-Drugs/Survey-of-Retail-Prices.html. Equivalent daily doses are based on data provided by the Ventura County Health Care Agency, http://www.vchca.org/docs/hospitals/fentanyl-patch-protocol-(1).pdf?sfvrsn=0.

3. http://hospicecare.com/resources/palliative-care-essentials/iahpc-essential-medicines-for-palliative-care.

REFERENCES

Amery, J., C. J. Rose, J. Holmes, J. Nguyen, and C. Byarugaba. 2009. "The Beginnings of Children's Palliative Care in Africa: Evaluation of a Children's Palliative Care Service in Africa." *Journal of Palliative Medicine* 12 (11): 1015–21.

Brennan, F., D. B. Carr, and M. Cousins. 2007. "Pain Management: A Fundamental Human Right." *Anesthesia and Analgesia* 105 (1): 205–21. doi:10.1213/01.ane.0000268145.52345.55.

Cherny, N. I., J. Baselga, F. de Conno, and L. Radbruch. 2010. "Formulary Availability and Regulatory Barriers to Accessibility of Opioids for Cancer Pain in Europe: A Report from the ESMO/EAPC Opioid Policy Initiative." *Annals of Oncology* 21 (3): 615–26. doi:10.1093/annonc/mdp581.

Cherny, N. I., J. Cleary, W. Scholten, L. Radbruch, and J. Torode. 2013. "The Global Opioid Policy Initiative (GOPI) Project to Evaluate the Availability and Accessibility of Opioids for the Management of Cancer Pain in Africa, Asia, Latin America and the Caribbean, and the Middle East: Introduction and Methodology." *Annals of Oncology* 24 (Suppl. 11): xi7–13. doi:10.1093/annonc/mdt498.

Clark, D., M. Wright, J. Hunt, and T. Lynch. 2007. "Hospice and Palliative Care Development in Africa: A Multi-Method Review of Services and Experiences." *Journal of Pain and Symptom Management* 33 (6): 698–710. doi:http://dx.doi.org/10.1016/j.jpainsymman.2006.09.033.

Cleary, J. F., and P. P. Carbone. 1997. "Palliative Medicine in the Elderly." *Cancer* 80 (7): 1335–47. http://www.ncbi.nlm.nih.gov/pubmed/9317188.

Cleary, J., L. De Lima, J. Eisenchlas, L. Radbruch, J. Torode, and others. 2013. "Formulary Availability and Regulatory Barriers to Accessibility of Opioids for Cancer Pain in Latin America and the Caribbean: A Report from the Global Opioid Policy Initiative (GOPI)." *Annals of Oncology* 24 (Suppl. 11): xi41–50. doi:10.1093/annonc/mdt502.

Cleary, J., R. A. Powell, G. Munene, F. N. Mwangi-Powell, E. Luyirika, and others. 2013. "Formulary Availability and Regulatory Barriers to Accessibility of Opioids for Cancer Pain in Africa: A Report from the Global Opioid Policy Initiative (GOPI)." *Annals of Oncology* 24 (Suppl. 11): xi14–23. doi:10.1093/annonc/mdt499.

Cleary, J., L. Radbruch, J. Torode, and N. I. Cherny. 2013. "Next Steps in Access and Availability of Opioids for the Treatment of Cancer Pain: Reaching the Tipping Point?" *Annals of Oncology* 24 (Suppl. 11): xi60–64. doi:10.1093/annonc/mdt504.

Cleeland, C. S., J. L. Ladinsky, R. C. Serlin, and N. C. Thuy. 1988. "Multidimensional Measurement of Cancer Pain: Comparisons of US and Vietnamese Patients." *Journal of Pain and Symptom Management* 3 (1): 23–27. http://linkinghub.elsevier.com/retrieve/pii/0885392488901340?showall=true.

Cleeland, C. S., Y. Nakamura, T. R. Mendoza, K. R. Edwards, J. Douglas, and others. 1996. "Dimensions of the Impact of Cancer Pain in a Four Country Sample: New Information from Multidimensional Scaling." *Pain* 67 (2–3): 267–73. doi:http://dx.doi.org/10.1016/0304-3959(96)03131-4.

Daut, R. L., and C. S. Cleeland. 1982. "The Prevalence and Severity of Pain in Cancer." *Cancer* 50 (9): 1913–18.

De Lima, L., and D. Doyle. 2007. "The International Association for Hospice and Palliative Care List of Essential Medicines for Palliative Care." *Journal of Pain and Palliative Care Pharmacotherapy* 21 (3): 29–36. doi:10.1080/J354v21n03_05.

De Lima, L., T. Pastrana, L. Radbruch, and R. Wenk. 2014. "Cross-Sectional Pilot Study to Monitor the Availability, Dispensed Prices, and Affordability of Opioids around the Globe." *Journal of Pain and Symptom Management.* doi:10.1016/j.jpainsymman.2013.12.237.

Ferlay, J., H.-R. Shin, F. Bray, D. Forman, C. Mathers, and others. 2010. "Estimates of Worldwide Burden of Cancer in 2008: GLOBOCAN 2008." *International Journal of Cancer* 127 (12): 2893–917. doi:10.1002/ijc.25516.

Foley, K. 1979. "Pain Syndromes in Patients with Cancer." In *Advances in Pain Research and Therapy*, edited by K. Foley, J. Bonica, and V. Ventafridda, 59–75. New York: Raven Press.

————. 1999. "Pain Assessment and Cancer Pain Syndromes." In *Oxford Textbook of Palliative Medicine*, 2nd ed., edited by D. Doyle, G. Hank, and N. MacDonald, 310–31. New York: Oxford University Press.

Foley, K., and H. Gelband. 2001. *Improving Palliative Care for Cancer*. Washington, DC: National Academies Press.

Foley, K. M., J. L. Wagner, D. E. Joranson, and H. Gelband. 2006. "Pain Control for People with Cancer and AIDS." In *Disease Control Priorities in Developing Countries*, 2nd ed., edited by D. Jamison, J. G. Breman, A. R. Measham, G. Alleyne, M. Claeson, D. B. Evans, P. Jha, A. Mills, and P. Musgrove, 981–93. Washington, DC: Oxford University Press and World Bank.

García-Pérez, L., R. Linertová, R. Martín-Olivera, P. Serrano-Aguilar, and M. A. Benítez-Rosario. 2009. "A Systematic Review of Specialised Palliative Care for Terminal Patients: Which Model Is Better?" *Palliative Medicine* 23 (1): 17–22. doi:10.1177/0269216308099957.

Gilson, A. M., M. A. Maurer, V. T. LeBaron, K. M. Ryan, and J. F. Cleary. 2013. "Multivariate Analysis of Countries' Government and Health-Care System Influences on Opioid Availability for Cancer Pain Relief and Palliative Care: More Than a Function of Human Development." *Palliative Medicine* 27 (2): 105–14. doi:10.1177/0269216312461973.

Gwyther, L., F. Brennan, and R. Harding. 2009. "Advancing Palliative Care as a Human Right." *Journal of Pain and Symptom Management* 38 (5): 767–74. doi:10.1016/j.jpainsymman.2009.03.003.

HAU (Hospice Africa Uganda). 2013. *Hospice Africa Uganda Annual Report 2012–2013*. Kampala: HAU.

INCB (International Narcotics Control Board). 1961. *Single Convention on Narcotic Drugs, 1961*. http://www.incb.org/incb/en/narcotic-drugs/1961_Convention.html.

International Pain Summit of the International Association for the Study of Pain. 2011. "Declaration of Montréal: Declaration that Access to Pain Management Is a Fundamental Human Right." *Journal of Pain and Palliative Care Pharmacotherapy* 25 (1): 29–31. doi:10.3109/15360288.2010.547560.

Lohman, D., R. Schleifer, and J. J. Amon. 2010. "Access to Pain Treatment as a Human Right." *BMC Medicine* 8: 8. doi:10.1186/1741-7015-8-8.

Lynch, T., S. Connor, and D. Clark. 2013. "Mapping Levels of Palliative Care Development: A Global Update." *Journal of Pain and Symptom Management* 45 (6): 1094–106. http://dx.doi.org/10.1016/j.jpainsymman.2012.05.011.

Miaskowski, C., J. Cleary, R. Burney, P. Coyne, R. Finley, and others. 2005. *Guidelines for the Management of Cancer Pain in Adults and Children*. Glenview, IL: American Pain Society.

Morrison, R. S., and D. E. Meier. 2011. "The National Palliative Care Research Center and the Center to Advance Palliative Care: A Partnership to Improve Care for Persons with Serious Illness and Their Families." *Journal of Pediatric Hematology/Oncology* 33 (Suppl. 2): S126–31. doi:10.1097/MPH.0b013e318230dfa.

National Cancer Institute. 2009. *SEER Cancer Statistics Review 1975–2010*. National Cancer Institute, Bethesda, MD. http://seer.cancer.gov/csr/1975_2010/browse_csr.php?sectionSEL=2&pageSEL=sect_02_table.09.html.

Seya, M.-J., S. F. A. M. Gelders, O. U. Achara, B. Milani, and W. K. Scholten. 2011. "A First Comparison between the Consumption of and the Need for Opioid Analgesics at Country, Regional, and Global Levels." *Journal of Pain and Palliative Care Pharmacotherapy* 25 (1): 6–18. doi:10.3109/15360288.2010.536307.

Simoens, S., B. Kutten, E. Keirse, P. Berghe, P. Vanden, and others. 2010. "The Costs of Treating Terminal Patients." *Journal of Pain and Symptom Management* 40 (3): 436–48. http://linkinghub.elsevier.com/retrieve/pii/S0885392410003635?showall=true.

Sloan, F. A., and H. Gelband. 2007. *Cancer Control Opportunities in Low- and Middle-Income Countries: Cancer Control*. Washington, DC: National Academies Press. http://books.google.com/books?hl=en&lr=&id=rJ6LAD7l8nMC&oi=fnd&pg=PA1&dq=Cancer+Control+Opportunities+in+Low-+and+Middle

+income+countries&ots=IypmpWQGQf&sig=1 DGx__xZ_SLYTB5fxNsRS2TI1PM.

Stjernsward, J., and D. Clark. 2003. "Palliative Medicine: A Global Perspective." In *Oxford Textbook of Palliative Medicine*, 3rd ed., edited by D. Doyle, G. Hanks, and N. I. Cherny, 1199–222. New York: Oxford University Press.

WHO (World Health Organization). 1986. *Cancer Pain Relief.* Geneva: WHO.

————. 1990. *Cancer Pain Relief and Palliative Care.* Report of a WHO expert committee. Geneva: WHO.

————. 2000. *Achieving Balance in National Opioids Control Policy: Guidelines for Assessment.* Geneva: WHO. http://apps.who.int/iris/bitstream/10665/66496/1/WHO_EDM_QSM_2000.4.pdf?ua=1.

————. 2011. "WHO Model List of Essential Medicines." 17th ed., WHO, Geneva.

————. 2013a. *Draft Comprehensive Global Monitoring Framework and Targets for the Prevention and Control of Noncommunicable Diseases.* Geneva: WHO.

————. 2013b. "WHO Model List of Essential Medicines." 18th ed., WHO, Geneva.

Global Hazards of Tobacco and the Benefits of Smoking Cessation and Tobacco Taxes

Prabhat Jha, Mary MacLennan, Frank. J. Chaloupka, Ayda Yurekli, Chintanie Ramasundarahettige, Krishna Palipudi, Witold Zatoński, Samira Asma, and Prakash C. Gupta

INTRODUCTION

Tobacco use kills approximately five million people annually worldwide, accounting for over 20 percent of all deaths of adult men and 5 percent of deaths of adult women. As death rates from causes not attributed to tobacco are falling, the proportion of all adult deaths due to smoking will rise. In the 20th century, 100 million tobacco deaths occurred; nearly 70 percent were in high-income countries (HICs) and the former socialist economies of Europe. In contrast, in the 21st century, tobacco is expected to kill about one billion people, mostly in low- and middle-income countries (LMICs).

Widespread use of a few powerful interventions affecting tobacco price, information, and regulations could prevent tens of millions of premature deaths over the next few decades.

This chapter starts with the epidemiology of smoking-related diseases, focusing on contemporary estimates of the hazards of smoking and the benefits of cessation, and then describes current and future smoking patterns, including the rapid emergence of electronic cigarettes. We next turn to interventions to rapidly raise cessation rates in LMICs, in particular, higher excise taxes on tobacco products. We discuss the cost-effectiveness, cost-benefit, and poverty considerations

of tobacco control and conclude by reviewing the current state of global tobacco control implementation.

EPIDEMIOLOGY OF SMOKING-ATTRIBUTABLE DISEASES

Approximately 1.3 billion people smoke worldwide; over 80 percent of smokers reside in LMICs. Smoked tobacco accounts for about 97 percent of all tobacco sales globally (Euromonitor International 2013), mostly in the form of cigarettes, or in the case of South Asia, in the form of bidis, which typically contain about one-fourth as much tobacco as cigarettes. Inhaling tobacco smoke causes a greater diversity and incidence of disease than chewing tobacco. Active smoking is also more hazardous than exposure to secondhand smoke, although secondhand smoke contributes significantly to some diseases (IARC 2004).

Substantial Delay from Smoking Uptake to Excess Mortality

After smoking becomes common in a population of young adults, it may take more than half a century to assess reliably the full risks of mortality (Jha and Peto 2014). Five recent studies in Japan, the United Kingdom,

Corresponding author: Prabhat Jha, Center for Global Health Research, St. Michael's Hospital and Dalla Lana School of Public Health, University of Toronto, Prabhat.Jha@utoronto.ca.

and the United States have examined large populations of men and women who began to smoke regularly when they were young and never quit. These five studies find a twofold to threefold increased risk of death among smokers, leading to a reduction in lifespan of at least one decade (Doll and others 2004; Jha, Ramasundarahettige, and others 2013; Pirie and others 2013; Sakata and others 2012; Thun and others 2013). The same studies included individuals who quit smoking. Those who stopped before age 40 avoided about 90 percent of the excess risk of death of those who continued. Smokers who do not start in early adult life have much smaller hazards in middle and old age. Table 10.1 summarizes the main findings for individuals, and figure 10.1 shows the risks by gender for Japan, the United Kingdom, and the United States, as well as comparable risks among men who smoke cigarettes in India.

Men born in the United Kingdom in the first quarter of the 20th century were the first major population to smoke regularly from early adult life; by 1970, the nation had the highest tobacco-attributable death rates in the world (Peto and others 1992). Sir Richard Doll's study of doctors born during the first half of the 20th century and followed for the second half showed a 10-year loss of life expectancy among those who continued to smoke (figure 10.1).

For women, smoking became common later in the United Kingdom and the United States, beginning with women born in the 1940s and 1950s. The full risks in women have been measured only early in the 21st century. By the 1980s, the lung cancer risk ratio in men who smoked versus men who never smoked rose substantially from 12-fold in the 1960s to 24-fold in the 1980s; it stabilized at 25-fold in the 2000s. By contrast, the risks of lung cancer for women who smoked versus never-smokers rose later (Thun and others 2013). In the 1960s, it was threefold; in the 1980s, 13-fold; and in the 2000s, 26-fold (with similar ratios in women in the United Kingdom in the 2000s). This is because the typical 60-year-old female smoker in the United States in the 2000s had smoked since early adult years, whereas those who were smokers in the 1960s had not.

Cancer and Other Diseases Caused by Smoking

More than two-thirds of the 47 million deaths among adults over age 25 years worldwide in 2012 were caused by cancer, vascular and respiratory diseases, and tuberculosis (WHO 2013a). Because smoking causes many of these diseases, overall mortality from smoking—rather than cause-specific mortality—is increasingly used as a measure of total smoking risk (U.S. Department of Health and Human Services 2014). About 50 percent of the current five million smoking-related deaths worldwide occur in LMICs, and about 80 percent of these smoking deaths occur in men, but this is chiefly because of the lag in women's uptake of smoking.

In 2012, 14 million new cases of cancer were diagnosed and about eight million cancer deaths occurred worldwide. Over 30 percent of the cancer deaths in middle-aged men and about 10 percent of those in women are due to smoking (Ferlay and others 2013). Smoking accounted for the vast majority of the 1.6 million deaths from lung cancer in 2012 (1.1 million in men and 0.5 million in women).

Table 10.1 Three Main Implications for Individuals Who Become Cigarette Smokers in Adolescence or Early Adult Life

---

1. The risk is big, if they continue smoking.

- Continued smoking eventually kills at least half of men and women who smoke. Among persistent cigarette smokers, whether men or women, the overall relative risk of death throughout middle age and well into old age is at least twofold higher than otherwise similar never-smokers. Among smokers of a given age, more than half of those who die in the near future would not have done so at never-smoker death rates.

- On average, smokers lose at least one decade of life. This average combines a zero loss for those not killed by tobacco with the loss of much more than one decade for those who are killed by it.

2. At least half of those killed are middle aged (ages 30–69 years), losing many years of life.

- Some of those killed in middle age might have died anyway, but others might have lived on for another 10, 20, 30, or more years.

- On average, those killed in middle age lose about 20 years of never-smoker life expectancy.

3. Stopping smoking works to reduce health risks.

- Those who stop before age 40 avoid more than 90 percent of the excess risk among those who continue to smoke. Those who stop before age 30 avoid nearly all of the smokers' excess risk.

- Those who have smoked cigarettes since early adult life but stop at 30, 40, 50, or 60 years of age gain, respectively, about 10, 9, 6, and 4 years of life expectancy, compared with those who continue smoking.

Sources: Doll and others 2004; Jha, Ramasundarahettige, and others 2013; Pirie and others 2013; Sakata and others 2012; Thun and others 2013.

Figure 10.1 Loss of a Decade of Life among Current Cigarette Smokers versus Never-Smokers Who Are Middle Aged: Men and Women in the United Kingdom and the United States, Men in Japan, and Men in India

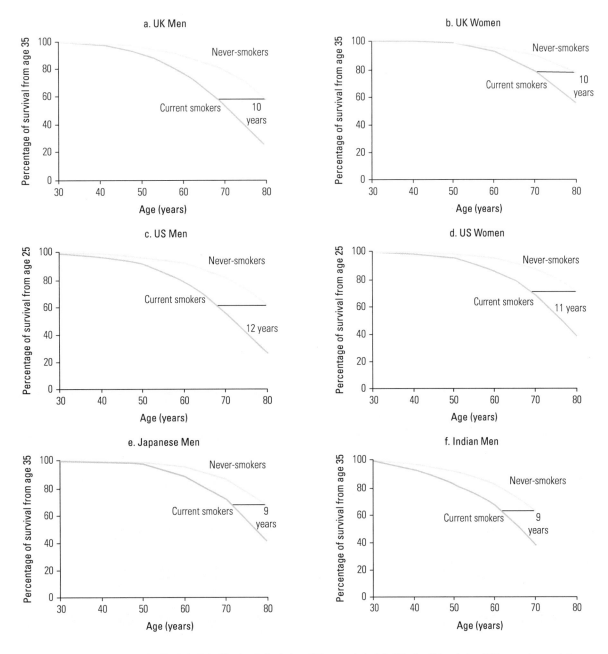

Sources: Data adapted from various studies. Men in the United Kingdom: Doll and others 2004; women in the United Kingdom: Pirie and others 2013; men and women in the United States: Jha Ramasundarahettige, and others 2013; men in Japan: Sakata and others 2012; men in India: Jha and others 2008.

The International Agency for Research on Cancer (IARC) cancer registry data reveal that the age-standardized mortality rate from lung cancer is highest in men in Europe, Northern America, Australia/New Zealand, and Japan and lower in LMICs, reflecting the long duration of smoking in the former populations and earlier age of initiation. Men in LMICs have not yet smoked for prolonged periods, and the lung cancer incidence and mortality rates are accordingly lower.

However, where reliably measured, the proportion of cancer deaths due to smoking is substantial in LMICs. In China, smoking caused about 40 percent of cancer deaths in men and 20 percent in women ages 35 or older in 2010 (Chen and others, forthcoming).

In India, smoking caused about 32 percent and 6 percent of cancer deaths at ages 30–69 years in men and women, respectively, in 2010. Smoking appears to have a synergistic effect on the chronic viral infections that cause liver and cervical cancers.

Smoking causes about three times as many noncancer deaths as it does cancer deaths. Cardiovascular disease is the leading cause of smoking-attributable deaths worldwide (Jha 2009). Smoking is a significant risk factor for fatal and nonfatal heart attack and stroke. In HICs, about one-half of the male and one-third of the female deaths at ages 35–69 years from chronic lung disease are due to smoking. In China, chronic lung disease accounted for a quarter of all tobacco deaths among men and women in 2010 (Chen and others, forthcoming). Among those ages 30–69 years in India in 2010, over 30 percent of deaths among men and 10 percent of deaths among women from chronic lung disease were due to smoking.

Increased risks of tuberculosis death and nonfatal tuberculosis among smokers have been observed in countries where tuberculosis remains common, most notably, in India. In India, nearly 40 percent of tuberculosis deaths among middle-aged males—about 120,000 deaths annually—are attributable to smoking. Tuberculosis is the leading cause of smoking deaths in rural areas; acute heart attack is the leading cause in urban areas. Subclinical infection with the tubercle bacillus is widespread, and smoking appears to facilitate the progression from silent to active clinical disease. Thus, smoking might contribute to the spread of tuberculosis (Gajalakshmi and others 2003; Jha and others 2008).

Effects of Cessation on Total Mortality in Individuals and Populations

Large numbers of adult males and fewer adult females have quit smoking in HICs, providing the opportunity to study the effect of quitting at various ages on subsequent mortality. The results of various studies indicate a 90 percent reduction in the excess risk of death among those who quit smoking by age 40; for those quitting by age 30, the benefit approaches the rates of never-smokers (figure 10.2, panel a) (Jha, Ramasundarahettige, and others 2013). The benefits of cessation are remarkably similar in studies in Japan, the United Kingdom, and the United States (table 10.1).

The large individual benefits of smoking cessation translate into major reductions in smoking-attributable deaths from all causes and from cancer in the overall population. In the United Kingdom, there are now twice as many ex-smokers as current smokers over age 50. Reliable indirect methods (Peto and others 2012) to calculate tobacco-attributable deaths demonstrate

a substantial reduction. Smoking-attributable deaths at ages 35–69 years in men declined by three-quarters from 1970 to 2010 (from 70,000 to 16,000 deaths). Men who died in 1970 had begun smoking between 1920 and 1940, near the peak of the smoking rate, when cessation was uncommon. The decline was caused by fewer men beginning to smoke from 1950 to 1970; a substantial proportion of this cohort ultimately quit smoking.

The cancer and all-cause death rates from smoking among women in the United Kingdom and the United States peaked much later, around 1995, and they have since reached a plateau. Similar declines have been seen in the proportion of all deaths due to tobacco. Notably, cancer death rates due to smoking have fallen substantially in men and have not risen in women. Death rates from cancers not caused by smoking have declined, due in part to screening and treatment of common cancers (Gelband and others 2015).

Comparably High Mortality Risks from Smoking Emerging in LMICs

Cigarette smoking rose substantially among men in many HICs in the first few decades of the 20th century and subsequently increased in women in most HICs and men in LMICs. Currently, there are about 1.3 billion smokers worldwide (Giovino and others 2012), although slightly lower estimates have been proposed (Ng and others 2014). A simple formula is that every metric tonne of tobacco produces about one million cigarettes, which leads to one death (Jha and Peto 2014).

The magnitude of the tobacco epidemic in a given country depends on the average daily consumption of cigarettes or bidis, which is generally lower in LMICs than in HICs; in India, about 80 percent of current smoking is of the lower-risk bidis, but these are being replaced by higher-risk cigarettes (Jha and others 2011). Relative to nonsmokers in India, male bidi smokers lose roughly six years, female bidi smokers lose about eight years, and male cigarette smokers lose about 10 years of life. The 10-year loss of life among Indian male cigarette smokers is about as extreme as that in the recent studies noted, despite the fact that Indian men smoke fewer cigarettes per day and start later in life than do men in HICs. The age at starting smoking is generally later in LMICs than HICs. Urban Chinese men, however, have begun to start as young as men in the United States (Chen and others, forthcoming). If similar shifts to smoking at younger ages occur in India and other populations, the eventual hazards of smoking might well be greater. Epidemiological studies have confirmed the elevated age-specific, smoking-attributable risks in Bangladesh (Alam and others 2013); China, and Hong

Figure 10.2 Effect of Smoking Cessation on Survival at Various Ages, Men and Women, United States, 2006–12

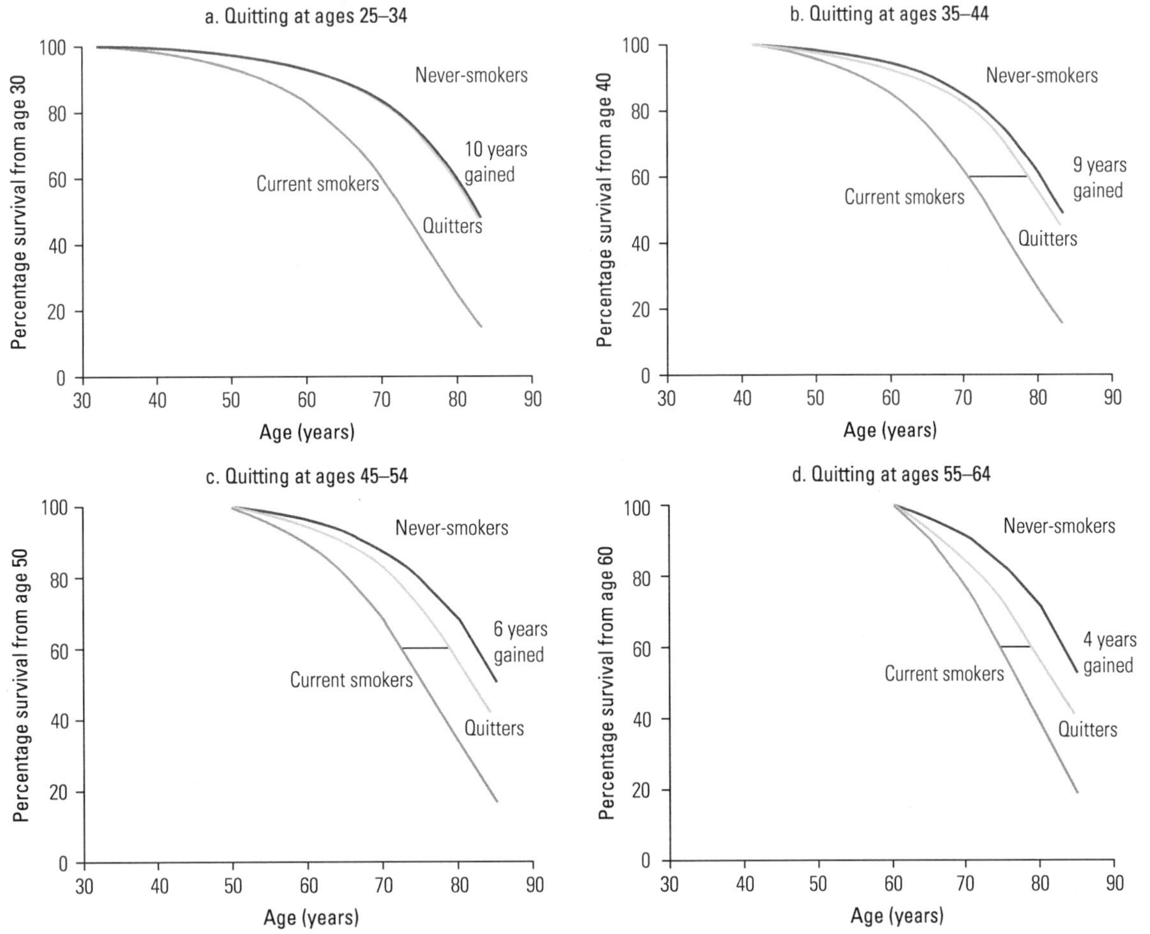

Source: Adapted from Jha, Ramasundarahettige, and others 2013.

Kong SAR, China (Gu and others 2009; Chen and others, forthcoming; Lam and others 1997); India (Jha and others 2008); and South Africa (Sitas and others 2013). Accordingly, the future mortality risks from 2010 to 2050 in many LMICs might be greater than those from 1940 to 1980 in the United Kingdom or the United States.

Overall global death rates have fallen sharply over the past four decades, particularly from 2000 to 2010 (Norheim and others 2014). Greater declines have been seen in childhood and infectious diseases than for diseases made more common by tobacco. Hence, while it is certain that tobacco will account for an increasing proportion of a falling overall total of premature deaths before age 70 years, the future projections of the absolute total from tobacco use are less certain.

Sir Richard Peto estimated that global tobacco deaths will total about 450 million between 2000

and 2050 (Peto and Lopez 2001). Further estimations are more uncertain, but based on current initiation and cessation rates and projected population growth, from 2050 to 2100, there would be, conservatively, an additional 550 million tobacco deaths, an average of 10 million deaths per year. Of the estimated one billion smoking-attributable deaths in this century, most will be in LMICs. In contrast, there were "only" 100 million tobacco deaths in the 20th century, mostly among those born before or around World War II in HICs and Eastern Europe. Already, 80–90 million smoking deaths will have occurred from 2000 to 2015. Peto's estimates of 50–60 million smoking deaths from 2000 to 2010 and about 400 million tobacco-attributable deaths from 2010 to 2050 remain plausible. Indeed, the chief uncertainty is not *if* tobacco deaths will reach about 10 million a year, but *when*, with the most likely scenario around 2030 to 2035 (Peto and Lopez 2001).

SMOKING AND CESSATION PATTERNS WORLDWIDE

The epidemiological data on the consequences of smoking help predict, with reasonable certainty, that deaths from smoking will be high in LMICs unless current smokers quit and potential new smokers do not start. This section reviews the statistics on current smoking and cessation across countries.

Current Smoking

The overall global volume of legal cigarette sales rose from 5.1 trillion in 1990 to 5.9 trillion in 2012, largely due to population growth. Although per-person consumption has fallen worldwide, it has risen in many LMICs (Euromonitor International 2013). About 80 percent of the 1.3 billion smokers age 15 years or older in the world live in LMICs; over half reside in eight regions or countries—Bangladesh, Brazil, China, the European Union, India, Indonesia, the Russian Federation, and the United States (table 10.2). The threefold hazards of lifelong smoking can be applied reliably to the cohort of roughly 620 million younger current and would-be smokers in selected countries. This application suggests that at least half, over 300 million, of this cohort will be killed by smoking unless they quit.

The Global Adult Tobacco Survey, of people ages 15 years and older in selected countries, indicates that the proportion of males who smoke ranges from over 67 percent in Indonesia to about 7 percent in Nigeria. In most LMICs, male smoking is far more common than female smoking. Among adult women, for example, the proportion of smokers ranges from 24 percent in Poland to less than 1 percent in Nigeria (Giovino and others 2012).

Smoking Cessation Patterns

To determine smoking prevalence in a population, individuals are divided into three categories: current smokers, ex-smokers, and never-smokers. Ex-smoking prevalence is a good measure of cessation at a population level. An increase in cessation, along with an increasing proportion of never-smokers, reduced adult smoking prevalence in the United Kingdom between 1950 and 2005, from 70 percent to 25 percent in men and from 40 percent to 20 percent in women. In the United States, among men ages 60–64, there are about four times as many ex-smokers as current smokers (Jha, Ramasundarahettige, and others 2013). Similar rates of cessation have been reported in most HICs.

The prevalence of male ex-smoking in LMICs is much lower. Even reported figures may be misleadingly high because they include people who quit either because they are too ill to continue smoking or because of early symptoms of tobacco-attributable illness, such as respiratory disease. A good measure of the success of tobacco control is a rising proportion of adults quitting in middle age (ages 45–64) when they can expect personal gains in health. In the European Union and the United States, where cessation has become common, about as many adults in this age group are former smokers as are current smokers. About 60 percent of all ex-smokers reside in HICs. By contrast, most LMICs, except Brazil, have far fewer former than current smokers at these ages. Cessation among women continues to lag men in nearly every country.

INTERVENTIONS TO RAISE CESSATION RATES RAPIDLY

Cessation by today's smokers is the only practicable way to avoid a substantial proportion of tobacco deaths worldwide before 2050. Halving the worldwide per capita adult consumption of tobacco by 2025 (akin to the declines in adult smoking in the United Kingdom over the past three decades) would prevent approximately 160 million to 180 million tobacco deaths over the next few decades. In contrast, halving the percentage of children who become prolonged smokers (from about 30 percent to 15 percent over two decades) would prevent 20 million deaths over the next few decades; its main effect would be to lower mortality rates by 2050 and beyond (Jha and Chaloupka 1999; Peto and Lopez 2001). Table 10.3 summarizes the effectiveness of the major interventions.

Tobacco Taxation

Aggressive taxation is the key strategy for LMICs to reduce smoking at a rate faster than that achieved by HICs. Tobacco taxes and consumption are strongly inversely related worldwide. Well over 100 studies demonstrate a strong negative relationship between cigarette pricing and consumption (Chaloupka, Yurekli, and Fong 2012; Jha and Chaloupka 1999). We review five key aspects of smart taxation:

- Price elasticity of demand for tobacco
- Affordability, the relationship of price to income growth
- Importance of smart tax structure, including excise taxes
- Implementation experience of large tax increases
- Signaling of prices to consumers.

Table 10.2 Prevalence and Number of Current and Future Smokers below age 35 and Expected Deaths, Selected Countries

Country	Current smoking prevalence, ages 15+ (percent)			Current smokers, ages 15+ (millions)	Current and future smokers, ages 0–34 (millions)	Approximate number of deaths in current and future smokers ages <35, unless smokers quit
	Male	Female	Total			
China (2010)[a]	53	2	28	317	193	97
India (2009)[a]	24	3	14	122	95	48
EU-28 (2012)[b]	32	22	27	115	54	27
Indonesia (2011)[a]	67	3	35	61	58	29
United States (2011)[c]	22	17	20	50	26	13
Russian Federation (2008)[a]	60	22	39	47	32	16
Brazil (2008)[a]	22	13	17	26	19	10
Bangladesh (2009)[a]	45	2	23	25	25	13
Philippines (2008)[a]	48	9	28	18	22	11
Turkey (2008)[a]	48	15	31	17	18	9
Vietnam (2010)[a]	47	1	24	17	14	7
Mexico (2009)[a]	25	8	16	14	14	7
Thailand (2009)[a]	46	3	24	13	8	4
Ukraine (2010)[a]	50	11	29	11	8	4
Egypt, Arab Rep. (2009)[a]	38	1	19	11	12	6
Argentina (2012)[a]	29	24	22	7	7	4
Canada (2011)[d]	20	16	17	5	2	1
Malaysia (2011)[a]	44	15	23	5	5	3
Nigeria (2012)[a]	7	1	4	4	6	3
Subtotal (HICs)				170	~80	~40
Subtotal (LMICs)				715	~540	~270
Total				885	~620	~310

Note: For future smokers in low- and middle-income countries (LMICs), we apply the smoking prevalence at ages 25–34 from the Global Adult Tobacco Survey to the United Nations 2012 population under age 25 years, plus current smokers at ages 25–34. For future smokers in high-income countries (HICs), we apply the smoking prevalence at ages 18–24 or 20–24 to the under-25 population, with an assumed 1 percent annual decline due to decreased uptake in these countries.

a. WHO-GATS, various years, various Country Reports.
b. EU-28: Zatoński and others 2012, ages 18+.
c. United States: Centers for Disease Control and Prevention 2009–11, ages 18+.
d. Canada: Health Canada 2012, ages 15+.

Price Elasticity of Demand for Tobacco

Raising tobacco taxes to achieve a 50 percent increase in tobacco prices decreases consumption by about 20 percent in HICs and by at least as much in most LMICs (that is, price elasticity of −0.4). Price elasticity estimates vary more in LMICs than in HICs, ranging from −0.15 to −0.9, but most studies find results to be concentrated in the −0.20 to −0.60 range. In theory, people in LMICs should be more sensitive to price and nonprice tobacco control interventions because the cost of cigarettes constitutes a larger relative proportion of income. However, in China and Russia, price elasticity estimates are closer to zero, in part due to a rapid rise in affordability.

Half or more of the effect of prices on demand results from increased quitting; the remaining effect results from reducing the amount of tobacco smoked. Higher taxes increase the number of attempts to quit smoking and the success of those attempts; in the United States, a 10 percent increase in price results in 11–13 percent

Table 10.3 Interventions and Their Effectiveness in Reducing Tobacco Consumption

Intervention	Effectiveness
Large, regular increases in excise taxes that reduce affordability	50 percent higher prices reduce consumption by approximately 20 percent (10 percent quit, 10 percent reduce the amount smoked)
Mass media counter-advertising; warning labels; plain packaging; and epidemiological studies, such as deaths from smoking on death records	Not quantified but does increase cessation rates
Complete bans on tobacco advertising, promotion, and sponsorship	Reduces consumption by approximately 15 percent in LMICs
Complete ban on smoking in public places, including workplaces	Reduces consumption by 3–14 percent
Cessation support for smokers, brief medical advice, pharmacotherapy	At six months unaided cessation is about 2–5 percent; brief medical advice doubles the quit rates (to 4–8 percent); medications triple the quit rates (to 8–12 percent)
Antismuggling technologies: local language labels, improved tax administration, and increased customs and international efforts to target smuggling	10 percent higher spending on antismuggling efforts reduces smuggling by 5 percent and consumption by 2 percent

shorter smoking duration, or a 3 percent higher probability of cessation (Tauras 1999). Recent analyses of the Global Adult Tobacco Survey data and the Global Youth Tobacco Survey find that cessation is generally price inelastic, but it is still significantly positively related to price, while initiation is generally price elastic (Kostova and others 2011; Shang and others 2014).

Higher cigarette prices are particularly effective in reducing consumption among less educated and lower-income individuals and in preventing young smokers from moving beyond experimentation into regular, addicted smoking. A comprehensive study using multiple waves of the Global Youth Tobacco Survey in 17 LMICs concluded that a 50 percent increase in cigarette prices would result in a reduction of youth prevalence of almost 40 percent. Furthermore, the estimated price elasticity of youth smoking was about −2.0 (Kostova and others 2011; Nikaj and Chaloupka 2014).

Affordability
Affordability is a concept that captures the interaction between consumers' income levels and tobacco prices. Typically, affordability is defined as per capita gross domestic product (GDP) relative to the wholesale price index for bidis or cigarettes. As income rises relative to price, affordability increases. From 1990 to 2006, cigarettes became less affordable in 59 percent of 32 HICs, but only in 38 percent of 45 LMICs. Particularly since 2003, cigarettes in some LMICs have quickly become more affordable. In India, bidis were nearly three times more affordable in 2011 than in 1990, while cigarettes were about twice as affordable (Blecher and van Walbeek 2009; Jha and others 2011). Thus, tax policy needs to take into account income

growth, particularly in fast-growing countries such as China and Vietnam.

Importance of Smart Excise Tax Structure
Most LMICs have low levels of taxation; they also have inefficient tax structures that contribute to increased consumption. For example, China has a relatively low price elasticity of demand for cigarettes; smokers are likely to switch to a wide range of cheaper brands rather than quit smoking. This low measured price elasticity in part reflects the underlying tax structure and income growth. Further, there are several types of taxes: *excises*, which are based on quantity or weight (for example, the tax per pack of 20 cigarettes); *ad valorem taxes*, which are based on the value of tobacco products (for example, a specific percentage of manufacturers' prices for tobacco products); and *other taxes* (for example, import duties).

Specific excise taxes are more important insofar as they differentiate tobacco product prices from other prices more than broader taxes do. A high reliance on ad valorem and similar taxes by most LMICs creates large price gaps and increases incentives to switch to cheaper products. China, like Indonesia, uses a complex tiered system with small specific, different ad valorem rates that rise with the cost of cigarettes (Barber and others 2008; Hu and others 2008). Indeed, the tobacco industry usually offers such advice to ministries of finance to promote complex, tiered taxation systems so as to decrease the impact of tax increases on sales (Jha 2015)

By contrast, empirical research from HICs finds that high uniform, specific excise taxes are more likely to discourage switching among different types of tobacco products, are easier to administer, and produce a steadier stream of excise revenue (Chaloupka and others 2010). The exact impact of high excises depends on market conditions, industry efforts to counter the tax hike, and the effectiveness of tax administration. Increases in the specific excise tax decrease the relative differences between higher- and lower-priced cigarettes, effectively increasing the public health impact. The main weakness is that such excise taxes need to be adjusted periodically for inflation, which is often higher in LMICs than in HICs. Thus, a complementary strategy is to raise the excise every year in excess of inflation and income growth to reduce affordability so that the number of ex-smokers increases every year.

Implementation of Large Tax Increases

Powerful policy interventions to tax and regulate consumption and to inform consumers have reduced consumption in most HICs. The United Kingdom and the United States each took about 35 years, and Canada about 25 years, to halve per adult cigarette consumption, from about 10 to about five per adult per day (Forey and others 2013). However, France took only 15 years to halve consumption. France's uptake of smoking was chiefly after World War II, and its prevalence rose until the mid-1980s. From 1990 to 2005, cigarette consumption fell from about six cigarettes per adult per day to three (figure 10.3). This sharp decline was mostly due to a sharp increase in excise tobacco taxation starting in 1990. These excise tax increases raised the inflation-adjusted price threefold. Among men, the corresponding lung cancer rates at ages 35–44, which are a good measure of recent smoking in the population, fell sharply from 1997 onward. During this period, revenues in real terms rose from about 6 billion to 12 billion euros.

In HICs, about 64 percent of the retail price of the most popular brands consists of the excise tax; in most LMICs, the proportion of the excise tax is well below 50 percent (figure 10.4).

Excise taxes tend to be higher and account for a greater share of retail prices in HICs, but LMICs are increasing the proportion of excise tax to retail prices, as seen in HICs. In Turkey, the excise share as a proportion of the retail price rose to 67 percent; in Thailand, it rose to 58 percent; the rise contributed to a decline in adult smoking prevalence rates in both countries (WHO 2013b; WHO-GATS, various years).

The Mexican government raised the tobacco excise in 2012 (WHO 2013b). This rise contributed to an estimated decrease in cigarette sales of 30 percent, which may avoid about 100,000 deaths over the next 30 years (Hernandez-Villa and others, personal communication). In South Africa, the excise tax as a percentage of the

Figure 10.3 Inverse Relationship of Consumption and Price in the United States, France, and South Africa, Various Years

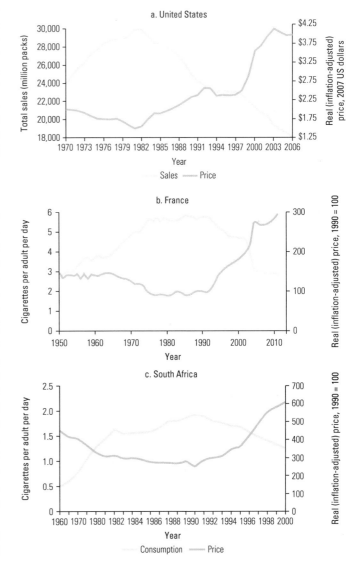

Sources: Based on data from the Tobacco Institute (United States) and personal communications from C. Hill (France) and C. van Walbeek (South Africa).

retail price fell to about 20 percent around 1990, but it subsequently rose to nearly 40 percent. Consumption fell from about four to two cigarettes per adult per day. Poland's tax increases have doubled the real price of cigarettes and decreased consumption. Mauritius has raised excise taxes by about 30 percent, which has reduced consumption. More recently, the doubling of excise taxes in the Philippines is expected to raise the average price by 70 percent and reduce consumption by about 40 percent (Jha and Peto 2014).

The World Health Organization (WHO) recommends that excise taxes account for 70 percent of the retail price

Figure 10.4 Retail Price of the Most Popular Brand and the Proportion Due to Excise Taxes by Country Income Levels, 2012 *(US$)*

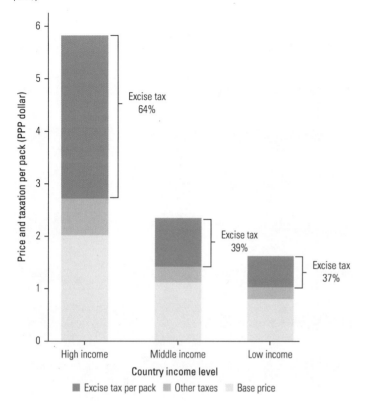

Source: Adapted from WHO 2013b.
Note: Prices are expressed in dollars adjusted for purchasing power parity (PPP). In low- and middle-income countries, tripling specific excise taxes on tobacco would approximately double street prices, because non-excise taxes and retailer mark-up would also rise. In the European Union, more complex variations of specific excise taxes on tobacco are used. Data are for 48 high-income countries, 95 middle-income countries, and 30 low-income countries.

of cigarettes and that countries raise excise levels more than inflation levels and income growth to reach that point (WHO 2010). Based on WHO data for the most popular brand, achieving this level of excise would result in the weighted price per pack rising from US$0.8 per pack to US$1.4 in low-income countries, from U$1.5 per pack to US$2.6 in middle-income countries, and from US$6.3 per pack to US$10.6 in HICs. Such excise tax increases, while large, have already been achieved in some countries, including Canada, France, the Philippines, Poland, and South Africa, and in some states in the United States.

An increase in cigarette taxes of 25 and 50 percent globally would raise cigarette tax revenues by 14 percent and 25 percent, respectively, as the fall in demand is less than proportional to the price increase in most countries (WHO 2013b). The overall increase in government revenue would be about US$100 billion (Jha and Peto 2014).

Signaling the Effects of Price Increases

Tobacco consumption changes in response to announced taxation changes (Becker, Grossman, and Murphy 1994; Chaloupka 1991; Gruber and Köszegi 2001). For example, even the debate on a tax increase in Switzerland, which was not adopted by popular vote, led to decreased consumption (Kenkel and Chen 2000). There are likely two mechanisms for this decline. The first is rational price expectations. Consumers respond to future price expectations for cigarettes, despite their addictive properties. Second is the signal that governments and peers give about the undesirability of smoking, leading people to reconsider cessation. In the United States, the higher price responsiveness by youth has been linked in part to peer effects, in which one quitter who might be more responsive to price increases influences other teenagers to do the same (Tauras and Chaloupka 2004).

Thus, governments can announce future tobacco tax targets to decrease current and future consumption, in much the same way that central banks announce inflation targets. For example, Australia and New Zealand have opted to raise tax rates to ensure that affordability decreases. France started a similar policy in 1991, increasing cigarette prices by 5 percent or more in excess of inflation every year. As a result, French ex-smoking prevalence at ages 45–64 is now well above the European Union average (Jha 2013; Zatoński and Mańczuk 2010).

Health Information and Counter-Advertising

With more than 40,000 studies on smoking and health published over the past five decades, it is easy to assume that the health consequences of tobacco are well known worldwide (IARC 2004; U.S. Department of Health and Human Services 2014). Although this is often the case in HICs, even in these countries many smokers minimize the personal relevance of these risks. Awareness of the hazards of smoking and the benefits of cessation is much lower in most LMICs. In India, few smokers know that 70 percent of smoking deaths occur during productive middle age or that the average number of years of life lost from cigarette smoking is nearly 10 years. The Global Adult Tobacco Survey revealed that only 23 percent of Chinese adults know that smoking causes strokes, heart attacks, and lung cancer. The survey also revealed the widespread belief in most countries that smoking *does not* cause strokes: over 50 percent in India, 39 percent in Mexico, 33 percent in Russia, 30 percent in Vietnam, and 27 percent in Brazil.

Smoking patterns in Western countries have changed in response to control policies and increased information.

Data on tobacco hazards help build public support for control measures, such as higher prices and bans on advertising and promotion. A systematic review found that nine of 11 mass media campaigns evaluated had reduced smoking prevalence or increased cessation rates (Bala and others 2013). Decreases in smoking prevalence were largest in HICs, where coverage of issues related to tobacco in the news media is consistent. For example, the 1962 report by the British Royal College of Physicians, and the 1964 U.S. Surgeon General's Report, in combination with the publicity that followed each publication, reduced consumption by 4–9 percent initially, and by 15–30 percent in the longer term in both countries, and indeed in other countries, such as Switzerland (Kenkel and Chen 2000).

Prominent, rotating pictorial warning labels on tobacco products are effective at portraying risks to smokers and can reach even illiterate individuals, which is important in countries such as India, where half the smoking deaths occur among the uneducated. Thailand changed the warnings from 30 percent text-only to 50 percent pictorial in 1996; subsequent surveys noted an increase from 34 percent to 54 percent of people who claimed that the warnings made them think about health risks "a lot," with 31–44 percent "a lot" more likely to quit (International Tobacco Control Project 2009). The impact has been similar in other countries.

In 2011, Australia became the first country to legislate plain packaging for tobacco products. Plain packaging aims to standardize the look of cigarette packages by mandating the removal of all brand imagery, including logos and trademarks. Manufacturers are required to print the brand name in a required size, font, and place and to include prominent pictorial health warnings. This goes beyond the pictorial warning labels used in Canada and introduced in the United States. The result is that smokers perceive their plain-packaged cigarettes to be lower quality and to experience lower satisfaction. Smokers were also more likely to consider quitting (Wakefield and others 2013). Experimental research demonstrates that plain packaging enhances the effectiveness of health warnings, helps dispel false beliefs, and reduces the appeal of smoking (Hammond 2010).

Reliable reporting of smoking deaths is possible with the simple addition of a smoking status question to South Africa's death certificates, for example, "Was the dead person a smoker five years ago?," which is asked of living respondents (Sitas and others 2013). A similar strategy in India obtains the smoking status of the deceased and the respondent during household surveys of the causes of death (Dikshit and others 2012; Jha and others 2008).

Bans on Advertising and Promotion

Cigarettes are among the most heavily advertised and promoted products in the world. Cigarette companies spend over US$9 billion annually on advertising and promotion in the United States alone, spending has risen in recent years (Federal Trade Commission 2015). The spending in the United States is relevant globally because it funds research and industry marketing strategies on advertisement and promotion of cigarettes globally.

In HICs, partial bans on tobacco advertising have had little effect on consumption, as the industry shifts to other media, price-reducing promotions, or sponsorship of events, such as rock concerts. However, comprehensive bans reduce consumption by 6–7 percent, taking into account differences in price and nonprice control interventions. For example, complete tobacco advertising bans in Norway and Finland reduced smoking demand by 9–16 percent and 7 percent, respectively. Such bans may be twice as effective in LMICs. In a study of 50 LMICs, comprehensive bans reduced consumption by 14.4–15.5 percent, and by about 5.5 percent in the broader sample of 76 countries. Limited bans still had some impact, in part because the marginal impact of bans is greater where no or little tobacco control has occurred (Blecher 2008).

Restrictions on Smoking in Public Places

Restrictions on smoking in public places are primarily intended to reduce nonsmokers' exposure to passive tobacco smoke. However, comprehensive restrictions in HICs also raise attempts to quit, so that overall consumption falls by 3–4 percent. Tobacco consumption significantly decreased after laws restricting smoking were implemented in Germany, Ireland, and the Netherlands, but not in France (Mons 2011).

According to a systematic review of studies (most from HICs), workplace and community smoke-free policies reduce tobacco use prevalence by a median of 14 percent. These policies are most effective when strong social norms help make smoking restrictions self-enforcing (IARC 2009). Reduced hospital admissions for cardiac events and an improvement in some health indicators consistently occur after smoking is banned in public places. This appears to be more related to increased cessation—in particular, among working-age adults, in whom smoking causes a large proportion of the acute heart attacks (Jha and others 2009)—and less related to reduced environmental smoke exposure triggering acute heart attacks.

Smoking Cessation Treatments

Most of the ex-smokers in the world have quit unaided. However, unaided quit rates are only about 2–3 percent at six months. Physician support or telephone- or Internet-based counseling and cessation support can increase these low rates. A systematic review noted that Internet and mobile telephone programs roughly doubled short- and long-term self-reported quitting (Whittaker and others 2012). Another systematic review from pooled data in 17 trials demonstrated a significant increase in the rate of quitting in those who received brief physician advice compared with no advice, increasing unaided quit rates by another 1–3 percent (Stead and others 2013). Pharmacological treatments, including nicotine replacement therapies, bupropion, and vareni-cline, further improve the likelihood of quitting, with success rates two to three times higher than when phar-maceutical treatments are not employed (Hartmann-Boyce and others 2014). In addition, over-the-counter access to such medications increases access and decreases cost. Cytisine, a cessation drug used commonly in the former socialist economies, was more effective than a placebo for smoking cessation in Poland. As cytosine is much less expensive than standard drugs, it might be practicable in LMICs (West and others 2011).

Electronic Cigarettes

In recent years, there has been rapid development of e-cigarettes or other noncombustible products. In the United States, e-cigarettes are now more commonly used than traditional cigarettes among high-school students (National Institute of Drug Abuse 2015). In most LMICs, these products are mostly unregulated and not subject to traditional tobacco control policies. It remains unknown whether these products result mostly in adult cessation, or whether they also are significant gateway or bridge prod-ucts that might increase the uptake of cigarette smoking by youth or diminish cessation by adults. No studies have yet reliably documented if young e-cigarette smokers actually quit after a few years. Clinical trials confirm that e-cigarettes, used as nicotine replacement, can raise adult cessation rates, comparable to other nicotine replacement products (Bullen and others 2013). Multinational tobacco companies are expanding into the nontobacco nicotine delivery business. However, access to e-cigarettes remains more limited in LMICs than HICs.

Much more epidemiological and economic research is needed in this rapidly changing field. The United States and other high-income countries are discussing nuanced regulation that would allow some promotion of e-cigarettes to adults, but not for children. Bearing in mind that most LMICs have far less regulatory capacity currently, interim policies should try to encourage ces-sation and avoid the pathways to use of manufactured cigarettes. Key policies include the following: (a) restrict advertising and promotion of e-cigarettes comparable to comprehensive bans on cigarette advertising, even though this is a more blunt instrument than ideally suited to helping adult smokers quit; (b) ensure that bans on smoking in public places also cover e-cigarettes; and (c) ensure, as much as possible, separation of the ownership of these companies by cigarette companies (Jha and Peto 2014). Taxation strategies for e-cigarettes are feasible (Huang, Tauras and Chaloupka 2014), but would need to raise the price of cigarettes even more, so as to encourage cessation.

Supply-Side Interventions

In contrast to the effective interventions designed to reduce demand, scant evidence exists to indicate that restricting supply can effectively reduce consump-tion. Limitation of youth access to tobacco products, cross-border trade restrictions, and crop substitution and diversification are largely ineffective in reducing consumption, given that supply will always respond to demand (Jacobs and others 2000). Recent debate has included phasing in outright bans on sales to birth cohorts, such as anyone born after 2000. These strate-gies have not yet been tested (Reuter 2013). Importantly, most of the deaths from smoking before 2050 will occur in current smokers, so to the extent these efforts draw political attention away from taxation and regulation aimed at encouraging cessation and reducing initiation, they could be counterproductive.

However, controlling cigarette smuggling is effec-tive. An estimated 6–11 percent of the 5.9 trillion cigarettes sold globally in 2006—about 600 billion cigarettes—enter the market without being taxed. This amounts to approximately US$50 billion in lost revenue, excess consumption, and increased deaths (Joossens and others 2009). The main determinant of smuggling is not price differences from different tax regimes, but corruption, organized criminal networks, and weak tax administration.

A common misconception by governments and pol-icy makers is that illicit trade will increase as cigarette taxes rise. Clearly, higher taxes increase the financial incentives for smugglers, but these claims ignore factors of equal or greater importance in making smuggling attractive, such as the following: (a) weak governance and lack of high-level commitment by governments; (b) ineffective customs and excise administration;

(c) corruption and complicity of cigarette manufacturers; (d) presence of informal sectors and distribution channels; and (e) population perceptions and socioeconomic status.

A study by Yurekli and Sayginsoy (2010) showed no clear correlation between the illicit trade market and the tax rate for the most popular cigarettes from a sample of 76 countries. By contrast, a stronger correlation was seen between illicit trade markets and weak governance; countries with strong governance experience lower illicit trade levels than those with weak governance.

In HICs, companies have been convicted in criminal courts for encouraging smuggling. In addition to harmonizing prices among countries, effective measures to counter smuggling include prominent tax stamps and warning labels in local languages, better methods for tracking cigarettes through the distribution chain, aggressive enforcement of antismuggling laws, and stronger penalties (IARC 2011).

Spain provides a good example of effective measures to reduce smuggling. Spain raised its investment in intelligence tenfold over five years, increased customs activity in border areas, and developed international collaborations to target smuggling (Joossens and Raw 2008). As a result, the market share of smuggled cigarettes fell from 16 percent to 2 percent, and tax revenues more than doubled, netting US$68 for every dollar spent on smuggling control. A 10 percent increase in price, paired with a 10 percent increase in spending on smuggling controls, would decrease smuggling by 5 percent, reduce consumption by 2 percent, and increase tax revenues by nearly 8 percent (Yurekli and Sayginsoy 2010). The Canadian government raised cigarette taxes in 2014, and also funded US$100 million for better police enforcement against smuggling (Jha 2014). Even in the presence of smuggling, tax increases will reduce consumption and increase revenue. For example, South Africa saw a rise in reported smuggling from 0 percent to 6 percent in the years when it raised excise taxes, but revenues continued to rise (Van Walbeek 2006).

COST-EFFECTIVENESS OF TOBACCO CONTROL

Costs

Tobacco is a major contributor to the large and increasing global burden of noncommunicable diseases (NCDs). A recent paper uses the value of lost output approach to estimate the impact of NCDs on worldwide GDP (Jha, Nugent, and others 2013). It employs the WHO's EPIC model to simulate the macroeconomic effects of NCDs (see DCP3 volume 5,

Cardiovascular, Respiratory, Renal, and Endocrine Disorders) on labor and capital, which determine economic output, from 2011 to 2030 (table 10.4). Using conservative estimates attributing about 33 percent of cardiovascular disease, about 50 percent of cancers, and 60 percent of chronic respiratory diseases to tobacco use, the total economic loss from tobacco is expected to be about US$12.7 trillion dollars over the next few decades. This loss translates to about 1.3 percent of GDP spent on tobacco-associated diseases every year, or approximately US$0.9 trillion in 2010 terms.

Cost-Effectiveness Analysis

Tobacco control is highly cost-effective. Significant price increases and comprehensive tobacco control measures are cost-effective in all WHO regions, according to 2002 analysis of data from 2000 (table 10.5).

For 23 LMICs, an increased real price of cigarettes to reduce smoking prevalence by 10 percent, in combination with mid-range estimates of nonprice interventions, would reduce the smoking prevalence rate by 20 percent. Over three decades, about three million deaths from cardiovascular disease would be averted: two million from respiratory disease and one million from cancer (assuming price elasticity ranges from −0.40 to −1.20). The cost of implementation would be US$0.04 to US$0.32 per person, which would be largely, if not completely, offset by the increased revenue from the tax (Asaria and others 2007).

A US$0.50 increase in the tax on cigarettes and small cigars, keeping pace with inflation and the growth of people's income, would reduce the federal budget deficit in the United States by about US$42 billion through 2021 (Baumgardner and others 2012). Tax revenues would be higher and spending on Medicare slightly lower, although spending on Social Security would rise slightly as more people would live longer. Even in the long run, there would be a net positive budgetary impact, given that the higher revenues from the tax would exceed any increase

Table 10.4 Economic Costs of Tobacco, 2010–30
US$ trillions

Region/disease	Vascular	Cancer	Chronic lung	Total	Total due to tobacco
Low and middle-income countries	9	5	2	16	7
High-income countries	7	3	3	13	6
World	16	8	5	29	13

Source: Adapted from Jha, Nugent, and others 2013.

Table 10.5 Range of Cost-Effectiveness Values for Price Increases, Nicotine Replacement Therapies, and Nonprice Interventions, by World Bank Regions, 2000
(2002 US$/DALY saved)

World Bank region	33% price increase	NRTs with effectiveness of 1–5%	Nonprice interventions with effectiveness of 2–10%
	Low and high estimate	Low and high estimate	Low and high estimate
East Asia and Pacific	2–30	65–864	40–498
Europe and Central Asia	3–42	45–633	55–685
Latin America and the Caribbean	6–85	53–812	109–1,361
Middle East and North Africa	6–89	47–750	115–1,432
South Asia	2–27	54–716	34–431
Sub-Saharan Africa	2–26	42–570	33–417
World	13–195	75–1,250	233–2,916

Source: Adapted from Jha, Chaloupka, and others 2006.

Note: Country economies are categorized according to 2002 World Bank regions. DALY = disability-adjusted life year; NRT = nicotine replacement therapy.

in longevity-related spending. Another study demonstrated that tobacco tax increases are cost-effective from the health care perspective, even factoring in the medical costs from years of life gained (van Baal and others 2007).

Poverty Considerations

Smoking in most countries is more common in lower-income and lower-education groups (Palipudi and others 2012), and smoking causes greater disease burdens in the poor than in the rich. In several HICs and Poland, smoking deaths account for at least one-half of the differences in the middle-age risk of death between men who are richer and more educated versus men who are poorer and less educated (Jha, Peto, and others 2006).

A recent report from the Asian Development Bank highlights the equity implications of tobacco taxation for five high-burden countries: China, India, the Philippines, Thailand, and Vietnam (ADB 2012). This study found that a 50 percent increase in price (resulting from excise tax increases of 75 percent to 122 percent) would decrease the number of current and future smokers by almost 67 million, save 27 million people from tobacco-related deaths, and generate in excess of US$24 billion in additional revenue annually (an increase of 143–178 percent above existing cigarette tax revenue). Importantly, each country's poorest socioeconomic groups would undertake a relatively small proportion of the extra tax burden but would gain a substantial proportion of the health benefits from smoking reduction.

The ratio of health benefits obtained by the poor to the additional taxes paid by the poor ranges from 1.4 to 9.5. Poorer income groups spend more of their income on tobacco than do richer groups, but the higher price responsiveness by the poor in China showed that after a 50 percent price increase, those in the lowest two quintiles of income would gain 5 and 1 percent in net income, whereas only the higher income quintiles would lose income after the tax increase on tobacco (Verguet and others 2015). Main and others (2008) conclude that tax and price policies reduce inequalities, but they find that cessation policies might increase inequities, given the greater likelihood of quitting among higher social groups. In LMICs with low levels of awareness of smoking risks and higher illiteracy levels, pictorial warning labels might help to reduce inequalities.

IMPLEMENTATION OF TOBACCO CONTROL INTERVENTIONS

Case Study: Tobacco Control in Uruguay

In Uruguay, smoking is a major cause of avoidable mortality; in 2004, smoking contributed to 14 percent of the country's total deaths (Sandoya and Bianco 2011).

Uruguay ratified the Framework Convention on Tobacco Control (FCTC) in 2004; by 2005, the country began to implement increasingly comprehensive tobacco control measures. Starting with banning tobacco advertising except at the point of sale and tobacco sponsorships, Uruguay outlawed smoking in enclosed public spaces and workplaces. It also required primary health care providers to give free diagnosis and treatment of tobacco dependence, and stipulated that pictograms with health warnings must cover 80 percent of the front and back of cigarette packages. Terms like *light*, *mild*, and *low in tar* were banned. Following a sequence of tax increases, the real consumer price of a pack of cigarettes rose by 88 percent from January 2003 to December 2010.

Abascal and others (2012) evaluated the impact of these tobacco control measures by comparing Uruguay with neighboring Argentina. Per-person consumption of cigarettes fell by 4.3 percent annually in Uruguay but increased by 0.6 percent in Argentina; the prevalence of tobacco use in adolescents decreased by 8 percent annually in Uruguay and decreased 2.5 percent in Argentina; and the prevalence of tobacco use by adults decreased by 3.3 percent annually in Uruguay and decreased by 1.7 percent in Argentina.

The impact of specific interventions is difficult to estimate, but studies suggest that comprehensive tobacco control policies should be adopted. Reductions in tobacco use of the size seen in Uruguay (approximately 23 percent over six years) would have a significant impact on the future global burden of tobacco-associated diseases.

Globalization and Tobacco Control

A new major challenge to tobacco control is the globalization of the tobacco industry. Globalization increasingly challenges strong domestic tobacco control policies under various trade and investment agreements (in addition to challenges in national courts). For example, the major multinational tobacco companies have sued the government of Uruguay for its aggressive tobacco control policies. Australia's plain packaging legislation is being challenged by Philip Morris Asia under the bilateral investment treaty between Hong Kong SAR, China, where the corporation is based, and Australia, as well as by the Dominican Republic, Honduras, and Ukraine through the World Trade Organization (WTO) (Oliver 2015). Similarly, Philip Morris International is challenging Uruguay's graphic warning labels and limit on brand variations under a bilateral investment treaty between Switzerland and Uruguay, while Indonesia won its WTO case against the United States' ban on clove-flavored cigarettes.

International Initiatives

The main vehicle to accelerate tobacco control is WHO's FCTC, the first global treaty on public health, which has been signed by 180 countries. The FCTC has specific provisions for the introduction of the strategies with proven effectiveness discussed in this chapter. The main limitation of the FCTC is that it is largely a statement of intent; the specific actions needed to implement the provisions in each country require ongoing

technical support. The highest priority is countering the active influence of the tobacco industry, which seeks to secure complex tax regimes favoring certain segments of the tobacco market, as well as to lobby for initiatives to confuse governments on tobacco taxes (Jha and Alleyne 2015).

The 2013 World Health Assembly called on governments to decrease the prevalence of smoking by one-third by 2025 (WHO 2011); doing so would avoid more than 200 million deaths from tobacco over the remainder of the century (Jha 2009; Jha and Peto 2014). However, few governments are investing resources in tobacco control measures. HICs spent the largest amount (US$1.4 per capita in 2010), which was less than 1 percent of the revenues from tobacco taxes. Middle-income countries spent a great deal less (a little more than US$0.1 per capita in 2010); low-income countries spent about US$0.1 per capita in 2010 (WHO 2013b).

Bloomberg Philanthropies and the Bill & Melinda Gates Foundation have pledged, collectively, nearly US$700 million to fund global tobacco control programs. Effective use of these funds could avoid a substantial number of deaths in the coming decades as a result of increased adult cessation, and even more deaths could be avoided in the second half of the 21st century from lower increases in youth smoking rates.

CONCLUSIONS: AVOIDABLE TOBACCO DEATHS BEFORE 2050

Earlier estimates (Jha 2009; Jha, Chaloupka, and others, 2006) have examined the potential impact of a 70 percent price increase and a 10 percent reduction in tobacco consumption from nonprice interventions, such as bans on public smoking and information measures, among the global cohort of 1.1 billion smokers in 2000. Price increases have the greatest impact on future tobacco mortality; a 70 percent higher price would prevent more than 110 million deaths, or one-fourth of all expected premature deaths from tobacco worldwide. Of the avoided deaths, about 25 million would be from cancer and 50 million would be from vascular disease. Nonprice interventions would prevent 35 million deaths.

Worldwide, a one-third reduction in smoking could be achieved by doubling the inflation-adjusted price of cigarettes; in many LMICs, this price increase could be realized by tripling the real excise tax on tobacco. Other nonprice interventions could help to reduce consumption and make the substantial increases in real excise taxes politically acceptable. The main challenge remains to try to bring forward the time when large numbers of current smokers quit.

NOTES

World Bank Income Classifications as of July 2014 are as follows, based on estimates of gross national income (GNI) per capita for 2013:

- Low-income countries (LICs) = US$1,045 or less
- Middle-income countries (MICs) are subdivided:
  - lower-middle-income = US$1,046 to US$4,125
  - upper-middle-income (UMICs) = US$4,126 to US$12,745
- High-income countries (HICs) = US$12,746 or more.

Acknowledgments: This chapter is dedicated to the late Sir Richard Doll, who would have turned 100 years of age on October 28, 2012. We thank Yul Dorothea, Cindy Gauvreau, Hellen Gelband, Emmanuel Guindon, Paul Isenman, Tricia Moser, and Ken Warner for comments; Joy Pader and Leslie Newcombe for their editorial assistance; and Catherine Hill for the French data and Corne van Walbeek for the South African data. Sources of support: Disease Control Priorities 3, the U.S. National Institutes of Health, the Canadian Institutes of Health Research, and the Canada Research Chairs Program.

REFERENCES

Abascal, W., E. Esteves, B. Goja, F. G. Mora, A. Lorenzo, and others. 2012. "Tobacco Control Campaign in Uruguay: A Population-Based Trend Analysis." *The Lancet* 380: 1575–82.

ADB (Asian Development Bank). 2012. *Tobacco Taxes: A Win–Win Measure for Fiscal Space and Health.* Manila: ADB.

Alam, D. S., P. Jha, C. Ramasundarahettige, P. K. Streatfield, L. W. Niessen, and others. 2013. "Smoking-Attributable Mortality in Bangladesh: Proportional Mortality Study." *Bulletin of the World Health Organization* 91 (10): 757–64.

Asaria, P., D. Chishom, C. Mathers, M. Ezzati, and R. Beaglehole. 2007. "Chronic Disease Prevention: Health Effects and Financial Costs of Strategies to Reduce Salt Intake and Control Tobacco Use." *The Lancet* 370: 2044–53.

Australian Bureau of Statistics. 2013. *Australian Health Survey (AHS) 2011–13: Tobacco Smoking.* Australian Bureau of Statistics. http://www.abs.gov.au/australianhealthsurvey.

Bala, M. M., L. Strzeszynski, R. Topor-Madry, and K. Cahill. 2013. "Mass Media Interventions for Smoking Cessation in Adults." *Cochrane Database of Systematic Reviews* 6: Cd004704. doi:10.1002/14651858.CD004704.pub3.

Barber, S., S. M. Adioetomo, A. Ahsan, and D. Setyonaluri. 2008. *Tobacco Economics in Indonesia.* Paris: International Union Against Tuberculosis and Lung Disease.

Baumgardner, J., L. T. Bilheimer, M. B. Booth, W. J. Carrington, N. J. Duchovny, and others. 2012. "Cigarette Taxes and the Federal Budget—Report from the CBO." *New England Journal of Medicine* 367: 2068–70.

Becker, G. S., M. Grossman, and K. M. Murphy. 1994. "An Empirical Analysis of Cigarette Addiction." *American Economic Review* 84 (3): 396–418.

Blecher, E. 2008. "The Impact of Tobacco Advertising Bans on Consumption in Developing Countries." *Journal of Health Economics* 27 (4): 930–42.

Blecher, E. H., and C. P. van Walbeek. 2009. "Cigarette Affordability Trends: An Update and Some Methodological Comments." *Tobacco Control* 18 (3): 167–75. doi:10.1136/tc.2008.026682.

Bullen, C., C. Howe, M. Laugesen, H. McRobbie, V. Parag, and others. 2013. "Electronic Cigarettes for Smoking Cessation: A Randomised Controlled Trial." *The Lancet* 382 (9905): 1629–37. doi:10.1016/s0140-6736(13)61842-5.

Centers for Disease Control and Prevention. 2009–11. *National Health Interview Survey (NHIS) 2009–11.* U.S. Centers for Disease Control and Prevention. http://www.cdc.gov/nchs/nhis.htm.

Chaloupka, F. J. 1991. "Rational Addictive Behaviour and Cigarette Smoking." *Journal of Political Economy* 99 (4): 722–42.

Chaloupka, F. J., R. Peck, J. A. Tauras, X. Xu, and A. Yurekli. 2010. *Cigarette Excise Taxation: The Impact of Tax Structure on Prices, Revenues and Cigarette Smoking.* NBER Working Paper 16287, National Bureau of Economic Research, Cambridge, MA. http://www.nber.org/papers/w16287.

Chaloupka, F. J., A. Yurekli, and G. T. Fong. 2012. "Tobacco Taxes as a Tobacco Control Strategy." *Tobacco Control* 21 (2): 172–80. doi:10.1136/tobaccocontrol-2011-050417.

Chen, Z., R. Peto, M. Smith, and others, for the China Kadoorie Biobank Collaborative Group. Forthcoming. "Chinese Mortality from Tobacco in the 21st century: Nationwide Prospective Study of 0.5 Million Adults." *The Lancet.*

Dikshit, R., P. C. Gupta, C. Ramasundarahettige, V. Gajalakshmi, L. Aleksandrowicz, and others. 2012. "Cancer Mortality in India: A Nationally Representative Survey." *The Lancet* 379 (9828): 1807–16. doi:10.1016/s0140-6736(12)60358-4.

Doll, R., R. Peto, J. Boreham, and I. Sutherland. 2004. "Mortality in Relation to Smoking: 50 Years' Observations on Male British Doctors." *British Medical Journal* 328 (7455): 1519. doi:10.1136/bmj.38142.554479.AE.

Euromonitor International. 2013. *Cigarettes: Global.* Euromonitor International 2012. http://www.euromonitor.com/tobacco.

Federal Trade Commission. 2015. *Federal Trade Commission Cigarette Report for 2012.* https://www.ftc.gov/system/files/documents/reports/federal-trade-commission-cigarette-report-2012/150327-2012cigaretterpt.pdf.

Ferlay, J., I. Soerjomataram, M. Ervik, R. Dikshit, S. Eser, and others. 2013. "GLOBOCAN 2012 v1.0." In *Cancer Incidence and Mortality Worldwide: IARC CancerBase No. 11* [Internet]. Lyon, France: International Agency for Research on Cancer.

Forey, B. A., J. Hamling, J. Hamling, A. Thorton, and P. N. Lee. 2013. *International Smoking Statistics (ISS): Web Edition.* http://www.pnlee.co.uk/ISS.htm.

Gajalakshmi, V., R. Peto, T. S. Kanaka, and P. Jha. 2003. "Smoking and Mortality from Tuberculosis and Other Diseases in India: Retrospective Study of 43,000 Adult Male Deaths and 35,000 Controls." *The Lancet* 362 (9383): 507–15. doi:S0140-6736(03)14109-8 [pii] 10.1016/S0140-6736(03)14109-8.

Gelband, H., P. Jha, R. Sankaranarayanan, C. L. Gauvreau, and S. Horton. 2015. "The Costs, Affordability and Feasibility of an Essential Package of Cancer Control Interventions in Low- and Middle-Income Countries." In *Disease Control Priorities* (third edition): Volume 3, *Cancer*, edited by H. Gelband, P. Jha, R. Sankaranarayanan, and S. Horton. Washington, DC: World Bank.

Giovino, G. A, S. A. Mirza, J. M. Samet, P. C. Gupta, M. J. Jarvis, and others. 2012. "Tobacco Use in 3 Billion Individuals from 16 Countries: An Analysis of Nationally Representative Cross-Sectional Household Surveys." *The Lancet* 380: 668–79.

Gruber, J., and B. Köszegi. 2001. "Is Addiction 'Rational'? Theory and Evidence." *The Quarterly Journal of Economics* 116 (4): 1261–303. doi:10.1162/003355301753265570.

Gu, D., T. N. Kelly, X. Wu, J. Chen, J. M. Samet, and others. 2009. "Mortality Attributable to Smoking in China." *New England Journal of Medicine* 360 (2): 150–59. doi:360/2/150 [pii] 10.1056/NEJMsa0802902.

Hammond, D. 2010. "'Plain Packaging' Regulations for Tobacco Products: The Impact, the Standardizing, the Color, and Design of Cigarette Packs." *Salud Publica de Mexico* 52 (Suppl.): 226–32.

Hartmann-Boyce, J., L. F. Stead, K. Cahill, and T. Lancaster. 2014. "Efficacy of Interventions to Combat Tobacco Addiction: Cochrane Update of 2013 Reviews." *Addiction* 109 (9): 1414–25. doi:10.1111/add.12633.

Health Canada. 2012. *Canadian Tobacco Use Monitoring Survey (CTUMS)*. http://www.hc-sc.gc.ca/hc-ps/tobac-tabac /research-recherche/stat/index-eng.php.

Hu, T-W., Z. Mao, J. Shi, and W. Chen. 2008. *Tobacco Taxation and Its Potential Impact in China*. Paris: International Union Against Tuberculosis and Lung Disease.

Huang J., J. Tauras, and F. J. Chaloupka. 2014. "The Impact of Price and Tobacco Control Policies on the Demand for Electronic Nicotine Delivery Systems." 2014. *Tobacco Control* 23 (suppl 3): iii41–47. doi:10.1136/ tobaccocontrol-2013-051515.

IARC (International Agency for Research on Cancer). 2004. IARC Monographs on the Evaluation of the Carcinogenic Risks of Chemicals to Humans. Volume 83, *Tobacco Smoke and Involuntary Smoking*. Lyon, France: IARC, WHO Press.

———. 2009. *Tobacco Control: Evaluating the Effectiveness of Smoke-Free Policies*. IARC Handbooks of Cancer Prevention. Lyon, France: IARC.

———. 2011. *Effectiveness of Tax and Price Policies for Tobacco Control*. Edited by International Agency for Research on Cancer. Volume 14, IARC Handbooks of Cancer Prevention. Lyon, France: IARC, WHO Press.

International Tobacco Control Policy Evaluation Project. 2009. *FCTC Article 11 Tobacco Warning Labels: Evidence and Recommendations from the ITC Project*. Waterloo, ON: International Tobacco Control Policy Evaluation Project.

Jacobs, R., H. F. Gale, T. C. Capehart, P. Zhang, and P. Jha. 2000. "The Supply-Side Effects of Tobacco Control Policies." In *Tobacco Control in Developing Countries*, edited by P. Jha and F. J. Chaloupka, 311–341. Oxford, UK: Oxford University Press.

Jha, P. 2009. "Avoidable Global Cancer Deaths and Total Deaths from Smoking." *Nature Reviews Cancer* 9: 655–64.

———. 2013. "The 21st Century Benefits of Smoking Cessation in Europe." *European Journal of Epidemiology* 28 (8): 617–19. doi:10.1007/s10654-013-9835-6.

Jha, P., and G. Alleyne. 2015. "Effective Global Tobacco Control in the Next Decade." *Canadian Medical Association Journal.* doi:10.1503/cmaj.150261.

Jha, P., and F. J. Chaloupka. 1999. *Curbing the Epidemic: Governments and the Economics of Tobacco Control*. Washington, DC: World Bank.

Jha, P., F. J. Chaloupka, J. Moore, V. Gajalakshmi, P. C. Gupta, and others. 2006. "Tobacco Addiction." In *Disease Control Priorities in Developing Countries*, 2nd ed., edited by D. T. Jamison, J. G. Breman, A. R. Measham, G. Alleyne, M. Claeson, D. Evans, P. Jha, A. Mills, and P. Musgrove, 869–86. Washington, DC: World Bank and Oxford University Press.

Jha, P., E. Guindon, R. A. Joseph, A. Nandi, R. M. John, and others. 2011. "A Rational Taxation System of Bidis and Cigarettes to Reduce Smoking Deaths in India." *Economic and Political Weekly* 46 (4.2): 44–51.

Jha, P., B. Jacob, V. Gajalakshmi, P. C. Gupta, N. Dhingra, and others. 2008. "A Nationally Representative Case-Control Study of Smoking and Death in India." *New England Journal of Medicine* 358 (11): 1137–47. doi:NEJMsa0707719 [pii] 10.1056/NEJMsa0707719.

Jha, P., P. Mony, J. A. Moore, and W. Zatoński. 2009. "Avoidance of World-Wide Vascular Deaths and Total Deaths from Smoking." In *Evidence-Based Cardiology*, 3rd ed., edited by S. Yusuf, J. Cairns, A. J. Camm, E. L. Fallen, and B. J. Gersh. Oxford, UK: Wiley-Blackwell.

Jha, P., R. Nugent, S. Verguet, D. E. Bloom, and R. J. Hum. 2013. "Chronic Disease Control and Prevention." In *Global Problems, Smart Solutions—Costs and Benefits*, edited by B. Lomborg. Cambridge, UK: Cambridge University Press.

Jha, P., and R. Peto. 2014. "Global Effects of Smoking, of Quitting, and of Taxing Tobacco." *The New England Journal of Medicine* 370 (1): 60–68. doi:10.1056/NEJMra1308383.

———. 2014. "Tax Hike on Tobacco Could Save 25,000 Lives." *The Star* [Toronto], February 25. http://www.thestar.com /opinion/commentary/2014/02/25/tax_hike_on_tobacco _could_save_25000_lives.html.

———. 2015. "Deaths and Taxes: Stronger Global Tobacco Control by 2025." *The Lancet* 385 (9972): 18–20.

Jha, P., R. Peto, W. Zatoński, J. Boreham, M. J. Jarvis, and A. D. Lopez. 2006. "Social Inequalities in Male Mortality and in Male Mortality from Smoking: Indirect Estimation from National Death Rates in England and Wales, Poland, and North America." *The Lancet* 368 (9533): 367–70.

Jha, P., C. Ramasundarahettige, V. Landsman, B. Rostron, M. Thun, and others. 2013. "21st-Century Hazards of Smoking and Benefits of Cessation in the United States." *The New England Journal of Medicine* 368 (4): 341–50. doi:10.1056/NEJMsa1211128.

Joossens, L., D. Merriman, H. Ross, and M. Raw. 2009. *How Eliminating the Global Illicit Cigarette Trade Would Increase*

Tax Revenue and Save Lives. Paris: International Union Against Tuberculosis and Lung Disease.

Joossens, L., and M. Raw. 2008. "Progress in Combating Cigarette Smuggling: Controlling the Supply Chain." *Tobacco Control* 17 (6): 399–404. doi:tc.2008.026567 [pii] 10.1136/tc.2008.026567.

Kenkel, D., and L. Chen. 2000. "Consumer Information and Tobacco Use." In *Tobacco Control in Developing Countries*, edited by P. Jha and F. J. Chaloupka, 177–214. Oxford, UK: Oxford University Press.

Kostova, D., H. Ross, E. Blecher, and S. Markowitz. 2011. "Is Youth Smoking Responsive to Cigarette Prices? Evidence from Low- and Middle-Income Countries." *Tobacco Control* 20: 419–24.

Lam, T. H., Y. He, L. S. Li, S. F. He, and B. Q. Liang. 1997. "Mortality Attributable to Cigarette Smoking in China." *Journal of the American Medical Association* 278: 1505–08.

Main, C., S. Thomas, D. Ogilvie, L. Stirk, M. Petticrew, and others. 2008. "Population Tobacco Control Interventions and Their Effects on Social Inequalities in Smoking: Placing an Equity Lens on Existing Systematic Reviews." *BMC Public Health* 8: 178. doi:10.1186/1471-2458-8-178.

Mons, U., G. E. Nagelhout, S. Allwright, R. Guignard, B. van den Putte, M. Willemsen, and others. 2011. "Adoption of Home Smoking Bans after the Implementation of National Smoke-Free Laws: Results from the ITC Europe Surveys." Paper presented at the meeting of the European Conference on Tobacco or Health, Amsterdam, the Netherlands, March.

National Institute of Drug Abuse. 2015. Monitoring the Future 2014 Survey Results. http://www.drugabuse.gov /related-topics/trends-statistics/infographics/monitoring -future-2014-survey-results.

Ng, M., M. K. Freeman, T. D. Fleming, M. Robinson, L. Dwyer-Lindgren, and others. 2014. "Smoking Prevalence and Cigarette Consumption in 187 Countries, 1980–2012." *JAMA* 311 (2): 183–92. doi:10.1001/jama.2013.284692.

Nikaj, S., and F. J. Chaloupka. 2014. "The Effect of Prices on Cigarette Use among Youths in the Global Youth Tobacco Survey." *Nicotine & Tobacco Research* 16 (Suppl. 1): S16–23. doi:10.1093/ntr/ntt019.

Norheim, O. F., P. Jha, K. Admasu, T. Godal, R. J. Hum, and others. 2014. "Avoiding 40% of the Premature Deaths in Each Country, 2010–30: Review of National Mortality Trends to Help Quantify the UN Sustainable Development Goal for Health." *The Lancet* 385 (9964): 239–52.

Oliver J. 2015. Last Week Tonight with John Oliver: Tobacco. https://www.youtube.com/watch?v=6UsHHOCH4q8.

Palipudi, K. M., P. C. Gupta, D. N. Sinha, L. J. Andes, S. Asma, and others. 2012. "Social Determinants of Health and Tobacco Use in Thirteen Low and Middle Income Countries: Evidence from Global Adult Tobacco Survey." *PLoS One* 7 (3): e33466. doi:10.1371/journal .pone.0033466.

Peto, R., and A. D. Lopez. 2001. "The Future Worldwide Health Effects of Current Smoking Patterns." In *Critical Issues in Global Health*, edited by E. C. Koop, C. E. Pearson, and M. R. Schwarz. New York: Jossey-Bass.

Peto, R., A. D. Lopez, J. Boreham, and M. Thun. 2012. "Mortality from Smoking in Developed Countries, 1950– 2005 (or later): United Kingdom." http://www.ctsu.ox.ac .uk/~tobacco/C4308.pdf.

Peto, R., A. D. Lopez, J. Boreham, M. Thun, and C. Heath, Jr. 1992. "Mortality from Tobacco in Developed Countries: Indirect Estimation from National Vital Statistics." *The Lancet* 339 (8804): 1268–78. doi:0140-6736(92)91600-D [pii].

Pirie, K., R. Peto, G. K. Reeves, J. Green, and V. Beral. 2013. "The 21st Century Hazards of Smoking and Benefits of Stopping: A Prospective Study of One Million Women in the UK." *The Lancet* 381 (9861): 133–41. doi:10.1016 /s0140-6736(12)61720-6.

Reuter, P. 2013. "Can Tobacco Control Endgame Analysis Learn Anything from the US Experience with Illegal Drugs?" *Tobacco Control* 22 (Suppl. 1): i49–51. doi:10.1136 /tobaccocontrol-2012-050809.

Sakata, R., P. McGale, E. J. Grant, K. Ozasa, R. Peto, and others. 2012. "Impact of Smoking on Mortality and Life Expectancy in Japanese Smokers: A Prospective Cohort Study." *British Medical Journal* 345: e7093. doi:10.1136 /bmj.e7093.

Sandoya, E., and E. Bianco. 2011. "Mortality from Smoking and Second-Hand Smoke in Uruguay." *Revista Uruguaya de Cardiologia* 26: 201–06.

Shang, C., F. J. Chaloupka, N. Zahra, and G. T. Fong. 2014. "The Distribution of Cigarette Prices Under Different Tax Structures: Findings from the International Tobacco Control Policy Evaluation (ITC) Project." *Tobacco Control* 23 (Suppl. 1): i23–29. doi:10.1136/tobaccocontrol-2013-050966.

Sitas, F., S. Egger, D. Bradshaw, P. Groenewald, R. Laubscher, and others. 2013. "Differences among the Coloured, White, Black, and Other South African Populations in Smoking-Attributed Mortality at Ages 35–74 Years: A Case-Control Study of 481,640 Deaths." *The Lancet* 382 (9893): 685–93. doi:10.1016/s0140-6736(13)61610-4.

Stead, L. F., D. Buitrago, N. Preciado, G. Sanchez, J. Hartmann-Boyce, and others. 2013. "Physician Advice for Smoking Cessation." *Cochrane Database of Systematic Reviews* 5: Cd000165. doi:10.1002/14651858.CD000165 .pub4.

Tauras, J. A. 1999. "The Transition to Smoking Cessation: Evidence from Multiple Failure Duration Analysis." NBER Working Paper 7412. National Bureau of Economic Research, Cambridge MA.

Tauras, J. A., and F. J. Chaloupka. 2004. "Impact of Tobacco Control Spending and Tobacco Control Policies on Adolescents' Attitudes and Beliefs about Cigarette Smoking." *Evidence-Based Preventive Medicine* 1 (2): 111–20.

Thun, M. J., B. D. Carter, D. Feskanich, N. D. Freedman, R. Prentice, and others. 2013. "50-Year Trends in Smoking-Related Mortality in the United States." *The New England Journal of Medicine* 368 (4): 351–64. doi:10.1056 /NEJMsa1211127.

U.S. Department of Health and Human Services. 2014. *The Health Consequences of Smoking: 50 Years of Progress. A Report of the Surgeon General*. Atlanta, GA: Centers for Disease Control and Prevention.

van Baal, P. H., W. B. Brouwer, R. T. Hoogenveen, and T. L. Feenstra. 2007. "Increasing Tobacco Taxes: A Cheap Tool to Increase Public Health." *Health Policy* 82 (2): 142–52.

Van Walbeek, C. P. 2006. "Industry Responses to the Tobacco Excise Tax Increases in South Africa." *South African Journal of Economics* 74: 110–22.

Verguet, S., C. L. Gauvreau, S. Mishra, M. MacLennan, S. M. Murphy, and others. 2015. "The Consequences of Raising Tobacco Tax on Household Health and Finances among Richer and Poorer Smokers in China: An Extended Cost-Effectiveness Analysis." *The Lancet Global Health* 3 (4): e206-e216. doi:10.1016/S2214-109X(15)70095-1.

Wakefield, M. A., L. Hayes, S. Durkin, and R. Borland. 2013. "Introduction Effects of the Australian Plain Packaging Policy on Adult Smokers: A Cross-Sectional Study." *BMJ Open* 3 (7): e003175. doi:10.1136/Bmjopen-2013-003175.

West, R., W. Zatoński, M. Cedzynska, D. Lewandowska, J. Pazik, and others. 2011. "Placebo-Controlled Trial of Cytisine for Smoking Cessation." *New England Journal of Medicine* 365 (13): 1193–200.

Whittaker, R., H. Mcrobbie, C. Bullen, R. Borland, A. Rodgers, and others. 2012. "Mobile Phone-Based Interventions for Smoking Cessation." *Cochrane Database of Systematic Reviews* 11: Cd006611. doi:10.1002/14651858.CD006611 .Pub3.

WHO (World Health Organization). 2010. *WHO Technical Manual on Tobacco Tax Administration.* Geneva: WHO.

———. 2011. *Scaling Up Action Against Non-Communicable Diseases: How Much Will It Cost?* Geneva: WHO.

———. 2013a. *Global Health Observatory 2013.* http://www .who.int/gho/mortality_burden_disease/en/.

———. 2013b. *WHO Report on the Global Tobacco Epidemic.* Geneva: WHO.

WHO-GATS (World Health Organization–Global Adult Tobacco Survey). Various years. *Global Adult Tobacco Survey.* WHO. http://www.who.int/tobacco/surveillance /gats/en/.

Yurekli, A., and O. Sayginsoy. 2010. "Worldwide Organized Cigarette Smuggling: An Empirical Analysis." *Journal of Applied Economics* 42 (5): 545–61.

Zatoński, W. A., and M. Mańczuk. 2010. "Tobacco Smoking and Tobacco-Related Harm in the European Union with Special Attention to the New EU Member States." In *Tobacco: Science, Policy, and Public Health,* edited by P. Boyle, N. Gray, J. Henningfield, J. Seffrin, and W. A. Zatoński. Oxford, UK: Oxford University Press.

Zatoński, W., K. Przewozniak, U. Sulkowska, R. West, and A. Wojtyla. 2012. "Tobacco Smoking in Countries of the European Union." *Annals of Agricultural and Environmental Medicine* 19 (2): 181–92.

Cancer Services and the Comprehensive Cancer Center

Mary Gospodarowicz, Joann Trypuc, Anil D'Cruz,
Jamal Khader, Sherif Omar, and Felicia Knaul

INTRODUCTION

Most countries and numerous global and local organizations are addressing the challenges of cancer (Blanchet and others 2013; Knaul, Alleyne, Atun, and others 2012), including the development of comprehensive national cancer control programs designed to reduce the number of cancer cases and deaths and to improve the quality of life of cancer patients through evidence-based strategies for prevention, early detection, diagnosis, treatment, and palliation. A national cancer control program addresses the *functions* and delivery of many *components* of cancer control (http://www.who.int/cancer /nccp/en/). The delivery of most services is anchored in comprehensive cancer centers (Gralow and others 2012; Hensher, Price, and Adomakoh 2006; Sloan and Gelband 2007).

This chapter describes an optimal framework for a comprehensive cancer center, which can be a freestanding dedicated institution, a program within an academic health science center or a community hospital, or a group of hospitals providing an integrated program.

The first section presents an overview of the framework for a comprehensive cancer center, which includes three levels that are embedded within a comprehensive cancer system. Detailed information on each level is presented, followed by a discussion of quality as an integrating theme for the framework. The chapter concludes by detailing the benefits that a comprehensive cancer center provides to a country's cancer control and health care efforts.

Cancer System Functions

Cancer system planning includes the development of population-based cancer plans, at the national or lower levels. Cancer plans address all aspects of cancer control, including cancer registries, practice and operating standards, research, health care education and practice standards, certification and accreditation of service providers, and system performance.

Cancer System Components

The World Health Organization (WHO) (2006b) recommends that all nations have a cancer control plan that includes these *components*: prevention, screening, diagnosis, treatment, survivorship, and palliative and end-of-life care (figure 11.1).

Many cancer control components are provided in comprehensive cancer centers, regardless of a country's resource level. WHO and others have recommended that every country aim to have at least one publicly supported cancer center that advances

Corresponding author: Mary Gospodarowicz, MD FRCPC FRCR (Hon), Princess Margaret Cancer Centre, University of Toronto Mary.Gospodarowicz@rmp.uhn.on.ca the broad objectives of control; provides exemplary patient care, appropriate to local circumstances and resources; and concentrates the specialized human and technical resources of the country (Gralow and others 2012; Knaul, Gralow, and others 2012; Sloan and Gelband 2007).

Comprehensive Cancer Centers in LMICs

Many low- and middle-income countries (LMICs) are developing comprehensive cancer centers with public or private resources. Patients can be managed directly at the centers; for many aspects of treatment, they can be managed in less specialized hospitals and local health clinics, with the center providing oversight and care plans. Comprehensive cancer centers educate health care professionals and the public, and they conduct research on the causes, prevention, diagnosis, and treatment of cancer (National Cancer Institute 2012).

Comprehensive cancer centers can act as focal points for cancer control nationally (Sloan and Gelband 2007) and influence cancer and health system development.

By strengthening health system capacity, cancer centers go beyond treating cancer as a vertical, disease-specific program, to enable a diagonal approach that cuts across horizontal initiatives that target system-wide constraints to address the overall goals of the health system (Knaul, Alleyne, Piot, and others 2012). The capacity to develop comprehensive cancer systems varies with available resources, national governance, management effectiveness, public accountability, engagement of civil society, and other factors (Knaul, Alleyne, Atun, and others 2012; WHO 2012).

Although this goal will take time to attain in many countries, it is being successfully achieved in multiple settings (Knaul, Gralow, and others 2012). For example, the King Hussein Cancer Center in Jordan, an upper-middle-income country, progressed from offering limited access to poorly organized, low-quality cancer services to providing internationally accredited cancer care, engaging in cancer-related education and research, leading national control planning efforts, and contributing to regional and global efforts (box 11.1).

Figure 11.1 Cancer Control Components

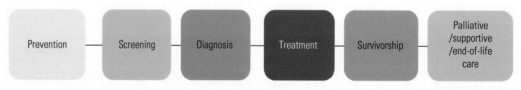

Source: Adapted from Cancer Care Ontario 2013.

Box 11.1

King Hussein Cancer Foundation and Center, Jordan

The King Hussein Cancer Foundation in Amman, Jordan, is an independent, nongovernmental, non-profit organization that oversees the operations of the cancer center. The hospital first opened in 1997 as the *Al-Amal Center* or *Center of Hope* and was renamed the King Hussein Cancer Center in September 2002. The center treats all types of cancer in adults and children from the Middle East and North Africa.

The center evolved by:

• Reversing the brain drain by convincing accomplished clinical and executive leaders working in high-income countries to return to the region to create the foundation for and expansion of excellent cancer care
• Designing and building a well-functioning and appropriately equipped physical facility

box continues next page

Box 11.1 (continued)

- Raising the standard of care in surgery, systemic/chemotherapy, radiation therapy, nursing oncology, bone marrow transplantation, and psycho-oncology
- Adopting policies and procedures to ensure effective, efficient, safe operations
- Establishing cancer education, training, and public awareness programs, including oncology fellowships and residency programs
- Developing a research program
- Collaborating with other centers to improve cancer care, training, and research; these include St. Jude Children's Research Hospital, H. Lee Moffitt Cancer Center, and MD Anderson Cancer Center in the United States; the Hospital for Sick Children and Princess Margaret Cancer Centre in Canada; National Cancer Institute in the Arab Republic of Egypt; American University of Beirut, Lebanon; Augusta Victoria Hospital in Israel; Stefan-Morsch Foundation in Germany; and Leeds Cancer Centre in the United Kingdom.

In 2006, the King Hussein Cancer Center was accredited as a hospital by Joint Commission International (JCI); in 2007, the center was certified by JCI's Clinical Care Program in cancer. The center helped organize the Ministry of Health's national early detection and awareness program. It is also leading an effort to establish a national cancer control planning program. Internationally, the European Arab Society of Oncology has recognized the center as a Cancer Center of Excellence for the training of cancer health workers from the region. The center has signed agreements with Petra University to establish the first diploma program in tobacco dependence treatment in the region, as well as with the German Jordan University to establish a diploma program in nursing oncology. The center is a WHO collaborating center. The center and foundation are active in the Union for International Cancer Control (UICC) and are helping other countries in the region to collaborate with UICC.

The center continues to develop to meet increasing patient demand from Jordan and the region. Construction is underway to double capacity by mid-2016. Capacity building is ongoing with recruitment of additional staff, including in cancer subspecialties, as is strengthening of cancer research and education activities.

FRAMEWORK FOR A COMPREHENSIVE CANCER CENTER

The comprehensive cancer center has three layers: clinical management, clinical services, and core services (figure 11.2).

The framework provides a reference point for planning for a comprehensive center, even if this is achieved incrementally as funding and capacity are built up.

Clinical Management

Patient Care Plans

Clinical management sets standards for clinical decision making and formulating patient care plans. Patient care plans are based on the histopathologic and/or molecular diagnosis identifying the type of cancer; the anatomic disease extent or stage; and the individual patient's characteristics, such as age, comorbidities, and performance status. Determining the best clinical management for cancer patients involves defining the goals of care—cure, disease control, symptom control—recommending appropriate interventions, and setting out the optimal timeframes for instituting and completing treatment. The patient care plans vary from simple to complex, and may require a range of services.

Errors in clinical decisions can lead to increased morbidity and disability, increased costs, and even premature death. For example, a recent study reported that almost one-quarter of children with acute myeloid leukemia in El Salvador, Guatemala, and Honduras died from largely avertable treatment-related mortality (Gupta and others 2012).

Clinical Practice Guidelines

Clinical practice guidelines are developed to assist practitioners and patients in deciding on appropriate care for their circumstances (Hensher, Price, and Adomakoh 2006). Comprehensive cancer centers play a leadership role in developing and promoting treatment guidelines locally and nationally. Center clinicians and researchers work with professional organizations to develop

Figure 11.2 Framework for a Comprehensive Cancer Center

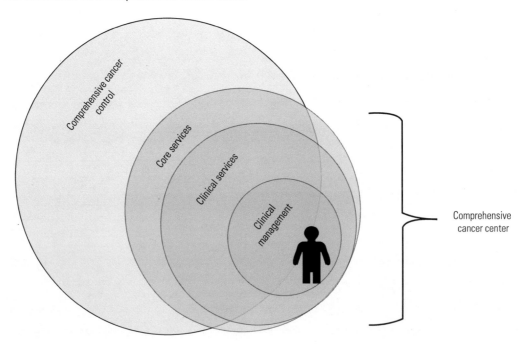

guidelines for a wide range of scenarios. Some examples include the U.S. Preventive Services Task Force for screening guidelines and Cancer Care Ontario's Program in Evidence-Based Care, which produces evidence-based guidance documents.[1] Guidelines are not limited to therapeutic interventions and include indications for medical imaging and other diagnostic interventions[2] and for symptom management. Nursing and other allied health professions develop guidelines to organize and direct care.[3] Guidelines must be adapted for use in resource-constrained settings (Anderson and others 2008; Kerr and Midgley 2010).

Many clinical practice guidelines have been adopted and adapted for use in LMICs (Gralow and others 2012; Konduri and others 2012). Although the focus of most of these initiatives is broader than the comprehensive cancer centers, their impact has influenced the care of patients within centers. A well-known international example is the Breast Health Global Initiative, which has developed evidence-based, economically feasible, and culturally appropriate guidelines for breast health and cancer control in LMICs (chapter 3, this volume [Anderson and others 2015]; El Saghir and others 2011; Varughese and Richman 2010). The matrix guideline spans the spectrum of breast health care, from early detection to treatment and palliation, and considers the available resources at each stage (Sloan and Gelband 2007). Another example is the

United States–based National Comprehensive Cancer Network, which collaborates to produce international adaptations and translations of its guidelines that may include modifications based on local circumstances.[4] Other examples include efforts in India to establish a wide range of guidelines adapted to local resource availability,[5] and consensus group recommendations for imaging techniques for head and neck cancers in Singapore and South Asia, as developed by Wee and colleagues depending on resource availability (Wee and others 2009). Mexico has developed a series of *Normas Officiales Mexicanas* (Official Mexican Standards) that guide cancer services and finance.

Clinical Services

Clinical service departments include facilities, equipment, skilled personnel, and policies and procedures to deliver diagnostic, treatment, or supportive care. The cancer center works to integrate these services effectively. For example, there is no point in offering screening if positive results cannot be followed up with definitive diagnostic tests and, if needed, treatment.

Access to the full range of clinical services is critical for timely and appropriate cancer diagnosis and treatment. A timely and accurate diagnosis is critical, because early detection makes the difference between a curable cancer and an untreatable one.

Many clinical service departments require special accreditation and are subject to external review and control, such as in radiation protection and safety for imaging and radiotherapy, external accreditation for laboratory services, and cell therapy. Accreditation standards may be regional or national, or they may be international (Econex 2010).[6]

Office- and Clinic-Based Ambulatory Care

The initial patient encounter with a cancer system often happens in an office or clinic, where cancer-related ambulatory procedures, such as clinical visits, physical examinations, Pap smears, blood samples, or endoscopies, can take place. Guidelines help to determine when and where these procedures should occur and how they should be provided properly and safely by trained staff. Ambulatory facilities may need special equipment to address the needs of various patient populations, for example, special examining tables for gynecologic malignancies, and chairs and special endoscopic equipment for assessing head and neck cancers. Depending on the activity and jurisdiction, special facilities to support these procedures may be required and should be accredited.

Medical Imaging (Diagnostic Radiology)

Imaging is a critical technology for diagnosis, to assess the effects of cancer treatment and complications, monitor for the recurrence of cancer, and screen the general population for cancerous conditions. It also is used to guide interventional procedures such as biopsies under ultrasound, computed tomography (CT), or magnetic resonance imaging (MRI); securing of vascular access; and therapeutic interventions, such as embolization and high frequency ultrasound tumor ablation. Imaging for cancer ranges from conventional X-rays to ultrasound, CT, MRI, and molecular imaging (nuclear medicine) with position emission tomography, frequently combined with CT.

Imaging services require equipment and specialized staff, such as radiologists and radiology technologists, to operate and maintain the equipment. International organizations, such as the International Atomic Energy Agency, the International Society of Radiology, and WHO, have developed and published standards and guidelines for the safe installation, operation, and use of imaging equipment. This information is used to create national and regional standards (for example, Radiation Safety Institute of Canada 2014; Zaidi 2010). Picture archiving and communication systems and web-based systems allow for offsite evaluation and reporting of images and are useful in management of care in remote communities, remote mentoring, and quality

control initiatives. These processes are especially useful in limited-resource settings.

Pathology and Laboratory Medicine

Pathology and laboratory medicine, including blood banking, are essential for diagnosing cancer by examining patient biologic specimens. Laboratory medicine services include pathology, hematology, biochemistry, microbiology, and, increasingly, cytogenetic and molecular testing, services that are not specific to cancer.

Pathology and laboratory medicine services require facilities equipped to handle biological specimens with appropriate precautions, and specialized equipment to process and analyze tissues, blood, serum, and body fluids. Basic pathology can include the capability for specimen fixation, embedding into paraffin, tissue slicing, and staining; modern facilities must include immunohistochemistry, flow cytometry, and molecular and cytogenetic testing (Gralow and others 2012). Given that the diagnosis of cancer, especially rare cancers, is complex, subspecialty expertise or access to such expertise via international networks is required. Collaborative or twinning initiatives have been developed to support pathology services in LMICs. Examples include a Ghana-Norway partnership as part of the Breast Health Global Initiative (Masood and others 2008) and Partners in Health, which includes clinics in a number of LMICs (Haiti and Rwanda) with close ties to the Brigham and Women's Hospital and Dana-Farber Cancer Institute (Carlson and others 2010). Laboratories require specialized accreditation to ensure that processes are in place to optimize the quality of specimen procurement and reporting.[7]

Surgery

Surgery is a fundamental element of cancer treatment and its pertinence to LMICs is the subject of chapter 13 of this volume (Dare and others 2015). Well-established interventions have proven effective in reducing surgical risk and provide promising strategies to improve outcomes (Weiser and Gawande 2015). The introduction of standardized practices, such as the Surgical Safety Checklist endorsed by WHO, has improved the outcomes of surgical procedures in countries at all economic levels (Farmer and others 2010; Gawande 2009; Haynes and others 2009; Lingard and others 2008; Lingard and others 2011; World Alliance for Patient Safety 2008). The use of comprehensive standard policies and procedures facilitates safe and efficient operations.

Radiation Therapy

Radiation therapy, or radiotherapy, involves the use of ionizing radiation for therapeutic purposes. It is the subject of chapter 14 in this volume. Strategies to improve access to radiotherapy in LMICs have been suggested, including offering basic treatment techniques and optimizing fractionation to increase the throughput on radiotherapy machines, encouraging competitive pricing, and supporting long-distance mentorship for programs in remote areas (Gralow and others 2012). For many reasons, cobalt machines have frequently been considered more appropriate for LMICs (IAEA 2008, 2010). These views are changing as access to more sophisticated technologies is improving. Although linear accelerators require a more reliable power supply, cobalt units present a higher radiation safety risk and require frequent source replacement, which presents a hazard and additional expense.

Systemic Cancer Therapy or Chemotherapy

In systemic cancer therapy or chemotherapy, drugs are distributed in the body through the bloodstream. These drugs include chemotherapy, administered intravenously or orally; hormones; and immune and molecular-targeted therapies. Systemic therapy is used alone or in combination with surgery and radiotherapy to reduce recurrence, improve survival (Gralow and others 2012; Valentini, Barba, and Gambacorta 2010), and help preserve organs. Chemotherapy alone is used in hematologic cancers and in most metastatic cancers. Chemotherapy facilities can be used for other intravenous treatments, transfusions, minor procedures such as bone marrow biopsies, thoracentesis, paracentesis, and lumbar puncture for cancer and noncancerous conditions. Systemic therapy can usually be delivered in specialized ambulatory facilities in hospital outpatient units and community-based medical offices or clinics.[8]

Chemotherapy drugs may be expensive, although a host of agents are now off patent and can be effective and used extensively in LMICs (Konduri and others 2012). Several of the cancers endemic to the lowest income settings are amenable to treatment with relatively low-cost chemotherapy, but treatment cost is still a major barrier for many in LMICs.

Palliative Care and Supportive Care

Palliative care aims to prevent or relieve suffering, provide early identification and assessment of symptoms, and address other physical, psychosocial, and spiritual issues (WHO 2006a). It is the subject of chapter 9 of this volume (Cleary, Gelband, and Wagner 2015).

Survivorship

Survivorship is defined as the care of persons diagnosed with cancer, from the time of diagnosis throughout their lives, as well as the impact of cancer on family members, friends, and caregivers of survivors (Centers for Disease Control and Prevention 2013).

Increasingly, as treatments become more successful and life expectancy increases, patients face new issues. With improvements in access to and quality of care, this will increasingly be the case in LMICs, where survivorship services are currently unavailable.

Psychosocial support can be provided to patients and their families by a broad range of people, depending on the level of need. Complex mental health issues and social matters can benefit from the engagement of other health professionals, including primary care providers, community health workers, spiritual guides, volunteers, friends, families, and other lay individuals. Comprehensive cancer centers should have a survivorship program with a range of professionals, including psychiatrists, psychologists, social workers, nurses, therapists, nutritionists, and educators, as well as patients in treatment and long-term survivors.

Core Services

Core services are delivered by departments of administration and management, human resources, information technology and management, physical facilities, pharmacy, infection prevention and control, quality assurance, and finance. The level of core services depends on the size of the center and whether it is a designated standalone facility, part of a larger hospital, or a consortium of providers. In the latter two instances, the core services may not be specific to cancer and may be used for the management of other diseases and injuries. Generally, the core services must meet accreditation and licensing standards and guidelines and are usually included in the hospital accreditation. The lack of investment in core services leads to poor access to and performance of clinical services (Grimes and others 2011), including poor quality, inefficient use of resources, and negative impacts on health (Mavalankar and others 2005).

External challenges to core service infrastructure can paralyze the best clinical service. For example, long-term increases in the price of petroleum needed for medical supplies; transportation of goods, personnel, and patients; and fuel for lighting, heating, cooling, and medical equipment may have significant adverse impacts on health sectors in LMICs (Dalglish, Poulsen, and Winch 2013). In addition, the absence of robust supply chain management may result in delays in pathology reporting because of the lack of reagents, and insufficient maintenance may result in equipment breakdowns that limit access to imaging or radiotherapy.

Administration and Management

Cancer care is complex and requires skilled and accountable leadership and management at all levels. Generally, hospitals with better management have better clinical outcomes, and good management practices help to preserve or enhance the quality of care (Carter, Dorgan, and Layton 2011). Useful frameworks exist to help guide the development and ongoing excellence of administration and management. For example, the United States–based Baldrige Performance Excellence Program focuses on performance excellence in leadership, strategic planning, customer focus, workforce focus, operations focus, results and measurement, and analysis and knowledge management (Baldrige Performance Excellence Program, National Institute of Standards and Technology, and U.S. Department of Commerce 2011); the program has a self-assessment tool.

Human Resources

Cancer centers require appropriately trained and licensed clinicians and administrative and support staff. Centers need to recruit and retain staff and provide professional and career development opportunities to maintain competence and develop new skills. Core human resource services include identifying the roles and responsibilities of the range of positions within the center, setting compensation and benefit levels, developing performance evaluations, setting up management and supervisory structures, and providing conflict resolution services.

Making the best use of human resources means maximizing their impact. Human resources can be increased in LMICs and remote areas by using nonspecialists or general medical professionals working under specific conditions. This practice promotes *task-shifting* and optimizes the use of sparse, highly skilled personnel. For example, the use of community health workers, expert patients, and clinical officers (Knaul, Bhadelia, and others 2012) and, in some countries, traditional healers who play an important role in influencing people's health care decisions (Price and others 2012) will enhance the capacity for health care delivery. Teleservices, such as telepathology, teleradiology, and virtual consultation can offer support and guidance in cancer to nonspecialists by tapping large international networks of highly trained professionals.

Information Technology and Management

Information technology (IT) refers to systems and their applications, for example, computer hardware and software and telecommunications that collect, store, use, and share information. Information management refers to organizing, linking, analyzing, and presenting data to guide decisions.

In cancer centers, IT includes health records; operational systems, such as human resources, pharmacy, supplies, and equipment; financing; and other systems. IT also includes telemedicine and mobile information and communication technologies, such as cell phones (mHealth), which improve access to services. Telemedicine initiatives have the potential to decrease disparities in cancer care between resource-poor and resource-rich institutions by developing resources— human capital and telecommunication infrastructure— that link institutions with different levels of funding and expertise (Hazin and Qaddoumi 2010).

Although IT requires funding for capital, training, ongoing maintenance, and technical backup, cancer centers need reliable electronic systems to manage the high volumes of information; inform safe, efficient, and effective care; and improve access. The systems can be especially important in LMICs for linking comprehensive centers to more remote areas and less specialized centers, as well as for linking to international expertise and networks (Knaul, Bhadelia, and others 2012; Shekelle, Morton, and Keeler 2006).

Pharmacy

Pharmacy services focus on safe and effective medication use and include managing practice; adhering to policies on medication use; optimizing medication therapy; procuring drug products and managing inventory; preparing, packaging, and labeling medications; delivering medications; monitoring medication use; evaluating the effectiveness of the medication-use system; and conducting research (American Society of Health-System Pharmacists 2013).

Cancer pharmacy services reflect specialized knowledge about the medications used for cancer, management of cancer complications, treatment side effects, and drug toxicities. The complexity of caring for patients with cancer; the costs of chemotherapy; the potential for severe drug toxicity and medication errors; and the requirements for safe preparation, administration, and disposal of cytotoxic drugs highlight the important role of pharmacies in cancer centers, regardless of a country's resource level (Wiernikowski 2013). The International Society of Oncology Pharmacy Practitioners has developed Standards of Oncology Pharmacy Practice that take into account realities from resource-rich and resource-poor settings.

Infection Control

Infection control is a core service that focuses on preventing and controlling infections in cancer patients, including advice on the care of patients with infections, especially those acquired in the cancer center.

Main infection prevention and control tactics include complying with hand hygiene, disinfecting and sterilizing surfaces and equipment, investigating and monitoring suspected infections, managing difficult cases and outbreaks, wearing personal protective equipment, and vaccinating and educating health care providers. For centers, this includes introducing prevention bundles,[9] improving compliance with hand hygiene, making prudent use of antimicrobials, translating research results into practice, and upgrading the capabilities of the microbiology laboratory (Raka 2010).

Quality Assurance

Cancer care has many potential risks. Complex clinical management using multiple treatment paths and multiple health care providers highlights the importance of a centerwide commitment to a quality and safety agenda and ongoing performance improvement.

Centers need to select appropriate indicators to monitor and assess the quality and effectiveness of their structures (for example, setting and facilities), processes (range of care), and outcomes (patients' recovery, restoration of function, and survival) (Donabedian 1966). Information systems should capture baseline performance measures for each indicator and track changes over time. Cancer centers should regularly monitor performance, identify problem areas, and focus improvement efforts in these areas.

Finance

All cancer centers need competent financial systems to monitor revenues and expenses. Sources of funding vary widely and can include national and subnational government funding; private user payments, either through health insurance or out of pocket; revenue-generating practices, for example, retail and parking; and philanthropic support from external donors. Available finances dictate the services that can be provided. Centers need systems that allow effective and efficient operations and ensure appropriate quality services to optimize the use of funds.

Additional Key Supports

Additional key supports required in the cancer center include the following: equipment and technology support services, supplies and materials management, supply chain processes, patient transport, fire safety and radiation protection, occupational health and safety, and security. In areas of violence or conflict, security services may be especially important for patients and their families, as well as for guaranteeing the safety of health inputs and avoiding robbery. National and regional bodies generally set policies and standards for areas such as fire safety and radiation protection, occupational health and safety, and infection prevention and control. Organizations and providers usually determine how the other ancillary services will be provided, depending on local circumstances and resources.

CANCER CENTERS AND QUALITY OF CARE: AN INTEGRATING THEME

Having well-developed and resourced centers and systems does not guarantee higher quality (Chalkidou and others 2014; WHO 2006c). Indeed, high-quality care can be achieved in centers with minimal resources.

Many organizations have highlighted issues and impacts of quality in health care (IOM 2000, 2001) and cancer care (IOM 2013). Poor quality of care can lead to increased injury, morbidity, disability, and death for patients. It also has financial, physical, and psychological impacts on patients and families; financial impacts on health care institutions and systems, especially if additional health services are needed; and economic impacts on societies (IOM 2000). Definitions and frameworks, along with quality measures, may also be influenced by a variable focus on structures, processes, and outcomes of quality.

A review of conceptual quality frameworks in six Organisation for Economic Co-operation and Development member countries (OECD, Kelley, and Hurst 2006) identified the most commonly used dimensions of quality:

- *Effectiveness:* The degree of achieving desirable outcomes, given the correct provision of evidence-based health care services to all who could benefit but not to those who would not benefit
- *Safety:* The degree to which health care processes avoid, prevent, and ameliorate adverse outcomes or injuries that stem from the processes of health care itself; closely related to effectiveness, albeit distinct in its emphasis on preventing unintentional adverse events for patients
- *Responsiveness:* The way a system treats people to meet their legitimate non-health expectations; also known as *patient-centeredness*
- *Accessibility:* The ease with which health services are reached; can be physical, financial, or psychological and requires health services to be a priority and available
- *Equity:* Closely related to accessibility but assesses health system financing and outcomes and health status

- *Efficiency:* The system's optimal use of available resources to yield maximum benefits or results; speaks to a system's ability to function at lower cost without diminishing attainable and desirable results.

Other dimensions of quality identified included acceptability (related to patient-centeredness), appropriateness (related to effectiveness), competency or capability (related to effectiveness), continuity (related to patient-centeredness), and timeliness (related to patient-centeredness).

External accreditation, regulatory, licensing, and professional and evidence-based clinical practice organizations and bodies require cancer centers to meet quality standards for organizations and how they should operate. Countries or regions may have general accreditation standards as well as service-specific credentialing bodies[10] (Econex 2010). These external organizations provide cancer centers with arm's-length quality reference points to guide their operations. Accreditation is also an external motivator for quality reform and is consistently seen as an effective driver for quality in LMICs (Barnett and Hort 2013).

Catalyzing the Development of Effective National Cancer Control Systems

A center's critical mass of clinical management expertise and clinical and core services results in effective and efficient quality cancer control. Cancer centers can lead the development of regional systems of cancer care, with care ranging from very complex to basic interventions and community-based care. Centers can contribute to national cancer control efforts by being a credible voice for public education on prevention and the signs, symptoms, and treatment of cancer. This contribution is especially important in LMICs, since many people present with advanced or metastatic disease. The establishment of regional cancer centers in every state of India illustrates the important contribution of these centers to supporting an effective national cancer control system (box 11.2).

Training Health Care Professionals

Comprehensive centers play a significant role educating a country's health care professionals. In addition to providing specialty training for individual professions, centers provide training on interprofessional

---

Box 11.2

Regional Cancer Centers in India

India's active National Cancer Control Program was launched by the government in 1975 and revised in 1984. The main focus is primary prevention and early detection of cancer, which includes the following:

- Tobacco control measures to prevent tobacco-related cancers
- Screening for cancers of the uterine cervix, mouth, and breast
- Extending and strengthening therapeutic services nationally through regional cancer centers (RCCs) and medical colleges, including dental colleges.

The objectives of the program are to be met by creating one RCC in every state and developing oncology units in existing medical colleges across the country.

The main functions of RCCs are cancer detection and diagnosis, treatment, aftercare and rehabilitation, education and training, cancer registration, and research. RCC core requirements include divisions of surgical oncology, radiation oncology, and medical oncology, with support from the departments of anesthesiology, pathology, cytopathology, hematology, biochemistry, and radiologic diagnosis, with appropriate equipment and staff.

Oncology units in medical colleges form an important link between RCCs and the more peripheral health infrastructure, that is, district hospitals, Tehsil (regional) hospitals, and primary health centers. This three-tier model will help to make cancer care accessible across all socioeconomic groups and geographical areas.

At the peripheral level, a district cancer control program was launched in 1990/91 with elements

box continues next page

Box 11.2 (continued)

of health education, early detection, training of medical and paramedic personnel, palliative treatment and pain relief, coordination, and monitoring.

Although the national cancer control program has been beneficial, given the geographic expanse and the vast population, cancer care facilities remain unavailable to the majority of the population from lower socioeconomic strata and those living in remote areas. For example, global standards require two radiotherapy treating units per 100,000 population; currently, India has 0.4 radiotherapy units per 100,000.

A wide disparity exists in the level of cancer care across various centers in India. Efforts are underway to create a national cancer grid linking major oncology centers across the country to facilitate the following:

- Development of a cooperative cancer management network for the transfer of standard treatment guidelines and expertise
- Facilitation of uniform standards for education, training, and human resource development in cancer care
- Creation of a cooperative oncology research network to conduct studies of national importance.

---

team-based care. Other hospitals, community clinics, and primary care can provide training placement opportunities (Debas and others 2006). Trained professionals can take on various roles and responsibilities throughout the country. LMICs that wish to train their own doctors need at least one teaching hospital (Hensher, Price, and Adomakoh 2006), which, in most instances, would include the comprehensive cancer center. Given that every developing country will not be able to train a full complement of health professionals on its own (Frenk and others 2010) or train staff in highly specialized skills, comprehensive cancer centers, especially in developed countries, can be part of education consortia that extend beyond national borders.

For example, when the treatment of pediatric malignancy was expanded in Chile to include bone marrow transplantation, clinical staff needed specialty training to support the development of this new program (Palma and others 2006). In collaboration with St. Jude Children's Research Hospital, Memphis, Tennessee, pediatric oncologists, nurses, and other specialists—immunologists, hematologists, intensivists, pathologists, and medical technologists—received training from international institutions, including St. Jude, Vall d'Hebron Hospital in Barcelona, and the Hospital de Clínicas in Curitiba, Brazil. The experiences and survival outcomes of the program have been positive.

Supporting the Development of Effective Health Care Systems

Comprehensive cancer centers guide and support the development of effective health systems. Centers model effective quality clinical management practices that are transferrable to all health care services. In addition, many of the clinical and core services in cancer centers—such as diagnostic imaging, pathology, surgery, and palliative care—can support other clinical programs. Similarly, the referral systems that cancer centers establish with a continuum of providers can meet other health needs.

Innovative financing of cancer services through comprehensive cancer centers can drive efforts to develop financial protection in health as part of universal health coverage. In Mexico, for example, pediatric and women's cancers were among the first to be included in *Seguro Popular*, the national public insurance program focused on the poor. The visibility and effectiveness of these efforts helped to develop confidence among citizens, legislators, and policy makers alike regarding the feasibility and importance of establishing financial protection in health (Atun and Knaul 2012; Knaul, González-Pier, and others 2012).

Contributing to Global Health

Comprehensive cancer centers can make important contributions to global health and health systems. Centers can contribute to broad global efforts to improve health (Frenk and Moon 2013). International health organizations that cross national boundaries can benefit from the participation of centers in such areas as research and development and sharing of information for ongoing learning (Blanchet and others 2013; Jamison, Frenk, and Knaul 1998).

Successfully developing comprehensive cancer centers in LMICs requires locally developed and driven approaches that consider national and subnational resources and circumstances. Gupta and others (chapter 7, this volume) identify the basic personnel and infrastructure requirements for the ideal dedicated childhood cancer treatment center in an LMIC setting. The authors note that satellite centers can be especially important for decreasing the abandonment of treatment for children and recognize that much treatment occurs despite the lack of ideal centers. Many LMICs have leveraged the experience, expertise, and resources of high-income countries to develop cancer services. For example, twinning relationships can facilitate the

development of cancer centers and help to achieve a country's cancer goals (Gralow and others 2012; Sloan and Gelband 2007). Furthermore, research suggests that twinning improves cancer survival in LMICs (Hazin and Qaddoumi 2010). Box 11.3 provides examples of beneficial twinning relationships.

Other LMICs have raised funds locally to finance the development of cancer center services. Box 11.4 presents the experience of establishing the Fakous Cancer Center in the Arab Republic of Egypt, which integrates cancer treatment with primary health care to help prevent and treat cancer in a low-resource setting.

Box 11.3

Twinning Relationships

St. Jude Children's Research Hospital's International Outreach Program and 20 Partners
The St. Jude Children's Research Hospital's International Outreach Program improves the survival rates of children with catastrophic illnesses worldwide by transferring knowledge, technology, and organizational skills to countries and regions, so they can become self-sufficient and successfully treat children close to home. The program involves local communities, supports the development of regional expertise and diagnostic capabilities, partners with medical institutions and fundraising organizations, and facilitates the involvement of other agencies and organizations to support key programs and the education of local personnel.

Located in Memphis, Tennessee, the program has pediatric oncology twinning programs with 20 partner sites in 14 countries, including Brazil, Chile, China, Costa Rica, Ecuador, El Salvador, Guatemala, Honduras, Jordan, Lebanon, Mexico, Morocco, the Philippines, and the República Bolivariana de Venezuela. The results have been significant; survival rates for childhood cancers increased and the rate of abandonment of treatment decreased. For example, the abandonment rate in El Salvador dropped from 13 percent to 3 percent from 2010 to 2012, and the five-year

survival rate for children with acute lymphoblastic leukemia increased from 10 percent to 70 percent.[a]

Fred Hutchinson Cancer Research Center and Uganda Cancer Institute
The Uganda Cancer Institute (UCI), the only cancer treatment and training facility in the country of 32 million people, partnered with the Fred Hutchinson Cancer Research Center in Seattle, Washington, to establish the UCI/Hutchinson Center Cancer Alliance in 2004. The alliance focuses on developing effective prevention and treatment strategies for infection-associated cancers through the following activities:

- Conducting advanced research in infection-related cancers to improve understanding of the pathogenesis of these diseases and to develop and test more effective and safer treatment and prevention regimens
- Improving clinical capacity by providing medical support and revised clinical protocols for those with infectious cancers
- Training cancer specialists, scientists, and support staff in Uganda to increase local human capacity for clinical care and research at UCI and providing a training environment for United States–based personnel in Uganda.[b]

box continues next page

Box 11.3 (continued)

Victoria Hospice and B. P. Koirala Memorial Cancer Hospital, Bharatpur, Nepal

The International Network for Cancer Treatment and Research established the Palliative Access Program to assist developing countries in initiating and sustaining palliative care programs. In 2007, the B. P. Koirala Memorial Cancer Hospital, Nepal's national cancer hospital, expressed a desire to twin with a hospice to help expand its patient care services, develop education and research, and introduce home and community-based palliative care services. The hospital—which has a 12-bed inpatient palliative care unit and provides inpatient and outpatient consultations—twinned with Victoria Hospice in Victoria, British Columbia,

Canada. Funds have been raised to help support the hospital's patient care services and increase health professional education. Medical supplies have been purchased, local staff have been hired and trained, travel funds have been provided for staff training opportunities, and educational material has been provided and adapted. In addition, the partners exchange mutually beneficial knowledge and expertise in palliative care.[c]

a. For additional information, see: http://www.stjude.org/stjude/v/index.jsp?vgnextoid=2f166f9523e70110VgnVCM1000001e0215acRCRD&vgnextchannel=e41e6fa0a9118010VgnVCM1000000e2015acRCRD.

b. For additional information, see: http://www.fredhutch.org/en/labs/vaccine-and-infectious-disease/international-programs/global-oncology/uganda/uci-fred-hutch.html.

c. For additional information, see https://sites.google.com/site/nepalhospicetwin.

Box 11.4

The Fakous Cancer Center

In Fakous district in the northeast of the Arab Republic of Egypt, breast cancer is the most common cancer. Until the center was opened in 1992, the closest cancer treatment for the largely poor population of 660,000 was the National Cancer Institute in Cairo. It was a three-hour trip and a world apart, and most cancer patients went untreated.

One of many challenges confronted in building the Fakous Cancer Center was financing. Using "crowd sourcing," one million Egyptian pounds (US$330,000) was raised in the first two months, and donations continued to come in. A second challenge was finding doctors to work in the center. In place of permanent staff, specialists from the National Cancer Institute and various universities come to the center to perform surgery and provide other specialized treatment. The Fakous Cancer Center has become a center of excellence in training as well as treatment. The third challenge, the retention of good nursing staff, was accomplished through the establishment of a nursing school.

The Fakous model integrates third-level services with primary health care, taking prevention and

treatment to less developed parts of the country. The center has 80 beds; three operating rooms; an eight-bed intensive care unit; basic diagnostic facilities with conventional X-ray; ultrasound for ultrasound-guided biopsy, mammography, and endoscopy; and a histopathology unit equipped to provide cytology, tissue analysis, and hormone receptor assays, as well as treatment modalities. Social support of cancer patients' families is also provided.

The center's outpatient facilities provide free clinical consultations for poor patients, who constitute the majority in this region—nearly 230,000 outpatients in the past 22 years. The inpatient wards have seen 29,000 patients admitted.

Care at the center is reflected in survival statistics: for women treated for breast cancer in 2008, the five-year survival is 89 percent for stage I, 77 percent for stage II, 71 percent for stage III, and 19 percent for stage IV. A recent study of the experience of the center also documents stage shift at diagnosis from the time the center was opened through 2007–08 (Omar and others 2013).

CONCLUSIONS

The optimal framework for establishing a comprehensive cancer center provides the nucleus around which an entire cancer control program can be developed. Many LMICs are developing comprehensive cancer centers supported with public and private resources, and these countries are using locally driven approaches appropriate to their local circumstances. Most important, they are having significant impacts on advancing cancer control and improving the health of their populations.

NOTES

World Bank Income Classifications as of July 2014 are as follows, based on estimates of gross national income (GNI) per capita for 2013:

- Low-income countries (LICs) = US$1,045 or less
- Middle-income countries (MICs) are subdivided:
  a) lower-middle-income = US$1,046–US$4,125
  b) upper-middle-income(UMICs)=US$4,126–US$12,745
- High-income countries (HICs) = US$12,746 or more.

1. For the Cochrane Collaboration, see http://www .cochrane.org/cochrane-reviews. For the U.S. Preventive Services Task Force, see http://www.uspreventiveservices taskforce.org/recommendations.htm. For Cancer Care Ontario, see https://www.cancercare.on.ca/cms/One .aspx?portalId=1377&pageId=10144.
2. For example, see the Royal College of Radiologists, http://www.rcr.ac.uk/index.aspx, and the American College of Radiology, http://www.acr.org/Quality-Safety /Standards-Guidelines.
3. For example, see the Oncology Nursing Society, http://www .ons.org/ClinicalResources; European Oncology Nursing Society, http://www.cancernurse.eu/education/guidelines .html; and Association of Oncology Social Work, http://www .aosw.org/aosw/Main/professionals/standards-of-practice /AOSWMain/Professional-Development/standards-of-practice. aspx?hkey=51fda308-28bd-48b0-8a75-a17d01251b5e.
4. See http://www.nccn.org/international/international _adaptations.asp.
5. See https://tmc.gov.in/clinicalguidelines/clinical.htm.
6. For example, see the Joint Commission International, http://www.jointcommissioninternational.org/achieve -accreditation/; National Accreditation Board for Hospitals and Healthcare Providers International, http://www.nabh .co/Index.aspx; and Accreditation Canada International, http://www.internationalaccreditation.ca/en/home.aspx.
7. For example, see the International Federation of Clinical Chemistry and Laboratory Medicine, http://www.ifcc .org/executive-board-and-council/regional-federations /efcc-european-federation-of-clinical-chemistry/; National Accrediting Agency for Clinical Laboratory Sciences, http://www.naacls.org/; and National Accreditation Board

for Testing and Calibration Laboratories, http://www .nabl-india.org/.
8. See, for example, http://www.asco.org/institute-quality /asco-ons-standards-safe-chemotherapy-administration.
9. Bundles focus on aseptic procedures that potentially carry a high risk of hospital-related infection, for example, catheter-associated bloodstream infection, catheter-associated urinary tract infection, ventilator-associated pneumonia, and surgical site infections.
10. A number of accreditation bodies have international accreditation programs to inform centers in countries where national accreditation does not exist. See, for example, Joint Commission International, http:// www.jointcommissioninternational.org/achieve -accreditation/; Accreditation Canada International, http://www.internationalaccreditation.ca/en/home.aspx; and National Accreditation Board for Hospitals and Healthcare Providers, http://www.nabh.co/.

REFERENCES

American Society of Health-System Pharmacists. 2013. "ASHP Guidelines: Minimum Standard for Pharmacies in Hospitals." *American Journal of Health-System Pharmacy* 70: 1619–30.

Anderson, B. O., J. Lipscomb, R. H. Murillo, and D. B. Thomas. 2015. "Breast Cancer." In *Disease Control Priorities* (third edition): Volume 3, *Cancer*, edited by H. Gelband, P. Jha, R. Sankaranarayanan, and S. Horton. Washington, DC: World Bank.

Anderson, B. O., C. H. Yip, R. A. Smith, R. Shyyan, S. F. Sener, and others. 2008. "Guideline Implementation for Breast Healthcare in Low-Income and Middle-Income Countries: Overview of the Breast Health Global Initiative Global Summit 2007." *Cancer* 113 (8 Suppl.): 2221–43. doi:10.1002 /cncr.23844.

Atun, R., and F. M. Knaul. 2012. "Innovative Financing: Local and Global Opportunities." In *Closing the Cancer Divide: An Equity Imperative*, edited by F. M. Knaul, J. Gralow, R. Atun, and A. Bhadelia, for the Global Task Force on Expanded Access to Cancer Care and Control in Developing Countries, chapter 8. Boston, MA: Harvard Global Equity Initiative.

Baldrige Performance Excellence Program, National Institute of Standards and Technology, and U.S. Department of Commerce. 2011. *2011–2012 Health Care Criteria for Performance Excellence*. Gaithersburg, MD: Baldrige. http:// www.nist.gov/baldrige/publications/archive/2011_2012 _healthcare_criteria.cfm.

Barnett, C., and K. Hort. 2013. "Approaches to Regulating the Quality of Hospital Services in Low- and Middle-Income Countries with Mixed Health Systems: A Review of Their Effectiveness, Context of Operation and Feasibility." Working Paper Series 32, The Nossal Institute for Global Health, University of Melbourne, Australia. http://ni.unimelb.edu.au/__data/assets/pdf _file/0010/834418/WP_32.pdf.

Blanchet, N., M. Thomas, R. Atun, D. T. Jamison, F. Knaul, and others. 2013. "Global Collection Action in Health: The WDR+20 Landscape of Core and Supportive Functions." Working Paper, The Lancet Commission on Investing in Health.

Cancer Care Ontario. 2013. "The Cancer Journey." https://www.cancercare.on.ca/ocs/csoverview/.

Carlson, J. W., E. Lyon, D. Walton, W.-C. Foo, A. C. Sievers, and others. 2010. "Partners in Pathology: A Collaborative Model to Bring Pathology to Resource Poor Settings." *American Journal of Surgical Pathology* 34 (1): 118–23.

Carter, K., S. Dorgan, and D. Layton. 2011. "Why Hospital Management Matters." Health International, McKinsey's Health Systems and Services Practice, McKinsey and Company, London.

Centers for Disease Control and Prevention. 2013. "Basic Information about Cancer Survivorship." http://www.cdc.gov/cancer/survivorship/basic_info/index.htm.

Chalkidou, K., P. Marquez, P. K. Dhillon, Y. Teerawattananon, T. Anothaisintawee, and others. 2014. "Evidence-Informed Frameworks for Cost-Effective Cancer Care and Prevention in Low, Middle, and High-Income Countries." *The Lancet Oncology* 15 (3): e119–31. http://dx.doi.org/10.1016/S1470-2045(13)70547-3.

Cleary, J., H. Gelband, and J. Wagner. 2015. "Cancer Pain Relief." In *Disease Control Priorities* (third edition): Volume 3, *Cancer*, edited by H. Gelband, P. Jha, R. Sankaranarayanan, and S. Horton. Washington, DC: World Bank.

Dalglish, S. L., M. N. Poulsen, and P. J. Winch. 2013. "Localization of Health Systems in Low- and Middle-Income Countries in Response to Long-Term Increases in Energy Prices." *Globalization and Health* 9: 56. http://www.globalizationandhealth.com/content/9/1/56.

Dare, A. J., B. O. Anderson, R. Sullivan, C. S. Pramesh, C.-H. Yip, and others. 2015. "Surgical Services for Cancer Care." In *Disease Control Priorities* (third edition): Volume 3, *Cancer*, edited by H. Gelband, P. Jha, R. Sankaranarayanan, and S. Horton. Washington, DC: World Bank.

Debas, H. T., R. Gosselin, C. McCord, and A. Thind. 2006. "Surgery." In *Disease Control Priorities in Developing Countries*, 2nd ed., edited by D. T. Jamison, J. G. Breman, A. R. Measham, G. Alleyne, M. Claeson, D. B. Evans, P. Jha, A. Mills, and P. Musgrove, 1245–59. Washington, DC: World Bank and Oxford University Press.

Donabedian, A. 1966. "Evaluating the Quality of Medical Care." *Milbank Memorial Fund Quarterly* 44 (3 Suppl.): 166–203.

Econex. 2010. *Accreditation of Healthcare Providers. Health Reform Note 2.* http://econex.co.za/publication/health-reform-note-2/.

El Saghir, N. S., C. A. Adebamowo, B. O. Anderson, R. W. Carlson, P. A. Bird, and others. 2011. "Breast Cancer Management in Low Resource Countries (LRCs): Consensus Statement from the Breast Health Global Initiative." *The Breast* 20 (Suppl. 2): S3–11.

Farmer, P., J. Frenk, F. M. Knaul, L. N. Shulman, G. Alleyne, and others. 2010. "Expansion of Cancer Care and Control in Countries of Low and Middle Income: A Call to Action." *The Lancet* 376 (9747): 1186–93. doi:10.1016/S0140-6736(10)61152-X.

Frenk, J., L. Chen, Z. A. Bhutta, J. Cohen, N. Crisp, and others. 2010. "Health Professionals for a New Century: Transforming Education to Strengthen Health Systems in an Interdependent World." *The Lancet* 376: 1923–58.

Frenk, J., and S. Moon. 2013. "Governance Challenges in Global Health." *The New England Journal of Medicine* 368 (10): 936–42.

Gawande, A. 2009. *The Checklist Manifesto: How to Get Things Right.* London: Metropolitan Books.

Gralow, J. R., E. Krakauer, B. O. Anderson, A. Ilbawi, P. Porter, and others. 2012. "Core Elements for Provision of Cancer Care and Control in Low and Middle Income Countries." In *Closing the Cancer Divide: An Equity Imperative*, edited by F. M. Knaul, J. Gralow, R. Atun, and A. Bhadelia, for the Global Task Force on Expanded Access to Cancer Care and Control in Developing Countries, 125–65. Boston, MA: Harvard Global Equity Initiative.

Grimes, C. E., K. G. Bowman, C. M. Dodgion, and C. B. D. Lavy. 2011. "Systematic Review of Barriers to Surgical Care in Low-Income and Middle-Income Countries." *World Journal of Surgery* 35: 941–50.

Gupta, S., M. Bonilla, P. Valverde, L. Fu, S. C. Howard, and others. 2012. "Treatment-Related Mortality in Children with Acute Myeloid Leukaemia in Central America: Incidence, Timing and Predictors." *European Journal of Cancer* 48: 1363–69.

Haynes, A. B., T. G. Weiser, W. R. Berry, S. R. Lipsitz, A. H. Breizat, and others. 2009. "A Surgical Safety Checklist to Reduce Morbidity and Mortality in a Global Population." *New England Journal of Medicine* 360: 491–99.

Hazin, R., and I. Qaddoumi. 2010. "Teleoncology: Current and Future Applications for Improving Cancer Care Globally." *The Lancet Oncology* 11 (2): 204–10.

Hensher, M., M. Price, and S. Adomakoh. 2006. "Referral Hospitals." In *Disease Control Priorities in Developing Countries*, 2nd ed., edited by D. T. Jamison, J. G. Breman, A. R. Measham, G. Alleyne, M. Claeson, D. B. Evans, P. Jha, A. Mills, and P. Musgrove, 1229–43. Washington, DC: World Bank and Oxford University Press.

IAEA (International Atomic Energy Agency). 2008. *Setting Up a Radiotherapy Programme: Clinical, Medical Physics, Radiation Protection and Safety Aspects.* Vienna: IAEA.

———. 2010. AGaRT (The Advisory Group on increasing access to Radiotherapy Technology in low and middle income countries). Brochure. http://cancer.iaea.org/documents/AGaRTBrochure.pdf.

IOM (Institute of Medicine). 2000. *To Err Is Human: Building a Safer Health System*, edited by L. T. Kohn, J. M. Corrigan, and M. S. Donaldson. Washington, DC: National Academies Press.

———. 2001. *Crossing the Quality Chasm: A New Health System for the 21st Century.* Washington, DC: National Academies Press.

———. 2013. *Delivering High-Quality Cancer Care: Charting a New Course for a System in Crisis.* Washington,

DC: National Academies Press. http://www.nap.edu/catalog .php?record_id=18359.

Jamison, D. T., J. Frenk, and F. Knaul. 1998. "International Collective Action in Health: Objectives, Functions, and Rationale." *The Lancet* 351: 514–17.

Kerr, D. J., and R. Midgley. 2010. "Can We Treat Cancer for a Dollar a Day? Guidelines for Low-Income Countries." *New England Journal of Medicine* 363 (9): 801–03.

Knaul, F. M., G. Alleyne, R. Atun, F. Bustreo, J. R. Gralow, and others. 2012. "Strengthening Stewardship and Leadership to Expand Access to Cancer Care and Control." In *Closing the Cancer Divide: An Equity Imperative*, edited by F. M. Knaul, J. Gralow, R. Atun, and A. Bhadelia, for the Global Task Force on Expanded Access to Cancer Care and Control in Developing Countries, 311–42. Boston, MA: Harvard Global Equity Initiative.

Knaul, F. M., G. Alleyne, P. Piot, R. Atun, J. R. Gralow, and others. 2012. "Health System Strengthening and Cancer: A Diagonal Response to the Challenge of Chronicity." In *Closing the Cancer Divide: An Equity Imperative*, edited by F. M. Knaul, J. Gralow, R. Atun, and A. Bhadelia, for the Global Task Force on Expanded Access to Cancer Care and Control in Developing Countries, 95–124. Boston, MA: Harvard Global Equity Initiative.

Knaul, F. M., A. Bhadelia, R. Bashshur, A. J. Berger, A. Binagwaho, and others. 2012. "Innovative Delivery of Cancer Care and Control in Low-Resource Scenarios." In *Closing the Cancer Divide: An Equity Imperative*, edited by F. M. Knaul, J. Gralow, R. Atun, and A. Bhadelia, for the Global Task Force on Expanded Access to Cancer Care and Control in Developing Countries, 165–95. Boston, MA: Harvard Global Equity Initiative.

Knaul, F. M., E. González-Pier, O. Gómez-Dantés, D. García-Junco, H. Arreola-Ornelas, and others. 2012. "The Quest for Universal Health Coverage: Achieving Social Protection for All in Mexico." *The Lancet* 380 (9849): 1259–79.

Knaul, F. M., J. R. Gralow, R. Atun, A. Bhadelia, J. Frenk, and others. 2012. "Closing the Cancer Divide: Overview and Summary." In *Closing the Cancer Divide: An Equity Imperative*, edited by F. M. Knaul, J. Gralow, R. Atun, and A. Bhadelia, for the Global Task Force on Expanded Access to Cancer Care and Control in Developing Countries, 3–28. Boston, MA: Harvard Global Equity Initiative.

Konduri, N., J. Quick, J. R. Gralow, M. Samiei, P. Castle, and others. 2012. "Access to Affordable Medicines, Vaccines, and Health Technologies." In *Closing the Cancer Divide: An Equity Imperative*, edited by F. M. Knaul, J. Gralow, R. Atun, and A. Bhadelia, for the Global Task Force on Expanded Access to Cancer Care and Control in Developing Countries, 197–256. Boston, MA: Harvard Global Equity Initiative.

Lingard, L., G. Regehr, C. Cartmill, B. Orser, S. Espin, and others. 2011. "Evaluation of a Preoperative Team Briefing: A New Communication Routine Results in Improved Clinical Practice." *BMJ Quality & Safety* 20: 475–82.

Lingard, L., G. Regehr, B. Orser, R. Reznick, G. R. Baker, and others. 2008. "Evaluation of a Preoperative Checklist and Team Briefing among Surgeons, Nurses, and Anesthesiologists to Reduce Failures in Communication." *Archives of Surgery* 143 (1): 12–17.

Masood, S., L. Vass, J. A. Ibarra, B. M. Ljung, H. Stalsberg, and others, on behalf of the Breast Health Global Initiative Pathology Focus Group. 2008. "Breast Pathology Guideline Implementation in Low- and Middle-Income Countries." *Cancer* 113 (Suppl. 8): 2297–304.

Mavalankar, D. V., K. V. Ramani, A. Patel, and P. Sankar. 2005. *Building the Infrastructure to Reach and Care for the Poor: Trends, Obstacles and Strategies to Overcome Them.* Ahmedabad, India: Center for Management of Health Services, Indian Institute of Management. http:// www.iimahd.ernet.in/publications/data/2005-03-01 mavalankar.pdf.

National Cancer Institute (National Institutes of Health, U.S. Department of Health and Human Services). 2012. *The National Cancer Program: Managing the Nation's Research Portfolio. An Annual Plan and Budget Proposal for Fiscal Year 2013.* Bethesda, MD: National Institutes of Health (NIH Publication No. 13-7957).

OECD (Organisation for Economic Co-operation and Development), E. Kelley, and J. Hurst. 2006. "OECD Health Care Quality Indicators Project Conceptual Framework Paper." OECD, Paris.

Omar, A., M. Abdelgawad, M. Aboserea, and O. Omar. 2013. "Breast Cancer Experience at Fakous Cancer Center (FCC)." *Pan Arab Journal Oncology* 6 (3): 12–17.

Palma, J., C. Mosso, C. Paris, M. Campbell, X. Tong, and others. 2006. "Establishment of a Pediatric HSCT Program in a Public Hospital in Chile." *Pediatric Blood Cancer* 46: 803–10.

Price, A. J., P. Ndom, E. Atenguena, J. P. M. Nouemssi, and R. W. Ryder. 2012. "Cancer Care Challenges in Developing Countries." *Cancer* 118: 3627–35.

Radiation Safety Institute of Canada. 2014. Canadian and Provincial Regulatory Documents. http://www.radiation safety.ca/resources/regulatory-documents.

Raka, L. 2010. "Prevention and Control of Hospital-Related Infections in Low and Middle Income Countries." *The Open Infectious Diseases Journal* 4: 125–31.

Shekelle P., S. C. Morton, and E. B. Keeler. 2006. "Costs and Benefits of Health Information Technology. Rockville (MD): Agency for Healthcare Research and Quality." Evidence Reports/Technology Assessments, 132. http:// www.ncbi.nlm.nih.gov/books/NBK37988/ and Benefits of Health Information Technology.

Sloan, F. A., and H. Gelband. 2007. *Cancer Control Opportunities in Low- and Middle-Income Countries.* Washington, DC: National Academies Press.

Valentini, V., M. C. Barba, and M. A. Gambacorta. 2010. "The Role of Multimodality Treatment in M0 Rectal Cancer: Evidence and Research." *European Review for Medical and Pharmacological Sciences* 14 (4): 334–41.

Varughese, J., and S. Richman. 2010. "Cancer Care Inequity for Women in Resource-Poor Countries." *Reviews in Obstetrics and Gynecology* 3 (3): 122–32.

Wee, J. T., B. O. Anderson, J. Corry, A. D'Cruz, K. C. Soo, and others. 2009. "Management of the Neck after Chemoradiotherapy for Head and Neck Cancers in Asia:

Consensus Statement from the Asian Oncology Summit 2009." *The Lancet Oncology* 10 (11): 1086–92.

Weiser, T. G., and A. Gawande. "Excess Surgical Mortality: Strategies for Improving Quality of Care." 2015. In *Disease Control Priorities* (third edition): Volume 1, *Essential Surgery*. Washington, DC: World Bank.

WHO (World Health Organization). 2006a. *Palliative Care: Cancer Control—Knowledge into Action. WHO Guide for Effective Programs: Module 5.* Geneva: WHO. http://www.who.int/cancer/publications/cancer_control _palliative/en/index.html.

———. 2006b. *Planning: Cancer Control—Knowledge into Action. WHO Guide for Effective Programmes: Module 1.* Geneva: WHO. http://www.who.int/cancer/publications /cancer_control_planning/en/index.html.

———. 2006c. *Quality of Care: A Process for Making Strategic Choices in Health Systems.* Geneva: WHO.

http://www.who.int/management/quality/assurance/ QualityCare_B.Def.pdf.

———. 2012. *Assessing National Capacity for the Prevention and Control of Noncommunicable Diseases: Report of the 2010 Global Survey.* Geneva: WHO.

Wiernikowski, J. T. 2013. "Equitable Access to Chemotherapy, Supportive Care Drugs and Pharmaceutical Care: A Challenge for Low- and Middle-Income Countries." *Cancer Control* 146. http://globalhealthdynamics.co.uk/cc2013 /wp-content/uploads/2013/04/146-isopp.pdf.

World Alliance for Patient Safety. 2008. *Implementation Manual: WHO Surgical Safety Checklist*, 1st ed. Geneva: World Health Organization. http://www.who.int/patientsafety /safesurgery/ss_checklist/en/index.html.

Zaidi, Z. 2010. "Accreditation Standards for Medical Imaging Services." *Indian Journal of Radiology and Imaging* 20 (2): 89–91.

Screening for Cancer: Considerations for Low- and Middle-Income Countries

Terrence Sullivan, Richard Sullivan, and Ophira M. Ginsburg

INTRODUCTION

The goal of cancer screening is to detect cancer or precancerous lesions in asymptomatic individuals at a point when cancer is more likely to be prevented or cured than if the patient waited for symptoms to develop (Morrison 1992). A screening intervention can be successful only if the disease is more likely to be cured when detected early, and for which effective treatment for early-stage disease is available, affordable, and acceptable to the individual, the community, and the jurisdiction of interest. This chapter briefly describes the principles and pitfalls of cancer screening, based largely on the experience in high-income countries (HICs); summarizes the evidence for screening "best buys" relevant to low- and middle-income countries (LMICs); and highlights opportunities to avoid some of the costly and vexatious problems associated with screening in HICs and LMICs. The chapter focuses principally on existing projects and recent literature on cancer screening in LMICs.

Policy considerations regarding whether and in what manner to implement a cancer screening program should be based on systematic evaluation of several factors, including at a minimum: the burden of the cancer in the population of interest (those at risk), the cost effectiveness of the proposed screening intervention, and how well a given screening test performs in the target population. How well the test works can be judged by how many individuals must be screened to prevent one death from that cancer, balanced with how many people who undergo screening have a positive or abnormal test result when they do not have cancer (false-positive test), and how many have a normal result when they in fact do have cancer (false-negative test). The number of individuals with positive results who will actually proceed to follow up and receive treatment is a critical issue to consider for a given population. Other critical considerations include the cost effectiveness of a screening intervention when moving from initial trials to scale and the health system requirements needed to ensure the success of a given program. (See chapters 11, 16, and 17 for more on health systems.)

In this chapter, we selected three cancer sites for which there is the most evidence for screening effectiveness in LMICs—breast, cervical, and colorectal—and three promising candidate conditions.

DEFINITIONS OF AND CRITERIA FOR CANCER SCREENING

Opportunistic versus Organized Screening

Opportunistic screening or *case finding* occurs when an asymptomatic individual actively seeks a screening procedure or a health professional offers a screening test to an asymptomatic individual.

Organized screening occurs when there is an organized, population-based program with a structured

Corresponding author: Terrence Sullivan, PhD, terrence.sullivan@utoronto.ca public health approach. Organized screening has six elements (IARC 2005):

- An explicit policy that specifies eligible age categories, methods, and screening intervals
- A defined target population
- A dedicated and responsible management team responsible for implementation
- Associated teams for decision and care
- Specified methods for quality assurance
- Screening methods to identify cancer occurrence in the target population.

In *population-based screening*, the elements of the screening pathway are planned for an entire population and are delivered, monitored, and evaluated for effectiveness and quality to ensure that the benefits are maximized in a cost-effective way. Although the approach to implementation may be phased or staged geographically or by age intervals, the intention for population screening is to capture all at-risk individuals in the appropriate age interval. Organized screening is expensive and can succeed only if adequate resources exist to achieve the full trajectory of screening, with program quality assurance, including effective reach to all in the target population group (appropriate age, gender, and risk category) and follow-up for disease assessment, diagnosis, and treatment if disease is discovered.

High-risk screening targets known subpopulations of men or women who may be at considerably higher risk for specific cancer because of their genetic or risk exposure backgrounds. In HICs, such high-risk screening has included known single-gene mutations associated with breast or ovarian cancer—such as BRCA1 and BRCA2 mutations, or family history of breast or ovarian cancer—as well as similarly rare forms of hereditary colon cancers. In LMICs, a pragmatic example of screening of high-risk groups in South and Southeast Asia for oral cancer could apply to heavy smokers and drinkers who chew betel, areca nut, paan, and gutka.

The target age range of a screening program depends on several factors, including the following:

- Burden of the cancer in a given population
- Age-specific trends of the cancer, which may vary widely between countries
- Screening modality, the type of test used, for example, visual inspection with acetic acid (VIA) versus human papilloma virus (HPV) testing or combinations of these for cervical cancer
- Considerations regarding the capacity of local health systems.

Cervical cancer screening should begin only after a woman has become sexually active. When considering the choice of screening method, HPV screening is not advised until a woman is 30 years of age, as younger women are more likely to naturally "clear" the virus through the immune system. Overtreatment, particularly of young women, may lead to fertility problems in the future (chapter 4 in this volume [Denny and others 2015]).

The optimal frequency or interval for cancer screening depends on the capacity of the health system, as well as the cancer's natural history, which includes the rate of growth. Fast-growing cancers are less amenable to screening, while slower-growing, indolent cancers with a more predictable natural history (for example, colonic polyps or cervical precancerous lesions) are more obvious candidates for a screening intervention (Esserman, Thompson, and Reid 2013). Breast cancer has many different subtypes (for example, estrogen and/or progesterone receptor positive and negative, her2neu positive and negative) with a broad range of growth rates, patterns of spread (metastases), and prognoses (Carey and others 2006; Van de Vijver and others 2002). This complex natural history of breast cancer and the expense of subtyping breast cancer are among the reasons for the ongoing debate regarding the utility of screening mammography in HICs.

It is important to consider potential sources of bias when evaluating the effectiveness of organized cancer screening programs. Three such forms of bias are lead-time bias, length bias, and overdiagnosis.

- **Lead-time bias**
  Survival time for cancer patients is usually measured from the day the cancer is diagnosed until the day they die. Patients are often diagnosed after they have symptoms. If a screening test leads to a diagnosis before symptoms develop, the survival time is increased because the date of diagnosis is earlier. This increase in survival time makes it seem as though screened patients are living longer when that may not be the case. This is called *lead-time bias*. Screened patients may die at the same time they would have without the screening test.

  Lead-time bias has been a particular challenge for screening with prostate specific antigen in HICs. As part of the American Board of Internal Medicine's Choosing Wisely campaign, the American Society of Clinical Oncology added prostate screening to its updated "Top Five List" of oncology practices that should be stopped because they are not supported by the evidence or are considered wasteful (Schnipper and others 2013).

- **Length bias**

  Another source of potential bias is apparent when screening detects mostly indolent, slowly progressive tumors while missing the more aggressive ones. As an example, some types of breast cancer are indolent and can be asymptomatic for years; others are much more aggressive and have a far shorter asymptomatic period. The latter are more likely to cause symptoms between screening intervals and may cause a patient to seek medical attention prior to ever participating in cancer screening. Consequently, a screening test will detect more slow-growing than fast-growing cancers, giving a false impression that screening lengthens survival, when in fact it is merely detecting a subset of a more treatable disease (Family Practice Notebook 2011).

- **Overdiagnosis**

  Interest in cancer screening in LMICs is growing at a time when concerns about overdiagnosis and overtreatment, with resulting costs to the health care system, as well as the psychosocial, physical, and economic risks incurred by individuals are increasingly a matter of concern in HICs. *Overdiagnosis* is the diagnosis of disease that will never cause symptoms or death during a patient's lifetime. It can be viewed as a side effect of testing for early forms of disease that may turn people into patients unnecessarily and may lead to treatments that do no good and perhaps do harm. This is especially relevant for breast and prostate cancer (Esserman, Thompson, and Reid 2013; Welch, Schwartz, and Woloshin 2011; Yaffe and Pritchard 2014). Overdiagnosis in breast screening is discussed further in the section on breast screening in this chapter.

  Another important debate in HICs is about how much screening causes harm from a false-positive screening test, which often leads to significant wait-times for additional imaging tests and/or a tissue biopsy for what ultimately proves to be a benign finding. False-positive screens must be balanced against the benefits conferred by finding screen-detected cancers that genuinely extend survival and reduce mortality.

Criteria for Cancer Screening

Screening for cancer can be effective if the criteria are met. The Wilson-Junger (1968) criteria (box 12.1) set out a series of considerations that, notwithstanding updates in an era of molecular and genetic diagnostics, remain worthy criteria to help make an assessment. Modern variants of the criteria extend to the consideration of genetic susceptibility, in addition to preclinical disease or precursors (Goel 2001).

Box 12.1

Principles of Early Disease Detection

Condition
- The condition should be an important health problem.
- There should be a recognizable latent or early symptomatic stage.
- The natural history of the condition, including development from latent to declared disease, should be adequately understood.

Test
- There should be a suitable test or examination.
- The test should be acceptable to the population.

Treatment
- There should be an accepted treatment for patients with recognized disease.

Screening Program
- There should be an established policy on whom to treat as patients.
- Facilities for diagnosis and treatment should be available. The cost of case-finding, including diagnosis and treatment, should be economically balanced in relation to possible expenditure on medical care as a whole.
- Case-finding should be a continuing process and not a "once and for all" project.

Source: Adapted from Wilson and Junger 1968.

SYSTEM REQUIREMENTS FOR ORGANIZED CANCER SCREENING

Infrastructure, Education, and Advocacy

The reality in many LMICs is quite different from that in HICs with longstanding cancer health promotion efforts and organized screening programs. Organized approaches to screening risk straining the burden on already thin health care and public health resources. Delayed presentation for cancer is the norm in many LMICs and within low-resource or geographically remote regions in upper-middle-income countries. This delay exists for a variety of structural, equity, and sociocultural reasons (Knaul, Frenk, and Shulman 2011; Story and others 2012). Structural obstacles include the following:

- Strained health infrastructure, for example, the lack of available human and technical resources for proper diagnosis and disease management
- Long distances and poor road conditions that render proper care inaccessible
- Sociocultural barriers, including extreme poverty, myths, and stigma about cancer
- Gender inequity, which is especially relevant to breast and cervical cancer (Errico and Rowden 2006; Ginsburg 2013; Price and others 2012; Vorobiof, Sitas, and Vorobiof 2001)

Such obstacles underscore the need to incorporate a range of decisions in LMICs to inform the optimal approach to screening. Options vary from an opportunistic case-finding approach, to a population-based screening model, to a high-risk screening approach. Regardless of the approach taken, a new cancer screening program will contribute to increasing the number of prevalent cases. This additional burden of disease can be substantial and should be viewed as a potential strain on local capacity at all levels—public health, primary care, diagnostic, and treatment facilities. In regions with severely constrained health infrastructure, the effects of the screening program must be carefully considered prior to planning and implementing an organized screening program. Decisions regarding the choice of cancer sites, screening strategies, and target populations should be informed not only by cost considerations, but also by an understanding of the local burden of disease, sociocultural contexts, health systems, infrastructure, human resource capacity, community acceptability, and local political will.

Irrespective of the approach to screening, to scale up organized screening projects, initial plans require rigorous evaluation as well as knowledge translation and exchange to all relevant stakeholders, including community agencies and patient advocacy groups. Whether in low-, middle-, or high-income settings, key factors for community acceptance and success include early and high levels of engagement with community and medical leaders, education, advocacy, and the establishment of adequate infrastructure and information systems to promote screening and capture initial diagnosis, treatment, and active follow-up information. Follow-up for those with a positive (for example, abnormal) screening test should include a well-developed care pathway to ensure timely referrals for further evaluation, which may include another imaging modality (for example, breast ultrasound), a biopsy, or surgery, as well as a timely and accurate pathology result. For those with a cancer diagnosis, appropriate referral for evidence-based and resource-appropriate treatment planning is essential, begging again the capacity to make it so in LMICs. Those with a negative screening test should be offered "invitations" for their next round of screening, according to local guidelines (for example, a woman age 60 years who is of average population risk can be invited by mail or telephone to schedule her next screening mammogram two years from the last negative screen).

Cost-Effectiveness Considerations

Cost considerations should include excess direct and indirect health care expenditures for cancers detected at an advanced stage, including out-of-pocket expenses and caregivers' time away from work. Any analysis should also consider the case for such investment, describing macroeconomic cost models and potential savings from treatment and prevention of cancer sites for which prevention or early detection can have the largest impact on morbidity and mortality (Knaul, Frenk, and Shulman 2011). Estimated losses are presented with more- or less-conservative estimates of avoidable deaths.

According to these models for 2010, global investments in cancer care and control might have saved from US$10 million to US$230 million in disability-adjusted life years (DALYs), or US$531 million to almost US$1 trillion in value of statistical life. Further, Knaul, Frenk, and Shulman (2011) highlight greater cost savings from adopting a prevention/early detection-and-treatment approach versus a treatment-only approach for breast and cervical cancer. Cancer screening policy may be framed in terms of *investments*, although the timeline to downstream benefits (such as DALYs saved or citizens remaining in the workforce longer) will certainly outspan the political cycle and will depend on how robust and effective the screening program becomes. Cost-effectiveness analysis should also consider the opportunity costs of not screening, specifically for cancers where early detection and appropriate treatment may significantly improve survival rates, such as breast, cervical, and colorectal cancer.

Ethical Considerations

In addition to economic considerations, ethical obligations require jurisdictions to ensure that benefits outweigh harms and that the diagnostic and treatment resources are sufficient to justify from the outset the initiation of a screening program. Recently, some investigators have suggested that the informed population's preference should also be a factor in such deliberations (Harris and others 2011). The informed population may have a fair say in the design and buy-in for new screening programs, but countries with established cancer screening policies may find it problematic to separate informed preferences from the popular view that earlier detection is invariably better.

This viewpoint is attributable in part to what Gilbert Welch refers to as the *popularity paradox*, whereby the very modest benefits of some forms of screening are interpreted by the individuals who have detected early-stage disease as having had their disease cured or survival improved as a function of screening (Welch, in Raffle and Gray 2007). Few cancer care professionals and few screening policy makers will counter this view publicly because there is no simple way other than the fullness of time to fully determine whether the disease is "cured." Nor is there much compassion to be earned for calling into question patients who optimistically, but in many cases mistakenly, believe they have had their disease cured. Counterintuitively, the greater the extent of overdiagnosis and overtreatment, the greater the number of screened individuals who believe they owe their lives to the screening program. While the popularity paradox has been identified in HICs, this experience may provide cautionary advice to LMICs that are contemplating establishing screening programs. By contrast, high-risk areas in LMICs consist of specific countries, regions, and subpopulations that bear the disproportionate burden of premature mortality in a range of lethal cancers, including liver, stomach, esophagus, and oral cancer.

CANCER SCREENING CANDIDATES IN LMICs

Overall and site-specific cancer mortality rates can be gender-specific. For women in LMICs, breast and cervical cancer are the leading causes of cancer death, followed by lung, stomach, and liver cancer. For men in these geographical areas, lung, liver, stomach, esophagus, and colon cancer represent the highest mortality burden. The following sections explore the value of screening among several of these candidate conditions.

Breast Cancer

Breast cancer, the most common cancer in women worldwide, is the leading cause of cancer deaths in women in most jurisdictions with reliable data. More than 50 percent of breast cancer deaths occur in LMICs.[1] These rates will continue to grow with development (Bray and others 2012), which has gone hand in hand with the Westernization of diets and reproductive

patterns—fewer children, later first childbirth, and shorter breastfeeding periods. These are factors that raise the risk of breast cancer (Corbex, Burton, and Sancho-Garnier 2012; Porter 2008).

The debate regarding overdiagnosis is of particular relevance to breast cancer screening; it is estimated that from 10 to 30 percent of breast cancer detected through population-based screening mammography may never have resulted in clinically significant disease but triggers full-scale treatment.

A moderate view is that despite some limitations in all screening studies, breast screening mammography has benefits that outweigh harms, and a frank discussion should take place between health care providers and their patients, so that each woman can make an informed decision. In 2012, the National Cancer Institute (U.S.) convened a task force to address overdiagnosis in cancer screening. The task force concluded that while screening is intended to detect early-stage cancer to improve the likelihood of cure, finding more indolent cancers with "better biology" also contributes to better outcomes. The task force suggested that policies be developed to help mitigate the problems of overdetection and over-treatment, "while maintaining those gains by which early detection is a major contributor to decreasing mortality and locally advanced disease," (Esserman, Thompson, and Reid 2013, p. 798) and recommend that health care providers and patients openly discuss the issues, which the media should better understand and communicate to the public.

Despite these controversies, breast cancer mortality has been declining in many HICs where mammogram screening programs have been in place for over 20 years (OECD 2011). Many agree that this reflects a combination of newer effective therapies, improved breast awareness, and advocacy campaigns, but the relative contribution of each of these factors is difficult to isolate (Kalager, Adami, and Bretthauer 2014). Of relevance to LMICs, Kalager, Adami, and Bretthauer's commentary on the Canadian National Breast Screening Study 25-year follow-up noted that the study lacked a "mammogram only" arm, which limited the ability to determine the effects of clinical breast examination (CBE) alone versus mammography alone. The authors allude to the potential risk of generalizing to other countries and suggest that early detection may be of greater benefit in communities where most breast cancers present clinically with more advanced disease. In regions where no such advocacy and awareness campaigns exist, it remains unclear how much early detection for breast cancer (or other cancers for which screening is promoted in HICs) can be achieved by a combination of advocacy and awareness campaigns to reduce stigma and overcome cancer myths, and by implementing lower-cost but potentially effective screening interventions such as CBE.

The use of mammography for mass screening for breast cancer requires expensive machinery, with its own measurable risk, adequate distribution of radiologists and radiographers, and complex quality controls. Moreover, as overall incidence rates remain lower in LMICs relative to HICs and the average age of women with breast cancer is lower than in HICs, the overall benefit-to-harm ratio will be correspondingly lower whether mammography or simpler techniques, such as CBE with a skilled trainee, are used.

A recent systematic review of economic analyses of breast cancer control in LMICs concludes that the evidence base for guidance on screening modality (for example, CBE versus mammography), the frequency of screening, and the target population is limited and of poor quality (Zelle and Baltussen 2013). Anderson and others in chapter 3 explore in detail the most promising of the early detection studies reviewed by Zelle and Baltussen and recommend that early detection programs in LMICs be carefully designed to facilitate early phase evaluation.

Self-screening or breast self-examination in LMICs appears to present greater harms than benefits based on one large Asian trial (Thomas and others 2002). A lower risk of mortality or advanced breast cancer was found in a meta-analysis of breast self-examination only in studies of women with breast cancer who reported practicing breast self-examination before diagnosis (Hackshaw and Paul 2003); no difference was found in the death rate in studies on women who detected their cancer during an examination. Despite conflicting evidence for CBE in some low-income and lower-middle-income country settings (Nguyen and others 2013; Pisani and others 2006), Anderson and others in chapter 3 of this volume note that a case remains to be made for CBE as a means of stage shifting, especially in populations where the average tumor size at presentation is considerably larger than that in most of the breast screening studies to date. Reasonable evidence suggests that formal training in CBE for primary care professionals can improve the sensitivity of the procedure and reduce the number of false positives (Vetto and others 2002).

The Breast Health Global Initiative has developed an evidence-based, resource-stratified approach to early detection and screening, as well as diagnosis, treatment, and most recently, supportive care and quality of life (Anderson 2013). Recommendations for resource allocation include not only the screening modalities such as CBE, mammography, and diagnostic ultrasound, but culturally-sensitive and linguistically-appropriate local programs to teach the value of early detection as well as risk factors and breast health (Anderson 2013). Evaluation goals are included for each resource level for public education and awareness, as well as detection methods. Recognizing that great differences in health systems and infrastructure often exist within countries, most notably from urban centers to rural areas, stratification is based on on-the-ground capacities, rather than a single country-level determination, such as gross domestic product per capita.

There is an important role for improved breast cancer awareness among the general population in LMICs as well as primary care practitioners; this can be an entry point to any early detection program. In the absence of evidence of the benefits from a systematic assessment of CBE-based organized screening, we will await the final results from the Mumbai trial (Mittra and others 2010) and the Trivandrum trial of CBE in India (Sankaranarayanan and Bofetta 2010) for any definitive story on CBE as an organized screening tool. Notwithstanding the absence of definitive experimental evidence for implementing organized CBE-based screening as a preferred approach to screen for breast cancer, there is value in trying to strengthen primary care skill in CBE to improve early case-finding and diagnostic activity among symptomatic women, since the large majority of breast cancers are diagnosed in women with breast lumps.

Cervical Cancer

Cervical screening may have the greatest potential for screening-detected reductions in cancer mortality in less developed regions, where about 85 percent of all new cases and 87 percent of deaths from cervical cancer occur (Ferlay and others 2013). The incidence of cervical cancer is highly correlated with country income group, the prevalence of high-risk subtypes of the causal agent HPV (particularly HPV 16 and 18, which account for approximately 70 percent of the case burden), and whether the country or region of interest has had a longstanding population-based screening program (see chapter 4 in this volume). In terms of DALYs, which depend also on the average age at which individuals are affected, cervical cancer ranks highest by, and is correlated with, a lower human development index, a composite measure that includes life expectancy, education, and income (Soerjomataram and others 2012).

Despite the efficacy of cytology-based mass screening programs, Papanicolaou, or Pap, testing is costly, complex, and requires robust health systems. Chapter 4 in this volume notes the poor penetration of widespread Pap testing owing to such costs. The unequal burden of mortality as a consequence reflects unequal access in less developed countries. Newer and less expensive strategies to prevent cervical cancer have been evaluated and the introduction of new HPV vaccines offers real prevention prospects for the first time.

VIA in combination with cryotherapy (screen-and-treat) was trialed in a demonstration project in Ghana and was well accepted by the communities involved (Blumenthal and others 2007). This effort underlines the value of simple and effective technologies for low-resource settings despite inadequate coverage and significant numbers lost to follow-up. A one-time screening at 35 years of age with VIA or HPV testing reduced the lifetime risk of cervical cancer by approximately 25 to 36 percent and cost less than US$500 per year of life saved (Goldie and others 2005).

Two exciting trials reporting on test-and-treat models in India (Sankaranarayanan and others 2009) and South Africa (Denny and others 2010) have highlighted the superiority of a screen-and-treat approach that uses relatively more expensive HPV testing over VIA, whether followed by colposcopy in the Indian trial or cryotherapy in the South African trial. The Indian trial showed that a single round of HPV testing can reduce the incidence of advanced cancers and deaths from cervical cancer. The South African study showed benefits in the VIA group, but HPV DNA testing most effectively reduced the incidence of advanced invasive cancer that developed more than 12 months after cryotherapy. HPV DNA testing, with or without VIA, shows the greatest promise; however, given the current state of pathology infrastructure and cost considerations for less developed regions and, in particular, for rural populations in LICs and lower-middle-income countries, the introduction of mass screening with VIA may be the most prudent real-world approach.

In addition, several combination modes of preventive HPV vaccination in preadolescent girls, combined with various screening measures in adult women, appear promising as a comprehensive method to reduce the burden of cervical cancer and reduce HPV infection. In Sub-Saharan Africa in particular, a strong case exists for screening with VIA and rapid HPV tests to ramp up prevention and detection services to screen, treat, or refer. This approach would allow for the opportunity to deal with any other gynecological issues. Populations with coterminous HPV and HIV infections are at highest risk and have the highest need for cervical cancer prevention focus (Sahasrabuddhe and others 2012).

With respect to the cost effectiveness of cervical screening programs, recent analyses demonstrate that there are promising opportunities to prevent cervical cancer in different world settings. As stated in chapter 4, HPV vaccination for preadolescent girls and/or screening

of adult women, even only three times per lifetime, can avert a significant proportion of cervical cancer cases in a cost-effective manner. In addition to many other critical inputs to health decisions, such as political will and cultural acceptability, evidence on the cost effectiveness and affordability of HPV vaccination and screening from rigorous model-based analyses can help to inform decision makers and stakeholders in their deliberations of how best to prevent cervical cancer worldwide.

Colorectal Cancer

Lambert, Sauvaget, and Sankaranarayanan (2009) advance a strong argument that the burden of colorectal cancer, while high and growing in HIC regions (about 12 percent of deaths from cancer), remains low on the list of common cancers and primary causes of cancer-related mortality in less developed regions (about 6 percent of deaths from cancer). Lambert, Sauvaget, and Sankaranarayanan argue that the expense of mounting a mass screening effort in most LMICs is not currently justified, given the significant costs of colonoscopy and follow-up services. The authors do allow that the growth of more Western lifestyles in large urban centers in upper-middle-income countries may represent areas where colon screening may be more justifiable.

By contrast, as noted in chapter 16 of this volume, at least one report suggests that screening colonoscopy may be cost effective in Sub-Saharan Africa (Ginsberg and others 2012), at least in the urban areas of upper-middle-income countries, where the incidence of colorectal cancer is increasing because of population aging and the adoption of Western lifestyles.

The International Colorectal Cancer Screening Network (2013), which works to document and standardize the best jurisdictional approaches to colorectal screening, identifies the need for screening program experience on every continent, although membership is currently limited to more developed regions. Research in progress may offer a range of promising and less invasive methods to detect early-stage colon cancer, which may offer better options to reduce colon cancer mortality in LMICs.

A phased introduction of colorectal cancer screening by immune sensitive fecal occult blood testing in Thailand, beginning with a pilot evaluation in Lampang province, shows promise for reducing colon cancer mortality. The program is based on a five-year interval for immune fecal testing, which is supportable by the health system infrastructure and appropriate, given the relatively lower colon cancer rates compared with other countries with screening programs (Khuhaprema and others 2014).

Promising New Candidates

Simple visual screening methods in high-risk areas for oral cancer in South Asia and Southeast Asia represent an excellent example of pragmatic screening (Sankaranarayanan and others 2005). These cancers are highly linked to tobacco and alcohol consumption, as well as to chewing betel and areca nut and paan and gutka (see chapter 5). Increasing evidence suggests that HPV is a risk factor in oral, head, and neck cancers. Most cost-effectiveness studies come from HICs, but one very promising study from India suggests that oral cancer screening by visual inspection has an incremental cost-effectiveness ratio of US$835 per life year saved (Subramanian and others 2009). Further, the authors note that the most prudent approach for limited resource settings should include only higher risk populations, such as heavy users of tobacco and alcohol. There is now some trial evidence that visual screening can reduce oral cancer mortality in users of tobacco and alcohol (Sankaranarayanan and others 2013).

By contrast, in HICs, a recent assessment from the U.S. Preventive Services Task Force has concluded that the case for mass screening for oral cancers in the relatively lower risk United States is insufficient to justify the harms of mass screening of asymptomatic adults (Moyer and U.S. Preventive Services Task Force 2014).

Gastric cancer is a close tie with liver cancer as the second leading cancer-related cause of death and is a particular challenge in the East Asia and Pacific region. Promising programs are being mounted in Japan and the Republic of Korea and in trials in China to screen for the bacterium *Helicobacter pylori*, the cause of a large fraction of gastric cancer, and to eradicate infections detected. However, *H. pylori* eradication, which reduces gastric cancer risk, is hampered by emerging regional antimicrobial resistance to antibiotics used to treat it and the lack of a means to target a high-risk population. Gastric cancer remains a screening and prevention candidate in need of more refined trials (Park and others 2013).

SPECIAL CONSIDERATIONS FOR CANCER SCREENING IN LMICs

Screening Priorities in LMICs

Promising cancer screening candidates in each of the less developed regions warrant attention. The joint report of the World Economic Forum/Harvard School of Public Health and the World Health Organization highlights a set of affordable, feasible, and cost-effective intervention strategies to reduce the economic impact of noncommunicable diseases in LMICs (WEF 2011).

The most promising evidence in LMICs suggests that the highest priorities are breast and cervical cancer screening, possibly followed by colorectal cancer or stomach cancer screening, if programmatic infrastructure can be established in a stepwise fashion. Carefully planned programs for breast screening, according to local context and resource capacity as highlighted in the Breast Health Global Initiative documents, and VIA with cryosurgery or colposcopy (with or without HPV testing, where available) can appropriately be recommended as first cancer screening priorities in LMICs.

Role of Innovation

Many opportunities already exist to exploit the potential impact of programs for early detection and screening. Considering a given screening strategy for which locally-sourced evidence demonstrates at least proof of concept in terms of efficacy and cost effectiveness, transition-to-scale projects can take advantage of a variety of innovative approaches to optimize participation, follow-up for an abnormal screening, as well as monitoring for treatment-related toxicities and survivorship care. These approaches include telemedicine; telepathology; institutional twinning; task-shifting; and "m-Health" (WHO 2011a, 2011b), models of care enhanced by the use of mobile phones, which are widely available and affordable in most LMICs (Ginsburg 2013). Large technical platforms can give way to cloud applications, which allow for easy and secure storage and compilation of information for screening programs. However, this still requires a basic information and communications technology infrastructure, computer availability, and up-to-date software, which are missing in many countries.

Similarly, not all screening activity needs to involve only primary care physicians or specialty care providers, if reliable evidence is used to build from project-to-scale programs. In this fashion, trained community care workers, nurses, and other care providers can assist in building capacity, promoting screening activities, and being effective screening agents in LMICs.

Diagonal Approach to Strengthen Health Systems

From a programmatic perspective, the breast and cervical cancer studies also indicate some merit in an integrated approach to screening under the umbrella of maternal or reproductive health policy, as suggested in the trial in Mumbai (Mittra and others 2010) and the approach taken in Morocco.[2] The Global Task Force on

Expanded Access to Cancer Care and Control (2011) has championed this diagonal approach, "the proactive, supply-driven provision of a set of highly cost-effective interventions on a large scale that bridges health clinics and homes" (Sepúlveda 2006). While the age intervals best chosen for a first screening intervention may not be an exact match, for women undergoing simultaneous screening efforts, there is at least the prospect of having both screening procedures performed during the same visit, a predictor of better participation than multiple visits, an observation now being mimicked in HICs. "Pink Ribbon Red Ribbon" (UNAIDS 2011) is an example of a program that added breast and cervical cancer screening to an existing program for another health condition, namely, HIV. HIV-positive women have a greater chance of developing invasive cervical cancer and higher mortality rates than their HIV-negative counterparts. This type of program can address the needs of a group at particularly high risk with a low marginal cost.

Such a diagonal approach is not limited to women's health services. Integrating cancer screening into existing health programs can also help to build primary care capacity. Harnessing the synergies between traditionally vertical programs can build platforms onto which additional preventive and wellness care (such as vaccinations, smoking cessation, and nutritional counseling) may be added to reduce the incidence and mortality from other cancers (such as lung, stomach, or oral), as well as other high-burden chronic noncommunicable diseases. Modeling such programs can also help to convince policy makers that cancer screening and cancer control in general will not necessarily siphon off scarce resources from competing health priorities.

Policy Considerations for Cancer Screening in LMICs

Cancer screening policies and the programs they create become part of established health care systems in governments and societies, each with its own norms and standards. Although the evidence base may be global for any particular cancer, policies and programs vary considerably across the globe, not just between countries according to level of wealth, but among countries of similar economic status. Some differences mirror the huge variation in the incidence of different cancers, but many are caused by differential weighting of evidence and other factors.

Developing a screening policy for cancer involves many decisions, including choice of diagnostic technologies and follow-up interventions, the age groups targeted, referral and enrollment strategies,

and quality assurance processes. The heterogeneity of cancer screening policies across LMICs reflects differences in health care structures as well as the political and cultural factors that shape policy. The governance mechanisms for the development of screening policy may also vary. Some countries use a legislative approach to mandate screening, thus opening policy development to political influence. In other countries, policy development is delegated to technocrats who rely on advice from expert committees or ad hoc groups. Screening policy in LMICs often involves several layers of organization, including transnational actors (for example, the United Nations Population Fund), national health ministries, and experts in various disciplines, as well as prominent domestic and global advocacy groups. The respective roles of authorities is another source of variation, as is the degree of reliance on or participation in the development of policy at the transnational level (for example, guidelines) and how this is shaped by the institutional processes of decision making (Flintcroft 2011).

Cancer screening policies sometimes run counter to what would seem to reflect the best evidence (Nutley, Walter, and Davies 2007). Knowing the diversity of factors (political, social, and economic) that contribute to the development of the health policies reinforces the understanding that the way that research influences policy is not linear and not necessarily determined by the quality of the research alone (Humpreys and Piot 2012; Nightingale and Scott 2007). In fact, many accepted models of public health policy making for cancer screening (research utilization) have likened the process to a complex dance (Edwards 2001), a garbage can of ideas waiting to be needed (Cohen, March, and Olsen 1972), and parallel streams awaiting a social, political, or economic reason to stimulate a convergence and therefore the formation of policy (Kingdon 2003). The policy process can become more transparent and outcomes more predictable (although still respecting national differences) with standardized decision making systems that encompass the principles of health technology assessment for all policy decisions that involve weighing evidence on effectiveness, costs, and societal factors.

Ultimately, the success of a cancer screening policy and its associated program depends not only on the evidence base, but also on the willingness of the public to take part in the screening process. This, in turn depends to a great extent on how the benefits and risks of the procedure are communicated (McCormack and others 2011) and how the program fits within the health care system and with other health messages, including cancer prevention.

ACKNOWLEDGMENT

The authors express special thanks to Signy Roland for her support in the compilation and extraction of the studies discussed in this chapter and to Sandra Hofstetter for her support in compiling the manuscript.

NOTES

World Bank income classifications as of July 2014 are as follows, based on estimates of gross national income per capita for 2013:

- Low-income countries: US$1,045 or less
- Middle-income countries:
  - Lower-middle-income: US$1,046–US$4,125
  - Upper-middle-income: US$4,126–US$12,745
- High-income countries: US$12,746 or more

1. http://www.who.int/cancer/detection/breastcancer/en /index1.html.
2. "Importance of the Screening," Fondation Lalla Salma Prévention et Traitement des Cancers, accessed March 8, 2014, http://www.contrelecancer.ma/en/importance_du _depistage.

REFERENCES

Anderson, B. 2013. "Context-Relevant Guidelines in Cancer Care: Breast Cancer Early Detection, Diagnosis, and Treatment in Low and Middle Income Countries." In *Cancer Control 2013*, edited by Ian McGrath, 36–40. http:// globalhealthdynamics.co.uk/cc2013/wp-content/uploads /2013/04/36-40-Benjamin-O-Anderson_2013.pdf.

Blumenthal, P. D., L. Gaffikin, S. Deganus, R. Lewis, M. Emerson, and others. 2007. "Cervical Cancer Prevention: Safety, Acceptability, and Feasibility of a Single-Visit Approach in Accra, Ghana." *American Journal of Obstetrics and Gynecology* 196 (4): 407.e1–9.

Bray, F., A. Jemal, N. Grey, J. Ferlay, and F. Forman. 2012. "Global Cancer Transitions According to the Human Development Index (2008–2030): A Population-Based Study." *The Lancet* 13: 790–801.

Carey, L. A., C. M. Perou, C. A. Livasy, L. G. Dressler, D. Cowan, and others. 2006. "Race, Breast Cancer Subtypes, and Survival in the Carolina Breast Cancer Study." *Journal of the American Medical Association* 295 (21): 2492–502.

Cohen, M. D., J. G. March, and J. P. Olsen. 1972. "A Garbage Can Model of Organizational Choice." *Administrative Science Quarterly* 17: 1–25.

Corbex, M., R. Burton, and H. Sancho-Garnier. 2012. "Breast Cancer Early Detection Methods for Low and Middle Income Countries." *The Breast* 21 (4): 428–34.

Denny, L., R. Herrero, C. Levin, and D. B. Thomas. 2015. "Cervical Cancer." In *Disease Control Priorities* (third edition): Volume 3, *Cancer*, edited by H. Gelband, P. Jha, R. Sankaranarayanan, and S. Horton. Washington, DC: World Bank.

Denny, L., L. Kuhn, C. C. Hu, W. Y. Tsai, and T. C. Wright Jr. 2010. "Human Papillomavirus-Based Cervical Cancer Prevention: Long-Term Results of a Randomized Screening Trial." *Journal of the National Cancer Institute* 102 (20): 1–11.

Edwards, M. 2001. Social Policy, Public Policy: From Problems to Practice. St. Leonards, NSW: Allen & Unwin.

Errico, K. M., and D. Rowden. 2006. "Experiences of Breast Cancer Survivor-Advocates and Advocates in Countries with Limited Resources: A Shared Journey in Breast Cancer Advocacy." *The Breast Journal* 12 (Suppl. 1): 111–16.

Esserman, L., I. Thompson Jr., and B. Reid. 2013. "Overdiagnosis and Overtreatment in Cancer: An Opportunity for Improvement." *Journal of the American Medical Association* 310 (8): 797–98. doi:10.1001/jama.2013.108415.

Family Practice Notebook. 2011. *Length Bias*. http://www .fpnotebook.com/Prevent/Epi/LngthBs.htm.

Ferlay J, Soerjomataram I, Ervik M, Dikshit R, Eser S, Mathers C, Rebelo M, Parkin DM, Forman D, Bray, F. GLOBOCAN 2012 v1.0, Cancer Incidence and Mortality Worldwide: IARC CancerBase No. 11 [Internet]. Lyon, France: International Agency for Research on Cancer; 2013. Available from: http:// globocan.iarc.fr, accessed on 23/11/2014.

Flintcroft, T. 2011. "Getting Evidence into Policy: The Need for Deliberative Strategies?" *Social Science & Medicine* 72: 1039–46.

Ginsberg, G. M., J. A. Lauer, S. Zelle, S. Baeten, and R. Baltussen. 2012. "Cost Effectiveness of Strategies to Combat Breast, Cervical, and Colorectal Cancer in Sub-Saharan Africa and South East Asia: Mathematical Modeling Study." *British Medical Journal* 344: e614.

Ginsburg, O. M. 2013. "Breast and Cervical Cancer Control in Low and Middle-Income Countries: Human Rights Meet Sound Health Policy." *Journal of Cancer Policy* 1 (3): e35–e41.

Global Task Force on Expanded Access to Cancer Care and Control in Developing Countries. 2011. *Closing the Divide: A Blueprint to Expand Access in Low- and Middle-Income Countries*. Boston, MA: Harvard Global Equity Initiative. http://ghsm.hms.harvard.edu/files/assets/Programs /NewbornHealth/files/ccd_report_bw.pdf.

Goel, V. 2001. "Appraising Organized Screen Programmes for Testing for Genetic Susceptibility to Cancer." *British Medical Journal* 322 (7295): 1174–78.

Goldie, S., G. Gaffikin, J. Goldhaber-Fiebert, A. Gordillo-Tobar, C. Levin, and others. 2005. "Cost-Effectiveness of Cervical-Cancer Screening in Five Developing Countries." *New England Journal of Medicine* 353: 2158–68.

Hackshaw, A. K., and E. A. Paul. 2003. "Breast Self-Examination and Death from Breast Cancer: A Meta-Analysis." *British Journal of Cancer* 88: 1047–53.

Harris, R., G. F. Sawaya, V. A. Moyer, and N. Calonge. 2011. "Reconsidering the Criteria for Evaluating Proposed Screening Programs: Reflections from 4 Current and Former Members of the U.S. Preventive Services Task

Force." *Epidemiologic Reviews* 33 (1): 20–35. doi:10.1093/epirev/mxr005.

Humpreys, K., and P. Piot. 2012. "Scientific Evidence Alone Is Not Sufficient Basis for Health Policy." *British Medical Journal* 344: e1316.

IARC (International Agency for Research on Cancer). 2005. *IARC Handbooks of Cancer Prevention: Cervix Cancer Screening.* Lyon, France: IARC. http://www.iarc.fr/en/publications/pdfs-online/prev/handbook10/HANDBOOK10.pdf.

International Colorectal Cancer Screening Network. 2013. "ICRCSN Publications." http://icrcsn.ceu.ox.ac.uk/publications.

Kalager, M., H. Adami, and M. Bretthauer. 2014. "Too Much Mammography." *British Medical Journal* 348: g1403. doi:http://dx.doi.org/10.1136/bmj.g1403.

Khuhaprema, T., S. Sangrajrang, S. Lalitwongsa, V. Chokvanitphong, T. Raunroadroong, and others. 2014. "Organised Colorectal Cancer Screening in Lampang Province, Thailand: Preliminary Results from a Pilot Implementation Programme." *British Medical Journal* 4: e003671. doi:10.1136/bmjopen-2013-003671.

Kingdon, J. 2003. *Agendas, Alternatives and Public Policies.* 2nd ed. New York: Longman.

Knaul, F., J. Frenk, and L. Shulman. 2011. *Closing the Cancer Divide: A Blueprint to Expand Access in Low and Middle Income Countries.* Boston, MA: Harvard Global Equity Initiative. http://gtfccc.harvard.edu/icb/icb.do?keyword=k69586&pageid=icb.page334798.

Lambert, R., C. Sauvaget, and R. Sankaranarayanan. 2009. "Mass Screening for Colorectal Cancer Is Not Justified in Most Developing Countries." *International Journal of Cancer* 125 (2): 253–56.

McCormack, L. A., K. Treiman, D. Rupert, P. Williams-Piehota, E. Nadler, and others. 2011. "Measuring Patient-Centered Communication in Cancer Care: A Literature Review and the Development of a Systematic Approach." *Social Science & Medicine* 72 (7): 1085–95.

Mittra, I., G. A. Mishra, S. Singh, S. Aranke, P. Notani, and others. 2010. "A Cluster Randomized, Controlled Trial of Breast and Cervix Cancer Screening in Mumbai, India: Methodology and Interim Results after Three Rounds of Screening." *International Journal of Cancer* 126 (4): 976–84. doi:10.1002/ijc.24840.

Morrison, A. S. 1992. *Screening in Chronic Disease.* New York: Oxford University Press.

Moyer, V. A., on behalf of the U.S. Preventive Services Task Force. 2014. "Screening for Oral Cancer: U.S. Preventive Services Task Force Recommendation Statement." *Annals of Internal Medicine* 160 (1): 55–60. doi:10.7326/M13-2568.

Nguyen, L. H., W. Laohasiriwong, J. F. Stewart, P. Wright, Y. T. B. Nguyen, and P. C. Coyte. 2013. "Cost-Effectiveness Analysis of a Screening Program for Breast Cancer in Vietnam." *Value in Health Regional Issues* 2 (1): 21–28.

Nightingale, P., and A. Scott. 2007. "Peer Review and the Relevance Gap: Ten Suggestions for Policymakers." *Science and Public Policy* 34: 543–553.

Nutley, S. M., I. Walter, and H. T. O. Davies. 2007. *Using Evidence: How Research Can Inform Public Services.* Bristol, UK: The Policy Press.

OECD (Organisation for Economic Co-operation and Development). 2011. *Screening, Survival and Mortality for Breast Cancer.* http://www.oecd-ilibrary.org/docserver/download/8111101ec048.pdf?expires=1394159448&id=id&accname=guest&checksum=2FC8D19B124E6033BD7AF114C1A8E2CB.

Park, J. Y., D. Forman, E. R. Greenberg, and R. Herrero. 2013. "Helicobacter Pylori Eradication in the Prevention of Gastric Cancer: Are More Trials Needed?" *Current Oncology Reports* 15 (6): 517–25.

Pisani, P., D. M. Parkin, C. Ngelangel, D. Esteban, L. Gibson, and others. 2006. "Outcome of Screening by Clinical Examination of the Breast in a Trial in the Philippines." *International Journal of Cancer* 118 (1): 149–54.

Porter, P. 2008. "'Westernizing' Women's Risks? Breast Cancer in Lower-Income Countries." *New England Journal of Medicine* 358: 213–16. doi:10.1056/NEJMp0708307.

Price, A. J., P. Ndom, E. Atenguena, J. P. Mambou Nouemssi, and R. W. Ryder. 2012. "Cancer Care Challenges in Developing Countries." *Cancer* 118 (14): 3627–35. doi:10.1002/cncr.26681.

Raffle, A., and M. Gray. 2007. *Screening: Evidence and Practice.* Oxford, UK: Oxford University Press.

Sahasrabuddhe, V. V., G. P. Parham, M. H. Mwanahamuntu, and S. H. Vermund. 2012. "Cervical Cancer Prevention in Low- and Middle-Income Countries: Feasible, Affordable, Essential." *Cancer Prevention and Research* 5 (1): 11–17.

Sankaranarayanan, R., and P. Bofetta. 2010. "Research on Cancer Prevention, Detection and Management in Low and Middle Income Countries." *Annals of Oncology* 21: 1935–43.

Sankaranarayanan, R., B. M. Nene, S. S. Shastri, K. Jayant, R. Muwonge, and others. 2009. "HPV Screening for Cervical Cancer in Rural India." *New England Journal of Medicine* 360: 1385–94.

Sankaranarayanan, R., K. Ramadas, S. Thara, R. Muwonge, G. Thomas, and others. 2013. "Long Term Effect of Visual Screening on Oral Cancer Incidence and Mortality in a Randomized Trial in Kerala, India." *Oral Oncology* 49 (4): 314–21.

Sankaranarayanan, R., K. Ramadas, G. Thomas, R. Muwonge, S. Thara, and others. 2005. "Effect of Screening on Oral Cancer Mortality in Kerala, India: A Cluster-Randomised Controlled Trial." *The Lancet* 365 (9475): 1927–33.

Schnipper, L. E., G. H. Lyman, D. W. Blayney, J. R. Hoverman, D. Raghavan, and others. 2013. "American Society of Clinical Oncology 2013 Top Five List in Oncology." *Journal of Clinical Oncology* 31 (34): 4362–70.

Sepúlveda, J. 2006. "Foreword." In *Disease Control Priorities in Developing Countries*, 2nd ed., edited by D. T. Jamison, J. G. Breman, A. R. Measham, G. Alleyne, M. Claeson, D. B. Evans, P. Jha, A. Mills, and P. Musgrove, xii–xv. Washington, DC: World Bank and Oxford University Press.

Soerjomataram, I., J. Lortet-Tieulent, D. M. Parkin, J. Ferlay, C. Mathers, and others. 2012. "Global Burden of Cancer in 2008: A Systematic Analysis of Disability-Adjusted Life Years in 12 World Regions." *The Lancet* 380 (9856): 125.

Story, H. L., R. R. Love, R. R. Salim, A. J. Roberto, J. L. Krieger, and others. 2012. "Improving Outcomes from Breast Cancer in a Low-Income Country: Lessons from Bangladesh." *International Journal of Breast Cancer.* doi:10.1155/2012/423562.

Subramanian, S., R. Sankaranarayanan, B. Bapat, T. Somanathan, G. Thomas, and others. 2009. "Cost-Effectiveness of Oral Cancer Screening: Results from a Cluster Randomized Controlled Trial in India." *Bulletin of the World Health Organization* 87 (3): 200–06.

Thomas, D. B., D. L. Gao, R. M. Ray, W. W. Wang, C. J. Allison, and others. 2002. "Randomized Trial of Breast Self-Examination in Shanghai: Final Results." *Journal of the National Cancer Institute* 94 (19): 1445–57.

UNAIDS (Joint United Nations Programme on HIV/AIDS). 2011. The George W. Bush Institute, the U.S. Department of State, Susan G. Komen for the Cure®, and UNAIDS Announce New Women's Health Initiative. http://www.unaids.org/en/resources/presscentre/pressreleaseandstatementarchive/2011/september/20110913pinkribbonredribbon/.

Van de Vijver, M. J., Y. D. He, L. J. van't Veer, H. Dai, A. A. M. Hart, and others. 2002. "A Gene-Expression Signature as a Predictor of Survival in Breast Cancer." *New England Journal of Medicine* 347: 1999–2009.

Vetto, J. T., J. K. Petty, N. Dunn, N. C. Prouser, and D. F. Austin. 2002. "Structured Clinical Breast Examination (CBE) Training Results in Objective Improvement in CBE Skills." *Journal of Cancer Education* 17 (3): 124–27.

Vorobiof, D. A., F. Sitas, and G. Vorobiof. 2001. "Breast Cancer Incidence in South Africa." *Journal of Clinical Oncology* 19 (Suppl. 18): 125–27.

WEF (World Economic Forum). 2011. *From Burden to Best Buys: Reducing the Economic Impact of Non-Communicable Disease in Low and Middle-Income Countries.* Geneva, Switzerland: WEF. http://www.who.int/nmh/publications/best_buys_summary.pdf.

Welch, G., L. Schwartz, and S. Woloshin. 2011. *Overdiagnosed: Making People Sick in the Pursuit of Health.* Boston, MA: Beacon Press.

WHO (World Health Organization). 2011a. *mHealth: New Horizons for Health through Mobile Technologies: Based on the Findings of the Second Global Survey on eHealth* (Global Observatory for eHealth Series, Volume 3). http://whqlibdoc.who.int/publications/2011/9789241564250_eng.pdf.

———. 2011b. *E-health in Low- and Middle-Income Countries: Findings from the Center for Health Market Innovations.* http://www.who.int/bulletin/volumes/90/5/11-099820/en/.

Wilson, J. M. G., and G. Junger. 1968. "Principles and Practice of Screening for Disease." Public Health Papers 34, WHO, Geneva.

Yaffe, M. J., and K. I. Pritchard. 2014. "Overdiagnosing Overdiagnosis." *The Oncologist* 19: 103–06. doi:10.1634/theoncologist.2014-0036.

Zelle, S., and R. Baltussen. 2013. "Economic Analyses of Breast Cancer Control in Low- and Middle-Income Countries: A Systematic Review." *Systematic Reviews* 2: 20. doi:10.1186/2046-4053-2-20.

Surgical Services for Cancer Care

Anna J. Dare, Benjamin O. Anderson, Richard Sullivan,
C. S. Pramesh, Cheng-Har Yip, Andre Ilbawi, Isaac F. Adewole,
Rajendra A. Badwe, and Cindy L. Gauvreau

Chapter **13**

INTRODUCTION

Surgery is a fundamental modality for curative and palliative treatment of most cancers in countries across all income settings. In high-income countries (HICs), where the most common solid organ malignant cancers, such as breast and colon cancers, are more likely to be successfully diagnosed at early stages, surgical resection provides definitive locoregional control of the primary tumor. This approach has significant curative potential when combined with appropriately selected adjuvant systemic treatment and radiotherapy. In low- and middle-income countries (LMICs), where locally advanced or metastatic cancer is a common initial disease presentation, surgical resection or debulking may be one of the few available modalities to achieve reasonable palliative disease control.

Surgery has not received sufficient attention in the cancer control discussion in LMICs (Goss and others 2014; Purushotham, Lewison, and Sullivan 2012). With many competing health priorities and significant financial constraints, surgical services in these settings are given low priority within national health plans and are allocated few resources from domestic accounts or international development assistance programs (Bae, Groen, and Kushner 2011; Farmer and Kim 2008). As a result, in most low-income countries (LICs), and many middle-income countries (MICs), access to safe, optimal surgical services for cancer is poor, and large proportions of the population are unable to access even the most basic surgical care (Funk and others 2010).

The projected increase in the cancer burden in LMICs over the next 20 years (see chapter 2 in this volume) necessitates that all countries give consideration to the establishment of surgical services with adequate capacity to meet current and future needs. In general, significant capital investment in surgical infrastructure, equipment, and personnel is needed in LICs, especially those in Sub-Saharan Africa (LeBrun and others 2014). In MICs, improved coordination, regulation, financial risk protection, and strategic planning for cancer and surgical services are requisites to improve service delivery and outcomes (Goss and others 2014). Surgical capacity building takes time, particularly with respect to developing the surgical workforce. Efforts to strengthen surgical services in LMICs should be strategically proactive to facilitate the provision of safe, effective, and accessible surgical cancer care for current and future patients.

This chapter discusses the public sector delivery of surgical cancer services in resource-constrained environments. We describe the current status of surgical services for cancer care in LMICs, analyze the barriers to care, and outline the surgical delivery platforms available to countries at different resource and income levels. Key considerations for policy makers relating to quality, safety, access, coverage, and economic and planning considerations in the scale-up of surgical cancer services are highlighted.

Corresponding author: Anna J. Dare, MBChB, PhD, St. Michael's Hospital and University of Toronto, Canada, DareA@smh.ca

BURDEN OF SURGICALLY TREATABLE CANCERS IN LMICs

As many LMICs transition to higher levels of social and economic development, with attendant greater population growth and improved longevity, the cancer burden amenable to surgical treatment is projected to increase dramatically (figure 13.1). Almost all of the common cancers require surgical services for histological diagnosis if radiology-guided biopsy is not available, for resection as the mainstay of curative treatment, and selectively for palliation.

Surgery is more effective, less complex, and less costly when performed for early-stage or locally advanced cancer. Curative treatment can often be delivered within a single clinical encounter and is achievable even in low-resource settings. Although surgery has less of a role in advanced stage cancer, in select cases it can provide improved quality and prolongation of life, for example,

for malignant bowel obstruction and fungating breast cancers. To realize the therapeutic benefit of surgical care in achieving cancer cure, stage-shifting is required to address the disease burden before it becomes locally advanced or metastatic—an objective particularly valid in LMICs, where more than 70 percent of patients present with advanced cancer (Adebamowo and Ajayi 2000; Anyanwu 2000, 2008).

STATUS OF SURGICAL CANCER SERVICES IN LMICs

The availability of, access to, and quality of surgical cancer care varies widely, leading to equally wide variations in outcomes among and within countries. Most LICs face profound shortages of surgeons, anesthesiologists, and pathologists; inadequate equipment and supplies; absent or severely dilapidated general and

Figure 13.1 Estimated Number of New Cancer Cases by Country-Income Group in LMICs for Four Common Surgically Treatable Cancers, 2010 and 2030

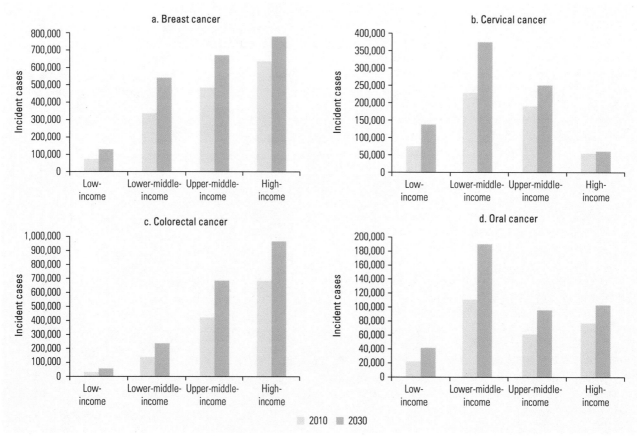

Source: Ferlay, Soerjomataram, and others 2013.

Note: All cases of breast, cervical, colorectal, and oral cancer require the input of a surgeon or gynecologist for diagnosis and clinical management. LMICs = low- and middle-income countries.

surgical infrastructure; and a lack of financing and strategic health services planning. The result is that a large proportion of the population is without access to even the most basic surgical services (Funk and others 2010; Weiser and others 2008). In most MICs, surgical services for cancer are more widely available, especially in major cities, but variations in quality, inequitable coverage and utilization, and poor central regulation and coordination (Pramesh and others 2014; Yip and others 2011) hamper the effective provision of care.

Access, Distribution, and Utilization

Access
Cancer surgery typically requires more complex infrastructure, training, support services, and referral networks than many basic surgical procedures. Gross inequities between HICs and LMICs exist in access to surgical services (Funk and others 2010; Weiser and others 2008) (table 13.1). An estimated two billion people lack access to any form of surgical care, including surgery for cancer (Funk and others 2010). Regional and national estimates of surgical services for cancer are not available, but access and coverage are likely to be significantly worse than for surgical services in general. Globally, approximately seven million to eight million patients require a major cancer operation each year, and at least three million additional patients require biopsies each year (Ferlay, Steliarova-Foucher, and others 2013).

Distribution
The distribution of surgical services within countries is also uneven in LMICs, compounding issues of access and coverage (Goss and others 2014). The surgical workforce and surgical facilities tend to cluster in urban areas (Ozgediz and others 2008). Surgical services for cancer, if present, typically are located at third-level facilities, often in the capital city, with poor or nonexistent referral networks. In settings in which a large proportion of the population lives in rural areas, accessing appropriate surgical cancer care can be an insurmountable challenge.

Utilization
Transportation costs and the time required to access diagnostic and treatment facilities may act as deterrents to receiving timely care. Even traveling relatively short distances can be a significant barrier in countries with poor transport infrastructure or challenging terrain. In a study of South African women presenting with breast cancer, the risk of presenting with an advanced stage cancer was 1.25 times higher for every 30 kilometers traveled to the diagnostic facility (Dickens and others 2014). In a

situational analysis of health facilities in 24 LICs and 27 MICs, the average patient had to travel 100 kilometers to reach a facility that could perform a basic biopsy diagnostic procedure (Ilbawi, Cherian, Mikkelson, Sankaranarayanan, and Sullivan, unpublished data).

Even where surgical cancer services are available and accessible, prohibitive user costs and perceptions that cancer cannot be successfully treated may prevent people from obtaining timely treatment (Ilbawi, Einterz, and Nkusu 2013).

Sociocultural belief systems and practices can affect cancer awareness and the uptake of surgical cancer services in LMICs (Goss and others 2014). Barriers to timely uptake of services include fear of surgery and hospital services in general, "cancer fatalism," cultural beliefs and social stigma related to being cut or having a body part removed, poor community experiences relating to outcomes, and costs (Daher 2012; Goss and others 2014; Yip and Anderson 2007).

Quality, Safety, and Outcomes

Wide variations exist globally in the quality and safety of surgical care (see Debas and others 2015, chapter 16). Quality issues are particularly concerning in the context of surgical treatment for cancer, where achieving adequate resection is fundamental to the success of the procedure.

Infrastructure and Training
In LMICs, quality and safety issues are often closely linked to basic resource deficits relating to infrastructure,

Table 13.1 Disparities in Surgical Capacity between High-Income and Low-Income Countries

Measure	High-income countries	Low-income countries
Number of surgeons (Hoyler and others 2014)	34–97 per 100,000[a]	0.13–1.57 per 100,000
Number of anesthesiologists (Hoyler and others 2014)	34–97 per 100,000[a]	0–4.9 per 100,000
Number of operating rooms (Funk and others 2010)	> 14 per 100,000	< 2 per 100,000
Volume of operations[b] (Weiser and others 2008)	172.3 million procedures per year (73.6 percent of global total, for 30.2 percent of the global population)	8.1 million procedures per year (3.5 percent of global total, for 34.8 percent of the global population)

a. High-income country data refer to "surgical providers" and include surgeons and anesthesiologists within the same estimate.
b. Data refer to high-health-expenditure countries and low-health-expenditure countries, which are correlated with income status.

equipment, supplies, and sterility, as well as a lack of appropriately trained providers. Poor outcomes reinforce community perceptions that cancer cannot be successfully treated with surgery. Although lumpectomy and modified radical mastectomy for breast cancer are not technically complex procedures, inadequate surgical resection of tumors can significantly undermine the effectiveness of these procedures. Incomplete or inadequate breast cancer resection following lumpectomy or mastectomy has been reported at rates as high as 15–45 percent in India and Nigeria (Agarwal and others 2009; Thorat and others 2008; Ukwenya and others 2008); almost 50 percent of patients who underwent incomplete surgery in nonspecialist centers in India had surgically excisable disease left behind (Thorat and others 2008). Postgraduate training, which covers modern surgical oncology practices and continuing medical education, is lacking in many LMICs. This deficit impacts not only proper surgical oncology technique but also appropriate decision-making, including whether surgery is indicated.

Standardization of Guidelines

The standardization of surgical care with guidelines, standards, and checklists can ensure a minimum level of quality and safety and reduce avoidable surgical morbidity and mortality (Haynes and others 2009), even in resource-constrained settings (see Debas and others 2015, chapter 16). Current use of guidelines and standards for surgical care in LMICs varies among countries and facilities. A recent study of health facilities in 24 LICs and 27 MICs reported that only 22 percent of facilities (n = 294/1,269) had established clinical management guidelines for surgical care and pain relief (Ilbawi, Cherian, Mikkelson, Sankaranarayanan, and Sullivan, unpublished data). Most clinical guidelines have been developed in and for HICs and are not necessarily applicable in resource-poor settings. However, for the past decade, Tata Memorial Centre, a national comprehensive cancer center in Mumbai, India, has published its own clinical guidelines and algorithms for all aspects of cancer care, including surgical and perioperative care. The guidelines are developed and updated through annual evidence-based management meetings, using international evidence and taking into account local resources and challenges. Tata's guidelines (freely available for reference on their institutional website, https://tmc.gov .in/clinicalguidelines/clinical.htm) are now used in other LMICs, including Bangladesh, Kenya, and Nigeria. There is also an initiative to categorize some of these guidelines as "minimum," "optimal," and "optional," with health care delivery platforms treating patients based on the platforms' individual infrastructural and trained human resource capabilities.

Partners in the Provision of Surgical Services

The safe provision of anesthesia is another often overlooked requirement of effective surgical cancer care. Profound differences exist in anesthetic mortality rates between low and high Human Development Index countries (Bainbridge and others 2012); anesthetic mortality rates are reported to be as high as one in 500 in several LMICs in Sub-Saharan Africa (Glenshaw and Madzimbamuto 2005; Hansen, Gausi, and Merikebu 2000; Maman and others 2005; Walker and Wilson 2008; see Debas and others 2015, chapter 15.)

Cancer surgery is also highly dependent on two other major areas of clinical care: pathology and imaging. Quality pathology services are central to making an accurate diagnosis and planning appropriate surgical care. Imaging is required for accurately staging early, curable cancers; for planning more complex operative resections; and, in some cases, for establishing the presence of metastatic disease. The role of these services in the delivery of quality comprehensive cancer is discussed further in chapter 11 in this volume.

DEVELOPING SURGICAL CANCER SERVICES AND DELIVERY PLATFORMS IN LMICs

Resource-Stratified Approaches

Resource-stratified approaches to screening, diagnosis, and treatment interventions for specific cancers, which can help countries assess the level at which they can provide effective cancer services, have been presented in previous chapters. However, policy makers developing cancer control strategies need to consider not only what services are required, but also the platforms through which these services can be most effectively delivered to those who need them.

In this section, we outline potential delivery platforms for surgical cancer services in resource-poor settings, using a level-of-care approach (box 13.1). We consider how surgical cancer services—diagnostic, curative, palliative, and adjuvant services—may be effectively delivered across different surgical platforms (community health center, first-level hospital, or third-level hospital), using breast, cervical, oral, and bowel cancers as examples. Where relevant, we consider the most appropriate surgical platform for service delivery for countries at different income levels and according to the resource-stratified interventions presented in earlier chapters.[1] Finally, we discuss how quality and efficiency demands can be balanced with access and coverage challenges in LMICs through the appropriate deployment of surgical cancer platforms, and the referral networks and service partnerships between them. Many countries are

Situational Analysis of Surgical Cancer Services: Key Questions

Key Questions for Policy Makers and Planners

- What is the burden of surgically treatable cancers in the country?
  - Current
  - Projected
- What stage of presentation is typical for each cancer (percent early, locally advanced, disseminated)?
- What surgical platforms are currently available within the country? Where are they located?
- Do any of these platforms currently provide surgical cancer care:
  - As part of a general surgical service?
  - As part of a dedicated cancer service?
- How well-resourced are these platforms?
  - Human resources, infrastructure, equipment, supporting services
- What adjuvant therapies are available and affordable for the country's resource level?
  - Where are these adjuvant therapies currently delivered, if anywhere?
  - Who delivers them?

- Are radiotherapy services available? Where?
  - Where are they available in relation to surgical and adjuvant treatment?
- Are palliative medicines, such as opioids, reliably available? Where?
- What referral networks exist? What are the barriers to referring patients between facilities?
- What are the barriers to receiving timely and appropriate surgical and cancer treatment?
  - Financial, geographic, sociocultural
  - Human resources, infrastructure, equipment and supplies
- Is it feasible to provide screening and early case detection, given the country's resource level and priorities?
  - Are there plans to do this in the medium-to-long term?
  - How will this affect surgical need?

---

only beginning to consider these issues; very little analysis or published country experience in LMICs is available to serve as an evidence base.

Guidelines for Surgical Platforms

Delivery platforms refer to the structural and organizational modes or channels of delivery for public health and clinical services. Platforms for delivery of surgical care can be defined across four levels:

- Community health center
- First-level hospital/district hospital
- Second-level hospital/regional hospital
- Third-level hospital/tertiary hospital

The basic resources required for each level are summarized in table 13.2. In practice, significant variations and overlap occur among levels of care.

Delivery platforms for surgical cancer services coexist with other platforms delivering general cancer and surgical services, inpatient services, and primary care. They are often co-located and operate synergistically

to support the effective delivery of clusters of health services.

Diagnostic, Curative, and Palliative Services

Diagnosis Surgical services play a key role in cancer diagnosis. Biopsy, which is required for the definitive diagnosis of cancer, involves taking a sample of suspicious tissue by using either a needle or an open surgical technique and then examining the removed cells under a microscope. The tissue sampling aspects of the biopsy procedure can be provided in most LMICs within a first-level hospital platform, as well as higher platforms, if the surgical providers are trained in the technique used and adequate means for sample fixation exist. Providing biopsy services at a first-level platform reduces delays between initial presentation and definitive diagnosis and improves access and coverage. Because lymphadenopathy has many non-neoplastic causes in LMICs (Kingham and others 2013), referral to a higher specialist service for the purposes of tissue sampling only is premature, increases losses to follow-up, delays diagnosis, and risks overwhelming limited specialist services with nonspecific referrals.

Table 13.2 Platforms for Delivering Surgical Cancer Care

Community health center	District/first-level hospital	Regional/second-level hospital	Tertiary/third-level hospital
• Community health center or small rural hospital	• District– or provincial-level hospital, with 50–300 beds	• Referral hospital of 200–800 beds	• Referral hospital of 300–1,500 beds
• May have a small number of inpatient and maternity beds	• Adequately equipped major and minor operating theaters	• Well-equipped major and minor operating theaters	• Well-equipped major and minor operating theaters
• Capable of performing minor surgical procedures under local anesthesia	• Trained nonphysician or medical officer anesthetists	• Supported by imaging, laboratory, and blood bank services, as well as basic intensive care facilities	• Advanced imaging, laboratory services
• Paramedical staff, nurses, midwives	• District medical officers in surgery, senior clinical (nonphysician) officers in surgery, nurses, midwives	• Adequately equipped major and minor operating theaters	• Intensive care facilities
• Visiting doctors	• +/– resident general surgeon and/or obstetrician-gynecologist	• General surgeons, obstetrician-gynecologists	• Highly specialized staff and technical equipment
	• Visiting specialists	• Anesthesiologists	• Clinical services highly differentiated by function
		• +/– specialist surgeons	• Often have teaching activities

Source: Adapted from WHO 2003 and Debas and others 2015, chapter 12.

Tissue sampling itself is not technically complex. Accurate and timely reporting of the biopsy sample by a trained pathologist is the main challenge in obtaining a diagnosis. In LICs, specimens may be taken at the first-level hospital level but processed and reported at a higher center, often within a third-level or national platform, because of the lack of trained histopathology technicians and pathologists. This approach can maximize available resources and also promote standardized, quality reporting. However, it requires coordination between the tissue sampling center, where the biopsy sample is taken, and the pathology center, where the biopsy is read and reported, to ensure timely feedback of the diagnosis.

In MICs, histopathology services may be more widely available, and basic pathology services may be provided within a first-level hospital platform. Centralized approaches to reading and reporting cancer biopsies are still important, however. These approaches can promote the efficient use of resources; increase the range of diagnostic tests able to be performed; and ensure standardized, quality reporting. For this reason, the use of second- or third-level platforms for biopsy reporting is encouraged.

Treatment with Curative Intent In LICs, surgical services for cancer are usually provided through second- or third-level platforms. Severe shortages of surgical infrastructure, equipment, surgeons, anesthesiologists, and supporting services preclude providing these services within a first-level platform. Cancer surgery is typically performed by generalist surgeons, as specialist cancer surgeons are not available.

In LICs with basic surgical resources at first-level facilities, a minimum package of surgical services for cancer can be delivered within this platform. This package includes biopsy, surgical treatment for precancerous cervical lesions and early-stage invasive cervical cancer, breast cancer surgery, and resection of small oral tumors (table 13.3). Provided there is a surgical provider familiar with cancer resection requirements, these procedures require little additional infrastructure, equipment, or supplies, compared with other major general surgical operations routinely performed at first-level facilities. Treatment of some precancerous lesions can be safely undertaken within a community or first-level platform, even where full general surgical services are not available. Rwanda has recently published its experience scaling up cervical screening and treatment services across the country using first-level or community-level facilities to screen, diagnose, and treat, often within a single clinical encounter (Binagwaho and others 2013).

In MICs, surgical services for early-stage breast, cervical, colon, and oral cancer can often be delivered within a first-level platform because of the greater availability of basic surgical resources, including surgeons. This delivery can improve access and may reduce the direct nonmedical costs associated with seeking surgical cancer care in many MICs. Appropriate training and continuing education of surgical providers at the first level is crucial, however, to reduce the risk of inadequate or incomplete resection.

Advanced breast, cervical, oral, and colorectal cancers require advanced surgical platforms in LMICs, typically a dedicated regional or national center providing cancer care. Advanced cancers are technically more

Table 13.3 Delivery Platforms for Priority Surgical Cancer Interventions in LICs and MICs

Intervention	Community health center	District (first-level) hospital	Regional (second-level) hospital	Tertiary (third-level) hospital
Breast cancer: LICs				
Diagnosis	Refer to higher center	Biopsy (send pathology to higher center)	Biopsy ± onsite pathology, imaging (XR, liver US), lab (CBC, LFT)	Biopsy + onsite pathology, imaging (XR, liver US), lab (CBC, LFT)
Curative surgical treatment	"	Referral to a higher center	MRM ± oophorectomy	MRM ± oophorectomy
Palliative surgical treatment	"	Referral to a higher center	Total mastectomy	Total mastectomy
Adjuvant therapy	"	Hormone therapy	Hormone therapy, chemotherapy	Hormone therapy, chemo, RT[a]
Breast cancer: MICs				
Diagnosis	Refer to higher center	FNA/US-guided FNAB, imaging (XR, liver US), lab (CBC, LFT)	FNA/US-guided FNAB + onsite pathology, imaging (XR, liver US), lab (CBC, LFT) BCS & SLNB (dye or radio[a,b])	FNA/US-guided FNAB + onsite pathology, imaging (XR, liver US), lab (CBC, LFT) BCS & SLNB (dye or radio[a,b])
Curative surgical treatment	"	MRM ± oophorectomy	MRM ± oophorectomy	MRM ± oophorectomy
Palliative surgical treatment	"	Total mastectomy	Total mastectomy	Total mastectomy
Adjuvant therapy	"	Hormone therapy, 1st-line chemo[b]	Hormone therapy, chemo, RT[a]	Hormone therapy, chemo, RT[a]
Cervical cancer: LICs				
Diagnosis	HPV test, VIA	HPV test, VIA	HPV test, VIA ± colposcopy, biopsy	HPV test, VIA ± colposcopy, biopsy
Curative surgical treatment				
Precancerous	Cryotherapy	Cryotherapy, LEEP	Cryotherapy, LEEP, cold knife	Cryotherapy, LEEP, cold knife
Invasive cancer	Refer to higher center	Refer to higher center	Simple and radical hysterectomy	Simple and radical hysterectomy
Palliative surgical treatment	"	"		
Adjuvant therapy	"	"	Chemo	Chemo, RT[a]
Cervical cancer: MICs				
Diagnosis	HPV test, VIA or cytology	HPV test, VIA or cytology, colposcopy, biopsy	HPV test, cytology, colposcopy, biopsy	HPV test, cytology, colposcopy, biopsy
Curative surgical treatment				
Precancerous	Cryotherapy	Cryotherapy, LEEP, cold knife	Cryotherapy, LEEP, cold knife	Cryotherapy, LEEP, cold knife
Invasive cancer	Refer to higher center	Simple hysterectomy; advanced cancer, refer to higher center	Simple and radical hysterectomy	Radical trachelectomy, hysterectomy, pelvic exenteration
Palliative surgical treatment	"			
Adjuvant therapy	"	Chemo[b]	Chemo, RT	Chemo, RT
Oral cancer: LICs				
Diagnosis	Refer to higher center	Biopsy	Biopsy + histopathology	Biopsy + histopathology
Curative surgical treatment	"	Resection of early-stage cancers	Resection of early and advanced	Resection of early and advanced
Palliative surgical treatment	"	Refer to higher center	For debulking/pain relief	For debulking/pain relief
Adjuvant therapy	"	"	RT[a] ± chemo	RT[a] ± chemo

table continues next page

Intervention	Community health center	District (first-level) hospital	Regional (second-level) hospital	Tertiary (third-level) hospital
Oral cancer: MICs				
Diagnosis	Refer to higher center	Biopsy	Biopsy + histopathology	Biopsy + histopathology
Curative surgical treatment	"	Resection of early-stage cancers	Resection of early and advanced ± oncoplastics	Resection of early and advanced ± oncoplastics
Palliative treatment	"	Refer to higher center	For debulking/pain relief	For debulking/pain relief
Adjuvant therapy	"	"	RT[a] ± chemo	RT[a] ± chemo
Colorectal cancer: LICs				
Diagnosis	Refer to higher center	gFOBT/FIT + referral for colonoscopy	Sigmoidoscopy/colonoscopy	Sigmoidoscopy/colonoscopy
Curative surgical treatment	"	Colectomy[b]	Colectomy, APR[b], LAR[b]	Colectomy, APR, LAR
Palliative surgical treatment	"	Colostomy for bowel obstruction	Colostomy for bowel obstruction	Colostomy for bowel obstruction
Adjuvant therapy	"	Refer to higher center	Chemo ± RT[a]	Chemo ± RT[a]
Colorectal cancer: MICs				
Diagnosis	FOBT + referral for colonoscopy	Colonoscopy + biopsy[b]	Colonoscopy + biopsy	Colonoscopy + biopsy
Curative surgical treatment	Refer to higher center	Colectomy	Colectomy, APR, LAR	Colectomy, APR, LAR
Palliative surgical treatment	"	Colostomy for bowel obstruction	Colostomy for bowel obstruction	Colostomy for bowel obstruction
Adjuvant therapy	"	Chemo[a,b]	Chemo ± RT	Chemo ± RT

Note: APR = abdominoperineal resection; BCS = breast-conserving surgery; CBC = complete blood count; FIT = fecal immunochemical test; FNA = fine needle aspiration; FNAB = fine-needle aspiration biopsy; FOBT = fecal occult blood test; gFOBT = guaiac fecal occult blood test; HPV = human papillomavirus; LAR = lower anterior resection; LEEP = loop electrocautery excision procedure; LFT = liver function test; LICs = low-income countries; MICs = middle-income countries; MRM = modified radical mastectomy; RT = radiotherapy; SLNB = sentinel lymph node biopsy; US = ultrasound; VIA = visual inspection of the cervix after acetic acid application; XR = x-ray; ± = with or without; " = repeats above.

a. If available within a country's resource level.

b. Provision at this level will be dependent on the availability of appropriate equipment, supplies, monitoring, and adequately trained providers.

complex to achieve adequate resection margins and wound closure. Platforms capable of delivering complex cancer and surgical care are often not available in LICs, especially outside the capital city. In addition to these priority cancers, other complex cancers (for example, musculoskeletal, thoracic, or hepatobiliary cancers) require surgical treatment within third-level platforms, usually by specialist surgeons.

Treatment with Palliative Intent Palliative surgery can significantly enhance the quality of life and allow patients to return home for end-of-life care. Palliative care for all patients with advanced-stage cancer hinges on access to appropriate analgesics, including opioids (see chapter 9). Surgery also has an important role in palliation, particularly in regions in which advanced presentations with very large, debilitating tumors are common. Palliative treatment should be provided within delivery platforms as close to patients' homes as possible.

Palliative surgical procedures commonly required in LMICs include mastectomy for bulky, fungating, or bleeding tumors and formation of a colostomy for obstructing colorectal tumors. In LICs, palliative colostomy formation or mastectomy can be performed within a second-level platform, or potentially at a first-level facility when resources permit. In MICs, most first-level platforms are equipped to provide this level of surgical care. Palliative surgical treatment must be undertaken cautiously. It should be made clear that the procedure is being done to improve the quality of life, rather than to extend it. Advanced disease has higher operative and postoperative risks; the risks and benefits of the procedure must be weighed carefully by providers and patients.

Adjuvant Treatment Considerations

Cancer treatment with surgery alone is only effective in early-stage disease. In resource-constrained settings, most patients tend to present with advanced disease, and adjuvant therapy is usually required in addition to surgical resection. Strong coordination of surgical services and adjuvant services is needed to maximize outcomes, and additional considerations present with respect to the most appropriate surgical platform for patients who require both surgical care and adjuvant therapy.

In LMICs, platforms for basic surgical cancer care are likely to be more widely available than for adjuvant treatment, particularly radiotherapy. When planning cancer services, policy makers need to consider not only where surgical services are provided, but also how these are distributed in relation to where adjuvant therapy—including hormonal therapy, chemotherapy, radiotherapy, and biologics—can be provided. The availability of these services may dictate whether surgical treatment is appropriate and the type of intervention to be performed.

In many LMICs, the surgical providers are often responsible for prescribing and/or administering adjuvant therapy. This is very common when adjuvant endocrine therapy is required in the setting of breast cancer, for example, tamoxifen. Adjuvant chemotherapy is also often given by general surgeons, physicians, and even patients' families in LMICs. Ideally, chemotherapy should be delivered in a comprehensive cancer center by specialist staff within a second- or third-level platform to ensure appropriate, high-quality care. However, these stipulations place chemotherapy out of reach for many LICs. Where significant barriers exist to accessing chemotherapy and prevent uptake, preoperative or postoperative first-line chemotherapy can be administered by trained surgeons, general physicians, or nurses at first- or second-level hospitals, using clinical guidelines and management algorithms to guide treatment selection, if appropriate blood tests are available to monitor complications. Such polyskilling (where a provider is trained to deliver more than one type of cancer care) can be used to overcome human resource shortages and minimize referral delays.

The delivery of radiotherapy is limited by its availability; in all LICs and most MICs, delivery requires referral to a regional or national platform. The availability and accessibility of radiotherapy at a higher center do not necessitate the delivery of surgical care at the same center, although there may be advantages in doing so.

Centralized versus Decentralized Delivery Models

Delivery platforms for surgical cancer services must necessarily be organized into an overall delivery model within a country. It is useful to consider the benefits and risks of different models of surgical cancer service

Table 13.4 Benefits and Risks of Centralized versus Decentralized Surgical Cancer Platforms

Centralized surgical platforms for cancer	Decentralized surgical platforms for cancer
Benefits	*Benefits*
• Standardization of care, higher operative volumes, and specialist surgical care for quality assurance	• Improved coverage and access for greater equity
• Economies of scale	• Reduced direct nonmedical and indirect costs to patients and families, because of reduced travel time and productivity loss
• "One-stop shop" for cancer services	
• Multidisciplinary practice for better outcomes	• Reduced referral delays between presentation and definitive care
• Research and training activities that drive practice forward	• Surgical platform more cost-effective at the first or second level (Debas and others 2006)
Risks	*Risks*
• Reduced access and increased inequity for rural versus urban populations	• Inefficient clinical services and duplication
• May encourage super-specialization and workforce maldistribution	• Poor coordination and access to higher-level centers and other cancer disciplines, causing delayed or missed adjuvant care
	• Poorer quality care

delivery; balancing quality and efficiency with access and coverage demands is a key challenge in delivering surgical cancer care in LMICs. Centralized, specialist surgical platforms for cancer services generally promote quality and efficiency, whereas strengthening delivery platforms peripherally tends to enhance access and coverage (table 13.4).

Referral Networks, Service Coordination, and Partnerships

The delivery of surgical cancer care requires functional clinical platforms, as well as strong referral networks and coordination between other cancer services and providers.

Strategies to improve the coordination and links among all platforms providing cancer services can promote high-quality, standardized, and efficient surgical cancer care. For example, India has developed a National Cancer Grid (Pramesh, Badwe, and Sinha 2014), funded by the Government of India, which links facilities providing cancer care, with the goal of standardizing the quality of care, developing uniform guidelines, reducing the variations in care, and facilitating exchanges of expertise and experience between larger and smaller centers. Such links also strengthen referral capabilities and provider coordination. This is particularly important when diagnostic, surgical, and adjuvant services are spread across different facilities.

Comprehensive cancer centers with multidisciplinary cancer teams have been shown to be the most effective strategy for ensuring high-quality, efficient, and appropriate cancer care in HICs (chapter 11 in this volume; Yip and others 2011). The severe shortage of specialist health workers makes it almost impossible to achieve comprehensive, multidisciplinary centers currently in LICs and difficult to achieve in a manner that ensures high coverage and equity in many MICs. However, even in the absence of a highly specialized cancer workforce, some LMICs are beginning to develop regional or national cancer centers, drawing on expertise within general second- or third-level hospitals. Often, one or two surgeons within a country become well known for providing cancer care and serve as references for the rest of the country, with high numbers of patients referred to them. These reference surgeons and the large urban hospitals in which they typically work can serve as a major focus to drive forward cancer care within countries, provided they are well supported. Although not all surgical cancer services need to be provided at this level, the presence of such centers may strengthen the surgical care provided at other locations through the exchange of knowledge and experience and the strengthening of referral networks.

International partnerships between LMICs or between LMICs and HICs also support the development and delivery of cancer care, including surgical cancer care in low-resource environments. The most effective international partnerships are those that seek to develop local cancer care capacity and that are closely aligned with local needs. The practice of short-term surgical trips that focus on operative resection only, use entirely foreign surgical teams to deliver care, and do not participate in teaching or local capacity-building efforts is not generally an effective model for cancer care.

STRENGTHENING SURGICAL SYSTEMS AND BUILDING CAPACITY

Conducting Baseline Assessment of Capacity

At the country level, policy makers will consider several key elements, especially when considering the most appropriate delivery platforms:

- Burden of cancer
- Stage at diagnosis
- Availability and distribution of surgical and cancer-specific resources in relation to the population and

the available resources, current and projected, for the scale-up of cancer care and surgical services

A situational analysis of current surgical and cancer capacity within a country should precede policy, planning, and scale-up efforts (box 13.1).

Developing the Surgical Workforce

Human resources are a crucial component of surgical cancer services, and the development of an effective workforce requires proactive strategic planning at the national level. LICs and many MICS require urgent investment in strengthening the surgical, anesthetic, and supporting cancer workforce—including pathologists, radiotherapists, and nurses trained in perioperative and wound care. The surgical and anesthetic workforce takes time to develop—a minimum of 10 years from entry into medical school to qualification as an accredited surgeon or anesthetist—and workforce planning must take into account projected as well as current needs. Many LICs lack postgraduate surgical training programs and must pay to send their doctors outside the country (and sometimes outside the region or continent) for further training after medical school. This requirement is costly and increases the likelihood that the home countries will not be able to retain the doctors upon training completion. Creating the capacity for accredited postgraduate surgical training in LICs has been shown to be effective and sustainable, allowing countries to achieve national health goals (Anderson and others 2014).

Task-shifting of general surgical procedures—for example, laparotomy, cesarean section, and fracture repair—to nonphysician providers is increasingly used to overcome critical surgical workforce shortages in many LMICs. In Malawi, 93 percent of the surgical workforce is composed of nonphysicians (Henry and others 2014). However, this process poses risks for developing surgical cancer services. It is generally agreed that task-shifting to nonphysicians for cancer surgery is not possible owing to case complexity and quality concerns. The failure to address the shortage of surgeons in LMICs and the overreliance on nonphysician surgical providers to deliver surgical services will significantly hamper the ability of countries to respond to the substantial projected increase in cancer requiring surgical treatment in the future. Attempts to address the surgical workforce crisis need to focus on increasing the number of surgeons through recruitment and retention to ensure long-term success in meeting surgical needs. Training of surgical nursing staff is also critical to ensure optimal postoperative care and surgical outcomes.

In settings with an adequate surgical workforce, as in some MICs, expanding the skills of the existing workforce to provide quality surgical cancer services through ongoing training will improve outcomes and maximize health gains.

Improving Infrastructure and Procurement Processes

The significant deficits in basic infrastructure, equipment, supplies, and procurement processes in many LMICs need to be addressed early in any scale-up plans. These deficits include an absence of reliable power, water, and oxygen, as well as insufficient or dilapidated operating theaters and surgical and sterility equipment and supplies. Attention to the development of sustainable supply chains and procurement practices is important. Improving and developing the surgical infrastructure within countries often requires capital outlays; in LICs, these costs may need to be met through development assistance.

Further research is needed as to the most appropriate and cost-effective infrastructure and equipment for surgical cancer care specific to the resource level. In some cases, the use of technology in LMICs, for example, human papillomavirus DNA testing, can lead to leapfrogging of cancer delivery models over

HICs and assist in detecting cases at stages amenable to curative surgical treatment. However, the greatest overall gains are likely to come from the planned development of more basic surgical infrastructure, with good population coverage, rather than the ad hoc purchasing or donation of state-of-the art technology or facilities that can be accessed by only a small percentage of the population. Maintenance and repair of surgical infrastructure and equipment are major challenges; an estimated 40 percent of the equipment in LMICs is out of service, compared with less than 1 percent in HICs (Howitt and others 2012). The inappropriate deployment of medical technologies from HICs to LMICs is a significant contributor to this problem.

Promoting Quality and Ensuring Safety

Prerequisite to the scale-up of surgical cancer services is consideration of how to promote and ensure quality and safety. These are fundamental components for achieving good outcomes and building community trust in cancer and surgical care. All countries can embrace the goal of high-quality and safe surgical care, regardless of development status. Specific strategies for LMICs are listed in box 13.2.

Box 13.2

Strategies to Improve the Quality of Surgical Cancer Services in LMICs

All LMICs
- Clinical management guidelines and surgical standards developed specifically for low-resource settings
- Collection of outcome data
  - Case fatality rates
  - Risk-adjusted postoperative mortality rates
- Morbidity and mortality meetings and clinical audits
  - Encouraged reflection on practice and identification of areas for improvement
- Multidisciplinary approach to diagnosis and treatment management
  - Local
  - International, for example, via telemedicine links

- CME for all surgical cancer providers
  - CME and regular courses for updates on surgical technique, patient selection, postoperative care, and systemic therapy

LIC-specific strategies
- Focus on developing strong general surgical services and referral mechanisms
- Operation within the limits of the human and infrastructural resources to reduce poor outcomes
- Establishment of formal links among centers providing surgical and cancer care within a country, especially between different referral levels
- Development of international twinning arrangements

box continues next page

Box 13.2 (continued)

- Support for training, diagnosis, and case management decisions in centers providing cancer care
  - ○ South-South
  - ○ North-South
  - ○ Local and international NGOs

MIC-specific strategies
- Development of regional and national comprehensive cancer centers
  - ○ Provision of locally appropriate management guidelines for own country
  - ○ Provision of training support and outreach clinical services for peripheral facilities

- Establishment of cancer grids or partnerships
  - ○ Encourage collaboration and standardization of surgical care
- Development of regional and national cancer registries to track outcomes
- Requirements for mandatory reporting of case volumes, procedures, and outcomes in all sectors providing surgical cancer services (government, private for-profit, and private not-for-profit)

Note: CME = continuing medical education; LICs = low-income countries; LMICs = low- and middle-income countries; MICs = middle-income countries; NGOs = nongovernmental organizations.

Scaling Up Surgical Services for Cancer

The requirements for the scale-up of surgical services to meet cancer needs are country specific, dependent on current and projected patterns of disease, available health resources and health systems capacity, amounts of domestic spending on health, and distribution of the population. Some general recommendations can be made, however, to guide policy makers based on the resource patterns, income level, and development status.

LICs should initially focus on building general surgical capacity and inpatient care within their health systems, including investing in human resources and hospital infrastructure and developing effective supply chains and referral networks. Without these fundamentals in place, it is not appropriate to embark on cancer surgery–specific treatment planning. Adequate general surgical capacity will allow countries to deliver the surgical components of the minimum cancer intervention package, such as diagnosis and treatment of breast cancer and treatment of precancerous cervical lesions, at the basic resource level. Importantly, it will also serve as a base for the effective scale-up of a range of cancer-specific services.

In MICs with basic or limited surgical resources in place, the focus should be on developing coordinated and context-specific cancer systems and services that improve the quality and standards and ensure equitable access to surgical cancer care through sound public policy and health governance. Many MICs have national health programs, services, and structures geared to the delivery of vertical programs, rather than horizontal health system–based approaches (Anderson and others 2014). Surgical care may be present, but coordination and delivery within a functioning health system may be weak. As countries move beyond the most basic package of cancer care delivered within a single clinical encounter, they will require complex and highly coordinated delivery systems, with surgical care embedded within. Improving governance and regulation around surgical service provision will assist MICs to improve quality, reduce waste and inefficiency, and promote equity. Large imbalances between private and public sector provision of surgical cancer services are seen in some MICs, such as India. Unregulated, these imbalances can drain resources (for example, higher salaries in the private sector drain surgeons away from the public sector), hinder quality and transparency (for example, through inappropriate, nonstandardized, or unwanted surgical treatment), increase medical impoverishment (for example, treating patients until finances have run out and then transferring them to the public sector), and create a two-tiered system of cancer care (Flores and others 2008; Pramesh and others 2014).

Complementing steps to improve surgical capacity is the need to simultaneously focus on removing patient barriers to the uptake of surgical cancer services to improve cancer outcomes and promote equity. Delayed presentation increases the morbidity, mortality, and micro- and macroeconomic costs associated with cancer. As countries move to introduce financial risk protection and progressive universal health coverage for their populations, there is a need to ensure coverage for a basic package of inpatient care, including surgical care, early in the expansion pathway (Jamison and others 2013).

Cancer care requires strong, coordinated health systems and services, rather than an isolated focus on surgical services. Early detection and comprehensive treatment improve cancer outcomes. Improving the rate of surgical cure in LMICs requires coordinated efforts across the health system to achieve stage-shifting, combined with efforts to improve surgical capacity to deliver effective treatment. For example, clinical breast examination provided at a community-level platform by trained allied health workers has led to stage-shifting of breast cancer in India, making it more amenable to surgical cure (Sankaranarayanan and others 2011).

ECONOMIC CONSIDERATIONS OF SURGICAL CANCER CARE IN LMICs

There have been few economic evaluations of cancer care in LMICs; among these, surgical interventions and surgical services have received almost no attention. Tables 16.3 to 16.8 in chapter 16 summarize the available cost-effectiveness evidence for the detection and treatment of the priority cancers considered in this volume. Notably, surgical interventions that are feasible at the basic, limited, and enhanced resource levels have barely been assessed, even in upper-middle-income countries. Chemotherapy, in comparison, is a far more studied treatment modality, given concerns about its high cost and poor accessibility, regardless of resource level. For example, in a systematic review of the Tufts Medical Center Cost-Effectiveness Analysis Registry of cancer-related studies set mainly in HICs, 53.3 percent of the studies were concerned with pharmaceutical interventions, compared with 13.3 percent with surgical interventions (Greenberg and others 2010).

Yet, surgery is the most significant life-saving intervention in cancer treatment. Coupled with their wider roles in the cancer care spectrum, as a diagnostic modality and in palliative care, surgery and surgical services have the potential to be good-value choices for health care investment in LMICs. The expansion of surgical interventions for solid tumors routinely found at early stages is recommended in this volume based on feasibility, at even basic and limited resource levels, and suggested cost-effectiveness evidence from higher resource levels (chapter 16 in this volume).

Economic Studies

In the enhanced resource settings of MICs, limited cost-effectiveness analyses of comparisons between simple and enhanced surgical techniques or between surgery and other treatment modalities are emerging (He and others 2011; Lu and others 2012; Tan and others 2013). The results are set in single hospitals and are very

specific to the local cost structure and, especially given the heterogeneity of health care financing in MICs, are not generalizable to other countries. The results often reflect the increasing ability and desire of individuals and governments to pay for a perceived (if unsupported) qualitative improvement in outcomes, balanced against increased costs of more expensive (often imported) equipment, more highly trained personnel, and more supporting services. However, these studies also often provide insights into and implications for the structuring of health care financing and equitable access.

In reviews of the literature, basic surgical services in a variety of low-resource settings were reported to be cost-effective or very cost-effective, according to the World Health Organization threshold definitions (Chao and others 2014; Grimes and others 2014). Local costing studies and partial economic evaluations (for example, where costs or effectiveness components are assessed but not directly linked) or evaluations from narrower perspectives (for example, from provider or patient perspectives rather than societal perspectives) can provide insights for inputs into fuller cost-effectiveness studies or for intervention adaptation in implementation. Detailed costing of surgery procedures, excluding preoperative and postoperative care, in a selection of hospitals of varying resources and settings in India showed that the salaries and benefits of operating theater staff formed 42 percent of the cost of a hysterectomy in a first-level hospital, compared with 48 percent in a third-level hospital (Chatterjee and Laxminarayan 2013). Overhead costs were higher at the first-level hospital, however, constituting 30 percent versus 20 percent of hysterectomy costs at the third-level hospital. This finding suggests that if the outcomes are similar, it may be equally or more cost-effective to perform simple hysterectomies at a first-level hospital, thereby improving access for a wider population in India.

In costing breast cancer care in central Vietnam, a lower-middle-income country, Lan and others (2013) found the surgical treatment, while a large cost component, was significantly less expensive than chemotherapy. Over a five-year course of care for breast cancer that included diagnosis, initial treatment, and follow-up care, surgery accounted for 8.4 percent of the total cost (Lan and others 2013).

Financing

In many LMICs, out-of-pocket payment for surgical cancer services may be the main form of financing (Ilbawi, Einterz, and Nkusu 2013). Lan and others (2013) found that the absence of health insurance or financial risk protection from the costs of cancer care in Vietnam was the main barrier to the uptake of breast cancer treatment services. The impoverishment impact of surgical conditions on a household is immense, especially in the context of cancer. In a study in rural Bangladesh, the impoverishment rates from cancer hospitalization and surgical procedures were four- to sevenfold higher than the impoverishment average of 3.4 percent for all health services (Hamid, Ahsan, and Begum 2014). High user fees and out-of-pocket payments also increase the likelihood that patients will not return at all for definitive surgical care. In a study of patients presenting at a first-level hospital in rural Cameroon, preoperative payment greater than US$310 and a recommended procedure for cancer significantly increased the likelihood of patients not returning for surgical care as advised following an initial assessment (Ilbawi, Einterz, and Nkusu 2013).

Gaps in the Economic Evidence

The dearth of economic evaluations for surgical cancer services means that many knowledge gaps exist in making investment decisions. This section identifies some of the fundamental areas that can be addressed to start an economic evidence base of cancer surgery interventions and surgical services.

Burden

Country-level estimates of the health burden of resectable cancer, refined by site, incidence, and stage, are unknown but required for the underlying foundation of an economic evidence base. Estimates of avertable burden help direct the considerable resources needed for economic evaluations to appropriate areas of research, identify proper comparators, and give a measure against which to weigh costs. In the United States, 61.4 percent of patients admitted to hospital with a cancer diagnosis required a surgical procedure (Rose and others 2014). Similar country-level estimates for operative cancer need in LMICs are not available. Given the increasing and changing burden of cancer (see chapter 2 in this volume) relative to communicable diseases and among sites and nations, the extent of the potential value of surgical treatments needs to be quantified.

Costing

There is a general lack of costing studies on which to build cost-effectiveness studies of surgical cancer services. As a first step, those that exist for general surgical services, such as the hospital-based studies of Chatterjee and Laxminarayan (2013), could be validated for surgical cancer services. This process requires the characterization and differentiation of cancer surgery costs versus general surgery costs, including the appropriate apportioning of overhead costs to cancer surgery and

the differential training of personnel. In LMICs in particular, there is need for costing of the surgical cancer systems, processes, and platforms that would allow the identification of minimized patient travel time and related productivity costs.

Effectiveness

The short- and long-term effectiveness of surgical services in cancer cure and control, measured at the national and sub-national level, could be estimated to better inform cost-effectiveness analyses. The efficacy of cancer surgery may be severely compromised by poor access to supporting cancer services, including chemotherapy and radiotherapy, or by poor quality surgical care. However, there has been little evaluation of the potential impact of this on cancer outcomes in LMICs.

CONCLUSIONS

Surgical services are a central component of cancer cure and control in all resource settings, playing a key role in the diagnosis, treatment, and palliation of most solid tumors. Basic surgical cancer care can be affordable and effective, even in countries with substantial resource constraints. This fact has not been well recognized in previous dialogues on cancer control in LMICs.

Major resourcing, geographic, financial, and sociocultural barriers to access to surgical cancer services exist in many LMICs. Given the high case-fatality rates from common malignancies such as breast cancer in LMICs, as well as the large projected increase in cancer incidence in these regions over the next 20 years, countries would benefit from strategic and proactive approaches to the planning and delivery of surgical cancer services. Unfortunately, very little is known about the most effective or cost-effective delivery platforms for surgical cancer care in LMICs to guide policy makers, or about how applicable or transferable models and lessons from HICs are to low-resource settings. Current models of care delivery in LMICs have been largely developed through experience, pragmatism, and consensus, rather than through rigorous academic or economic evaluation.

Key considerations in the scale-up of surgical cancer care in LMICs that are supported by evidence include the urgent need to develop the surgical workforce, improve basic general and surgical infrastructure, and strengthen supporting services. Coordinated integration of surgical services with other cancer services and the development of cancer networks and partnerships are also required to promote quality and standards.

Most important, efforts to improve surgical capacity in LMICs need to be coupled with strategies to promote cancer stage-shifting. Resource-appropriate efforts across the health system to facilitate the early detection of surgically treatable cancers and reduce barriers to timely service uptake are required to realize fully the curative benefits—as well as the associated social and economic gains—that surgery can offer.

NOTES

World Bank income classifications as of July 2014 are as follows, based on estimates of gross national income per capita for 2013:

- Low-income countries: US$1,045 or less
- Middle-income countries:
  a) Lower-middle-income: US$1,046–US$4,125
  b) Upper-middle-income: US$4,126–US$12,745
- High-income countries: US$12,746 or more

1. Typically, a country's income level and development status track with its health resource level. However, this is not always the case; there may be significant variation within countries in resource availability, according to geography and income quintile.

REFERENCES

Adebamowo, C. A., and O. O. Ajayi. 2000. "Breast Cancer in Nigeria." *West African Journal of Medicine* 19 (3): 179–91.

Agarwal, G., P. Ramakant, E. R. Forgach, J. C. Rendón, J. M. Chaparro, and others. 2009. "Breast Cancer Care in Developing Countries." *World Journal of Surgery* 33 (10): 2069–76.

Anderson, F. W., S. A. Obed, E. L. Boothman, and H. Opare-Ado. 2014. "The Public Health Impact of Training Physicians to Become Obstetricians and Gynecologists in Ghana." *American Journal of Public Health* 104 (Suppl. 1): S159–65. doi:10.2105/Ajph.2013.301581.

Anyanwu, S. N. 2000. "Breast Cancer in Eastern Nigeria: A Ten Year Review." *West African Journal of Medicine* 19 (2): 120–25.

———. 2008. "Temporal Trends in Breast Cancer Presentation in the Third World." *Journal of Experimental and Clinical Cancer Research* 27: 17. doi:10.1186/1756-9966-27-17.

Bae, J. Y., R. S. Groen, and A. L. Kushner. 2011. "Surgery as a Public Health Intervention: Common Misconceptions versus the Truth." *Bulletin of the World Health Organization* 89 (6): 395.

Bainbridge, D., J. Martin, M. Arango, and D. Cheng. 2012. "Perioperative and Anaesthetic-Related Mortality in Developed and Developing Countries: A Systematic Review and Meta-Analysis." *The Lancet* 380: 1075–81.

Binagwaho, A., F. Ngabo, C. M. Wagner, C. Mugeni, M. Gatera, and others. 2013. "Integration of Comprehensive Women's Health Programmes into Health Systems: Cervical Cancer Prevention, Care and Control in Rwanda." *Bulletin of the World Health Organization* 91 (9): 697–703. doi:10.2471/Blt.12.116087.

Chao, T. E., K. Sharma, M. Mandigo, L. Hagander, S. C. Resch, and others. 2014. "Cost-Effectiveness of Surgery and Its Policy Implications for Global Health: A Systematic Review and Analysis." *The Lancet Global Health* 2 (6): E334–45.

Chatterjee, S., and R. Laxminarayan. 2013. "Costs of Surgical Procedures in Indian Hospitals." *British Medical Journal Open* 3 (6).

Daher, M. 2012. "Cultural Beliefs and Values in Cancer Patients." *Annals of Oncology* 23 (Suppl. 3): 66–69.

Debas, H. T., P. Donkor, A. Gawande, D. T. Jamison, M. Kruk, and C. Mock. 2015. *Essential Surgery*. Volume 1 of *Disease Control Priorities in Developing Countries*, 3rd ed., edited by D. T. Jamison, H. Gelband, S. Horton, P. Jha, R. Laxminarayan, and R. Nugent. Washington, DC: World Bank.

Debas, H., R. Gosselin, C. McCord, and A. Thind. 2006. "Surgery." In *Disease Control Priorities in Developing Countries*, 2nd ed., edited by D. T. Jamison, J. Breman, A. R. Measham, G. Alleyne, M. Claeson, D. B. Evans, P. Jha, A. Mills, and P. Musgrove, 1245–59. Washington, DC: World Bank and Oxford University Press.

Dickens, C., M. Joffe, J. Jacobson, F. Venter, J. Schüz, and others. 2014. "Stage at Breast Cancer Diagnosis and Distance from Diagnostic Hospital in a Periurban Setting." *International Journal of Cancer* 135 (9): 2173–82. doi:10.1002/Ijc.28861.

Farmer, P. E., and J. Y. Kim. 2008. "Surgery and Global Health: A View from beyond the OR." *World Journal of Surgery* 32 (4): 533–36.

Ferlay J., I. Soerjomataram, M. Ervik, R. Dikshit, S. Eser, and others. 2013. GLOBOCAN 2012 v1.0, Cancer Incidence and Mortality Worldwide: IARC CancerBase No. 11. [Internet]. International Agency for Research on Cancer, Lyon, France. http://globocan.iarc.fr, accessed on 01/September/2014.

Ferlay, J., E. Steliarova-Foucher, J. Lortet-Tieulent, S. Rosso, J. W. W. Coebergh, and others. 2013. "Cancer Incidence and Mortality Patterns in Europe: Estimates for 40 Countries in 2012." *European Journal of Cancer* 49 (6): 1374–403.

Flores, G., J. Krishnakumar, O. O'Donnell, and E. Van Doorslaer. 2008. "Coping with Health-Care Costs: Implications for the Measurement of Catastrophic Expenditures and Poverty." *Health Economics* 17: 1393–412.

Funk, L. M., T. G. Weiser, W. R. Berry, S. R. Lipsitz, A. F. Merry, and others. 2010. "Global Operating Theatre Distribution and Pulse Oximetry Supply: An Estimation from Reported Data." *The Lancet* 376 (9746): 1055–61.

Glenshaw, M., and F. D. Madzimbamuto. 2005. "Anaesthesia Associated Mortality in a District Hospital in Zimbabwe." *Central African Journal of Medicine* 51: 39–44.

Goss, P. E., K. Strasser-Weippl, B. L. Lee-Bychkovsky, L. Fan, J. Li, and others. 2014. "Challenges to Effective Cancer Control in China, India and Russia." *The Lancet Oncology* 15: 489–538.

Greenberg, D., C. Earle, C. H. Fang, A. Eldar-Lissai, and P. J. Neumann. 2010. "When Is Cancer Care Cost-Effective?

A Systematic Overview of Cost-Utility Analyses in Oncology." *Journal of the National Cancer Institute* 102 (2): 82–88.

Grimes, C. E., J. A. Henry, J. Maraka, N. C. Mkandawire, and M. Cotton. 2014. "Cost-Effectiveness of Surgery in Low- and Middle-Income Countries: A Systematic Review." *World Journal of Surgery* 38 (1): 252–63.

Hamid, S. A., S. M. Ahsan, and A. Begum. 2014. "Disease-Specific Impoverishment Impact of Out-of-Pocket Payments for Health Care: Evidence from Rural Bangladesh." *Applied Health Economics and Health Policy* 12 (4): 421–33.

Hansen, D., S. C. Gausi, and M. Merikebu. 2000. "Anaesthesia in Malawi: Complications and Deaths." *Tropical Doctor* 30: 146–49.

Haynes, A. B., T. G. Weiser, W. R. Berry, S. R. Lipsitz, A.-H. S. Breizat, and others. 2009. "A Surgical Safety Checklist to Reduce Morbidity and Mortality in a Global Population." *New England Journal of Medicine* 360 (5): 491–99.

He, J., W. Shao, C. Cao, T. Yan, D. Wang, and others. 2011. "Long-Term Outcome and Cost-Effectiveness of Complete versus Assisted Video-Assisted Thoracic Surgery for Non-Small Cell Lung Cancer." *Journal of Surgical Oncology* 104 (2): 162–68.

Henry, J. A., E. Frenkel, E. Borgstein, N. C. Mkandawire, and C. Goddia. 2014. "Surgical and Anaesthetic Capacity of Hospitals in Malawi: Key Insights." *Health Policy and Planning* doi:10.1093?heapol/czu102.

Howitt, P., A. Darzi, G.-Z. Yang, H. Ashrafian, R. Atun, and others. 2012. "Technologies for Global Health." *The Lancet* 380 (9840): 507–35.

Hoyler, M., S. R. Finlayson, C. D. McClain, J. G. Meara, and L. Hagander. 2014. "Shortage of Doctors, Shortage of Data: A Review of the Global Surgery, Obstetrics, and Anesthesia Workforce Literature." *World Journal of Surgery* 38 (2): 269–80.

Ilbawi, A. M., E. M. Einterz, and D. Nkusu. 2013. "Obstacles to Surgical Services in a Rural Cameroonian District Hospital." *World Journal of Surgery* 37 (6): 1208–15.

Jamison, D. T., L. H. Summers, G. Alleyne, K. J. Arrow, S. Berkley, and others. 2013. "Global Health 2035: A World Converging within a Generation." *The Lancet* 382 (9908): 1898–955.

Kingham, P., O. I. Alatise, V. Vanderpuye, C. Casper, F. A. Abantanga, and others. 2013. "Treatment of Cancer in Sub-Saharan Africa." *The Lancet Oncology* 14: E158–67.

Lan, N. H., W. Laohasiriwong, J. F. Stewart, N. Dinh Tung, and P. C. Coyte. 2013. "Cost of Treatment for Breast Cancer in Central Vietnam." *Global Health Action* 6: 18872.

Lebrun, D. G., S. Chackungal, T. E. Chao, L. M. Knowlton, A. F. Linden, and others. 2014. "Prioritizing Essential Surgery and Safe Anesthesia for the Post-2015 Development Agenda: Operative Capacities of 78 District Hospitals in 7 Low- and Middle-Income Countries." *Surgery* 155 (3): 365–73.

Lu, Z., X. Yi, W. Feng, J. Ding, H. Xu, and others. 2012. "Cost-Benefit Analysis of Laparoscopic Surgery versus Laparotomy for Patients with Endometrioid Endometrial

Cancer: Experience from an Institute in China." *Journal of Obstetrics and Gynaecology Research* 38 (7): 1011–17.

Maman, A. F., A. Ouro-Bang'na, K. Tomta, S. Ahouangbévi, and M. Chobli. 2005. "Deaths Associated with Anaesthesia in Togo, West Africa." *Tropical Doctor* 35: 220–22.

Ozgediz, D., M. Galukande, J. Mabweijano, S. Kijjambu, C. Mijumbi, and others. 2008. "The Neglect of the Global Surgical Workforce: Experience and Evidence from Uganda." *World Journal of Surgery* 32 (6): 1208–15.

Pramesh, C. S., R. A. Badwe, B. B. Borthakur, M. Chandra, E. H. Raj, and others. 2014. "Delivery of Affordable and Equitable Cancer Care in India." *The Lancet Oncology* 15: E223–33.

Pramesh, C. S., R. A. Badwe, and R. K. Sinha. 2014. "The National Cancer Grid of India." *Indian Journal of Medical and Paediatric Oncology* 35: 226–27.

Purushotham, A. D., G. Lewison, and R. Sullivan. 2012. "The State of Research and Development in Global Cancer Surgery." *Annals of Surgery* 255 (3): 427–32.

Rose, J., D. C. Chang, T. G. Weiser, N. J. Kassebaum, and S. W. Bickler. 2014. "The Role of Surgery in Global Health: Analysis of United States Inpatient Procedure Frequency by Condition Using the Global Burden of Disease 2010 Framework." *Plos One* 9 (2): E89693. doi:10.1371/Journal.Pone.0089693.

Sankaranarayanan, R., K. Ramadas, S. Thara, R. Muwonge, J. Prabhakar, and others. 2011. "Clinical Breast Examination: Preliminary Results from a Cluster Randomized Controlled Trial in India." *Journal of the National Cancer Institute* 103 (19): 1476–80.

Tan, C., L. Peng, X. Zeng, J. Li, X. Wan, and others. 2013. "Economic Evaluation of First-Line Adjuvant Chemotherapies for Resectable Gastric Cancer Patients in China." *Plos One* 8 (12): e83396.

Thorat, M. A., A. Rangole, M. S. Nadkarni, V. Parmar, and R. A. Badwe. 2008. "Revision Surgery for Breast Cancer." *Cancer* 113 (Suppl. 8): 2347–52.

Ukwenya, A. Y., L. M. Yusufu, P. T. Nmadu, E. S. Garba, and A. Ahmed. 2008. "Delayed Treatment of Symptomatic Breast Cancer: The Experience from Kaduna, Nigeria." *South African Journal of Surgery* 46: 106–10.

Walker, I. A., and I. H. Wilson. 2008. "Anaesthesia in Developing Countries: A Risk for Patients." *The Lancet* 371 (9617): 968–69.

Weiser, T. G., S. E. Regenbogen, K. D. Thompson, A. B. Haynes, S. R. Lipsitz, and others. 2008. "An Estimation of the Global Volume of Surgery: A Modelling Strategy Based on Available Data." *The Lancet* 372 (9633): 139–44.

WHO (World Health Organization). 2003. *Surgical Care at the District Hospital*. Geneva: WHO.

Yip, C. H., and B. O. Anderson. 2007. "The Breast Health Global Initiative: Clinical Practice Guidelines for Management of Breast Cancer in Low- and Middle-Income Countries." *Expert Reviews in Anticancer Therapy* 7 (8): 1095–104.

Yip, C. H., E. Cazap, B. O. Anderson, K. L. Bright, M. Caleffi, and others. 2011. "Breast Cancer Management in Middle-Resource Countries (MRCs): Consensus Statement from the Breast Health Global Initiative." *The Breast* 20: S12–19.

Radiation Therapy for Cancer

David A. Jaffray and Mary K. Gospodarowicz

INTRODUCTION

More than 14 million new cases of cancer are diagnosed globally each year; radiation therapy (RT) has the potential to improve the rates of cure of 3.5 million people and provide palliative relief for an additional 3.5 million people. These conservative estimates are based on the fact that approximately 50 percent of all cancer patients can benefit from RT in the management of their disease (Barton, Frommer, and Shafiq 2006; Barton and others 2014; Tyldesley and others 2011); of these, approximately half present early enough to pursue curative intent.

Soon after Roentgen's discovery of X-rays in 1895, ionizing radiation was applied to the treatment of cancer, with remarkable results. Carefully controlled doses of ionizing radiation induce damage to the DNA in cells, with preferential effects on cancer cells compared with normal tissues, providing treatment benefits in most types of cancer and saving lives.

RT is now recognized as an essential element of an effective cancer care program throughout the world, regardless of countries' economic status. RT is used to cure cancers that are localized; it also can provide local control—complete response with no recurrence in the treated area—or symptom relief in cancers that are locally advanced or disseminated (Gunderson and Tepper 2012). It is frequently used in combination with surgery, either preoperatively or postoperatively, as well as in combination with systemic chemotherapy before,

during, or subsequent to the course of RT (Barton and others 2014).

Because radiation affects normal tissues and tumors, achieving an acceptable therapeutic ratio—defined as the probability of tumor control versus the probability of unacceptable toxicity—requires that the radiation dose be delivered within very tightly controlled tolerances with less than 5 percent deviation. This controlled production and precise application of radiation requires specialized equipment that is maintained and operated by a team of trained personnel. The team includes, at a minimum, radiation oncologists to prescribe the appropriate dose, medical physicists to ensure accurate dose delivery, and radiation technologists to operate the equipment and guide patients through the radiation process. Radiation oncologists work within multidisciplinary teams with medical and surgical oncologists to coordinate a multidisciplinary approach to the management of cancer. A comprehensive cancer center provides the full scope of RT services, ranging from externally applied beams of X-rays to the placement of radiation-emitting sources within tumors (see chapter 11 in this volume [Gospodarowicz and others 2015]).

RT is one of the more cost-effective cancer treatment modalities, despite the need for substantial capital investment in the facilities and equipment. Concerns about the initial investment, however, have resulted in severely limited access in most low- and middle-income countries (LMICs). Increasing the supply of RT services is critical to expanding effective cancer treatment in

Corresponding author: David A. Jaffray, University of Toronto, Princess Margaret Cancer Centre, and TECHNA Institute, David.Jaffray@rmp.uhn.on.ca.

USES OF RADIATION THERAPY

RT is an essential element of curative treatment of cancers of the breast, prostate, cervix, head and neck, lung, and brain, as well as sarcomas. The first four cancers are common in LMICs (Barton and others 2014; Delaney, Jacob, and Barton 2005b; Engstrom and others 2010; Gregoire and others 2010; Petrelli and others 2014; Pfister and others 2013; Ramos, Benavente, and Giralt 2010; Souchon and others 2009; Tyldesley and others 2011). RT is also used extensively in the management of prostate cancer (Delaney, Jacob, and Barton 2005a; Tyldesley and others 2011).

Patients with hematologic malignancies are primarily treated with chemotherapy, but they also access RT resources (Barton and others 2014). Total body irradiation is used in the treatment of leukemia in the context of bone marrow transplantation. Localized RT is applied in many lymphomas to optimize local disease control and cure; palliative RT is extremely useful in multiple myeloma and lymphomas. RT is increasingly used to control selected metastases. In short, RT both saves lives and alleviates suffering associated with cancer.

Radiation Therapy Alone

RT as the sole therapy is used in the treatment of localized tumors, such as early-stage cancer of the larynx or prostate; non-melanoma skin cancer; head and neck cancers; and radiosensitive tumor types, such as seminoma and lymphomas (Hoppe and others 2012; Motzer and others 2009). In more advanced disease stages, RT is used before, during, or after surgery and is frequently combined with chemotherapy, either as concurrent or adjuvant treatment.

Prior to the development of sophisticated computerized treatment planning systems, RT was planned using clinical information and conventional X-rays (2D RT) for field placement verification. This approach resulted in the use of large radiotherapy fields that assured coverage of the tumor, but also resulted in limiting toxicity. With the introduction of computerized tomography (CT) scanners and computerized treatment planning, fields were shaped (3D conformal radiation therapy, 3D CRT) to correspond to the tumors; the use of smaller fields resulted in less toxicity and the ability to escalate the radiation dose, with resulting improved outcomes and reduced toxicity. Now 3D CRT is the standard approach in most countries. However, in some low-income countries, the introduction of basic 2D radiotherapy would still save many lives and reduce suffering in thousands of patients with advanced cancers.

The use of high-dose RT has been limited by the dose delivered to adjacent normal tissues, especially those areas with limited radiation tolerance, called *critical normal structures*. Continued progress in computerization of RT planning and delivery allows shaping the radiation field to deposit higher doses to tumors and further sparing the surrounding normal tissues. These newer techniques—intensity modulated radiation therapy (IMRT) and stereotactic RT—allow a therapeutic dose of RT to be delivered in a few high-dose treatments and result in a higher probability of tumor eradication; they have been successfully applied in the management of brain metastasis and lung, bone, and paraspinal tumors. IMRT is being gradually introduced in many centers and is the preferred treatment for cancers of the prostate, as well as, head and neck, where it has been shown to improve outcomes significantly.

Concurrent Chemotherapy and Radiation Therapy

The use of concurrent chemotherapy and RT has significantly improved tumor eradication and survival in several cancers. It may improve local control, result in organ preservation, and eradicate distant microscopic metastases. This combination therapy has proven beneficial in treating cancers of the lung, cervix, head and neck, vulva, and anal canal (Benson and others 2012; Chen and others 2013; Glynne-Jones and Renehan 2012; Gregoire and others 2010; Koh and others 2013; Petrelli and others 2014).

Radiation Therapy as Adjuvant Treatment

RT is commonly used as adjuvant treatment following surgery, especially in the case of incomplete resection. Postoperative radiation is commonly used in cancers of the head and neck, rectum, breast, and lung, as well as soft tissue sarcomas (Gunderson and Tepper 2012). RT is also used after chemotherapy as the mainstay of treatment when chemotherapy alone was not expected to result in cure, such as for locally advanced breast cancer or bladder cancer, or as adjuvant treatment to potentially curative chemotherapy, such as for Hodgkin and non-Hodgkin lymphomas.

these settings and improving equity in access (Abdel-Wahab and others 2013; Fisher and others 2014; Goss and others 2013; Jaffray and Gospodarowicz 2014; Rodin and others 2014; Rosenblatt and others 2013).

Radiation Therapy in Metastatic Disease

RT is beneficial in providing palliation to patients with metastatic disease. It is highly effective in controlling bleeding and pain, as well as the symptoms resulting from compression of the nerves, spinal cord, or airways. The use of RT for pain relief is particularly valuable; a single moderate dose (8–10 Gy) achieves significant pain relief in 60–80 percent of patients. This benefit is of particular importance in LMICs, where many patients present with advanced and metastatic disease.

DELIVERING RADIATION THERAPY

RT is delivered in three ways:

- *External beam radiation therapy:* applied externally through directed beams of radiation to treat the cancer deep within the body.
- *Brachytherapy:* applied through the insertion of radiation-emitting sources directly within the tumor or adjacent body cavity.
- *Radioisotope therapy:* applied through the systemic injection of a radioisotope that has been designed to target disease.

Externally applied radiation beams can be produced by several approaches: radioactive sources, such as cobalt-60, that emit gamma rays; high-energy X-rays or photons produced by linear accelerators; or particle beams—electrons, protons, or heavier ions—accelerated by other types of accelerators. These machines are equipped with accessories that are able to shape dynamically the radiation beam according to beam direction, as well as onboard imaging devices that can verify the accuracy of treatment delivery. Linear accelerators are currently the backbone of external beam RT; multiple companies manufacture the technologies, offering a range of high-energy X-rays (4–25 MV) to enable treatment of deep-seated tumors.

Brachytherapy involves either temporarily or permanently placing radiation-emitting sources directly within tissues or body cavities. Permanent sources decay rapidly, depositing the dose and remaining in the body; temporary placement uses higher-activity sources that are electromechanically guided to tumors within preplaced interstitial or intracavitary catheters. The source and applicators are removed after delivery of the prescribed dose of radiation. These removable radiation sources can provide either *low-dose rate brachytherapy*, where the source remains in the tissues for

several days, or *high-dose rate brachytherapy*, where the single dose of radiation is delivered within minutes.

Radioisotope therapy may be applied in the radiotherapy department or in the nuclear medicine department. The most common application of radioisotope therapy is in the treatment of thyroid cancer using radioactive iodine or in the palliation of pain from bone metastasis using a radioactive isotope of strontium. Less common indications employ a conjugated radioisotope such as lutetium (^{177}Lu) DOTA-TATE to target somatostatin-expressing neuroendocrine tumors.

Facilities

RT is delivered in a specially designed facility that contains specialized equipment for imaging, treatment planning, and radiation delivery. Modern RT departments are designed to optimize patient flow through the process and contain the following elements:

- Waiting areas
- Examination rooms
- Imaging suites with simulators/CT-simulators
- Computer planning workrooms
- Shielded treatment rooms for linear accelerators or ^{60}Co treatment units
- Shielded high-dose rate brachytherapy suites.

Additional support space is required for a physics testing laboratory, equipment storage, and dedicated environmentally controlled computer server rooms.

External beam RT is delivered using machines that produce high-energy X-ray or electron beams. The two main types of photon beams are ^{60}Co machines or X-ray-generating linear accelerators. Cobalt units contain radioactive cobalt sources in the head of the unit that emit photons with a mean energy of 1.25 MeV. The source is constantly emitting and requires constant radiation protection; it decays gradually and requires replacement every three to five years. Linear accelerators use electric power to generate an electron beam that is accelerated to produce a high-energy photon beam. Linear accelerators require a stable power supply for reliable operation. Both units have collimators and filters to shape the radiation beam, including multileaf collimators that allow motorized shaping and/or modulation of the beam shape and intensity during treatment delivery, thereby producing more conformal irradiation of the target tissues while minimizing normal tissue exposure. In the past 10 years, X-ray and CT imaging capabilities have been added to these machines to allow therapists to guide the placement of the radiation with increased precision and accuracy.

Personnel

RT requires a specially trained team of professionals that includes radiation oncologists to prescribe the dose; medical physicists, trained to commission and maintain the equipment and develop treatment plans; radiation technologists or therapists to operate the treatment units; and nurses experienced in managing patients undergoing therapy. Biomedical engineers and computer or information technology experts complement the team.

Once a decision to treat a patient has been made, the team develops a treatment plan and proceeds with delivery. The plan is based on accepted clinical guidelines that describe the indications for RT; the target tissues to be irradiated; the dose and fractionation prescriptions; support for patients during treatment; and management of patients after treatment, including acute and late complications of treatment.

The safe and effective management of the RT system requires a high level of communication and coordination of the processes and systems employed in the prescription, design, and delivery of radiation. Local, national, and international bodies provide regulations and guidelines for radiation safety, dose calibration, and quality assurance of devices, clinical practice, and monitoring of compliance.

Process

The *process* refers to all the steps from the decision to treat a patient with radiation to the completion of the course of radiation treatment.

- *Prescription.* The first step is completion of the radiation prescription, which indicates the exact part of the body to be treated, as well as the dose/fractionation schedule, including the total radiation dose to be delivered in how many fractions, at what intervals, and in what overall time period.
- *Planning.* The second step is initiation of the planning process. Patients are positioned on an X-ray imaging machine that simulates the geometry of the treatment machine, or in more modern settings, on a specially adapted CT scanner (CT simulator). A desired position is determined (supine, prone, arms up or by the side of the body); if needed, the patient is immobilized with a specifically designed device to secure the reproducibility of the position. The set-up

information is documented in the RT chart or electronic medical record. Images of the part of the body to be treated are obtained and stored.

- *Treatment plan.* Once the set-up and imaging are complete, the radiation oncologist outlines the tissues that must be irradiated on images and a radiation technologist/dosimetrist or a medical physicist develops the treatment plan, using specialized planning software that models the placement of radiation beams and the dose contributed by each beam to ensure that the prescribed dose is delivered to the disease, while the dose to other tissues is minimized, especially critical and particularly sensitive organs. The individualized treatment plan is independently verified, and the total dose is delivered through a series of treatments (fractions) in a prearranged schedule of sessions, usually daily over several weeks, as specified in the prescription.
- *Treatment delivery.* Once the treatment plan is developed by a medical physicist and dosimetrist and reviewed and approved by a radiation oncologist, the treatment can begin. In each session, the patient is positioned exactly as during the simulation. After verifying the prescription, treatment plan, and patient's position, the radiation dose is delivered. Treatments are frequently given five days per week; in curative settings, they may continue for four to six weeks. Daily treatments are commonly delivered during a session lasting 10–20 minutes.

In specific circumstances, RT is applied in a shorter schedule consisting of one to three high-dose fractions. These hypofractionated treatments can be applied with generous margins for symptom relief for palliation rather than local disease control. Alternatively, they can be applied for curative intent, using high-precision (also called *stereotactic*) methods, wherein the targeted volume is very small and surrounding normal tissues are avoided.

During each session, specific verification steps are taken before the dose is applied. During the course of RT, the patient is monitored daily by technologists and at least weekly by a physician; patients with acute side effects receive supportive care, as needed. The radiation records are kept for decades and made available for review in case further RT or other interventions, such as surgery, are planned for the previously irradiated part of the body.

Safe and Effective Operation

The staff processes and equipment need to be well managed to ensure safe and effective care that adheres to best practices and evidence-based medicine. Specially trained and certified personnel are essential for safe and effective treatments, as well as safe operation of the facility. The medical specialization requires a residency in radiation oncology to learn evidence-based practice, radiation biology, and the principles of radiation physics. Typically, an experienced radiation oncologist oversees the operations of the RT department. The technological and treatment design activities are supported by specially trained physicists, called *medical physicists,* with a degree in physics and additional training to acquire the specific skills required to practice RT. Trained technologists interact with patients and operate the treatment machines to deliver the radiation doses. Dedicated education programs have been developed to train these staff members in a range of topics, including patient care, technology, and radiation physics.

The operational team of the department has several key responsibilities:

- Ensuring that the radiation systems are safe for patients, the public, and staff members
- Ensuring that the radiation equipment is appropriately calibrated, tested, and maintained
- Ensuring that the each patient receives appropriate care through peer review of the treatment plan and independent checks of the calculations
- Monitoring and responding to errors or variations in the delivery of care.

Depending on the local, national, and international context, these activities may need to comply with regulations.

Integration into Cancer Centers

RT departments collaborate closely with departments of pathology and laboratory medicine, diagnostic imaging, surgery or surgical oncology, medical oncology, and palliative care to ensure that treatment plans are created based on correct diagnosis, full assessment of disease extent (stage), and the medical condition of the patient. Modern clinical practice ensures the physical and operational infrastructure is in place to allow multidisciplinary cancer care. This infrastructure may include multidisciplinary clinics and conferences where the management of the patient is discussed with all appropriate experts—for example, oncologists, pathologists, and radiologists—and the amalgamation of medical records to facilitate communication and coordination of care.

RT has evolved from the direct application of a single beam of ionizing radiation to a cancerous lesion to image-guided, computer-optimized, robotically controlled systems that work to maximize the therapeutic ratio for each patient. This evolution has resulted in significant increases in the complexity of the treatment, which is characterized by hundreds of megabytes of treatment data and detailed quality control activities to ensure that the prescription is applied not only accurately, but also appropriately for each patient. In the interest of reducing costs and standardizing interventions, the field is developing automated methods that allow high-quality treatment plans to be designed in a few minutes. These approaches promise to "bury the complexity" of the current RT process, while still providing a high degree of safety and personalization (Jaffray 2012).

The adoption of expert systems and machine learning methods allows the treatment team to design and deliver highly personalized RT (Purdie and others 2014). This degree of automation provides a valuable form of peer review that is inexpensive and can learn from experts around the world by drawing on the clinical expertise that has gone into large databases of existing treatment plans. The emergence of cloud-based treatment planning and peer review is likely to fuse with modern telemedicine approaches to create more efficient delivery and learning platforms. An additional advantage of these cost-saving methods is that they require a standardization in the nomenclature used to describe the treatment intent and treatment record—a benefit that is highly synergistic with the adoption of medical and bioinformatics efforts that promise to advance clinical practice (Lambin and others 2013).

EQUITABLE ACCESS TO RADIATION THERAPY

The World Health Organization recommends that all countries develop and implement a population-based cancer control plan. These plans are based on the information provided by cancer registries and include plans for prevention; screening and early detection; timely access to high-quality treatment, including surgery, radiotherapy, and chemotherapy; and palliative and supportive care.

Planning RT resource provision requires detailed knowledge of the patterns of cancer, including different disease entities and distribution by stage. National cancer plans should define the number of departments and treatment machines that are appropriate for the current and projected cancer burden. The distribution of cancer facilities needs to consider not only the burden, but also the geographic distribution of the population to facilitate access.

Requisite elements of effective RT include medical and professional education, training programs for support staff, and ongoing refreshment of equipment and infrastructure. Specific elements that need attention include the following:

- *Medical education system.* The training of radiation oncologists, medical physicists, and radiation therapists is a critical element. Without this foundation, shortages of professionals will lead to long waiting lists, treatment delays, and compromised outcomes. In addition, the lack of local training programs prevents the establishment of a stable supply of staff to operate the facilities. This lack is not only a challenge during initiation of a program; it will persist as cancer services are ramped up to reach the level of appropriate use.
- *Regulatory structure.* The presence of external accreditation and regulation frameworks helps to standardize the operation of RT departments and secure high-quality practice. Establishing these frameworks can be particularly challenging in resource-constrained economies, where infrastructure is limited and political stability is an issue.
- *Societal infrastructure.* Limitations in access to a reliable supply of electric power, climate control, service infrastructure, and complex procurement settings affected by such factors as political instability and transportation are problematic.

Innovative approaches need to be pursued to address the numerous challenges that impede capacity building. These innovations need to come from the technological, educational, operational, and clinical practice domains to avoid unnecessary suffering and loss of human life.

Efforts to Address the Equity Gap

Ample evidence indicates severe gaps in access to RT in large areas of the world. The International Atomic Energy Agency (IAEA) maintains a directory of all RT facilities (http://www-naweb.iaea.org/nahu/dirac/).

Significant inequity exists in access to RT across the world. Map 14.1 shows one descriptor. By comparison, access rates in high-income countries would correspond to approximately 100,000 people served by one radiation treatment machine.

IAEA has brought attention to the lack of adequate RT resources for several decades. Comprehensive reviews of the resources in Europe, Latin America and the Caribbean, and Sub-Saharan Africa describe the limitations in centers, equipment, and staff. One publication on cancer in Sub-Saharan Africa stated that 29 of 52 countries have no RT facilities; those that have facilities face severe shortages. Less than 10 percent of the population in the region has access (Zubizarreta and others 2015).

The barriers to the implementation of RT are numerous. They include perceptions that it is expensive, complex, and unlikely to succeed because of the

Map 14.1 Number of People Served by One Radiotherapy Unit

IBRD 41687 I JULY 2015

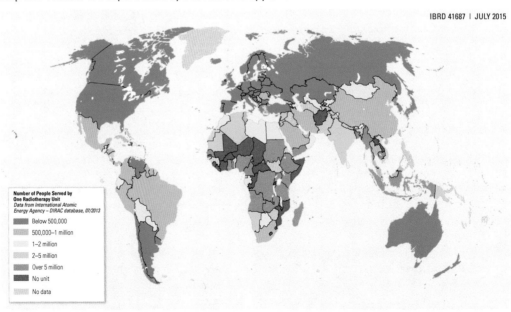

Source: Based on data from the Directory of Radiotherapy Centres (DIRAC) database of radiation therapy equipment, International Atomic Energy Agency, Vienna, http://www-naweb.iaea.org/nahu/dirac/.

shortage of qualified personnel and funding. With many competing demands for cancer control activities, there is a risk that the appropriate investment in RT may not be made, leaving countries and patients to wrestle with dysfunctional cancer services.

IAEA has provided technical assistance, training and education, and financing for equipment. Unfortunately, these efforts have not resolved the severe limitations in access. The IAEA Programme of Action for Cancer Therapy, established in 2004 (http://cancer.iaea.org/), organized a large number of missions to assess the readiness of a country to develop new RT facilities. These missions assess all aspects of cancer control, since the potential benefit offered by RT can be realized only in the presence of adequate diagnostic facilities, surgery, chemotherapy, and supportive and palliative care. IAEA can advise governments on the optimal ways to proceed, but the implementation depends on the political will and resources devoted to cancer control.

Effective cancer planning has improved access in a number of areas, including Brazil; Ireland; Ontario, Canada; and Poland (Chalubinska-Fendler and others 2014). Overall, however, such progress is lacking in LMICs, and international partnerships and assistance are needed to accelerate progress to close the access gap. The U.S.-based AMPATH Program is building a new cancer center in Eldoret, Kenya, and has included plans to implement RT as soon as possible (http://www.ampathkenya.org/our-programs/primary-care-chronic-diseases/oncology/).

In Latin America and the Caribbean, a unique network of national cancer institutes has embarked on an initiative to improve the quality of RT in the region (http://www2.rinc-unasur.org/wps/wcm/connect/rinc/site/home). The Network of National Cancer Institutions of Latin America (RINC) initiative draws together 18 countries to organize a regional community of best practices; exchange information and knowledge; identify needs, opportunities, and common interests; foster coordination among member countries; and promote the commitment of every country's corresponding levels of government, with emphasis on the availability of the financial, human, and legislative resources necessary for the development of cancer control.

Ongoing efforts in India and Turkey offer promise, but to date fall short of addressing the limited access to effective RT for their populations (Banerjee, Mahantshetty, and Shrivastava 2014; Goksel and others 2011).

Although ample data describe the benefits of RT for cancer control, the cost of equipment and development of skills seem an overwhelming challenge. This does not need to be the case; any return begins with an investment. Real effort needs to be put into calculating the true cost and the resultant benefits of RT so that decision makers can make informed choices. Such approaches have been applied in advancing the global HIV/AIDS effort and are being pursued by the Union for International Cancer Control Global Task Force on Radiotherapy for Cancer Control (http://www.gtfrcc.org). Such approaches are the key to articulating the importance and value of financial investments in cancer control. Moreover, these approaches immediately lead to the development of novel financing schemes to overcome the reluctance to commit the funds for the capital investment required to improve access globally (chapter 17 in this volume [Knaul and others 2015]).

CONCLUSIONS

Cancer is projected to become the number one cause of death across the globe in the next 20 years. The evidence demonstrates that more than 40 percent of patients with cancer would benefit from RT; the lack of access will compromise the care of millions of people suffering from cancer if not addressed through immediate action. The global community has been working hard to ensure quality through standardization in RT practices and provide guidance in the establishment of new treatment capacity (IAEA 2008). It is now critical that RT be acknowledged as an essential element of an effective cancer control plan—and that the critical equipment, operations, and educational investments be provided to ensure that RT is in place to respond to the growing cancer burden.

NOTE

World Bank income classifications as of July 2014 are as follows, based on estimates of gross national income per capita for 2013:

- Low-income countries (LICs): US$1,045 or less
- Middle-income countries are subdivided:
  a) Lower-middle-income: US$1,046–US$4,125
  b) Upper-middle-income (UMICs): US$4,126–US$12,745
- High-income countries (HICs): US$12,746 or more.

REFERENCES

Abdel-Wahab, M., J. M. Bourque, Y. Pynda, J. Izewska, D. Van der Merwe, and others. 2013. "Status of Radiotherapy Resources in Africa: An International Atomic Energy Agency Analysis." *The Lancet Oncology* 14 (4): e168–75. doi:10.1016/s1470-2045(12)70532-6.

Banerjee, S., U. Mahantshetty, and S. Shrivastava. 2014. "Brachytherapy in India: A Long Road Ahead." *Journal of Contemporary Brachytherapy* 6 (3): 331–35.

Barton, M. B., M. Frommer, and J. Shafiq. 2006. "Role of Radiotherapy in Cancer Control in Low-Income and Middle-Income Countries." *The Lancet Oncology* 7 (7): 584–95. doi:10.1016/s1470-2045(06)70759-8.

Barton, M. B., S. Jacob, J. Shafiq, K. Wong, S. R. Thompson, and others. 2014. "Estimating the Demand for Radiotherapy from the Evidence: A Review of Changes from 2003 to 2012." *Radiotherapy & Oncology* 112 (1): 140–44. doi:10.1016/j.radonc.2014.03.024. Epub May 12.

Benson, A. B., 3rd, J. P. Arnoletti, T. Bekaii-Saab, E. Chan, Y. J. Chen, and others. 2012. "Anal Carcinoma, Version 2.2012: Featured Updates to the NCCN Guidelines." *Journal of the National Comprehensive Cancer Network* 10 (4): 449–54.

Chalubinska-Fendler, J., W. Fendler, J. Luniewska-Bury, W. Mlynarski, M. Spych, and others. 2014. "Tackling the Turmoil of Transformation: Radiation Oncology in Poland." *International Journal of Radiation Oncology, Biology, Physics* 90 (3): 480–86. doi:10.1016/j.ijrobp.2014.05.031.

Chen, R. C., W. U. Shipley, J. A. Efstathiou, and A. L. Zietman. 2013. "Trimodality Bladder Preservation Therapy for Muscle-Invasive Bladder Cancer." *Journal of the National Comprehensive Cancer Network* 11 (8): 952–60.

Delaney, G., S. Jacob, and M. Barton. 2005a. "Estimating the Optimal External-Beam Radiotherapy Utilization Rate for Genitourinary Malignancies." *Cancer* 103 (3): 462–73. doi:10.1002/cncr.20789.

———. 2005b. "Estimation of an Optimal External Beam Radiotherapy Utilization Rate for Head and Neck Carcinoma." *Cancer* 103 (11): 2216–27. doi:10.1002/cncr.21084.

Engstrom, P. F., J. P. Arnoletti, A. B. Benson, 3rd, J. D. Berlin, J. M. Berry, and others. 2010. "NCCN Clinical Practice Guidelines in Oncology: Anal Carcinoma." *Journal of the National Comprehensive Cancer Network* 8 (1): 106–20.

Fisher, B. J., L. C. Daugherty, J. P. Einck, G. Suneja, M. M. Shah, and others. 2014. "Radiation Oncology in Africa: Improving Access to Cancer Care on the African Continent." *International Journal of Radiation Oncology, Biology, Physics* 89 (3): 458–61. doi:10.1016/j.ijrobp.2013.12.032.

Glynne-Jones, R., and A. Renehan. 2012. "Current Treatment of Anal Squamous Cell Carcinoma." *Hematology/Oncology Clinics of North America* 26 (6): 1315–50. doi:10.1016/j.hoc.2012.08.011.

Goksel, F., O. Koc, N. Ozgul, M. Gultekin, M. Abacioglu, and others. 2011. "Radiation Oncology Facilities in Turkey: Current Status and Future Perspectives." *Asian Pacific Journal of Cancer Prevention* 12: 2157–62.

Gospodarowicz, M., J. Trypuc, A. D'Cruz, J. Khader, S. Omar, and F. Knaul. 2015. "Cancer Services and the Comprehensive Cancer Center." In *Disease Control Priorities* (third edition): Volume 3, *Cancer*, edited by H. Gelband, P. Jha, R. Sankaranarayanan, and S. Horton. Washington, DC: World Bank.

Goss, P. E., B. L. Lee, T. Badovinac-Crnjevic, K. Strasser-Weippl, Y. Chavarri-Guerra, and others. 2013. "Planning Cancer Control in Latin America and the Caribbean." *The Lancet Oncology* 14 (5): 391–436. doi:10.1016/s1470-2045(13)70048-2.

Gregoire, V., J. L. Lefebvre, L. Licitra, E. Felip, and Ehns-Esmo-Estro Guidelines Working Group. 2010. "Squamous Cell Carcinoma of the Head and Neck: EHNS-ESMO-ESTRO Clinical Practice Guidelines for Diagnosis, Treatment and Follow-Up." *Annals of Oncology* 21 (Suppl. 5): v184–86. doi:10.1093/annonc/mdq185.

Gunderson, L. L., and J. E. Tepper. 2012. *Clinical Radiation Oncology*. 3rd ed. Philadelphia, PA: Saunders; London: Elsevier.

Hoppe, R. T., R. H. Advani, W. Z. Ai, R. F. Ambinder, P. Aoun, and others. 2012. "Hodgkin Lymphoma, Version 2.2012: Featured Updates to the NCCN Guidelines." *Journal of the National Comprehensive Cancer Network* 10 (5): 589–97.

IAEA (International Atomic Energy Agency). 2008. *Setting Up a Radiotherapy Programme: Clinical, Medical Physics, Radiation Protection and Safety Aspects.* Vienna: IAEA.

Jaffray, D. A. 2012. "Image-Guided Radiotherapy: From Current Concept to Future Perspectives." *Nature Reviews Clinical Oncology* 9 (12): 688–99. doi:10.1038/nrclinonc.2012.194.

Jaffray, D. A., and M. Gospodarowicz. 2014. "Bringing Global Access to Radiation Therapy: Time for a Change in Approach." *International Journal of Radiation Oncology, Biology, Physics* 89 (3): 446–47. doi:10.1016/j.ijrobp.2014.05.019.

Knaul, F., S. Horton, P. Yerramilli, H. Gelband, and R. Atun. 2015. "Financing Cancer Care in Low-Resource Settings." In *Disease Control Priorities* (third edition): Volume 3, *Cancer*, edited by H. Gelband, P. Jha, R. Sankaranarayanan, and S. Horton. Washington, DC: World Bank.

Koh, W. J., B. E. Greer, N. R. Abu-Rustum, S. M. Apte, S. M. Campos, and others. 2013. "Cervical Cancer." *Journal of the National Comprehensive Cancer Network* 11 (3): 320–43.

Lambin, P., R. G. Van Stiphout, M. H. Starmans, E. Rios-Velazquez, G. Nalbantov, and others. 2013. "Predicting Outcomes in Radiation Oncology: Multifactorial Decision Support Systems." *Nature Reviews Clinical Oncology* 10 (1): 27–40. doi:10.1038/nrclinonc.2012.196.

Motzer, R. J., N. Agarwal, C. Beard, G. B. Bolger, B. Boston, and others. 2009. "NCCN Clinical Practice Guidelines in Oncology: Testicular Cancer." *Journal of the National Comprehensive Cancer Network* 7 (6): 672–93.

Petrelli, F., A. De Stefani, F. Raspagliesi, D. Lorusso, and S. Barni. 2014. "Radiotherapy with Concurrent Cisplatin-Based Doublet or Weekly Cisplatin for Cervical Cancer: A Systematic Review and Meta-Analysis." *Gynecologic Oncology* 134 (1): 166–71. doi:10.1016/j.ygyno.2014.04.049.

Pfister, D. G., K. K. Ang, D. M. Brizel, B. A. Burtness, P. M. Busse, and others. 2013. "Head and Neck Cancers, Version 2.2013. Featured Updates to the NCCN

Guidelines." *Journal of the National Comprehensive Cancer Network* 11 (8): 917–23.

Purdie, T. G., R. E. Dinniwell, A. Fyles, and M. B. Sharpe. 2014. "Automation and Intensity Modulated Radiation Therapy for Individualized High-Quality Tangent Breast Treatment Plans." *International Journal of Radiation Oncology, Biology, Physics* 90 (3): 688–95. doi:10.1016/j.ijrobp.2014.06.056.

Ramos, M., S. Benavente, and J. Giralt. 2010. "Management of Squamous Cell Carcinoma of the Head and Neck: Updated European Treatment Recommendations." *Expert Review of Anticancer Therapy* 10 (3): 339–44. doi:10.1586/era.10.6.

Rodin, D., D. Jaffray, R. Atun, F. M. Knaul, M. Gospodarowicz, and others. 2014. "The Need to Expand Global Access to Radiotherapy." *The Lancet Oncology* 15 (4): 378–80. doi:10.1016/s1470-2045(14)70121-4.

Rosenblatt, E., J. Izewska, Y. Anacak, Y. Pynda, P. Scalliet, and others. 2013. "Radiotherapy Capacity in European Countries: An Analysis of the Directory of Radiotherapy Centres (DIRAC) Database." *The Lancet Oncology* 14 (2): e79–86. doi:10.1016/s1470-2045(12)70556-9.

Souchon, R., F. Wenz, F. Sedlmayer, W. Budach, J. Dunst, and others. 2009. "DEGRO Practice Guidelines for Palliative Radiotherapy of Metastatic Breast Cancer: Bone Metastases and Metastatic Spinal Cord Compression (MSCC)." *Strahlentherapie und Onkologie* 185 (7): 417–24. doi:10.1007/s00066-009-2044-2.

Tyldesley, S., G. Delaney, F. Foroudi, L. Barbera, M. Kerba, and others. 2011. "Estimating the Need for Radiotherapy for Patients with Prostate, Breast, and Lung Cancers: Verification of Model Estimates of Need with Radiotherapy Utilization Data from British Columbia." *International Journal of Radiation Oncology, Biology, Physics* 79 (5): 1507–15. doi:10.1016/j.ijrobp.2009.12.070.

Zubizarreta, E. H., E. Fidarova, B. Healy, and E. Rosenblatt. 2015. "Need for Radiotherapy in Low and Middle Income Countries: The Silent Crisis Continues." *Clinical Oncology* 27 (2): 107–14. doi:10.1016/j.clon.2014.10.006.

Chapter 15

Need for National Commitments to Cancer Research to Guide Public Health Investment and Practice

Edward L. Trimble, Preetha Rajaraman, Ann Chao,
Thomas Gross, Carol Levin, You-Lin Qiao, Timothy Rebbeck,
Lisa Stevens, and Fang-hui Zhao

INTRODUCTION

This chapter is addressed primarily to potential funders of health research at the national, provincial, and state levels. Health research in general, and cancer research in particular, is not a luxury reserved for high-income countries (HICs); it is a necessity for all countries across the income spectrum. The extent and depth of that research may vary by a country's financial situation, and the topics may vary by a country's specific burden of cancers and associated risk factors. Nevertheless, a comprehensive health research plan is foundational to the ability to allocate resources efficiently and effectively, develop human capacity and infrastructure, and identify the appropriate technologies and medicines for health and health services delivery. In short, robust research is essential to building evidence-based cancer prevention and control programs.

In recognition of the foundational nature of research, ministers and representatives of ministries of health, science and technology, agriculture, education, foreign affairs, and international cooperation from 53 countries convened in 2008 in Mali at the Bamako Global Ministerial Forum on Research in Health. Of the 53 participating countries, 38 were low- and middle-income countries (LMICs), according to

World Bank criteria. The group issued its Call to Action, which articulates the rationale for supporting research to inform public policy, and sent the Call to Action to the World Health Organization (WHO 2008). The Call to Action recommends that national governments allocate at least 2 percent of the budgets of ministries of health to research and that international development agencies invest at least 5 percent of development assistance funds earmarked for the health sector in research. Box 15.1 highlights many of the principles applicable to cancer research.

Subsequent white papers and policy statements have made clear the importance of research on noncommunicable diseases and cancer to guide public policy and public investment (See Annotated Select Bibliography).

STAKEHOLDERS AND THEIR KNOWLEDGE NEEDS IN CANCER RESEARCH

There are many stakeholders in cancer prevention and control, including researchers, ministers of health, physicians, other providers, and patients.

The most important stakeholders are the individuals with cancer, their families, patient advocates, and those at risk of cancer. Ministers of health and their colleagues

Corresponding author: Edward L. Trimble, MD, MPH, trimblet@nih.org

Box 15.1

Highlights of the 2008 Bamako Call to Action for Research on Health

- *Adopting comprehensive approaches.* Ensure that research and innovations are interdisciplinary and intersectoral; engage the public sector, private sector, and civil society associations in collaborations.
- *Setting priorities.* Develop the global research agenda in light of national and regional priorities, and encourage national governments to make the development of policies for health research and innovation a priority.
- *Building capacity.* Improve capacity at all relevant levels to foster research and technology transfer, improve the education and training of researchers, integrate research into health systems, and establish systems to evaluate the impact of research.
- *Improving equity.* Make greater equity a key element in the process.

Source: WHO 2008.

are also important stakeholders, as are physicians and other members of the health care team who provide care on a daily basis. Additional ministries at the national and state levels often play roles (albeit some of them minor), including the ministries responsible for finance, education, science and technology, agriculture, energy, customs, and foreign affairs. Universities and other academic units, as well as hospitals and clinics in the public and private sectors, have major roles in research.

Nongovernmental organizations are also crucial partners in fostering cancer research. Specialists from many disciplines of research and health are involved, including physicians, nurses, pharmacists, psychologists, social workers, epidemiologists, biostatisticians, basic and translational research scientists, information technologists, and data managers.

The needs of national stakeholders should guide cancer research in each country. One way to recognize those needs is by determining what ministries of health need to know (box 15.2) and what patients and their doctors need to know (box 15.3).

RESEARCH PRIORITIES IN CANCER

Health Surveillance and Cancer Surveillance

Making cancer surveillance an integral part of public health surveillance, which collects information on other risk factors and diseases, will greatly facilitate efforts to improve cancer outcomes. More than 20 percent of cancers in LMICs, for example, are associated with chronic viral, bacterial, or helminthic infection (De Martel and others 2012). Comprehensive cancer surveillance, accordingly, requires surveillance of relevant preventive practices, including vaccinations, that can influence the incidence and prevalence of infections linked to cancer. Similarly, cancer and other noncommunicable diseases, such as cardiovascular disease, diabetes, and chronic obstructive pulmonary disease, share a number of common risk factors, such as tobacco use, obesity, poor diet, physical inactivity, alcohol consumption, and environmental pollution. Surveillance for these common risk factors is critical to effective cancer control.

The Institute for Health Metrics and Evaluation (2011) has developed a framework for integrating surveillance systems across health information sources to help decision makers allocate resources and evaluate interventions. The World Health Organization also collects data on a variety of health indicators across diseases through its Global Health Observatory (WHO 2013). Table 15.1 sets out the range of health surveillance systems with relevance for cancer prevention and control. Few countries can afford to collect such health surveillance data on 100 percent of their populations. Nonetheless, through judicious use of cross-sectional surveys in representative populations, cohort studies, and disease and death registries, health policy makers can draft, implement, evaluate, and modify cancer control plans.

A national system that assigns unique individual identifying numbers or biometrics can be used routinely at all health system encounters and vital registrations of births and deaths to strengthen national health surveillance systems. Such a national identification system can facilitate the linkage of medical records, including records from clinic visits and hospitalizations, immunization records, pathology reports, operative notes, health insurance reimbursement information, and death registration.

Cancer Registries and Pathologic Diagnosis

Cancer Registries The most basic public health oncology question is what is the burden of cancer in a city, a state, a country, or a region? The answer begins with pathology laboratories, where biological specimens for individuals—including blood tests, diagnostic biopsies,

Box 15.2

What Do Ministries of Health Need to Know?

The answers to the following questions are relevant to ministries of health from low-, middle-, and high-income countries.

What is the burden of cancer in the country?
- How many cancers are diagnosed each year?
- How many people die from cancer?
- Which are the most common cancers?
- Which geographic regions and populations bear the greatest cancer burden?
- How does the burden of cancer compare with that of other diseases?
- What are the risk factors for cancer in the country?

What resources are now in place for cancer control?
- What can be done in the context of the existing health care system to prevent cancer and other common diseases?
- What can be done to screen for and treat cancer?
- How can we help cancer survivors return to being productive members of society?
- What palliative care can we provide?

What could we do by redeploying existing resources? What else should we be doing and what will it cost?
- What are the "best buys" for the country in the context of currently available health resources?

and surgical specimens—are evaluated. To these data are added cancers diagnosed on the basis of imaging studies, as well as cancers diagnosed on the basis of physical signs and patient symptoms. The data for individuals diagnosed with cancer can then be added up to give a picture of the overall cancer burden. Cancer registry data can provide descriptive and trend information about the burden of cancer in a population and enable the formation of hypotheses about etiology that can be tested in analytic studies. Cancer registry data also inform the need for cancer diagnosis and treatment facilities and allow the evaluation of cancer control interventions in a population.

Obtaining such data at the country level is difficult and expensive. The traditional approach has been to start small, with one hospital, then expand to a city or county, then to a state or province, and finally to other representative or high-risk populations of interest. Population-based registries may cover a representative portion of the geographic region of interest from which the larger (for example, countrywide) cancer burden can be estimated. Furthermore, population-based registries can be used to evaluate community health interventions in the region.

In the United States, for example, the National Cancer Institute's Surveillance, Epidemiology, and End Results (SEER) Program began to capture information on cancer incidence from 14 percent of the country's population in 1973. The scope was subsequently expanded to track additional areas with low-income

Box 15.3

What Do Patients and Doctors Need to Know?

The answers to these questions are relevant for patients, families, and health care providers in low-, middle-, and high-income countries.

- What type of cancer does the patient have?
- What is the extent or stage of the cancer?
- What are the options for treating the cancer and its symptoms?
- How can the patient gain access to appropriate and affordable cancer therapy, treatment of symptoms, survivorship counseling, and supportive care?
- If the treatment works as hoped and the patient is cured of cancer, what steps are needed to help the patient reintegrate into family and work life?
- If the cancer is too advanced for curative therapy or if treatment does not cure the patient, will the patient benefit from palliative care, including pain control?
- How can the patient best gain access to palliative care?

Table 15.1 Health Surveillance Systems for Noncommunicable Diseases and Cancer Control Planning

Infections

- Incidence and prevalence of infections linked to cancer, such as hepatitis B virus (HBV) and C, human papillomavirus (HPV), human immunodeficiency virus (HIV), human T-lymphotropic virus-1, Epstein-Barr virus, human herpesvirus, *Helicobacter pylori*, and liver flukes
- Uptake of prophylactic HBV and HPV vaccines

Common risk factors for noncommunicable diseases

- Tobacco use (smoked and oral), including exposure to secondhand smoke
- Lack of proper diets, such as those with more fruits and vegetables and whole grains; exposure to known carcinogens, such as nitrates and high-temperature beverages
- Alcohol intake
- Obesity
- Low activity level

Availability of, access to, and uptake of cancer screening

- Preinvasive cervical cancer
- Breast cancer
- Colon cancer

Cancer registries

- Type and stage of cancer annotated with demographic data
- Primary treatment and cancer outcome

Death registries

- Deaths occurring due to cancer or concurrent disease after diagnosis of cancer

---

and minority populations; as of 2013, it included approximately 28 percent of the population. The SEER Program collects high-quality, individual-level data on patient demographics, primary tumor site, morphology, stage at diagnosis, first course of treatment, and follow-up for vital status (Howlader and others 2013). A complementary program established through the U.S. Centers for Disease Control and Prevention in 1992 has expanded cancer registries to cover 96 percent of the U.S. population.

Role of Laboratories and Anatomic Pathology Accuracy in histopathologic diagnosis of tumor specimens from surgery or biopsy is required to make the correct diagnosis for any one person's cancer and help that person and health care providers make the appropriate treatment decision. In addition, accuracy in histopathologic diagnosis is also required to ensure the accuracy of cancer incidence data in cancer registries. Biological specimens must be processed promptly, shortly after removal from the human body. Pathology laboratories require trained histotechnicians and cytotechnicians, as well as functioning instrumentation and a reliable supply chain for the equipment needed to process specimens, such as formalin, glass slides, and diagnostic reagents. Trained

pathologists must be available to review the processed material, whether onsite, at central laboratories, or from remote sites via telepathology.

When a person is diagnosed with cancer, it is important to determine the aggressiveness of the specific cancer and whether the cancer has spread from the original site of origin to other parts of the body. This additional information is used to assign a stage to the cancer, which generally ranges from stage I (the earliest stage, which in many cases can be cured with standard therapy) to stage IV (the most advanced stage, which is most difficult to treat effectively). The ability to assign a stage to newly diagnosed cases requires linking the pathology report to clinical data. Without data on the extent of the disease or stage, it is not possible to provide appropriate treatment or determine the success of interventions intended to diagnose cancer at earlier stages when the cancer is more successfully treated.

Biobanking Biobanks and biological resource centers constitute key components of cancer research. To understand the biological basis of cancer; to develop biomarkers for cancer risk, early detection, and prognosis; and to determine the most appropriate cancer treatment based on precise diagnosis of tumor characteristics, it is necessary to have access to clinically annotated biologic specimens of cancer and normal tissue (Vaught, Henderson, and Compton 2012). Until recently, some analyses required special preparation of specimens, such as fresh frozen tissue. More recent developments in molecular pathology permit many studies to be done on formalin-fixed, paraffin-embedded tissue.

To make progress in cancer research as quickly as possible, it is important to be able to facilitate the collection and analysis of such specimens. Some specimens may need to be shipped to global or regional core laboratories for analysis using standardized protocols. In other cases, the primary analysis may be done in the country of origin, with a small number of samples exchanged among countries for standardization and quality control of the laboratory techniques. National or state regulations that prohibit any shipment of specimens outside the country or region of origin may preclude efficient analysis of those specimens and delay progress in research needed for cancer control.

Given the increasing need to pool data and biospecimens from consortia of studies around the world to achieve adequate sample size and statistical power, countries with rigid rules for data- and biospecimen-sharing will be at a disadvantage in the ability to participate in cutting-edge cancer research (NRC 2011; Thun, Hoover, and Hunter 2012). Although it is clear that regulations must be in place for the appropriate use of all samples when shared outside national boundaries, facilitating processes for the timely sharing of biological specimens will enhance research for all.

Linking Death Registration Systems to Cancer Registration Systems

Functioning national, regional, or sample-area death registration systems are critical to a country's ability to monitor its burden of all diseases. In areas covered by cancer registries, accurate death registration information may serve as an important source of cancer-case finding. In general, cancer registrars routinely search hospital medical records for the initial diagnosis and pathology report of medically certified cancer deaths.

Linking information on individuals diagnosed with cancer to death registries also greatly facilitates the computation of rates of cancer survival (for example, case-fatality rates) by tumor site and stage of disease, which otherwise would require expensive and time-consuming active follow-up of individuals diagnosed with cancer. As noted, the use of unique individual patient identifiers can help to link the diagnosis of cancer with patient follow-up and, ultimately, the death of that individual. In the absence of cancer registries, the cancer burden of a country can be estimated by the cancer mortality rate, if cause-of-death data are available (Boyle and Levin 2008; Jensen and others 1991).

A less costly and less precise alternative approach to obtaining the medically certified cause of death is that of the verbal autopsy, in which trained health workers interview the members of a household in which a death has occurred about the symptoms of the deceased person (Institute for Health Metrics and Evaluation 2011). Dikshit and others (2012) have reported the successful use of the verbal autopsy in the Million Death Study in India to estimate mortality from cancer and other diseases.

Cancer Epidemiology

The application of sound epidemiologic methods is indispensable in cancer research. Experimental and observational studies have yielded much of the current knowledge about causation, prevention, and intervention; epidemiologic studies conducted using cancer registry data have made significant contributions to the understanding of rates and trends. Cancer registries provide descriptive data that reveal important patterns and trends in the burden of cancer in defined populations. Registry data help to generate hypotheses that guide epidemiologic investigations that can identify potential causative factors, rule out false associations, define the nature of the dose-response relationship, identify co-factors and, in some cases, identify explanations for late-stage diagnosis. Increasingly, epidemiology studies incorporate molecular biology in their design to help better define outcome (cancer subtypes at a given site can vary greatly) and exposure with relevant biomarkers and to identify genetic and other molecular risk factors.

Case-Control Studies

A great deal of knowledge on cancer epidemiology is generated by case-control studies, which identify cancer cases using cancer registries or hospitals and other points of care and sample controls from the source population of cases. These epidemiologic investigations may require rapid case finding by study personnel, in-depth interviews of cases, and controls by trained interviewers to assess exposure information, environmental sampling, and collection and analysis of biospecimens at core laboratories. Case-control studies are efficient and generally less costly than cohort studies, particularly in the study of rare outcomes (Rothman, Greenland, and Lash 2008). Challenges include the potential for biases, such as differential recall, and the challenge of measuring exposures or assessing biomarkers of environmental exposure before the time of cancer diagnosis, thereby making it difficult to assess temporality (Wild 2009).

Cohort Studies

Cohort studies can overcome some of the limitations of case-control and cross-sectional study designs by enabling the measurement of exposures at the time of cohort enrollment, often years or decades before cancer development and diagnosis (Breslow and Day 1987; Rothman and Greenland 2008). Exposure assessment can be determined before the onset of disease and thereby limit the potential for recall bias and other types of bias inherent to case-control studies.

Cohort studies also contribute to health surveillance by providing the opportunity to obtain repeated measures of multiple exposures and potential confounding factors and to measure changes in these factors over time. Cohort studies enable estimation of the incidence of outcomes of interest, including infections, premalignant lesions, cancers, and comorbid conditions. Follow-up of cohorts requires long-term commitment, for supporting the study infrastructure and team, as well as for building and maintaining trust between the research team and the participants in the cohort. Recent developments in information technology, including the increased uptake of mobile telephones and Internet access, have facilitated the development and maintenance of study cohort enrollment and follow-up.

A cohort may be used to study multiple health endpoints and multiple exposures; new endpoints may be added over time, and data and biospecimens from multiple cohorts can be pooled to obtain greater statistical power. Thun and others (2013), for example, pooled data from seven cohorts to analyze the long-term impact of cigarette smoking in the United States. Another example is the 2004 formation of the International Childhood Cancer Cohort Consortium to assemble birth and child cohorts around the world to prospectively collect information on early life exposures and childhood cancers. This effort resulted from the recognition that single studies lacked the statistical power to study childhood cancers that are rare. It also provided evidence that pre-conception and in utero exposures may be important determinants of subsequent risk of childhood and adult cancers (Brown and others 2007).

Some adult cohorts that have made seminal contributions to cancer epidemiology include the following:

- The prospective cohort study of British doctors (Doll and Hill 1954)
- The American Cancer Society Cancer Prevention Studies (Calle and others 2002; Hammond 1966; Thun and others 1997)
- The United Kingdom Million Women Study (Million Women Study Collaborative Group 1999)
- The Japan Life Span Study (Sakata and others 2012)
- The Nurses' Health Study (Colditz, Manson, and Hankinson 1997) (box 15.4)

More recently formed cohorts in LMICs include the following:

- The China Kadoorie Biobank, which includes 500,000 adults from urban and rural areas in China (Chen and others 2011) (box 15.5)
- A separate cohort of 220,000 men in China (Chen and others 2012)
- A cohort of 150,000 women and men in Mexico City (Kuri-Morales and others 2009)
- The Chennai Prospective Study of 500,000 adults in Tamil Nadu, India (Gajalakshmi and others 2007; Gajalakshmi, Whitlock, and Peto 2012)

Box 15.4

Cohort Study: The Nurses' Health Studies

The Nurses' Health Study (2014a) comprises two cohorts of registered female nurses that enrolled more than 115,000 nurses in the United States. The first cohort began in 1976 and the second in 1989. These long-term epidemiologic studies were originally designed to assess risk factors for two major chronic diseases in women, namely, cancer and cardiovascular disease. Due to the large sample size, the extensive data available on each participant, and associated biological specimens, the investigators have also been able to study risk factors for many other chronic diseases, including diabetes mellitus, stroke, osteoporosis, mental health, and connective tissue disease. The Nurses' Health Study coordinating center is recruiting a third cohort of 100,000 nurses. Participant registration and follow-up will be conducted entirely via Internet communication (Nurses' Health Study 2014b).

Cohort Study: The China Kadoorie Biobank

The China Kadoorie Biobank includes 500,000 adults recruited between 2004 and 2008 from 10 regions in China, urban and rural (Chen and others 2011). All participants are being followed for hospital admissions, as well as cause-specific morbidity and mortality. Already, studies have been published on respiratory disease, depression, anxiety, diabetes, cardiovascular disease, alcohol consumption, physical activity, and obesity, and interactions among these factors within the cohort (Bragg and others 2014; Chen and others 2014; Du and others 2013; Lewington and others 2012; Mezuk and others 2013; Millwood and others 2013; Zhang and others 2013).

The studies have found, for example, that self-reported diabetes was associated with a doubling

of the odds of prevalent cardiovascular disease (Bragg and others 2014); that only one in three individuals with prior cardiovascular disease was routinely treated with any proven secondary preventive drugs (Chen and others 2014); that drinking alcohol was positively correlated with regular smoking, increased blood pressure, and increased heart rate (Millwood and others 2013); that major depression and generalized anxiety disorder are associated with type 2 diabetes mellitus (Mezuk and others 2013); and that exhaled carbon monoxide can be used as a biomarker for assessing current smoking and exposure to indoor household air pollution (Zhang and others 2013).

Health Communications

Health communications contribute in a number of critical areas needed in cancer research (National Cancer Institute 2004). First is the need to communicate the importance of health research to the media, policy makers, and the general public. Without community recognition of the need for health research, without appropriate levels of funding, and without a regulatory framework that facilitates the health research needed to guide public policy and public investment in health, health research cannot take place.

Second is the need to understand how best to communicate to individuals, families, and communities that research findings support public health recommendations and guidance. One clear example is how best to communicate the health risks associated with tobacco use, alcohol abuse, and physical inactivity. Ideally, such communication should lead to changes in behavior that reduce the risk of cancer and other chronic diseases. Other examples are communication regarding recommended regimens for approved vaccines that prevent chronic infections associated with cancer, such as those for hepatitis B virus (HBV) and human papillomavirus (HPV), and recommendations for routine cancer screening.

Third is the need to identify ways to help communities understand cancer. This includes understanding

that some cancers can be prevented, that some cancers are amenable to screening, and that many cancers can be treated successfully if diagnosed early. Such education and communication may help to overcome the stigma of cancer, particularly in settings where cancers are typically diagnosed at late stages with poor prognoses.

Different communication strategies may be needed for different populations, based on language, levels of literacy and health literacy, access to health care, socioeconomic status, cultural sensitivities, and other factors. The development and validation of effective cancer-related health communication strategies is key to developing and implementing research that can facilitate cancer prevention and control.

Implementation Science

Effective means of implementing cancer prevention; population-based screening; and timely and accurate cancer diagnosis, treatment, and symptom management are needed to improve cancer control. The U.S. National Cancer Institute has developed a website (http://cancercontrolplanet.cancer.gov) with links to effective cancer control interventions, including a database of research-tested intervention programs developed in partnership with the Substance Abuse

What Questions Can Implementation Science Answer?

Implementation science can help obtain answers to the following questions for cancer prevention and control:

- Which tobacco control programs are most effective for specific populations?
- What are the most cost-effective ways to ensure that as many children as possible are vaccinated for HBV and HPV?
- What is the most effective way to screen for and treat preinvasive HPV-related cervical neoplasia?
- What is the most effective way to screen for colon cancer?
- What is the most effective way to provide palliative care, including pain control?
- What are the most effective ways to ensure quality control across the cancer spectrum, from screening to treatment to survivorship care?

and Mental Health Services Administration (National Cancer Institute 2013).

Different approaches may be needed for different regions in the same country and between countries, based on existing health resources, cultural norms, and other factors. In some cases, task shifting of responsibilities from doctors to nurses, other health professionals, and lay community health workers or from nurses to community health workers may be required. The principles of implementation science can guide public health interventions for cancer control and facilitate their routine evaluation and modification, as needed, to achieve the goals (Madon and others 2007). Although more research is needed in all the areas mentioned, much is already known to be able to implement cancer control strategies to reduce the burden of cancer (box 15.6).

Cancer Research Collaboration

National Level

To optimize country-level outcomes, national policy makers will need to consider the essential elements of and necessary conditions for health research that require a comprehensive approach that includes the following:

- Achieving a consensus that health research deserves the appropriate funding and strategies

for implementation, as the Bamako Call to Action advocates

- Developing and implementing mechanisms for transparent and objective evaluation and prioritization of clinical research studies
- Establishing systems for ethical, regulatory, and scientific reviews so that research can be conducted in a timely manner and clinical studies can be completed expeditiously
- Revising customs inspections and policies to remove restrictions on the importation of drugs, devices, and reagents for health research
- Developing mechanisms and resources for the efficient and inexpensive acquisition of drugs, devices, and reagents for health research
- Providing financial support—possibly from national governments, state governments, nongovernmental organizations, or a combination—for the infrastructure for public clinical trials, including protocol development, regulatory management, routine medical expenses of patients, data management, quality assurance, biobanking, biostatistics, and informatics
- Integrating clinical research into national health systems
- Integrating education about clinical research into education and training of health care providers

Local Level

It is important to assist the institutional leadership at the local level—whether hospital, clinic, or university—to appreciate the importance of health research. Doctors, nurses, pharmacists, and specialists from other relevant disciplines need protected time to conduct clinical research. Academic tracks could be established to foster research and reward individuals for conducting clinical research. In some cases, money could be earmarked to pay for the additional costs associated with research. These costs may include additional imaging studies or specimen processing that may not be required for routine clinical care. The local study sites also need the appropriate financial and technical resources for clinical research management, biobanking, and informatics.

Research Training

For research to have a significant impact on health, governments in LMICs and HICs need to invest in training future scientists, clinicians, public health professionals, and physician-scientists. Such investments in training professionals in the range of relevant disciplines and helping them to maintain and strengthen their research skills require effective coordination that may involve government ministries responsible for education, health, science and technology, and human resources, as well as academic institutions, hospitals, clinics, nongovernmental organizations, and professional societies.

Principles of health research can be integrated into the core curriculums of schools of medicine, nursing, public health, pharmacy, and allied health sciences, as well as university programs for basic sciences and social sciences. This integration will ensure that all individuals involved in research with relevance for health learn about the conduct of health research and appreciate the need for such research.

Biostatisticians are a critical component of the research team, as are basic and translational research scientists, social scientists, health economists, and health communicators. There is a great need, particularly among young scientists in low-resource settings, for opportunities to participate in high-quality cancer research and to have access to nurturing mentors, whether local or remote.

Other allied areas in which training and mentorship are critically needed are the ethical conduct of cancer research, research subject protection, scientific writing for preparation of research proposals and manuscripts, and responsible study and financial management.

International Collaboration

International collaboration in cancer research spans capacity building and joint research projects. There are many examples of North-South and South-South projects to build capacity in health and cancer research. Institutional "twinning" has been particularly successful in this regard. Joint research projects can facilitate training opportunities for investigators in LMICs. Two recent reports from the Organisation for Economic Co-operation and Development's Global Science Forum highlight the need for international collaboration in clinical research to address many important health questions (OECD 2011, 2013).

The facilitation of such collaboration requires an effective national commitment to health research as well as a commitment to facilitate international collaboration (Trimble and others 2009). International research collaboration may require allowing specimens to be shipped to a regional or global core laboratory, as well as pooling relevant information in an international database. Timely scientific and ethical review is critical for national studies, particularly for international collaboration (Abrams and others 2013). International partnerships in cancer research require the timely recognition of scientific opportunities, available resources and study conditions, strengths of research partners, integrity, persistence, and commitment of all partners in jointly overcoming barriers to accomplish research objectives.

Industry Collaboration

Many aspects of cancer control, including prevention with vaccines, screening, diagnosis, treatment, and symptom management, require reliable drugs, devices, and reagents. Many areas of cancer need better, more effective, more accessible, and less costly drugs, devices, and reagents. Partnering with industry will facilitate the development and validation of novel products, as well as help to ensure a reliable supply chain to bring products shown to be beneficial to routine clinical practice. Once a product is developed and tested, it will be important to work with industry partners to make the product available and affordable on a population basis. Such public-private partnering is an integral component of developing and translating innovations in cancer research to clinical care and public health.

CERVICAL CANCER: EXEMPLAR OF INTEGRATED RESEARCH

Cervical cancer provides a sterling example of how cancer research in virology, immunology, epidemiology, clinical care, behavioral sciences, and implementation science has led to effective cancer prevention and control. Much of this work occurred because of international collaborations that allowed appropriate sharing of research material, data, and expertise.

Epidemiology and Biology

The link between chronic HPV infection and cervical cancer was established by zur Hausen and colleagues in the early 1990s, building on earlier experimental work that strongly suggested the possibility that the two were linked (Reid 1983; zur Hausen and de Villiers 1994). Muñoz and others (2002) confirmed that HPV was responsible for more than 99 percent of cervical cancers globally. Epidemiologic studies have also permitted the identification of additional co-risk factors for cervical cancer, including exposure to tobacco smoke, both firsthand and secondhand, chronic immunosuppression, multiparity, long-term use of oral contraceptives, and high-risk male partners (Schiffman and Hildesheim 2006).

Development of Vaccines to Prevent HPV Infection

The identification of HPV as a necessary causative agent led to the development of vaccines to prevent HPV infection and cervical cancer. Two vaccines to prevent HPV infection demonstrated efficacy and safety in phase III and IV studies (Schiller, Castellsagué, and Garland 2012). Both agents have been widely approved by drug regulatory authorities, including the U.S. Food and Drug Administration and the European Medicines Agency. The rollout of these vaccines to prevent HPV infection required a progression of clinical research studies, first to confirm primary efficacy, then to validate in different populations, followed by public health investigations to determine how best to deliver and encourage uptake of the new vaccines to prevent HPV infection and cervical cancer (Program for Appropriate Technology in Health 2012).

These investigations incorporated studies of messaging, including how best to communicate to parents the health benefits that the new vaccine offers to their daughters; studies comparing on-the-ground vaccine delivery programs, such as school-based versus clinic-based HPV vaccination programs; and comparisons and studies of different dosing schedules for HPV vaccines (Galagan and others 2013; Lamontagne, Barge, and others 2011; Lamontagne, Thiem, and others 2013). Australia, which has a national reporting system for HPV-associated warts in addition to a national registry for vaccinations, has been able to document significant decreases in HPV infection and genital warts among teenagers and young adults following the widespread introduction of the vaccine (Read and others 2011; Tabizi and others 2012). Several second-generation vaccines to prevent HPV infection are under development, with the goal of addressing the issue of type-restricted protection and decreasing the cost of production.

HPV Diagnostics for Cervical Cancer Screening

Based on the understanding of the link between chronic oncogenic HPV infection and cervical neoplasia, new diagnostic tests have been developed to target the virus, including evidence of active infection with high-risk HPV types, as well as evidence of HPV integration. DNA-based tests detect the presence or absence of the HPV virus genome. DNA testing for high-risk HPV types has a high sensitivity for the detection of high-grade cervical intraepithelial neoplasia and cervical cancer (Arbyn and others 2012). The great advantages are that HPV detection assays are automated and objective and have a greater reproducibility than cytology; as such, they are a promising screening test in LMICs, which may lack skilled personnel. Sankaranarayanan and others (2009) found that a single round of testing for HPV was associated with a significant reduction in the risk of advanced cervical cancer and death from cervical cancer among rural women in India. In this study, which accrued 131,746 women ages 30–59 years in 52 villages, the other two screening arms—cytologic testing and visual inspection of the cervix with acetic acid—did not demonstrate significant reductions in the risk of advanced cervical cancer and deaths from cervical cancer.

Unanswered Questions in HPV-Associated Neoplasia and Cervical Cancer Control

Based on the body of research to date, as well as the extensive programs for control of HPV-associated neoplasia, many critical research questions remain unanswered (Schiller and Lowy 2014) (box 15.7). These questions span a variety of scientific areas, including the following:

- Behavioral sciences
- Health communications
- Health services research
- Immunology
- Implementation science
- Prevention

Box 15.7

Ongoing Research Questions in HPV and Cervical Cancer Control

The tremendous progress in HPV and cervical cancer control can be taken even further as these still outstanding research questions are addressed. The following cervical cancer research agenda provides opportunities for scientists in all interested countries.

- *Prevention, health services research, and immunology.* How can the cost of the currently available prophylactic HPV vaccine regimen be reduced? Are one or two doses as effective as three? Will additional booster doses be needed and when?
- *Prevention, implementation science, and health communications.* What combination of feasibility and affordability would convince policy makers in LMICs to introduce and fund population-based prophylactic HPV vaccination?

box continues next page

Box 15.7 (continued)

- *Health communications, prevention, behavioral sciences, and implementation science.* What are the critical components in educational programs for parents considering whether to permit their daughters and sons to undergo prophylactic HPV vaccination?
- *Prevention, virology, and immunology.* What is needed to develop second-generation prophylactic HPV vaccines that provide protection against infection from more HPV subtypes than included in the first-generation HPV vaccines?
- *Screening and virology.* What is needed to develop effective screening strategies for HPV-associated neoplasia of the oropharynx and anus?
- *Screening, health services research, and implementation science.* What types of infrastructure, human resource capacity, and logistical support are needed to scale up existing and new cervical neoplasia screening and treatment services at multiple levels of the health system to meet the needs of urban and rural populations?
- *Screening and virology.* What is the feasibility of developing inexpensive, highly sensitive, and highly specific HPV-based tests to use as a primary screen for cervical neoplasia and chronic HPV infection in low-resource settings?
- *Screening, health services research, and implementation science.* How can population-based screening for cervical neoplasia or chronic HPV infection be more effectively integrated into maternal-child health programs, programs

caring for HIV-positive individuals, well-woman programs, and programs screening for other noncommunicable diseases, such as diabetes, hypertension, and breast cancer?
- *Health communications, screening, behavioral sciences, and implementation science.* What measures can be taken to ensure that no woman found to have an abnormal screening result is lost to follow-up?
- *Treatment.* What can be done to improve current ablative therapy for preinvasive cervical and anal cancer?
- *Immunology and treatment.* Can therapeutic HPV immunization strategies be developed to prevent the development of neoplasia in individuals already infected with HPV, as well as to complement or replace ablative therapy for HPV-associated neoplasia?
- *Treatment and implementation science.* How can current therapy, including surgery, radiation, chemoradiation, and neoadjuvant chemotherapy, be improved for women with invasive cervical cancer?
- *Treatment, behavioral sciences, and implementation science.* How can the quality of life best be maintained and enhanced in cervical cancer survivors, including bowel, bladder, and sexual function, as well as physical intimacy?
- *Symptom management, behavioral sciences, and implementation science.* How can palliative care be delivered most effectively to women diagnosed with late-stage or recurrent cervical cancer?

- Screening
- Symptom management
- Treatment
- Virology.

CONCLUSIONS: "BEST BUYS" FOR CANCER RESEARCH

What are the "best buys" for cancer research in LMICs? Where should ministers of health, ministers of science and technology, and other funders of research begin?

- Robust health surveillance systems, including surveillance of cancer risk factors, cancer registries,

and cancer-associated deaths, are critical to effective decision making for prevention and control, as well as priorities in cancer research.
- Next is implementation science focused on how to deliver interventions that have been shown to be effective. Perhaps the most effective method of cancer prevention is tobacco control. Countries at all levels of income could sponsor research focused on how best to reduce or eliminate use of tobacco. This research should include public policy, public education, and smoking cessation initiatives.
- For LMICs burdened with liver cancer or cervical cancer, implementation science focused on expanding routine administration of HBV and HPV vaccinations is appropriate. For countries at all levels of development,

implementation science in effective methods to deliver palliative care is critical. Educational and training programs for health care professionals and community health workers would benefit from the inclusion of the principles of health research. How best to educate and retain health care workers at all levels is also an appropriate area for research.

- Countries with the ability to conduct programs for cancer screening, early diagnosis, and treatment could expand implementation science research to cover these areas, as well as tobacco control and preventive vaccines. Timely topics for research also include cost-effective strategies to screen for cervical, colon, oral, esophageal, stomach, and skin cancers; to evaluate breast masses; and to provide potentially curative therapy for preinvasive and invasive cancer.

- The next area for research, as national resources permit, encompasses cancer epidemiology and biology. Improved understanding of the risk and protective factors for specific cancers, as well as their molecular biology, is essential to design effective interventions for prevention, screening, early diagnosis, and treatment. For example, the epidemiology and biology of prostate cancer is not sufficiently well understood to prevent it, screen for it, or know how best to treat it. Similarly, the ability to make progress on cancer control for many cancers linked to chronic infection and inflammation requires better elucidation of the salient biology, natural history, co-factors, and protective factors.

NOTE

World Bank income classifications as of July 2014 are as follows, based on estimates of gross national income per capita for 2013:

- Low-income countries: US$1,045 or less
- Middle-income countries:
  a) Lower-middle-income: US$1,046–US$4,125
  b) Upper-middle-income: US$4,126–US$12,745
- High-income countries: US$12,746 or more

REFERENCES

Abrams, J. S., M. M. Mooney, J. A. Zwiebel, E. L. Korn, S. H. Friedman, and others. 2013. "Implementation of Timeline Reforms Speeds Initiation of National Cancer Institute–Sponsored Trials." *Journal of the National Cancer Institute* 105 (13): 954–59.

Arbyn, M., G. Ronco, A. Anttila, C. J. Meijer, M. Poljak, and others. 2012. "Evidence Regarding Human Papillomavirus Testing in Secondary Prevention of Cervical Cancer." *Vaccine* 30 (Suppl. 5): F88–99.

Boyle, P., and B. Levin, eds. 2008. *World Cancer Report*. Lyon: IARC Press.

Bragg, F., L. Li, M. Smith, Y. Guo, Y. Chen, and others. 2014. "Associations of Blood Glucose and Prevalent Diabetes with Risk of Cardiovascular Disease in 500,000 Adult Chinese: The China Kadoorie Biobank." *Diabetic Medicine* 31 (5): 540–51.

Breslow, N. E., and N. E. Day. 1987. *Statistical Methods in Cancer Research, Volume II: The Design and Analysis of Cohort Studies*. Scientific Publications 82. Lyon: IARC Press.

Brown, R. C., T. Dwyer, C. Kasten, D. Krotoski, Z. Li, and others. 2007. "International Childhood Cancer Cohort Consortium (I4C)." *International Journal of Epidemiology* 36 (4): 724–30.

Calle, E. E., C. Rodriguez, E. J. Jacobs, L. Almon, A. Chao, and others. 2002. "The American Cancer Society Cancer Prevention Study II Nutrition Cohort: Rationale, Study Design, and Baseline Characteristics." *Cancer* 94 (9): 2490–501.

Chen, Y., L. Li, Q. Zhang, R. Clarke, J. Chen, and others. 2014. "Use of Drug Treatment for Secondary Prevention of Cardiovascular Diseases in Urban and Rural Communities of China: China Kadoorie Biobank Study of 0.5 Million People." *International Journal of Cardiology* 172 (1): 88–95.

Chen, Z., J. Chen, R. Collins, Y. Guo, R. Peto, and others. 2011. "China Kadoorie Biobank of 0.5 Million People: Survey Methods, Baseline Characteristics and Long-Term Follow-Up." *International Journal of Epidemiology* 40 (6): 1652–66.

Chen, Z., G. Yang, A. Offer, M. Zhou, M. Smith, and others. 2012. "Body Mass and Mortality in China: A 15-Year Prospective Study of 220,000 Men." *International Journal of Epidemiology* 41 (2): 472–81.

Colditz, G. A., J. E. Manson, and S. E. Hankinson. 1997. "The Nurses' Health Study: 20-Year Contribution to the Understanding of Health among Women." *Journal of Women's Health* 6 (1): 49–62.

De Martel, C., J. Ferlay, S. Franceschi, J. Vignat, F. Bray, and others. 2012. "Global Burden of Cancers Attributable to Infections in 2008: A Review and Synthetic Analysis." *The Lancet Oncology* 13 (6): 607–15.

Dikshit, R., P. C. Gupta, C. Ramsundarahettige, V. Gajalakshmi, L. Aleksandrowicz, and others. 2012. "Cancer Mortality in India: A Nationally Representative Survey." *The Lancet* 379 (9828): 1807–16.

Doll, R., and A. B. Hill. 1954. "The Mortality of Doctors in Relation to Their Smoking Habits: A Preliminary Report." *British Medical Journal* 1 (4877): 1451–55.

Du, H., D. Bennett, L. Li, G. Whitlock, Y. Guo, and others. 2013. "Physical Activity and Sedentary Leisure Time and Their Associations with BMI, Waist Circumference, and Percentage Body Fat in 0.5 Million Adults: The China Kadoorie Biobank Study." *American Journal of Clinical Nutrition* 97 (3): 487–96.

Gajalakshmi, V., R. Peto, V. C. Kanimozhi, G. Whitlock, and D. Veeramani. 2007. "Cohort Profile: The Chennai Prospective Study of Mortality among 500,000 Adults in Tamil Nadu, South India." *International Journal of Epidemiology* 36 (6): 1190–95.

Gajalakshmi, V., G. Whitlock, and R. Peto. 2012. "Social Inequalities, Tobacco Chewing, and Cancer Mortality in South India: A Case-Control Analysis of 2,580 Cancer Deaths among Non-Smoking Non-Drinkers." *Cancer Causes and Control* 23 (Suppl. 1): 91–98.

Galagan, S. R., P. Paul, L. Menezes, and D. S. LaMontagne. 2013. "Influences on Parental Acceptance of HPV Vaccination in Demonstration Projects in Uganda and Vietnam." *Vaccine* 31 (30): 3072–78.

Hammond, E. C. 1966. "Smoking in Relation to the Death Rates of One Million Men and Women." *National Cancer Institute Monographs* 19: 127–204.

Howlader, N., A. M. Noone, M. Krapcho, J. Garshell, N. Neyman, and others, eds. 2013. "SEER Cancer Statistics Review, 1975–2010." National Cancer Institute, Bethesda, MD, based on November 2012 SEER data submission, posted to the SEER website, April 2013, http://seer.cancer.gov/csr/1975_2010.

Institute for Health Metrics and Evaluation. 2011. Verbal Autopsy Series. http://www.healthmetricsandevaluation .org/publications/verbal-autopsy-series.

Jensen, O. M., D. M. Parkin, R. MacLennan, C. S. Muir, and R. G. Skeet, eds. 1991. *Cancer Registration: Principles and Methods.* Scientific Publications 95. Lyon: IARC Press.

Kuri-Morales, P., J. Emberson, J. Alegre-Diaz, R. Tapia-Conyer, R. Collins, and others. 2009. "The Prevalence of Chronic Diseases and Major Disease Risk Factors at Different Ages among 150,000 Women Living in Mexico City: Cross-Sectional Analyses of a Prospective Study." *BioMed Central Public Health* 9: 9.

Lamontagne, D. S., S. Barge, N. T. Le, E. Mugisha, M. E. Penny, and others. 2011. "Human Papillomavirus Vaccine Delivery Strategies That Achieved High Coverage in Low- and Middle-Income Countries." *Bulletin of the World Health Organization* 89 (11): 821–30B.

Lamontagne, D. S., V. D. Thiem, V. M. Huong, Y. Tang, K. M. Neuzil, and others. 2013. "Immunogenicity of Quadrivalent HPV Vaccine among Girls 11 to 13 Years of Age Vaccinated Using Alternative Dosing Schedules: Results 29 to 32 Months after Third Dose." *Journal of Infectious Diseases* 208 (8): 1325–34.

Lewington S., L. Li, P. Sherliker, Y. Guo, I. Millwood, and others. 2012. "Seasonal Variation in Blood Pressure and Its Relationship with Outdoor Temperature in 10 Diverse Regions of China: The China Kadoorie Biobank." *Journal of Hypertension* 30 (7): 1383–91.

Madon, T., K. J. Hofman, L. Kupfer, and R. I. Glass. 2007. "Public Health: Implementation Science." *Science* 318 (5857): 1728–29.

Mezuk, B., Y. Chen, C. Yu, Y. Guo, Z. Bian, and others. 2013. "Depression, Anxiety, and Prevalent Diabetes in the Chinese Population: Findings from the China Kadoorie Biobank of 0.5 Million People." *Journal of Psychosomatic Research* 75 (6): 511–17.

Million Women Study Collaborative Group. 1999. "The Million Women Study: Design and Characteristics of the Study Population." *Breast Cancer Research* 1 (1): 73–80.

Millwood, I. Y., L. Li, M. Smith, Y. Guo, L. Yang, and others. 2013. "Alcohol Consumption in 0.5 Million People from 10 Diverse Regions of China: Prevalence, Patterns, and Socio-Demographic and Health-Related Correlates." *International Journal of Epidemiology* 42 (3): 816–27.

Muñoz, N., S. Franceschi, C. Bosetti, V. Moreno, R. Hererro, and others. 2002. "Role of Parity and Human Papillomavirus in Cervical Cancer: The IARC Multicentric Case-Control Study." *The Lancet* 359 (9312): 1093–101.

National Cancer Institute. 2004. *Making Health Communications Programs Work.* Bethesda, MD: National Institutes of Health, U.S. Department of Health and Human Services.

———. 2013. Cancer Control P.L.A.N.E.T. http:// cancercontrolplanet.cancer.gov

NRC (National Research Council). 2011. *Toward Precision Medicine: Building a Knowledge Network for Biomedical Research and a New Taxonomy of Disease.* Committee on a Framework for Developing a New Taxonomy of Disease. Washington, DC: National Academies Press.

Nurses' Health Study. 2014a. *The Nurses' Health Study.* http:// www.channing.harvard.edu/nhs.

———. 2014b. *Nurses' Health Study 3.* http://www.nhs3.org.

OECD (Organisation for Economic Co-operation and Development). 2011. "Facilitating International Cooperation in Non-Commercial Clinical Trials." Global Science Forum, OECD. http://www.oecd.org/science /sci-tech/49344626.pdf.

———. 2013. "Recommendation on the Governance of Clinical Trials." http://www.oecd.org/sti/sci-tech/oecd -recommendation-governance-of-clinical-trials.pdf.

Program for Appropriate Technology in Health. 2012. "Evaluating HPV Vaccination Pilots: Practical Experience from PATH." Program for Appropriate Technology in Health, Seattle. http://www.rho.org/HPV-evaluating-pilots.htm.

Read, T. R., J. S. Hocking, M. Y. Chen, B. Donovan, and C. S. Bradshaw. 2011. "The Near Disappearance of Genital Warts in Young Women 4 Years after Commencing a National Human Papillomavirus (HPV) Vaccination Programme." *Sexually Transmitted Infections* 87 (7): 544–47.

Reid, R. 1983. "Genital Warts and Cervical Cancer: Is Human Papillomavirus Infection the Trigger to Cervical Carcinogenesis?" *Gynecologic Oncology* 15 (2): 239–52.

Rothman, D. J., and S. Greenland. 2008. "Cohort Studies." In *Modern Epidemiology,* edited by K. J. Rothman, S. Greenland, and T. Lash, 3rd edition, 100–10. Philadelphia, PA: Lippincott Williams and Wilkins.

Rothman, K. J., S. Greenland, and T. L. Lash. 2008. "Case-Control Studies." In *Modern Epidemiology,* edited by K. J. Rothman, S. Greenland, and T. Lash, 3rd edition, 111–27. Philadelphia, PA: Lippincott Williams and Wilkins.

Sakata, R., P. McGale, E. J. Grant, K. Ozasa, R. Peto, and others. 2012. "Impact of Smoking on Mortality and Life Expectancy in Japanese Smokers: A Prospective Cohort Study." *British Medical Journal* 345: e7093.

Sankaranarayanan R., B. M. Nene, S. S. Shastri, K. Jayant, R. Muwonge, and others. 2009. "HPV Screening for Cervical Cancer in Rural India." *New England Journal of Medicine* 360 (14): 1385–94.

Schiffman, M. H., and A. Hildesheim. 2006. "Cervical Cancer." In *Cancer Epidemiology and Prevention*, edited by D. Schottenfeld and J. F. Fraumeni, 1044–67. New York: Oxford University Press.

Schiller, J. T., X. Castellsagué, and S. M. Garland. 2012. "A Review of Clinical Trials of Human Papillomavirus Prophylactic Vaccines." *Vaccine* 30 (Suppl. 5): F123–38.

Schiller, J. T., and D. R. Lowy. 2014. "Virus Infection and Human Cancer: An Overview." *Recent Results in Cancer Research* 193: 1–10.

Tabizi, S. N., J. M. Brotherton, J. M. Kaldor, S. R. Skinner, E. Cummins, and others. 2012. "Fall in Human Papillomavirus Prevalence Following a National Vaccination Program." *Journal of Infectious Diseases* 206 (11): 1645–51.

Thun, M. J., B. D. Carter, D. Feskanich, N. D. Freedman, R. Prentice, and others. 2013. "50-Year Trends in Smoking-Related Mortality in the United States." *New England Journal of Medicine* 368 (4): 351–64.

Thun, M. J., R. N. Hoover, and D. J. Hunter. 2012. "Bigger, Better, Sooner: Scaling Up for Success." *Cancer Epidemiology, Biomarkers, and Prevention* 21 (4): 571–75.

Thun, M. J., C. A. Lally, J. T. Flannery, E. E. Calle, W. D. Flanders, and others. 1997. "Cigarette Smoking and Changes in the Histopathology of Lung Cancer." *Journal of the National Cancer Institute* 89 (21): 1580–86.

Trimble, E. L., J. S. Abrams, R. M. Meyer, F. Calvo, E. Cazap, and others. 2009. "Improving Cancer Outcomes through International Collaboration in Academic Cancer Treatment Trials." *Journal of Clinical Oncology* 27 (30): 5109–14.

Vaught, J. B., M. K. Henderson, and C. C. Compton. 2012. "Biospecimens and Biorepositories: From Afterthought to Science." *Cancer Epidemiology, Biomarkers, and Prevention* 21 (2): 253–55.

WHO (World Health Organization). 2008. "The Bamako Call to Action for Research on Health." WHO, Geneva. http://www.who.int/rpc/news/BAMAKOCALLTOACTIONFinalNov24.pdf.

———. 2013. "Global Health Observatory." WHO, Geneva. http://www.who.int/gho/database/en/.

Wild, C. P. 2009. "Environmental Exposure Measurement in Cancer Epidemiology." *Mutagenesis* 24 (2): 117–25.

Zhang, Q., L. Li, M. Smith, Y. Guo, G. Whitlock, and others. 2013. "Exhaled Carbon Monoxide and Its Associations with Smoking, Indoor Air Pollution and Chronic Respiratory Diseases among 512,000 Chinese Adults." *International Journal of Epidemiology* 42 (5): 1464–75.

zur Hausen, H., and E. M. de Villiers. 1994. "Human Papillomaviruses." *Annual Review of Microbiology* 48: 427–47.

ANNOTATED SELECT BIBLIOGRAPHY

Farmer, P., J. Frenk, F. M. Knaul, L. N. Shulman, G. Alleyne, L. Armstrong, and others. 2010. "Expansion of Cancer Care and Control in Countries of Low and Middle Income: A Call to Action." *The Lancet* 376: 1186–93.

This policy paper includes the need for implementation science research in low- and middle-income countries to guide effective cancer preventions and control in these settings.

Hunter, D. J., and K. S. Reddy. 2013. "Noncommunicable Diseases." *New England Journal of Medicine* 369: 1336–43.

The authors emphasize the need for global research efforts to inform the prevention, detection, and treatment of noncommunicable diseases.

Institute of Medicine. 2011. "The National Cancer Policy Summit: Opportunities and Challenges in Cancer Research and Care." National Academies Press, Washington, DC.

———. 2013a. *Delivering High-Quality Cancer Care: Charting a New Course for a System in Crisis*. Washington, DC: National Academies Press.

———. 2013b. "Delivering Affordable Cancer Care in the 21st Century-Workshop Summary." National Academies Press, Washington, DC.

Together these three reports from the Institute of Medicine outline the essential elements for effective cancer research, as well as priorities for implementation science to guide cancer control.

Lozano, R., M. Naghvai, K. Foreman, S. Lim, K. Shibuya, V. Aboyans, and others. 2012. "Global and Regional Mortality from 235 Causes of Death for 20 Age Groups in 1990 and 2010: A Systematic Analysis for the Global Burden of Disease Study 2010." *The Lancet* 380: 2095–28.

This analysis makes clear the burden of cancer, compared with other causes of death.

Varmus, H., and H. S. Kumar. 2013. "Addressing the Growing International Challenge of Cancer: A Multi-National Perspective." *Science Translational Medicine* 175.

The authors summarize the recommendations, including priorities for research, of representatives of institutions and organizations that fund and perform cancer research in 15 countries that include more than half of the world's population.

WHO (World Health Organization). 1996. "Ad Hoc Committee on Health Research Relating to Future Intervention Options: Investing in Health Research and Development." Document TDR/Gen/96.1, WHO, Geneva.

This document was developed to assist decision making by government, industry, and other investors on the allocation of funds for health research and development.

———. 2013. *Global Action Plan for the Prevention and Control Of Non-Communicable Diseases*. 2013–2020. ISBN 978 92 4 150623 6.

This action provides guidance on public health priorities and thus key implementation science issues related to cancer prevention and control, developed as part of follow-up to the 2011 United Nations High-Level Meeting on Non-communicable Diseases.

Wild, C. P. 2012. "The Role of Cancer Research in Noncommunicable Disease Control 2012." *Journal of the National Cancer Institute* 104 (14): 5109–14.

Cancer in Low- and Middle-Income Countries: An Economic Overview

Chapter 16

Susan Horton and Cindy L. Gauvreau

INTRODUCTION

Health care is informed first and foremost by scientific and medical understanding of how to treat and prevent disease. Economics can, however, provide useful insights to inform policy in the design and implementation of the systems to provide health care, as well as in the process of prioritizing interventions to make the best use of scarce resources. Treating a single cancer patient may require the coordination of many inputs and may cost tens or even hundreds of thousands of dollars in high-income countries (HICs). Ongoing population cancer screening and early detection also require considerable coordination, including treatment for cases detected, and costs. Finally, although knowledge of cancer prevention is inadequate, prevention can be a costly endeavor—as demonstrated by the large sums spent on behavior change promotion (such as smoking cessation) or on vaccines to prevent cancer, such as against human papilloma virus to prevent cervical cancer and hepatitis B virus to prevent liver cancer—and economics can be informative.

The second section of this chapter reviews how the availability of resources for cancer care varies by economic status, using the World Bank's categories of low-income countries (LICs), middle-income countries (MICs) (comprising lower-middle-income countries and upper-middle-income countries), and HICs. At the same time, economy is not destiny. Countries

at the same level of economic development differ because other factors intervene. Urbanization affects the patterns of cancer and the ability to access care. Local champions, governmental political leadership, and international partnerships can all loosen the constraints of local economic resources. Conversely, some countries are underachievers in cancer care despite their income level, perhaps because of leadership failures.

The third section reviews the cost-effectiveness of interventions for cancer care, where care is here defined to include prevention. The cost-effectiveness of interventions has been well studied in HICs, but much less so in low- and middle-income countries (LMICs). This section summarizes the literature on the economics of cancer care in LMICs; the section also draws on the literature from HICs, particularly for cancer treatment, in areas where reliable studies for LMICs are particularly scarce. It may be possible to make inferences for one country using results from another country; the validity of these inferences rises with the extent of the similarities in the two countries. Where possible, we separate out the findings for high-income economies in Asia, since they are likely to be more relevant for LMICs in this region than the results from North America or Western Europe.

We use the resource grouping suggested by Anderson and others (see chapter 3) for the Breast Health Global

Corresponding author: Susan Horton, PhD, sehorton@uwaterloo.ca

Initiative and apply this to other cancers. In this framework, facility resource environments fall into four categories of resource availability:

- Basic
- Limited
- Enhanced
- Maximal

These categories are correlated with the World Bank income groupings. LICs have a preponderance of Basic facilities, rural areas in MICs have more facilities with Limited capabilities, urban areas in MICs have more facilities with Enhanced capabilities, and much of the population in HICs has access to facilities with Maximal capabilities. The implications for the availability of resources specific to cancer care are described. This section requires some interpolation on the authors' part because of the paucity of previous work in the area and is subject to further validation by experts.

The fourth and final section contains conclusions, consisting of summary recommendations of packages of cancer care appropriate for each of the four resource environments, as well as priority areas where further research is required. The appropriateness of a package is defined by feasibility (those resources can be expected to exist or could exist with reasonable investments) and by likely cost-effectiveness (within the limits of available data). Although there are internationally validated resource-specific care guidelines for breast cancer (the Breast Health Global Initiative), no such guidelines are available as yet for other cancers. The packages presented here have been validated in consultation with the chapter authors of this volume (chapters 3 through 8), but need to be further refined by expert consultation.

AVAILABILITY OF CANCER CARE RESOURCES ACROSS COUNTRIES

Patterns of cancer vary across countries of different income levels (chapter 2 in this volume). Countries also have different capabilities for cancer care, depending on resource availability. Some of the resources for cancer care are specific to individual cancers, for example, the availability of a specific drug or test kit. Other resources are specific to cancer in general, for example, radiation therapy or the need for specialized medical personnel trained in oncology. Still others are not specific to cancer but affect many kinds of medical care, including imaging facilities, surgical facilities, pathology, and laboratory medicine services. Finally, there are broader

factors that affect health care generally, such as the availability of health insurance (public, private, or mixed) and general administrative capability for the requisite health care systems.

LMICs generally have inadequate resources for health care, which conditions what is available specifically for cancer care and, hence, mortality rates. From a policy perspective, it is important to identify the priorities for investment to make maximum health gains with the available budgetary resources. We use cost-effectiveness analysis to provide some guidelines, for areas where additional recurrent expenditures would benefit care (such as buying additional drugs) and for areas where large investments in fixed costs are required (such as setting up a specialized cancer hospital).

Some resource constraints can be overcome. Even low-income Sub-Saharan African countries can acquire and maintain radiation facilities, although ensuring access for patients from remote rural areas may be difficult. It is more challenging, however, to advocate treatments that require sophisticated pathology and laboratory facilities. Such facilities are important for a wide range of medical conditions, for which cancer forms only a small percent, and they require a much larger effort and investment to set up and maintain, particularly the training of skilled personnel. It may be completely infeasible in such countries to consider certain types of organized screening if no insurance system is in place to finance the screening costs, much less the treatment of the cases diagnosed.

Table 16.1 provides examples of availability, by income grouping, of some specific resources relevant to cancer treatment; each resource is discussed in turn. Information about the availability of radiation therapy and cancer registries is available elsewhere (and not included in the table); quantitative data on the availability of skilled personnel and laboratories are not easily obtained.

Surgery

Surgery is the cornerstone of treatment for many solid tumors. The level of surgical skill and associated resources required varies by type of cancer. Surgery for earlier stage colon cancer or mastectomy for early-stage breast cancer can be undertaken at reasonably well-equipped first-level hospitals. More sophisticated facilities and skills are required for such procedures as breast-conserving surgery and rectal surgery. Surgery for certain precancerous conditions may be possible at lower-level facilities; cryotherapy for cervical cancer, for example, can be undertaken in clinics. Table 16.1 shows that HICs have more than 12 times as many operating

Table 16.1 Resource Availability Affecting Cancer Care by Country Income Groups

Resource	Low-income countries	Lower-middle-income countries	Upper-middle-income countries	High-income countries
Surgical facilities per 1,000 population,[a] 2007–08	1.3	4.7	9.9	16.4
Out-of-pocket health expenditure (% of health expenditures),[b] 2011	48.1	52.8	33.3	13.7
Availability of tamoxifen (% of countries where it is generally available, according to knowledgeable respondents),[c,d] 2010	34	53	80	85
Availability of oral morphine (% of countries where it is generally available, according to knowledgeable respondents),[c,d] 2010	27	28	57	81
Income range,[e] 2012 (US$)	1,036 and below	1,036–4,087	4,087–12,615	12,616 and above

a. Funk and others 2010.
b. World Bank 2013.
c. WHO 2012.
d. The question asked whether the medication was generally available in the public sector.
e. World Bank 2013.

theaters per capita as LICs (chapter 13 in this volume). Countries may face difficult choices as to how much surgical capacity to utilize for palliation for patients for whom there is no chance of cure, compared with those for whom there is the possibility of cure.

Radiotherapy

Radiotherapy is a key to improving survival for certain cancers. In Afghanistan, Iraq, and Sub-Saharan Africa, 25 countries lack any radiation unit; other countries have one unit per five million people (IAEA 2013). Clearly, the radiation unit alone is not the only constraint; sufficient trained staff members are also required. Not surprisingly, greater availability of radiotherapy is correlated with country income. Low-income countries can provide radiotherapy, but the main issue is that the capacity in many countries is completely insufficient to meet the need. Typically, facilities need, at a minimum, the Limited level of resources to be able to provide radiotherapy.

Medications

Pharmaceuticals of various kinds are vital to improve cancer survival rates, yet country income is associated with the availability of these agents. Access to tamoxifen for breast cancer is limited in LICs, as is access to pain control using oral morphine (table 16.1, using survey data from WHO 2012). The case is similar for chemotherapy agents, although no quantitative data were readily available. The budget constraints in LICs

and rural areas of MICs often mean that these areas can only afford the lowest cost (usually older, off-patent) regimens. In addition to the cost of the agents, chemotherapy requires multiple visits to a health facility each month to obtain the supporting blood chemistry. Facilities need the Limited level of resources to support chemotherapy, effectively restricting its use to MICs and HICs.

Some effective but modest-cost cancer medications should be available, even from Basic level facilities. As long as a single laboratory test can be undertaken per patient to determine hormone receptor status, tamoxifen can be used, even in rural areas and LICs. Pain control medication, including morphine, should be available in all environments as long as access can be controlled.

Laboratories

Laboratories are an essential component of screening, diagnosis, and treatment options. They are required for rapid, accurate results from cytology or biopsies, or from the analysis of blood chemistry for chemotherapy. These services are typically not available in Basic, or even Limited, facilities. Although it is possible to send specimens collected from rural residents to a major city, the results are often not obtained in a sufficiently timely manner to provide optimal treatment. Hence, treatments involving extensive laboratory support are often not feasible in settings without facilities with Enhanced resources, as in urban areas of MICs (see Fleming in DCP3 volume 9, *Disease Control Priorities*).

Cancer Registries

Cancer registries, which form the basis for understanding and documenting patterns of cancer, are a basic tool in health care service provision. In LMICs, the percentage of the population covered by a high-quality registry, such as those in the International Agency for Research on Cancer's series on Cancer Incidence in Five Continents (Curado and others 2007), is in the single digits; this level rises to double digits in Europe; it is 80 percent or more only in Australia, New Zealand, and North America. Although it is not essential to have 100 percent population coverage, country planning and policy setting are much more difficult in the absence of a cancer registry of reasonable quality that covers at least one region.

Skilled Medical Personnel

The lack of adequate numbers of skilled medical personnel in LICs affects the ability to screen for, as well as to treat, cancer. LICs have few oncologists and oncology nurses, which limits treatment ability. Although some of the tests involved in cancer screening are often deceptively low-technology interventions (for example, Pap smears, clinical breast exams, and fecal occult blood tests), the organizational skills and infrastructure to conduct them successfully at scale and ensure appropriate referral make screening a high-technology intervention. Accordingly, organized screening programs become feasible in urban areas of MICs. Opportunistic screening, however, can occur in countries at all levels, provided that the screening test involved is not too demanding; clinical breast examination, visual inspection with acetic acid of the cervix, and the rapid DNA test for human papillomavirus (HPV) in low-resource environments are all possibilities. Campaign-style screening has been successfully used in LMICs, for example, in the Arab Republic of Egypt for breast cancer and in India for oral cancer; a rapid DNA test for cervical cancer is being piloted in low-resource provinces in China. In a campaign, the effort is made to screen a large number of the vulnerable groups in a short period of time, sometimes in local health facilities and sometimes using outreach, for example, using mobile facilities.

Health Insurance

Health insurance conditions access to all services, including treatment and screening. Individuals, who often underinvest in preventive health measures, may not see the value of paying for screening tests, particularly if they cannot afford treatment if they are subsequently diagnosed. The proportion of the population covered by health insurance typically increases with the level of development. In the poorer countries, only those people working in the formal sector or for the government may be covered; coverage in rural areas is minimal. Out-of-pocket spending on health constituted 48.1 percent of health expenditures in LICs, 52.8 percent in lower-middle income countries, 33.3 percent in upper-middle income countries, and only 13.7 percent in HICs (table 16.1, using data for the most recent years available from World Bank 2013). Expansion of insurance coverage in Mexico since 2003 through Seguro Popular—the scheme that covers those working outside the formal sector—was accompanied by an increase in coverage of cervical cancer screening and a reduction in the proportion of those abandoning breast cancer treatment (Knaul and others 2012). Chapter 17 elaborates further on the role of health financing in cancer care.

Although the importance of country resource levels for the inputs required for different aspects of cancer care has been documented, some countries underperform despite relatively high levels of income. The dislocation of public health systems in the Russian Federation following the economic system change, combined with adverse risk factors that include the relatively high consumption of fat, tobacco, and alcohol, is associated with high rates of incidence as well as overall cancer mortality. For example, 25 percent of the cases of colon cancer are diagnosed at stage 4 and 33 percent of newly diagnosed patients die within a year of diagnosis (Avksentyeva 2010). Many of those diagnosed are not eligible to receive reimbursement for drugs; of those who are eligible, drug supply problems inhibit the success of treatment. A cancer registry has existed since 1939 and, in theory, screening programs exist for at least five cancers. In practice, however, the lack of resourcing and lack of political will are associated with poor outcomes in cancer care (Avksentyeva 2010).

International Partnerships

Local champions can enable countries to outperform others at similar income levels. Local champions—key individuals willing to exert their influence in advocacy and/or leadership—can draw on substantial international resources that can make a difference, whether through partnership with a single other country or hospital or through membership in international networks. Partnerships have been used extensively for pediatric cancer in particular (Sloan and Gelband 2007, chapter 7). Although international financial resources can be important in saving lives, such as the radiation facilities provided by the International Atomic Energy Authority (IAEA) to selected Sub-Saharan African countries, the true value of these resources lies in access to expertise and support for developing guidelines and systems.

Cancer care works best in the context of a national cancer plan, and political leadership and the will to provide the funding for the plan are keys. The World Health Organization reports that, although increasing numbers of countries surveyed have developed cancer plans over the past decade, many countries still have not dedicated resources to fund these plans (WHO 2012).

The role of partnerships with or membership in international networks matters at all levels, including the following examples:

- **For clinicians:** World Endoscopy Society, http://www.worldendo.org
- **For guideline-setting:** Breast Health Global Initiative, http://portal.bhgi.org/Pages/Default.aspx or Asia Pacific Working Group on Colorectal Cancer
- **For screening:** International Cancer Screening Network, http://appliedresearch.gov.icsn
- **For training:** IAEA's support of radiation personnel training in eight LICs and MICs through its Programme of Action for Cancer Therapy model demonstration sites project, http://cancer.iaea.org/pmds.asp

Partnerships between institutions, such as twinning arrangements between cancer hospitals, serve a similar function.

COST-EFFECTIVENESS

Cost-Effectiveness Methods

Cost-effectiveness methods are described in standard texts (such as Drummond and others 2005); these methods have been applied widely in LMICs for infectious disease, for example, where there are large flows of international assistance. These methods have been much less well used for cancer interventions in LMICs, with the exception of vaccines for hepatitis B (HBV) and HPV and new DNA tests for HPV.

For this volume, a systematic literature search was undertaken to identify studies from LMICs for all aspects of care for six cancers; the literature on tobacco control is addressed separately in chapter 10. The search covered English language articles contained in PubMed and EconLit from 2000 to 2013. The detailed search terms, inclusion criteria, and full table of results are available in annex 16A. The articles are also graded for quality using a checklist based on Drummond and others (2005).

Fewer than 15 articles were found for the cost-effectiveness of interventions for breast, colon, liver, oral, and pediatric cancers in LMICs—including four

for HBV. In contrast, 16 articles were found that satisfied the inclusion criteria for the cost-effectiveness of vaccination and/or screening for cervical cancer. This result may reflect the fact that international funding has been available to investigate and promote the vaccines, principally through Gavi, the Vaccine Alliance. An additional six articles for breast and colon cancer were found for HICs in Asia. These six were included, since they may provide some guidance for MICs in this region.

Another reason that may explain the thin literature is that there are very few articles (whether for LMICs or HICs) on the cost-effectiveness of surgery, the cornerstone of cancer treatment. The effectiveness of basic surgery was established long before economic cost-effectiveness methods were developed and surgery became "usual care."

Given the lack of cost-effectiveness data for LMICs, the literature from other countries might prove helpful. The literature from HICs may provide guidance and the literature from HICs in Asia may be useful for other countries in the region. The cost-effectiveness literature has to be used cautiously, since the greater the difference in context (including disease patterns, prevalence, usual care alternatives, costs, and comorbidities), the less reliable the comparison is likely to be. We utilized cost-effectiveness findings from HICs from the web appendix of Greenberg and others (2010). Greenberg and colleagues undertook a systematic review of interventions for several cancers in HICs. Their approach yielded some useful studies, primarily for breast cancer, that have relevance for LMICs.

In tables 16.3 through 16.8, we indicate generally whether an intervention is "very cost-effective," "cost-effective," or "not cost-effective" in a given study. A few countries have set their own decision criteria, for example, the National Institute for Health and Care Excellence in the United Kingdom. In a comprehensive study of cost-effectiveness in Australia, Vos and others (2010) categorize interventions that cost less than US$10,000 per quality-adjusted life year (QALY) as very cost-effective; those interventions between US$10,000 and US$50,000 per QALY are cost-effective; and those over $50,000 per QALY are not cost-effective. A similar limit (US$50,000) is often used in the United States as the dividing line between what is and is not cost-effective. For countries that have not established their own threshold, the Commission on Macroeconomics and Health (2001) suggests that interventions costing less than one times the per capita gross national product per DALY averted are very cost-effective and those between one and three times per capita gross national product are cost-effective.

What is very cost-effective in HICs might merit consideration in LICs and what is cost-effective in HICs might be considered in MICs. This approach presupposes that the underlying model is similar, namely, the interventions are similar and the "no intervention" or "standard care" alternative scenarios are also similar, as are other key parameters. Country-specific data would be better in the future to guide policy.

The results summarized in the following section draw on the cost-effectiveness analyses in other chapters of this volume: Anderson and others (chapter 3), Denny and others (chapter 4), Sankaranarayanan and others (chapter 5), Rabeneck and others (chapter 6), Gupta and others (chapter 7), and Gelband and others (chapter 8). These analyses, in turn, utilize systematic literature surveys for the LMICs described in annex 16A.

Cost-Effectiveness Results

Table 16.2 summarizes the specific resources likely to be available at each of the four facility environments: Basic, Limited, Enhanced, and Maximal. Cancer care feasible in facilities with Basic resources is likely to be the norm in LICs, care feasible in facilities with Limited resources predominates for the rural population in MICs, care

feasible in facilities with Enhanced resources is likely to be available for urban populations in MICs, and facilities with Maximal resources are broadly available only in some HICs. Almost all countries, irrespective of income, have some facilities with Maximal resources to which a minority of the population has access or can be referred.

These resource categories are used as an organizing framework for five of the six major cancers covered. The exception is pediatric cancer, which has a similar ranking of feasibility but is determined differently. Patients with pediatric cancers, which are relatively rare, are often referred to specialized facilities. Specialized facilities with the least expertise can successfully treat a limited range of pediatric cancers; the range increases as experience grows.

Tables 16.3 through 16.8 summarize by resource environment the feasibility of various interventions for the six cancers considered: breast, cervical, colorectal, liver, oral, and pediatric. The cost-effectiveness evidence is provided where it exists, along with the country context in which the data were obtained. For surgery, the cost-effectiveness data are virtually nonexistent, even for HICs, except for new techniques, such as laparoscopic surgery. Data are most abundant for pharmaceuticals,

Table 16.2 Cancer Care Tools in Four Resource Environments

Basic	• Resources for organized screening and treatment of precancer conditions do not exist; vertical programs, such as mobile services for screen-and-treat options in one or two visits, may be feasible.
	• Basic surgery is available but in limited supply; specialized surgery skills may be available only by referral to another facility.
	• Radiation therapy is very scarce or unavailable.
	• Chemotherapy is not feasible because of the lack of laboratory facilities for required blood work.
Limited	• Mobile screening units are an option; rapid DNA testing is possible, if cost is sufficiently low.
	• Availability of surgery is better but still limited.
	• Radiation therapy is scarce and patients may need to travel long distances for access.
	• Chemotherapy may be possible, using off-patent drugs and "classical" therapies; new techniques, such as metronomics, may be considered. Laboratory facilities are limited.
	• Limited treatment of precancer conditions occurs at lower-level health facilities and first-level hospitals.
Enhanced	• Organized screening can be considered, along with treatment of precancer conditions at facilities at different levels.
	• Radiotherapy and surgery are widely available.
	• Chemotherapy is possible and newer generations of drugs can be considered, although typically not those still on-patent. Laboratory facilities are available on site to support use of chemotherapy.
	• The most advanced hospitals can offer most of the care options available in high-income countries, but budgets are insufficient to make such care broadly available.
Maximal	• State-of-the-art treatment is available; however, even in high-income countries, health budgets still require hard choices, and private insurers or public systems may carefully ration access to the most costly therapies.

Note: Resource typology based on Breast Health Global Initiative (Anderson and others, chapter 3). Most facilities in low-income countries have Basic levels of resources, facilities in rural areas in middle-income countries generally have Limited resources, most facilities in urban areas of middle-income countries have Enhanced resources, and facilities with Maximal resources are widespread only in some industrial countries.

since these data are often required in HICs as part of the approval process for new drugs.

Interventions listed as options in the Basic environment are limited to those that the evidence suggests are very cost-effective in HICS or cost-effective in LMICs. The range of options is broadened a little in the Limited environment to include items that are "close to being very cost-effective" in HICs, or "possibly cost-effective in LMICs," and the greater feasibility of radiation and chemotherapy options broadens the range for consideration.

In the Enhanced environment, more interventions are feasible because of the greater availability of resources and because a larger percent of the population is located in urban areas and able to undertake treatments that require regular visits, for example, for preoperative radiotherapy, or require more intensive follow-up,

for example, for organized screening. Options that are not recommended in this environment are those that are not cost-effective even in HICs.

Finally, in the Maximal environment, an even broader range of options is available, some of which are cost-effective in those environments. Those that are currently not cost-effective—for example, some new chemotherapy agents—may well eventually become cost-effective once they no longer have patent protection.

CONCLUSIONS

Feasibility and cost-effectiveness data suggest that cancer care can and should be expanded in LMICs. Table 16.9 summarizes the interventions, by cancer and by resource level, which are supported by feasibility and cost-effectiveness data, noting that virtually no

Table 16.3 Breast Cancer: Summary of Feasibility and Likely Cost-Effectiveness of Interventions, by Resource Level

Resource level	Intervention type	Intervention details	Cost-effectiveness (if available)
Basic	Detection	Clinical history and CBE	• CBE **cost-effective** in Ghana (Zelle and others 2012)
	Treatment, stages I and II	Modified radical mastectomy; ovarian ablation in premenopausal (stage I) or all (stage II)	—
		Test for ER and add tamoxifen if feasible; add chemotherapy (classical CMF or AC, EC, or FAC if blood chemistry and CBC available)	• Either tamoxifen or chemotherapy **very cost-effective** after surgery in United states for younger women (Hillner and Smith 1991; Malin and others 2002) • Tamoxifen **very cost-effective** in the Republic of Korea (Yang and others 2010)
	Treatment, locally advanced	Same options as for stages I and II; add preoperative chemotherapy if resources available	—
Limited	Detection	CBE with diagnostic ultrasound or mammography in target group	• Single lifetime CBE **very cost-effective** in India • Every three years or every five years **cost-effective** (Okonkwo and others 2008) • Annual CBE **very cost-effective** in Vietnam (Nguyen and others 2013)
	Treatment, stages I and II	Breast-conserving surgery; add irradiation of chest wall for high-risk stage II	• Breast-conserving surgery versus modified radical mastectomy **cost-effective** in United States (Norum and others 1997)
		Chemotherapy (classical CMF or AC, EC, or FAC if blood chemistry and CBC available)	• **Very cost-effective** after surgery in United States for younger women (Hillner and Smith 1991; Malin and others 2002) • **Cost-effective** in United States for older women (Desch and others 1993; Hillner, Smith, and Desch 1993; Malin and others 2002; Naeim and Keeler 2005)
	Treatment, locally advanced	Same options as for stages I and II; add irradiation of chest wall	—

table continues next page

Table 16.3 Breast Cancer: Summary of Feasibility and Likely Cost-Effectiveness of Interventions, by Resource Level (continued)

Resource level	Intervention type	Intervention details	Cost-effectiveness (if available)
Enhanced	Detection	Mammography every two years for women ages 55–69 years; every 12–18 months for women ages 40–54 years	• Mammography every year for women over age 50 years and every two years in high-risk women ages 40–49 years **cost-effective** in Mexico (Salomon and others 2012)
	Treatment, stages I and II	Breast-conserving surgery and whole-breast irradiation	—
		Aromatase inhibitors or LH-RH agonists (hormones) and taxanes (chemo) to replace tamoxifen and classical chemo, respectively	• Using raloxifene (taxane) instead of tamoxifen **cost-effective** for some women in United States (Armstrong and others 2001) • Using letrozole instead of tamoxifen **cost-effective** in United States (Delea and others 2007). Using anastrozole (aromatase) instead of tamoxifen **cost-effective** in Brazil (Fonseca, Araújo, and Saad 2009); **very cost-effective** in United States (Moeremans and others 2006); **not cost-effective** in Spain (Gil and others 2006)
	Treatment, locally advanced	Add trastuzumab for HER2/neu+ disease	• Short-course trastuzumab **very cost-effective** in United States compared with usual treatment for women with HER2+ disease (Malin and others 2002). Using letrozole (aromatase) instead of tamoxifen **very cost-effective** in United States for advanced disease (Dranitsaris, Verma, and Trudeau 2003; Karnon and others 2003)
Maximal	Detection	Mammography every year for women ages 40 years and older	• Mammography every three years in the Republic of Korea for women ages 45–65 years **not cost-effective** (Lee and others 2009) • Mammography every two years in Hong Kong SAR, China, for women ages 40–69 years **cost-effective** (Wong and others 2007)
	Treatment, stages I and II	Add trastuzumab for HER2/neu+ disease	• **Very cost-effective** in Singapore (de Lima Lopes 2011) • **Cost-effective** in Belgium (van Vlaenderen and others 2009), Canada (Hedden and others 2012), Italy and United States (Liberato and others 2007), Netherlands (Essers and others 2010)
	Treatment, stages I and II, locally advanced	Add growth factors and dose-dense chemotherapy	• Growth factors **cost-effective** in Japan for high-risk early cancer (Ishiguro and others 2010) • **Not cost-effective** in United States for early stage (Ramsey and others 2009)
	Metastatic	Use bevacizumab (chemo), fulvestrant (hormone), and growth factors (supportive)	• Bevacizumab **not cost-effective** in United Kingdom (Rodgers and others 2011), United States (Montero and others 2012) • Fulvestrant **cost-effective** in United Kingdom (Cameron and others 2008)

Note: See individual studies for further details, such as age and hormone status, for which cost-effectiveness results were obtained. Screening and treatment typically become less cost-effective for women ages 60 years and older. Resource typology based on Breast Health Global Initiative (Anderson and others, chapter 3). Most facilities in low-income countries have Basic levels of resources, facilities in rural areas in middle-income countries generally have Limited resources, most facilities in urban areas of middle-income countries have Enhanced resources, and facilities with Maximal resources are widespread only in some industrial countries. The table is cumulative, for example, treatments that are feasible in facilities with Basic environments are also feasible in facilities with Limited, Enhanced, and Maximal resources. AC = doxorubicin (Adriamycin) and cyclophosphamide (Cytoxan); CBC = complete blood count; CBE = clinical breast examination; CMF = cyclophosphamide, methotrexate, and fluorouracil; EC = epirubicin and cyclophosphamide; ER = estrogen receptor; FAC = fluorouracil, doxorubicin (Adriamycin), and cyclophosphamide (Cytoxan); LH-RH = luteinizing hormone–releasing hormone; — = not available.

cost-effectiveness data are available for surgery. The interventions provide suggestions to policy makers as to the sequence in which to add publicly funded interventions as country income increases, as part of a cancer plan.

Table 16.9 suggests that LMICs have cost-effective options in cancer control. More can be done in all countries in prevention, particularly tobacco control, and

expansion of HPV vaccine and DNA testing for cervical cancer, provided that the costs can be reduced sufficiently. There are methods to reduce the risk of liver cancer. The large expansion of HBV vaccination is a success story in preventing cancer.

The cost-effectiveness results suggest that a sustained expansion of cancer treatment is appropriate in

Table 16.4 Cervical Cancer: Summary of Feasibility and Likely Cost-Effectiveness of Interventions, by Resource Level

Resource level	Intervention type	Intervention details	Cost-effectiveness (if available)
Basic	Prevention	HPV vaccination of adolescent girls	**Cost-effective** in LMICs if the following three conditions apply: 1. Cost per vaccinated girl is low enough (US$10–25): Gavi-eligible countries can likely achieve this 2. Incidence is high 3. Vaccine protection is long-lasting (chapter 4)
	Detection	VIA starting at age 35 years, one to three times per lifetime, or rapid DNA test starting at age 35 years, two or three times per lifetime, assuming cost per HPV test is less than US$10	• **Very cost-effective** (Praditsitthikorn and others 2011, Thailand) • Rapid DNA is **very cost-effective** in LMICs with screen-and-treat in single visit (Goldie and others 2005) but difficult to undertake in practice • **Cost-effective** in MICs with two visits required (Kim and others 2008; Levin and others 2010)
	Diagnosis	Colposcopy	—
	Treatment, precancer	Cryotherapy for suspicious precancerous lesions	—
	Treatment, early-stage cancer	LEEP, CKC, simple hysterectomy	—
Limited	Treatment, more advanced stage cancer	Surgery and/or radiation therapy	—
Enhanced	Screening	Cytology every two to three years, starting at time of initiation of sexual activity; DNA test 1–3 times per lifetime	• Cytology may be **cost-effective** if quality control is good (Kim and others 2008) • DNA testing **cost-effective** depending on test cost, frequency of testing (Campos and others 2012)
	Prevent and screen	HPV vaccination combined with screening	Can be **cost-effective** in all countries, depending on cost per vaccinated girl and cost of screening strategy chosen (Denny and others, chapter 4)
	Treatment options	Add chemotherapy (cisplatin) where warranted	—
Maximal	Treatment options	Trachelectomy (fertility-sparing surgery), brachytherapy, intensity-modulated radiotherapy	—

Note: Resource typology based on Breast Health Global Initiative (Anderson and others, chapter 3). Most facilities in low-income countries have Basic levels of resources, facilities in rural areas in middle-income countries generally have Limited resources, most facilities in urban areas of middle-income countries have Enhanced resources, and facilities with Maximal resources are widespread only in some industrial countries. The table is cumulative, for example, treatments that are feasible in facilities with Basic environments are also feasible in facilities with Limited, Enhanced, and Maximal resources. CKC = cold knife conization; HPV = human papillomavirus; LEEP = loop electrosurgical excision procedure; LMICs = low- and middle-income countries; MICs = middle-income countries; VIA = visual inspection with acetic acid; — = not available.

Table 16.5 Colorectal Cancer: Summary of Feasibility and Cost-Effectiveness of Interventions, by Resource Level

Resource level	Intervention type	Intervention details	Cost-effectiveness (if available)
Basic	Prevention	Tax cigarettes	**Very cost-effective** for various cancers
	Detect/diagnose	Use barium enema where colonoscopy not available	—
	Treatment, stages I, II, III colon	Hemicolectomy and regional lymph node dissection	—
	Treatment, stages I, II, III rectal	Abdominal perineal resection with lymph node dissection	—
	Treatment, stage IV colorectal	Consider palliative surgery	—
Limited	Treatment, stages I and II colon	Hemicolectomy and regional lymph node dissection	—
	Treatment, stage I rectal	Abdominal perineal resection with lymph node dissection	—
	Treatment, stage III colon	Hemicolectomy and regional lymph node dissection plus adjuvant 5-fluorouracil	• Adjuvant chemotherapy **close to being very cost-effective** in United States versus no adjuvant after surgery for colorectal cancer (Nostrum and others 1997) • Adjuvant chemotherapy **close to being very cost-effective** in United States versus no adjuvant after surgery for colorectal cancer, colon cancer (Smith and others 1993)
	Treatment, stages II and III rectal	Abdominal perineal resection with lymph node dissection plus preoperative short course radiotherapy; add 5-fluorouracil	• Adjuvant chemotherapy **close to being very cost-effective** in United States versus no adjuvant after surgery for colorectal cancer (Nostrum and others 1997) • Preoperative radiotherapy **very cost-effective** in United States versus no preoperative radiotherapy (van den Brink and others 2004)
	Treatment, stage IV colorectal	Consider palliative surgery; consider palliative 5-fluorouracil-based chemotherapy	—
Enhanced	Detection	Organized screening (beginning with pilot)	• **Very cost-effective** in United States (gFOBT) (Pignone, Russell, and Wagner 2005) • **Cost-effective** in United States (colonoscopy) (Pignone, Russell, and Wagner 2005) • **Very cost-effective** in high-income Asia (gFOBT, sigmoidoscopy, colonoscopy) (Park, Yun, and Kwon 2005; Tsoi and others 2008; Wong, Leong, and Leong 2004; Wu and others 2006)
	Treatment, stages I and II colon	Hemicolectomy with en bloc removal of at least 12 lymph nodes	—
	Treatment, stage I rectal	Total mesorectal excision	—
	Treatment, stage III colon	Hemicolectomy plus removal of at least 12 lymph nodes plus adjuvant FOLFOX	FOLFOX **very cost-effective** in United Kingdom versus 5-fluorouracil plus leucovorin (Aballéa and others 2007)

table continues next page

Table 16.5 Colorectal Cancer: Summary of Feasibility and Cost-Effectiveness of Interventions, by Resource Level (continued)

Resource level	Intervention type	Intervention details	Cost-effectiveness (if available)
Maximal	Treatment, stages II and III rectal	Total mesorectal excision; preoperative chemo-radiotherapy; capecitabine or infusional 5-fluorouracil; adjuvant FOLFOX	—
	Treatment, stage IV colorectal	Consider palliative surgery; palliative radiation; FOLFOX/FOLFIRI; possibly aggressive surgery for cure	—
	Treatment, stages I and II colon	Surgery: can use polypectomy for selected stage I cancers; consider adjuvant 5-fluorouracil or capecitabine in high-risk stage II; can consider LAC	• LAC **not cost-effective** in United States (Hayes and Hansen 2007) • **Not cost-effective** in United States for colorectal cancer (de Verteuil, Hernández, and Vale 2007)
	Treatment, stage I rectal	Total mesorectal excision	—
	Treatment, stage III colon	Hemicolectomy plus removal of at least 12 lymph nodes plus adjuvant FOLFOX	FOLFOX **very cost-effective** in United Kingdom versus 5-fluorouracil plus leucovorin (Aballéa and others 2007)
	Treatment, stages II and III rectal	Total mesorectal excision; preoperative chemo-radiotherapy; capecitabine or infusional 5-fluorouracil; adjuvant FOLFOX	—
	Treatment, stage IV colorectal	As for stage IV (Enhanced); plus biological options (bevucizumab, aflibercept; if K-Ras wild-type cetuximab, panitumumab; regorafenib)	• Cetuximab plus irinotecan versus active or best support care **not cost-effective** in United States (Starling and others 2007) • Bevucizumab plus irrotecan and 5-fluorouracil plus leucovorin versus irrotecan and 5-fluorouracil plus leucovorin **not cost-effective** in United States (Tappenden and others 2007)

Note: Resource typology based on Breast Health Global Initiative (Anderson and others 2014). Most facilities in low-income countries have Basic levels of resources, facilities in rural areas in middle-income countries generally have Limited resources, most facilities in urban areas of middle-income countries have Enhanced resources, and facilities with Maximal resources are widespread only in some industrialized countries. The table is cumulative, for example, treatments that are feasible in facilities with Basic environments are also feasible in facilities with Limited, Enhanced, and Maximal resources. FOLFIRI = folinic acid, fluorouracil, and irinotecan; FOLFOX = folinic acid, fluorouracil, and oxalipatin; gFOBT = guaiac fecal occult blood test; K-Ras = Kirsten rat sarcoma viral oncogene homolog; LAC = laparoscopically-assisted colectomy; — = not available.

Table 16.6 Liver Cancer: Summary of Feasibility and Likely Cost-Effectiveness of Interventions, by Resource Level

Resource level	Intervention type	Intervention details	Cost-effectiveness (if available)
Basic	Prevention	Hepatitis B vaccination of neonates (East and Southeast Asia); infants (Sub-Saharan Africa)	**Cost-effective/very cost-effective** in intermediate- and high-prevalence countries (Beutels 2001; Ozawa and others 2012)
		Aflatoxin reduction through better post-harvest handling and storage	**Cost-effective** in Guinea (Khlangwiset and Wu, 2010)
Limited	Prevention	Hepatitis B vaccination of infants or adolescents	**Cost-effective/very cost-effective** in intermediate- and high-prevalence countries (Beutels 2001; Ozawa and others 2012)
		Aflatoxin reduction through biocontrol (different seed strains)	**Very cost-effective** in Nigeria (Wu and Khlangwiset 2010), but validation needed; however, analysis did not take account of cost of diffusion of technology

table continues next page

Table 16.6 Liver Cancer: Summary of Feasibility and Likely Cost-Effectiveness of Interventions, by Resource Level (continued)

Resource level	Intervention type	Intervention details	Cost-effectiveness (if available)
		Prevention programs for hepatitis C through reducing unsafe injections (for example, auto-disposable syringes) and screening blood donors	Using auto-disposable syringes is **very cost-effective** in India (Reid 2012)
		Prevention programs for liver flukes through education regarding food habits and hygiene	—
Enhanced	Prevention	Hepatitis B vaccination of infants, children, and adolescents	**Cost-effective** in intermediate and high-prevalence countries (Beutels 2001; Ozawa and others 2012)
	Treatment	Screening for and treatment with praziquantel for liver flukes in high-prevalence regions	—
Maximal	Prevention	Hepatitis B vaccination of adolescents	**Possibly cost-effective or not cost-effective** in low-prevalence countries (Beutels 2001)
	Treatment	Hepatitis B virus treatment with antivirals or immune system modulators	**Possibly cost-effective** in HICs (chapter 8)
	Treatment	Hepatitis C: pegylated interferon treatment plus ribavirin	**Cost-effective only in select patients** in HICs (chapter 8)
	Treatment	Various treatments of hepatocellular carcinoma or cholangiocarcinoma	**Not cost-effective** even in HICs because of poor survival even with treatment (chapter 8)

Note: Resource typology based on Breast Health Global Initiative (Anderson and others, chapter 3). Most facilities in low-income countries have Basic levels of resources, facilities in rural areas in middle-income countries generally have Limited resources, most facilities in urban areas of middle-income countries have Enhanced resources, and facilities with Maximal resources are widespread only in some industrial countries. The table is cumulative, for example, treatments that are feasible in facilities with Basic environments are also feasible in facilities with Limited, Enhanced, and Maximal resources. HICs = high-income countries; — = not available.

Table 16.7 Oral Cancer: Summary of Feasibility and Likely Cost-Effectiveness of Interventions, by Resource Level

Resource level	Intervention type	Intervention details	Cost-effectiveness (if available)
Basic	Prevention	Tobacco and alcohol taxes	**Cost-saving** (cannot be separated from impact on other cancers) (chapter 10)
	Screening	Visual screening by trained personnel (for example, dentist or nurse) of high-risk groups (known or self-declared tobacco and alcohol users) or by all at risk (for example, over 35 years of age) in high-prevalence regions; screening is sporadic rather than organized	• **Cost-effective** where prevalence is reasonably high; **very cost-effective** for screening high-risk groups (India: Subramanian and others 2009) • Cost-effective in three HICs with prevalence of 30 or more per 100,000 in men, age-adjusted population (Netherlands: van der Meij, Bezemer, and van der Waal 2002; United Kingdom: Speight and others 2006; United States: Dedhia and others 2011)
	Diagnosis	Visual inspection; biopsy; X-ray to diagnose spread	—
	Treatment	Surgery, no adjuvant treatment, for stages I, II, III; availability of surgery for oral reconstruction very limited	—
		Pain control, stage IV	

table continues next page

Table 16.7 Oral Cancer: Summary of Feasibility and Likely Cost-Effectiveness of Interventions, by Resource Level (continued)

Resource level	Intervention type	Intervention details	Cost-effectiveness (if available)
Limited	Treatment	Add postoperative radiotherapy if indicated (stage II or III, depending on type and location of tumor) or radical radiotherapy instead of surgery (stage II or II, depending on type/location of tumor)	—
		Palliative radiotherapy, stage IV	
Enhanced	Screening	Organized screening is possible	**Cost-effective** (Dedhia and others 2011; Speight and others 2006; Subramanian and others 2009; van der Meij, Bezemer, and van der Waal 2002)
	Diagnosis	CT scan to confirm spread	—
	Treatment	Surgery and/or radiotherapy or brachytherapy and/or off-patent chemotherapy, stages II, III and IV, depending on type/location of tumor; reconstructive surgery possible	—
		Palliative chemotherapy, stage IV	
Maximal	Diagnosis	PET, MRI to determine spread if bone/soft tissue potentially involved; can consider chemotherapy with patent drugs	—

Note: Resource typology based on Breast Health Global Initiative (Anderson and others, chapter 3). Most facilities in low-income countries have Basic levels of resources, facilities in rural areas in middle-income countries generally have Limited resources, most facilities in urban areas of middle-income countries have Enhanced resources, and facilities with Maximal resources are widespread only in some industrialized countries. The table is cumulative, for example, treatments that are feasible in facilities with Basic environments are also feasible in facilities with Limited, Enhanced, and Maximal resources. CT = computerized tomography; HICs = high-income countries; MRI = magnetic resonance imaging; PET = positron emission tomography; — = not available.

Table 16.8 Pediatric Cancer: Summary of Likely Cost-Effectiveness of Interventions, by Experience Level

Experience level	Cancer treated	Cost-effectiveness (if available)
Center with least expertise	Burkitt lymphoma	**Very cost-effective** (Malawi: Bhakta and others 2013)
	Hodgkin lymphoma (adolescents and adults)	**Very cost-effective** (Norway: Norum and others 1996)
Center with more expertise	Wilms tumor	**Cost-effective** (Brazil: Bhakta and others 2013)
	Acute lymphoblastic leukemia	**Very cost-effective** (Netherlands: van Litsenburg and others 2011); **cost-effective** (China: Luo and others 2009)
	Intraocular retinoblastoma	—
Center with most expertise	Sarcomas, brain tumors, acute myeloid leukemia, high-risk neuroblastoma, other retinoblastomas	—

Note: Sequencing of cancer is illustrative rather than exhaustive. Feasibility of treatment of pediatric cancer does not follow the same pattern as adult cancers. Pediatric cancers are rare and many low-income countries have used the approach of treatment in specialized centers. Prevention is not an important issue (other than via hepatitis B vaccination); because incidence is very low, population-level screening is not an option. — = not available.

all LMICs. The expansion of capacity for surgery and radiation is a priority throughout. The use of tamoxifen is feasible and cost-effective for breast cancer in LICs, and newer hormone treatments can be cost-effective in MICs. In MICs, the use of classical chemotherapy regimens for breast and cervical cancer is cost-effective; in areas where Enhanced facilities predominate. Chemotherapy can be expanded to include newer regimens for breast and cervical cancers and chemotherapy regimens for colon and oral cancers.

As treatment is scaled up, screening is more important to stage-shift treatment. LICs with largely Basic

Table 16.9 Summary Recommendations Based on Feasibility and Cost-Effectiveness, by Resource Level

Cancer	Intervention by resource level
Primary prevention	
Tobacco-related	Taxation of cigarettes, legislation, regulation (ALL)
Cervical	HPV vaccine (ALL: cost-effectiveness depends on price)
Liver	• HBV vaccination integrated with expanded program for immunization (B)
	• Neonatal (L, E); adolescent (E, M)
	• Screening blood donors (E, M); reducing unsafe injections (L, E, M)
	• Education to prevent liver fluke infection (L, E, M)
	• Aflatoxin reduction: post-harvest storage (B); biocontrol (L)
Screening and detection (to stage-shift treatment)	
Breast	• Clinical breast exam (B, L)
	• Mammography (E, M)
Cervical	• Visual inspection with acetic acid (B, L)
	• Rapid DNA test and treat in two visits (L)
	• DNA test, cytology (E, M)
Colorectal	Fecal immunochemical test (E); fecal immunochemical or endoscopy (M)
Liver cancer	Screen and treat for liver flukes in high-prevalence regions (E, M)
Oral cancer	Visual inspection (L, high-prevalence countries only)
Treatment with curative intent	
Breast	• Surgery (ALL); radiation (L, E, M)
	• Hormones: tamoxifen (B, L); aromatase inhibitors, LH-RH agonists (E); fulvestrant (M)
	• Chemotherapy: CMF or AC (B); EC or FAC (L); taxanes (E); trastuzumab (E, M)
	• Growth factors (M); bevacizumab (M)
Cervical	• Surgery (ALL); trachelectomy (M)
	• Cryotherapy (B, L); radiotherapy (L, E, M); brachytherapy, intensity modulated brachytherapy (M)
	• Chemotherapy (cisplatin) (E, M)
Colorectal	• Surgery: colon (ALL); rectal (L, E, M)
	• Radiation: preoperative, rectal (L); chemo-radiotherapy preoperative, rectal (E, M)
	• Chemotherapy: classical 5-fluorouracil (L); FOLFOX (E, M)
Liver	• Antivirals or immune system modulators for hepatitis B (M)
	• Hepatitis C (M, cost-effective only in select patients)
	• Treatment of liver cancer (M, although not generally cost-effective)
Oral	Surgery (ALL); radiotherapy (L, E, M); brachytherapy (E, M); chemotherapy (E, M)
Pediatric	• Burkitt lymphoma, Hodgkin lymphoma (specialized center, least expertise)
	• Wilms tumor (specialized center, more expertise)
	• Sarcomas, brain tumors, acute myeloid leukemia, high-risk neuroblastoma (specialized center, most expertise)

table continues next page

Table 16.9 Summary Recommendations Based on Feasibility and Cost-Effectiveness, by Resource Level (continued)

Cancer	Intervention by resource level
Advanced disease	
All	• Pain control (ALL)
	• Home or hospice care (ALL)
	• Palliative radiotherapy (L, E, M, as resources allow)
	• Palliative surgery (as resources allow)
	• Palliative chemotherapy (L, classical; E, next generations; M, on-patent, as resources allow)
	• Aggressive treatment with curative intent (M)

Note: Resource typology based on Breast Health Global Initiative (Anderson and others, chapter 3). Most facilities in low-income countries have Basic levels of resources, facilities in rural areas in middle-income countries generally have Limited resources, most facilities in urban areas of middle-income countries have Enhanced resources, and facilities with Maximal resources are widespread only in some industrial countries. Higher resource–level countries can consider any of the options from lower resource levels. The table is cumulative, for example, treatments that are feasible in facilities with Basic environments are also feasible in facilities with Limited, Enhanced, and Maximal resources. AC = doxorubicin (Adriamycin) and cyclophosphamide (Cytoxan); ALL = all resource levels; B = Basic resource level; CMF = cyclophosphamide, methotrexate, and fluorouracil; E = Enhanced resource level; EC = epirubicin and cyclophosphamide; FAC = fluorouracil, doxorubicin (Adriamycin), and cyclophosphamide (Cytoxan); FOLFOX = folinic acid, fluorouracil, and oxalipatin; HBV = hepatitis B virus; HPV = human papillomavirus; L = Limited resource level; LH–RH = luteinizing hormone–releasing hormone; M = Maximal resource level. Recommendations are based on existing cost-effectiveness data and expected availability of resources. Recommendations for basic surgery, radiation therapy, hormone therapy, and classical chemotherapy are based on expert opinion, where cost-effectiveness studies are not available, and are subject to development of infrastructure where it does not yet exist.

facilities are not readily able to undertake organized screening. Opportunistic screening in LICs and organized screening in MICs can help to identify cancer earlier to increase the chance of a cure. In LICs, cost-effective screening choices include clinical breast examination, visual inspection of the cervix with acetic acid, and visual inspection for oral cancer in high-prevalence countries, with rapid DNA test-and-treat for cervical cancer potentially feasible as country income increases or the cost of the test falls. Urban areas in MICs can consider mammography and fecal immunochemical testing for colon cancer, where prevalence patterns dictate. MICs can screen in rural areas for liver flukes, if prevalent.

For the common pediatric cancers, a case can be made for centralizing treatment, either in-country or in-region. Evidence suggests that many pediatric cancers can be treated cost-effectively, even in LMICs, and scale-up is feasible.

To support countries as they develop cancer plans, more work on costing is needed. Experience with other global health concerns facing LMICs (for example, HIV-AIDS and nutrition) suggests that credible estimates of total costs are important. These estimates can help to convince the international community that action is possible and may motivate the substantial mobilization of resources required. Estimating resource requirements will be a key next step for the global fight against cancer.

Further research is needed to validate the recommendations for cervical, colorectal, liver, oral, and pediatric cancer made in table 16.9, including expert consultations and updating of the systematic literature reviews. The literature search was conducted only in English,

but groups are undertaking cost-effectiveness studies in Brazil and China, and some literature is not yet categorized in PubMed. Table 16.9 also does not include studies after 2007 for HICs, except for breast cancer.

It is clear that the literature on cost-effectiveness in LMICs is thin. More studies need to be done using best practice methodology, such that findings can be compared across countries. Multi-country studies with common assumptions are valuable to help identify the types of situations where a particular intervention is cost-effective. For screening, there are good multi-country studies for cervical cancer using a common model, but almost none for the other cancers. Although the WHO's Choosing Interventions That Are Cost-Effective multi-country work has been done for cervical, breast, and colon cancer screening (for example, Ginsberg and others 2012), this needs to be updated using state-of-the-art models similar to the large ones used in HICs. Future economics work on cancer is to cost out the ingredients required for the priority interventions, such that costs of resource-appropriate care can be estimated in individual countries. This approach can help countries to plan for and mobilize the resources needed to implement a cancer plan.

ACKNOWLEDGMENTS

The authors thank Hellen Gelband, Carol Levin, Joe Lipscomb, and Rachel Nugent for helpful suggestions on earlier drafts, and Benjamin Anderson, Craig Earle, Surendra Shastri, and Rengaswamy Sankaranarayanan for useful inputs regarding specific cancers.

ANNEX 16A

The annex to this chapter is as follows. It is available at http://www.dcp-3.org/cancer.
• Annex 16A. Search terms, Inclusion Criteria, and Results

NOTE

World Bank income classifications as of July 2014 are as follows, based on estimates of gross national income per capita for 2013:

• Low-income countries: US$1,045 or less
• Middle-income countries:
  • Lower-middle-income: US$1,046–US$4,125
  • Upper-middle-income: US$4,126–US$12,745
• High-income countries: US$12,746 or more

REFERENCES

Aballéa, S., A. Boler, A. Craig and H. Wasan. 2007. "An economic evaluation of oxaliplatin for the Adjuvant Treatment of Colon Cancer in the United Kingdom." *European Journal of Cancer* 43(11): 1687–93.

Armstrong, K., T. M. Chen, D. Albert, T. C. Randall, and J. S. Schwartz. 2001. "Cost-Effectiveness of Raloxifene and Hormone Replacement Therapy in Postmenopausal Women: Impact of Breast Cancer Risk." *Obstetrics Gynecology* 98 (6): 996–1003.

Avksentyeva, M. 2010. "Colorectal Cancer in Russia." *European Journal of Health Economics* 1: S91–S98.

Beutels, P. 2001. "Economic Evaluations of Hepatitis B Immunization: A Global Review of Recent Studies (1994–2000)." *Health Economics* 10: 751–74.

Bhakta, N., A. L. C. Martiniuk, S. Gupta, and S. C. Howard. 2013. "The Cost-Effectiveness of Treating Paediatric Cancer in Low-Income and Middle-Income Countries: A Case-Study Approach Using Acute Lymphocytic Leukaemia in Brazil and Burkitt Lymphoma in Malawi." *Archives of Disease in Children* 98 (2): 155–60.

Cameron, D. A., D. R. Camidge, J. Oyee, and M. Hirsch. 2008. "Economic Evaluation of Fulvestrant as an Extra Step in the Treatment Sequence for ER-Positive Advanced Breast Cancer." *British Journal of Cancer* 99 (12): 1984–90.

Campos, N. G., J. J. Kim, P. E. Castle, J. Ortendahl, M. O'Shea, and others. 2012. "Health and Economic Impact of HPV 16/18 Vaccination and Cervical Cancer Screening in Eastern Africa." *International Journal of Cancer* 130 (11): 2672–84.

Commission on Macroeconomics and Health. 2001. WHO. *Macroeconomics and Health: Investing in Health for Economic Development.* Geneva: World Health Organization. http://whqlibdoc.who.int/publications/2001/924154550x.pdf.

Curado, M. P., B. Edwards, H. R. Shim, H. Storm., J. Ferlay, and others, eds. 2007. *Cancer Incidence in Five Continents,*

vol. IX. Scientific Publications 160. Lyon: International Agency for Research on Cancer.

de Lima Lopes, G. 2011. "Societal Costs and Benefits of Treatment with Trastuzumab in Patients with Early HER2neu-Overexpressing Breast Cancer in Singapore." *BMC Cancer* 11: 178–85.

de Verteuil, R. M., R. A. Hernández, and L. Vale. 2007. "Economic Evaluation of Laparoscopic Surgery for Colorectal Cancer." *International Journal of Technology Assessment in Health Care* 23 (4): 464–72.

Dedhia, R. C., K. J. Smith, J. T. Johnson, and M. Roberts. 2011. "The Cost-Effectiveness of Community-Based Screening for Oral Cancer in High-Risk Males in the United States: A Markov Decision Analysis Approach." *Laryngoscope* 121 (5): 952–60.

Delea, T.E., J. Karnon, O. Sofrygin, S. K. Thomas, N. L. Papo and V. Barghout. 2007. "Cost-effectiveness of Letrozole versus Tamoxifen as Initial Adjuvant Therapy in Hormone-receptor-positive Postmenopausal Women with Early-stage Breast Cancer." *Clinical Breast Cancer* 7 (8): 608–18.

Desch, C. E., B. E. Hillner, T. J. Smith, and S. M. Retchin. 1993. "Should the Elderly Receive Chemotherapy for Node-Negative Breast Cancer? A Cost-Effectiveness Analysis Examining Total and Active Life-Expectancy Outcomes." *Journal of Clinical Oncology* 11 (4): 777–82.

Dranitsaris, G., S. Verma and M. Trudeau. 2003. "Cost Utility Analysis of First-line Hormonal Therapy in Advanced Breast Cancer: Comparison of Two Aromatase Inhibitors to Tamoxifen." *American Journal of Clinical Oncology* 26(3): 289–96.

Drummond, M. F., M. J. Schulpher, G. W. Torrance, D. J. O'Brien, and G. L. Stoddart. 2005. *Methods for the Economic Evaluation of Health Care Programmes.* 3rd edition. New York: Oxford University Press.

Essers, B. A., S. C. Seferina, V. C. Tjan-Heijnen, J. L. Severens, A. Novák, and others. 2010. "Transferability of Model-Based Economic Evaluations: The Case of Trastuzumab for the Adjuvant Treatment of HER2-Positive Early Breast Cancer in the Netherlands." *Value in Health* 13 (4): 375–80.

Fonseca, M., G. T. B. Araújo, and E. D. Saad. 2009. "Cost-Effectiveness of Anastrozole, in Comparison with Tamoxifen, in the Adjuvant Treatment of Early Breast Cancer in Brazil." *Revista Da Associação Medica Brasileira* 55: 410–15.

Funk, L. M., T. G. Weiser, W. R. Berry, S. R. Lipsitz, A. F. Merry, and others. 2010. "Global Operating Theatre Distribution and Pulse Oximetry Supply: An Estimation from Reported Data." *Lancet* 376 (9746): 1055–61.

Gil, J. M., C. Rubio-Terres, C.A. Del, P. Gonzalez and F. Canorea. 2006. "Pharmacoeconomic Analysis of Adjuvant Therapy with Exemestane, Anastrozole, Letrozole or Tamoxifen in Postmenopausal Women with Operable and Estrogen Receptor-Positive Breast Cancer" *Clinical Transl Oncology* 8 (5): 339–48.

Ginsberg, G. M., J. A Lauer, S. Zelle, S. Baetan and R. Baltussen. 2012. "Cost Effectiveness of Strategies to Combat Breast, Cervical, and Colorectal Cancer in sub-Saharan Africa and

South East Asia: Mathematical Modelling Study." *British Medical Journal* 344: eb14. doi:10.1136/bmj.e614.

Goldie, S. J., L. Gaffikin, J. D. Goldhaber-Fiebert, A. Gordillo-Tobar, C. Levin, and others. 2005. "Cost-Effectiveness of Cervical-Cancer Screening in Five Developing Countries." *New England Journal of Medicine* 353: 2158–68.

Greenberg, D., C. Earle, C. H. Fang, A. Eldar-Lissai, and P. J. Neumann. 2010. "When Is Cancer Care Cost-Effective? A Systematic Overview of Cost-Utility Analyses in Oncology." *Journal of the National Cancer Institute* 102 (2): 82–88.

Hayes, J. L., and P. Hansen. 2007. "Is Laparoscopic Colectomy for Cancer Cost-Effective Relative to Open Colectomy?" *Australia and New Zealand Journal of Surgery* 77 (9): 782–86.

Hedden, L., S. O'Reilly, C. Lohrisch, S. Chia, C. Speers, and others. 2012. "Assessing the Real-World Cost-Effectiveness of Adjuvant Trastuzumab in HER-2/neu Positive Breast Cancer." *Oncologist* 17 (2): 164–71.

Hillner, B. E., and T. J. Smith. 1991. "Efficacy and Cost Effectiveness of Adjuvant Chemotherapy in Women with Node-Negative Breast Cancer. A Decision-Analysis Model." *New England Journal of Medicine* 324 (3): 160–68.

———. 1993. "Assessing the Cost Effectiveness of Adjuvant Therapies in Early Breast Cancer Using a Decision Analysis Model." *Breast Cancer Research and Treatment* 25 (2): 97–105.

IAEA (International Atomic Energy Authority). 2013. "Radiotherapy Availability." Programme of Action for Cancer Therapy (PACT), Programme Office. http://cancer.iaea.org/agart.asp.

Ishiguro, H., M. Kondo, S. L. Hoshi, M. Takada, S. Nakamura, and others. 2010. "Economic Evaluation of Intensive Chemotherapy with Prophylactic Granulocyte Colony-Stimulating Factor for Patients with High-Risk Early Breast Cancer in Japan." *Clinical Therapeutics* 32 (2): 11–26.

Karnon, J., R. Delea, S. R. Johnston, R. Smith, J. Brandman, J. Sung and others 2003. "Cost-effectiveness of Extended Adjuvant Letrozole in Postmenopausal Women after Adjuvant Tamoxifen Therapy: the UK Perspective. *Pharmacoeconomics* 24 (3): 237–50.

Kim, J. J., K. E. Kobus, M. Diaz, V. Van Minh, and S. J. Goldie. 2008. "Exploring the Cost-Effectiveness of HPV Vaccination in Vietnam: Insights for Evidence-Based Cervical Cancer Prevention Policy." *Vaccine* 26: 4015–24.

Khlangwiset, P. and F. Wu. 2010. "Costs and Efficacy of Public Health Interventions to Reduce Aflatoxin-induced Human Disease." *Food Additives and Contaminants Part A Chemical Analysis, Control of Exposure and Risk Assessment* 27(7): 998–1014.

Knaul, F. M., E. E. González-Pier, O. Gómez-Dantés, D. García-Junco, H. Arreola-Ornelas, and others. 2012. "The Quest for Universal Health Coverage: Achieving Social Protection for All in Mexico." *Lancet* 350: 1259–79.

Lee, S. Y., S. H. Jeong, Y. N. Kim, J. Kim, D. R. Kang, and others. 2009. "Cost-Effective Mammography Screening in Korea: High Incidence of Breast Cancer in Young Women." *Cancer Science* 100: 1105–1111.

Levin, C. E., J. Sellors, J.-F. Shi, L. Ma, Y.-L. Qiao, J. Ortendahl, M. K. H. O'Shea, and S. J. Goldie. 2010. "Cost-effectiveness Analysis of Cervical Cancer Prevention based on a Rapid Human Papillomavirus Screening Test in a High-Risk Region of China." *International Journal of Cancer* 127: 1404–11.

Liberato, N. L., M. Marchetti, and G. Barosi. 2007. "Cost-Effectiveness of Adjuvant Trastuzumab in Human Epidermal Growth Factor Receptor 2-Positive Breast Cancer." *Journal of Clinical Oncology.* 25(6): 625–33.

Luo, X. Q., Z. Y. Ke, L. B. Huang, X. Q. Guan, Y. C. Zhang, and others. 2009. "Improved Outcome for Chinese Children with Acute Promyelocytic Leukemia: A Comparison of Two Protocols." *Pediatric Blood and Cancer* 53: 325–28.

Malin, J. L., E. Keeler, C. Wang, and R. Brook. 2002. "Using Cost-Effectiveness Analysis to Define a Breast Cancer Benefits Package for the Uninsured." *Breast Cancer Research and Treatment* 74 (2): 143–53.

Montero, A. J., K. Avancha, S. Glück, and G. Lopes. 2012. "A Cost-Benefit Analysis of Bevacizumab in Combination with Paclitaxel in the First-Line Treatment of Patients with Metastatic Breast Cancer." *Breast Cancer Research and Treatment* 132 (2): 747–51.

Naeim, A., and E. B. Keeler. 2005. "Is Adjuvant Therapy for Older Patients with Node (-) Early Breast Cancer Cost-Effective?" *Critical Reviews in Oncology/Hematology* 53 (1): 81–89.

Nguyen, L. H., W. Laohasiriwong, J. F. Stewart, P. Wright, Y. T. B. Nguyen, and P. C. Coyte. 2013. "Cost-effectiveness Analysis of a Screening Program for Breast Cancer in Vietnam." *Value in Health Regional Issues* 2: 21–28.

Norum, J., V. Angelsen, E. Wist, and J. A. Olsen. 1996. "Treatment Costs in Hodgkin's Disease: A Cost-Utility Analysis." *European Journal of Cancer* 32A (9): 1510–17.

Norum, J., J. A. Olsen and E. A. Wist. 1997. "Lumpectomy or mastectomy? Is breast conserving surgery too expensive?" *Breast Cancer Research and Treatment* 45 (1): 7–14.

Okonkwo, Q. L., G. Draisma, A. der Kinderen, M. L. Brown, and H. J. de Koning. 2008. "Breast Cancer Screening Policies in Developing Countries: A Cost-Effectiveness Analysis for India." *Journal of the National Cancer Institute* 100 (18): 1290–1300.

Ozawa, S., A. Mirelman, M. L. Stacka, D. G. Walker, and O. S. Levine. 2012. "Cost-Effectiveness and Economic Benefits of Vaccines in Low- and Middle-Income Countries: A Systematic Review." *Vaccine* 31: 108–96.

Park, S. M., Y. H. Yun, and S. Kwon. 2005. "Feasible Economic Strategies to Improve Screening Compliance for Colorectal Cancer in Korea." *World Journal of Gastroenterology* 11: 1587–93.

Pignone, M., L. Russell, and J. Wagner, eds. 2005. *Economic Models of Colorectal Cancer Screening in Average-Risk Adults.* Washington, DC: National Academies Press.

Praditsitthikorn, N., Y. Teerawattananon, S. Tantivess, S. Limwattananon, A. Riewpaiboon, and others. 2011. "Economic Evaluation of Policy Options for Prevention and Control of Cervical Cancer in Thailand." *Pharmacoeconomics* 29 (9): 781–806.

Ramsey, S. D., Z. Liu, R. Boer, S. D. Sullivan, J. Malin, and others. 2009. "Cost-Effectiveness of Primary versus Secondary Prophylaxis with Pegfilgrastim in Women with Early-Stage Breast Cancer Receiving Chemotherapy." *Value in Health* 12 (2): 217–25.

Reid, S. 2012. "Estimating the Burden of Disease from Unsafe Injections in India: A Cost-Benefit Assessment of the Auto-Disable Syringe in a Country with Low Blood-Borne Virus Prevalence." *Indian Journal of Community Medicine* 37 (2): 89–94. doi:10.4103/0970-0218.96093.

Rodgers, M., M. Soares, D. Epstein, H. Yang, D. Fox, and others. 2011. "Bevacizumab in Combination with a Taxane for the First-Line Treatment of HER2-Negative Metastatic Breast Cancer." *Health Technology Assessment* 1: 1–12.

Salomon, J. A., N. Carvalho, C. Gutiérrez-Delgado, R. Orozco, A. Mancuso, and others. 2012. "Intervention Strategies to Reduce the Burden of Non-Communicable Diseases in Mexico: Cost Effectiveness Analysis." *British Medical Journal* 344: e355.

Sloan, F. A., and H. Gelband, eds. 2007. *Opportunities for Cancer Control in Low- and Middle-Income Countries.* Washington, DC: National Academies Press.

Smith, R. D., J. Hall, H. Gurney, and P. R. Harnett. 1993. "A Cost-Utility Approach to the Use of 5-Fluorouracil and Levamisole as Adjuvant Chemotherapy for Dukes' C Colonic Carcinoma." *Medical Journal of Australia* 158 (5): 319–22.

Speight, P. M., S. Palmer, D. R. Moles, M. C. Downer, D. H. Smith, and others. 2006. "The Cost-Effectiveness of Screening for Oral Cancer in Primary Care." *Health Technology Assessment* 10 (14): 1–144.

Starling, N., D. Tilden, J. White, and D. Cunningham. 2007. "Cost-Effectiveness Analysis of Cetuximab/Irinotecan vs Active/Best Supportive Care for the Treatment of Metastatic Colorectal Cancer Patients Who Have Failed Previous Chemotherapy Treatment." *British Journal of Cancer* 96 (2): 206–12.

Subramanian, S., R. Sankaranarayanan, B. Bapat, T. Somanathan, G. Thomas, and others. 2009. "Cost-Effectiveness of Oral Cancer Screening: Results from a Cluster Randomized Controlled Trial in India." *Bulletin of the World Health Organization* 87 (3): 200–06.

Tappenden, P., R. Jones, S. Paisley, and C. Carroll. 2007. "The Cost-Effectiveness of Bevacizumab in the First-Line Treatment of Metastatic Colorectal Cancer in England and Wales." *European Journal of Cancer* 17 (2487): 2494.

Tsoi, K. K. F., S. S. M. Ng, M. C. M. Leung, and J. J. Y. Sung. 2008. "Cost-Effectiveness Analysis on Screening for Colorectal Neoplasm and Management of Colorectal Cancer in Asia." *Alimentary Pharmacology and Therapeutics* 28 (3): 353–63.

van den Brink, M., W. B. van den Hout, A. M. Stiggelbout, E. Klein Kranenbarg, C. A. Marijnen, and others. 2004. "Cost-Utility Analysis of Preoperative Radiotherapy in Patients with Rectal Cancer Undergoing Total Mesorectal Excision: A Study of the Dutch Colorectal Cancer Group." *Journal of Clinical Oncology* 22 (2): 244–53.

van der Meij, E. H., P. D. Bezemer, and I. van der Waal. 2002. "Cost-Effectiveness of Screening for the Possible Development of Cancer in Patients with Oral Lichen Planus." *Community Dentistry and Oral Epidemiology* 30 (5): 342–52.

van Litsenburg, R. R., C. A. Uyl-de Groot, H. Raat, G. J. Kaspers, and R. J. Gemke. 2011. "Cost-Effectiveness of Treatment of Childhood Acute Lymphoblastic Leukemia with Chemotherapy Only: The Influence of New Medication and Diagnostic Technology." *Pediatric Blood and Cancer* 57 (6): 1005–10.

van Vlaenderen, I., J. L. Canon, V. Cocquyt, G. Jerusalem, J. P. Machiels, and others. 2009. "Trastuzumab Treatment of Early Stage Breast Cancer Is Cost-Effective from the Perspective of the Belgian Health Care Authorities." *Acta Clinica Belgica* 64 (2): 100–12.

Vos, T., R. Carter, J. Barendregt, C. Mihalopoulos, L. Veerman, A. Magnus, L. Cobiac, M. Bertram, and A. Wallace. 2010. Assessing Cost-Effectiveness in Prevention: Final Report. University of Queensland, Brisbane and Deakin University, Melbourne.

WHO (World Health Organization). 2012. Assessing National Capacity for the Prevention and Control of Noncommunicable Diseases: Report of the 2010 Global Survey. Geneva: WHO.

Wong, I. O. L., K. M. Kuntz, B. J. Cowling, C. L. K. Lam, and G. M. Leung. 2007. "Cost Effectiveness of Mammography Screening for Chinese Women." *Cancer* 110 (885): 895.

Wong, S. S., A. P. K. Leong, and T. Z. Leong. 2004. "Cost-Effectiveness Analysis of Colorectal Cancer Screening Strategies in Singapore: A Dynamic Decision Analytic Approach." *Studies in Health Technology Information* 107 (Pt 1): 104–10.

World Bank. 2013. *World Databank.* World Bank, Washington, DC. http://databank.worldbank.org/data/home.aspx.

Wu, G. H.-M., Y.-M. Wang, A. M.-F. Yen, J.-M. Wong, H.-C. Lai, and others. 2006. "Cost-Effectiveness Analysis of Colorectal Cancer Screening with Stool DNA Testing in Intermediate-Incidence Countries." *BMC Cancer* 6: 136–48.

Yang, J. J., S. K. Park, L. Y. Cho, W. Han, B. Park, and others. 2010. "Cost-Effectiveness Analysis of 5 Years of Postoperative Adjuvant Tamoxifen Therapy for Korean Women with Breast Cancer: Retrospective Cohort Study of the Korean Breast Cancer Society Database." *Clinical Therapeutics* 32: 1122–38.

Zelle, S. G., K. M. Nyarko, W. K. Bosu, M. Aikins, L. M. Niëns, and others. 2012. "Costs, Effects and Cost-Effectiveness of Breast Cancer Control in Ghana." *Tropical Medicine and International Health* 17: 1031–43.

Chapter 7

Financing Cancer Care in Low-Resource Settings

Felicia Knaul, Susan Horton, Pooja Yerramilli,
Hellen Gelband, and Rifat Atun

INTRODUCTION

Cancer accounts for a rapidly growing health and economic burden in low- and middle-income countries (LMICs) (Knaul and others 2014). The long-term nature of chronic and noncommunicable diseases that characterizes many cancers inflicts repeated financial onslaughts on families, intensifying the poverty-illness cycle. Inadequately treated illnesses deepen poverty, leading to a cycle of loss of health, lack of treatment, higher morbidity, lost income, and deeper impoverishment (Atun and Knaul 2012).

Many LMICs are working to achieve greater, and even universal, financial protection in health care, with funding from domestic sources that combines public insurance and prepayment. Establishing universal entitlement to key services through guaranteed benefits packages is a cornerstone of these efforts. These countries face challenges as they strive to include cancer and other chronic and noncommunicable diseases in the package of covered services. The inclusion of cancer interventions poses a specific set of challenges because of the chronic nature of the illness and the high costs of treatment.

An effective response to cancer requires strengthening all health system functions—stewardship, financing, service provision and delivery, and resource generation—along the entire, six-component, care-control continuum—primary and secondary prevention,

diagnosis, treatment, survivorship, rehabilitation, and palliative care and pain control (Hewitt, Greenfield, and Stovall 2005; Knaul, Alleyne, and others 2012). The failure to adequately manage one of the components can jeopardize the entire response, resulting in premature deaths, unnecessary pain, and wasted resources. Although responding to all facets of the continuum is a daunting task, several countries have included cancer care in recent reforms designed to achieve universal health coverage (UHC); these reforms provide useful lessons for other countries.

This chapter analyzes one health system function—financing—in relation to cancer, focusing on treatment. The analysis draws on experiences from several middle-income countries (MICs) in which domestic finance is used and efforts are underway to achieve universal coverage. We draw lessons for other components of cancer care and control and highlight the importance of developing strategies for financing that consider all aspects of the care continuum and strengthening of health systems.

Our analysis focuses on how domestic sources of funding are deployed to finance cancer care; we leave for later work the issues of how these funds are sourced and collected. Domestic funding in the vast majority of LMICs does, and will inevitably continue to, pay for the bulk of cancer care. We do not focus on global and regional financing and platforms; this is a topic for future research. These platforms are especially important

Corresponding author: Felicia Knaul, PhD, Director, Miami Institute for the Americas, and Professor, Miller School of Medicine, University of Miami, Florida, United States, fknaul@miami.edu.

sources of finance for the poorest countries, for catalyzing discovery and innovation and for aggregating demand to reduce the costs of medicines and vaccines.

FINANCIAL PROTECTION, HEALTH FINANCING, AND CANCER CARE[1]

The set of diseases that we call *cancer* leads to some of the most problematic financial issues in providing care for chronic and noncommunicable diseases. Some cancers can be prevented by changing behaviors or by controlling cancer-associated infections. For other cancers whose causes are unknown, the only effective control comes from early detection and treatment. Even where the causes are known and somewhat controllable, early detection and treatment remain the best course for cancers that are not prevented. For some cancers, especially those detected at later stages, even the most advanced treatments are not effective and palliation is the appropriate course of action (Gralow and others 2012).

Cancer often requires relatively expensive, complex, multimodal medical treatment for extended periods, leading to household impoverishment, treatment abandonment, and, too often, poor outcomes, especially if the disease is detected at a later stage or patients cannot adhere to a full regime of treatment. Yet many interventions for cancer are both effective and cost-effective according to today's global metrics. Recent discoveries have made it possible to prevent several of the infection-associated cancers that disproportionately affect poor people because of their exposure to communicable diseases and lack of access to early detection of precancerous lesions. For example, vaccinating against the human papillomavirus (HPV) can prevent the most common cervical cancers, the vast majority of which occur in LMICs.

Need for Financial Protection

Acute care costs, even for simple ailments, can push already poor families deeper into poverty. The repeated and ongoing costs of a chronic illness are more devastating. India provides an example of the substantial financial vulnerability of households to noncommunicable diseases, especially cancer. In India, the share of out-of-pocket health expenditure devoted to noncommunicable diseases increased from 33 percent to almost 50 percent from 1995 to 2004. The cost of a single stay for cancer or heart disease in a public hospital is the equivalent of 40–50 percent of gross domestic product (GDP) per capita (Mahal, Karan, and Engelgau 2010). As a result, cancer-affected households derive over 30 percent of annual inpatient expenditures from borrowing and asset sales, which is significantly greater than the reliance on these funding mechanisms by unaffected households (Mahal and others 2013). In South Asia, the probability of incurring catastrophic health expenditure from hospitalization is 1.6 times higher for cancer than for a communicable disease, such as pneumonia (Engelgau and others 2010; Nikolic, Stanciole, and Zaydman 2011).

One of the most insidious aspects of this illness-impoverishment cycle is that for many patients, out-of-pocket spending is wasted because it contributes nothing to improved health. Especially in LMICs, cancer is often detected so late that even the most effective treatment will not effect a long-term cure. Second, a substantial proportion of what is spent by patients buys low-quality or inappropriate care that is ineffective. Third, care may be coupled with prohibitive transportation costs and investments of time that include long waits to access care. These difficulties are more likely to occur with a disease such as cancer, where care often requires repeated travel and months-long treatment.

Cancer Care Financing

In all LMICs, most of the financing for cancer care and control is, and will continue to be, from domestic sources. This is especially true for MICs where external financing is 1 percent or less of total health expenditure. An important exception is the poorest and most aid-dependent countries. However, even countries as poor as Ethiopia, Haiti, and Niger rely on domestic funding for more than 50 percent of their total health expenditures. The World Health Organization (WHO) estimated that in 2008, external sources covered 16.4 percent of total health expenditure in LMICs (WHO 2011a).

Domestic finance of health care comes from two primary sources: (1) out-of-pocket spending by families, either at the point of service or via private insurance (the latter being much less common in LMICs), and (2) public spending for health or broader social protection organized as public insurance. Out-of-pocket spending by families is the least equitable and efficient means of financing health systems and often leads to impoverishment. Out-of-pocket expenditures as a share of total health expenditures is highest in LMICs—about 50 percent—and lowest in high-income countries (HICs), averaging 14 percent (World Bank 2013). By contrast, public financing or insurance schemes that enable prepayment and pooling offer financial protection from excessive expenditures for health care and can create more effective and equitable ways of organizing health system financing (Knaul and others 2006; WHO 2010).

The movement toward UHC is a transition to pooled, publicly financed health care that offers financial protection to families and constitutes the scaffolding that will support cancer coverage in LMICS. Achieving UHC involves a process with overlapping stages, beginning with enrollment and legal coverage, which entitles all people to health services funded by publicly organized insurance. The second stage is coverage that seeks to guarantee access to a comprehensive package of health services. The third stage is universal effective coverage that guarantees the maximum attainable health results from an appropriate package of high-quality services for the evolving health needs of a population. UHC implies financial protection that promotes equity and efficiency and reduces the risk of financial shocks to families by reducing out-of-pocket payments (Knaul, González-Pier, and others 2012).

Financial protection toward UHC can expand in three ways and is often tied to growth in resources allocated to health and overall growth of country income:

- Expansion of prepayment and risk pooling over time to cover entire populations, in some cases on a group-by-group basis
- Provision of a more comprehensive benefit package of health interventions and covered conditions
- Expansion of risk pooling and financial risk protection through the elimination of out-of-pocket expenses at the point of service delivery for the poor and for those interventions considered of high value where use should not be deterred (Jamison and others 2013)

These three dimensions of coverage are summarized in WHO's (2010) financing "cube" as *height, breadth, and depth*. For a health system to achieve universal coverage, the height (proportion of the service cost covered), breadth (covered services), and depth (proportion of the population covered) must be taken into account (WHO 2010). The goal of UHC, according to WHO, is to ensure that all people are able to obtain the health services that they need without suffering financial hardship because they cannot afford to pay for them (WHO 2012, 2013).

Country Approaches

The country-specific roadmap to UHC can take several routes. One approach that has been strongly advocated in the literature is what Gwatkin and Ergo term "progressive universalism" (2011), which refers to the determination to include people who are poor from the outset as programs and policies to promote UHC are introduced.

Two major paths of progressive universalism have been identified, both of which use prepayment and pooling of funds to extend publicly financed insurance. The first route drives the expansion of population coverage and targets the poor by insuring health interventions for diseases that place a high burden on this group, with no co-payment for anyone. The second variant begins with a larger package for the poor. The definition of the package is pivotal and based on burden of disease. Recommendations include highly cost-effective interventions for infectious diseases and reproductive, maternal, newborn, and child health, as well as chronic conditions and noncommunicable diseases. For cancer, the package includes interventions for prevention, early detection, treatment, and palliation, focusing on those cancers of highest burden and interventions of greatest potential effectiveness, especially for the poor (Jamison and others 2013).

In practice, countries have tended to apply a combined or iterative approach, depending on the point of departure to UHC. The point of departure is often a political issue and largely determined by existing institutional arrangements and the availability of resources. Mexico's Seguro Popular design, for example, is based on universal population coverage with no co-payment for community services, sliding scale prepayment for personal health services that exempts the poor, and universal population coverage without prepayment for catastrophic illness; all of these elements are anchored in an expanding benefit package of cost-effective services that includes an increasing number of cancers. A related approach focused on enhancing equity in Turkey has been analyzed in detail (Atun and others 2013).

Cancer—because it encompasses a set of chronic and complex diseases—challenges the limits of UHC and the pathways to progressive universalism. A defining characteristic of most cancers and many other chronic diseases is the need, on a population level, for a series of interventions along the care-control continuum and illness lifecycle.

Analyzing the extent to which effective interventions for specific cancers are covered along the continuum provides insights into the depth and breadth of the overall package, as well as the balance between prevention and treatment. To ensure effective coverage, the benefits package needs to be guaranteed with permanent revenue sources and capacity-building commitments. Low effective coverage—particularly of early detection—is common, even in countries with relatively complete benefit packages. This situation compromises final outcomes (Knaul, Chertorivski Woldenberg, and Arreola-Ornelas 2012).

PATHS TO UNIVERSAL HEALTH CARE FINANCING

Countries are following different paths to UHC. Some countries, mostly of middle income, in Latin America and the Caribbean (Colombia, the Dominican Republic, Mexico, and Peru, for example) have extended public insurance to nonsalaried workers, the unemployed, those out of the labor force, and the poor; these countries are making adjustments to equalize benefits across groups. Thailand has followed a similar path, beginning in 2002, and India is beginning this process. China has extended coverage of the national medical insurance program widely, but with a high co-payment and no coverage for catastrophic expenditures. LMICs in Sub-Saharan Africa (such as Ghana) face much greater resource constraints, and UHC tends to be associated with a more restricted package of services. We illustrate some of the differences and similarities among countries in their paths to UHC by considering the specific case of introducing coverage for cancer, focusing on treatment.

This section draws on case studies of eight countries: China (Yerramilli and Jiang 2013), Colombia (Guerrero, Amaris, and Yerramilli 2013), the Dominican Republic (Rathe, Knaul, and Yerramilli 2013), Ghana (Yerramilli and Ataguba 2013), India (Yerramilli 2013), Mexico (Knaul, Chertorvski Woldenberg, and Arreola-Ornelas 2012), Peru (Seinfeld and Pleic 2013), and Thailand (Yerramilli and Firestone 2013). The four case studies from Latin America and the Caribbean are updates of earlier case studies from Atun and Knaul (2012). Salient details for the eight countries are summarized in table 17.1. Common themes and lessons emerge from these experiences. Each country faces the challenge of including chronic, catastrophic illnesses such as cancer in the package for rich and poor.

Health Insurance Coverage by Population Group

Health systems have historically built their financing schemes around sources of funding rather than health needs, often leaving the poor without access to pooled, public financing systems or opportunities for prepayment. One of the core ideas of UHC and progressive universalism is the determination to cover the poor first and relieve this group of the burden of impoverishing and catastrophic health spending.

In countries that finance their health systems through health or social insurance, salaried workers and government employees are typically the first to be covered, financed by payroll deductions supplemented by employer contributions. In many countries, this group has access to superior social security health

facilities, while all other groups (nonsalaried workers, the unemployed, those outside the labor force, and agricultural workers, all of whom tend to be poorer) are limited to usually lower quality, public facilities (or those provided by nongovernmental organizations) that may have user fees and that often ration care by availability and expertise. In such cases, medication costs are frequently paid out of pocket.

The path from this pattern of segmented coverage to universal coverage has varied. Canada and many countries in Europe (the United Kingdom and the Nordic countries, for example) rely heavily on general taxation revenue to finance the system; others more strongly emphasize the contribution of private health insurance, either voluntary or mandatory (Singapore and the United States). Some countries, for example, Germany, have brought together coverage of distinct groups to reach comprehensive coverage.

The Lancet Commission on Investing in Health evaluated the extent to which the path toward increasing coverage of different groups is universal and progressive (Jamison and others 2013). In Latin America and the Caribbean, where health care provision has been highly segmented between those covered by social security and those not, several countries have moved to invest in publicly financed programs to extend pooled coverage, focusing on the poor and nonsalaried workers, and to reduce coverage differentials progressively.

Colombia adopted a universal social insurance plan in the 1990s, with gradual implementation, and reached universal coverage in 2011. This approach combined the contributory plan for the formal sector (including the self-employed) with coverage for the poor and the informal sector. The cost for the subsidized scheme is partly funded through general taxation, with some cross-subsidization from contributions from salaried workers and employers, with a convergence in per capita expenditures between the two sectors (Guerrero, Amaris, and Yerramilli 2013).

Mexico has more recently followed a similar path. The health reform of 2003 led to the Seguro Popular de Salud (SPS), which, by 2012, provided health coverage to more than 52 million Mexicans who had been ineligible for health care through the existing social security systems, with coverage of a progressively expanding number of interventions (Knaul, Chertorivski Woldenberg, and Arreola-Ornelas 2012). The expansion of coverage began with the poorest segments of the population. SPS deliberately built on the platform of the anti-poverty program Oportunidades and enhanced the coverage of a package of covered services for the poor by expanding the package (Frenk 2006; Knaul, González-Pier, and others 2012).

Table 17.1 Summary of Health Insurance Initiatives: China, Colombia, Dominican Republic, Ghana, India, Mexico, Peru, and Thailand

Country (World Bank income group)	Program/legal underpinning	Population coverage	Interventions covered	Percentage of cost covered	Current cancer provisions	Impact
China (upper-middle-income)	Launched in early 2000s • New Cooperative Medical Scheme (NCMS) • Urban Employee Basic Medical Insurance Scheme (UEBMI) • Urban Residents Basic Medical Insurance Scheme (URBMI) • Medical Financial Assistance Program (MFA) for the poor, covers premiums, extra expenses for programs 1–3 • Various directives from the Ministry of Health	87% coverage in 2008 (72% urban, 93% rural) MFA: 93.37 million poor covered as of 2010	All included catastrophic diseases	• Varies by county: 25% to 40% of cost for cancer covered in rural counties • UEBMI and URBMI reimburse 70% and 50%, respectively, of inpatient expenditures	Required coverage by catastrophic disease insurance (per Ministry of Health 2012 decree): childhood leukemia, breast cancer, cervical cancer, chronic lymphoid leukemia, lung cancer, esophageal cancer, colon cancer, and rectal cancer	• Increased access by NCMS to health services but no improvement of financial protection, potentially because of increasing costs of care • Supplementary insurance program too new to be evaluated
Colombia (upper-middle-income)	• Universal social health insurance system introduced in early 1990s, with two schemes: 1. Contributory for formal sector 2. Subsidized for informal sector, unemployed, and poor • High-cost subaccount created to pool risk among insurers across entire population	Universal as of 2011 • Subsidized plan: 51% • Contributory plan: 39%	• Child vaccination, cervical cancer screening, hospitalization, chemotherapy, radiotherapy, and most cancer drugs • Coverage of catastrophic illness expanded gradually, now including some cancers, with others under consideration		• Screening: cervical, breast, prostate, colorectal • Treatment: hospitalization; chemotherapy; radiotherapy; and most cancer drugs, including tamoxifen and paclitaxel, rituximab, and trastuzumab	• Has protected against catastrophic expenditures (no details in case study) • Access still limited: 78% of breast cancers diagnosed in advanced stages

table continues next page

Table 17.1 Summary of Health Insurance Initiatives: China, Colombia, Dominican Republic, Ghana, India, Mexico, Peru, and Thailand (continued)

Country (World Bank income group)	Program/legal underpinning	Population coverage	Interventions covered	Percentage of cost covered	Current cancer provisions	Impact
Dominican Republic (upper-middle-income)	Seguro Familiar de Salud: 2001 (full implementation in 2007) Compulsory, contributory, and subsidized parts	2013: 29% covered by contributory plan, 25% by subsidized plan; intention to reach universal coverage	Explicit and comprehensive package of community and personal health goods and services	• Up to 1 million pesos/person/year (US$25,000 in 2013), with 20% to 30% co-payment • Contributory scheme: up to US$2,250 additional for outpatient cancer drugs	• Screening: Pap smear and mammography • Diagnosis, treatment, physiotherapy, rehabilitation, and palliative care for adult and pediatric cancers	• No evaluation; no registry, so not possible to evaluate impact on survival • Intended to provide financial protection, but not yet clear whether it has • Almost half the population without coverage, so pay out of pocket for all health care
Ghana (lower-middle-income)	National Health Insurance Act (2003) established the National Health Insurance Scheme (NHIS)	• All eligible, but only 34% enrolled as of 2010 • Premiums: sliding scale with no payment from poorest, but not implemented in practice	Common, relatively inexpensive interventions, but breast and cervical cancer included		Breast and cervical cancer, with Parliament considering adding prostate and childhood cancers	• Has had relatively little effect on reducing impoverishment caused by medical care • In 2005, 45% of financing out of pocket, including for services that should be free
India (lower-middle-income)	• Rashtriya Swasthya Bima Yojana (RSBY) (national) and several similar state programs, for example, in Andhra Pradesh, Karnataka, and Tamil Nadu • Rajeev Aarogyasri Scheme (RAS): 2007, state of Andhra Pradesh, for high-cost treatments mainly for NCDs; contributory health insurance schemes run by RAS for employed people • National Programme for Prevention and Control of Cancer, Diabetes, Cardiovascular Diseases, and Stroke (NPCDCS): 2010	• RSBY and RAS-like programs targeted to poorest, with per family per year limits • NPCDCS: intention to cover all by 2017; more public health focus, optimized spending on prevention, diagnosis, treatment, and palliation	• 100% covered, including premiums • Treatment covered up to Rs150,000 (US$2,430) per family for subsidized coverage • Limits higher for contributory schemes		• RAS: Some treatments for head and neck cancers, gastrointestinal tract cancers, genitourinary system cancers, gynecological cancers, soft tissue/bone tumors, thoracic and mediastinum cancers, breast cancer, skin cancer, multiple myeloma, hepatoblastoma, Wilms tumor, childhood B-cell lymphomas, AML, ALL, ocular cancers, histiocytosis, and rhabdomyosarcoma • Includes palliative care	No evaluation of coverage or financial protection

table continues next page

Table 17.1 Summary of Health Insurance Initiatives: China, Colombia, Dominican Republic, Ghana, India, Mexico, Peru, and Thailand (*continued*)

Country (World Bank income group)	Program/legal underpinning	Population coverage	Interventions covered	Percentage of cost covered	Current cancer provisions	Impact
Mexico (upper-middle-income)	• Seguro Popular de Salud (SPS): 2004, for basic package for all not eligible for preexisting coverage through social security (formal sector employees) • Fund for Protection against Catastrophic Expenses (FPCE) national program • Health Insurance XXI Century (2013), for children under five years of age	2012: 52 million previously uninsured covered	June 2013: • Basic package covers 285 interventions • FPCE covers 59 interventions for 19 disease groups		Through FPCE: all childhood cancers and cervical, breast, testicular, prostate, NHL, ovarian, and colorectal cancers	• Catastrophic spending decrease of more than 20% among SPS enrollees; overall out-of-pocket spending decrease for poorest households • 2006–09: increase of treatment of childhood cancers from 3% to 55%; three-year survival, 55% for ALL and 75% for HL • Low abandonment rates
Peru (upper-middle-income)	Universal Health Insurance Law (Law 29,344, 2009) with mandatory health insurance for all through one of three plans: contributory, semi-contributory, and subsidized	Plan Esperanza (Project Hope) for cancer to cover all poor and vulnerable	• Essential Health Plan (no high-cost treatment) for all • Health Solidarity Intangible Fund (FISSAL): covers common cancers, ESRD, rare diseases	No out-of-pocket payment for cancer services	Plan Esperanza (Project Hope), cancer plan: 2012 • All costs covered for select group of cancers: cervix, breast, colon, stomach, prostate, leukemia, and lymphoma • Includes health promotion, prevention, early detection, diagnosis, treatment, and palliative care	• 21,000 cancers treated in first year at no personal cost for subsidized population • Decrease of out-of-pocket costs from 34% in 2012 to 11% in the first trimester of 2013, for those in contributory scheme

table continues next page

Table 17.1 Summary of Health Insurance Initiatives: China, Colombia, Dominican Republic, Ghana, India, Mexico, Peru, and Thailand (continued)

Country (World Bank income group)	Program/legal underpinning	Population coverage	Interventions covered	Percentage of cost covered	Current cancer provisions	Impact
Thailand (upper-middle-income)	• 2002: National Health Security Act, establishing the Universal Coverage Scheme (UCS) • Prior to 2002: a. Civil Servants Medical Benefits Scheme (CSMBS) b. Social Security Scheme (SSS) c. Worker Compensation Scheme (WCS)	• UCS: 76% of population covered • CSMBS: 7% of population covered • SSS and WCS together: 15% of population covered	• UCS: inpatient and outpatient services, such as free prescription medicines, ambulatory care, hospitalization, disease prevention, and health promotion	• 100% of services covered	• Cervical cancer screening (Pap smear and VIA): special FFS payment to incentivize use • Breast self-examination promotion • UCS coverage of radiotherapy and chemotherapy, as well as surgeries and critical care for emergency patients • Royal Thai Government issuance of compulsory licenses for four cancer drugs: letrozole, docetaxel, erlotinib, and imatinib	• No increase in hospital sales of anti-cancer drugs after five years, despite increases in other NCD drugs (for example, for diabetes, blood pressure, and cholesterol) • Screening rates for cervical and breast cancer quite low

Sources: Based on Guerrero, Amaris, and Yerramilli 2013; Knaul, Chertorivski Woldenberg, and Arreola-Ornelas 2012; Rathe, Knaul, and Yerramilli 2013; Seinfeld and Pleic 2013; Yerramilli 2013; Yerramilli and Ataguba 2013; Yerramilli and Firestone 2013; Yerramilli and Jiang 2013.

Note: ALL = acute lymphoblastic leukemia; AML = acute myeloid leukemia; ESRD = end-stage renal disease; FFS = fee-for-service; HL = Hodgkin's lymphoma; NCD = noncommunicable disease; NHL = non-Hodgkin's lymphoma; VIA = visual inspection with acetic acid.

Peru's Health Insurance Law of 2009 provided coverage for nonsalaried workers through a semi-contributory plan and for the poor through a highly subsidized plan that includes vulnerable groups, such as children and elderly persons. Salaried workers continue to be covered through a preexisting plan (Seinfeld and Pleic 2013).

Similarly, the Dominican Republic introduced a law in 2001 (establishing the Seguro Familiar de Salud) and commenced implementation in 2007, with the aim of comprehensive coverage within a decade. As of 2013, 54 percent of the population had achieved coverage, with slightly over 54 percent of this group in the contributory scheme and the remaining 46 percent in the subsidized scheme (Rathe, Knaul, and Yerramilli 2013).

Many other countries in Latin America and the Caribbean have not yet adopted pro-poor health insurance policies and programs, and coverage remains more segmented.

In the MICs of Asia included in our review, coverage is less complete than in many countries in Latin America and the Caribbean. Singapore, now an HIC, has a scheme with greater reliance on private insurance, including a separate catastrophic insurance scheme (Medishield) in addition to the mandatory regular insurance (Medisave) and the scheme for the poor (Medifund) (Haseltine 2013). The Singapore scheme has been held up as a good example. However, Shanghai briefly experimented with a similar model and discontinued it (Dong 2003). The problems in Shanghai included poor control of incentives for doctors and hospitals to provide expensive treatments and extreme cases where households exhausted the limits of their insurance and were unable to pay hospital bills and bury their deceased relatives. These experiences suggest that what can work in a small, high-income urban country or city is not necessarily replicable in other settings.

Thailand passed the National Health Security Act in 2002, integrating five existing schemes and extending coverage to workers in the informal sector (Yerramilli and Firestone 2013). The scheme covering the poor, the Voluntary Health Card, was expanded following the financial crisis in 1997.

In 2003, the Chinese government began covering rural residents and nonworking urban residents (including students, children, and elderly and disabled persons) by adding programs to existing schemes for urban public and private sector employees. This expansion increased national insurance coverage from 23 percent in 2003 to 87 percent in 2008 (72 percent of urban residents and 93 percent of rural residents) (Yerramilli and Jiang 2013) and to 97 percent by 2011 (Goss and others 2014). The main group remaining uncovered consists of rural migrants to urban areas,

who do not have rights of residence. They are covered by medical insurance in their place of origin but do not have access to doctors where they work (Goss and others 2014). The scheme for the formal sector is financed by payroll taxes; the other schemes require individual fixed contributions, supplemented by contributions from various levels of government. The local autonomy in program design has resulted in some variations in the services covered by county (Yerramilli and Jiang 2013).

In India, as elsewhere, schemes have existed to cover salaried workers and their families. A national scheme for the poor was instituted in 2008, covering treatment up to a relatively low annual expenditure limit. However, there is no national program for informal sector workers. Some states, such as Andhra Pradesh, Karnataka, and Tamil Nadu, have developed schemes with broader entitlement (Yerramilli 2013).

Ghana is one of the few Sub-Saharan African countries with a national health insurance system, which was introduced in 2003. In theory, coverage is comprehensive, with payroll contributions from formal sector workers, contributions from informal sector workers on a sliding scale, contributions from the poor, and exemptions for the core poor (Yerramilli and Ataguba 2013). In practice, informal sector workers pay the minimum contribution and a small percentage of the poor is exempted from contributions. With donor contributions, the scheme ran at a deficit in 2010 and 2011 (Yerramilli and Ataguba 2013). The Ghana case illustrates some of the issues facing ambitious schemes in LMICs.

Health Insurance Coverage by Services and Conditions Covered

The second dimension of coverage is breadth—by services and diseases included. All health insurance schemes have restrictions on which medical services are eligible for coverage; how these are determined crucially affects the equity and efficiency of a health system. Cost-effectiveness, population health needs, and funding should define the package of covered services. In turn, the package defines entitlement, especially once universal enrollment is achieved, which tends to become less restrictive as country income increases. A shallow package, even if it covers a large proportion of the population, is unlikely to offer protection from financial catastrophe or to lower financial barriers to accessing care, particularly for cancer.

Cancer coverage often comes later in the development of these schemes. In LMICs, coverage has tended to start with cancers that affect children and women and that are curable with access and adherence to treatment.

Poor quality of care, incomplete services, or waiting times can force many patients to seek care in the private sector and pay out of pocket, especially for medications, even though these are officially covered by insurance. Because treatment typically involves the repeated use of chemotherapeutic agents, waiting can severely reduce the effectiveness of treatment or block access entirely. Further, the package of covered services may not include components that are important for accessing or managing care, such as transport costs or medications to control symptoms. Similarly, some essential treatments or services (for example, radiotherapy) may be unavailable in the public sector, preventing patients from accessing a complete package of care. This situation can severely reduce the efficacy of the package of provided treatment.

In Colombia, for example, cancer was not included when the program started in 1994. A year later, some cancer interventions were added. Screening for four cancers was added in 2000, radiotherapy was added in 2010, and mammography and breast biopsies were added in 2012. Until 2012, fewer services were covered under the subsidized scheme than under the contributory scheme, and access to treatment has often been an issue because of geographic isolation (Guerrero, Amaris, and Yerramilli 2013).

Mexico has a fund for protection against catastrophic expenses that has gradually covered more cancer interventions since 2003 (Knaul, Chertorivski Woldenberg, and Arreola-Ornelas 2012; Knaul, González-Pier, and others 2012). Initially, coverage was provided for acute lymphoblastic leukemia in children; this coverage has subsequently been extended to certain cervical, breast, and prostate cancers in adults. The package of covered services is based on cost-effectiveness criteria but includes some expensive components (breast cancer treatment, for example, includes trastuzumab for HER2-positive patients).

Peru, which has a separate fund to provide for catastrophic illnesses, launched Project Hope as part of a national cancer plan in 2012 (Seinfeld and Pleic 2013). In the Dominican Republic, coverage of cancer is at an early stage and specifies a fixed per capita sum for financial protection. The more advanced treatments are provided in the private sector; although there is some coverage from the new insurance scheme, co-payments remain relatively high (25–30 percent). New public sector facilities are under development (Rathe, Knaul, and Yerramilli 2013).

In Thailand, the government has aimed to expand access to cancer treatment and, in addition to coverage, has obtained compulsory licenses for four cancer medications: letrozole, docetaxel, erlotinib, and imatinib (Yerramilli and Firestone 2013). Thailand also has proactive policies to tax alcohol and tobacco; it uses the proceeds to help fund the Thai Health Promotion Foundation (ThaiHealth), which has been involved in comprehensive campaigns to reduce smoking (Yerramilli and Firestone 2013).

China is at an earlier stage of expanding cancer treatment packages. The central government required local schemes to provide coverage for treatment of specified catastrophic illnesses, including six types of cancer, as of February 2013 (Yerramilli and Jiang 2013). However, because medications are not generally covered by insurance, and because of high co-payments, the extent of financial protection remains limited.

Although publicly funded insurance in India, particularly for the poor, is expanding, coverage in practice remains limited. In several states, including Andhra Pradesh, Karnataka, and Tamil Nadu, coverage is limited to third-level care and the treatments included in the packages may not be the most effective or cost-effective for the condition (Yerramilli 2013). Primary and secondary cancer prevention is largely piecemeal and organized by hospitals and nongovernmental organizations. However, a national program that aims to expand access to and coverage of noncommunicable disease prevention, including cancer education and screening, is in the initial stages of implementation (Yerramilli 2013). Several cancer drugs are available at modest cost in India, for historic reasons and because of the large domestic pharmaceutical industry (Goss and others 2014), providing some relief to cancer patients.

In Sub-Saharan Africa, coverage for cancer is more limited still. The Ghana National Health Insurance Scheme is restricted to the more common and inexpensive procedures, and the only cancer coverage is for breast and cervical cancer (Blanchet, Fink, and Osei-Akoto 2012). Ghana signed a memorandum with aid partners in 2007 to commence screening for breast cancer using mammograms; however, this screening program has not yet been implemented (Bosu 2012).

Level of Financial Protection for Cancer Services

The third dimension of coverage is whether (and how much) patients and families contribute out of pocket for services covered. Financial protection—based on prepayment, risk pooling, and public funding for the poor—is a cornerstone of efforts to achieve UHC and is the goal of many health system reforms.

Most countries recognize that public and community health services are of the highest priority and should be universally available and fully and publicly funded. Following experiences with reforms where basic public health services, such as vaccination, suffered because funding was not explicitly protected (as in Colombia), countries have developed strategies to offer protected financing for all covered interventions in this rubric (Estevez 2012). In Mexico, Seguro Popular includes a separate and protected fund (Knaul, González-Pier, and others 2012). Still, it has been challenging to build into UHC the mechanisms through which these funds grow in tandem with public and community health services, especially with the availability of new interventions to treat or prevent disease. A clear example is the HPV vaccine, which is essential to the future prevention of cervical and several other cancers that are infection associated and much more common in LMICs.

Offering public financing for disease prevention and health-promoting services is important, given the importance of lifestyle and early detection in managing many cancers, including those that most burden LMICs. Patients tend to underuse these services, especially patients who are not fully informed or aware of the risks of unhealthy behavior or late detection; this underuse is exacerbated if they also face significant barriers to access.

Co-payments

The effectiveness of co-payments has been debated for decades, because any degree of co-payment can deter patients from seeking care. Further, implementing exemptions that target the poor sounds simple but, in fact, it is difficult to achieve. For these reasons, many proponents advocate the use of taxes as the more effective and equitable means of generating revenue for financing health. UHC initiatives tend to promote sliding-scale prepayments rather than co-payment at point of service.

Co-payments generally fall as country per capita income increases, but they exist even in HICs. Many LMICs, especially the poorest countries, rely heavily on co-payments. In the LICs of Sub-Saharan Africa—with some notable and recent exceptions, such as Rwanda—public resources for cancer treatment and care are severely limited and co-payments are the norm.

Co-payments often vary by type of service, being smaller (or zero) for services at facilities, but very large (even 100 percent) for medications. In China, the design varies by county, but co-payments of 60–80 percent can be required (Yerramilli and Jiang 2013). Many countries set explicit limits on annual coverage per person or per household (for example, India's national scheme for the poor and China), such that treatment for cancer is likely to exhaust benefits and require large out-of-pocket expenditures.

Thailand is unusual in that services provided by the government sector do not require co-payment, including prescription drugs (Yerramilli and Firestone 2013).

China has begun to identify priority diseases for the reduction of co-payments, focusing on inpatient services. As of 2013, childhood and chronic myeloid leukemia, as well as breast, cervical, lung, esophageal, gastric, and colorectal cancers, were included in these programs (Goss and others 2014).

COVERAGE OF CANCER CARE: EARLY RESULTS

For cancer especially, it takes time for the benefits of improved coverage to translate into increased use of services and then to improvements in health. Unlike adding a vaccination or a medication for an infectious disease, adding cancer services to meet new demand may require new facilities and infrastructure, specially trained medical personnel, and the trust of patients and providers. Without these elements, access to care will not improve, even if it is formally part of an insurance or health care program. We report on a few results of improved coverage that have been recorded in the case study countries.

It is important to note that data on the impacts on health—cancer survival or years of healthy life lived—are almost impossible to obtain for the financing of cancer treatment. In some cases, reforms are too recent to show this degree of impact. In most cases, a major limiting factor is the lack of data in the form of cancer registries and a dearth of formal evaluation efforts.

Outcomes

Improvements in access and financial protection have been documented for the more comprehensive reforms and those of longer duration, although few formal evaluations have assessed health outcomes.

Thailand has made explicit efforts to increase care availability, for example, by issuing compulsory licenses for some cancer drugs, expanding the number of medical school graduates, and offering incentives to doctors to practice in rural areas (WHO 2011b). Thailand also explicitly allocates a fixed per capita amount to prevention, which is given to communities for local efforts, in addition to national programs undertaken by the Thai Health Promotion Foundation (Yerramilli and Firestone 2013). Despite these efforts, less than 20 percent of eligible women have been screened for cervical cancer (Leetongin 2011).

In Mexico, improved coverage has translated to improved survival rates for some pediatric cancers and lower treatment abandonment rates than elsewhere in the region. For breast cancer, the introduction of SPS was associated with reduced treatment abandonment rates at the National Cancer Institute. Incidence of catastrophic spending has decreased, as has out-of-pocket expenditure by the poor (Knaul, Chertorivski Woldenberg, and Arreola-Ornelas 2012; Knaul, González-Pier, and others 2012).

There is a clear need for evaluation of programs as they mature, measuring health outcomes as well as process outcomes.

Incentives

The design of a financing system may create unintended or intended incentives. In India, the annual cap on payments in the scheme covering the poor means that private cancer care providers have an incentive to move patients to the public sector once the benefits have been exhausted (Yerramilli 2013). In Latin America and the Caribbean, the relatively high payroll taxes on formal sector employment were a concern in the 1980s and blamed for holding down the size of the formal employment sector and increasing informal employment. Similar issues can arise if nonsalaried and own-account workers become entitled to the same health benefits as salaried workers, without being required to pay similar payroll taxes. These pitfalls need to be recognized in system design to meet efficiency needs as well as to improve equity.

In Colombia, the access to and use of health services by the poor have improved (Giedion and Uribe 2009). A concerning development, however, is that patients and their families are successfully suing the government to demand coverage of expensive but ineffective cancer treatments, including those for late-stage cancers (Guerrero, Amaris, and Yerramilli 2013). Open-ended constitutional and programmatic rights, combined with the desperation of patients and families, and the financial benefits for producers of on-patent drugs and expensive services provide strong financial incentives. These costly interventions may deplete available funding for the national cancer fund and undermine the financing of the health system (Guerrero, Amaris, and Yerramilli 2013).

Incentives to provide care are also affected by whether payments to service providers are made on a capitation or fee-for-service basis. Some insurance schemes pay on a fee-for-service basis for interventions that the government wishes to promote, for example, cervical cancer screening in Thailand (Srithamrongswat and others 2010). Private sector providers are reimbursed for other services on a capitation basis, with a global budget ceiling based on Diagnosis Related Groups to contain costs (Garebedian and others 2012). In China in the past, fee-for-service payment provided hospitals with the incentive to offer expensive treatments to end-stage cancer patients, although the treatments were futile. In the Republic of Korea, fee-for-service payments for screening tests for colorectal cancer are used, but the reimbursement rates are not consistent with the pattern of cost. Reimbursement rates for colonoscopy are set too low relative to fecal occult blood tests, making colonoscopy, on the one hand, more cost-effective than it would otherwise be, but, on the other hand, providing a disincentive for its provision by service providers (Park, Yun, and Kwon 2005).

CONCLUSIONS

In many LMICs, health financing reform efforts have much in common. Key elements include developing contributory and subsidized plans for various population groups, meeting the challenges of incorporating and financing nonsalaried workers and the poor, and building on basic services associated with social welfare programs.

Countries working toward UHC have established universal entitlements to key services through guaranteed benefits packages. The countries are striving to include interventions for common cancers and other chronic and noncommunicable diseases for which there are effective interventions.

Our review of the experiences in several LMICs suggests that these challenges can be met with well-designed financing reform. Prevention, early detection, treatment, and palliative care interventions for cancer can be effectively integrated into basic service packages covered by a combination of social insurance and tax-financed schemes. Invariably, cancer comes after other basic services have been covered, but this can happen relatively quickly—within a decade of program initiation.

In several countries, for example, Mexico and Singapore, specific and distinct funds were established to cover personal health services and catastrophic expenses. In China and India, the design of public insurance provides for some coverage, yet treatment expense ceilings leave the population vulnerable to catastrophic health expenses. Some countries, such as Ghana, have used earmarked taxes or levies to derive resources for health. In all cases, UHC coverage is built up over time, adding covered populations and services and covering a greater proportion of costs, particularly catastrophic costs.

Cancer epitomizes why investment in a systems approach to chronic diseases in LMICs is strategic. The expansion of services and interventions discussed in other chapters can be realized only if countries develop appropriate financing and insurance systems.

Linking each component of the cancer care control continuum in an integrated financing plan is challenging but necessary to guarantee the effectiveness of national cancer programs.

NOTES

World Bank Income Classifications as of July 2014 are as follows, based on estimates of gross national income (GNI) per capita for 2013:

- Low-income countries (LICs) = US$1,045 or less
- Middle-income countries (MICs) are subdivided:
  a) lower-middle-income = US$1,046 to US$4,125
  b) upper-middle-income (UMICs) = US$4,126 to US$12,745
- High-income countries (HICs) = US$12,746 or more

1. This section is based on Atun and Knaul (2012).

REFERENCES

Atun, R., S. Aydin, S. Chakraborty, S. Sümer, M. Aran, and others. 2013. "Universal Health Coverage in Turkey: Enhancement of Equity." *The Lancet* 382 (9886): 65–99. doi: 10.1016/S0140-6736(13)61051-X.

Atun, R., and F. M. Knaul. 2012. "Innovative Financing: Local and Global Opportunities." In *Closing the Cancer Divide: An Equity Imperative*, edited by F. M. Knaul, J. R. Gralow, R. Atun, and A. Bhadalia, 257–88. Cambridge, MA: Harvard Global Equity Initiative and Harvard University Press.

Blanchet, N. J., G. Fink, and I. Osei-Akoto. 2012. "The Effect of Ghana's National Health Insurance Scheme on Health Care Utilisation." *Ghana Medical Journal* 46 (2): 76–84.

Bosu, W. K. 2012. "A Comprehensive Review of the Policy and Programmatic Response to Chronic Non-Communicable Disease in Ghana." *Ghana Medical Journal* 46 (2 Suppl): 69–78.

Dong, W. 2003. "Healthcare-Financing Reforms in Transitional Society: A Shanghai Experience." *Journal of Health, Population and Nutrition* 21 (3): 223–34.

Engelgau, M., K. Okamoto, K. Navaratne, and S. Gopalan. 2010. "Prevention and Control of Selected Chronic NCDs in Sri Lanka: Policy Options and Action Plan." Health, Nutrition and Population Discussion Paper, World Bank, Washington, DC. http://siteresources.worldbank.org/HEALTHNUTRITIONANDPOPULATION/Resources/281627-1095698140167/NCDsSriLanka.pdf.

Estevez, R. 2012. "The Quest for Equity in Latin America: A Comparative Analysis of the Health Care Reforms in Brazil and Colombia." *International Journal of Equity and Health* 11 (6). http://www.equityhealthj.com/content/11/1/6. doi: 10.1186/1475-9276-11-6.

Frenk, J. 2006. "Bridging the Divide: Global Lessons from Evidence-Based Health Policy in Mexico." *The Lancet* 368 (9539): 954–61.

Garebedian, L. F., D. Ross-Degnan, S. Ratanawijitrasin, P. Stephens, and A. K. Wagner. 2012. "Impact of Universal Health Insurance Coverage in Thailand on Sales and Market Share of Medicines for Non-Communicable Diseases: An Interrupted Time Series Study." *British Medical Journal Open* 1: e001686.

Giedion, U., and M. Uribe. 2009. "Colombia's Universal Health Insurance System." *Health Affairs* 28 (3): 853–63.

Goss, P. E., K. Strasser-Weippl, B. L. Lee-Bychkovsky, L. Fan, J. Lie, and others. 2014. "Challenges to Effective Cancer Control in China, India and Russia." *Lancet Oncology* 15: 489–538.

Gralow, J. R., E. Krakauer, B. O. Anderson, A. Ilbawi, P. Porter, and others. 2012. "Core Elements for Provision of Cancer Care and Control in Low and Middle Income Countries." In *Closing the Cancer Divide: An Equity Imperative*, edited by F. M. Knaul, J. R. Gralow, R. Atun, and A. Bhadalia, 123–65. Cambridge, MA: Harvard Global Equity Initiative and Harvard University Press.

Guerrero, R., A. M. Amaris, and P. Yerramilli. 2013. "Colombia Study." Harvard University Global Health Equity Initiative, updated from R. Guerrero, "Case 2: Colombia," in R. Atun and F. M. Knaul, 2012, and "Innovative Financing: Local and Global Opportunities," in *Closing the Cancer Divide: An Equity Imperative*, edited by F. M. Knaul, J. R. Gralow, R. Atun, and A. Bhadalia, 257–88. Cambridge, MA: Harvard Global Equity Initiative and Harvard University Press. http://hgei.harvard.edu/fs/docs/icb.topic910623.files/DCP3%20Input%20-Colombia.pdf.

Gwatkin, D. R., and A. Ergo. 2011. "Universal Health Coverage: Friend or Foe of Equity?" *The Lancet* 377: 2160–61.

Haseltine, W. A. 2013. *Affordable Excellence: The Singapore Healthcare Story*. Washington, DC: Brookings Institution Press.

Hewitt, M., S. Greenfield, and E. Stovall, eds. 2005. *From Cancer Patient to Cancer Survivor: Lost in Transition*. Washington, DC: Institute of Medicine and National Research Council of the National Academics, The National Academies Press.

Jamison, D. T., L. H. Summers, G. Alleyne, K. J. Arrow, S. Berkley, and others. 2013. "Global Health 2035: A World Converging within a Generation." *The Lancet* 382 (9908): 1898–55.

Knaul, F. M., G. Alleyne, P. Piot, R. Atun, J. Gralow, and others. 2012. "Health System Strengthening and Cancer: A Diagonal Response to the Challenge of Chronicity." In *Closing the Cancer Divide: An Equity Imperative*, edited by F. M. Knaul, J. R. Gralow, R. Atun, and A. Bhadalia, 95–122. Cambridge, MA: Harvard Global Equity Initiative and Harvard University Press.

Knaul, F. M., H. Arreola-Ornelas, O. Méndez, M. Alsan, J. Seinfeld, and others. 2014. "The Global Economic Burden of Cancer." In *World Cancer Report 2014*, edited by B. W. Stewart and C. P. Wild, chapter 6.7. Lyon, France: IARC. http://www.iarc.fr/en/publications/books/wcr/index.php.

Knaul, F. M., H. Arreola-Ornelas, O. Mendez-Carniado, C. Bryson-Cahn, J. Barofsky, and others. 2006. "Evidence Is Good for Your Health System: Policy Reform to Remedy Catastrophic and Impoverishing Health Spending in Mexico." *The Lancet* 368 (9549): 1828–41.

Knaul, F. M., S. Chertorivski Woldenberg, and H. Arreola-Ornelas. 2012. "Case 4: Mexico." In *Closing the Cancer Divide: An Equity Imperative*, edited by F. M. Knaul, J. R. Gralow, R. Atun, and A. Bhadalia, 269–70. Cambridge, MA: Harvard Global Equity Initiative and Harvard University Press.

Knaul, F. M., E. González-Pier, O. Gómez-Dantés, D. Garcia-Junco, H. H. Arreola-Ornelas, and others. 2012. "The Quest for Universal Health Coverage: Achieving Social Protection for All in Mexico." *The Lancet* 380 (9849): 1259–79.

Knaul, F. M., J. R. Gralow, R. Atun, and A. Bhadalia, eds. 2012. *Closing the Cancer Divide: An Equity Imperative.* Cambridge, MA: Harvard Global Equity Initiative and Harvard University Press.

Leetongin, G. 2011. "Results Based Financing: Screening for Cervical Cancer in Thailand." World Bank Presentation. http://siteresources.worldbank.org/INTHSD/Resources/topics/415176-1217510876610/5259033-1333544225723/Day5_3_Grits_Thailand_NHSO_EN.pdf.

Mahal, A., A. Karan, and M. Engelgau. 2010. "The Economic Implications of Non-Communicable Disease for India." Health, Nutrition and Population Discussion Paper, World Bank, Washington, DC. http://siteresources.worldbank.org/HEALTHNUTRITIONANDPOPULATION/Resources/281627-1095698140167/EconomicImplicationsofNCDforIndia.pdf.

Mahal, A., A. Karan, V. Fan, and M. Engelgau. 2013. "The Economic Burden of Cancers on Indian Households." *PLOS One* 8 (8): e71853. doi: 10.1371/journal.pone.0071853.

Nikolic I., A. Stanciole, and M. Zaydman. 2011. "Chronic Emergency: Why NCDs Matter." Health, Nutrition and Population Discussion Paper, World Bank, Washington, DC. http://siteresources.worldbank.org/HEALTHNUTRITIONANDPOPULATION/Resources/281627-1095698140167/ChronicEmergencyWhyNCDsMatter.pdf.

Park, S. M., Y. H. Yun, and S. Kwon. 2005. "Feasible Economic Strategies to Improve Screening Compliance for Colorectal Cancer in Korea." *World Journal of Gastroenterology* 11 (11): 1587–93.

Rathe, M., F. M. Knaul, and P. Yerramilli. 2013. "Dominican Republic Case Study." Harvard Global Equity Initiative, updated from M. Rathe, "Case 3: The Dominican Republic,"

in R. Atun and R. M. Knaul, 2012. http://hgei.harvard.edu/fs/docs/icb.topic910623.files/DCP3%20Input%20-Dominican%20Republic.pdf.

Seinfeld, J., and M. Pleic. 2013. "Peru Case Study." Harvard Global Equity Initiative, updated from J. Seinfeld, "Case 4: Peru," in R. Atun and F. M. Knaul, 2012. http://hgei.harvard.edu/fs/docs/icb.topic910623.files/DCP3%20Input%20-Peru.pdf.

Srithamrongswat, S., W. Aekplakorn, P. Jongudomsuk, J. Thammatach-aree, W. Patcharanarumol, and others. 2010. "Funding Health Promotion and Prevention: The Thai Experience." Background Paper 45 for the *World Health Report 2010*, World Health Organization. http://www.who.int/healthsystems/topics/financing/healthreport/ThailandNo45FINAL.pdf.

WHO (World Health Organization). 2010. *World Health Report 2010: Health Systems Financing: The Path to Universal Coverage.* WHO, Geneva. http://www.who.int/whr/2010/whr10_en.pdf?ua=1

———. 2011a. "World Health Statistics, 2011." WHO, Geneva. http://www.who.int/whosis/whostat/EN_WHS2011_Full.pdf.

———. 2011b. "Country Cooperation Strategy: Thailand." http://www.who.int/countryfocus/cooperation_strategy/listofccs/en/index.html.

———. 2012. "What Is Universal Health Coverage? Online Q&A." http://www.who.int/features/qa/universal_health_coverage/en/index.html.

———. 2013. *World Health Report 2013: Research for Universal Health Coverage.* Geneva: WHO.

World Bank. 2013. *World Development Indicators 2013.* Washington, DC: World Bank. http://data.worldbank.org/indicator/NY.GNP.PCAP.CD/countries/SG--XR?page=1&display=default.

Yerramilli, P. 2013. "The Financing of Cancer Care and Control in Andhra Pradesh, India." MSc thesis, London School of Tropical Medicine and Hygiene and London School of Economics.

Yerramilli, P., and J. Ataguba. 2013. "Ghana Case Study." Harvard Global Equity Initiative. http://hgei.harvard.edu/fs/docs/icb.topic910623.files/DCP3%20Input%20-Ghana.pdf.

Yerramilli, P., and R. Firestone. 2013. "Thailand Case Study." Harvard Global Equity Initiative. http://hgei.harvard.edu/fs/docs/icb.topic910623.files/DCP3%20Input%20-%20Thailandt.pdf.

Yerramilli, P., and X. X. Jiang. 2013. "China Case Study." Harvard University Global Equity Initiative. http://hgei.harvard.edu/fs/docs/icb.topic910623.files/DCP3%20Input%20-%20China.pdf.

Chapter 18

An Extended Cost-Effectiveness Analysis of Publicly Financed HPV Vaccination to Prevent Cervical Cancer in China

Carol Levin, Monisha Sharma, Zachary Olson, Stéphane Verguet,
Ju-Fang Shi, Shao-Ming Wang, You-Lin Qiao, Dean T. Jamison,
and Jane J. Kim

INTRODUCTION

Disproportionate Burden of Disease

Cervical cancer is one of the 10 most common diseases affecting women in China. Although the average national estimates of the cervical cancer burden in China are low, the burden may be underestimated because the prevalence of the human papillomavirus (HPV) is high. Cervical cancer mortality is heterogeneous across geographic settings (Li, Kang, and Qiao 2011); it is highest among poor women living in Gansu, Shanxi, and Shaanxi, the least developed provinces in central and western China.

The low national cervical cancer estimates may be the result of the lack of a nationwide cancer registry. Most registries are located in urban areas, where the socioeconomic status of women is higher and the cancer disease burden is likely to be lower than in rural areas (Shi and others 2011). The HPV prevalence has been found to be similar in rural and urban regions, but cervical cancer mortality is significantly higher among women in rural areas. This disproportionate disease burden is likely attributable to the unequal availability and utilization of health services, such as screening and treatment.

Inadequate Screening Services

Screening in China is opportunistic in the absence of a national cervical cancer screening program. From 2009 to 2011, the national government initiated a program to provide free cervical cancer screening for 10 million rural women between ages 35 and 59 years; the program covered only 7 percent of women because of the shortages of gynecologists and cytologists and an overburdened health care system (Colombara and Wang 2013; Qiao 2010; *The Lancet* 2009). China has an estimated 500 million women in rural areas; scaling up preventive services constitutes a significant public health challenge (Li, Kang, and Qiao 2011), and national cervical cancer screening coverage remains low (Gakidou, Nordhagen, and Obermeier 2008; WHO 2012). Additional reasons for low screening coverage include weak health system infrastructure to support screening, diagnosis, and treatment; limited access to health services; and limited knowledge of cervical cancer among women in less developed regions (Jia and others 2013; Qiao and others 2008).

China's health care system has been evolving to respond to the pervasive inequity in access to health services. In 2009, China began to introduce

Corresponding author: Carol Levin, PhD, University of Washington, clevin@uw.edu.

universal health coverage (Yip and others 2012), reaching relatively high coverage in urban and rural areas with two government-sponsored schemes. Despite the high coverage, the benefits are minimal and reimbursement is limited to inpatient expenses. It is unclear how recent health insurance schemes and opportunistic screening programs have affected women's cervical cancer treatment rates, health outcomes, and costs. Recent studies that focused on prevention indicate that existing cancer prevention services do not reach women in poorer rural and urban areas (Jia and others 2013; Li, Kang, and Qiao 2011; Shi, Canfell, and others 2012). This trend is likely to continue until insurance schemes cover outpatient services, including treatment of pre-cancer and early-stage cancer.

Although widespread screening with cytology has dramatically reduced the cervical cancer burden in high-income countries, low-resource settings have been unable to achieve similar cancer reductions. Newer screening technologies are cheaper and easier to implement and scale up than cytology and can reduce the cervical cancer burden among Chinese women, protecting them from the future costs and consequences of the disease. For example, a study of cervical cancer screening that evaluated strategies using cervical cytology and HPV DNA testing found that screening women three times in their lives (between the ages of 25 and 45 years) reduced the risk of cancer by 50 percent at a cost of US$150 per life-year saved (LYS). The most efficient strategy used a two-visit rapid HPV DNA test, with screening and diagnostic assessment at a county hospital and treatment provided during the second visit (Levin and others 2010; Li and others 2013; Shi, Canfell, and others 2012; Wang and others 2013; Zhang, Pan, and others 2013; Zhao and others 2013).

HPV Vaccination

In addition to screening, HPV vaccination presents a promising primary prevention strategy against cervical cancer. Several studies have concluded that screening women and vaccinating preadolescent girls against HPV are cost-effective interventions in reducing the burden of cervical cancer in China (Canfell and others 2011; Goldie and others 2008; Levin and others 2010; Shi and others 2011). Canfell and others (2011) showed that vaccination strategies were cost effective up to US$55 per vaccinated girl, with incremental cost-effectiveness ratios (ICERs) of US$2,746 per LYS when vaccination was combined with screening once in a lifetime; the ICER was up to US$5,963 per LYS when combined with five screenings in a lifetime. Goldie and others (2008) found an ICER of US$1,360 per LYS when total vaccine costs were US$25 per vaccinated girl. Chapter 4 in this volume (Denny and others 2015) provides a fuller description of the cost-effectiveness of cervical cancer prevention in China and other settings.

Extended Cost-Effectiveness Analysis

Recent attention to attaining the goal of universal health coverage provides a strong rationale for exploring mechanisms to expand access to the prevention and treatment of cervical cancer in China, without increasing the financial burden of the women seeking care and paying for services (WHO 2013b). We conducted an extended cost-effectiveness analysis (ECEA) to evaluate public financing of HPV vaccination to prevent cervical cancer. Importantly, the ECEA approach adds new dimensions to conventional cost-effectiveness analysis through a more explicit treatment of equity and impact on financial risk protection—prevention of medical impoverishment (Verguet and others 2015; Verguet, Laxminarayan, and Jamison 2015; Verguet and others 2013). Specifically, ECEA can evaluate publicly financed programs by measuring program impact along four main dimensions:

- Health benefits
- Household private expenditures averted (household cost savings)
- Financial risk protection provided to households
- Distributional consequences across the wealth strata of country populations.

As a result, ECEA enables the quantitative inclusion of information on equity and on how much financial risk protection is bought per dollar expenditure on health policy, in addition to how much health is bought (Verguet, Laxminarayan, and Jamison 2015; Verguet and others 2013).

As a consequence, the distribution of health and financial benefits resulting from health interventions—and, by extension, from the policy instruments that finance them—can be examined to answer the question of whether the interventions are pro-poor. In practice, the ECEA approach can also be used to examine the financial effects of interventions and policies on individuals or families by income group and in aggregate. Health policies and interventions typically involve costs to the public sector and to households. Even if a specific intervention is provided at no cost, users often incur time costs if they are required to travel or wait at health facilities to receive information, treatment, or test results; the value placed on these costs differs according to income level.

Publicly financed health interventions can help users to avoid future costs. For example, HPV vaccination and cancer screening programs reduce the risk of cervical cancer, which might otherwise lead to medical impoverishment, devastating health consequences (for example, the death of a mother increases the mortality risk for children), or both (for example, the death of the primary household income earner could impoverish the family).

The objective of this analysis is to evaluate the consequences of public finance of HPV vaccination in China, using the ECEA methodology. Public finance increases the uptake of the HPV vaccine, which can improve health, reduce household medical expenditures related to cervical cancer treatment, and prevent subsequent impoverishment. Finally, public finance can have differential impacts among populations of different income levels. We estimate the level and distribution across income groups of the cervical cancer deaths averted, the households' expenditures related to cervical cancer treatment averted and the costs needed to sustain the HPV program, and the financial risk protection that the program provides, using a combination of indicators.

MATERIALS AND METHODS

Model

We synthesized the available epidemiological, clinical, and economic data from China, using a previously described individual-based Monte Carlo simulation model of cervical cancer (Goldhaber-Fiebert and others 2007; Goldie and others 2007; Kim and others 2007). The model consists of health states representing important clinical stages of disease, including HPV infection, grade of precancerous lesions, and stage of invasive cancer. We evaluated vaccination and screening as a combined strategy in a single cohort, such that preadolescent girls who are vaccinated will also eventually receive screening.

Cervical cancer can be detected through symptoms or screening, and women with cancer survive according to stage-specific survival rates for local, regional, and metastatic disease. This model does not consider screening strategies alone for the current cohort of older women. Individual girls enter the model at age nine years, before sexual debut and free of HPV infection, and they transition between health states throughout their lifetimes. Each month, women face a risk of acquiring HPV infection; once infected, they can clear their infection or develop low- or high-grade lesions, categorized as cervical intraepithelial neoplasia, grade 1 (CIN 1) or grade 2,3 (CIN 2,3). Low-grade lesions can regress; CIN 2,3 can progress to invasive cancer. These transitions are determined by age, HPV type, and type-specific natural

immunity after clearance of HPV infections. The natural history and model transitions have been well described elsewhere (Kim and Goldie 2008; Kim, Ortendahl, and Goldie 2009). For a more extensive discussion of the natural history of cervical cancer, see chapter 4 in this volume (Denny and others 2015).

All women are subject to mortality from the competing causes listed in the World Health Organization (WHO) life table estimates for China (WHO 2011). Our approach was to calibrate the model for the cervical cancer burden of the country as a whole and also for the HPV 16/18 type distribution in cervical cancer, which has been found in previous meta-analyses to be stable for 16/18 at 70 percent, regardless of country. De Sanjose and others (2010) found that more than 30 types of HPV are sexually transmitted and may lead to cervical cancer, most notably HPV 16 and 18, which together contribute to approximately 70 percent of cervical cancers worldwide. Accordingly, HPV is categorized as follows:

- High-risk type 16 (HR-16)
- High-risk type 18 (HR-18)
- Other high-risk types (HR-other), including 31, 33, 35, 39, 45, 51, 52, 56, 58, 59, 66, 68, 73, and 82
- Low-risk (LR) types, including 6, 11, 26, 32, 34, 40, 42, 44, 53, 54, 55, 57, 61, 62, 64, 67, 69, 70, 71, 72, 81, 83, and 84.

We initially established model parameters using the best available information on the natural history of HPV infection and cervical carcinogenesis. The model was adapted to the context in China using likelihood-based methods to fit the parameters to epidemiological data (figure 18A.1 in online annex 18A). Age-specific cervical cancer estimates were obtained from the GLOBOCAN (2008); data on HPV 16 and 18–type distribution in CIN 2,3 and cervical cancer were from a meta-analysis of primary data from Asia (Bao and others 2008) (figure 18A.2 in online annex 18A). The baseline natural history parameters were allowed to vary over plausible ranges. We identified sets of parameter values that achieved close fit to the empirical data and conducted the analysis using the parameter set with the maximum likelihood. Additional details of the model structure, calibration process, and calibration results are available online in annex 18A.

Strategies, Data, and Assumptions

To model the impact of cervical cancer prevention on distributional benefits and financial risk protection, we simulated screening with cytology and visual inspection with acetic acid (VIA) at five-year intervals, beginning at age 35 years, for a cohort of one million women in each of the income quintiles. We assumed that the screening frequency progressively increases with income; women in the lowest two quintiles would be screened once in a lifetime, those in the next two income quintiles would be screened three times in a lifetime, and those in the highest quintile would be screened five times in a lifetime. Consistent with assumptions made in previous analyses (Goldie and others 2001; Goldie and others 2005), cytology was assumed to occur in three visits: the initial screening (visit 1); colposcopy and possible biopsy for screen-positive women (visit 2); and treatment of precancerous lesions or invasive cancer (visit 3), including loop electrosurgical excision procedure (LEEP), cold knife conization, simple hysterectomy, or simple radiotherapy, depending on lesion size or cancer stage. The VIA screening incorporated same-day screening and treatment for all women with positive screening results as described in the Comprehensive Cervical Cancer Control guidelines (WHO 2006).

Vaccination was assumed to occur before age 12 (prior to sexual debut), with full adherence to the three doses, affording complete and lifelong protection against HPV 16 and 18. HPV vaccine coverage was assumed at 70 percent, based on current immunization rates of over 95 percent for childhood vaccines and recent evidence on the feasibility of reaching preadolescent girls with HPV vaccination using facility, school-based, and outreach strategies (La Montagne and others 2011; WHO 2013a). We used screening coverage estimates by quintile from the WHO Study of Global AGEing and Adult Health (WHO 2012). In the absence of patient health utilization data for screen-positive women, we assumed that loss to follow-up from screening to subsequent visits for diagnosis and treatment was inversely related to income, with loss to follow-up rates ranging from 62 to 5 percent from lowest to highest quintile, respectively. Recognizing that service utilization and loss to follow-up will be influenced by heterogeneity in health system, spatial, and socioeconomic factors across China's provinces, we conducted a sensitivity analysis on screening coverage rates and the loss to follow-up assumptions by quintile. Table 18.1 summarizes the point estimates for the model input parameters.

Using output data from the simulation model, we estimated the level and distribution of deaths averted by income quintile, comparing vaccination plus screening against screening at current coverage rates. We also estimated the reduction in cervical cancer, incremental costs to the government equal to HPV vaccination costs minus cervical cancer treatment costs averted, and patient cost savings, as well as the incremental government health care costs per death averted. Financial risk protection

Table 18.1 Summary of Parameters Used for Modeling the Impact and Costs of a Publicly Financed HPV Vaccination Policy in China

Parameter	Estimate
Screening with cytology: frequency[a] and coverage[b] (%)	
Quintile I: Once per lifetime	21
Quintile II: Once per lifetime	34
Quintile III: Three times per lifetime	43
Quintile IV: Three times per lifetime	47
Quintile V: Five times per lifetime	51
Loss to follow-up[c] (%)	
Quintile I	62
Quintile II	40
Quintile III	22
Quintile IV	13
Quintile V	5
Vaccine characteristics[c]	
Vaccination coverage (%)	70
HPV vaccine price per dose (US$)	13
Incremental vaccine program delivery cost per fully immunized girl (US$)	5
Vaccine cost per fully immunized girl, including wastage and handling (US$)	46
Income and wages[d]	
Average GDP per capita (US$)	3,749
Average GDP per capita[e] (US$)	
Quintile I	783
Quintile II	1,633
Quintile III	2,567
Quintile IV	3,888
Quintile V	7,896
Mean wage rate[f] (US$)	
Quintile I	3
Quintile II	6
Quintile III	10
Quintile IV	15
Quintile V	30

Note: Income quintiles are from lowest (I) to highest (V). Monetary values are in 2009 U.S. dollars. GDP = gross domestic product; HPV = human papillomavirus.

a. Frequency of screening was estimated at one time and five times per lifetime for all income quintiles in the sensitivity analysis.

b. Estimates from Gakidou, Nordhagen, and Obermeyer (2008) and WHO (2012).

c. Estimates are assumed values.

d. Estimates from WHO Global Health Observatory.

e. Estimates from WHO (2012) and WHO Global Health Observatory.

f. Estimates from WHO Global Health Observatory and Shi, Chen, and others (2012).

was estimated using a combination of indicators, including the number of women who would avoid cervical cancer treatment expenses and the average out-of-pocket expenses averted as a share of average per capita income, measured by gross domestic product (GDP). We present all results by income quintile.

Cost Data Sources

To estimate direct medical and nonmedical costs associated with screening, diagnosis, and treatment, we used published cost data from two studies conducted in China (Levin and others 2010; Shi, Chen, and others 2012), where all costs were expressed in 2009 U.S. dollars. Since these studies provided cost estimates by type of facility in urban and rural settings, we assumed an average health-seeking behavior by income quintile and geographic setting, where in the lowest three income quintiles rural and urban women were screened at the levels of township (primary health center) and county hospital, respectively, and all women in these lower quintiles received diagnosis and treatment at the county hospital. We assumed that in the highest two income quintiles, rural and urban women were screened and treated at prefecture or provincial level hospitals, respectively.

We then applied a weighted average unit cost for screening, diagnosis, and cancer treatment, based on urban and rural population proportions by income quintile. To estimate the consequences for household and government costs, we assumed that 35 percent of cancer screening and treatment costs are still privately financed in China (WHO Global Health Observatory), reflecting that many services, including outpatient services, are not covered, despite mandatory health insurance schemes. Direct nonmedical patient time costs for transportation and waiting were based on time estimates from Shi, Chen, and others (2012), using an updated national average wage rate in China ranging from US$3 to US$30 per day for the lowest to highest quintile, respectively. The average wage rate is equal to average per capita income divided by 255 workdays per year at eight hours per day (Shi, Chen, and others 2012). We obtained GDP data from the World Bank and used the consumer price index to deflate all costs to 2009 U.S. dollars. Per capita income for each quintile is the proportion of GDP accrued to each income quintile using estimates from the World Bank and PovCalNet, an online poverty analysis tool, divided by the total population per quintile (World Bank 2013a, 2013b).

Although Merck and GlaxoSmithKline's commercially available HPV vaccines are not yet approved in China, both are offered at low prices for public sector programs that range from less than US$5 for countries eligible for Gavi, the Vaccine Alliance, to US$13 for Pan American Health Organization (PAHO) countries (Gavi 2013). Given the likelihood that China could negotiate lower public sector prices (Colombara and Wang 2013), we assumed a public sector cost of US$46 per fully immunized girl, which includes the vaccine price (three doses at US$13 per dose), vaccine wastage (2 percent), freight (6 percent), and program administration cost (US$5). The program administration cost captures the average cost of new delivery strategies to reach preadolescent girls who fall outside existing routine immunization programs. The program administration costs are lower than the average incremental costs in recent studies in Latin America and the Caribbean and Sub-Saharan Africa, but they are likely to reflect economies of scale that are found in more densely populated Asian countries (Levin and others 2013). Tables 18A.2 and 18A.3, in online annex 18A, summarize the cost data by quintile.

Sensitivity Analysis

We performed a sensitivity analysis of the findings and evaluated the robustness of the results to changes in screening frequency per lifetime, screening coverage, loss to follow-up rates, and the cost per fully vaccinated girl. To accommodate the uncertainty around the uptake of the vaccine and vaccine delivery costs in the case of China, we conducted a sensitivity analysis and varied the cost between US$10 and US$100 per fully immunized girl to allow for either higher vaccine prices or higher service delivery costs. Table 18.2 provides the estimates or ranges used in the sensitivity analysis for these parameters and the way they varied by income quintile. Not shown are the estimates for cancer treatment costs, which were uniformly increased by 50 and 100 percent for all income quintiles.

RESULTS

We estimate that adding preadolescent HPV vaccination at 70 percent coverage to current screening will yield a 44 percent cancer reduction across all income quintiles, as shown in table 18.3. Although the relative cancer reduction is constant across income groups, the absolute numbers of cervical cancer deaths averted and the financial risk protection from HPV vaccination are highest among women in the lowest quintile; women in the bottom income quintiles received relatively higher benefits compared with those in the upper income quintiles. HPV vaccination averts 15 percent more detected cancer cases and 18 percent more deaths in the

Table 18.2 Sensitivity Analysis Parameter Estimates and Ranges for HPV Vaccine and Service Delivery Costs

(US$)

Parameter	Point estimate	Estimate or range
Screening with cytology: frequency[a,b] and coverage (%)		
Quintile I: Once per lifetime	21	21–70
Quintile II: Once per lifetime	34	34–70
Quintile III: Three times per lifetime	43	43–70
Quintile IV: Three times per lifetime	47	47–70
Quintile V: Five times per lifetime	51	51–70
Loss to follow-up[c] (%)		
Quintile I	62	15, 39
Quintile II	40	15, 24
Quintile III	22	15, 22
Quintile IV	13	15, 17
Quintile V	5	11, 15
Vaccine cost per fully immunized girl, including wastage and handling (US$)	46	10–100

Note: Income quintiles are from lowest (I) to highest (V). Monetary values are in 2009 U.S. dollars. HPV = human papillomavirus.

a. The frequency of screening is estimated at one time and five times per lifetime for all income quintiles in the sensitivity analysis.

b. Estimates from Gakidou, Nordhagen, and Obermeyer (2008) and WHO (2012).

c. Estimates are assumed.

lowest compared with the highest quintile. Although in absolute dollars patient savings were higher in the top income quintile compared with the lowest quintile (US$7,041,335 and US$1,633,160, respectively), the cost savings from HPV vaccination constituted a larger share of per capita income among women in the bottom income quintiles, ranging from 60 percent among the lowest income quintile to 30 percent among the highest quintile.

At a vaccine cost of US$46 per fully immunized girl and 70 percent coverage, the incremental cost is approximately US$160 million for a single cohort of five million girls. At the relatively low levels of cancer screening and treatment in China, government intervention costs do not vary by wealth strata, since these medical savings are offset by the publically financed HPV vaccination costs.

Given China's low reported rates of cervical cancer screening, the model results and relative relationships across income quintiles are robust to changes in assumptions about screening frequency, screening coverage, and loss to follow-up (table 18.4). As expected, changes in the cost per fully immunized girl do not have an impact on deaths averted, cancer reduction, or financial risk protection, assuming that 70 percent coverage is maintained. At US$10 per fully vaccinated girl, the cost per death averted ranges from US$2,161 for the lowest income quintile to US$2,608 for the highest income quintile. At US$100 per vaccinated girl, the cost per death averted increases to US$24,000 for the lowest income quintile to more than US$29,000 for the highest income quintile (table 18.4). Universal coverage of the HPV vaccination becomes even more favorable for individuals in the lower income quintiles and provides greater relative financial risk protection when treatment costs are increased by an additional 50 or 100 percent (table 18.5).

DISCUSSION

Despite worldwide progress in reducing the burden of cervical cancer, more than 270,000 women still die from the disease each year; the majority of these deaths occur

Table 18.3 Benefits and Costs of a Publicly Financed HPV Vaccination Policy in China

Benefit or cost	Quintile				
	I	II	III	IV	V
Deaths averted per million women	2,877	2,854	2,667	2,604	2,362
Government cost per million women (incremental) (US$)	31,417,285	31,420,191	31,440,420	31,446,679	31,359,970
Government cost per death averted (US$)	3,540	3,511	3,312	3,256	2,999
Treatment-seeking cases of cancer averted per million women	3,540	3,511	3,312	3,256	2,999
Patient cost savings per million women (US$)	1,633,160	2,240,688	2,785,626	4,417,303	7,041,335
Savings as percentage of total income	59	39	33	35	30
Cancer reduction (%)	44	44	43	43	44

Note: Income quintiles are from lowest (I) to highest (V). Monetary values are in 2009 U.S. dollars. HPV = human papillomavirus.

Table 18.4 Results of Sensitivity Analysis for HPV Vaccination Costs at US$10, US$46, and US$100 per Fully Vaccinated Girl

Result	Quintile				
	I	II	III	IV	V
HPV vaccination at US$10 per fully vaccinated girl					
Deaths averted	2,877	2,854	2,667	2,604	2,362
Government cost (incremental) (US$)	6,217,285	6,220,191	6,240,420	6,246,679	6,159,970
Government cost per death averted (US$)	2,161	2,179	2,340	2,399	2,608
Treatment-seeking cases of cancer averted	3,540	3,511	3,312	3,256	2,999
Patient cost savings (US$)	1,633,160	2,240,688	2,785,626	4,417,303	7,041,335
Savings as percentage of income	59	39	33	35	30
Cancer reduction (%)	44	44	43	43	44
HPV vaccination at US$46 per fully vaccinated girl					
Deaths averted	2,877	2,854	2,667	2,604	2,362
Government cost (incremental) (US$)	31,417,285	31,420,191	31,440,420	31,446,679	31,359,970
Government cost per death averted (US$)	10,920	11,009	11,789	12,076	13,277
Treatment-seeking cases of cancer averted	3,540	3,511	3,312	3,256	2,999
Patient cost savings (US$)	1,633,160	2,240,688	2,785,626	4,417,303	7,041,335
Savings as percentage of income	59	39	33	35	30
Cancer reduction (%)	44	44	43	43	44
HPV vaccination at US$100 per fully vaccinated girl					
Deaths averted	2,877	2,854	2,667	2,604	2,362
Government cost (incremental) (US$)	69,217,285	69,220,191	69,240,420	69,246,679	69,159,970
Government cost per death averted (US$)	24,059	24,254	25,962	26,592	29,280
Treatment-seeking cases of cancer averted	3,540	3,511	3,312	3,256	2,999
Patient cost savings (US$)	1,633,160	2,240,688	2,785,626	4,417,303	7,041,335
Savings as percentage of income	59	39	33	35	30
Cancer reduction (%)	44	44	43	43	44

Note: Income quintiles are from lowest (I) to highest (V). Monetary values are in 2009 U.S. dollars. HPV = human papillomavirus.

in Asia, Latin America and the Caribbean, and Sub-Saharan Africa. China accounts for 12 percent of new cervical cancer cases each year (Ferlay and others 2013), with higher incidence and death rates in the country's poorest provinces. The factors contributing to the disproportionate distribution of cervical cancer disease include low coverage and poor quality of screening programs, differential access to services for screening and treatment, poverty, and lack of awareness. The availability of HPV vaccines can complement existing cervical cancer prevention efforts, accelerating the equity and health impacts by overcoming many of these barriers (Tsu and Levin 2008).

The HPV vaccine holds great promise for reducing the burden of cervical cancer, but the vaccine is not yet available in China. Delaying the introduction of the HPV vaccine will result in a lost opportunity to prevent cervical cancer cases and deaths. A national vaccination program from 2006 to 2012 of all girls ages 9–15 years could have prevented 381,000 cervical cancer cases and 212,000 related deaths in the coming decades (Colombara and Wang 2013). It is expected that China could negotiate HPV vaccine prices to cost-effective levels of approximately US$9 to US$13 per dose, but many Chinese women—at least 33 percent—are not willing to pay more than US$3 (Li and others 2009). A successful program is likely to depend on government financing.

We applied an ECEA approach to evaluate the impact of a publically financed policy for HPV vaccination in China on the distribution of health consequences and

Table 18.5 Results of Sensitivity Analysis Assuming Treatment Costs Increase by 50 Percent and 100 Percent Compared with Baseline

Result	Quintile				
	I	II	III	IV	V
Baseline strategy					
Deaths averted	2,877	2,854	2,667	2,604	2,362
Government cost (incremental) (US$)	31,417,285	31,420,191	31,440,420	31,446,679	31,359,970
Government cost per death averted (US$)	10,920	11,009	11,789	12,076	13,277
Treatment-seeking cases of cancer averted	3,540	3,511	3,312	3,256	2,999
Patient cost savings (US$)	1,633,160	2,240,688	2,785,626	4,417,303	7,041,335
Savings as percentage of income	59	39	33	35	30
Cancer reduction (%)	44	44	43	43	44
Treatment costs increased by 50%					
Deaths averted	2,877	2,854	2,667	2,604	2,362
Government cost (incremental) (US$)	31,035,156	31,057,311	31,085,113	31,103,101	30,939,508
Government cost per death averted (US$)	10,787	10,882	11,655	11,944	13,099
Treatment-seeking cases of cancer averted	3,540	3,511	3,312	3,256	2,999
Patient cost savings (US$)	1,899,093	2,506,089	3,040,532	4,714,290	7,310,555
Savings as percentage of income	69	44	36	37	31
Cancer reduction (%)	44	44	43	43	44
Treatment costs increased by 100%					
Deaths averted	2,877	2,854	2,667	2,604	2,362
Government cost (incremental) (US$)	30,647,484	30,682,085	30,728,534	30,760,469	30,550,290
Government cost per death averted (US$)	10,653	10,751	11,522	11,813	12,934
Treatment-seeking cases of cancer averted	3540	3511	3312	3256	2999
Patient cost savings (US$)	2,165,026	2,771,490	3,295,438	5,011,276	7,579,775
Savings as percentage of income	78	48	39	40	32
Cancer reduction (%)	44	44	43	43	44

Note: Income quintiles are from lowest (I) to highest (V). Monetary values are in 2009 U.S. dollars.

financial risk protection benefits across income levels. Our analysis showed that preadolescent HPV vaccination, added to current cervical cancer screening, could reduce cancer by over 40 percent across all income groups, while providing relatively higher financial protection to households in the bottom income quintiles. The low screening coverage rates reported for China affect the government and patient screening and treatment costs, but with differential results.

- From the governmental perspective, a publically financed HPV vaccination program would increase net costs, with little offset from averted cervical-related treatment costs, because of the low levels of screening.

- Although HPV vaccination led to patient cost savings that were small relative to the increase in government costs, all income groups experienced cost savings; importantly, there was a powerful equity effect, with higher financial risk protection in the poorest groups.
- Patient cost savings represent a large proportion of poor women's average per capita income, reaching 60 percent among women in the bottom income quintile and declining to 30 percent among women in the wealthiest quintile.

We also estimated standard cost-effectiveness ratios (results available from the authors) and, similar to previous studies conducted in China, found that HPV vaccination is cost effective across all income groups when the cost is less than US$50 per vaccinated girl.

Since the vaccine is not yet available in China, we assumed a cost of US$46 per vaccinated girl, using US$13 per dose, based on the manufacturers' offer price to PAHO for public vaccination programs in Latin America and the Caribbean. The financial cost of vaccinating 70 percent of China's current cohort of 6.6 million 10-year-old girls is US$213 million. This estimate, which accounts for less than 0.5 percent of projected health care spending of US$357 billion in 2011, would have a large financial impact on China's current Expanded Program for Immunization (EPI). The introduction of the HPV vaccine would require a change in policy to finance the vaccine publicly, through current health insurance schemes or inclusion in EPI, which provides free childhood vaccines for measles, diphtheria/tetanus/pertussis, Bacille Calmette–Guérin, polio, and hepatitis B. EPI manages non-EPI vaccines, such as those for Japanese encephalitis, mumps, and rubella, but patients pay for these vaccines via user fees. A third type of "optional" vaccines, such as hepatitis A, *Haemophilus* influenza type B, and rotavirus, are procured and delivered outside EPI and paid for by patients without government subsidies (Liu and others 2006).

Limitations of the Analysis

This analysis has several limitations:

- First, the analysis is an illustrative application of the ECEA method using the best available published data from selected provinces, which do not fully capture the heterogeneity in disease burden, health systems, socioeconomic development, and GDP per capita across China's provinces. For example, we used data from different regions in China to estimate the cervical cancer burden and costs for the whole country, leading to results that may not hold for a country as large as China. Accordingly, in this application, the results should be considered suggestive, rather than evidence based, but the estimates can be refined for specific subregions as improved data become available.
- Second, the ECEA method simulates the costs and impacts of HPV vaccination by income quintile; however, there are limited data on the variation of HPV incidence, mortality rates, loss to follow-up rates for screening, and out-of-pocket health expenses related to cancer prevention or treatment by wealth or income category.
- Third, there is limited information on health service utilization; screening and treatment costs; and the

impact of mandatory health insurance by prefecture, province, and other geographic settings or across wealth strata. Our assumptions were based on aggregate national estimates of private expenses, which may be out of date, given the recent rapid growth in GDP per capita.
- Fourth, we estimated women's time using a wage rate derived from a national estimate of GDP per capita income, which may overestimate income in the lowest quintile, where some rural communities are likely to live on US$2 per day or less.
- Fifth, this analysis does not include women's transport costs in seeking screening, treatment, or vaccination; these costs are expected to be small components of patient costs based on previous analyses in China (Canfell and others 2011; Levin and others 2010; Shi, Chen, and others 2012).
- Sixth, we did not conduct an exhaustive evaluation of scenarios, including increasing screening to higher levels, since the objective of the analysis was to illustrate the potential of an HPV vaccination program to address equity and financial risk protection and not to identify optimal cervical cancer prevention approaches.

An ECEA approach yields new and essential information on a policy's ability to reduce inequity and catastrophic expenses. The approach complements information on value for money from traditional cost-effectiveness analyses. Future applications of this approach will benefit from improved information on public and private health financing, as well as from disaggregated data on disease burden and health service utilization by key socioeconomic, demographic, and geographic variables.

CONCLUSIONS

HPV vaccines have not yet been approved in China, and concern is growing that the use of HPV vaccines in the country is still a long way off (Lu 2013). A recent editorial recognizing the burden of cervical cancer in China, as well as its unequal impact among women in lower income groups, proposes a semi-mandatory HPV vaccination program in China targeted to low-income, high-risk women living in regions with historically high prevalence of cervical cancer (Zhang, Li, and others 2013). This illustrative application of the ECEA approach to a publicly financed HPV vaccination policy provides decision makers with the potential distributional consequences and financial risk protection of including cervical cancer in future health care reform investments to provide insight to policy debates in China. An ECEA can provide policy makers with additional evidence beyond evidence of effectiveness, costs, and cost-effectiveness for selective resource allocation to the populations and provinces most in need in the context of public financing and the strengthening of Chinese health reform.

Previous research has demonstrated that HPV vaccination in China can be cost-effective at a cost of US$50 per vaccinated girl. A targeted program may even be affordable, given China's plans for dramatically increasing health care spending in the near future (Le Deu and others 2012; Zhang, Li, and others 2013). Ensuring high and uniform HPV vaccine uptake will likely also contribute to more equitable gains with respect to the reduction of morbidity and mortality from cervical cancer and has the potential to protect women in poor households against catastrophic cervical cancer medical expenses.

NOTE

This chapter was previously published in a shorter form in *Vaccine*; the original publication may be found at doi: 10.1016/j.vaccine.2015.02.052. It is reprinted here under the Creative Commons CC-BY 4.0 License (https://creativecommons.org/licenses/by/4.0/). Reprinting in this volume does not indicate Elsevier's endorsement. doi:10.1016/j.vaccine.2015.02.052

World Bank Income Classifications as of July 2014 are as follows, based on estimates of gross national income (GNI) per capita for 2013:

- Low-income countries (LICs) = US$1,045 or less
- Middle-income countries (MICs) are subdivided:
  a) lower-middle-income = US$1,046 to US$4,125
  b) upper-middle-income (UMICs) = US$4,126 to US$12,745
- High-income countries (HICs) = US$12,746 or more.

REFERENCES

Bao, Y. P., N. Li, J. S. Smith, Y. L. Qiao, and Asian Cervical Cancer Prevention Supervisory Board. 2008. "Human Papillomavirus Type Distribution in Women from Asia: A Meta-Analysis." *International Journal of Gynecological Cancer* 18 (1): 71–79.

Canfell, K., J. F. Shi, J. B. Lew, R. Walker, F. H. Zhao, and others. 2011. "Prevention of Cervical Cancer in Rural China: Evaluation of HPV Vaccination and Primary HPV Screening Strategies." *Vaccine* 29 (13): 2487–94.

Colombara, D. V., and S.-M. Wang. 2013. "The Impact of HPV Vaccination Delays in China: Lessons from HBV Control Programs." *Vaccine* 31 (38): 4057–59.

Denny, L., R. Herrero, C. Levin, and J. T. Kim. 2015. "Cervical Cancer." In *Disease Control Priorities* (third edition): Volume 3, *Cancer*, edited by H. Gelband, P. Jha, R. Sankaranarayanan, and S. Horton. Washington, DC: World Bank.

de Sanjose, S., W. G. V. Quint, L. Alemany, D. T. Geraets, J. E. Klaustermeier, and others. 2010. "Human Papillomavirus Genotype Attribution in Invasive Cervical Cancer: A Retrospective Cross-Sectional Worldwide Study." *The Lancet Oncology* 11 (11): 1048–56.

Ferlay, J., H. R. Shin, F. Bray, D. Forman, C. Mathers, and others. 2010. "Estimates of Worldwide Burden of Cancer in 2008: GLOBOCAN 2008." *International Journal of Cancer* 127 (12): 2893–917. doi:10.1002/ijc.25516.

Ferlay, J., I. Soerjomataram, M. Ervik, R. Dikshit, S. Eser, and others. 2013. GLOBOCAN 2012 v1.0, Cancer Incidence and Mortality Worldwide: IARC CancerBase No. 11 [Internet]. Lyon: IARC. http://globocan.iarc.fr.

Gakidou, E., S. Nordhagen, and Z. Obermeyer. 2008. "Coverage of Cervical Cancer Screening in 57 Countries: Low Average Levels and Large Inequalities." *PLoS Medicine* 5 (6): e132.

Gavi (Vaccine Alliance). 2013. "Human Papillomavirus Vaccine Support." http://www.gavialliance.org/support/nvs/human-papillomavirus-vaccine-support.

Goldhaber-Fiebert, J. D., N. K. Stout, J. Ortendahl, K. M. Kuntz, S. J. Goldie, and others. 2007. "Modeling Human Papillomavirus and Cervical Cancer in the United States for Analyses of Screening and Vaccination." *Population Health Metrics* 5: 11. doi:10.1186/1478-7954-5-11.

Goldie, S. J., M. Diaz, S. Y. Kim, C. E. Levin, H. Van Minh, and others. 2008. "Mathematical Models of Cervical Cancer Prevention in the Asia Pacific Region." *Vaccine* 26 (Suppl. 12): M17–29.

Goldie, S. J., L. Gaffikin, J. D. Goldhaber-Fiebert, A. Gordillo-Tobar, C. Levin, and others. 2005. "Cost-Effectiveness of Cervical-Cancer Screening in Five Developing Countries." *New England Journal of Medicine* 353 (20): 2158–68.

Goldie, S. J., J. J. Kim, K. Kobus, J. D. Goldhaber-Fiebert, J. Salomon, and others. 2007. "Cost-Effectiveness of HPV 16, 18 Vaccination in Brazil." *Vaccine* 25 (33): 6257–70.

Goldie, S. J., L. Kuhn, L. Denny, A. Pollack, and T. C. Wright. 2001. "Policy Analysis of Cervical Cancer Screening Strategies in Low-Resource Settings: Clinical Benefits and Cost-Effectiveness." *Journal of the American Medical Association* 285 (24): 3107–15.

IARC (International Agency for Research on Cancer). 2012. http://www.iarc.fr/.

Jia, Y., S. Li, R. Yang, H. Zhou, Q. Xiang, and others. 2013. "Knowledge about Cervical Cancer and Barriers of Screening Program among Women in Wufeng County, a High-Incidence Region of Cervical Cancer in China." *PLoS One* 8 (7): e67005.

Kim, J. J., and S. J. Goldie 2008. "Health and Economic Implications of HPV Vaccination in the United States." *New England Journal of Medicine* 359 (8): 821–32.

Kim, J. J., K. M. Kuntz, N. K. Stout, S. Mahmud, L. L. Villa, and others. 2007. "Multiparameter Calibration of a Natural History Model of Cervical Cancer." *American Journal of Epidemiology* 166 (2): 137–50.

Kim, J. J., J. Ortendahl, and S. J. Goldie 2009. "Cost-Effectiveness of Human Papillomavirus Vaccination and Cervical Cancer Screening in Women Older than 30 Years in the United States." *Annals of Internal Medicine* 151 (8): 538–45.

LaMontagne, D. S., S. Barge, N. T. Le, E. Mugisha, M. E. Penny, and others. 2011. "Human Papillomavirus Vaccine Delivery Strategies That Achieved High Coverage in Low- and Middle-Income Countries." *Bulletin of the World Health Organization* 89 (11): 821–30.

Le Deu, F., R. Parekh, F. Zhange, and G. Zhou. 2012. "Healthcare in China: Entering Unchartered Waters." McKinsey & Co. http://www.mckinsey.com/insights/health_systems_and _services/health_care_in_china_entering_uncharted _waters.

Levin, C. E., H. V. Minh, J. Odaga, S. S. Rout, N. T. N. Diep, and others. 2013. "Incremental Costs of Strategies to Deliver Human Papillomavirus Vaccine to Young Adolescent Girls in Peru, Uganda, and Viet Nam." *Bulletin of the World Health Organization* 91: 585–92.

Levin, C. E., J. Sellors, J. F. Shi, L. Ma, Y. L. Qiao, and others. 2010. "Cost-Effectiveness Analysis of Cervical Cancer Prevention Based on a Rapid Human Papillomavirus Screening Test in a High-Risk Region of China." *International Journal of Cancer* 127 (6): 1404–11.

Li, J., L.-N. Kang, and Y.-L. Qiao. 2011. "Review of the Cervical Cancer Disease Burden in Mainland China." *Asian Pacific Journal of Cancer Prevention* 12: 1149–53.

Li, J., L. K. Li, J.-F. Ma, L. H. Wei, M. Niyazi, and others. 2009. "Knowledge and Attitudes about Human Papillomavirus (HPV) and HPV Vaccines among Women Living in Metropolitan and Rural Regions of China." *Vaccine* 27 (8): 1210–15.

Li, R., Q. Zhou, M. Li, S. M. Tong, M. He, and others. 2013. "Evaluation of Visual Inspection as the Primary Screening Method in a Four-Year Cervical (Pre-) Cancer Screening Program in Rural China." *Tropical Doctor* 43 (3): 96–99.

Liu, W., J. D. Clemens, J. Yang, and Z. Xu. 2006. "Immunization against Japanese Encephalitis in China: A Policy Analysis." *Vaccine* 24: 5178–82.

Lu, Y. 2013. "HPV Vaccines among Chinese Women Still a Long Way Off." *People's Daily Online*, July 24. http://english .people.com.cn/90882/8339695.html.

Qiao, Y. L. 2010. "Perspective of Cervical Cancer Prevention and Control in Developing Countries and Areas." *Chinese Journal of Cancer* 29 (1): 1–31.

Qiao, Y. L., J. W. Sellors, P. S. Eder, Y. B. Bao, J. M. Lim, and others. 2008. "A New HPV-DNA Test for Cervical Cancer Screening in Developing Regions: A Cross-Sectional Study of Clinical Accuracy in Rural China." *The Lancet Oncology* 9 (10): 929–36.

Shi, J. F., K. Canfell, J. B. Lew, and Y. L. Qiao. 2012. "The Burden of Cervical Cancer in China: Synthesis of the Evidence." *International Journal of Cancer* 130 (3): 641–52.

Shi, J. F., K. Canfell, J. B. Lew, F. H. Zhao, R. Legood, and others. 2011. "Evaluation of Primary HPV-DNA Testing in Relation to Visual Inspection Methods for Cervical Cancer Screening in Rural China: An Epidemiologic and Cost-Effectiveness Modelling Study." *BMC Cancer* 11: 239. doi:10.1186/1471–2407–11–239.

Shi, J. F., J. F. Chen, K. Canfell, X. X. Feng, J. F. Ma, and others. 2012. "Estimation of the Costs of Cervical Cancer Screening, Diagnosis and Treatment in Rural Shanxi Province, China: A Micro-Costing Study." *BMC Health Services Research* 12: 123.

The Lancet. 2009. "Women's Health in Rural China." *The Lancet* 374 (9687): 358. doi:10.1016/S0140-6736(09)61394-5.

Tsu, V., and C. Levin. 2008. "Making the Case for Cervical Cancer Prevention: What about Equity?" *Reproductive Health Matters* 16 (32): 104–12.

Verguet, S., C. Gauvreau, S. Mishra, M. MacLennan, S. Murphy, and others. 2015. "The Consequences of Tobacco Tax on Household Health and Finances in Rich and Poor Smokers in China: An Extended Cost-Effectiveness Analysis." *The Lancet* Global Health 3 (4): e206-16. doi:10.1016 /s2214-109x(15)70095-1.

Verguet, S., R. Laxminarayan, and D. T. Jamison. 2015. "Universal Public Finance of Tuberculosis Treatment in India: An Extended Cost-Effectiveness Analysis." *Health Economics* 24: 318–22.

Verguet, S., S. Murphy, B. Anderson, K. A. Johansson, R. Glass, and others. 2013. "Public Finance of Rotavirus Vaccination in India and Ethiopia: An Extended Cost-Effectiveness Analysis." *Vaccine* 31 (42): 4902–10.

Wang, J. L., Y. Z. Yang, W. W. Dong, J. Sun, H. T. Tao, and others. 2013. "Application of Human Papillomavirus in Screening for Cervical Cancer and Precancerous Lesions." *Asian Pacific Journal of Cancer Prevention* 14 (5): 2979–82.

WHO (World Health Organization). 2006. *Comprehensive Cervical Cancer Control: A Guide to Essential Practice.* Geneva: WHO.

———. 2011. "WHO Life Tables." http://www.who.int/gho /mortality_burden_disease/life_tables/life_tables/en.

———. 2012. Study on Global AGEing and Adult Health— 2007/2010, WAVE 1. Geneva: WHO. http://apps.who.int /healthinfo/systems/surveydata/index.php/catalog/13.

———. 2013a. *WHO Vaccine-Preventable Diseases: Monitoring System 2013 Global Summary.* Geneva: WHO.

———. 2013b. *The World Health Report 2013: Research for Universal Health Coverage.* Geneva: WHO.

———. "Global Health Observatory (GHO) data." http:// www.who.int/gho/en/.

World Bank. 2013a. *World Development Indicators 2013.* Washington, DC: World Bank.

———. 2013b. "PovCalNet: An Online Analysis Tool for Global Poverty Monitoring." Development Research Group, World Bank, Washington, DC. http://iresearch.worldbank.org/PovcalNet/index.htm.

Yip, W. C., W. C. Hsiao, W. Chen, S. Hu, J. Ma, and others. 2012. "Early Appraisal of China's Huge and Complex Health Care Reforms." *The Lancet* 379 (9818): 833–42.

Zhang, S. K., X. F. Pan, S. M. Wang, C. X. Yang, X. H. Gao, and others. 2013. "Perceptions and Acceptability of HPV Vaccination among Parents of Young Adolescents: A Multicenter National Survey in China." *Vaccine* 31 (32): 3244–49.

Zhang, W. J., F. Li, Y. H. Wang, D. Simayi, A. Saimaiti, and others. 2013. "The Case of Semi-Mandatory HPV Vaccination in China." *Nature Biotechnology* 31: 590–91.

Zhao, F. H., J. Jeronimo, Y. L. Qiao, J. Schweizer, W. Chen, and others. 2013. "An Evaluation of Novel, Lower-Cost Molecular Screening Tests for Human Papillomavirus in Rural China." *Cancer Prevention Research* 6 (9): 938–48.

DCP3 Series Acknowledgments

Disease Control Priorities, third edition *(DCP3)* compiles the global health knowledge of institutions and experts from around the world, a task that required the efforts of over 500 individuals, including volume editors, chapter authors, peer reviewers, advisory committee members, and research and staff assistants. For each of these contributions we convey our acknowledgement and appreciation. First and foremost, we would like to thank our 31 volume editors who provided the intellectual vision for their volumes based on years of professional work in their respective fields, and then dedicated long hours to reviewing each chapter, providing leadership and guidance to authors, and framing and writing the summary chapters. We also thank our chapter authors who collectively volunteered their time and expertise to writing over 160 comprehensive, evidence-based chapters.

We owe immense gratitude to the institutional sponsor of this effort: The Bill & Melinda Gates Foundation. The Foundation provided sole financial support of the Disease Control Priorities Network. Many thanks to Program Officers Kathy Cahill, Philip Setel, Carol Medlin, and (currently) Damian Walker for their thoughtful interactions, guidance, and encouragement over the life of the project. We also wish to thank Jaime Sepúlveda for his longstanding support, including chairing the Advisory Committee for the second edition and, more recently, demonstrating his vision for *DCP3* while he was a special advisor to the Gates Foundation. We are also grateful to the University of Washington's Department of Global Health and successive chairs King Holmes and Judy Wasserheit for providing a home base for the *DCP3* Secretariat, which included intellectual collaboration, logistical coordination, and administrative support.

We thank the many contractors and consultants who provided support to specific volumes in the form of economic analytical work, volume coordination, chapter drafting, and meeting organization: the Center for Disease Dynamics, Economics, & Policy; Center for Chronic Disease Control; Center for Global Health Research; Emory University; Evidence to Policy Initiative; Public Health Foundation of India; QURE Healthcare; University of California, San Francisco; University of Waterloo; University of Queensland; and the World Health Organization.

We are tremendously grateful for the wisdom and guidance provided by our advisory committee to the editors. Steered by Chair Anne Mills, the advisory committee assures quality and intellectual rigor of the highest order for *DCP3*.

The U.S. Institute of Medicine, in collaboration with the Interacademy Medical Panel, coordinated the peer-review process for all *DCP3* chapters. Patrick Kelley, Gillian Buckley, Megan Ginivan, and Rachel Pittluck managed this effort and provided critical and substantive input.

The World Bank External and Corporate Relations Publishing and Knowledge division provided exceptional guidance and support throughout the demanding production and design process. We would particularly like to thank Carlos Rossel, the publisher; Mary Fisk, Nancy Lammers, Devlan O'Connor, Rumit Pancholi, and Deborah Naylor for their diligence and expertise. Additionally, we thank Jose de Buerba, Mario Trubiano, Yulia Ivanova, and Chiamaka Osuagwu of the World Bank for providing professional counsel on communications and marketing strategies.

Several U.S. and international institutions contributed to the organization and execution of meetings that supported the preparation and dissemination of *DCP3*.

We would like to express our appreciation to the following institutions:

- University of Bergen, consultation on equity (June 2011)
- University of California, San Francisco, surgery volume consultations (April 2012, October 2013, February 2014)
- Institute of Medicine, first meeting of the Advisory Committee to the Editors ACE (March 2013)
- Harvard Global Health Institute, consultation on policy measures to reduce incidence of noncommunicable diseases (July 2013)
- Institute of Medicine, systems strengthening meeting (September 2013)
- Center for Disease Dynamics, Economics, and Policy (Quality and Uptake meeting September 2013, reproductive and maternal health volume consultation November 2013)
- National Cancer Institute cancer consultation (November 2013)
- Union for International Cancer Control cancer consultation (November 2013, December 2014)

Carol Levin provided outstanding governance for cost and cost-effectiveness analysis. Stéphane Verguet added invaluable guidance in applying and improving the extended cost-effectiveness analysis method. Shane Murphy, Zachary Olson, Elizabeth Brouwer, and Kristen Danforth provided exceptional research assistance and analytic assistance. Brianne Adderley ably managed the budget and project processes. The efforts of these individuals were absolutely critical to producing this series and we are thankful for their commitment.

Volume and Series Editors

VOLUME EDITORS

Hellen Gelband is Associate Director for Policy at the Center for Disease Dynamics, Economics & Policy (CDDEP). Her work spans infectious disease, particularly malaria and antibiotic resistance, and noncommunicable disease policy, mainly in low- and middle-income countries. Before joining CDDEP, then Resources for the Future, she conducted policy studies at the (former) Congressional Office of Technology Assessment, the Institute of Medicine of the U.S. National Academies, and a number of international organizations.

Prabhat Jha is the founding director of the Centre for Global Health Research at St. Michael's Hospital and holds Endowed and Canada Research Chairs in Global Health in the Dalla Lana School of Public Health at the University of Toronto. He is lead investigator of the Million Death Study in India, which quantifies the causes of death and key risk factors in over two million homes over a 14-year period. He is also Scientific Director of the Statistical Alliance for Vital Events, which aims to expand reliable measurement of causes of death worldwide. His research includes the epidemiology and economics of tobacco control worldwide.

Rengaswamy Sankaranarayanan is head of the Early Detection and Prevention Section and the Screening Group at the World Health Organization's International Agency for Research on Cancer (IARC) in Lyon, France. He was trained in radiation oncology at the University of Pittsburgh and the University of Cambridge. He is an expert in evaluating early detection strategies and has conducted trials of screening interventions for cervical, oral, and breast cancers in a number of low- and middle-income countries. Aided by collaborative relationships with other international and national organizations and individual researchers, he provides technical assistance to countries developing public health policies that include cancer. His manuals on early detection of cervical cancer have been translated into several languages, including Chinese, French, Hindi, Portuguese, Spanish and Turkish, and others.

Susan Horton is Professor at the University of Waterloo and holds the Centre for International Governance Innovation (CIGI) Chair in Global Health Economics in the Balsillie School of International Affairs there. She has consulted for the World Bank, the Asian Development Bank, several United Nations agencies, and the International Development Research Centre, among others in work carried out in over 20 low- and middle-income countries. She led the work on nutrition for the Copenhagen Consensus in 2008, when micronutrients were ranked as the top development priority. She has served as associate provost of graduate studies at the University of Waterloo, vice-president academic at Wilfrid Laurier University in Waterloo, and interim dean at the University of Toronto at Scarborough.

SERIES EDITORS

Dean T. Jamison

Dean Jamison is a Senior Fellow in Global Health Sciences at the University of California, San Francisco, and an Emeritus Professor of Global Health at the University of Washington. He previously held academic appointments at Harvard University and the

University of California, Los Angeles; he was an economist on the staff of the World Bank, where he was lead author of the World Bank's *World Development Report 1993: Investing in Health*. He was lead editor of DCP2. He holds a PhD in economics from Harvard University and is an elected member of the Institute of Medicine of the U.S. National Academy of Sciences. He recently served as Co-Chair and Study Director of The Lancet's Commission on Investing in Health.

Rachel Nugent

Rachel Nugent is a Research Associate Professor in the Department of Global Health at the University of Washington. She was formerly Deputy Director of Global Health at the Center for Global Development, Director of Health and Economics at the Population Reference Bureau, Program Director of Health and Economics Programs at the Fogarty International Center of the National Institutes of Health, and senior economist at the Food and Agriculture Organization of the United Nations. From 1991–97, she was associate professor and department chair in economics at Pacific Lutheran University. She has advised the World Health Organization, the U.S. government, and nonprofit organizations on the economics and policy environment of noncommunicable diseases.

Hellen Gelband

See the list of Volume Editors.

Susan Horton

See the list of Volume Editors.

Prabhat Jha

See the list of Volume Editors.

Ramanan Laxminarayan

Ramanan Laxminarayan is Vice President for Research and Policy at the Public Health Foundation of India, and he directs the Center for Disease Dynamics, Economics & Policy in Washington, D.C., and New Delhi. His research deals with the integration of epidemiological models of infectious diseases and drug resistance into the economic analysis of public health problems. He was one of the key architects of the Affordable Medicines Facility for malaria, a novel financing mechanism to improve access and delay resistance to antimalarial drugs. In 2012, he created the Immunization Technical Support Unit in India, which has been credited with improving immunization coverage in the country. He teaches at Princeton University.

Contributors

Isaac F. Adewole
University of Ibadan, Ibadan, Nigeria

Hemantha Amarasinghe
Institute of Oral Health, Maharagama, Sri Lanka

Benjamin O. Anderson
Fred Hutchinson Cancer Research Center, University of Washington, Seattle, Washington, United States

Federico G. Antillon
Universidad Francisco Marroquin, Guatemala City, Guatemala

Samira Asma
Centers for Disease Control and Prevention, Atlanta, Georgia, United States

Rifat Atun
Harvard University, Cambridge, Massachusetts, United States

Rajendra A. Badwe
Tata Memorial Centre, Mumbai, India

Freddie Bray
International Agency for Research on Cancer, Lyon, France

Frank J. Chaloupka
University of Illinois at Chicago, Chicago, Illinois, United States

Ann Chao
National Cancer Institute, Bethesda, Maryland, United States

Chien-Jen Chen
National Taiwan University, Taipei, Taiwan, China

Wendong Chen
University of Toronto, Toronto, Canada

James Cleary
University of Wisconsin, Madison, Wisconsin, United States

Anil D'Cruz
Tata Memorial Hospital, Mumbai, India

Anna J. Dare
Centre for Global Health Research, St. Michael's Hospital, University of Toronto, Toronto, Canada

Lynette Denny
University of Cape Town, Groote Schuur Hospital, Cape Town, South Africa

Craig Earle
Cancer Care Ontario, Ontario Institute for Cancer Research, University of Toronto, Toronto, Canada

Silvia Franceschi
International Agency for Research on Cancer, Lyon, France

Cindy L. Gauvreau
Centre for Global Health Research, St. Michael's Hospital, University of Toronto, Toronto, Canada

Hellen Gelband
Center for Disease Dynamics, Economics & Policy, Washington, DC, United States

Ophira M. Ginsburg
Dalla Lana School of Public Health, University of Toronto, Toronto, Canada; BRAC University, Dhaka, Bangladesh

Mary K. Gospodarowicz
Princess Margaret Cancer Centre, Toronto, Canada

Thomas Gross
National Cancer Institute, Bethesda, Maryland,
United States

Prakash C. Gupta
Healis Sehksaria Institute for Public Health, Mumbai,
India

Sumit Gupta
Toronto Hospital for Sick Children, Toronto, Canada

Sir Andrew Hall
International Agency for Research on Cancer, Lyon,
France

Mhamed Harif
CHU Mohammed VI, Marrakesh, Morocco

Rolando Herrero
International Agency for Research on Cancer, Lyon, France

Susan Horton
University of Waterloo, Waterloo, Ontario, Canada

Scott C. Howard
University of Tennessee Health Sciences Center,
Memphis, Tennessee, United States

Stephen P. Hunger
Children's Hospital of Philadelphia, Philadelphia,
Pennsylvania, United States

Andre Ilbawi
MD Anderson Cancer Center, Houston, Texas,
United States

Trijn Israels
Academisch Medisch Centrum, Amsterdam, the
Netherlands

David A. Jaffray
Princess Margaret Cancer Centre, TECHNA Institute,
Toronto, Ontario

Dean T. Jamison
University of California, San Francisco, and University
of Washington, Seattle, Washington, United States

Prabhat Jha
Centre for Global Health Research, St. Michael's
Hospital, Dalla Lana School of Public Health,
University of Toronto, Toronto, Canada

Newell Johnson
Griffith University, Gold Coast, Australia

Jamal Khader
King Hussein Cancer Center, Amman, Jordan

Jane J. Kim
Harvard University, Cambridge, Massachusetts,
United States

Felicia Knaul
Miami Institute for the Americas, and Miller School of
Medicine, University of Miami, Florida, United States

Carol Levin
University of Washington, Seattle, Washington,
United States

Joseph Lipscomb
Emory University, Atlanta, Georgia, United States

W. Thomas London
Fox Chase Cancer Center, Philadelphia, Pennsylvania,
United States

Mary MacLennan
Centre for Global Health Research, St. Michael's
Hospital, University of Toronto, Toronto, Canada

Katherine A. McGlynn
National Cancer Institute, Bethesda, Maryland,
United States

Monika L. Metzger
St. Jude Children's Research Hospital, Memphis,
Tennessee, United States

Raul H. Murillo
National Cancer Institute of Colombia, Bogotá,
Colombia

Zachary Olson
University of Washington, Seattle, Washington,
United States

Sherif Omar
Cairo University, Cairo, Arab Republic of Egypt

Krishna Palipudi
Centers for Disease Control and Prevention, Atlanta,
Georgia, United States

C. S. Pramesh
Tata Memorial Centre, Mumbai, India

You-Lin Qiao
Cancer Hospital, Chinese Academy of Medical Sciences,
Peking Union Medical College, Beijing, China

Linda Rabeneck
Cancer Care Ontario, University of Toronto, Toronto,
Canada

Preetha Rajaraman
National Cancer Institute, Bethesda, Maryland,
United States

Kunnambath Ramadas
Regional Cancer Centre, Trivandrum, India

Chinthanie Ramasundarahettige
Centre for Global Health Research, St. Michael's Hospital, University of Toronto, Toronto, Canada

Timothy Rebbeck
University of Pennsylvania, Philadelphia, Pennsylvania, United States

Carlos Rodriguez-Galindo
Harvard University, Cambridge, Massachusetts, United States

Rengaswamy Sankaranarayanan
International Agency for Research on Cancer, Lyon, France

Monisha Sharma
University of Washington, Seattle, Washington, United States

Ju-Fang Shi
Cancer Institute, Chinese Academy of Medical Sciences, Peking Union Medical College, Beijing, China

Isabelle Soerjomataram
International Agency for Research on Cancer, Lyon, France

Lisa Stevens
National Cancer Institute, Bethesda, Maryland, United States

Sujha Subramanian
RTI International, Waltham, Massachusetts, United States

Richard Sullivan
Kings College London, King's Health Partners, London, United Kingdom

Terrence Sullivan
University of Toronto, Canadian Partnership Against Cancer, Toronto, Canada

David B. Thomas
Fred Hutchinson Cancer Research Center, University of Washington, Seattle, Washington, United States

Edward L. Trimble
National Cancer Institute, Bethesda, Maryland, United States

Joann Trypuc
Princess Margaret Cancer Centre, Toronto, Canada

Stéphane Verguet
Department of Global Health and Population, Harvard T. H. Chan School of Public Health, Boston, Massachusetts, United States

Judith Wagner
Independent economic consultant, Bethesda, Maryland, United States

Shao-Ming Wang
Cancer Institute, Chinese Academy of Medical Sciences, Peking Union Medical College, Beijing, China

Christopher P. Wild
International Agency for Research on Cancer, Lyon, France

Pooja Yerramilli
Harvard Global Equity Initiative, Harvard University, Cambridge, Massachusetts, United States

Cheng-Har Yip
University of Malaya Medical Centre, Kuala Lumpur, Malaysia

Ayda Yurekli
Independent economist, Ithaca, New York, United States

Witold Zatoński
Maria Sklodowska-Curie Cancer Centre, Warsaw, Poland

Ann G. Zauber
Memorial Sloan-Kettering Cancer Center, New York, New York, United States

Fang-Hui Zhao
Cancer Institute/Hospital, Chinese Academy of Medical Sciences, Beijing, China

Advisory Committee to the Editors

Reviewers

Nicolas Andre, MD, PhD
Pediatric Oncology, Children's Hospital of La Timone, AP-HM Marseille, France

Ronald D. Barr, MD
Professor of Pediatrics, Pathology, and Medicine, McMaster University, Hamilton, Ontario, Canada

Nazmi Bilir, MD
Professor of Public Health, Faculty of Medicine, Hacettepe University, Ankara, Turkey

Miguela A. Caniza, MD
Associate Member, Director of Infectious Diseases, International Outreach, Department of Infectious Diseases, International Outreach Program, St. Jude Children's Research Hospital, Memphis, Tennessee, United States

Phaik-Leng Cheah, MBBS, MRC Path, FRC Path, MPath, MD
Professor, Department of Pathology, Faculty of Medicine, University of Malaya, Kuala Lumpur, Malaysia

Maria Paula Curado, MD, PhD
Senior Researcher, International Prevention Research Institute, and Epidemiologist, Accamargo Cancer Center, International Research Center, Sao Paulo, Brasil

Henry Ddungu, MD, consultant
Uganda Cancer Institute, Kampala, Uganda

Nagi S. El Saghir, MD, FACP
Professor of Clinical Medicine, Director, Breast Center of Excellence, NK Basile Cancer Institute, Division of Hematology/Oncology, Department of Internal Medicine, American University of Beirut Medical Center, Beirut, Lebanon

Dan Greenberg, PhD
Associate Professor and Chairman, Department of Health Systems Management, Guilford Glazer Faculty of Business Management & Faculty of Health Sciences, Ben-Gurion University of the Negev, Beersheba, Israel

Raymond Hutubessy, PhD
Senior Health Economist, Initiative for Vaccine Research, World Health Organization, Geneva, Switzerland

M. Tezer Kutluk, MD, PhD
Professor of Pediatrics and Pediatric Oncologist, Hacettepe University Cancer Institute, Ankara, Turkey

Cédric Mahé, PhD
Senior Director, Global Epidemiology, Sanofi Pasteur, Lyon, France

Donald Maxwell Parkin, MD, PhD
Senior Epidemiologist, Centre for Cancer Prevention, Wolfson Institute of Preventive Medicine, Queen Mary University of London, London, United Kingdom

Aloka Pathirana MS, FRCS (Eng), FRCS (Edin)
Professor in Surgery, University of Sri Jayewardenepura, Nugegoda, Sri Lanka

Sevket Ruacan, MD
Professor of Pathology, Koc University School of Medicine, Istanbul, Turkey

Vikash Sewram, PhD (Medicine, Chemistry, and Physiology), MPH (Cancer Epidemiology), PhD (Public Health)
Director, African Cancer Institute, Stellenbosch University, Stellenbosch, South Africa

Frank A. Sloan, PhD
J. Alexander McMahon Professor of Health Policy
and Management and Professor of Economics, Duke
University, Durham, North Carolina, United States

Verna Dnk Vanderpuye, MBCHB, FWACS
Consultant Radiation and Clinical Oncologist,
Department of Radiation Oncology, Korle Bu Teaching
Hospital, Accra, Ghana

**Katsuri Warnakulasuriya, Oral Med BDS, FDSRCS,
PhD, Dip, DSc**
Professor of Oral Medicine and Experimental
Oral Pathology, King's College London, London,
United Kingdom

Sidney J. Winawer, MD
Paul Sherlock Chair in Medicine,
Gastroenterology and Nutrition
Service, Department of Medicine, Memorial
Sloan-Kettering Cancer Center; Professor
of Medicine, Weill Medical College,
Cornell University, Ithaca, New York,
United States

Cheng-Har Yip, MBBS, FRCSEd, FRCS
Consultant breast surgeon, Breast Centre, Sime Darby
Medical Centre, Selangor, Malaysia

Index

Boxes, figures, maps, notes, and tables are indicated by b, f, m, n, and t respectively.

cost-effectiveness and DALYs averted, 13, 214
liver cancer and, 150
Disease Control Priorities
HPV (human papillomavirus) vaccination in essential package of, 8
publication background of, 5*b*
DNA testing for HPV. *See* HPV (human papillomavirus) infection
Doll, Richard, 176
Dominican Republic
childhood cancer treatment in, 130
universal health care in, 284, 286*t*, 289
drug costs. *See* affordability of cancer services
drug therapy. *See also* chemotherapy; pain relief
breast cancer, 55–56*t*, 55–57
comprehensive cancer centers, 201
constraints on, 265
as risk factor, 105
smoking cessation treatment, 186
universal health care, coverage of, 290
Dutch Childhood Oncology Group, 130–31

E
Earle, Craig, 101
East Asia and Pacific
aflatoxins in, 153
HBV infection in, 151
HCV infection in, 155
liver cancer in, 147, 149
stomach cancer in, 218
Eastern Europe
colorectal cancer in, 102
oral cancer in, 85, 87
types of cancer in, 29
e-cigarettes, 186
Egypt
breast cancer in, 206*b*
cervical cancer in, 71
Fakous Cancer Center, 206*b*
HCV infection in, 151, 153
incidence of HBV vs. HCV in, 151, 152*f*
liver cancer in, 149
National Cancer Institute, 206*b*
endrocrine therapy, 54–55, 55–56*t*
environmental factors, 38
epidemiologic studies, 253–57, 260
Epstein-Barr virus, 36, 131
Ergo, A., 283
erythroplakia, 90
esophagus. *See* oral cancer
estrogen receptor protein, testing for, 11, 12*b*, 45
ethical considerations of cancer screening, 214–15
Ethiopia

cervical cancer screening in, 74
domestic funding in, 282
opioid accessibility in, 168–69
European Guidelines for Quality Assurance in Colorectal Cancer Screening and Diagnosis (IARC), 107, 108, 109
European Medicines Agency, 258
Europe/European Union. *See also specific regions and countries*
alcohol consumption in, 157
cancer registries in, 266
cervical cancer in, 69
HPV vaccination in, 79
liver cancer in, 150
lung cancer in, 177
radiation therapy in, 244
smoking in, 180

F
Fakous Cancer Center (Egypt), 206*b*
false-positive screening tests, 213
farming practices. *See* aflatoxins
FCTC (Framework Convention on Tobacco Control), 10, 89, 188, 189
fee-for-service payments, 292
fentanyl patch, 168, 169, 170
Ferlay, J., 25
financing, 281–94. *See also* health insurance
cancer care and, 15, 282–83
co-payments, 291
country approaches, 283
domestic funding, 282
need for financial protection, 282
out-of-pocket spending by families, 282, 290
overview, 281–82
progressive universalism, 283
public financing, 282, 290–91
research support and, 256
surgery and, 235–36
Finland, ban on advertising of cigarettes in, 185
first-level hospitals
intervention packages, 9*t*
surgery in, 227, 228*t*
flukes. *See* liver fluke infection
Foley, K. M., 166
Fonseca, M., 60
Food and Drug Administration (U.S.), 258
food and grain storage. *See* aflatoxins
Framework Convention on Tobacco Control (FCTC), 10, 89, 188, 189
France
HCV treatment in, 156
liver cancer in, 149

oral cancer in, 85
smoking in
cigarette taxes, 10, 184
inverse relationship of consumption and price,
183, 183f
restrictions in public places, 185
Franceschi, Silvia, 147
Fred Hutchinson Cancer Research Center (Seattle,
Washington), 205b
Frenk, J., 214

G

Gakidou, E., 74
Gambia, liver cancer in, 149
Gardasil Access Program, 78
gastric cancer. See stomach cancer
Gauvreau, Cindy L., 1, 223, 263
Gavi (The Vaccine Alliance), 10, 16, 36, 78–80, 155, 299
Gelband, Hellen, 1, 147, 165, 268, 281
gender differences
cancer incidence and mortality by geographical
region, 29, 215
delay in screening for women, 214
liver cancer, 148m, 149
lung cancer, 29
most common cancers by gender, 30m, 215
oral cancer, 86t, 87–88m
smoking and associated cancer risks, 35–36, 176,
177f, 180
genetic factors
colorectal cancer, 105
high-risk screening and, 212
liver cancer, 149
oral cancer, 89–90
retinoblastoma, 137
Georgia, opioid accessibility in, 169
Germany
opioid accessibility in, 170
smoking restrictions in public places in, 185
Ghana
breast cancer screening in, 290
cervical cancer screening in, 217
Ghana-Norway partnership as part of Breast Health
Global Initiative, 199
HPV vaccination in, 78
liver cancer in, 149
universal health care in, 284, 286t, 289, 290
taxes to finance, 292
Ginsburg, Ophira M., 211
GlaxoSmithKline, 299
Global Adult Tobacco Survey, 180, 182, 184
Global Fund for AIDS, TB and Malaria, 16
Global Initiative for Cancer Registry Development, 39

globalization
comprehensive cancer centers, contribution to,
204–5
initiatives for cancer control, 16–17
tobacco use and, 189
Global Monitoring Framework for Noncommunicable
Diseases (WHO), 166
Global Opioid Policy Initiative (GOPI), 168, 170–71
Global Task Force on Expanded Access to Cancer Care
and Control, 218–19
Global Task Force on Radiotherapy for Cancer
Control, 16
Global Youth Tobacco Survey, 182
Goldie, S. J., 80, 296
Gospodarowicz, Mary K., 195, 239
Greenberg, D., 111, 267
Gross, Thomas, 249
Guatemala
childhood cancer treatment in, 127b, 130, 197
Unidad Nacional de Oncología Pediátrica
(UNOP), 140
opioid accessibility in, 170
Guinea
cervical cancer in, 71
liver cancer in, 149
Guinea-Bissau, liver cancer in, 149
Gupta, Prakash C., 175
Gupta, Sumit, 121, 205
Guyana, cervical cancer in, 71
Gwatkin, D. R., 283

H

Haiti
domestic funding in, 282
HPV vaccination in, 78
Hall, Andrew, 147
Harif, Mhamed, 121
HBV. See hepatitis B and C viruses
HCC (hepatocellular carcinoma). See liver cancer
HCV. See hepatitis B and C viruses
HDI (Human Development Index), 31, 71, 81n2,
166, 226
HDV (hepatitis D virus), 149
head and neck cancers
imaging techniques for, 198
radiation therapy for, 240
health care professionals
research support role of, 250, 251b
screening by community care workers
and nurses, 218
shortage of skilled medical personnel, 232–33, 266
training of, 203–4
health communications, 255

oral cancer in, 88
taxation to finance universal health coverage
in, 284
Northern Africa. *See* Middle East and North Africa
Northern Ireland's greenways urbanization project,
effect on chronic diseases, 38
North-South collaborations, 16, 257
Norway
advertising of cigarettes, ban on, 185
Ghana-Norway partnership as part of Breast
Health Global Initiative, 199
opioid accessibility in, 170
Nurses' Health Study, 254, 254b
nut chewing, as oral cancer risk, 85, 87, 88–89
nutrition as risk factor for oral cancer, 89

O

Obermeyer, Z., 74
obesity. *See also* lifestyle
relationship to cancer, 37–38
liver cancer, 147, 154
occult blood test. *See* colorectal cancer (CRC)
occupational risk factors, 38
Olson, Zachary, 295
Omar, Sherif, 195
opioid accessibility in, 168
opioid medications, 11, 165–69, 167f. *See also* pain relief
Opioid Price Watch (IAHPC), 167, 170
Opisthorchis viverrini, 36
Oportunidades program (Mexico), 284
oral cancer, 85–99
alcohol consumption associated with, 37, 89
chemotherapy, 94, 275
chronic trauma as risk factor, 90
cost-effectiveness assessments of interventions,
94–96
cost-effectiveness of interventions, 94–96, 95t, 268,
274–75t
defined, 85
early diagnosis and staging of, 92, 93t
future research needs, 96
genetic factors, 89–90
high-risk screening, 212
HPV infection and, 87, 88, 90, 218
incidence and death rates, 6t, 28f, 85–88
by gender, 86t, 87–88m, 215
by income group, 87f, 224f
intervention packages, 9t
management of, 92
natural history of, 90
nutrition as risk factor, 89
oral potentially malignant disorders (OPMDs),
screening for, 91

overview, 85
posttreatment follow-up, 94
prognosis, 94
radiation therapy for, 92–94, 240
research support for, 260
risk factors, 85–90, 218
screening for, 11, 90, 91–92, 218
health care personnel performing visual
screening, 91
high-risk screening, 212
self-examination, 91–92
visual screening, 90–91, 277
surgery, 92–94, 228, 229–30t
complications of, 94
survival rates, 88
treatment of, 92–94
viruses as risk factor, 90
oral submucous fibrosis (OSMF), 89, 90
Organisation for Economic Co-operation and
Development's Global Science Forum, 257
ovarian cancer
death rates from, 6t
high-risk screening, 58, 212
overdiagnosis concerns, 213, 215
oxycodone, 168, 170

P

PAF (population attributable fraction), 26–27
pain relief, 165–73
availability of broadly defined palliative care
services, 167
barriers in LMICs to, 167–69
cancer patients' need for, 166
comprehensive cancer center services, 200
cost-effectiveness of, 9, 169
costs of, 14t, 169–70
Global Opioid Policy Initiative (GOPI), 168,
170–71
as human right, 165
International Narcotics Control Board (INCB), 168
in LMICs, 166–67
opioid medications, availability of, 11, 166–67, 167f
Opioid Price Watch (IAHPC), 167, 170
overzealous regulation restricting access to, 168
patient perspective, 170
Pakistan
acute lymphoblastic leukemia (ALL) in, 128
HCV infection in, 151
incidence of HBV vs. HCV in, 151, 152f
oral cancer in, 87, 88, 94
Palestinian Authority, breast cancer screening in, 58
Palipudi, Krishna, 175
palliative care. *See also* pain relief

radiation therapy and, 165, 240, 241
surgery with palliative intent, 230
pancreas cancer, 28f
Pap smears, 69, 73, 74, 216
Papua New Guinea, oral cancer in, 85
Partners in Health, 199
pathology
comprehensive cancer center services, 199
research role of, 252
surgery's reliance on, 226
telepathology, 218
PBCRs (population-based cancer registries), 25, 39, 251
pediatric cancer. *See* childhood cancer
Pediatric Oncology in Developing Countries (PODC) committee of International Society of Pediatric Oncology (SIOP), 125
Peru
cervical cancer prevention approaches in, 80
universal health care in, 284, 287t, 289, 290
Peto, Richard, 179
pharmacotherapy. *See* chemotherapy
pharmacy services. *See also* drug therapy
comprehensive cancer centers, 201
pharynx. *See* oral cancer
Philip Morris, 189
Philippines
colorectal cancer incidence rates in, 103
opioid accessibility in, 170
smoking in
implementation of excise tax increases, 184
implications of tobacco taxation, 10, 188
inverse relationship of consumption and price, 183
physical inactivity. *See* lifestyle
"Pink Ribbon Red Ribbon" program, 219
Poland
opioid accessibility in, 170
radiation therapy in, 245
smoking in
cessation treatments, 186
implementation of excise tax increases, 184
inverse relationship of consumption and price, 183
popularity paradox, 215
population attributable fraction (PAF), 26–27
population-based cancer registries (PBCRs), 25, 39, 251
population-based randomized trial, 62
Pramesh, C. S., 223
prevention strategies, 1, 10. *See also specific types of cancer*
primary health clinic or mobile outreach, 9t
priorities for international support, 16–17

cost reduction for essential intervention packages, 16
research support, 17
technical assistance, 16–17
progressive universalism, 283
prostate cancer
early detection as factor, 29
by geographical region, 29
incidence and death rates, 6t, 27, 28f
by income group, 32f
transitions in low- and middle-income countries, 29
overdiagnosis concerns, 213
physical inactivity, relationship to, 38
radiation therapy for, 240
research support for, 260
screening for, 10
lead-time bias and, 212
prostate-specific antigen (PSA) testing, 10–11
psychosocial support, 200
public awareness of cancer control interventions, 16, 255
public places, restrictions on smoking in, 185, 188

Q
Qiao, You-Lin, 249, 295
quality-adjusted life years (QALYs), 7b

R
Rabeneck, Linda, 101, 268
Radiation Safety Institute of Canada, 199
radiation therapy (RT), 239–47. *See also specific types of cancer*
access to, 243–45, 244m
as adjuvant treatment, 231, 240
adoption of expert systems and machine learning methods, 243
brachytherapy, 241
comprehensive cancer center services, 199–200, 243
concurrent chemotherapy and, 240
constraints on, 265
cost-effectiveness of, 239
critical normal structures, limited tolerance of, 240
delivery methods, 241–43
equipment specialized for, 239, 265
externally applied radiation beams, 241
facilities designed for, 241–42
infrastructure requirements, 244, 265
integration into cancer centers, 243
intensity modulated radiation therapy (IMRT), 240
in multidisciplinary approach to cancer management, 239
oral cancer, 94

premature death, goal to reduce, 1

smoking, goal to reduce, 189

World Health Organization (WHO). *See also*
International Agency for Research on Cancer
(IARC)

on breast cancer guidelines, 48

cervical cancer screening, VIA demonstration
project, 75

Choosing Interventions That Are Cost-Effective
(WHO-CHOICE) framework, 59, 60, 277

on cigarette excise taxes, 183–84

collection of cancer incidence, 39

on cost-effective intervention strategies for NCDs in
LMICs, 218

cost effectiveness recommendations, 60, 138, 235

on effectiveness of tobacco control, HPV and HBV
vaccination, and opportunistic cervical cancer
screening, 17

EPIC model to simulate the macroeconomic effects
of noncommunicable diseases, 187, 187*t*

Essential Medicines List, 156, 166, 170

Framework Convention on Tobacco Control
(FCTC), 10, 89, 188, 189

Global Health Estimates, 7*b*

Global Health Observatory, 250

Global Monitoring Framework for
Noncommunicable Diseases, 166

on HBV vaccine, 155

on HCV infection, 151

on health expenditures covered by external sources,
282, 283

on imaging guidelines, 199

on life table estimates for China, 297

mortality databank, 26

MPOWER report on global tobacco epidemic, 36

on national cancer control planning, 195, 243, 267

on noncommunicable disease best buys for LMICs, 8

on palliative care, 165, 168

Study of Global AGEing and Adult Health, 298

Surgical Safety Checklist, 199

Three-Step Analgesic Ladder, 166

*WHO Action Plan for the Global Strategy for the
Prevention and Control of Noncommunicable
Diseases,* 39

World Trade Organization (WTO), 189

Y

Yerramilli, Pooja, 281

Yip, Cheng-Har, 223

youth smoking, 10, 182, 184, 186

Yurekli, Ayda, 175, 187

Z

Zambia, cervical cancer in, 71, 75

Zatońksi, Witold, 175

Zauber, Ann G., 101

Zelle, S. G., 59, 60, 216

Zhao, Fang-hui, 249

Zimbabwe

cancer trends in, 29

cervical cancer, increases in, 23

zur Hausen, H., 257

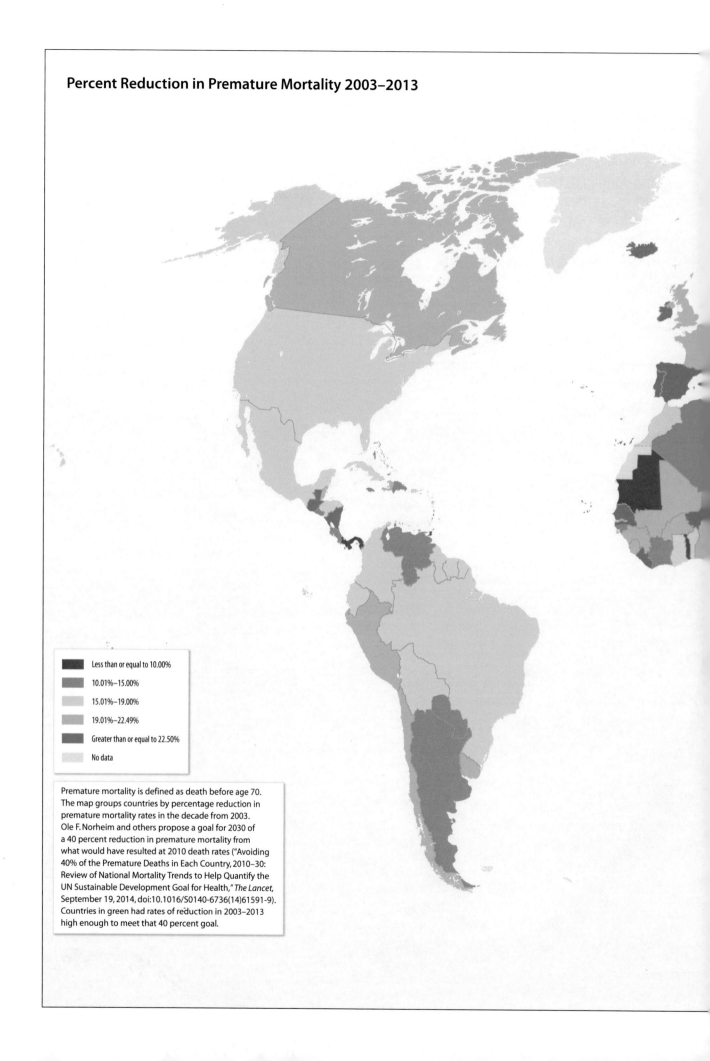

Percent Reduction in Premature Mortality 2003–2013

Less than or equal to 10.00%

10.01%–15.00%

15.01%–19.00%

19.01%–22.49%

Greater than or equal to 22.50%

No data

Premature mortality is defined as death before age 70.
The map groups countries by percentage reduction in
premature mortality rates in the decade from 2003.
Ole F. Norheim and others propose a goal for 2030 of
a 40 percent reduction in premature mortality from
what would have resulted at 2010 death rates ("Avoiding
40% of the Premature Deaths in Each Country, 2010–30:
Review of National Mortality Trends to Help Quantify the
UN Sustainable Development Goal for Health," *The Lancet,*
September 19, 2014, doi:10.1016/S0140-6736(14)61591-9).
Countries in green had rates of reduction in 2003–2013
high enough to meet that 40 percent goal.